D1232076

THE DEVELOPMENT OF PROPULSION TECHNOLOGY
FOR U.S. SPACE-LAUNCH VEHICLES, 1926–1991

NUMBER
SEVENTEEN:

Centennial of
Flight Series

Roger D.
Launius,
*General
Editor*

THE DEVELOPMENT OF PROPULSION TECHNOLOGY FOR U.S. SPACE-LAUNCH VEHICLES, 1926–1991

J. D. HUNLEY

Texas A&M University Press
College Station

The paper used in this book meets the minimum requirements
of the American National Standard for Permanence of Paper for
Printed Library Materials, Z39.48-1984.
Binding materials have been chosen for durability.
∞

The frontispiece shows a Delta 1910 vehicle launching *Orbiting
Solar Observatory 8* (Photo courtesy of NASA)

Library of Congress Cataloging-in-Publication Data

Hunley, J. D., 1941–
    The development of propulsion technology for U.S. space-
launch vehicles, 1926–1991 / J. D. Hunley.—1st ed.
        p. cm.—(Centennial of flight series ; no. 17)
    Includes bibliographical references and index.
    ISBN-13: 978-1-58544-588-2 (cloth : alk. paper)
    ISBN-10: 1-58544-588-6 (cloth : alk. paper)
    1. Space vehicles—Propulsion systems—History. 2. Rocket
engines—Research—United States—History. 3.   Launch
vehicles (Astronautics)—United States—History. I. Title.
    TL781.8.U5H87 2007
    629.47'520973—dc22   2006039178

CONTENTS

List of Illustrations   vii

Preface   ix

Introduction   1

CHAPTER 1
German and U.S. Missiles and Rockets, 1926–66   7

CHAPTER 2
U.S. Space-Launch Vehicles, 1958–91   48

CHAPTER 3
Propulsion with Alcohol and Kerosene Fuels, 1932–72   100

CHAPTER 4
Propulsion with Storable Fuels and Oxidizers, 1942–91   145

CHAPTER 5
Propulsion with Liquid Hydrogen and Oxygen, 1954–91   173

CHAPTER 6
Solid Propulsion: JATOs to Minuteman III, 1939–70   222

CHAPTER 7
Titan and Shuttle Boosters, Other Solid Propulsion, 1958–91   259

CHAPTER 8
Conclusions and Epilogue   288

Notes   299

A Note on Sources   263

Index   371

ILLUSTRATIONS

FIG. 1.1 Robert H. Goddard and the first known liquid-propellant rocket **10**

FIG. 1.2 Goddard's 1926 liquid-propellant rocket **11**

FIG. 1.3 Robert Goddard with his principal technical assistants **12**

FIG. 1.4 Launch of a Bumper-WAC with a V-2 first stage **24**

FIG. 1.5 A Juno I launch vehicle with the *Explorer I* satellite **29**

FIG. 1.6 Launch of final Vanguard rocket **31**

FIG. 2.1 A Mercury-Redstone launching *Freedom 7* **50**

FIG. 2.2 Launch of a Mercury-Atlas **52**

FIG. 2.3 Gemini-Titan 12 launch **53**

FIG. 2.4 A Thor-Able launch vehicle **55**

FIG. 2.5 Agena upper stage serving as Gemini 8 target vehicle **58**

FIG. 2.6 A Delta 1910 vehicle launching an *Orbiting Solar Observatory* **61**

FIG. 2.7 An Atlas-Centaur launch vehicle undergoing radio-frequency interference tests **65**

FIG. 2.8 Launch of a Titan-Centaur **66**

FIG. 2.9 Launch of Scout ST-5 (Scout Test 5) **71**

FIG. 2.10 Wernher von Braun explaining the Saturn launch system to John F. Kennedy **81**

FIG. 2.11 The static test of Solid-Rocket Booster (SRB) Demonstration Model 2 **95**

FIG. 3.1 Models of the Mercury-Atlas, Saturn C-1, and Saturn C-5 **101**

FIG. 3.2 Walt Disney, a model of the V-2 rocket, and Wernher von Braun in 1954 **111**

FIG. 3.3 A Vanguard launch vehicle undergoing a static test **115**

FIG. 3.4 Technical drawing of a baffled injector **124**

FIG. 3.5 Technical drawing showing components of an MA-5 engine **125**

FIG. 3.6 Technical drawing of an injector for an MA-5 engine **126**

FIG. 3.7 Atlas-Agena launch **130**

FIG. 3.8 H-1 engines **131**

FIG. 3.9 Launch of a Saturn IB vehicle **133**

FIG. 3.10 Diagram of the engines used on the Saturn IB and Saturn V 134

FIG. 3.11 Diagram of the Saturn IB 135

FIG. 3.12 The huge first stage of the Saturn V launch vehicle 136

FIG. 3.13 Fuel tank assembly for the Saturn V S-IC (first) stage 139

FIG. 3.14 Launch of the giant Saturn V on the Apollo 11 mission 142

FIG. 4.1 Technical drawing with description of the Agena upper stage 160

FIG. 4.2 Generic technical drawing of a liquid-propellant rocket 162

FIG. 5.1 Technical drawing of an RL10 engine 182

FIG. 5.2 The second (S-II) stage of the Saturn V launch vehicle 202

FIG. 5.3 The Space Shuttle *Columbia* launching 212

FIG. 5.4 The space shuttle main engine firing during a test 213

FIG. 5.5 Technical drawing of the Space Shuttle vehicle 216

FIG. 5.6 The Space Shuttle *Discovery* being rolled out 221

FIG. 6.1 An Ercoupe aircraft taking off with a solid-propellant jet-assisted takeoff unit 224

FIG. 6.2 Technical drawing of an early solid-propellant rocket 227

FIG. 6.3 Technical drawing of the Jupiter C (actually, Juno I) 238

FIG. 6.4 An unidentified solid-rocket motor being tested in an altitude wind tunnel 242

FIG. 7.1 Launch of a Delta E rocket 260

FIG. 7.2 Example of a filament-wound case for a solid-propellant stage 267

FIG. 7.3 Space Shuttle solid-rocket booster in a test stand 269

FIG. 7.4 Technical drawing of the Space Shuttle solid-rocket booster 271

FIG. 7.5 Testing of a developmental motor following the *Challenger* accident 275

FIG. 7.6 Scout S-131R with a new Castor II second stage 280

FIG. 7.7 The Inertial Upper Stage attached to the Magellan spacecraft 286

FIG. 8.1 Monkey Baker posing with a model of a Jupiter vehicle 289

FIG. 8.2 A static test of a Space Shuttle solid-rocket booster 293

PREFACE

THIS BOOK ATTEMPTS TO FILL A GAP IN THE LITERATURE about space-launch vehicles (and in the process, strategic missiles, from which launch vehicles borrowed much technology). There are many excellent books about rocketry. (The Note on Sources discusses many of them.) But none covers the ways in which the technology in the United States developed from its beginnings with Robert Goddard and the German V-2 project through the end of the cold war. This book concentrates on propulsion technology to keep its length manageable, but it occasionally mentions structures and guidance/control in passing, especially in chapters 1 and 2. ·

Besides the lack of coverage of the evolution of rocket technology in the existing literature, there is a severe problem with accuracy of details. Apparently reputable sources differ about matters as simple as lengths and diameters of vehicles and details about thrust. I cannot claim to have provided definitive measurements, but I have tried to select the most plausible figures and have provided various references in endnotes that readers can consult to find for themselves the many discrepancies.

I have been working on some aspects of this book since 1992. I initially wrote a much longer manuscript, organized by project, that covered the entire gamut of major technologies. I have organized this much shorter volume by types of propulsion with overviews in chapters 1 and 2 to provide context and cover factors in technology development that do not fit comfortably in chapters 3–7.

In researching and writing both manuscripts, I received help from a huge number of people. I apologize in advance for any I inadvertently neglect to mention or whose names I have forgotten. I especially want to thank Roger Launius. As my boss at the NASA History Office, he provided unfailing encouragement and support for my initial research. Now as editor for the series in which this book will appear, he has continued that support. Michael Neufeld at the Smithsonian National Air and Space Museum (NASM) shared his own research on the V-2 with me and arranged for me to consult the captured documents held by his institution. He also read many chapters in draft and offered suggestions for improvement. I am further greatly indebted to NASM for granting me the Ramsey Fellowship for 1991–92 and allowing me to continue my research there with the support of archivists, librarians, curators, docents, and volunteers, including John Anderson, Tom Crouch, David DeVorkin, Marilyn Graskowiak, Dan Hagedorn, Gregg Herken, Peter Jakab,

Mark Kahn, Daniel Lednicer, Brian Nicklas, George Schnitzer, Paul Silbermann, Leah Smith, Larry Wilson, Frank Winter, and Howard S. Wolko.

Special thanks are due to Glen Asner of the NASA History Division, who read an earlier version of this book and offered detailed editorial advice at a time when NASA intended to publish the book. Glen's advice was extremely valuable, as was that of three anonymous NASA readers. Then Texas A&M University Press accepted the book for publication. Glen and Steven Dick, NASA chief historian, graciously relinquished the manuscript to Texas A&M.

Chapters 1, 2, 6, and 7 contain material I published earlier in chapter 6 of *To Reach the High Frontier: A History of U.S. Launch Vehicles*, ed. Roger D. Launius and Dennis R. Jenkins (Lexington: University Press of Kentucky, 2002). The material in the present book results from much research done since I wrote that chapter, and it is organized differently. But I am grateful to Mack McCormick, rights manager, the University Press of Kentucky, for confirming my right to reuse the material that appeared in the earlier version his press published.

A number of people read earlier versions of the material in this book and offered suggestions for improvement. They include Matt Bille, Roger Bilstein, Trong Bui, Virginia Dawson, Ross Felix, Pat Johnson, John Lonnquest, Ray Miller, Fred Ordway, Ed Price, Milton Rosen, David Stumpf, and Jim Young. Many other people provided documents or other sources I would otherwise have been unable to locate easily, including Nadine Andreassen, Liz Babcock, Scott Carlin, Robert Corley, Dwayne Day, Bill Elliott, Robert Geisler, Robert Gordon, Edward Hall, Charles Henderson, Dennis Jenkins, Karl Klager, John Lonnquest, Ray Miller, Tom Moore, Jacob Neufeld, Fred Ordway, Ed Price, Ray Puffer, Karen Schaffer, Ronald Simmons, Ernst Stuhlinger, Ernie Sutton, Robert Truax, and P. D. Umholtz. Archivists, historians, and librarians at many locations were unfailingly helpful. Here I can only single out Air Force Historical Research Agency archivist Archangelo Difante and Air Force Space and Missile Systems Center historian and archivist (respectively) Harry Waldron and Teresa Pleasant; China Lake historian Leroy Doig; Laguna Niguel archivist Bill Doty; Clark University Coordinator of Archives & Special Collections Dorothy E. Mosakowski; NASA archivists Colin Fries, John Hargenrader, Jane Odom, and Lee Saegesser; and JPL archivists John Bluth, Barbara Carter, Dudee Chiang, Julie Cooper, and Margo E. Young for their exceptional assistance. Several reference librarians at the Library of Congress should be added to the list, but I do not know their names.

I also want to thank everyone who consented to be interviewed (included in endnote references) for their cooperation and agreement to allow me to use the information in the interviews. In addition, many people discussed technical issues with me or provided other technical assistance. These include Ranney Adams, Wil Andrepont, Stan Backlund, Rod Bogue, Al Bowers, George Bradley, Robert Corley, Daniel Dembrow, Mike Gorn, Mark Grills, John Guilmartin, Burrell Hays, J. G. Hill, Ken Iliff, Fred Johnsen, Karl Klager, Franklin Knemeyer, Dennis B. Mahon, Jerry McKee, Ray Miller, Ed Price, Bill Schnare, Neil Soderstrom, Woodward Waesche, Herman Wayland, and Paul Willoughby. Finally, I offer my deep appreciation to my excellent copyeditor, Cynthia Lindlof; my in-house editor, Jennifer Ann Hobson; editor-in-chief Mary Lenn Dixon; and everyone else at Texas A&M University Press for their hard work in getting this book published and marketed. To all of the people above and others whose names I could not locate, I offer my thanks for their assistance.

It goes (almost) without saying that these people bear no responsibility for the interpretation and details I provide in the following pages. I hope, however, that they will approve of the uses I have made of their materials, suggestions, comments, and information.

THE DEVELOPMENT OF PROPULSION TECHNOLOGY
FOR U.S. SPACE-LAUNCH VEHICLES, 1926–1991

INTRODUCTION

ALTHOUGH ROCKETS BURNING BLACK POWDER HAD existed for centuries, only in 1926 did Robert H. Goddard, an American physicist and rocket developer, launch the first known liquid-propellant rocket. It then took the United States until the mid-1950s to begin spending significant sums on rocket development. The country soon (January 1958) began launching satellites, and by the end of the cold war (1989–91), the United States had developed extraordinarily sophisticated and powerful missiles and launch vehicles. From the Atlas to the Space Shuttle, these boosters placed an enormous number of satellites and spacecraft into orbits or trajectories that enabled them to greatly expand our understanding of Earth and its universe and to carry voices and images from across the seas into the American living room almost instantaneously. What allowed the United States to proceed so quickly from the comparatively primitive rocket technology of 1955 to almost routine access to space in the 1980s?

This book provides answers to that question and explains the evolution of rocket technology from Goddard's innovative but not fully successful rockets to the impressive but sometimes problematic technology of the Space Shuttle. Although propulsion technology has often challenged the skills and knowledge of its developers, by and large, its achievements have been astonishing.

This combination of complexity and sophistication caused some inventive soul to coin the term "rocket science." But often in the history of rocketry, so-called rocket scientists ran up against problems they could not fully understand. To solve such problems, they often had to resort to trial-and-error procedures. Even as understanding of many problems continually grew, so did the size and performance of rockets. Each increase in scale posed new problems. It turns out that rocketry is as much art as science. As such, it best fits the definitions of engineering (not science) that students of technology, including Edwin Layton, Walter Vincenti, and Eugene Ferguson, have provided. (Besides engineering as art, they have discussed the discipline's emphasis on doing rather than just knowing, on artifact design instead of understanding, and on making decisions about such design in a context of imperfect knowledge.)[1]

In the light of their findings and the details of rocket development discussed in the present book, I will argue that designers and developers of missiles and space-launch vehicles were fundamentally engineers, not scientists, even though some of them were trained as scientists. For instance, Ronald L. Simmons received a B.A. in chemistry from the University of Kansas in 1952 and worked for 33 years as a propulsion and explosive chemist at Hercules Powder Company, a year with Rocketdyne, and 13 years for the U.S. Navy, contributing to upper stages for Polaris, Minuteman, and other missiles. He considered himself to be a chemist and as such, a scientist, but admitted that he had done "a lot of engineering." Unconsciously underlining points made about engineering by Vincenti and Layton, he added that it was "amazing how much we don't know or understand, yet we launch large rockets routinely . . . and successfully." He believed that we understood enough "to be successful . . . yet may not understand why."[2]

This is not to suggest any lack of professional expertise on the part of rocket engineers. Rocketry remains perplexingly complex. In the early years, engineers' knowledge of how various components and systems interacted in missiles and launch vehicles was necessarily limited. But quickly data, theory, and technical literature grew to provide them a huge repository of information to draw upon. Some processes nevertheless remained only partially understood. But when problems occur, as they still do, the fund of knowledge is great, permitting designers and developers to focus their efforts and bring their knowledge to bear on specific kinds of solutions.

Yet often there are no clear answers in the existing literature. Engineers must try out likely solutions until one proves to be effective, whether sooner or later. In the chapters that follow, I sometimes refer to this approach as cut-and-try (cutting metal and trying it out in a rocket) or trial-and-error. Neither term implies that practitioners were experimenting blindly. They brought their knowledge and available literature (including science) to bear on the problem, measured the results as far as possible, and made informed decisions. Limited funding and rigorous schedules often restricted this process. Given these circumstances, it is remarkable that they succeeded as often and well as they did. Not rocket science, this cut-and-try methodology was part of a highly effective engineering culture.

This book is about launch-vehicle technology. Because much of it originated in missile development, there is much discussion of missiles. These missiles launch in similar fashion to launch vehicles. But they follow a ballistic path to locations on Earth rather than somewhere in space. Their payloads are warheads rather than satellites or spacecraft. Especially in the discipline of propulsion, they have employed similar technology to that used in launch vehicles. Many launch vehicles, indeed, have been converted missiles or have used stages borrowed from missiles.

Both types of rockets use a variety of technologies, but this book focuses on propulsion as arguably more fundamental than such other fields as structures and guidance/control. The book starts with Goddard and his Romanian-German rival Hermann Oberth. It follows the development of technology used on U.S. launch vehicles through the end of the cold war. Because the German V-2 influenced American technology and was *a* (not *the*) starting place for the Saturn launch vehicles in particular, there is a section on the German World War II missile and its developers, many of whom, under Wernher von Braun's leadership, came to this country and worked on the Saturns.

Chapters 1 and 2 provide an overview of missile and rocket development to furnish a context for the technical chapters that follow. Chapters 3 through 7 then cover the four principal types of chemical propulsion used in the missiles and launch vehicles covered in chapters 1 and 2. Chapter 8 offers some general conclusions about the process of rocket engineering as well as an epilogue pointing to major developments that occurred after the book ends at the conclusion of the cold war. (There is no discussion of attempts at harnessing nuclear [and other nonchemical types of] propulsion—sometimes used in spacecraft—because funding restraints and technical risks precluded their use in production missiles and launch vehicles.)[3]

The book stops about 1991 because after the cold war ended, development of launch vehicles entered a new era. Funding became much more restricted, and technology began to be borrowed from the Russians, who had followed a separate path to launch-vehicle development during the Soviet era.

Most readers of this book presumably have watched launches of the Space Shuttle and other space-launch vehicles on television, but maybe a discussion of the fundamentals of rocketry will be useful to some. Missiles and launch vehicles lift off through the thrust produced by burning propellants (fuel and oxidizer). The combustion produces expanding, mostly gaseous exhaust products that a nozzle with a narrow throat and exit cone cause to accelerate, adding to the thrust. Nozzles do not work ideally at all altitudes because of changing atmospheric pressure. Thus, exit cones require different angles at low and higher altitudes for optimum performance. For this reason, rockets typically use more than one stage both to allow exit cones to be designed for different altitudes and to reduce the amount of weight each succeeding stage must accelerate to the required speed for the mission in question. As one stage uses up its propellants, it drops away and succeeding stages ignite and assume the propulsion task, each having less weight to accelerate while taking advantage of the velocity already achieved.

Most propellants use an ignition device to start combustion, but so-called hypergolic propellants ignite on contact and do not need an igniter. Such propellants usually have less propulsive power than such nonhypergolic fuels and oxidizers as the extremely cold (cryogenic) liquid hydrogen and liquid oxygen. But they also require less special handling than cryogenics, which will boil off if not loaded shortly before launch. Hypergolics can be stored for comparatively long periods in propellant tanks and launched almost instantly. This provided a great advantage for missiles and for launches that had only narrow periods of time in which to be launched to line up with an object in space that was moving in relation to Earth.

Solid-propellant motors also allowed rapid launches. They were simpler than and usually not as heavy as liquid-propellant engines. Solids did not need tanks to hold the propellants, high pressure or pumps to deliver the propellant to the combustion chamber, or extravagant plumbing to convey the liquids. Normally, rocket firms loaded the solid propellant in a case made of thin metal or composite material. Insulation between the propellant and the case plus an internal cavity in the middle of the propellant protected the case from the heat of combustion, the propellant burning from the cavity outward so that the propellant lay between the burning surface and the insulation. The design of the internal cavity provided optimal thrust for each mission, with the extent of the surface facing the cavity determining the amount of thrust. Different designs provided varying thrust-time curves. Solid propellants did pose the problem that they could not easily accommodate stopping and restarting of combustion, as liquids could do by using valves. Consequently, solids usually served in initial stages (called stage zero) to provide large increments of thrust for earth-escape, or in upper stages. For most of the period of this book, the Scout launch vehicle was unique in being a fully solid-propellant vehicle.

Liquid propellants typically propelled the core stages of launch vehicles, as in the Atlas, Titan, Delta, and Space Shuttle. Upper stages needing to be stopped and restarted in orbit (so they could insert satellites and spacecraft into specific orbits or trajectories after coasting) also used liquid propellants, as did stages needing high performance. But in liquid-propellant engines, the injection of fuels and oxidizers into combustion chambers remained problematic in almost every new design or upscaling of an old design. Mixing the two types of propellants in optimal proportions often produced instabilities that could damage or destroy a combustion chamber.

This severe problem remained only partly understood, and although engineers usually could find a solution, doing so often took much trial and error in new or scaled-up configurations. Solid propellants were by no means immune to combustion instability, although the problems they faced were somewhat different from those occurring in liquid-propellant engines. And often, by the time solid-propellant instabilities were discovered, design was so far along that it became prohibitively expensive to fix the problem unless it was especially severe.

Besides propulsion, missiles and launch vehicles required structures strong enough to withstand high dynamic pressures during launch yet light enough to be lifted into space efficiently; aerodynamically effective shapes (minimizing drag and aerodynamic heating); materials that could tolerate aerothermodynamic loads and heating from combustion; and guidance/control systems that provide steering through a variety of mechanisms ranging from vanes, canards, movable fins, vernier (auxiliary) and attitude-control rockets, and fluids injected into the exhaust stream, to gimballed engines or nozzles.[4]

With these basic issues to deal with, how did the United States get involved in developing missiles and rockets on a large scale? What sorts of problems did developers need to overcome to permit a rapid advance in missile and launch-vehicle technology? The chapters that follow answer these and other questions, but maybe a brief summary of how the process worked will guide the reader through a rather technical series of projects and developments.

Launch-vehicle technology emerged from the development and production of missiles to counter a perceived threat by the Soviet Union. In this environment, heavy cold-war expenditures to develop the missiles essentially fueled progress. In addition, many other factors (not always obvious to contemporaries) helped further the process. No short list of references documents the complex development discussed in this book, but one element of the effort was an innovative and flexible engineering culture that brought together a variety of talents and disciplines in a large number of organizations spanning the nation. People from different disciplines joined together in cross-organizational teams to solve both unanticipated and expected problems.

Likewise, supporting problem solving and innovation was a gradually developing network that shared data among projects. Although military services, agencies, and firms often competed for roles and missions or contracts, the movement of people among the competing entities, actual cooperation, professional organizations, partnering, federal intellectual-property arrangements, and umbrella organizations such as the Chemical Propulsion Information Agency promoted technology transfers of importance to rocketry. At the same time, the competition spurred development through the urge to outperform rivals.

A further factor helping to integrate development and keep it on schedule (more or less) consisted of numerous key managers and management systems. In some instances, managers served as heterogeneous engineers, managing the social as well as the technical aspects of missile and launch-vehicle development, stimulating support for rocketry in general from Congress, the administration, and the Department of Defense. By creating this support, they practiced what some scholars have defined as social construction of the technologies in question. At times, managers engaged in both technical direction and heterogeneous engineering, while in other cases technical managers and heterogeneous engineers were separate individuals.[5]

Although rocket technology is complex, I have tried to present it in a way that will be comprehensible to the general reader. The primary audience for this book will tend to be scholars interested in the history of technology or propulsion engineers seeking an overview of the history of their discipline. I have included many examples of problems encountered in the development of missiles and launch vehicles and explained, as far as I could determine, the way they were resolved. Even though I have not written in the technically rigorous language of engineering (or in some cases because of that), I hope my discussion of the evolution of propulsion technology will engage the interest of everyone from rocket enthusiasts to technical sophisticates.

CHAPTER 1

SPACE-LAUNCH-VEHICLE TECHNOLOGY
evolved from the development of early rockets and
missiles. The earliest of these rockets that led to
work on launch vehicles themselves was Robert
Goddard's in 1926, generally regarded as the first

German and U.S. Missiles and Rockets, 1926–66

liquid-propellant rocket to fly. But it was not until the mid-1950s that significant progress on large missiles occurred in the United States, greatly stimulated by the cold war between the United States and the Soviet Union. (Of course, the Germans had already developed the A-4 [V-2] in the 1940s, and the United States launched a series of reconstructed German V-2s in the New Mexico desert from 1946 to 1952.) Missile development was especially important in furthering the development of launch vehicles because many missiles became, with adaptations, actual stages for launch vehicles. In other cases, engines or other components for missiles became the bases for those on launch vehicles. By 1966 large, powerful, and comparatively sophisticated launch vehicles had already evolved from work on early missiles and rockets.

The Beginnings, Goddard and Oberth, 1926–45

The history of space-launch-vehicle technology in the United States dates back to the experimenting of U.S. physicist and rocket developer Robert H. Goddard (1882–1945). A fascinating character, Goddard was supremely inventive. He is credited with 214 patents, many of them submitted after his death by his wife, Esther. These led to a settlement in 1960 by the National Aeronautics and Space Administration (NASA) and the three armed services of $1 million for use of more than 200 patents covering innovations in the fields of rocketry, guided missiles, and space exploration. In the course of his rocket research, Goddard achieved many technological breakthroughs. Among them were gyroscopic control of vanes in the exhaust of the rocket engine, film cooling of the combustion chamber, parachutes for recovery of the rocket and any instruments on it, streamlined casing, clustered engines, a gimballed tail section for stabilization, lightweight centrifugal pumps to force propellants into the combustion chamber, a gas generator, igniters, injection heads, and launch controls, although he did not use them all on any one rocket.[1]

Despite these impressive achievements, Goddard had less demonstrable influence on the development of subsequent missiles and space-launch vehicles than he could have had. One reason was that he epitomized the quintessential lone inventor. With exceptions, he pursued a pattern of secrecy throughout the course of his career. This secretiveness hindered his country from developing missiles and rockets as rapidly as it might have done had he devoted his real abilities to the sort of cooperative development needed for the production of such complex devices.

Educated at Worcester Polytechnic Institute (B.S. in general science in 1908) and Clark University (Ph.D. in physics in 1911), Goddard seems to have begun serious work on the development of rockets February 9, 1909, when he performed his first experiment on the exhaust velocity of a rocket propellant. He continued experimentation and in 1916 applied to the Smithsonian Institution for $5,000 to launch a rocket within a short time to extreme altitudes (100–200 miles) for meteorological and other research. He received a grant for that amount in 1917. From then until 1941 he received a total of more than $200,000 for rocket research from a variety of civilian sources.[2]

In 1920 he published "A Method of Reaching Extreme Altitudes" in the *Smithsonian Miscellaneous Collections*. As Frank Winter has stated, this "publication established Goddard as the preeminent researcher in the field of rocketry" and "was unquestionably very influential in the space travel movement. . . ."[3] However, important and pathbreaking as the paper was, it remained largely theoretical, calling for "necessary preliminary experiments" still to be performed.[4] Following the paper's publication, with partial hiatuses occasioned by periods of limited funding, Goddard spent the rest of the interwar period performing these experiments and trying to construct a rocket that would achieve an altitude above that reached by sounding balloons.

After experiencing frustrating problems using solid propellants, Goddard switched to liquid propellants in 1921. But it was not until March 26, 1926—nine years after his initial proposal to the Smithsonian—that he was able to achieve the world's first known flight of a liquid-propulsion rocket at the farm of Effie Ward, a distant relative, in Auburn, Massachusetts. Goddard continued his rocket research in the desert of New Mexico after 1930 for greater isolation from human beings, who could reveal his secrets as well as be injured by his rockets. But when he finally turned from development of high-altitude rockets to wartime work in 1941, the highest altitude one of his rockets had reached (on March 26, 1937) was estimated at between 8,000 and 9,000 feet—still a long way from his stated goals.[5]

One reason he had not achieved the altitudes he originally sought was that he worked with a small number of technicians instead of cooperating with other qualified rocket engineers. He achieved significant individual innovations, but he never succeeded in designing and testing all of them together in a systematic way so that the entire rocket achieved the altitudes he sought. Trained as a scientist, Goddard failed to follow standard engineering practices.[6]

More important than this shortcoming was his unwillingness to publish technical details of his rocket development and testing. At the urging of sponsors, he did publish a second paper, titled "Liquid-Propellant Rocket Development," in 1936 in the *Smithsonian Miscellaneous Collections*. There, Goddard addressed, much more explicitly than in his longer and more theoretical paper of 1920, the case for liquid-propellant rockets, stating their advantages over powder rockets—specifically their higher energy. Although he did discuss some details of the rockets he had developed and even included many pictures, in general the rather low level of detail and the failure to discuss many of the problems he encountered at every step of his work made this paper, like the earlier one, of limited usefulness for others trying to develop rockets.[7]

FIG. 1.1
Robert H. Goddard and the first known liquid-propellant rocket ever to have been launched, Auburn, Massachusetts, March 16, 1926. (Photo courtesy of NASA)

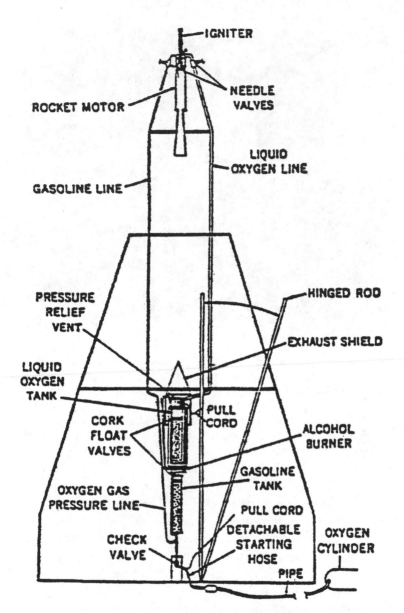

IGNITER

NEEDLE VALVES

ROCKET MOTOR

LIQUID OXYGEN LINE

GASOLINE LINE

PRESSURE RELIEF VENT

HINGED ROD

EXHAUST SHIELD

LIQUID OXYGEN TANK

CORK FLOAT VALVES

PULL CORD

ALCOHOL BURNER

GASOLINE TANK

OXYGEN GAS PRESSURE LINE

PULL CORD

CHECK VALVE

DETACHABLE STARTING HOSE

OXYGEN CYLINDER

PIPE

Dr. Goddard's 1926 Rocket

FIG. 1.2 Technical drawing of Goddard's 1926 liquid-propellant rocket. (Photo courtesy of NASA)

In 1948, Esther Goddard and G. Edward Pendray did publish his notes on rocket development. These contained many specifics missing from his earlier publications, but by that time the Germans under Wernher von Braun and his boss, Walter Dornberger, had developed the A-4 (V-2) missile, and a group at the Jet Propulsion Laboratory (JPL) in Pasadena, California, had also advanced well be-

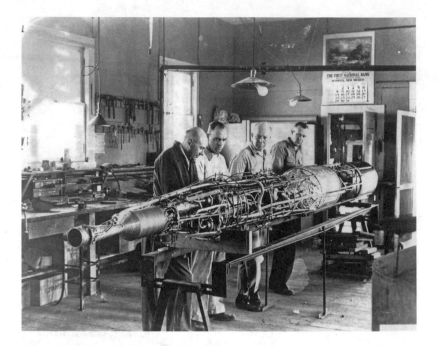

FIG. 1.3 Robert Goddard (*left*) with his principal technical assistants (*left to right:* Nils Ljungquist, machinist; Albert Kisk, brother-in-law and machinist; and Charles Mansur, welder) in 1940 at Goddard's shop in New Mexico. Shown is a rocket without its casing, with (*right to left*) the two propellant tanks and the extensive plumbing, including turbopumps to inject the propellants into the combustion chamber, where they ignite and create thrust by exhausting through the expansion nozzle (far *left*). (Photo courtesy of NASA)

yond Goddard in developing rockets and missiles. He patented and developed a remarkable number of key innovations, and the two papers he did publish in his lifetime significantly influenced others to pursue rocket development. But both the Germans under von Braun and Dornberger and the U.S. effort at JPL demonstrated in varying degrees that it took a much larger effort than Goddard's to achieve the ambitious goals he had set for himself.

Because of Goddard's comparative secrecy, Romanian-German rocket theoretician Hermann Oberth (1894–1989), oddly, may have contributed more to U.S. launch-vehicle technology than his American counterpart. Unlike Goddard, Oberth openly published the details of his more theoretical findings and contributed to their popularization in Germany. Because of these efforts, he was significantly responsible for the launching of a spaceflight movement that directly influenced the V-2 missile. Then, through the immigration of Wernher von Braun and his rocket team to the United States after World War II, Oberth contributed indirectly to U.S. missile and spaceflight development.

Born almost 12 years after Goddard on June 25, 1894, in the partly Saxon German town of Hermannstadt, Transylvania, Oberth attended a number of German universities but never earned a Ph.D. because none of his professors would accept his dissertation on rocketry. Undaunted by this rejection, Oberth nevertheless "refrained from writing another" dissertation on a more acceptable and conventional topic.[8]

He succeeded in publishing *Die Rakete zu den Planetenräumen* (The Rocket into Interplanetary Space) in 1923. Although Goddard always suspected that Oberth had borrowed heavily from his 1920 paper,[9] in fact Oberth's book bears little resemblance to Goddard's paper. Not only is *Die Rakete* much more filled with equations but it is also considerably longer than the paper—some 85 pages of smaller print than the 69 pages in Goddard's paper as reprinted by the American Rocket Society in 1946. Oberth devoted much more attention than Goddard to such matters as liquid propellants and multiple-stage rockets, whereas the American dealt mostly with solid propellants and atmospheric studies but did mention the efficiency of hydrogen and oxygen as propellants. Oberth also set forth the basic principles of spaceflight to a greater extent than Goddard had done in a work much more oriented to reporting on his experimental results than to theoretical elaboration. Oberth discussed such matters as liquid-propellant rocket construction for both alcohol and hydrogen as fuels; the use of staging to escape Earth's atmosphere; the use of pumps to inject propellants into the rocket's combustion chamber; employment of gyroscopes for control of the rocket's direction; chemical purification of the air in the rocket's cabin; space walks; microgravity experiments; the ideas of a lunar orbit, space stations, reconnaissance satellites; and many other topics.[10]

The book itself was influential. Besides writing it, Oberth collaborated with Max Valier, an Austrian who wrote for a popular audience, to produce less technical writings that inspired a great deal of interest in spaceflight.[11] According to several sources, Oberth's first book directly inspired Wernher von Braun (the later technical director of the German Army Ordnance facilities at Peenemünde where the V-2 was developed, subsequently director of NASA's Marshall Space Flight Center) to study mathematics and physics, so necessary for his later work. Von Braun had already been interested in rocketry but was a poor student, especially in math and physics, in which he had gotten failing grades. However, in 1925 he had seen an ad for Oberth's book and ordered a copy. Confronting its mathematics, he took it to his secondary school math teacher, who told him the only way he could understand Oberth was to study his two worst subjects. He did and ultimately earned a Ph.D. in physics.[12] Without Oberth's stimulation, who knows whether von Braun would have become a leader in the German and U.S. rocket programs?

Similarly, von Braun's boss at Peenemünde, Walter Dornberger, wrote to Oberth in 1964 that reading his book in 1929 had opened up a new world to him. And according to Konrad Dannenberg, who had worked at Peenemünde and come to the United States in 1945 with the rest of the von Braun team, many members of the group in Germany had become interested in space through Oberth's books. Also in response to Oberth's first book, in 1927 the German Society for Space Travel (*Verein für Raumschiffart*) was founded to raise money for him to perform rocket experiments. He served as president in 1929–30, and the organization provided considerable practical experience in rocketry to several of its members (including von Braun). Some of them later served under von Braun at Peenemünde, although they constituted a very small fraction of the huge staff there (some 6,000 by mid-1943).[13]

Both Goddard and Oberth exemplified the pronouncement of Goddard at his high school graduation speech "that the dream of yesterday is the hope of today and the reality of tomorrow."[14] But ironically it appears to have been Oberth who made the more important contribution to the realization of both men's dreams.[15] In any event, both men made extraordinary, pioneering contributions that were different but complementary.

Kummersdorf, Peenemünde, and the V-2

Because the German V-2 missile's technology became available to U.S. missile and rocket programs after the end of World War II, it helped stimulate further development of American rocket technology. The V-2 was by no means the only contributor to that technology. More or less purely American rocket efforts also occurred between the beginnings of the rocket development work by Germans working under von Braun and 1945 when some of those Germans and V-2s began to arrive in the United States. But in view of the importance of the V-2 to the development of American missiles and launch vehicles after World War II, this section considers the work of the Germans. A later section will trace the separate American efforts leading to U.S. ballistic missiles and, ultimately, launch vehicles.

Research leading to the V-2 began in 1932 when von Braun started working under Dornberger at the German army proving grounds in

Kummersdorf. The young man and his assistants experienced numerous failures, including burnthroughs of combustion chambers. They proceeded through test rockets labeled A-1, A-2, A-3, and A-5—the A standing for Aggregat (German for "assembly"). But as the size of their rockets (and the workforce) increased, they moved their operations to a much larger facility at Peenemünde on the German Baltic coast. There, they could launch their test rockets eastward along the Pomeranian coast.[16]

All of the test rockets contributed in various ways to the A-4, as did considerable collaboration with German universities, technical institutes, and industrial firms, showing that, as later in the United States, multiple organizations and skills were needed to develop missiles and rockets. Despite a truly massive amount of research-and-development work both at Peenemünde and at such associated entities, the A-4 still required a lot of modifications after its initial launch on October 3, 1942, with many failed launches after that. Even when actually used in the German war effort, the V-2 was neither accurate nor reliable. Nevertheless, at about 46 feet long, 5 feet 5 inches in diameter, an empty weight of 8,818 pounds, and a range of close to 200 miles, it was an impressive technological achievement whose development contributed much data and experience to later American missile and rocket development.[17]

Von Braun himself was a key factor in the relative success of the V-2. Born in the east German town of Wirsitz (later, Wyrzysk, Poland) to noble parents on March 23, 1912, Freiherr (Baron) Wernher Magnus Maximilian von Braun earned a prediploma (Vordiplom) in mechanical engineering at the Berlin–Charlottenburg Institute of Technology in 1932, followed by a Ph.D. in physics from the University of Berlin in 1934.[18] Both his boss, Walter Dornberger, and von Braun played the role of heterogeneous engineers, meeting with key figures in the government and Nazi Party, from successive Armaments Ministers Fritz Todt and Albert Speer, on up to Adolf Hitler himself, to maintain support for the missile.[19]

Von Braun also excelled as a technical manager after overcoming some initial lapses attributable to his youth and inexperience. He played a key role in integrating the various systems for the V-2 so that they worked effectively together. He did this by fostering communication between different departments as well as within individual elements of the Peenemünde organization. He met individually with engineers and perceptively led meetings of technical personnel to resolve particular issues. According to Dieter Huzel, who held a variety of positions at Peenemünde in the last two years of the war, von Braun "knew most problems at first hand. . . . He

15

German and U.S. Missiles and Rockets, 1926–66

repeatedly demonstrated his ability to go coherently and directly to the core of a problem or situation, and usually when he got there and it was clarified to all present, he had the solution already in mind—a solution that almost invariably received the wholehearted support of those present."[20] This described technical management of the first order and also a different kind of heterogeneous engineering from that discussed previously, the ability not only to envision a solution but to get it willingly accepted.

As another Peenemünder, Ernst Stuhlinger, and several colleagues wrote in 1962, "Predecessors and contemporaries of Dr. von Braun may have had a visionary genius equal or superior to his, but none of them had his gift of awakening in others such strong enthusiasm, faith and devotion, those indispensable ingredients of a successful project team." They added, "It is his innate capability, as a great engineer, to make the transition from an idea, a dream, a daring thought to a sound engineering plan and to carry this plan most forcefully through to its final accomplishment." Finally, Stuhlinger and Frederick Ordway, who knew von Braun in the United States, wrote in a memoir about him, "Regardless of what the subject was—combustion instability, pump failures, design problems, control theory, supersonic aerodynamics, gyroscopes, accelerometers, ballistic trajectories, thermal problems—von Braun was always fully knowledgeable of the basic subject and of the status of the work. He quickly grasped the problem and he formulated it so that everyone understood it clearly."[21] These qualities plus the hiring of a number of able managers of key departments contributed greatly to the development of the V-2.

GALCIT and JPL

Meanwhile, a much smaller American effort at rocket development began at the California Institute of Technology (Caltech) in 1936. A graduate student of aerodynamicist Theodore von Kármán, Frank J. Malina, together with Edward S. Forman and John W. Parsons—described respectively by Malina as "a skilled mechanic" and "a self-trained chemist" without formal schooling but with "an uninhibited fruitful imagination"—began to do research for Malina's doctoral dissertation on rocket propulsion and flight.[22] Gradually, the research of these three men expanded into a multifaceted, professional rocket development effort. As with the work under von Braun in Germany, there were many problems to be overcome. The difficulty of both endeavors lay partly in the lack of previous, detailed research-and-development reports. It also resulted from the many disciplines involved. In May 1945, Homer E. Newell, then a theoretical physicist and mathematician at the U.S. Naval Research Laboratory, wrote that the "design, construction, and operational use of guided missiles requires intimate knowledge of a vast number of subjects. Among these . . . are aerodynamics, kinematics, mechanics, elasticity, radio, electronics, jet propulsion, and the chemistry of fuels."[23] He could easily have added other topics such as thermodynamics, combustion processes, and materials science.

Malina and his associates consulted existing literature. Malina paid a visit to Goddard in 1936 in a fruitless attempt to gather unpublished information and cooperation from the secretive New Englander.[24] Initially as part of the Guggenheim Aeronautical Laboratory at Caltech (GALCIT), directed by von Kármán (and after 1943–44 as the Jet Propulsion Laboratory [JPL]), Malina and his staff used available data, mathematics, experimentation, innovations by other U.S. rocketeers, and imagination to develop solid- and liquid-propellant JATOs (jet-assisted takeoff devices), a Private A solid-propellant test rocket, and a WAC Corporal liquid-propellant sounding rocket before Malina left JPL in 1946 and went to Europe. He ultimately became an artist and a promoter of international cooperation in astronautics.[25] (Incidentally, in 1942 several of the people at GALCIT founded the Aerojet Engineering Corporation, later known as Aerojet General Corporation, to produce the rocket engines they developed. It became one of the major rocket firms in the country.)[26]

Under the successive leadership of Louis Dunn and William Pickering, JPL proceeded to oversee and participate in the development of the liquid-propellant Corporal and the solid-propellant Sergeant missiles for the U.S. Army. Their development encountered many problems, and they borrowed some engine-cooling technology from the V-2 to solve one problem with the Corporal, illustrating one case where the V-2 influenced U.S. missile development. The Corporal became operational in 1954 and deployed to Europe beginning in 1955. Although never as accurate as the army had hoped, it was far superior in this respect to the V-2. At 45.4 feet long, the Corporal was less than a foot shorter than the V-2, but its diameter (2.5 feet) was slightly less than half that of the German missile. However, even with a slightly higher performance than the V-2, its range (99 statute miles) was only about half that of the earlier missile, making it a short-lived and not very effective weapon.[27]

In 1953, JPL began working on a solid-propellant replacement for the Corporal, known as the Sergeant. In February 1956, a Sergeant contractor-selection committee unanimously chose the Sperry Gyroscope Company (a division of Sperry Rand Corp.) as a co-contractor for the development and ultimate manufacture of the missile. Meanwhile, on April 1, 1954, the Redstone Arsenal, which controlled development of the missile for the army, had entered into a supplemental agreement with the Redstone Division of Thiokol Chemical Corporation to work on the Sergeant's solid-propellant motor. The program to develop Sergeant began officially in January 1955.[28]

The Sergeant missile took longer to develop than originally planned and did not become operational until 1962, by which time the U.S. Navy had completed the much more capable and important Polaris A1 and the U.S. Air Force was close to fielding the significant and successful Minuteman I. The technology of the Sergeant paled by comparison. JPL director Louis Dunn had warned in 1954 that if the army did not provide for an orderly research and development program for the Sergeant, "ill-chosen designs . . . [would] plague the system for many years." In the event, the army did fail to provide consistent funding and then insisted on a compressed schedule. This problem was complicated by differences between JPL and Sperry and by JPL's becoming a NASA instead of an army contractor in December 1958. The result was a missile that failed to meet its in-flight reliability of 95 percent. It met a slipped ordnance support readiness date of June 1962 but remained a limited-production weapons system until June 1968. However, it was equal to its predecessor, Corporal, in range and firepower while being only half as large and requiring less than a third as much ground support equipment. Its solid-propellant motor could be ready for firing in a matter of minutes instead of the hours required for the liquid-propellant Corporal. An all-inertial guidance system on Sergeant made it virtually immune to enemy countermeasures, whereas Corporal depended on a vulnerable electronic link to guidance equipment on the ground.[29]

Thus, Sergeant was far from a total failure. In fact, although not at the forefront of solid-propellant technology by the time of its completion, the army missile made some contributions to the development of launch-vehicle technology—primarily through a smaller, test version of the rocket. JPL had scaled down Sergeant motors from 31 to 6 inches in diameter for performing tests on various solid propellants and their designs. By 1958, the Lab had performed static tests on more than 300 of the scaled-down motors and had flight-tested 50 of them—all without failures. Performance had accorded well with predictions. These reliable motors became the basis for upper stages in reentry test vehicles for the Jupiter missile (called Jupiter C) and in the launch vehicles for Explorer and Pioneer satellites, which used modified Redstone and Jupiter C missiles as first stages.[30]

Because von Braun's group of engineers developed the Redstone and Jupiter C, this was an instance where purely American and German-American technology blended. It is instructive to compare management at JPL with that in von Braun's operation in Germany. At JPL, the dynamic von Kármán served as director of the project until the end of 1944, when he left to establish the Scientific Advisory Board for the U.S. Army Air Forces. Malina held the title of chief engineer of the project until he succeeded von Kármán as (acting) director. But according to Martin Summerfield, head of a liquid-propellant section, there was no counterpart at GALCIT/JPL to von Braun at Peenemünde. Instead, Summerfield said, the way the professionals in the project integrated the various components of the rockets and the various developments in fields as disparate as aerodynamics and metallurgy was simply by discussing them as colleagues. He seemed to suggest that much of this was done informally, but like Peenemünde, JPL also had many formal meetings where such issues were discussed. In addition, a research analysis section did a good deal of what later was called systems engineering for JPL.[31]

Dunn succeeded Malina as acting director of JPL on May 20, 1946, becoming the director (no longer acting) on January 1, 1947. Whereas Malina operated in an informal and relaxed way, Dunn brought more structure and discipline to JPL than had prevailed previously. He was also cautious, hence concerned about the growth of the Lab during his tenure. From 385 employees in June 1946, the number grew to 785 in 1950 and 1,061 in 1953, causing Dunn to create division heads above the section heads who had reported to him directly. There were four such division heads by September 1950, with William Pickering heading one on guided-missile electronics.

In August 1954, Dunn resigned from JPL to take a leading role in developing the Atlas missile for the recently established Ramo-Wooldridge Corporation. At Dunn's suggestion, Caltech appointed Pickering as his successor. A New Zealander by birth, Pickering continued the tradition of having foreign-born directors at JPL (von Kármán coming from Hungary and Malina, Czechoslovakia). Easier to know than the formal Dunn, Pickering was also less stringent as a manager. Whereas Dunn had favored a project form of organization, Pickering returned to one organized by disciplines. He remained as director until 1976. Howard Seifert, who had come to GALCIT in 1942 and worked with Summerfield on liquid-propellant developments, characterized the three JPL directors in terms of an incident when some mechanics cut off the relaxed Malina's necktie because *he* was too formal. Seifert said they would never have cut Dunn's necktie off without losing their jobs, and they would not have cut Pickering's necktie either, but he would not have fired them for that offense alone. He added that Dunn had a rigid quality but undoubtedly was extremely capable.[32]

Despite all the changes in personnel and management from Malina and von Kármán, through Dunn to Pickering, and despite the differences in personalities and values, one constant seems to have been a not-very-structured organization, not well suited for dealing with outside industry and the design and fielding of a weapon system, as distinguished from a research vehicle. Even Dunn's project organization seems not to have been compatible with the kind of systems engineering soon common in missile development.[33]

It may be, however, that JPL's rather loose organization in this period was conducive to innovations that it achieved in both liquid- and solid-propellant rocketry (to be discussed in ensuing chapters). In addition to the direct influence they had upon rocketry, many people from JPL besides Louis Dunn later served in positions of importance on other missile and rocket projects, carrying with them, no doubt, much that they had learned in their work at JPL, as well as their talents. Thus, in a variety of ways—some of them incalculable—the early work at JPL contributed to U.S. rocketry, even though the Lab itself got out of the rocket propulsion business in the late 1950s.[34]

The American Rocket Society, Reaction Motors, and the U.S. Navy

While JPL's rocket development proceeded, there were several other efforts in the field of rocketry that contributed to the development of U.S. missile and launch-vehicle technology. Some of them started earlier than Malina's project, notably those associated with what became (in 1934) the American Rocket Society. This organization, first called the American Interplanetary Society, had its birth on April 4, 1930. Characteristically, although Goddard became a member of the society, founding member Edward Pendray wrote, "Members of the Society could learn almost nothing about the technical details of his work." Soon, society members were testing their own rockets with the usual share of failures and partial successes. But their work "finally culminated in . . . a practical liquid-cooled regenerative motor designed by James H. Wyld." This became the first American engine to apply regenerative cooling (described by Oberth) to the entire combustion chamber. Built in 1938, it was among three engines tested at New Rochelle, New York, December 10, 1938. It burned steadily for 13.5 seconds and achieved an exhaust velocity of 6,870 feet per second. This engine led directly to the founding of America's first rocket company, Reaction Motors, Inc., by Wyld and three other men who had been active in the society's experiments. Also, it was from Wyld that Frank Malina learned about regenerative cooling for the engines developed at what became JPL, one example of shared information contributing to rocket development.[35]

Reaction Motors incorporated as a company on December 16, 1941. It had some successes, including engines for tactical missiles; the X-1 and D-558-2 rocket research aircraft; and an early throttleable engine for the X-15 rocket research airplane that flew to the edge of space and achieved a record speed of 6.7 times the speed of sound (Mach 6.7). Reaction Motors had never been able to develop many rockets with large production runs nor engines beyond the size of the X-15 powerplant. On April 30, 1958, Thiokol, which had become a major producer of solid-propellant rocket motors, merged with Reaction Motors, which then became the Reaction Motors Division of the Thiokol Chemical Corporation. In 1970, Thiokol decided to discontinue working in the liquid-propellant field; and in June 1972, Reaction Motors ceased to exist.[36]

Despite its ultimate failure as a business, the organization had shown considerable innovation and made lasting contributions to U.S. rocketry besides Wyld's regenerative cooling. A second important legacy was the so-called spaghetti construction for combustion chambers, invented by Edward A. Neu Jr. Neu applied for a patent on the concept in 1950 (granted in 1965) but had developed the design earlier. It involved preforming cooling tubes so that they became the shells for the combustion chamber when joined together, creating a strong yet light chamber. The materials used for the tubes and the methods of connecting them varied, but the firm used the basic technique on many of its engines on up through the XLR99 for the X-15. By the mid-1950s, other firms picked up on the technique or developed it independently. Rocketdyne used it on the Jupiter and Atlas engines, Aerojet on the Titan engines. Later, Rocketdyne used it on all of the combustion chambers for the Saturn series, and today's space shuttle main engines still use the concept.[37]

Another important early contribution to later missile and launch-vehicle technology came from a group formed by naval officer Robert C. Truax. He had already begun developing rockets as an ensign at the Naval Academy. After service aboard ship, he reported to the navy's Bureau of Aeronautics from April to August 1941 at "the first jet propulsion desk in the Ship Installation Division." There, he was responsible for looking into jet-assisted takeoff for seaplanes. He then returned to Annapolis, where he headed a jet propulsion project at the Naval Engineering Experiment Station (where Robert Goddard was working separately on JATO units nearby). Truax's group worked closely with Reaction Motors and Aerojet on projects ranging from JATOs to tactical missiles. Among the officers who worked under Truax was Ensign Ray C. Stiff, who discovered that aniline and other chemicals ignited spontaneously with nitric acid. This information, shared with Frank Malina, became critical to JPL's efforts to develop a liquid-propellant JATO unit. In another example of the ways technology transferred from one organization or firm to another in rocket development, once Stiff completed his five years of service with the navy, he joined Aerojet as a civilian engineer. He rose to become vice president and general manager of Aerojet's liquid rocket division (1963) and then (1972) president of the Aerojet Energy Conversion Company. In 1969 he became a Fellow of the American Institute of Aeronautics and Astronautics (into which the American Rocket Society had merged) for "his notable contributions in the design, development and production of liquid rocket propulsion systems, including the engines for Titan I, II, and III." [38]

The U.S. Army and Project Hermes

Meanwhile, at the end of World War II, U.S. Army Ordnance became especially interested in learning more about missile technology from the German engineers under von Braun; from their technical documents; and from firing actual V-2 missiles in the United States. According to von Kármán, the army air forces (AAF) had a chance to get involved in long-range missile development before Army Ordnance stepped into the breach. In 1943, Col. W. H. Joiner, liaison officer for the AAF Materiel Command at Caltech, suggested a report on the possibilities for long-range missiles. Frank Malina and his Chinese colleague Hsue-shen Tsien prepared the report, stating that a 10,000-pound liquid-propellant rocket could carry a projectile 75 miles. Issued November 20, 1943, this was the first report to bear the rubric JPL, according to von Kármán. But the AAF did not follow up on the opportunity. Army Ordnance then contracted with JPL to conduct research resulting in the Corporal missile; it also initiated Project Hermes on November 15, 1944.

Under contract to the army for this effort, the General Electric Company (GE) agreed to perform research and development on guided missiles. The Ordnance Department sought to provide the company's engineers with captured V-2s for study and test firing. Through Project Overcast, which became Project Paperclip in 1946, von Braun and a handful of his associates flew to the United States on September 18, 1945. Three groups (about 118) who had worked at Peenemünde arrived in the United States by ship between November 1945 and February 1946, ending up at Fort Bliss in Texas, across the state border from White Sands Proving Ground in New Mexico, where the V-2s would be launched once they were assembled from parts captured in Germany.[39]

Using U.S.-manufactured parts when German ones were damaged or not available in sufficient quantity, between April 16, 1946, and September 19, 1952, GE and the army launched 73 V-2s at White Sands. The last GE flight was on June 28, 1951, with the ensuing five flights conducted by the army alone. Depending upon the criteria of failure, some 52 to 68 percent of the flights conducted under GE auspices succeeded, but many of the failures still yielded useful information. Many of the V-2 flights carried scientific experiments, with the areas of experimentation ranging from atmospheric physics to cosmic radiation measurements. The explorations helped spawn the field of space science that blossomed further after the birth of NASA in 1958.[40]

One of the major contributions to launch-vehicle technology by Project Hermes came from the Bumper-WAC project. This combined the V-2s with JPL's WAC Corporal B rockets in a two-stage configuration. The flights sought to provide flight tests of vehicle separation at high speeds, to achieve speeds and altitudes higher than could then otherwise be obtained, and to investigate such phenomena as aerodynamic heating at high speeds within the atmosphere. Since a number of groups were already looking into launching satellites, these matters were of some near-term importance because more than one rocket stage was commonly required to put a satellite in orbit.[41]

On the fifth Bumper-WAC launch from White Sands (February 24, 1949), the second stage reached a reported altitude of 244 miles and a maximum speed of 7,553 feet per second. These constituted the greatest altitude and the highest speed reached by a rocket or missile until that date. The highly successful launch demonstrated the validity of the theory that a rocket's velocity could be increased with a second stage. Also shown was a method of igniting a rocket engine at high altitude, offering a foundation for later two- and multiple-

FIG. 1.4 Launch of a Bumper-WAC with a V-2 first stage, July 24, 1950, at Cape Canaveral, showing the rather primitive launch facilities, although they were much more sophisticated than the ones Robert Goddard had used in the 1930s in New Mexico. (Photo courtesy of NASA)

stage vehicles. The final two launches of the Bumper program occurred at the newly activated Joint Long Range Proving Grounds in Florida, which later became Cape Canaveral Air Force Station and had previously been the site of the Banana River Naval Air Station until taken over by the air force on September 1, 1948.[42]

While preparations were being made for the Bumper-WAC project, six GE engineers assisted in launching a V-2 from the fantail of the aircraft carrier USS *Midway* on September 6, 1947. The missile headed off at an angle from the vertical of 45 degrees even though the ship had almost no pitch or roll. After the missile nearly hit the bridge and then straightened out momentarily, it began tumbling. This test, called Operation Sandy, could hardly have been encouraging for those in the Bureau of Aeronautics who wanted the navy to develop ballistic missiles for shipboard use. Even less so were the results of two other V-2s, loaded with propellants, that were knocked over on purpose aboard the *Midway* in part of what was called Operation Pushover. They detonated, as expected. Finally, on December 3, 1948, a V-2 with propellants burning was also toppled at White Sands on a mocked-up ship deck. This produced a huge blast during which structural supports cracked. There was a rupture in the deck itself, whereupon alcohol and liquid oxygen ran through the hole and ignited. These tests contributed significantly to the navy's negative attitude toward the use of liquid propellants aboard ship in what became the Polaris program.[43]

With two exceptions (discussed later), the tactical Hermes missiles GE developed appear not to have had a large influence on launch-vehicle technology. They began as weapons projects but became simply test vehicles in October 1953 and were canceled by 1954. Nevertheless, according to a GE publication written in 1965, the engineers who worked on Project Hermes "formed a unique nucleus of talent that was fully realized when they took over many top management slots in General Electric missile and space efforts in later years." GE also later supplied the first-stage engine for the Vanguard launch vehicle and the second stage for the short-lived Atlas-Vega vehicle, among others. Finally, once Project Hermes ended in 1954–55, the people who worked on it shifted their focus to a ballistic reentry vehicle for the air force.[44]

Even apart from GE's direct role in launch-vehicle technology, clearly there was a technical legacy of considerable importance from Project Hermes, including the firing of the V-2s. But opinions have been mixed about the significance of this legacy.[45] One emphatic proponent of its importance, Julius H. Braun, had worked on the project while serving in the army. He spoke of "a massive technology transfer to the U.S. rocket and missile community" from the V-2. "There was a steady flow of visitors from industry, government labs, universities and other services," he added. Referring to the Germans under von Braun's leadership, he observed, "Propulsion experts from the team traveled to North American Aviation [NAA] in Southern California to assist in formulating a program to design, build and test large liquid propellant rocket engines. This program led to the formation of the NAA Rocketdyne division." Braun opined that "the rapid exploitation and wide dissemination of captured information" from the Germans "saved the U.S. at least ten years during the severe R&D [research and development] cutbacks of the postwar period." He listed a great many U.S. missiles and rockets that "incorporated components . . . derived from the V-2 and its HERMES follow-on programs."[46]

As the quotations from Braun suggest, the V-2 technology was a starting point for many efforts by both the Germans and U.S. engineers to develop more advanced technology for the rockets and missiles that followed. But the Americans did not simply copy V-2 technology; they went beyond it. Even in assembling the V-2s for firing in this country, GE engineers and others had to develop modifications to German technology in making replacement parts. Firms that contracted to make the parts undoubtedly learned from the effort.

Although many visitors surely picked up a great deal of useful information from the Germans, as did the GE engineers themselves, JPL propellant chemist Martin Summerfield, who questioned von Braun and others about the rocket engine for the V-2 on April 19, 1946, evidently learned little from the interchange. Summerfield had already learned from his own research at JPL the kinds of technical lessons that the Germans imparted. Others from JPL had a good chance to look over the V-2s while testing the Corporal and firing the Bumper-WAC. According to Clayton Koppes, "They concluded there was relatively little they wanted to apply to their projects."[47] Of course, even the Corporal did borrow some technology from the V-2, but JPL had developed much else independently.

Other visitors to the German engineers had less experience with rocketry and probably benefited greatly from talking with them, as Braun said. Projects like the Bumper-WAC added to the fund of engineering data. However, as Braun had mentioned, funding for rocket-and-missile development was limited in the immediate post–World War II United States. Firing the V-2s had cost about $1 million per year through 1951, but until the United States became alarmed about a threat from the Soviet Union's missiles and warheads, there would not be a truly major U.S. effort to go much beyond the technologies already developed.[48]

The Redstone Missile

One Hermes test missile that did lead to a follow-on effort was the C1. General Electric envisioned it as a three-stage vehicle. However, the company did not continue immediately with its original conception in 1946 because at that time it had insufficient data to design such a missile. In October 1950, Army Ordnance directed the firm to proceed with a feasibility study of Hermes C1 in conjunction with the Germans under von Braun. Meanwhile, in April 1948 Col. Holger Toftoy, heading the Rocket Branch in the Army Ordnance Department, recommended establishment of a rocket laboratory. The result was the reactivation of the World War II Redstone Arsenal in Huntsville, Alabama, announced by the chief of ordnance on November 18, 1948.[49] This became the site for most of the development of the C1 missile as well as the reason for renaming it Redstone.

On October 28, 1949, the secretary of the army approved a move of the guided missile group—formerly known as the Ordnance Research and Development Division Sub-Office (Rocket)—from Fort Bliss, Texas, to Redstone Arsenal. It became the Ordnance Guided Missile Center. The army officially established the center on April 15, 1950. It took about six months for the people and equipment to be transferred. Those who moved included the German rocket group and some 800 other people, among them civil servants, GE employees, and about 500 military personnel.[50]

Despite the outbreak of the Korean War in June 1950, the C1/Redstone missile initially lacked significant funding. On July 10, 1950, Army Ordnance had told the center to study the possibility of developing a tactical missile with a 500-mile range and an accuracy that would place half of the warheads in a circle of 1,000 yards in radius (circular error probable, or CEP). Von Braun served as project engineer and put together a preliminary study, which he presented to the Department of Defense's Research and Development Board in the fall of 1950. Army Ordnance did not send the center the missile's initial funding in the amount of $2.5 million until May 1, 1951. Once development began in May, it continued for seven and a half years until the flight test of the last research-and-development vehicle. Proposed military characteristics for the missile changed over time. Using a modified North American Aviation (NAA) engine originally designed for the U.S. Air Force's Navaho missile (canceled in 1958), the Redstone incorporated much American as well as German rocket technology. With other American companies besides North American working on the missile, it became substantially different vehicle from the V-2.[51]

Following the usual high number of failures for early rockets during flight testing, the army deployed the 69-foot, 4-inch Redstone on June 18, 1958, and deactivated it in June 1964, when the faster and more mobile Pershing, also developed at Redstone Arsenal, replaced it. Costing more per missile than the Corporal and Sergeant, the Redstone also had much higher performance in terms of range, thrust, and payload than its older cousins among army missiles (see table 1.1).[52]

More than just a missile, however, the Redstone also became the basis for the first stage of the first U.S. true launch vehicle. Known as the Jupiter C because of its use in testing Jupiter-missile components, the variant of the elongated Redstone used in this launch vehicle incorporated larger fuel and oxidizer tanks and a change from alcohol to hydyne (unsymmetrical dimethylhydrazine and diethylene triamine) as the fuel to increase performance. For the upper stages, a combined Redstone Arsenal–JPL team employed six-inch-diameter scale models of the Sergeant missile already used as upper

TABLE 1.1. *Comparison of Corporal, Sergeant, and Redstone Missiles*

	Corporal	Sergeant	Redstone
Length	45.4 feet	34.5 feet	69.3 feet
Thrust	20,000 pounds	50,000 pounds	78,000 pounds
Range	99 miles	75–100 miles	175 miles
Payload	1,500 pounds	1,500 pounds	6,305 pounds
Nos. produced	1,101	475	120
Cost/missile	$0.293 million	$1.008 million	$4.266 million

stages in the Jupiter C tests. With three scaled-down-Sergeant upper stages, the Jupiter C became the Juno I launch vehicle. On January 31, 1958, it lifted off from Cape Canaveral and placed the first U.S. satellite, the *Explorer I*, into orbit. Subsequently, somewhat modified Juno Is placed *Explorer III* and *Explorer IV* in orbit, with three other Explorer launches failing for various reasons.[53]

Explorer I was the United States' rejoinder to the shocking launch by the Soviet Union on October 4, 1957, of *Sputnik I*, the world's first artificial satellite. Soon after *Sputnik*, the United States entered a competition with the Soviets to place a human being in orbit as part of an emerging space race between the two superpowers. Known as Project Mercury, the U.S. effort planned to use the air force's Atlas missiles as launch vehicles for the orbiting capsules containing astronauts, but testing of the capsules in suborbital flight employed modified Redstones as launchers. For these early launches, the Redstone was the only trustworthy booster in the American inventory. The military was still testing the Atlas as well as the Thor and Jupiter missiles. However, it required extensive modifications—some 800 in all—to make the Redstone safe for an astronaut in the Mercury capsule. Called the Mercury-Redstone, this version of the missile boosted Astronaut Alan Shepard into a successful suborbital flight on May 5, 1961, followed by Virgil I. Grissom on July 21 of the same year, concluding the involvement of Redstone in Project Mercury and its role as a launch vehicle.[54]

Viking and Vanguard

In the meantime, two other rocket programs had contributed to launch-vehicle technology. The Viking sounding rocket made its own contributions and was also, in a sense, the starting point for the second U.S. launch vehicle, Vanguard. Although often regarded

FIG. 1.5 A Juno I launch vehicle with the *Explorer I* satellite launched on January 31, 1958, almost four months after the Soviet launch of *Sputnik*. The Juno I was a modified liquid-propellant Jupiter C developed by the Army Ballistic Missile Agency plus second, third, and fourth stages that featured solid-propellant motors developed by the Jet Propulsion Laboratory. (Photo courtesy of NASA)

as a failure, Vanguard did launch three satellites. Together with Viking, it pioneered use of gimbals for steering in large rockets. In addition, its upper stages contributed significantly to the evolution of launch-vehicle technology.[55]

Milton W. Rosen, who was responsible for the development and firing of the Viking rockets, went on to become technical director of Project Vanguard and then director of launch vehicles and propulsion in the Office of Manned Space Flight Programs for NASA. Rosen had been working at the Naval Research Laboratory (NRL) during World War II and suggested that his group implement an idea of G. Edward Pendray of the American Rocket Society to use rockets for exploration of the upper atmosphere. To prepare himself, he spent about eight months working at JPL in 1946–47. Drawing on what he learned there, some conversations with Wernher von Braun, and other sources, Rosen oversaw the design and testing of a totally new rocket, the Viking,[56] another example of information sharing that contributed to rocket development.

Reaction Motors designed the engine, drawing on its own experience as well as data from the V-2, with the Glenn L. Martin Company designing and building the overall rocket. Martin engineers conceived Viking's innovative gimballing engine. But to make it work, the Martin staff had to develop careful adjustments, using the advice of Albert C. Hall, who wrote his Ph.D. thesis at MIT on negative feedback. A successful program with 12 launches, Viking prepared Rosen and the Martin engineers for Vanguard.[57]

Developed under the auspices of the NRL to launch a satellite for the United States during the International Geophysical Year (July 1, 1957, to December 31, 1958), Vanguard became a NASA responsibility near the end of the project (on November 30, 1958). NRL appointed astronomer John Hagen as overall director, with Rosen becoming technical director. The navy contracted with Martin on September 23, 1955, to design, build, and test Vanguard in preparation for flight. Martin, in turn, contracted with GE on October 1, 1955, to develop the first-stage engine and with Aerojet on November 14, 1955, for the second-stage engine. There were two contracts for alternative versions of a stage-three solid-propellant motor. One in February 1956 went to the Grand Central Rocket Company, with a second going to the Allegany Ballistics Laboratory (ABL), operated by the Hercules Powder Company, Inc., in West Virginia.[58]

Hampered by a low priority, which caused Martin to split up the experienced Viking team between it and the higher-priority Titan I missile (for which Martin had also contracted), Rosen and his Vanguard engineers had other difficulties, including substantially new technology for all three stages. Contributions from a wide variety of organizations were necessary to develop the three stages. Problems with the first- and second-stage engines caused delays in development and testing; *Sputnik* and the cold-war desire to catch up with the Soviets led to unexpected publicity for the first test launch, in which both the problematical second stage and the complete guidance/control system were operational. Although three previous tests had been successful, this attempted launch with a small satellite onboard was a spectacular failure. The press did not react charitably but called the vehicle "Kaputnik, Stayputnik, or Flopnik" while Americans, in one historian's words, "swilled the Sputnik Cocktail: two parts vodka, one part sour grapes."[59]

Between March 17, 1958, and September 18, 1959, Vanguard launch vehicles orbited three satellites in nine attempts, the last of which used the solid third stage developed at ABL. This hardly constituted a successful record, but Vanguard nevertheless made important technological contributions. The air force's Thor-Able launch vehicle used the Thor intermediate-range ballistic missile as a first stage plus modified Vanguard second and third stages, the last

FIG. 1.6
Launch of
final Vanguard
rocket, Septem-
ber 18, 1959,
from Cape
Canaveral.
(Photo courtesy
of NASA)

being the original third stage developed by Grand Central Rocket
Company. The air force also learned from the problems Vanguard
had experienced and thereby avoided them, illustrating a transfer
of information from a navy project to a competing military service.
Despite interservice rivalries, the federal government encouraged
this sort of transfer, limiting the rights of individual contractors to
protect discoveries made under federal contract in order to facilitate
technology transfer. But the emphasis in the literature on competition rather than cooperation often masks the importance of transferred data.

In January 1959, Rosen proposed to Abe Silverstein, NASA's director of Space Flight Programs, that the Thor-Able be evolved into
what became the Delta launch vehicle. Rosen suggested designing

more reliable control electronics than used on Vanguard, substitution of a stainless-steel combustion chamber for the aluminum one used in the second stage of Vanguard, and incorporation of Bell Telephone Laboratories' radio guidance system then being installed in the Titan ballistic missile, among other changes. Silverstein commissioned Rosen to develop the Delta launch vehicle along those lines, and it became highly successful. A variant of the ABL third stage for Vanguard, known as the Altair I (X248 A5), became a third stage for Delta and a fourth stage for the Scout launch vehicle. A follow-on, also built by Hercules Powder Company (at ABL), became the third stage for Minuteman I. And a fiberglass casing for the ABL third stage was also a feature in these later stages and found many other uses in missiles and rockets. In these and other ways, Vanguard made important contributions to launch-vehicle technology and deserves a better reputation than it has heretofore enjoyed.[60]

The Atlas, Thor, and Jupiter Missiles

Following Redstone and Vanguard, the Atlas, Thor, and Jupiter missiles brought further innovations in rocket technology and became the first stages of launch vehicles themselves, with Atlas and Thor having more significance in this role than Jupiter. All three programs illustrated the roles of interservice and interagency rivalry and cooperation that were both key features of rocket development in the United States. They also showed the continued use of both theory and empiricism in the complex engineering of rocket systems. "It was not one important 'breakthrough' that enabled this advance; rather, it was a thousand different refinements, a hundred thousand tests and design modifications, all aimed at the development of equipment of extraordinary power and reliability," according to Milton Rosen, writing in 1962.[61]

Atlas was a much larger effort than Vanguard, and it began to create the infrastructure in talent, knowledge, data, and capability necessary for the maturation of launch-vehicle technology in the decade of the 1960s. However, until the air force became serious about Atlas, that service had lagged behind the army and the navy in the development of purely ballistic missiles.[62]

The process began in a significant way on January 23, 1951, when the air force awarded the Consolidated Vultee Aircraft Corporation (Convair) a contract for MX-1593, the project that soon became Atlas. (MX-1593 had been preceded by MX-774B and a number of other air force missile contracts in the late 1940s, with a total of $34 million devoted to missile research in fiscal year 1946, much reduced in subsequent years.) But the specifications for the MX-1593 missile changed drastically as technology for nuclear warheads evolved to fit more explosive power into smaller packages. This new technology plus the increased threat from the Soviets provided one condition for greater air force support of Atlas and other ballistic missiles.

But it also took two heterogeneous engineers to nudge the newest armed service and the Department of Defense (DoD) in a new direction. One of them was Trevor Gardner, assistant for research and development to Secretary of the Air Force Harold Talbott in the Eisenhower administration. The other key promoter of ballistic missiles was the "brilliant and affable" polymath, John von Neumann, who was research professor of mathematics at Princeton's Institute for Advanced Study and also director of its electronic computer project. In 1953, he headed a Nuclear Weapons Panel of the Air Force Scientific Advisory Board, which confirmed beliefs that in the next six to eight years, the United States would have the capability to field a thermonuclear warhead weighing about 1,500 pounds and yielding 1 megaton of explosive force. This was 50 times the yield of the atomic warhead originally planned for the Atlas missile, fit in a much lighter package. This and a report (dated February 1, 1954) for von Neumann's Teapot Committee set the stage for extraordinary air force support for Atlas.[63]

In May 1954 the air force directed that the Atlas program begin an accelerated development schedule, using the service's highest priority. The Air Research and Development Command within the air arm created a new organization in Inglewood, California, named the Western Development Division (WDD), and placed Brig. Gen. Bernard A. Schriever in charge. Schriever, who was born in Germany but moved to Texas when his father became a prisoner of war there during World War I, graduated from the Agricultural and Mechanical College of Texas (since 1964, Texas A&M University) in 1931 with a degree in architectural engineering. Tall, slender, and handsome, the determined young man accepted a reserve commission in the army and completed pilot training, eventually marrying the daughter of Brig. Gen. George Brett of the army air corps in 1938. Placed in charge of the WDD, Schriever in essence took over from Gardner and von Neumann the role of heterogeneous engineer, promoting and developing the Atlas and later missiles.[64]

Gardner had been intense and abrasive in pushing the development of missiles. Schriever was generally calm and persuasive. He selected highly competent people for his staff, many of them becoming general officers. An extremely hard worker, like von Braun he demanded much of his staff; but unlike von Braun he seemed somewhat aloof to most of them and inconsiderate of their time—frequently late for meetings without even realizing it. Good at planning and organizing, gifted with vision, he was poor at management, often overlooking matters that needed his attention—not surprising because he spent much time flying back and forth to Washington, D.C. His secretary and program managers had to watch carefully over key documents to ensure that he saw and responded to them. One of his early staff members (later a lieutenant general), Otto J. Glasser, said Schriever was "probably the keenest planner of anybody I ever met" but he was "one of the lousiest managers."

Later Lt. Gen. Charles H. Terhune Jr., who became Schriever's deputy director for technical operations, called his boss a "superb front man" for the organization, "very convincing. . . . He had a lot of people working for him [who] were very good and did their jobs, but Schriever was the one who pulled it all together and represented them in Congress and other places." Glasser added, "He was just superb at . . . laying out the wisdom of his approach so that the Congress *wanted* to ladle out money to him." Glasser also said he was good at building camaraderie among his staff.[65]

To facilitate missile development, Schriever received from the air force unusual prerogatives, such as the Gillette Procedures. Designed by Hyde Gillette, a budgetary expert in the office of the secretary of the air force, these served to simplify procedures for managing intercontinental ballistic missiles (ICBMs). Schriever had complained that there were 40 different offices and agencies he had to deal with to get his job done. Approval of his annual development plans took months to sail through all of these bodies. With the new procedures (granted November 8, 1955), Schriever had to deal with only two ballistic missile committees, one at the secretary-of-defense and the other at the air-force level. Coupled with other arrangements, this gave Schriever unprecedented authority to develop missiles.[66]

Another key element in the management of the ballistic missile effort was the Ramo-Wooldridge Corporation. Simon Ramo and Dean Wooldridge, classmates at Caltech, each had earned a Ph.D. there at age 23. After World War II, they had presided over an electronics team that built fire-control systems for the air force at Hughes Aircraft. In 1953, they set up their own corporation, with the Thompson Products firm buying 49 percent of the stock. For a variety of reasons, including recommendations of the Teapot Committee, Schriever made Ramo-Wooldridge into a systems engineering–technical direction contractor to advise his staff on the management of the Atlas program. The air force issued a contract to the firm for this task on January 29, 1955, although it had begun working in May 1954 under letter contract on a study of how to redirect the Atlas program. This unique arrangement with Ramo-Wooldridge caused considerable concern in the industry (especially on the part of Convair) that Ramo-Wooldridge employees would be in an unfair position to use the knowledge they gained to bid on other contracts, although the firm was not supposed to produce hardware for missiles. To ward off such criticism, the firm created a Guided Missile Research Division (GMRD) and kept it separate from other divisions of the firm. Louis Dunn, who had served on the Teapot Committee, became the GMRD director, bringing several people with him from JPL. This arrangement did not put an end to controversy about Ramo-Wooldridge's role, so in 1957, GMRD became Space Technology Laboratories (STL), an autonomous division of the firm, with Ramo as president and Dunn as executive vice president and general manager.[67]

Some air force officers on Schriever's staff objected to the contract with Ramo-Wooldridge, notably Col. Edward Hall, a propulsion expert. Hall had nothing good to say about Ramo-Wooldridge (or Schriever), but several engineers at Convair concluded that the firm made a positive contribution to Atlas development.[68]

The Ramo-Wooldridge staff outnumbered the air force staff at WDD, but the two groups worked together in selecting contractors for components of Atlas and later missiles, overseeing their performance, testing, and analyzing results. For such a large undertaking as Atlas, soon joined by other programs, there needed to be some system to inform managers and allow them to make decisions on problem areas. The WDD, which became the Air Force Ballistic Missile Division on June 1, 1957, developed a management control system to collect information for planning and scheduling.

Schriever and his program directors gathered all of this data in a program control room, located in a concrete vault and kept under guard at all times. At first, hundreds of charts and graphs covered the walls, but WDD soon added digital computers for tracking information. Although some staff members claimed Schriever used the control room only to impress important visitors, program managers benefited from preparing weekly and monthly reports of status, because they had to verify their accuracy and thereby keep abreast of events. Separate reports from a procurement office the Air Force Air Materiel Command assigned to the WDD on August 15, 1954, provided Schriever an independent check on information from his own managers. The thousands of milestones—Schriever called them inchstones—in the master schedule kept him and his key managers advised of how development matched planning. All of the information came together on "Black Saturday" meetings once a month starting in 1955. Here program managers and department heads presented problem areas to Schriever, Ramo, and Brig. Gen. Ben I. Funk, commander of the procurement office. As problems arose, discussion sometimes could resolve them in the course of the meeting. If not, a specific person or organization would be assigned to come up with a solution, while the staff of the program control room tracked progress. Sometimes, Ramo brought in outside experts from industry or academia to deal with particularly difficult problems.[69]

Because the process of developing new missile systems entailed considerable urgency when the Soviet threat was perceived as great and the technology was still far from mature, Schriever and his team used a practice called concurrency that was not new but not routinely practiced in the federal government. Used on the B-29 bomber, the Manhattan Project, and development of nuclear vessels for the U.S. Navy, it involved developing all subsystems and the facilities to test and manufacture them on overlapping schedules; likewise, the systems for operational control and the training system for the Strategic Air Command, which took over the missiles when they became operational.

Schriever claimed that implementing concurrency was equivalent to requiring a car manufacturer to build the automobile and also to construct highways, bridges, and filling stations as well as teach drivers' education. He argued that concurrency saved money, but this seems doubtful. Each model of the Atlas missile from A to F involved expensive improvements, and the F models were housed in silos. Each time the F-model design changed, the Army Corps of Engineers had to reconfigure the silo. There were 199 engineering change orders for the silos near Lincoln, Nebraska, and these raised the costs from $23 million to more than $50 million dollars—to give one example of costs added by concurrency. What concurrency did achieve was speed of overall development and the assurance that all systems would be available on schedule.[70]

A further tool in WDD's management portfolio was parallel development. To avoid being dependent on a single supplier for a system, Schriever insisted on parallel contractors for many of them. Eventually, when Thor and Titan I came along, the testing program became overwhelming, and Glasser argued that Ramo-Wooldridge just ignored the problem. He went to Schriever, who directed him to come up with a solution. He decided which systems would go on

Atlas, which on Titan and Thor, in the process becoming the deputy for systems management and the Atlas project manager.[71]

A final component of the management structure for Schriever's west-coast operation consisted of the nonprofit Aerospace Corporation. It had come into existence on June 4, 1960, as a solution to the problems many people saw in Space Technology Laboratories' serving as a systems-engineering and technical-direction contractor to the air force while part of Thompson Ramo Wooldridge (later, just TRW), as the company had become following an eventual merger of Ramo-Wooldridge with Thompson Products. STL continued its operations for programs then in existence, but many of its personnel transferred to the Aerospace Corporation for systems engineering and technical direction of new programs. Further complicating the picture, a reorganization occurred within the air force on April 1, 1961, in which Air Force Systems Command (AFSC) replaced the Air Research and Development Command. On the same date, within AFSC, the Ballistic Missile Division split into a Ballistic Systems Division (BSD), which would retain responsibility for ballistic missiles (and would soon move to Norton Air Force Base [AFB] east of Los Angeles near San Bernardino); and a Space Systems Division (SSD), which moved to El Segundo, much closer to Los Angeles, and obtained responsibility for military space systems and boosters. There would be further reorganizations of the two offices, but whether combined or separated, they oversaw the development of a variety of missiles and launch vehicles, ranging from the Atlas and Thor to Titans I through IV.[72]

To return specifically to the Atlas program, under the earlier (1946–48) MX-774B project, Convair had developed swiveling of engines (a precursor of gimballing); monocoque propellant tanks that were integral to the structure of the rockets and pressurized with nitrogen to provide structural strength with very little weight penalty (later evolving into what Convair called a steel balloon); and separable nose cones so that the missile itself did not have to travel with a warhead to the target and thus have to survive the aerodynamic heating from reentering the atmosphere.[73]

Other innovations followed under the genial leadership of Karel (Charlie) Bossart. Finally, on January 6, 1955, the air force awarded a contract to Convair for the development and production of the Atlas airframe, the integration of other subsystems with the airframe and one another, their assembly and testing. The contractor for the Atlas engines was North American Aviation, which built upon earlier research done on the Navaho missile. NAA's Rocketdyne Division, formed in 1955 to handle the requirements of Navaho, Atlas, and

German and U.S. Missiles and Rockets, 1926–66

Redstone, developed one sustainer and two outside booster engines for the Atlas under a so-called stage-and-a-half arrangement, with the boosters discarded after they had done their work. Produced in 1957 and 1958, the early engines ran into failures of systems and components in flight testing that also plagued the Thor and Jupiter engines, which were under simultaneous development and shared many component designs with the Atlas.[74]

But innovation continued, partly through engineers making "the right guess or assumption" or simply learning from problems. Despite repeated failures and (trial-and-error) modifications to eliminate their causes, development proceeded from Atlas A through Atlas F with a total of 158 successful launches for all models against 69 failures—a success rate of only 69.6 percent. The Atlas D became the first operational version in September 1959, with the first E and F models following in 1961. All three remained operational until 1965, when they were phased out of the missile inventory, with many of them later becoming launch-vehicle stages.[75]

Meanwhile, fearing (unnecessarily) that an ICBM like the Atlas could not be deployed before 1962, a Technology Capabilities Panel headed by James R. Killian Jr., president of MIT, issued a report in mid-February 1955 recommending the development of both sea- and land-based intermediate-range ballistic missiles (IRBMs). In November 1955, the Joint Chiefs of Staff recommended, in turn, that the air force develop the land-based version while the army and navy collaborate on an IRBM that could be both land and sea based. Thus were born the air force's Thor and the army's Jupiter, with the navy eventually developing the solid-propellant Polaris after initially trying to adapt the liquid-propellant Jupiter to shipboard use.[76]

Arising out of this decision was the "Thor-Jupiter Controversy," which the House of Representatives Committee on Government Operations called a "case study in interservice rivalry." The Thor did not use the extremely light, steel-balloon structure of Atlas but a more conventional aluminum airframe. Its main engine consisted essentially of half of the booster system for Atlas. In 1957 and 1958, it experienced 12 failures or partial successes out of the first 18 launches. Before the air force nevertheless decided in September 1958 that Thor was ready for operational deployment, problems with the turbopumps (common to the Atlas, Thor, and Jupiter) and differences of approach to these problems had led to disagreement between the Thor and Jupiter teams.[77]

Von Braun's engineers, working on the Jupiter for the army, diagnosed the problem first and had Rocketdyne design a bearing retainer for the turbopump that solved the problem, which the Thor program would not admit at first, suspecting another cause. Once the Jupiters resumed test flights, they had no further turbopump problems. Meanwhile, failures of an Atlas and a Thor missile in April 1958, plus subsequent analysis, led the air force belatedly to accept the army's diagnosis and a turbopump redesign. The first Thor squadron went on operational alert in Great Britain in June 1959, with three others following by April 1960. When the Atlas and Titan ICBMs achieved operational readiness in 1960, the last Thors could be removed from operational status in 1963, making them available for space-launch activities.[78]

While the Western Development Division and the successor Air Force Ballistic Missile Division were developing the Thor in conjunction with contractors, von Braun's group at what had become the Army Ballistic Missile Agency (ABMA) in Alabama and its contractors were busily at work on Jupiter without a clear indication whether the army or the air force would eventually deploy the missile. At ABMA, the forceful and dynamic Maj. Gen. John B. Medaris enjoyed powers of initiative roughly analogous to those of Schriever for the air force. On December 8, 1956, the navy left the Jupiter program to develop Polaris, but not before the sea service's requirements had altered the shape of the army missile to a much shorter and somewhat thicker contour than the army had planned. With Chrysler the prime contractor (as on the Redstone), Medaris reluctantly accepted the same basic engine North American Rocketdyne was developing for the Thor except that the Jupiter engine evolved from an earlier version of the powerplant and ended as somewhat less powerful than the air force counterparts.[79]

With a quite different vernier engine and guidance/control system, the Jupiter was a decidedly distinct missile from the Thor. The first actual Jupiter (as distinguished from the Jupiter A and Jupiter C, which were actually Redstones) launched on March 1, 1957, at Cape Canaveral. Facing the usual developmental problems, including at least one that Medaris blamed on the thicker shape resulting from the navy's requirements, the Jupiter nevertheless achieved 22 satisfactory research-and-development flight tests out of 29 attempts. The air force, instead of the army, deployed the missile, with initial operational capability coming on October 20, 1960. Two squadrons of the missile became fully operational in Italy as of June 20, 1961. A third squadron in Turkey was not operational until 1962, with all of the missiles taken out of service in April of the following year. Three feet shorter, slightly thicker and heavier, the Jupiter was more accurate but less powerful than the Thor, with a comparable range. The greater average thrust of the Thor may have contributed to its becoming a standard first-stage launch vehicle, whereas Jupiter served in that capacity to only a limited degree. Another factor may have been that there were 160 production Thors to only 60 Jupiter missiles.[80]

Although much has rightly been made of the intense interservice rivalry between the army and the air force over Thor and Jupiter, even those two programs cooperated to a considerable extent and exchanged much data. Medaris complained about the lack of information he received from the air force, but Schriever claimed that his Ballistic Missile Division had transmitted to ABMA a total of 4,476 documents between 1954 and February 1959. By his count, BMD withheld only 28 documents for a variety of reasons, including contractors' proprietary information.[81] This was one of many examples showing that—although interservice and interagency rivalry helped encourage competing engineers to excel—without sharing of information and technology, rocketry might have advanced much less quickly than in fact it did.

Polaris and Minuteman

Jupiter, Thor, and Atlas marked a huge step forward in the maturation of U.S. rocketry, but before the technology from those missiles came to significant use in launch vehicles, the navy's development of the Polaris inaugurated a solid-propellant breakthrough in missile technology that also profoundly affected launch vehicles.[82] Until Polaris A1 became operational in 1960, all intermediate-range and intercontinental missiles in the U.S. arsenal had employed liquid propellants. These had important advantages in terms of performance but required extensive plumbing and large propellant tanks that made protecting them in silos difficult and expensive. Such factors also virtually precluded their efficient use onboard ships, especially submarines. Once Minuteman I became operational in 1962, the U.S. military began to phase out liquid-propellant strategic missiles. To this day, Minuteman III and the solid-propellant fleet ballistic missiles continue to play a major role in the nation's strategic defenses because they are simpler and cheaper to operate than liquid-propellant missiles.

Because of the higher performance of some liquid propellants and their ability to be throttled as well as turned off and on by the use of valves, they remained the primary propellants for space-launch vehicles. However, since solid-propellant boosters could be strapped on the sides of liquid-propellant stages for an instant addition of high thrust (because their thrust-to-weight ratio is higher, allowing faster liftoff), solid-propellant boosters became important parts of launch-vehicle technology. The technologies used on Polaris and Minuteman transferred to such boosters and also to upper stages of rockets used to launch satellites. Thus, the solid-propellant break-through in missiles had important implications for launch-vehicle technology. By the time that Polaris got under way in 1956 and Minuteman in 1958, solid-propellant rocketry had already made tremendous strides from the use of extruded double-base propel-lants in World War II tactical missiles. But there were still enor-mous technical hurdles to overcome before solid-propellant missiles could hope to launch strategic nuclear warheads far and accurately enough to serve effectively as a deterrent or as a retaliatory weapon in case of enemy aggression.[83]

With a much smaller organization than the army or air force, a navy special projects office under the leadership of Capt. (soon-to-be Rear Adm.) William F. Raborn pushed ahead to find the right tech-nologies for a submarine-launched, solid-propellant missile, a daunt-ing task since a solid propellant with the necessary performance did not yet exist. Capt. Levering Smith—who, at the Naval Ord-nance Test Station (NOTS), had led the effort to develop a 50-foot solid-propellant missile named "Big Stoop" that flew 20 miles in 1951—joined Raborn's special projects office in April 1956. Smith contributed importantly to Polaris, but one key technical discovery came from the Atlantic Research Corporation (ARC), a chemical firm founded in 1949 with which the Navy Bureau of Ordnance had contracted to improve the specific impulse of solid propellants (the ratio of thrust a rocket engine or motor produced to the amount of propellant needed to produce that thrust).[84]

ARC's discovery that the addition of comparatively large quan-tities of aluminum to solid propellants significantly raised perfor-mance, together with the work of Aerojet chemists, led to successful propellants for both stages of Polaris A1. The addition of aluminum to Aerojet's binder essentially solved the problem of performance for both Polaris (and, as it turned out, with a different binder, for Minuteman). Other key technical solutions relating to guidance and an appropriate warhead led to the directive on December 8, 1956, that formally began the Polaris program.[85]

Flight testing of Polaris at the air force's Cape Canaveral (be-ginning in 1958 in a series designated AX) revealed a number of problems. Solutions required considerable interservice cooperation. On July 20, 1960, the USS *George Washington* launched the first functional Polaris missile. The fleet then deployed the missile on November 15, 1960.[86]

The navy quickly moved forward to Polaris A2. It increased the range of the fleet ballistic missile from 1,200 to 1,500 miles. Flight testing of the A2 missiles started in November 1960, with the first successful launch from a submerged submarine occurring on October 23, 1961. The missile became operational less than a year later in June 1962. Polaris A3 was still more capable, with a range of 2,500 miles. It incorporated many other new technologies in both propulsion and guidance/control, becoming operational on September 28, 1964. All three versions of Polaris made significant contributions to launch-vehicle technology, such as the Altair II motor, produced by the Hercules Powder Company under sponsorship of the Bureau of Naval Weapons and NASA and used as a fourth stage for the Scout launch vehicle.[87]

While Polaris was still in development, the air force had officially begun work on Minuteman I. Its principal architect was Edward N. Hall, a heterogeneous engineer who helped begin the air force's involvement with solid propellants as a major at Wright-Patterson AFB in the early 1950s. As Karl Klager, who worked on both Polaris and Minuteman, has stated, Hall "deserves most of the credit for maintaining interest in large solid rocket technology [during the mid-1950s] because of the greater simplicity of solid systems over liquid systems." Hall's efforts "contributed substantially to the Polaris program," Klager added, further illustrating the extent to which (unintended) interservice cooperation and shared information contributed to the solid-propellant breakthrough. Hall moved to the WDD as the chief for propulsion development in the liquid-propellant Atlas, Titan, and Thor programs, but he continued his work on solids, aided by his former colleagues back at Wright-Patterson AFB.[88]

Despite this sort of preparatory work for Minuteman, the missile could not begin its formal development until the air force secured final DoD approval in February 1958, more than a year later than Polaris. Hall and others at WDD had a difficult job convincing Schriever in particular to convert to solids. Without their heterogeneous engineering, the shift to solids might never have happened. They were aided, however, by development of Polaris because it provided what Harvey Sapolsky has dubbed "competitive pressure" for the air force to develop its own solid-propellant missile.[89]

Soon after program approval, Hall left the Ballistic Missile Division. From August 1959 to 1963, the program director was Col. (soon promoted to Brig. Gen.) Samuel C. Phillips. Hall and his coworkers deserve much credit for the design of Minuteman and its support by the air force, whereas Phillips brought the missile to completion.

Facing many technical hurdles, Phillips succeeded as brilliantly as had Levering Smith with Polaris in providing technical management of a complex and innovative missile. Often using trial-and-error engineering, his team working on the three-stage Minuteman I overcame problems with materials for nozzle throats in the lower stages, with firing the missile from a silo, and with a new binder for the first stage called polybutadiene–acrylic acid–acrylonitrile (PBAN), developed by the contractor, Thiokol Chemical Corporation. Incorporating substantial new technology as well as some borrowed from Polaris, the first Minuteman I wing became operational in October 1962.[90]

Minuteman II included a new propellant in stage two, known as carboxy-terminated polybutadiene and an improved guidance/control system. The new propellant yielded a higher specific impulse, and other changes (including increased length and diameter) made Minuteman II a more capable and accurate missile than Minuteman I. The newer version gradually replaced its predecessor in missile silos after December 1966.[91]

In Minuteman III, stages one and two did not change from Minuteman II, but stage three became larger. Aerojet replaced Hercules as the contractor for the new third stage. With the larger size and a different propellant, the third stage more than doubled its total impulse. These and other modifications allowed Minuteman IIIs to achieve their initial operational capability in June 1970. As a result of the improvements, the range of the missile increased from about 6,000 miles for Minuteman I to 7,021 for Minuteman II, and 8,083 for Minuteman III.[92]

The deployment of Minuteman I in 1961 marked the completion of the solid-propellant breakthrough in terms of its basic technology, though innovations and improvements continued to occur. But the gradual phaseout of liquid-propellant missiles followed almost inexorably from the appearance on the scene of the first Minuteman. The breakthrough in solid-rocket technology required the extensive cooperation of a great many firms, government laboratories, and universities, only some of which could be mentioned here. It occurred on many fronts, ranging from materials science and metallurgy through chemistry to the physics of internal ballistics and the mathematics and physics of guidance and control, among many other disciplines. It was partially spurred by interservice rivalries for roles and missions. Less well known, however, was the contribution of interservice cooperation. Necessary funding for advances in and the sharing of technology came from all three services, the Advanced Research Projects Agency, and NASA. Technologies such as aluminum fuel, methods of thrust vector control, and improved guidance and control transferred from one service's missiles to another. Also crucial were the roles of heterogeneous engineers like Raborn, Schriever, and Hall. But a great many people with more purely technical skills, such as Levering Smith and Sam Phillips, ARC, Thiokol, and Aerojet engineers made vital contributions.

The solid-propellant breakthrough that these people and many others achieved had important implications for launch vehicles as well as missiles. The propellants for the large solid-rocket boosters on the Titan III, Titan IVA, and the Space Shuttles were derived from the one used on Minuteman, stage one. Without ARC's discovery of aluminum as a fuel and Thiokol's development of PBAN as a binder, it is not clear that the huge Titan and shuttle boosters would have been possible. Many other solid-propellant formulations also used aluminum and other ingredients of the Polaris and Minuteman motors. Although some or all of them might have been developed even if there had been no urgent national need for solid-propellant missiles, it seems highly unlikely that their development would have occurred as quickly as it did without the impetus of the cold-war missile programs and their generous funding.

Titan I and Titan II

Simultaneously with the development of Polaris and then Minuteman, the air force continued work on two liquid-propellant missiles, the Titans I and II. The Titan II introduced storable propellants into the missile inventory and laid the groundwork for the core portion of the Titans III and IV space-launch vehicles. Titan I began as essentially insurance for Atlas in case the earlier missile's technology proved unworkable. The major new feature of the first of the Titans was demonstration of the ability to start a large second-stage engine at a high altitude.[93] The WAC Corporal had proved the viability of the basic process involved, and Vanguard would develop it further (after Titan I was started). But in 1955, using a full second stage on a ballistic missile and igniting it only after the first-stage engines had exhausted their propellants seemed risky.

The air force approved development of Titan I on May 2, 1955. Meanwhile, the Western Development Division had awarded a contract on January 14, 1955, to Aerojet for engines burning liquid oxygen and a hydrocarbon fuel for possible use on Atlas. These soon evolved into engines for the two-stage missile. Even though the Aerojet engines burned the same propellants as Atlas, there were problems with development, showing that rocket engineers still did not have the process of design "down to a science." Despite the change in propellants, the Titan II used a highly similar design for its engines, making Aerojet's development for that missile less problematic than it might otherwise have been (although still not without difficulties), with technology then carrying over into the Titans III and IV core launch vehicles. Meanwhile, the air force deployed the Titan Is in 1962. They quickly deactivated in 1965 with the deployment of Minuteman I and Titan II, but Titan I did provide an interim deterrent force.[94]

The history of the transition from Titan I to Titan II is complicated. One major factor stimulating the change was the 15 minutes or so it took to raise Titan I from its silo, load the propellants, and launch it. Another was the difficulty of handling Titan I's extremely cold liquid oxygen used in Titan I inside a missile silo. One solution to the twin problems would have been conversion to solid propellants like those used in Polaris and Minuteman, but another was storable propellants. Under a navy contract in 1951, Aerojet had begun studying hydrazine as a rocket propellant. It had good performance but could detonate. Aerojet came up with a compromise solution, an equal mixture of hydrazine and unsymmetrical dimethyl hydrazine, which it called Aerozine 50. With nitrogen tetroxide as an oxidizer, this fuel mixture ignited hypergolically (upon contact with the oxidizer, without the need for an ignition device), offering a much quicker response time than for Titan I.[95] As a result of this and other issues and developments, in November 1959 the Department of Defense authorized the air force to develop the Titan II. The new missile would use storable propellants, in-silo launch, and an all-inertial guidance system.[96]

On April 30, 1960, the Air Force Ballistic Missile Division's development plan for Titan II called for it to be 103 feet long (compared to 97.4 feet for Titan I), have a uniform diameter of 10 feet (whereas Titan I's second stage was only 8 feet across), and have increased thrust over its predecessor. This higher performance would increase the range with the Mark 4 reentry vehicle from about 5,500 nautical miles for Titan I to 8,400. With the new Mark 6 reentry vehicle, which had about twice the weight and more than twice the yield of the Mark 4, the range would remain about 5,500 nautical miles. Because of the larger nuclear warhead it could carry, the Titan II served a different and complementary function to Minuteman I's in the strategy of the air force, convincing Congress to fund them both. It was a credible counterforce weapon, whereas Minuteman I served primarily as a countercity missile, offering deterrence rather than the ability to destroy enemy weapons in silos.[97]

In May 1960, the air force signed a letter contract with the Martin Company to develop, produce, and test the Titan II. It followed this with a contract to General Electric to design the Mark 6 reentry vehicle. In April 1959, AC Spark Plug had contracted to build an inertial guidance system for a Titan missile, although it was not clear at the time that this would be the Titan II.[98]

Although the Titan II engines were based on those for Titan I, the new propellants and the requirements in the April 30 plan necessitated considerable redesign. Because the new designs did not always work as anticipated, the engineers had to resort to empirical solutions until they found the combinations that provided the necessary performance. Even with other changes to the Titan I engine designs, the Titan II propulsion system had significantly fewer parts than its Titan I predecessor, reducing chances for failure during operation. Despite the greater simplicity, the engines had higher thrust and higher performance, as planned.[99]

Flight testing of the Titan II had its problems, complicated by plans to use the missile as a launch vehicle for NASA's Project Gemini, leading to the Project Apollo Moon flights. However, the last 13 flights in the research-and-development series were successful, giving the air force the confidence to declare the missile fully operational on the final day of 1963. Between October and December 1963, the Strategic Air Command deployed six squadrons of nine Titan IIs apiece. They remained a part of the strategic defense of the United States until deactivated between 1984 and 1987. By that time, fleet ballistic missiles and smaller land-based, solid-propellant ballistic missiles could deliver (admittedly smaller) warheads much more accurately than could the Titan IIs. Deactivation left the former operational Titan II missiles available for refurbishment as space-launch vehicles.[100]

Development of Titan I and Titan II did not require a lot of new technology. Instead, it adapted technologies developed either earlier or simultaneously for other missile or launch-vehicle programs. Nevertheless, the process of adaptation for the designs of the two Titan missiles generated problems requiring engineers to use their fund of knowledge to find solutions. These did work, and Titan II became the nation's longest-lasting liquid-propellant missile with the greatest throw weight of any vehicle in the U.S. inventory.

Analysis and Conclusions

The development of missiles and rockets for DoD needs arguably contributed to national defense and, through deterrence, kept the cold war from becoming hotter than it actually got in Korea, Vietnam, and Afghanistan, among other places. For the purposes of this book, however, the importance of the missiles and rockets discussed in this chapter lay in the technology that could transfer to launch-vehicle uses. In many cases, actual missiles, with some adaptations, became either launch vehicles or stages in larger combinations of rockets used to place satellites or spacecraft on their trajectories. Without the perceived urgency created by cold-war concerns and without the heterogeneous engineering of missile proponents, it conceivably would have taken much longer for launch vehicles to develop, although many satellites themselves were high on the DoD's priority lists.

Quite apart from their contributions to launch-vehicle technology, the missiles and rockets discussed in this chapter also illustrate many of the themes that will be further explored in subsequent chapters. Missiles such as the Titan II and Minuteman showed the ways in which technology for earlier missiles contributed to their successors. Although this chapter provides only an overview of missile development, it shows several examples of trial-and-error engineering that was necessary to overcome often unforeseen problems. Clearly, the missiles discussed here required a wide range of talents and a huge number of different organizations to design and develop them. Also important was a considerable sharing of information, even between competing organizations and firms. Finally, management systems such as the one Schriever adopted at WDD (and a similar system called Program Evaluation and Review Technique [PERT] adopted by Raborn for the Polaris program) enabled very complicated missiles and launch vehicles to be developed reasonably on time and in such a way that all component systems (such as propulsion, structures, guidance and control) worked together effectively.

CHAPTER 2

U.S. Space-Launch Vehicles, 1958–91

LAUNCH VEHICLES FREQUENTLY USED MISsiles as first stages, but these required many modifications, particularly when they had to boost humans into space. Even for satellite and spacecraft launches, technology for the booster stages frequently represented modification of technologies missiles needed for their ballistic paths from one part of Earth to another. Thus, the history of the Thor-Delta, Atlas, Scout, Saturn, Titan, and Space Shuttle launch vehicles differed from, but remained dependent on, the earlier development of the missiles discussed in chapter 1. Missiles and launch vehicles represented a continuum, with many of the same people contributing to both. But they remained different enough from one another to require separate treatment in this chapter.

Despite the differences, launch-vehicle development exhibited many of the same themes that characterized missiles. It featured the same engineering culture that relied heavily on extensive testing on the ground. But this did not always succeed in revealing all problems that occurred in flight. When unexpected problems occurred, it was not always possible for engineers to understand the exact causes. But they were able to arrive at fixes that worked. There continued to be a wide range of organizations and disciplines that contributed to launch-vehicle development, including the solution of unanticipated problems. Also characteristic of launch vehicles was a competitive environment that nevertheless featured sharing of information among organizations involved in development. In part, this sharing occurred through the movement of knowledgeable engineers from one organization to another. More often, the information sharing (plus its recording and validation) occurred through professional societies, papers delivered at their meetings, and publication of reports in professional journals.[1] Finally, missiles and launch vehicles shared the use of management systems that tracked development of components to ensure that all of them occurred on schedule and that they all worked together effectively.

"Man-Rating"

One major area of difference between missile and launch-vehicle development lay in the requirement for special safeguards on launch vehicles that propelled humans into space. Except for Juno I and Vanguard, which were short-lived, among the first U.S. space-launch vehicles were the Redstones and Atlases used in Project Mercury and the Atlases and Titan IIs used in Project Gemini to prepare for the Apollo Moon Program. Both Projects Mercury and Gemini required a process called "man-rating" (at a time before there were women serving as astronauts). This process resulted in adaptations of the Redstone, Atlas, and Titan II missiles to make them safer for the human beings carried in Mercury and Gemini capsules.

Man-rating was but one of the ways missiles had to be modified for use as launch vehicles, but the practice carried over to later launch vehicles initially designed as such (rather than as missiles). For Mercury-Redstone, Wernher von Braun's Development Opera-

FIG. 2.1
A Mercury-
Redstone
launching
Freedom 7
with Astronaut
Alan Shepard
onboard,
May 5, 1961,
from Pad
5 at Cape
Canaveral.
(Photo courtesy
of NASA)

tions Division of the Army Ballistic Missile Agency was responsible for the process. Von Braun established a Mercury-Redstone
Project Office to aid in redesigning the Jupiter C version of the Redstone to satisfy the requirements of the Mercury project. To direct
the effort, he chose Joachim P. Kuettner, a flight engineer and test
pilot who had worked for Messerschmitt during the Nazi period in
Germany.[2]

Kuettner's group recognized that the Redstone missile could not
satisfy the mission requirements for Project Mercury. These necessitated sufficient performance and reliability to launch a two-
ton payload with an astronaut aboard into a flight path reaching

an apogee of 100 nautical miles (115 statute miles). The Jupiter C, with its elongated propellant tanks and a lighter structure, had the required performance but not the safety features necessary for human flight. To add these, Kuettner's group reverted from the toxic hydyne to alcohol as a fuel. Other changes included an automatic, in-flight abort system with an escape rocket and parachutes to carry the astronauts to a safe landing. To ferret out potential sources of failure, Chrysler, as prime contractor, instituted a special test program to promote greater reliability. The overall process proved successful, resulting in the two flights of Alan Shepard and Virgil (Gus) Grissom in May and July 1961.[3]

Thereafter, Project Mercury switched to Atlas D missiles to propel the astronauts and their capsules into orbit. For this function, the missile required strengthening in its upper section to handle the greater loads the capsule created. Following an explosion on Mercury-Atlas (MA) 1 (July 29, 1960), whose cause investigators could not determine, engineers developed an improved structure linking the booster and capsule, resulting in a successful flight of MA-2 on February 21, 1961.[4] MA-2 also tested the Atlas abort sensing and implementation system (ASIS) and "escape tower" that were key features in man-rating the Atlas. Besides these two features, there had to be numerous other modifications to convert Atlas to its Mercury-Atlas configuration. For example, the Mercury capsule's separation rockets potentially could damage the thin "steel-balloon" skin on the liquid-oxygen dome of the Atlas, so General Dynamics (formerly Convair) engineers had to add a fiberglass layer covering the dome. This and other changes, plus increased quality control, caused the Mercury-Atlas launch vehicle to cost 40 percent more than the Atlas missile. After a failure on MA-3 (due to guidance/ control problems), Atlas launch vehicles placed John Glenn, Scott Carpenter, Walter Schirra, and Gordon Cooper in orbit between February 20, 1962, and May 15, 1963.[5]

For Titan II-Gemini, there were major problems with longitudinal oscillations in the engines, known as pogo (from their resemblance to the gyrations of the then-popular plaything, the pogo stick). These never occurred in flight but appeared in a severe form during static testing of second-stage engines. Surges in the oxidizer feed lines were causing the problem, which Martin engineers and others solved with suppression mechanisms. There was also the issue of combustion instability that occurred on only 2 percent of the ground tests of second-stage engines. But for man-rating, even this was too high. Aerojet (the Titan engine contractor) solved the problem with a new injector.[6]

FIG. 2.2
Launch of
a Mercury-
Atlas vehicle
from Cape
Canaveral on
February 20,
1962. (Photo
courtesy of
NASA)

For other aspects of man-rating Titan II for Gemini, procedures developed for Project Mercury offered a strong influence, especially as many NASA and Aerospace Corporation engineers who had worked on Mercury also worked on Gemini. Gemini engineers also benefited from Titan II test launches. As George E. Mueller, NASA's associate administrator for manned spaceflight from 1963 to 1969, stated in February 1964, the 28 launches of Titan II missiles to that date "provide[d] invaluable launch operations experience and actual space flight test data directly applicable to the Gemini launch vehicle which would [have] be[en] unobtainable otherwise,"[7] one example of the symbiotic (though not homogeneous) relationship between missiles and launch vehicles.

FIG. 2.3
Gemini-Titan
12 launch on
November 11,
1966, showing
the exhaust
plume from the
engines on the
Titan II launch
vehicle. (Photo
courtesy of
NASA)

In addition to a malfunction detection system, features added to the Titan II missile for astronaut safety included redundant components of the electrical systems. To help compensate for all the weight from the additional components, engineers also deleted vernier and retro-rockets, which were not necessary for the Gemini mission.[8] From March 23, 1965, to November 11, 1966, Gemini 3 through 12 all carried two astronauts on the Gemini spacecraft. These missions had their problems as well as their triumphs. But with them, the United States finally assumed the lead in the space race with its cold-war rival, the Soviet Union. Despite lots of problems, Gemini had prepared the way for the Apollo Moon landings and achieved its essential objectives.[9]

Following its successful Gemini missions, the Titan II did not serve again as a space-launch vehicle until the mid-1980s after it was taken out of service as a missile. Meanwhile, subsequent launch vehicles that required [hu]man-rating, notably the Saturn launch vehicles and the shuttle, included equipment for accommodating humans in their original designs, capitalizing on the experiences with Mercury-Redstone, Mercury-Atlas, and Gemini-Titan, which NASA passed on to the subsequent programs.

The Thor and Delta Family of Launch Vehicles, 1958–90

The Thor missiles did not remain in operational use very long, but even before the air force retired them in 1963, it had begun to use the Thor's airframe and propulsive elements (including its vernier engines) as the first stages of various launch vehicles. With a series of upratings and modifications, the Thor remained in use with such upper stages as the Able, Able-Star, Agena, Burner I, Burner II, and Burner IIA until 1980. In addition, NASA quickly chose the Thor as the first stage of what became its Thor-Delta (later, just Delta) launch-vehicle family, which has had an even longer history than the air force's Thor series. The Delta launch vehicles initially drew upon Vanguard upper stages, as did the Thor-Able used by the air force.[10]

Throughout its history, the Delta evolved by uprating existing components or adopting newer ones that had proven themselves. It used a low-risk strategy to improve its payload capacity through the Delta II at the end of the period covered by this history. But it did not stop there, evolving through a Delta III, first launched (unsuccessfully) in 1998, and a Delta IV that finally had its successful first launch on November 20, 2002. (To be sure, the Delta IV used an entirely new first stage, making it in some senses a new launch vehicle, but the design emphasized reliability and low cost, hallmarks of the Delta program from the beginning.) The unsuccessful first (and second) launch(es) of the Delta III and numerous delays in the launch of Delta IV because of both software and hardware problems suggested, however, that the design of new launch vehicles was still not something engineers had "down to a science," even in the 21st century.[11]

For the Able upper stage, the air force and its contractors used many features of the Vanguard second stage but added a control compartment, skirts and structural elements to mate it with the Thor, a tank venting and pressurization safety system, new electrical components, and a roll-control system. Used for reentry testing, the first Thor-Able failed because of a faulty turbopump in the Thor, but the second launch on July 9, 1958, was successful.[12]

FIG. 2.4
A Thor-Able
launch vehicle
with the
Pioneer 1
spacecraft as
its payload.
(Photo courtesy
of NASA)

Succeeding versions of Thor-Able modified both second and third stages of Vanguard. The final Thor-Able launch on April 1, 1960, placed the *Tiros 1* meteorological satellite in orbit. In the 16 Thor-Able launches, all of the stages worked satisfactorily on 10 of the missions, whereas at least one stage failed or was only partly successful on 6 flights. Although this was only a 62.5 percent success rate, it was sufficiently good for this early period that the air force could refer to Thor-Able as "an extremely capable and reliable vehicle combination."[13]

Long before the final launch of the Thor-Able, nevertheless, the Department of Defense's Advanced Research Projects Agency had issued an order on July 1, 1959, calling for the development of the Able-Star upper stage, derived from the Able but possessing two and one half times its total impulse plus the capability to shut down its propulsion in space, coast, and restart. This ability would permit a more precise selection of the orbit for a satellite than was possible before. Once Able-Star became operational in January 1960, it effectively replaced the Able as an upper stage.[14]

The Able-Star engine was a derivative of the several Able engines except that it had the added restart capability plus the capacity to provide attitude control during coasting periods and to burn longer than the earlier engines. Following a rapid but not unproblematic development, an Able-Star upper stage on a Thor booster launched the *Transit 1B* navigation satellite on April 13, 1960, marking the first programmed restart of a rocket engine in flight. Although the coast attitude-control system worked, a malfunction in the Able-Star ground guidance system resulted in a still-useful elliptical rather than a circular orbit. Sloshing in stage-two propellant tanks for *Transit 2A*—launched on June 22, 1960—again produced an elliptical orbit because it caused roll forces that the guidance/control system could not overcome. Again the orbit was useful. Following placement of anti-slosh baffles in both Able-Star propellant tanks, the Thor booster failed on the attempted launch of *Transit 3A*, November 30, 1960. Then on February 21, 1961, a Thor/Able-Star failed to place *Transit 3B* in a usable orbit because a part malfunctioned in the programmer before it could signal the restart of stage two from its coasting orbit. Substantially the same launch vehicle as on *Transit 3A* successfully launched *Transit 4A* into a nearly circular orbit on June 28, 1961.[15] Through August 13, 1965, including the launches just discussed, the Thor/Able-Star completed a total of 20 missions with 5 failures, for a success rate of 75 percent. Quite successful for an early launch vehicle, the Thor/Able-Star also marked a step forward in satellite-launching capability.[16]

Even before the first launch of Thor/Able-Star, the air force had begun using an Agena upper stage with the Thor, and this combination became a preferred choice for a great many often-classified missions, including those to place a family of reconnaissance satellites in orbit under what began as the WS-117L program. Initially, the Agena upper stages flew on basic Thors, but in three versions from A to D (without a C), the Agena also operated with uprated Thors, Atlases, and Titan IIIs to orbit a great many military and NASA spacecraft until 1987.[17]

The air force began developing the Agena in July 1956. On October 29, 1956, that service selected Lockheed Missile Systems

Division as the prime contractor for both the WS-117L reconnaissance satellite system and an associated upper stage that became the Agena. The engine for the Lockheed upper stage was a modified version of the Hustler propulsion unit (model 117) that Bell Aerospace had developed for the B-58 bomber's air-to-surface missile, designated the Powered Disposable Bomb Pod. The air force canceled the missile, but Lockheed contracted with Bell in the fall of 1957 to develop the engine for Agena.[18]

One change from the Hustler engine was the addition of gimballing. Another was a nozzle closure to ensure that the Agena started in space after cutoff of the first-stage engine. The Agena stage with this engine, known as the Bell 8001, flew only once, on February 28, 1959, for the launch of *Discoverer 1* by a Thor-Agena A. (Discoverer was the name publicly released for the secret Corona reconnaissance satellites, which had separated from the WS-117L program by this time.) Accounts differ as to the outcome of this first launch into a polar orbit from Vandenberg AFB, California—some claiming the launch itself was successful, and others that it was not.[19]

The Agena nevertheless had an extensive career as an upper stage. The Agena A operated successfully on 78 percent of its 14 launches by September 13, 1960 (all by Thors; all but one with a new Bell model 8048 engine for the Agena), with 3 failures. A more capable Thor-Agena B appears to have had 39 successful performances on 48 launches from October 26, 1960, to May 15, 1966, an 81 percent success rate, mostly launching Corona satellites. With a thrust-augmented Thor, the Agena B could launch much heavier satellites, added thrust coming from solid-propellant strap-on boosters.[20]

Meanwhile, in the fall of 1959 Bell began designing the engine for the Agena D, which became the standard Agena propulsion unit. From June 28, 1962, to May 25, 1972, a large number of Thor-Agena D launches occurred, but because of the classified nature of many of the payloads, a reliable and precise tally is not available. During this period, the basic booster changed from the thrust-augmented to the long-tank, thrust-augmented Thor (called Thorad) with increased burning time and improved strap-on boosters.[21]

Another series of upper stages used with the Thor first stage included Burner I, Burner II, and Burner IIA. Burner I actually bore little relation to Burners II and IIA. Information about it is sparse, but sources refer to it as the Altair, a derivative of the Vanguard third stage developed by Hercules Powder Company at the Allegany Ballistics Laboratory. The first launch of the Thor-Burner I occurred on January 18, 1965, with the last one taking place on March 30, 1966. There apparently were only four such launches, all from Van-

FIG. 2.5
An Agena
upper stage,
used also for
many satellite
launches,
serving here as
the Gemini 8
target vehicle
for docking.
(Photo courtesy
of NASA)

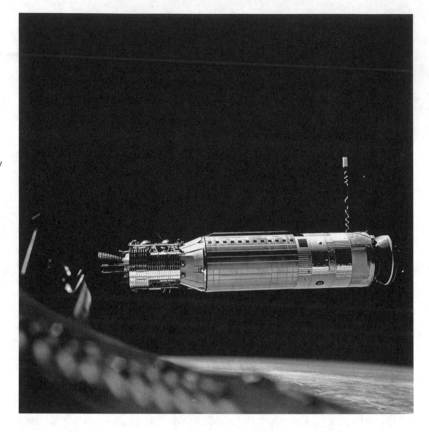

denberg AFB into sun-synchronous orbits, one of them a mission failure. The spacecraft were classified at the time but appear to have been Block 4A Defense Satellite Applications Program weather satellites used to inform the U.S. military of weather conditions for launching reconnaissance satellites and other defense purposes, such as mission planning during the conflict in Vietnam. In 1973, the program became the Defense Meteorological Satellite Program (DMSP) and was no longer classified.[22]

Burner I was little used because of the development of Burner II. Conceiving a need for a guided upper stage that would be low in cost and usable with more than one first-stage vehicle, on September 2, 1961, the air force's Space Systems Division (SSD) awarded study contracts to the Boeing Company and Ling-Temco-Vought, Inc., pursuant to development of what became Burner II. As a result of its initial work, Boeing won a fixed-price contract on April 1, 1965, to provide one ground-test and three flight versions of the new upper stage. By September 15, Maj. Gen. Ben I. Funk, commander of SSD, could announce the development of the new stage, which became the smallest maneuverable upper-stage vehicle in the air force inventory.[23]

The primary propulsion for Burner II came from the Thiokol TE-M-364-2 (Star 37B) motor, a spherical design promoted by NASA engineer Guy Thibodeaux. Between September 15, 1966, and February 17, 1971, Thor-Burner II vehicles launched four Block 4A, three Block 4B, and three Block 5A Defense Satellite Applications Program weather satellites from the Western Test Range. During this same general period, the Thor-Burner II also launched scientific satellites as part of the Department of Defense's Space Experiments Support Program managed by SSD.[24]

The Block 5B versions of the Defense Satellite Applications Program weather satellites were about twice as heavy as the 5A versions, necessitating increased thrust for Burner II. So the air force's Space and Missile Systems Organization (created July 1, 1967, to bring the SSD and its sister Ballistics Systems Division into a single organization headquartered in Los Angeles at the former SSD location) contracted with Boeing for an uprated Burner II that became Burner IIA. Boeing did the uprating with a minimum of modifications by adding a Thiokol TE-M-442-1 motor to form a second upper stage. With the Burner IIA, a Thor first stage launched five Block 5B and two Block 5C meteorological satellites (in what became the DMSP) from October 14, 1971, to May 24, 1975. A final Thor-Burner IIA launch on February 18, 1976, failed because the Thor prematurely ceased firing. This last use of the Burner IIA did not spell the end of the DMSP program, however, because a Thor coupled with a Thiokol TE-M-364-15 (Star 37S) motor that had a titanium case (rather than the steel used on the Star 37B) launched 4 improved Block 5D weather satellites between September 11, 1976, and June 6, 1979. Then Atlas Es and Titan IIs launched 10 more DMSP satellites by 1999.[25]

A final major Thor launch vehicle was the Thor-Delta. Whereas the other Thor-based launch vehicles were primarily air force assets sometimes used by NASA, Delta was a NASA-developed space-launch vehicle used on occasion by the air force until near the end of the period covered by this book, when the air force began to make extensive use of Delta IIs. Since it was conceived by NASA in 1959 as an interim vehicle to lift medium payloads by using existing technology, modified only as needed for specific missions, Delta has enjoyed a remarkably long career, attesting to its success.[26]

The initial idea for Thor-Delta apparently came from Milton Rosen. He was working at NASA Headquarters in the Office of Space Flight Development, headed by Abe Silverstein. His immediate supervisor was Abraham Hyatt, who had become the assistant director for propulsion following a decade of work at the navy's Bureau of Aeronautics. At Silverstein's behest, Rosen worked with Douglas Aircraft Company to develop the vehicle. Using components already proven in flight, NASA and Douglas eliminated the need for developmental flights. Their contract set a very ambitious goal (for 1959) of an initial 50 percent reliability with a final rate of 90 percent.[27]

An important asset in Delta's development consisted of the personnel from the Vanguard program, including Rosen, who brought their experience to decision-making positions at the new Goddard Space Flight Center within NASA, as well as at NASA Headquarters. At Goddard, William R. Schindler, who had worked on Vanguard, headed a small technical group that provided direction and technical monitoring for the Delta program, which initially borrowed technology from the Vanguard, Thor-Able, and Titan programs. On November 24, 1962, NASA converted this technical direction to formal project management for Delta.[28]

On May 13, 1960, an attempt to launch the spherical, passive reflector satellite Echo with the first Thor-Delta failed when the third-stage propellants did not ignite because a small chunk of solder in a transistor broke loose in flight and shorted out a semiconductor that had passed all of its qualification tests. A similar but less costly problem with another transistor on the third Delta launch led NASA to change its specifications and testing of such components. Meanwhile, on August 12, 1960, the second Delta launch successfully placed *Echo 1* into orbit. And the remainder of the original 12 Deltas all had successful launches of a variety of payloads from the *Tiros 2* through 6 weather satellites to the *Telstar 1* communications satellite, the first commercial spacecraft launched by NASA (on July 10, 1962, the last of the original 12 launches by a Delta).[29]

From this beginning, the Delta went through a long and complicated series of modifications and upgrades. The initial Delta could launch 100 pounds of payload to geostationary (also called geosynchronous) transfer orbit. Starting in 1962, Delta evolved through a series of models with designations such as A, B, C, D, E, J, L, M, M-6, N, 900, 904, 2914, 3914, 3910/PAM (for Payload Assist Module), 3920/PAM, 6925 (Delta II), and 7925 (also a Delta II), the last of them introduced in 1990. The payload capabilities of these versions of the vehicle increased, at first gradually and then more rapidly, so that the 3914 introduced in 1975 could lift 2,100 pounds to geostationary transfer orbit and the 7925 could lift 4,010 pounds (40.1 times the original capability).[30]

FIG. 2.6
A Delta
1910 vehicle
launching
*Orbiting Solar
Observatory
8* on June 21,
1975, showing
the Castor II
strap-on
boosters at the
base of the
vehicle to add
to the thrust.
(Photo courtesy
of NASA)

To achieve this enormous growth in payload from 1960 to 1990, the Delta program augmented the capabilities of the booster and upper stages, lengthened and enlarged the tanks of the first two liquid-propellant stages, enlarged and upgraded third-stage motors, improved guidance systems, and introduced increasingly large and numerous strap-on solids to provide so-called zero-stage boost. During this period, the program generally continued to follow Rosen's initial approach of introducing only low-risk modifications or ones involving proven systems. This enabled, on average, a launch every 60 days with a reliability over the 30 years of 94 percent (189 successes out of 201 attempts, the last one through the end of 1990 occurring on November 26, 1990).[31]

Delta launches and improvements continued beyond this period. Because the Thor and Delta rockets were not so much innovators as borrowers of new technology from other programs, they experienced fewer birth pangs than other missiles and rockets, showing the value of shared information. They nevertheless did experience some unexpected problems that required redesign. But by (mostly) using components already tested and proven, the Delta achieved a high reliability that made it an enduring member of the launch-vehicle family. From an interim launch vehicle in 1959, it became one of the few that lasted into the 21st century, a distinction shared with the Atlas family.[32]

The Atlas Space-Launch Vehicle and Its Upper Stages, 1958–90

Even before it began service as a missile, the Atlas had started to function as a launch vehicle. In December 1958, an entire Atlas (less two jettisoned booster engines) went into orbit carrying a repeater satellite in Project Score. Then, simultaneously with their role in Project Mercury, modified Atlas missiles served as space-launch vehicles for both the air force and NASA in a variety of missions. The basic Atlas was standardized, uprated, lengthened, and otherwise modified in a variety of configurations, often individually tailored for specific missions. Engineers mated the vehicle with a number of different upper stages, of which the Agena and Centaur were the best known and most important. In these various configurations, Atlas space boosters launched satellites and spacecraft for such programs as Samos, Midas, Ranger, Mariner, Pioneer, International Telecommunications Satellite Consortium (Intelsat), the Fleet Satellite Communications System (FLTSATCOM), the Defense Meteorological Satellite Program, and the Navstar Global Positioning System. Following the end of the period covered in this book, some Atlases even used strap-on solid motors to supplement their thrust at liftoff.[33]

After initial failures of three Atlas-Ables in 1959–60, Atlas-Agena had a number of problems but became a successful launch combination. From February 26, 1960, until June 27, 1978, Atlas-Agenas flew approximately 110 missions, many of them classified. Meanwhile, in 1962 NASA urged the air force to upgrade the Atlas D basic launch vehicle to a standardized launch configuration known as Space Launch Vehicle 3 (SLV-3), which was much more reliable than the Atlas D (96 versus 81 percent successful). A further upgrade after 1965 known as SLV-3A featured longer tanks, allowing heavier payloads in conjunction with other modifications. Because of the classified nature of many Agena missions, precise and reliable statistics are not available, but by May 1979, on Thor, Atlas, and Titan boosters, Agena had proved itself to be a workhorse of space, achieving a reported success rate of higher than 93 percent.[34]

With the exception of Agena, most of the upper stages used with Atlas were derivatives from other programs. The Centaur, however, was a derivative, in a sense, of Atlas in that it used the steel-balloon tank structure envisioned by Charlie Bossart and developed for the Atlas missile. Adapting that structure to the liquid-hydrogen fuel used on the Centaur proved to be a major challenge, however. It required a lot of engineering changes when problems occurred, a major reorganization of the way Centaur was managed, and a great deal of testing. But after initial delays, it worked well.[35]

If Agena was the workhorse of space, Centaur was the Clydesdale. Its powerful engines enabled it to carry heavier payloads into orbit or farther into space than Agena could manage. The Centaur could do this because it burned liquid hydrogen as well as liquid oxygen. Hydrogen offered more thrust per pound of fuel burned per second than any other chemical propellant then available—about 35 to 40 percent more than RP-1 (kerosene) when burned with liquid oxygen.[36]

This added performance allowed various versions of Atlas-Centaur to support such NASA missions as landing on the lunar surface in the Surveyor project and orbiting High-Energy Astronomy Observatories, as well as placing 35 communications satellites into orbit through 1989. As with other upper stages flying on Atlas vehicles, not all of the Centaur missions were successful, but most were.[37]

The intellectual push for Centaur came from Convair Division of General Dynamics engineer Krafft Ehricke, who had worked for von Braun at Peenemünde and Huntsville and for Bell Aircraft before moving to Convair. When General Dynamics managers asked him to design an upper stage for Atlas, he and some other engineers, including Bossart, decided that liquid hydrogen and liquid oxygen were the propellants they needed. Aware to some degree that liquid hydrogen's very low density, extremely cold boiling point (–423°F), low surface tension, and wide range of flammability made it unusually difficult to work with, Ehricke faced funding limitations under an air force contract that precluded performing as many tests as the propellant required—an important restriction on normal rocket-engineering practice.[38]

This, among other issues, prevented Convair engineers from discovering problems occasioned by liquid hydrogen's unique properties as early as they otherwise might have done, necessitating redesign.

Other problems arose with Centaur engines, designed by Pratt & Whitney Division of United Aircraft Corporation. The extreme cold of liquid hydrogen required completely new design features, including the use of aluminum coated with Teflon in place of rubber gaskets to seal pipe joints. Despite such problems plus burnthroughs of the combustion chamber that necessitated redesigns, Pratt & Whitney engineers conducted a successful engine run in September 1959, less than a year from the date of the initial contracts with their company and Convair.[39]

However, explosions in engines in late 1960–early 1961 revealed other problems. One of these required an adjustment to the method of feeding the hydrogen to the combustion chamber. Because of such difficulties and resultant delays, an Atlas-Centaur did not launch on a test flight until May 8, 1962, 15 months later than planned. At the point of maximum dynamic pressure, 54.7 seconds into the launch, an explosion occurred as the liquid-hydrogen tank split open. Engineers did not discover the real cause of the problem until five years later, but meanwhile the delays and problems resulted in a complete reorganization of the Centaur program to provide better control and coordination. Funding also improved.[40]

Solutions to further problems and programmatic changes followed, but finally, on May 30, 1966, an Atlas-Centaur successfully launched *Surveyor 1* to the Moon on the first operational Atlas-Centaur flight. Atlas-Centaur performed satisfactorily on all of the Surveyor launches, although two of the spacecraft had problems. But five of the seven missions were successful, providing more than 87,000 photographs and much scientific information valuable both for Apollo landings and for lunar studies. On *Surveyors 5–7* the Atlases used longer tanks with greater propellant volumes and payload capacity than the earlier versions. With the longer tanks, the weight of payload that the Atlas-Centaur combination could place in 300-nautical-mile orbit rose from 8,500 pounds on the shorter version to 9,100 pounds.[41]

The longer-tank Atlas (SLV-3C) and the original Centaur (known as Centaur D) launched on March 2, 1972, with a Delta third-stage solid-propellant motor, the Thiokol TE-M-364-4 (Star 37E), on the spectacular *Pioneer 10* mission that was NASA's first to the outer planets and the first to reach escape velocity from the solar system. Well before this launch, NASA, which had taken over the program from the air force, had decided to upgrade the Centaur with an improved guidance/control computer. The new computer allowed General Dynamics to simplify the Atlas to the SLV-3D configuration by removing the autopilot, programming, and telemetry units

FIG. 2.7
An Atlas-Centaur launch vehicle with the *Mariner 9* space probe undergoing radio-frequency interference tests at Kennedy Space Center in 1971. (Photo courtesy of NASA)

from the earlier, long-tank SLV-3C and having the Centaur perform those functions. The new Centaur had two configurations, the D-1A for use with Atlas and the D-1T for use with Titan space-launch vehicles. The differences between the two configurations involved details of external insulation, payload-fairing diameter, battery capacity, and the like.[42]

The first use of the Centaur D-1A and SLV-3D was on the launch of *Pioneer 11*, which had the same mission as *Pioneer 10* plus making detailed observations of Saturn and its rings. As on *Pioneer 10*, the mission also employed the Star 37 motor in a third stage. Launched on April 5, 1973, *Pioneer 11* returned much data about Saturn, including discoveries of Saturn's 11th moon and two new rings. Between 1973 and May 19, 1983, 32 SLV-3Ds launched with Centaur

FIG. 2.8
Launch of a
Titan-Centaur
vehicle from
Cape Canaveral
Air Force
Station, Febru-
ary 11, 1974.
The two solid-
rocket motors
and the core
stages of the
Titan appear
below the
Centaur upper
stage. (Photo
courtesy of
NASA)

D-1A upper stages. With the first launch of the *Intelsat V* with more relay capacity (and weight) on December 6, 1980, the Centaur began to use engines that were adjusted to increase their thrust. Of the total 32 SLV-3D/D-1A (and the slightly modified D-1AR) launches, only 2 failed. This marked a 93.75 percent success rate, with no failures caused by the Centaur stage.[43]

During the early 1980s, General Dynamics and Pratt & Whitney converted to new versions of Atlas and Centaur. The Atlas G was 81 inches longer than the SLV-3D because of additions to the lengths of the propellant tanks. It developed 438,000 pounds of thrust. Pratt & Whitney made several changes to the Centaur. The first Atlas G-Centaur launched on June 9, 1984, attempting to place an *Intelsat V* into orbit. It did so, but the orbit was not the intended one and was unusable for communications purposes. After a modification to fix the problem, there were four successes and one failure (caused by a lightning strike). Then, on September 25, 1989, an Atlas G-Centaur launched the 5,100-pound *FLTSATCOM F-8* satellite into geosynchronous transfer orbit. This was the last in a series of such navy ultra-high-frequency satellites, part of a worldwide communications system for the DoD.[44]

Meanwhile, forces had been building for commercializing launch-vehicle services. The air force had become unhappy with the idea, promoted by NASA, that all DoD payloads should be transported on the Space Shuttles instead of expendable launch vehicles. There was already competition from the Ariane launch vehicle in Europe, with prospects that other countries would sell launch-vehicle services to communications-satellite purveyors and other users. On January 28, 1986, the explosion of the shuttle *Challenger* grounded the remaining shuttles for more than two years. Early in 1987, General Dynamics announced that it would sell Atlas-Centaur as a commercial launch vehicle. NASA then signed a commercial contract with the company. General Dynamics decided to designate the commercial vehicles with Roman numerals, the first being Atlas I. All would have Centaur upper stages. On July 25, 1990, the first Atlas I successfully launched the joint NASA/Air Force *Combined Release and Radiation Effects Satellite* into a highly elliptical geosynchronous transfer orbit.[45]

Through this launch, the Centaur had had a 95 percent success rate on 76 flights. This included 42 successes in a row for Centaur D-1 and D-1A between 1971 and 1984. The Centaur had led to the use of liquid-hydrogen technology on both upper stages of the Saturn launch vehicle and in the space shuttle main engines (SSMEs). It had thus made major contributions to U.S. launch-vehicle technology.[46]

Partway through the history of Centaur and the various Atlas models used to launch it, the air force contracted with General Dynamics, beginning on February 14, 1966, to modify Atlas Es and Fs that had been in storage since their decommissioning as missiles in 1965. The process began with the newer F models. Rocketdyne inspected each of the MA-3 engines and fixed or replaced any part that failed to meet specifications. In 1969, the rocket division started a more extensive program of refurbishment to ensure that the engines in storage would work when called upon. After two launch failures in 1980–81, Rocketdyne rebuilt the engines at its plant, performing static tests before installing them on a launch vehicle.[47]

Six Atlas Ds and four Fs joined forces in launching Orbiting Vehicle One (OV-1) spacecraft, beginning with a failed launch on

January 21, 1965, by a D model and ending on August 6, 1971, with the successful launch of *OV-1 20* and *OV-1 21* by an F model. A number of the Atlas launch vehicles carried multiple OV-1 satellites, each of which included an FW-4S solid-propellant rocket motor built by the Chemical Systems Division (CSD) of United Technologies Corporation, the organization that also provided the solid-rocket motors (SRMs) for the Titan III. Although the satellite failed to orbit for a variety of causes on four of the OV-1 launches, the air force's Aerospace Research Support Program placed 117 space experiments in orbit to study a variety of phenomena.[48]

An Atlas F successfully launched a radar calibration target and a radiation research payload for the air force's Space Test Program on October 2, 1972, using the Burner II solid-propellant upper stage that usually paired with the Thor booster. Another solid-propellant upper stage that operated only once with an Atlas E or F was the Payload Transfer System (PTS), which used the same basic TE-M-364-4 Thiokol motor as the Stage Vehicle System (SVS), employed multiple times (as a different upper-stage system from PTS) with Atlas Fs and Es. On July 13, 1974, an Atlas F and the PTS successfully launched *Navigation Technology Satellite* (*NTS*) *1* to test the first atomic clocks placed in space to confirm their design and operation and provide information about signal propagation to confirm predictions for the Navstar Global Positioning System (GPS). GPS was then in development and destined to become a vital navigational aid, far more sophisticated and accurate than anything that preceded it.[49]

SVS, built by Fairchild Space and Electronics Company of Germantown, Maryland, used two TE-M-364-4 motors in two upper stages to place *NTS-2* and six Navigation Development System (NDS) spacecraft into orbit between June 23, 1977, and April 26, 1980. The NDS-7 launch failed on December 18, 1981, when the Atlas E launch vehicle went out of control. The other seven satellites all supported the development of GPS.[50]

The air force used a different upper stage, known as SGS-II, together with the Atlas E to launch *NDS-8* through *NDS-11* between July 14, 1983, and October 8, 1985, all four launches being successful. McDonnell Douglas Astronautics Company made the upper stage, using two Thiokol TE-M-711-8 (Star 48) motors, also featured on the Payload Assist Module (PAM), which the Space Shuttle and Delta launch vehicle had employed since 1980. Thiokol began developing the motor in 1976. It used the same hydroxy-terminated polybutadiene (HTPB)-based propellant as Thiokol's Antares III rocket motor, a third-generation, third-stage propulsion unit for the Scout launch vehicle.[51]

The Atlas Es and Fs used other upper stages to launch satellites, including one Agena D. On June 26, 1978, an Atlas F—modified to mate with the Agena and to carry the Seasat-A oceanographic satellite—placed its payload into orbit. The other major upper stage used by the Atlas Es and Fs was the Integrated Spacecraft System (ISS), with a Thiokol TE-M-364-15 motor (Star 37S). In 1977–78, this was the latest in the Star 37 series of motors, also used as an upper stage on the Thor for launching weather satellites. Beginning with a launch of *Tiros N* from an Atlas F on October 13, 1978, the ISS served as an upper stage for launching the *NOAA-6* through *NOAA-11* polar orbiting meteorological satellites plus a number of DMSP satellites. The only failure in the series was NOAA-B on May 29, 1980.[52]

In February 1983, the air force began operating a derivative of the SLV-3D known as the Atlas H. It used most of the basic systems on the SLV but employed GE radio-inertial guidance. The particular solid-propellant upper stage used with the Atlas H and previous Atlas Es and Fs to launch the White Cloud Naval Ocean Surveillance System (NOSS) satellites was classified. The White Cloud NOSS satellites provided the DoD (primarily the navy) with ocean surveillance. Overall, the Atlas E and F launch vehicles had only 4 failures in 41 launches by the end of 1990, yielding a success rate of more than 90 percent. All 5 launches with the Atlas H were successful.[53]

Conceived as a missile, the Atlas became a successful and versatile launch vehicle, mated with a great variety of upper stages. Featuring a controversial but "brilliant, innovative, and yet simple" concept (the steel-balloon tank design), both the Atlas and the Centaur proved to be flexible and effective. With commercialization, the Atlas and the Centaur continued to provide launch-vehicle services beyond the period of this book and into the 21st century. The Centaur proved to be especially difficult to develop because of the peculiar properties of liquid hydrogen. But it was also hampered by initial funding arrangements and other avoidable problems. As with many rocket programs, engineers found that the existing fund of knowledge was inadequate to predict all of the problems that would occur in developing and launching an extraordinarily complex machine. Unforeseen problems continued into the 1990s, and engineers had to relearn the lesson that continual and sophisticated testing was the price of success, even if it did not always preclude unanticipated failures.[54]

The Scout Family of Space-Launch Vehicles, 1958–91

With its development overlapping that of Atlas and other launch vehicles, the Scout series of boosters was unique in being the first multistage booster to operate exclusively with solid-propellant motors. It remained the smallest multistage vehicle in long-term use for orbital launches. And it was the only launch vehicle developed under the auspices of Langley Research Center, which made many contributions to space efforts but, as the oldest of NASA's component organizations, had a long heritage of aeronautical rather than space-related research. Like the Delta, with which it shared many stages, Scout proved to be long-lasting and reliable. But in contrast with Delta, it suffered through a difficult gestation and childhood.[55]

Because, like Delta, it used much technology that had already been developed elsewhere, Scout's problems lay less in the design-and-development area than was true with many other rockets, although there *were* several developmental difficulties. But Scout's problems were primarily matters of systems engineering and quality control. Following a series of early failures, the program underwent a reliability improvement and recertification process, after which one Scout engineer stated that he and his colleagues had "all underestimated the magnitude of the job" when they had undertaken its development. "The biggest problem we had was denying the existence of problems that we did not understand." Once the project accepted that it had such problems and examined them, it learned from the process and went on to produce a long-lived, reliable, small launcher used by NASA, the DoD, and foreign countries.

Scout's payload capability increased almost fourfold by its final flight in 1994. At that time, it had launched a great variety of scientific and applications payloads, Transit navigation satellites, and experiments to help understand the aerodynamics of reentry, among other types of missions. Counting two partial successes as failures, Scout had 103 successful missions out of 118 for an overall 87 percent success rate, according to one source. The 15 failures were mostly in the early years, with 12 of them occurring by June 1964. In the 91 missions since that time, only 6 failures or partial failures occurred for a 94 percent success rate.[56]

During 1956, the idea for Scout arose at Langley's Pilotless Aircraft Research Division (PARD) on remote Wallops Island in the Atlantic Ocean off Virginia's Eastern Shore. There, several engineers conceived of a four-stage solid-propellant launch vehicle. Between July 1, 1960, and March 29, 1962, Scout had nine developmental flights from Wallops, with six of them counted as successes. Several

FIG. 2.9
Launch of
Scout ST-5
(Scout Test 5)
on June 30,
1961, from
Wallops Island,
Virginia—a
failure because
the third
stage of the
Scout did not
ignite, which
prevented the
satellite from
going into
orbit. (Photo
courtesy of
NASA)

developmental problems led to upgrades of the third- and fourth-stage motors.[57]

While NASA was in the process of developing Scout, the air force worked with the civilian agency on a military version called the Blue Scout. Meetings with the air force had begun before the creation of NASA, as early as June 4, 1958. By the end of February 1959, the air force had assigned primary responsibility for the development of the Blue Scout to its Ballistic Missile Division, with a project office at BMD being set up under Maj. (soon-to-be Lt. Col.) Donald A. Stine. Because of the payloads the air force expected to launch, its vehicle required thicker walls and more mounting studs for the third and fourth stages. By September 1960, the air force had evolved its designs to include a Blue Scout 1, Blue Scout 2, and

Blue Scout Junior. All of them used the Castor I (the regular Scout second-stage motor) in place of the usual Algol I in the first stage, and the Antares I (the regular Scout third-stage motor) in the second stage. The third stage used the Aerojet 30-KS-8000 motor, also known as Alcor. The motor for the fourth stage of most Blue Scout Juniors was a unit designed by the Naval Ordnance Test Station, known as NOTS model 100A. The B version of the same motor later became the fifth-stage propulsion unit for NASA Scouts using that many stages.[58]

The first Blue Scout Junior launched on September 21, 1960, before the fourth-stage motor's development was complete, but apparently the vehicle did use a NOTS 100A. In all, there were 25 known Blue Scout Junior launches from Cape Canaveral, Vandenberg (or the navy's nearby Point Arguello), and Wallops Island, with the last one on November 24, 1970. All were suborbital, 22 of them successful, for an 88 percent success rate, although the telemetry and payloads sometimes failed. The configurations of the vehicles varied, depending on the mission, with some launches using only three stages and a supersonic combustion ramjet test employing only one.[59]

The Blue Scout 1 was a three-stage version of the Scout. Its first (successful) launch occurred at Cape Canaveral on January 7, 1961. Blue Scout 2 was a four-stage vehicle. Most sources list only three flights in 1961. But other sources continue to list launch vehicles as Blue Scouts, so the precise history of the vehicle is quite nebulous. The navy procured some of them at least as late as fiscal year 1967, and the air force, until fiscal year 1976. Of the first 92 Scouts, NASA paid for 54; the navy, 19; and the air force, 14, with the other 5 being funded by the Atomic Energy Commission or European users. Whereas earlier Blue Scout vehicles had been launched by uniformed ("blue suit") air force personnel, on January 10, 1970, an agreement between NASA and the DoD stated that NASA would contract for Scout launches from Vandenberg AFB for both itself and the DoD. Thus, it appears that there was a gradual blurring of the lines between Blue and NASA Scouts. But whichever they were called, they continued to perform launch services for the armed forces as well as the civilian space agency.[60]

Meanwhile, a number of Scout failures in the early years led in 1963 to a major review of the program. This revealed that no two Scout failures had been caused by the same problem. But the large number of failures, including many recent ones, suggested a need for greater procedural consistency and for requalifying all Scout vehicles then in storage awaiting launch. As Eugene Schult, head of the Langley Scout Project Office in 1990, remembered, "We did things differently at Wallops than at the Western Test Range. The Air Force had its own way of doing things; the contractor had his ways; and we had our ways. It was a problem trying to coordinate them."[61]

To address these problems, a team from NASA, the LTV Missile Group of the Chance Vought Corporation (the airframe and prime contractor for Scout), and the air force initiated procedures that brought the manufacturing and launch teams in closer contact to improve coordination and quality control. (Obviously, this entailed exchange of information as well.) In addition, all 27 existing Scout vehicles went back to the LTV plant for disassembly and X-ray or microscope inspection. Standardization became the order of the day. The first recertified Scout, S-122R, with the *R* indicating that it had been refurbished and recertified, launched from Vandenberg December 19, 1963. It was the beginning of a series of 26 launches through October 1966 with only 1 failure, for a 96 percent success rate.[62] Standardization and quality control had greatly improved reliability, showing the value of improved management and better systems engineering.

In this period and after, Scout continued to develop, with new stages replacing those already in use. These changes increased the payload and other capabilities of the Scout system. Beginning on April 26, 1967, Scout also began launching (under agreement with Italy) from the San Marcos platform off the coast of Kenya, Africa, on the equator. From there, Scout could place satellites into orbits not achievable by launches from Cape Canaveral, let alone Wallops and Vandenberg, the three U.S. launch sites for the vehicle. As a result of a long series of improvements, the payload capacity of Scout increased from only 131 pounds into a 300-mile circular orbit for the original Scout in 1960 to 454 pounds by October 30, 1979. The Scout continued in operation through August 5, 1994, with all of the remaining launches using this last (G-1) configuration.[63]

Operating for nearly three and a half decades, Scout obviously was successful. Neither its payload capacity nor reliability matched those of the Delta. But it filled a niche in the launch-vehicle spectrum, or it would not have lasted so long. In the process, it had to overcome some initial growing pains. Many of its motors and other components experienced developmental problems, including the Castor I, Antares I, and Altair II, as well as heat shields, a fourth-stage frangible diaphragm, and the nozzles on the Algol IIA and IIB. Thus, like other missiles and launch vehicles, Scout also suffered from the frequent inability of designers to foresee problems their handiwork might face. But as in so many other cases, engineers were able to correct the problems once they understood them and/or brought their experience and knowledge to bear on available data.

Saturn I through Saturn V, 1958–75

Soon after the engineers at Wallops began developing Scout, those at the Redstone Arsenal started work on the Saturn family of launch vehicles. Whereas the solid-propellant Scout was the runt among American launch vehicles, the liquid-fueled Saturn became the giant. The standard Scout at the end of its career was a four-stage vehicle about 75 feet in height, but the Saturn V, with only three stages, stood almost 5 times as tall, about 363 feet. This made the Saturn taller than the Statue of Liberty—equivalent in height to a 36-story building and taller than a football field was long. Composed of some 5 million parts, it was a complex mass of propellant tanks, engines, plumbing fixtures, guidance/control devices, thrust structures, and other elements. Its electrical components, for example, included some 5,000 transistors and diodes, all of which had to be tested both individually and in conjunction with the rest of the vehicle to ensure that they would work properly when called upon. The Scout could launch only 454 pounds into a 300-mile orbit, but the Saturn V sent a roughly 95,000-pound payload with three astronauts on board toward six successful lunar orbits.[64]

Using clustering of rocket engines in its lower stages to achieve its massive initial thrust, the Saturn V was based on the earlier development of vehicles that ultimately came to be designated the Saturn I and the Saturn IB. These two interim space boosters were, in turn, based upon technologies developed for the Redstone, Jupiter, Thor, Atlas, Centaur, and other vehicles and stages. Thus, although the Saturn family constituted the first group of rockets developed specifically for launching humans into space, it did not so much entail new technologies as it did a scaling up in size of existing or already developing technology and an uprating of engine performance. Even so, this posed significant technological hurdles and, often, a need to resort to empirical solutions to problems they raised. Existing theory and practice were inadequate for both the massive scale of the Saturns and the need to make them sufficiently reliable to carry human beings to an escape trajectory from Earth's immediate vicinity out toward the Moon.[65]

The organization under Wernher von Braun at the Army Ballistic Missile Agency (ABMA)—which became NASA's Marshall Space Flight Center (MSFC) in mid-1960—began the initial research and development of the Saturn family of vehicles. In response to DoD projections of a need for a very large booster for communication and weather satellites and space probes, ABMA had begun in April 1957 to study a vehicle with 1.5 million pounds of thrust in its first stage. Then the formation of the Advanced Research Projects Agency (ARPA) on February 7, 1958, led ABMA to shift from initial plans to use engines still under development. Despite the crisis resulting from *Sputnik*, ARPA urged the use of existing and proven engines so that the new booster could be developed as quickly as possible at a minimal cost. ABMA then shifted to use of eight uprated Thor-Jupiter engines in a cluster to provide the 1.5 million pounds of thrust in the first stage, calling the new concept the Juno V. This led to an ARPA order on August 15, 1958, initiating what von Braun and others soon started calling the Saturn program, a name ARPA officially sanctioned on February 3, 1959.[66]

Under a contract signed on September 11, 1958, the Rocketdyne Division of North American Aviation in fact supplied an H-1 engine that was actually more than an uprated Thor-Jupiter powerplant. It resulted from research and development on an X-1 engine that the Experimental Engines Group at Rocketdyne began in 1957. Meanwhile, the engineers at ABMA did some scrounging in their stock of leftover components to meet the demands of ARPA's schedule within their limited budget. The schedule called for a full-scale, static firing of a 1.5-million-pound cluster by the end of 1959. Instead of a new, single tank for the first stage, which would have required revised techniques and equipment, the ABMA engineers found rejected or incomplete 5.89-foot (in diameter) Redstone and 8.83-foot Jupiter propellant tanks. They combined one of the Jupiter tanks with eight from the Redstone to provide a cluster of propellant reservoirs for the first-stage engines. In such a fashion, the Saturn program got started, with funding gradually increased even before the transfer of the von Braun group to NASA.[67]

Initially called the Saturn C-1, the Saturn I (properly so-called after February 1963) was at first going to have a third stage, but between January and March 1961, NASA decided to drop the third stage and to use Pratt & Whitney RL10 engines in the second stage. These were the same engines being developed for Centaur. Meanwhile, on April 26, 1960, NASA had awarded a contract to the Douglas Aircraft Company to develop the Saturn I second stage, which confusingly was called the S-IV. Unlike the Centaur, which used only two RL10s, the S-IV held six of the engines, requiring considerable scaling up of the staging hardware. Using its own experience as well as cooperation from Centaur contractors Convair and Pratt &

Whitney, Douglas succeeded in providing an SL-IV stage in time for the January 29, 1964, first launch of a Saturn I featuring a live second stage. This was also the first launch with 188,000-pound-thrust H-1 engines in the first stage, and it succeeded in orbiting the second stage.[68]

Development of the Saturn I posed problems. Combustion instability in the H-1 engines, stripped gears in an H-1 turbopump, sloshing in first-stage propellant tanks, and an explosion during static testing of the S-IV stage all required redesigns. But apart from the sloshing on the first Saturn I launch (SA-1), the 10 flights of Saturn I (from October 27, 1961, to July 30, 1965) revealed few problems. There were changes resulting from flight testing, but NASA counted all 10 flights successful, a tribute to the thoroughness and extensive ground testing of von Braun's engineers and their contractors.[69]

At 191.5 feet tall (including the payload), Saturn I was still a far cry from Saturn V. The intermediate version, Saturn IB, consisted of a modified Saturn I with its two stages (S-IB and S-IVB) redesigned to reflect the increasing demands placed upon them, plus a further developed instrument unit with a new computer and additional flexibility and reliability. The S-IVB would serve as the second stage of the Saturn IB and (with further modifications) the third stage of the Saturn V, exemplifying the building-block nature of the development process. The first stage of the Saturn IB was also a modified S-I, built by the same contractor, Chrysler. The cluster pattern for the eight H-1 engines did not change, although uprating increased their thrust to 200,000 and then 205,000 pounds per engine. In its second stage, the Saturn IB had a new and much larger engine, the J-2, with thrust exceeding that of the six RL10s used on the Saturn I. Like the RL10s, it burned liquid hydrogen and liquid oxygen.[70]

Rocketdyne won a contract (signed on September 10, 1960) to develop the J-2, with specifications that the engine ensure safety for human flight yet have a conservative design to speed up availability. By the end of 1961, it had become evident that the engine would power not only stage two of Saturn IB but both the second and third stages of the Saturn V. In the second stage of Saturn V, there would be a cluster of five J-2s; on the S-IVB second stage of Saturn IB and the S-IVB third stage of Saturn V, there would be a single J-2 a piece. Rocketdyne engineers had problems with injectors for the new engine until they borrowed technology from the RL10, a further example of shared information between competing contractors, facilitated by NASA.[71]

After completion of its development, the Saturn IB stood 224 feet high. Its initial launch on February 26, 1966, marked the first flight tests of an S-IVB stage, a J-2 engine, and a powered Apollo space-craft. It tested two stages of the launch vehicle plus the reentry heat shield of the spacecraft. Except for minor glitches like failures of two parachutes for data cameras, it proved successful. Other flights also succeeded, but on January 27, 1967, a ground checkout of the vehicle for what would have been the fourth flight test led to the disastrous Apollo fire that killed three astronauts. The test flights of Saturn IB concluded with the successful launching and operation of the command and service modules (CSM), redesigned since the fire. Launched on October 11, 1968, the Saturn IB with a 225,000-pound-thrust J-2 in the second stage performed well in this first piloted Apollo flight. This ended the Saturn IB flights for Apollo, although the vehicle would go on to be used in the Skylab and Apollo-Soyuz Test Projects from 1973 to 1975.[72]

Development of some parts used exclusively for the Saturn V began before design of other components common to both the Saturn IB and the Saturn V. For instance, on January 9, 1959, Rocketdyne won the contract for the huge F-1 engine used on the Saturn V (but not the IB); however, not until May 1960 did NASA select Rocket-dyne to negotiate a contract for the J-2 common to both launch vehicles. Configurations were in flux in the early years, and NASA did not officially announce the C-1B as a two-stage vehicle for Earth-orbital missions with astronauts aboard until July 11, 1962, renaming it the Saturn IB the next February. (NASA Headquarters had already formally approved the C-5 on January 25, 1962.) Thus, even though the Saturn IB served as an interim configuration between the Saturn I and the Saturn V, development of both vehicles over-lapped substantially, with planning for the ultimate moon rocket occurring even before designers got approval to develop the interim configuration.[73]

Burning RP-1 as its fuel with liquid oxygen as the oxidizer, the F-1 did not break new technological ground—in keeping with NASA guidelines to use proven propellants. But its thrust level required so much scaling up of the engine as to mark a major advance in the state of the art of rocket making. Perhaps the most intricate design feature of the F-1, and certainly one that caused great difficulty to engineers, was the injection system. As with many other engines, combustion instability was the problem. On June 28, 1962, during an F-1 hot-engine test at the rocket site on Edwards AFB, combustion instability led to the meltdown of the engine. Using essentially trial-and-error methods coupled with high-speed instrumentation and careful analysis, a team of engineers had to test perhaps 40 or 50 design modifications before they eventually found a combination of baffles, enlarged fuel-injection orifices, and changed impingement angles that worked.[74]

Despite all the effort that went into the injector design, according to Roger Bilstein, it was the turbopump that "absorbed more design effort and time for fabrication than any other component of the engine." There were 11 failures of the system during the development period. All of them necessitated redesign or a change in manufacturing procedures. The final turbopump design provided the speed and high volumes needed for a 1.5-million-pound-thrust engine with a minimal number of parts and high ultimate reliability. However, these virtues came at the expense of much testing and frustration.[75]

There were many other engineering challenges during design and development of the Saturn V. This was especially true of the S-II second stage built by the Space and Information Systems Division of North American Aviation. Problems with that segment of the huge rocket delayed the first launch of the Saturn V from August until November 9, 1967. But on that day the launch of *Apollo 4* (flight AS-501) without astronauts aboard occurred nearly without a flaw.[76]

After several problems on the second Saturn V launch (including the pogo effect on the F-1 engines) prevented the mission from being a complete technical success, engineers found solutions. As a result, the third Saturn V mission (AS-503, or *Apollo 8*) achieved a successful circumlunar flight with astronauts aboard in late 1968. Following two other successful missions, the *Apollo 11* mission between July 16, 1969, and July 24, 1969, achieved the first of six successful lunar landings with the astronauts returning to Earth, fulfilling the goals of the Apollo program.[77]

With Saturns I and IB as interim steps, Saturn V was the culmination of the rocket development work von Braun's engineers had been carrying on since the early 1930s in Germany. In the interim, the specific engineers working under the German American baron had included a great many Americans. There had been a continual improvement of technologies from the V-2 through the Redstone, Jupiter, and Pershing missiles to the three Saturn launch vehicles.

Not all of the technologies used on Saturn V came from von Braun's engineers, of course. Many technologies in the Saturn V resulted from those developed on other programs in which von Braun's team had not participated or for which it was only partly responsible. This is notably true of much liquid-hydrogen technology, which stemmed from contributions by Lewis Research Center, Convair, Pratt & Whitney, Rocketdyne, and Douglas, among others—showing the cumulative effects of much information sharing. But Marshall engineers worked closely with the contractors for the J-2, S-II, and S-IVB stages in overcoming difficulties and made real contributions of their own. This was also true in the development of the Saturn engines. Rocketdyne had started its illustrious career in engine development by examining a V-2 and had worked with von Braun and his engineers on the Redstone engine, a process that continued through Jupiter and the Saturn engines. But a great many of the innovations that led to the F-1 and J-2 had come more or less independently from Rocketdyne engineers, and even on the major combustion-instability and injector problems for the F-1, Rocketdyne's contributions seem to have been at least as great as those from Marshall engineers. In other words, it took teamwork, not only among Americans and Germans at Marshall but among Marshall, other NASA centers, industry, universities, and the U.S. military to create the Apollo launch vehicles. Air force facilities and engineers at Edwards AFB, Holloman AFB, and the Arnold Engineering Development Center also made key contributions to facets of Saturn development.

Another key ingredient in the success of Saturn rocket development was the management system used at ABMA and the NASA Marshall Space Flight Center. As at Peenemünde, von Braun retained his role as an overall systems engineer despite other commitments on his time. At frequent meetings he chaired, he continued to display his uncanny ability to grasp technical details and explain them in terms everyone could understand. Yet he avoided monopolizing the sessions, helping everyone to feel part of the team. Another technique to foster communication among key technical people was his use of weekly notes. Before each Monday, he required his project managers and laboratory chiefs to submit one-page summaries of the previous week's developments and problems. Each manager had to gather and condense the information. Then von Braun wrote marginal comments and circulated copies back to the managers. He might suggest a meeting between two individuals to solve a problem or himself offer a solution. Reportedly, the roughly 35 managers were eager to read these notes, which kept them all informed about problems and issues and allowed them to stay abreast of overall developments, not just those in their separate areas. In this way, the notes integrated related development efforts and spurred efforts to solve problems across disciplinary and organizational lines.[78]

Superficially, these "Monday notes" seemed quite different from Schriever's "Black Saturdays" and Raborn's PERT system. They were certainly less formal and more focused on purely technical solutions than on cost control. But in the technical arena, von Braun's system served the same systems-engineering function as the other systems.

While the Saturn I was undergoing development and flight testing, significant management changes occurred in NASA as a whole. From November 18, 1959 (when NASA assumed technical direction of the Saturn effort), through March 16, 1960 (when the space agency took over administrative direction of the project and formal transfer took place), to July 1, 1960 (when both the Saturn program and the von Braun team of engineers transferred to the Marshall Space Flight Center), the administrator of NASA remained the capable and forceful but conservative T. Keith Glennan. Glennan had organized NASA, adding JPL and Marshall to the core centers inherited from the National Advisory Committee for Aeronautics, NASA's predecessor.[79]

Once John F. Kennedy became president in early 1961 and appointed the still more forceful and energetic but hardly conservative James E. Webb to succeed Glennan, there were bound to be management changes. This was further ensured by Kennedy's famous exhortation on May 25, 1961, "that this nation . . . commit itself to achieving the goal, before this decade is out, of landing a man on the Moon and returning him safely to earth." The commitment that followed gave an entirely new urgency to the Saturn program. To coordinate it and the other aspects of the Apollo program, NASA reorganized in November 1961. Even before the reorganization, Webb chose as head of a new Office of Manned Space Flight (OMSF) an engineer with Radio Corporation of America who had been project manager for the Ballistic Missile Early Warning System (BMEWS). D. Brainerd Holmes had finished the huge BMEWS project on time and within budget, so he seemed an ideal person to achieve a similar miracle with Apollo.[80]

Holmes headed one of four new program offices in the reorganized NASA Headquarters, with all program and center directors now reporting to Associate Administrator Robert C. Seamans Jr., who also took over control of NASA's budget. Webb apparently had not fully grasped Holmes's character when he appointed him. The second NASA administrator had previously considered Abe Silverstein to head OMSF and rejected him because he wanted too much authority, especially vis-à-vis Seamans. Holmes, however, turned out to be "masterful, abrasive, and determined to get what he needed to carry out his assignment, even at the expense of other programs." Within two weeks of joining NASA, the confrontational

FIG. 2.10
Wernher von
Braun (*center*)
showing the
Saturn launch
system to
Pres. John F.
Kennedy and
Deputy NASA
Administrator
Robert
Seamans
(*left*) at Cape
Canaveral,
November 16,
1963. (Photo
courtesy of
NASA)

new manager demanded independence of Seamans. Webb refused. In the summer of 1962, Holmes believed Apollo was getting behind schedule and demanded more funding from Webb to put it back on track, again without success. Holmes had also requested (in vain) that center directors report directly to him rather than to Seamans. In frustration, Holmes finally resigned in June 1963.[81]

Webb selected another highly regarded engineer, who turned out to be less confrontational (at least with his bosses) and more "bureaucratically adept." George E. Mueller (pronounced "Miller") had a background in electrical engineering. After working at Bell Telephone Laboratories and teaching at Ohio State University, he earned his Ph.D. in physics there in 1951 and became a professor in 1952. In 1957 he joined Ramo-Wooldridge's organization as director of the Electronics Laboratories and advanced quickly to become vice president for research and development before formally joining NASA as associate administrator for manned space flight on September 1, 1963.[82]

As a result of a headline in the *New York Times* on July 13, 1963, "Lunar Program in Crisis," Mueller obtained Webb's agreement to manage Apollo with some freedom. But he really showed his bureaucratic astuteness when he assigned John H. Disher in advanced projects and Adelbert O. Tischler, assistant director for propulsion in the Office of Manned Space Flight, to assess how long it would now take to land on the Moon. On September 28, they reported as unlikely that a lunar landing could be achieved during Kennedy's decade "with acceptable risk." They believed it would be late 1971 before a landing could occur. Mueller took the two men to Seamans's office to repeat the findings. Seamans then told Mueller privately to find out how to get back on schedule, exactly the authority and leverage Mueller had evidently sought.[83]

On November 1, 1963, Mueller then instituted two major changes that offered a way to land on the Moon by the end of the decade and greatly strengthened his position. One change was all-up testing. In 1971 Mueller claimed he had been involved with the development of all-up testing at Space Technology Laboratories, although he may or may not have known that his organization had opposed the idea when Otto Glasser introduced it as the only way he could conceive to cut a year from development time for Minuteman at the insistence of the secretary of the air force. In any event, all-up testing had worked for Minuteman and obviously offered a way to speed up testing for the Saturn vehicles.[84]

NASA defined all-up testing to mean a vehicle was "as complete as practicable for each flight, so . . . a maximum amount of test information is obtained with a minimum number of flights." This conflicted with the step-by-step procedures preferred by the von Braun group, but on November 1, Mueller sent a priority message to Marshall, the Manned Spacecraft Center (MSC) in Houston, and the Launch Operations Center (LOC) in Florida. In it he announced a deletion of previously planned Saturn I launches with astronauts aboard and directed that the first Saturn IB launch, SA-201, and the first Saturn V flight, AS-501, should use "all live stages" and include "complete spacecraft." In a memorandum dated October 26, 1963, Mueller wrote to Webb via Seamans, enclosing a proposed NASA press release about all-up testing: "We have discussed this course of action with MSFC, MSC, and LOC, and the Directors of these Centers concur with this recommendation," referring specifically to eliminating "manned" Saturn I flights but by implication, to the all-up testing. The press release stated that "experience in other missile and space programs" had shown it to be "the quickest way of reaching final mission objectives" (a further example of how shared information was important to missile and launch-vehicle programs).[85]

If Mueller had really discussed all-up testing with the center directors, this was not apparent at Marshall, where von Braun went over the message with his staff on November 4, creating a "furor." Staff members recalled numerous failed launches in the V-2, Redstone, and Jupiter programs. William A. Mrazek believed the idea of all-up testing was insane; other lab heads and project managers called it "impossible" and a "dangerous idea." Although von Braun and his deputy, Eberhard Rees, both had their doubts about the idea, in the end they had to agree with Mueller that the planned launches of individual stages would prevent landing on the Moon by the end of the decade. All-up testing prevailed despite von Braun's doubts.[86] And once again, it worked.

The second change introduced on November 1 entailed a reorganization of NASA, placing the field centers under the program offices once again, rather than under Seamans. Mueller obtained authority over Marshall, the MSC, and the LOC (renamed Kennedy Space Center in December).[87]

One aspect of the Marshall effort that did not fit with Mueller's management concepts was the proclivity for technical decisions in Huntsville to be based on their merits instead of schedule or cost. This was true even though project managers were supposed to get jobs done "on time and within budget." A concern with time, budget, and what had come to be called configuration control, however, had become very important in the Minuteman program and quickly spread to NASA when Mueller arranged for Brig. Gen. Samuel Phillips to come to NASA as deputy director and then director (after October 1964) of the Apollo program. The slender, handsome Phillips had moved from his post as director of the Minuteman program in August 1963 to become vice commander of the Ballistic Systems Division. He arrived at NASA Headquarters in early January 1964 and soon arranged for the issue in May of a NASA *Apollo Configuration Management Manual*, adapted from an air force manual.[88]

Phillips had expected resistance to configuration management from NASA. He was not disappointed. Mueller had formed an Apollo Executive Group consisting of the chief executives of firms working on Apollo plus directors of NASA field centers, and in June 1964, Phillips and a subordinate who managed configuration control for him presented the system to the assembled dignitaries. Von Braun objected to the premises of Phillips's presentation on the ground that costs for development programs were "very much unknown, and configuration management does not help." He contended that it was impossible for the chairman of a configuration control board to know enough about all the disciplines involved to decide intelligently about a given issue. Phillips argued that if managers were doing their jobs, they were already making such decisions.

Von Braun retorted that the system tended to move decisions higher in the chain of management. William M. Allen of Boeing countered that this was "a fundamental of good management." When von

Braun continued to argue the need for flexibility, Mueller explained that configuration management did not mean that engineers had "to define the final configuration in the first instance before [they knew] that the end item [was] going to work." It meant defining the expected design "at each stage of the game" and then letting everyone know when it had to be changed. Center directors like von Braun did not prevail in this argument, but resistance continued in industry as well as NASA centers, with the system not firmly established until about the end of 1966.[89]

Mueller and Phillips introduced other management procedures and infrastructure to ensure control of costs and schedules. Phillips converted from a system in which data from the field centers came to Headquarters monthly to one with daily updates. He quickly contracted for a control room in NASA Headquarters similar to the one he had used for Minuteman, with data links to field centers. A computerized system stored and retrieved the data about parts, costs, and failures. Part of this system was a NASA version of the navy's Program Evaluation and Review Technique (PERT), developed for Polaris, which most prime contractors had to use for reporting cost and scheduling data.[90]

Despite von Braun's resistance to configuration management, Phillips recalled in 1988, "I never had a single moment of problem with the Marshall Space Flight Center. [Its] teamwork, cooperation, enthusiasm, and energy of participation were outstanding." Phillips added, "Wernher directed his organization very efficiently and participated in management decisions. When a decision had been made, he implemented it—complied, if you will, with directives." In part, no doubt, Phillips was seeing through the rose-colored glasses of memory. But in part, this reflected von Braun's propensity to argue until he was either convinced that the contrary point of view was correct or until he saw that argument was futile. Then he became a team player.

Phillips had been at the receiving end of V-2s in England during World War II, and he was prepared to dislike the German baron who had directed their development. But the two became friends. He commented that von Braun "could make a person feel personally important to him and that [his or her] ideas were of great value." When asked about von Braun's contributions to the space program, Phillips observed that a few years before, he probably would have said that American industry and engineering could have landed on the Moon without German input. But in 1988 he said, "When I think of the Saturn V, which was done so well under Wernher's direction and which was obviously . . . essential to the lunar mission, . . . I'm not sure today that we could have built it without the ingenuity of Wernher and his team."[91]

The contributions of Mueller and Phillips were probably more critical to the ultimate success of Apollo than even von Braun's. Phillips hesitated about characterizing Mueller but did say that "his perceptiveness and ability to make the right decision on important and far-reaching [as well as] complex technical matters" was "pretty unusual." On the other hand, Mueller's biggest shortcoming, according to Phillips, was "dealing with people." John Disher, who admired Silverstein but characterized Mueller as the "only bona-fide genius I've ever worked with," had to observe that although his boss was "always the epitome of politeness, . . . deep down he [was] just as hard as steel." Also, human space program director of flight operations, Chris Kraft, who dealt with a great many people and frequently clashed with Mueller, had to say that "I've never dealt with a more capable man in terms of his technical ability." Difficult though Mueller was, without him and Phillips, American astronauts probably would not have gotten to the Moon before the end of the decade.[92]

Both men brought to NASA some of the culture and many of the management concepts used in the air force, plus the navy's PERT system. These added to the amalgam of cultures already present in the space agency. Inherited from the National Advisory Committee for Aeronautics (NACA) was a heavy research orientation coupled with a strong emphasis on testing. Von Braun's Germans had brought a similar culture from their V-2 and army experience, together with a tendency to over-engineer rocket systems to ensure against failure. JPL had added its own blend of innovation plus a strong reliance on theory and use of mathematics that was also part of the V-2 experience. The Lewis Research Center brought to the mix its experience with liquid hydrogen, and the Langley Research Center brought the testing of rockets at Wallops Island and a wind-tunnel culture (present also at Ames Research Center). All of these elements (and the management styles that accompanied them) contributed to the Saturn-Apollo effort.

Titan Space-Launch Vehicles, 1961–91

While NASA was just getting started with the massive development effort for the Saturn launch vehicles, the air force began work on what became the Titan family of launch vehicles, beginning with the Titan IIIs and ending with Titan IVBs. Essentially, most of these vehicles consisted of upgraded Titan II cores with a series of upper stages plus a pair of huge segmented, solid-propellant, strap-on motors to supplement the thrust of the Titan II core vehicle. And after September 1988, a limited number of actual Titan IIs, refurbished and equipped with technology and hardware from the Titan III program, joined the other members of the Titan family of launch vehicles. Beginning in June 1989, the Titan IV with a stretched core and seven (instead of Titan III's five or five and a half) segments in its solid-rocket motors became the newest member of the Titan family.[93]

By September 1961, the DoD had agreed to the concept of combining a suitably modified Titan II with strap-on solid motors to satisfy military requirements; and the following month, a DoD-NASA Large Launch Vehicle Planning Group recommended the Titan III, as the vehicle had come to be designated. It would feature 120-inch-diameter solid motors and would serve both DoD and NASA needs "in the payload range of 5,000 to 30,000 pounds, low-Earth orbit equivalent."[94]

Although the air force's Space Systems Division, which oversaw development of the Titan III, was later to complain about "daily redirection" of the program from the office of the director of defense, research and engineering, initially the launch vehicle got off to a quick start. Titan II contractor Martin Marietta Company (so-named since October 10, 1961, as a result of Martin's merger with the American Marietta Company) won a contract on February 19, 1962. A second contract, highly significant in its requirements for development of new technology, covered the large solid-propellant rocket motors to boost the Titan III. On May 9, 1962, the air force selected a new firm, named United Technology Corporation (UTC), to develop the solid-rocket motors.[95]

Not long after the founding of UTC in 1958 (under the name United Research Corporation), United Aircraft Corporation purchased a one-third interest in the rocket firm, later becoming its sole owner. When United Aircraft changed its name to United Technologies Corporation in 1975, its solid-propellant division became Chemical Systems Division (CSD). Formerly a contributor to Minuteman, UTC's second president, Barnet R. Adelman, had been an early proponent of segmentation for large solid-rocket motors to permit easier transportation. Other firms, including Aerojet, Lockheed, and Thiokol, participated in the early development of the technology, but UTC developed its own clevis joint design to connect the segments of such boosters and its own variant on the propellant used for Minuteman to provide the propulsion.[96]

Because there was a Titan IIIA that did not include the solid-rocket motors, some of the Titan III first-stage engines would fire at ground level, whereas those used on the Titan IIIC would start at altitude after the solid-rocket motors lifted the vehicle to about 100,000 feet. Titan III also featured a new third stage known as Transtage.[97] This featured a pressure-fed engine using the same propellants as stages one and two. Aerojet won this contract in addition to those for the first two stages, with a two-phase agreement signed in 1962 and 1963. Aerojet designed the Transtage engine to feature two ablatively cooled thrust chambers and a radiatively cooled nozzle assembly.[98]

The Transtage engine could start and stop in space, allowing it to place multiple satellites into different orbits on a single launch or to position a single satellite in a final orbit without a need for a separate kick motor. In August 1963, tests at the simulated-altitude test chamber of the air force's Arnold Engineering Development Center (AEDC) in Tullahoma, Tennessee, confirmed earlier suspicions that the combustion chamber would burn through before completing a full-duration firing. How Aerojet solved this and other problems is not explained in the sources for this book, only that it required "extensive redesign and testing."[99] Obviously, Aerojet engineers had not anticipated these problems in their initial design. Clearly, this was another example of the roles of testing and problem solving in rocket development as well as the involvement of multiple organizations in the process.

In any event, engine deliveries did not occur in mid-December, as initially planned, but in April 1964. Additionally, Aerojet had to test the engine at sea level and extrapolate the data to conditions at altitude. When the data from the simulated-altitude tests at AEDC came back, the extrapolated data were 2.5 percent higher than the Arnold figures. This might seem a small discrepancy to the casual reader. But since the program needed exact performance data to project orbital injection accurately, Aerojet had to investigate the discrepancy. The explanation proved to be simple, but it illustrates the difficulty of pulling together all relevant data for development of something as complex as a rocket engine, even within the same firm. It also meant that engineers did not have their procedures "down to a science" but sometimes operated with an incomplete understanding of the phenomena they were testing in programs where funding and schedules precluded thorough and meticulous research. It turned out that other engineers working on a solid rocket had already learned to decrease the calculations by 2.5 percent to extrapolate for conditions at altitude. Once aware of this, Transtage engineers found several references to this correction in the literature. But obviously, they initially had failed to find those references.[100]

There were several problems with the Titan IIIC, resulting in 4 failures in 18 launches from September 1, 1964, to April 8, 1970.[101] In ensuing years, there were many versions of the Titan III. Besides the Titan IIIA, there was a Titan 23C with uprated thrust for the core liquid stages and a simplified and lightened thrust-vector-control system for the solid-rocket motors. The 23C flew 22 times by March 6, 1982, with 19 successful missions and 3 failures. Overall, between the original Titan IIIC and the Titan 23C versions, Titan IIIC had 33 successful launches and 7 failures for a success rate of 82.5 percent. Four of the 7 failures were due to Transtage problems, without which the overall vehicle would have had a much more successful career.[102]

Another version of the Titan III was the Titan IIIB with an Agena D replacing the Transtage in the core stack of three stages. The Titan IIIB did not use solid-rocket boosters. With the Agena D's 5,800 pounds of thrust compared with Transtage's roughly 1,600, the Titan IIIB could launch a 7,920-pound payload to a 115-mile Earth orbit compared with 7,260 pounds for the Titan IIIA. At some point, certainly by 1976, a stretched version of the first stage converted the vehicle to a 24B configuration. And in 1971 a Titan 33B version first operated, featuring an "Ascent Agena"—so-called because it became purely a launch stage instead of staying attached to the payload to provide power and attitude control while it was in orbit. Between June 29, 1966, and February 12, 1987, various versions of the Titan IIIB (including 23B and 34B) with Agena D third stages launched some 68 times with only 4 known failures—a 94 percent success rate.[103]

On November 15, 1967, the Titan III Systems Program Office began designing, developing, and ultimately producing the Titan IIID, which essentially added Titan IIIC's solid-rocket motors to the Titan IIIB. Perhaps more accurately, it can be considered a Titan IIIC without the Transtage. By this time, Air Force Systems Command had inactivated Ballistic and Space Systems Divisions (BSD and SSD) and reunited the two organizations into the Space and Missile Systems Organization (SAMSO), headquartered in the former SSD location at Los Angeles Air Force Station. The D models carried many photo-reconnaissance payloads that were too heavy for the B models. The Titan IIID could carry a reported 24,200 pounds of payload to a 115-mile orbit, compared with only 7,920 for the B model.[104] The D model appears to have launched 22 heavy-imaging satellites from June 15, 1971, to November 17, 1982. All 22 launches seem to have been successful, giving the Titan IIID a perfect launch record.[105]

On June 26, 1967, NASA contracted with Martin Marietta to study the possibility of using a Titan-Centaur combination for missions such as those to Mars and the outer planets in the solar system. When this possibility began to look promising, in March 1969, NASA Headquarters assigned management of the vehicle to the Lewis Research Center, with follow-on contracts going to Martin Marietta (via the air force) and General Dynamics/Convair (directly) to study and then develop what became the Titan IIIE and to adapt the Centaur D-1 for use therewith.[106] The Titan IIIE and Centaur D-1T were ready for a proof flight on February 11, 1974. Unfortunately, the upper stage failed to start. But from December 10, 1974, to September 5, 1977, Titan IIIE-Centaurs launched two Helios solar probes, two Viking missions to Mars, and two Voyager missions to Jupiter and Saturn, all successful.[107]

By the mid- to late 1970s, air force planners perceived a need for still another Titan configuration to carry increasingly large payloads such as the Defense Satellite Communication System III (DSCS III) satellites into orbit before the Space Shuttle was ready to assume such responsibilities. (The first DSCS III weighed 1,795 pounds, a significant jump from the DSCS II weight of 1,150 pounds.) Even after the shuttle became fully operational, the Titan 34D, as the new vehicle came to be called, would continue in a backup role in case the shuttle was unavailable for any reason. The air force contracted with Martin Marietta in July 1977 for preliminary design, with a production contract for five Titan 34D airframes following in January 1978. SAMSO retained program responsibility for the Titan family of vehicles, and it contracted separately with suppliers of the component elements. It appears that the long-tank first stage was the driving element in the new vehicle. This seems to be the premise of a 1978 article in *Aviation Week & Space Technology* stating that CSD's solid-rocket motors (SRMs) would add half a segment "to make them compatible with the long-tank first stage." Thus, the SRMs contained five and a half segments in place of the five used on previous Titans.[108]

Equipped with these longer solid-rocket motors and an uprated Transtage, the Titan 34D could carry 32,824 pounds to a 115-mile orbit, as compared with 28,600 pounds for the Titan IIIC. The 34D could lift 4,081 pounds to geosynchronous orbit, which compared favorably with 3,080 pounds for the IIIC but not with the 7,480 pounds the Titan IIIE-Centaur could carry to the same orbit.[109]

A quite different but important upper stage had its maiden launch on the first Titan 34D and later launched on several Titan IVs. This was the Inertial Upper Stage (IUS) that sat atop stage two on the first Titan 34D launch. Unlike the rest of the booster, this stage was anything but easy to develop. In August 1976, the air force selected Boeing Aerospace Company as the prime IUS contractor. Soon afterward, Boeing subcontracted with CSD to design and test the solid motors to be used in the IUS. CSD chose to use a hydroxy-terminated polybutadiene propellant (also being used by Thiokol in the Antares IIIA motor for Scout, developed between 1977 and 1979). Problems with the propellant, case, and nozzles delayed development of IUS. Various technical and managerial problems led to more than two years of delay in the schedule and cost overruns that basically doubled the originally projected cost of the IUS. These problems showed that despite more than two and a half decades of rocket development, rocket engineering still often required constant attention to small details and, where new technology was involved, a certain amount of trial and error. Including its first (and only) IUS mission, the Titan 34D had a total of 15 launches from both the Eastern and Western Test Ranges between October 1982 and September 4, 1989. There were 3 failures for an 80 percent success rate.[110]

By the mid-1980s, the air force had become increasingly uncomfortable with its dependence on the Space Shuttle for delivery of military satellites to orbit. Eventually, this discomfort would lead to the procurement of a variety of Titan IV, Delta II, and Atlas II expendable launch vehicles, but the air service also had at its disposal 56 deactivated Titan II missiles in storage at Norton AFB. Consequently, in January 1986 Space Division contracted with Martin Marietta to refurbish a number of the Titan IIs for use as launch vehicles. Designated as Space Launch Vehicle 23G, the Titan II had only two launches during the period covered by this book, on September 5, 1988, and the same date in 1989, both carrying classified payloads from Vandenberg AFB. For a polar orbit from Vandenberg, the Titan II could carry only about 4,190 pounds into a 115-mile orbit, but this compared favorably with the Atlas E. Although the Atlas vehicle could launch about 4,600 pounds into the same orbit, it required two Thiokol TE-M-364-4 solid-rocket motors in addition to its own thrust to do so.[111]

The Titan IV grew out of the same concern about the availability of the Space Shuttle that had led to the conversion of Titan II missiles to space-launch vehicles. In 1984 the air force decided that it needed to ensure access to space in case no Space Shuttle was available when a critical DoD payload needed to be launched. Consequently, Space Division requested bids for a contract to develop a new vehicle. Martin Marietta proposed a modified Titan 34D and won a development contract on February 28, 1985, for 10 of the vehicles that became Titan IVs. Following the *Challenger* disaster, the air force amended the contract to add 13 more vehicles.[112]

The initial version of the new booster (later called Titan IVA) had twin, 7-segment solid-rocket motors produced by CSD as a subcontractor to Martin Marietta. These contained substantially the same propellant and grain configuration as the Titan 34D but with an additional 1.5 segments, bringing the length to about 122 feet and the motor thrust to 1.394 million pounds per motor at the peak (vacuum) performance. The Aerojet stages one and two retained the same configurations as for the Titan 34D except that stage one was stretched about 7.9 feet to allow for more propellant and thus longer burning times. Stage two, similarly, added 1.4 feet of propellant tankage.[113]

The first launch of a Titan IV took place at Cape Canaveral on June 14, 1989, using an IUS as the upper stage. There were four more Titan IV launches during the period covered by this book, but the vehicle went on to place many more satellites into orbit into the first years of the 21st century.[114] Including the 14 Titan II missiles reconfigured into launch vehicles after the missiles themselves were retired, 12 of which had been launched by early 2003, there had been 214 Titan space-launch vehicles used by that point in time. Of them, 195 had succeeded in their missions and 19 had failed, for a 91.1 percent success rate.[115] This is hardly a brilliant record, but with such a variety of types and a huge number of components that could (and sometimes did) fail, it is a creditable one. It shows a large number of missions that needed the capabilities of the Titan family members for their launch requirements.

However, if the handwriting was not yet quite on the wall by 1991, it had become clear by 1995 that even in its Titan IVB configuration, the Titan family of launch vehicles was simply too expensive to continue very far into the 21st century as a viable launch vehicle. Based on studies from the late 1980s and early 1990s, the air force had come up with what it called the Evolved Expendable Launch Vehicle (EELV) program to replace the then-existing Delta II, Atlas II, Titan II, and Titan IV programs with a family of boosters that would cost 25 to 50 percent less than their predecessors but could launch 2,500 to 45,000 pounds into low-Earth orbit with a 98 percent reliability rate, well above that achieved historically by the Titan family.[116]

The Space Shuttle, 1972–91

Meanwhile, the Space Shuttle marked a radical departure from the pattern of previous launch vehicles. Not only was it (mostly) reusable, unlike its predecessors, but it was also part spacecraft, part airplane. In contradistinction to the Mercury, Gemini, and Apollo launch vehicles, in which astronauts had occupied the payload over the rocket, on the shuttle the astronauts rode in and even piloted from a crew compartment of the orbiter itself. The mission commander also landed the occupied portion of the Space Shuttle and did so horizontally on a runway. The orbiter had wings like an airplane and set down on landing gear, as airplanes did. Indeed, the very concept of the Space Shuttle came from airliners, which were not discarded after each mission the way expendable launch vehicles had been but were refurbished, refueled, and used over and over again, greatly reducing the cost of operations.

Because of the complex character of the Space Shuttles, their antecedents are much more diverse than those of the expendable launch vehicles and missiles discussed previously. Given the scope and length of this book, it will not be possible to cover all of the various aspects of the orbiters in the same way as other launch vehicles.[117]

Studies of a reusable launch vehicle like the shuttle—as distinguished from a winged rocket or orbital reconnaissance aircraft/bomber—date back to at least 1957 and continued through the 1960s. But it was not until the early 1970s that budgetary realism forced planners to accept a compromise of early schemes. Grim fiscal reality led to NASA's decision in the course of 1971–72 to change from a fully reusable vehicle to an only partly reusable stage-and-a-half shuttle concept. Gradually, NASA and its contractors shifted their focus to designs featuring an orbiter with a nonrecoverable external propellant tank. This permitted a smaller, lighter orbiter, reducing the costs of development but imposing a penalty in the form of additional costs per launch. McDonnell Douglas and Grumman separately urged combining the external tank with strap-on solid-rocket boosters that would add their thrust to that of the orbiter's engines. Despite opposition to the use of solids by Marshall Space Flight Center (responsible for main propulsion elements) and in spite of their higher overall cost, solid-rocket boosters with a 156-inch diameter offered lower developmental costs than other options, hence lower expenditures in the next few years, the critical ones from the budgetary perspective.

On January 5, 1972, Pres. Richard M. Nixon had announced his support for development of a Space Shuttle that would give the country "routine access to space by sharply reducing costs in dollars and preparation time." By mid-March 1972, the basic configuration had emerged for the shuttle that would actually be developed. It included a delta-winged orbiter attached to an external tank with two solid-rocket boosters on either side of the tank.[118] Meanwhile, in February 1970, Marshall released a request for proposals for the study of the space shuttle main engine. Study contracts went to Rocketdyne, Pratt & Whitney, and Aerojet General. The engine was to burn liquid hydrogen and liquid oxygen at a combustion-chamber pressure well above that of any other production engine, including the Saturn J-2. In July 1971, NASA announced the selection of Rocketdyne as the winner of the competition.[119]

The SSME featured "staged combustion." This meant that unlike the Saturn engines, whose turbine exhaust contributed little to thrust, in the shuttle the turbine exhaust—having burned with a small amount of oxygen and thus still being rich in hydrogen—flowed back into the combustion chamber where the remaining hydrogen burned under high pressure and contributed to thrust. This was necessary in the shuttle because the turbines had to burn so much fuel to produce the high chamber pressure critical to performance.[120]

Timing for such an engine was delicate and difficult. As a result, there were many problems during testing—with turbopumps as well as timing. Disastrous fires and other setbacks delayed development, requiring much analysis and adjustment to designs. In 1972, the shuttle program had expected to launch a flight to orbit by the beginning of March 1978. By then, the expected first-flight date had slipped to March 1979, but various problems caused even a September 1979 launch to be postponed. Not until early 1981 was the space shuttle main engine fully qualified for flight. Finally on April 12, 1981, the first Space Shuttle launched, and the main engines performed with only a minor anomaly, a small change in mixture ratio caused by radiant heating in the vacuum of space. Some insulation and a radiation shield fixed the problem on subsequent flights. It had taken much problem solving and redesign, but the main engines had finally become operational.[121]

The sophistication of the SSME explained all its problems. "In assessing the technical difficulties that have been causing delays in the development and flight certification of the SSME at full power, it is important to understand that the engine is the most advanced liquid rocket motor ever attempted," wrote an ad hoc committee of the Aeronautics and Space Engineering Board in 1981. "Chamber pressures of more than 3,000 psi, pump pressures of 7,000–8,000 psi, and an operating life of 7.5 hours have not been approached in previous designs of large liquid rocket motors."[122]

Although more advanced, the SSMEs (producing 375,000 pounds of thrust at sea level and 470,000 pounds at altitude) were considerably less powerful than the Saturn V's F-1s (with 1.522 million pounds of thrust). At a length of 13.9 feet and a diameter of 8.75 feet, the SSMEs were also smaller than the F-1s, with a length of 19.67 feet and diameter of 12.25 feet. Nevertheless, they were impressively large, standing twice as tall as most centers in the National Basketball Association.[123]

Because they ignited before launch, the SSMEs did perform some of the same functions for the shuttle that the F-1s did for the Saturn V, but in most respects the twin solid-rocket boosters served as the principal initial sources of thrust. They provided 71.4 percent of the shuttle's thrust at liftoff and during the initial stage of ascent until about 75 seconds into the mission, when they separated from the orbiter to be later recovered and reused.[124]

Even before the decision in March 1972 to use solid-rocket boosters, Marshall had provided contracts of $150,000 each to the Lockheed Propulsion Company, Thiokol, United Technology Center, and Aerojet General to study configurations of such motors. Thiokol emerged as winner of the competition, based on its cost and managerial strengths. NASA announced the selection on November 20, 1973.[125] The design for the solid-rocket boosters (SRBs) was intentionally conservative, using a steel case of the same type employed on Minuteman and the Titan IIIC. The Ladish Company of Cudahy, Wisconsin, made the cases for each segment without welding. Each booster consisted of four segments plus fore and aft sections. The propellant used the same three principal ingredients employed in the first stage of the Minuteman missile. One place shuttle designers departed from the Marshall mantra to avoid too much innovation lay in the tang-and-clevis joints linking the segments of the SRBs. Although superficially the shuttle joints resembled those for Titan IIIC, they were different in orientation and the use of two O-rings instead of just one.[126]

In part because of its simplicity compared with the space shuttle main engine, the solid-rocket booster required far less testing than the liquid-propellant engine. Testing nevertheless occasioned several adjustments in the design. The SRBs completed their qualification testing by late May 1980, well before the first shuttle flight.[127] Of course, this was well after the first planned flight, so if the main-engine development had not delayed the flights, presumably the booster development would have done so on its own.

The third part of the main shuttle propulsion system was the external tank (ET), the only major nonreusable part of the launch vehicle. It was also the largest component at about 154 feet in length and 27.5 feet in diameter. On August 16, 1973, NASA selected Mar-

FIG. 2.11
The static test of Solid Rocket Booster (SRB) Demonstration Model 2 (DM-2) at the Thiokol test site near Brigham City, Utah. (Photo courtesy of NASA)

tin Marietta (Denver Division) to negotiate a contract to design, develop, and test the ET. Larry Mulloy, who was Marshall's project manager for the solid-rocket booster but also worked on the tank, said that the ET posed no technological challenge, although it did have to face aerodynamic heating and heavy loads on ascent. But it had to do so within a weight limit of about 75,000 pounds. As it turned out, this was in fact a major challenge. It came to be fully appreciated only after loss of Space Shuttle *Columbia* on February 1, 2003, to a "breach in the Thermal Protection System on the leading edge of the left wing" resulting from its being struck by "a piece of insulating foam" from the ET. During reentry into the atmosphere, this breach caused aerodynamic superheating of the wing's aluminum structure, its melting, and the subsequent breakup of the orbiter under increasing aerodynamic forces.[128]

The air force had a great deal of influence on the requirements for the shuttle because its support had been needed to get the program approved and make it viable economically. NASA needed a commitment from the military that all of its launch needs would be carried on the shuttle. To satisfy DoD requirements, the shuttle had to handle payloads 60 feet long with weights of 40,000 pounds for polar orbits or 65,000 pounds for orbits at the latitude of Kennedy Space Center. On July 26, 1972, NASA announced that the Space Transportation Systems Division of North American Rockwell had won the contract for the orbiters.[129]

That firm subcontracted much of the work. The design, called a double-delta planform, derived from a Lockheed proposal. The term referred to a wing in which the forward portion was swept more heavily than the rear part. Throughout the development of the shuttle, wind-tunnel testing at a variety of facilities, including those at NASA Langley and NASA Ames Research Centers plus the air force's Arnold Engineering Development Center, provided data, showing the continuing role of multiple organizations in launch-vehicle design. Before the first shuttle flight in 1981, there was a total of 46,000 hours of testing in various wind tunnels.[130]

An elaborate thermal protection system (designed primarily for reentry and passage through the atmosphere at very high speeds) and the guidance, navigation, and control system presented many design problems of their own. The launch vehicle that emerged from the involved and cost-constrained development of its many components was, as the Columbia Accident Investigation Board noted, "one of the most complex machines ever devised." It included "2.5 million parts, 230 miles of wire, 1,060 valves, and 1,440 circuit breakers." Although it weighed 4.5 million pounds at launch, its solid-rocket boosters and main engines accelerated it to 17,500 miles per hour (Mach 25) in slightly more than eight minutes. The three main engines burned propellants fast enough to drain an average swimming pool in some 20 seconds.[131]

From the first orbital test flight on April 12, 1981, to the end of 1991, there were 44 shuttles launched with 1 failure, an almost 98 percent success rate. On these missions, the shuttles had launched many communications satellites; several tracking and data relay satellites to furnish better tracking of and provision of data to (and from) spacecraft flying in low-Earth orbits; a number of DoD payloads; many scientific and technological experiments; and several key NASA spacecraft.[132]

Before launching some of these spacecraft, such as *Magellan*, *Ulysses*, and the *Hubble Space Telescope*, however, NASA had endured the tragedy of losing the Space Shuttle *Challenger* and all of its seven-person crew to an explosion. Since this is not an operational history, it is not the place for a detailed analysis, but because the accident reflected upon the technology of the solid-rocket boosters and resulted in a partial redesign, it requires some discussion. On the 25th shuttle launch, *Challenger* lifted off at 11:38 A.M. on January 28, 1986. Even that late in the day, the temperature had risen to only 36°F, 15° below the temperature on any previous shuttle launch. Engineers at Morton Thiokol (the name of the firm after 1982 when the Morton Salt Company took over Thiokol Corporation) had voiced reservations about launching in cold temperatures, but under pressure to launch in a year scheduled for 15 flights (6 more than ever before), NASA and Morton Thiokol agreed to go ahead. Almost immediately after launch, smoke began escaping from the bottommost field joint of one solid booster, although this was not noticed until postflight analysis. By 64 seconds into the launch, flames from the joint began to encounter leaking hydrogen from the ET, and soon after 73 seconds from launch, the vehicle exploded and broke apart.[133]

On February 3, 1986, Pres. Ronald Reagan appointed a commission to investigate the accident, headed by former Nixon-administration secretary of state William P. Rogers. The commission determined that the cause of the accident was "the destruction of the seals [O-rings] that are intended to prevent hot gases from leaking through the joint during the propellant burn of the rocket motor." It is possible to argue that the cause of the *Challenger* accident was faulty assembly of the particular field joint that failed rather than faulty design of the joint. But it seems clear that neither NASA nor Morton Thiokol believed the launch would lead to disaster. The fact that they went ahead with it shows (in one more instance) that rocket engineers still did not have launching such complex vehicles completely "down to a science." Some engineers had concerns, but they were not convinced enough of their validity to insist that the launch be postponed.[134]

Following the accident there was an extensive redesign of many aspects of the shuttle, notably the field joints. This new design allegedly ensured that the seals would not leak under twice the anticipated structural deflection. Following *Challenger*, both U.S. policy and law changed, essentially forbidding the shuttle to carry commercial satellites and largely restricting the vehicle to missions *both* using the shuttle's unique capabilities *and* requiring people to be onboard. A concomitant result was the rejuvenation of the air force's expendable launch-vehicle program. Although the Delta II was the only launcher resulting directly from the 32-month hiatus in shuttle launches following the accident, the air force also ordered more Titan IVs and later, other expendable launch vehicles. The shuttle became a very expensive launch option because its economic viability had assumed rapid turnaround and large numbers of launches every year. Yet in 1989 it flew only five missions, increased to six in 1990 and 1991.[135]

As further demonstrated by the *Columbia* accident, the shuttle clearly was a flawed launch vehicle but not a failed experiment. Its flaws stemmed largely from its nature as an outgrowth of heterogeneous engineering, involving negotiations of NASA managers with the air force, the Office of Management and Budget, and the White House, among other entities. Funding restrictions during development and other compromises led to higher operational costs. For example, compromises on reusability (the external tank) and employment of solid-rocket motors plus unrealistic projections of many more flights per year than the shuttles ever achieved virtually ensured failure in this area from the beginning. Also, as the Columbia Accident Investigation Board pointed out, "Launching rockets is still a very dangerous business, and will continue to be so for the foreseeable future as we gain experience at it. It is unlikely that launching a space vehicle will ever be as routine an undertaking as commercial air travel."[136]

Yet for all its flaws, the shuttle represents a notable engineering achievement. It can perform significant feats that expendable launch vehicles could not. These have ranged from rescue and relaunch of satellites in unsatisfactory orbits to the repair of the *Hubble Space Telescope* and the construction of the *International Space Station*. These are remarkable accomplishments that yield a vote for the overall success of the shuttle, despite its flaws and tragedies.

Analysis and Conclusions

Launch vehicles progressed greatly in both payload and sophistication from the early uses of Redstone, Vanguard, Atlas, and Titan II to Saturn V, Titan IV, and the Space Shuttles. In large part because of their greater thrust and complexity, though, the vehicles still in use at the end of the cold war did not reflect a mature science of rocket development. Designers and operators could not always predict failures, although when failures did occur, engineers could usually find a way to fix what had gone wrong.

Many launch vehicles built upon foundations laid by earlier missile development or by earlier launch vehicles like Vanguard. Because the missions of launch vehicles were different from those of missiles, directed at some location in the skies rather than a place on Earth, missiles used as launch vehicles required modifications to guidance/control systems and other components. This was especially true of "man-rated" vehicles, but the rule also applied to other launchers because of the changed nature of payloads. Upper stages in particular often required a restart capability to place satellites in a desired orbital path or to launch spacecraft in a designed trajectory for space exploration.

Like missiles, launch vehicles required extensive testing both on the ground and in flight. When unexpected problems occurred, rocket engineers had to design modifications to correct them, often in the absence of a full understanding of why the problem had occurred, necessitating guesses informed by available information and theory. Sometimes corrections worked. In other cases, an extensive trial-and-error process was required before arriving at a satisfactory fix. Multiple organizations typically contributed to resolving problems, with extensive sharing of information prominent in the process. Final ingredients in the development of launch-vehicle technology consisted of good management and heterogeneous engineering.

CHAPTER 3

Propulsion with Alcohol and Kerosene Fuels, 1932–72

ARGUABLY, THE PROPULSION SYSTEM CONSTI-
tutes the most basic component of a missile or
launch vehicle. Each rocket required a strong, light
structure to fly very high or far, and it needed a
guidance/control system to reach its intended destination. But without an adequate propulsion system, its structure and guidance systems were use-
less. Goddard and Oberth had both recognized the
superiority of liquid hydrogen as a rocket fuel, but
the difficulty of using this cryogenic (extremely
cold) substance delayed its employment for a long
time. Thus, the first practical missiles and rockets
had alcohol or hydrocarbons (especially kerosene)
as their fuels.

ADVANCED SATURN C-5

S-IVB

S-II

UNITED STATES

S-IC

SATURN C-1

S-IV

UNITED STATES

S-I

ATLAS-MERCURY

UNITED STATES

M-MS-G-35-2-62

FIG. 3.1
Models of the Mercury-Atlas, Saturn C-1 (later the Saturn I), and the Saturn C-5 (later the Saturn V) launch vehicles, showing their shapes and relative sizes. (Photo courtesy of NASA)

The major examples of missiles and launch vehicles that burned alcohol or kerosene included the German V-2, the Viking, Vanguard, the Redstone missile, the Atlas missile and launch vehicle, and the first stages of the giant Saturn launch vehicles. (Other examples—such as Thor and Jupiter—are not included in this discussion for reasons of brevity and because the Thor and Jupiter used essentially the same engines as the Atlas.) The histories of the propulsion systems for these rockets illustrate some of the same themes discussed in previous chapters of this book. In designing and developing these systems, engineers used available theory and existing knowledge from previous rocket development plus extensive testing both on the ground and in flight. But inevitably, unexpected problems occurred, and sometimes, even when problems were expected, existing theory and data were inadequate to forestall them. As a result, designers had to find innovative solutions and sometimes use cut-and-try methods to arrive at fixes that eventually worked, even when the full nature of the problems remained unclear.

In diagnosing and solving problems, individuals of varied backgrounds from many different organizations collaborated. Too often, we do not know which of them contributed which parts of specific solutions. But it seems clear that it was the synergy of their individual contributions rather than eureka moments on the parts of one or the other of the participants that often spelled the difference, although in some cases we do know the source of a key suggestion. Another ingredient in the process of successful rocket development was the transfer of individuals and information from one project to another. The most famous example of such technology transfer was the emigration of the von Braun team from Germany to the United States after World War II. This group, its documents, and actual V-2 rockets provided one (but far from the only) starting point for some postwar U.S. rocket technology. And the original immigrants continued to play important roles in developing the Redstone, Jupiter, and Saturn rockets.

But it is also important to note that U.S. rocket technology soon surpassed that of the V-2. In many cases, the German team contributed to improvements. But in others, Americans independently produced innovations for the Redstone, Atlas, and Saturn rockets. In still other cases, the advances resulted from collaborations between original members of the von Braun team and Americans or other immigrants. But in any event, the history of alcohol/hydrocarbon-fueled rockets began in important ways in Germany.

Propulsion for the A-4 (V-2)

Soon after he began working for German Army Ordnance at Kummersdorf in late 1932, Wernher von Braun began experimenting with rocket engines, which developed burnthroughs, "ignition explosions, frozen valves, fires in cable ducts and numerous other malfunctions." Learning "the hard way," von Braun called in "welding experts, valve manufacturers, instrument makers and pyrotechnicists . . . and with their assistance a regeneratively-cooled motor of 300 kilograms [about 660 pounds] thrust and propelled by liquid oxygen and alcohol was static tested and ready for flight in the A-1 rocket which had been six months a-building." Von Braun's boss, Walter Dornberger, added that the "650-pound-thrust chamber . . . gave consistent performance" but yielded an exhaust velocity slower than needed even after the developers "measured the flame temperature, took samples of the gas jet, analyzed the gases, [and] changed the mixture ratio."[1]

As the staff at Kummersdorf grew, bringing in additional expertise, engine technology improved. But only with the hiring of Walter Thiel did truly significant progress occur in the propulsion field. Thiel was "a pale-complexioned man of average height, with dark eyes behind spectacles with black horn rims." Fair-haired with "a strong chin," he joined the experimental station in the fall of 1936. Born in Breslau in 1910, the son of an assistant in the post office, he matriculated at the Technical Institute of Breslau as an undergraduate and graduate student in chemistry, earning his doctorate in 1935. He had served as a chemist at another army lab before coming to Kummersdorf.[2]

Dornberger said Thiel assumed "complete charge of propulsion, with the aim of creating a 25-ton motor" (the one used for the A-4, providing 25 metric tons of thrust). Because Thiel remained at Kummersdorf until 1940 instead of moving to Peenemünde with the rest of the von Braun group in 1937, testing facilities limited him to engines of no more than 8,000 pounds of thrust from 1936 to 1940. Although Thiel was "extremely hard-working, conscientious, and systematic," Dornberger said he was difficult to work with. Ambitious and aware of his abilities, he "took a superior attitude and demanded . . . devotion to duty from his colleagues [equal to his own]." This caused friction that Dornberger claimed he had to mollify. Martin Schilling (chief of the testing laboratory at Peenemünde for Thiel's propulsion development office and, later, head of the office after Thiel died in a bombing raid in 1943) noted that Thiel was "high strung." He said, "Thiel was a good manager of such a great and risky development program. He was a competent and dynamic leader, and a pusher. At the same time, he was no match to von Braun's or Steinhoff's vision and optimism." (Ernst Steinhoff was chief of guidance and control.)[3]

A memorandum Thiel wrote on March 13, 1937, after he had been on the job about six months, gives some idea of the state of development of a viable large engine at that time. It also suggests the approach he brought to his task. Although he certainly lacked optimism at some points in his career at Kummersdorf and Peenemünde, he did not betray that failing in his memo. He referred to "a certain completion of the development of the liquid rocket" that had been achieved "during the past years," surely an overstatement in view of the major development effort that remained. "Combustion chambers, injection systems, valves, auxiliary pressure systems, pumps, tanks, guidance systems, etc. were completely developed from the point of view of design and manufacturing techniques, for various nominal sizes. Thus, the problem of an actually usable liquid rocket can be termed as having been solved."

Despite this assessment, he listed "important items" requiring further development. One was an increase in performance of the rocket engine, using alcohol as its fuel. He noted that the engines at Kummersdorf were producing a thermal efficiency of only 22 percent, and combustion-chamber losses were on the order of 50 percent. Thus, about half of the practically usable energy was lost to incomplete combustion. The use of gasoline, butane, and diesel oil theoretically yielded an exhaust velocity only some 10 percent higher, but measurements on these hydrocarbon fuels showed actual exhaust velocities no higher than those with alcohol. Thiel felt that "for long range rockets, alcohol will always remain the best fuel," because hydrocarbons increased the danger of explosion, produced coking in the injection system, and presented problems with cooling.

He said the way to improved performance lay in exploiting the potential 50 percent energy gain available with alcohol and liquid oxygen. Fuller combustion could come from improving the injection process, relocating the locus for mixing oxygen and fuel into a premixing chamber, increasing the speed of ignition and combustion, and increasing chamber pressure by the use of pumps, among other improvements. He knew about the tremendous increases in performance available through the use of liquid hydrogen, but he cited the low temperature of this propellant (−423°F), its high boil-off rate, the danger of explosion, and huge tank volume resulting from its low specific weight (as the lightest element of all), plus a requirement to insulate its tanks, as "strong obstacles" to its use (as indeed, later proved to be the case).

He made repeated reference to the rocket literature, including a mention of Goddard, but noted that "the development of practically usable models in the field of liquid rockets . . . has far outdistanced research." Nevertheless, he stressed the need for cooperation between research and development, a process he would follow. He concluded by stating the need for further research in materials, injection, heat transfer, "the combustion process in the chamber," and "exhaust processes."[4]

Despite Thiel's optimism here, Martin Schilling referred in a postwar discussion of the development of the V-2 engine to the "mysteries of the combustion process." Thiel, indeed, said the combustion process needed further research but did not discuss it in such an interesting way. Dornberger also failed to use such a term, but his account of the development of the 25-ton engine suggests that indeed there were mysteries to be dealt with. He pointed out that to achieve complete combustion of the alcohol before it got to the nozzle end of the combustion chamber, rocket researchers before Thiel had elongated the chamber. This gave the alcohol droplets more time to burn than a shorter chamber would, they thought, and their analysis of engine-exhaust gases seemed to prove the idea correct. "Yet performance did not improve." They realized that combustion was not "homogeneous," and they experienced frequent burnthroughs of chamber walls.

Dornberger said he suggested finer atomization of both oxygen and alcohol by using centrifugal injection nozzles and igniting the propellants after mixing "to accelerate combustion, reduce length of the chamber, and improve performance." Thiel, he said, developed this idea, then submitted it to engineering schools for research while he used the system for the 1.5-ton engine then under development. It took a year, but he shortened the chamber from almost 6 feet to about a foot. This increased exhaust speed to 6,600 and then 6,900 feet per second (from the roughly 5,300 to 5,600 feet per second in early 1937). This was a significant achievement, but with it came a rise in temperature and a decrease in the chamber's cooling surface. Thiel "removed the injection head from the combustion chamber" by creating a "sort of mixing compartment," which removed the flames from the brass injection nozzles. This kept *them*, at least, from burning.[5]

In conjunction with the shortening of the combustion chamber, Thiel also converted the shape from cylindrical to spherical to encompass the greatest volume in available space. This also served to reduce pressure fluctuations and increase the mixing of the propellants. Until he could use a larger test stand at Peenemünde, however, Thiel was restricted in scaling up these innovations in the 1.5-ton engine to the full 25 tons. He thus went to an intermediate size of 4.2 tons that he could test at Kummersdorf, and he moved from one injector in the smaller engine to three in the larger one. Each had its own "mixing compartment" or "pot," and the clustering actually increased the efficiency of combustion further. But to go from that arrangement to one for the 25-ton engine created considerable problems of scaling up and of arranging the 18 "pots" that the researchers designed for the A-4 combustion chamber. At first, Thiel and his associates favored an arrangement of six or eight larger injectors around the sides of the chamber, but von Braun suggested 18 pots of the size used for the 1.5-ton engine, arranged in concentric circles on the top of the chamber. Schilling said this was a "plumber's nightmare" with the many oxygen and alcohol feed lines that it required, but it avoided the problems of combustion instability—as we now call it—that other arrangements had created.[6]

Cooling the engine remained a problem. Regenerative cooling used on earlier, less efficient engines did not suffice by itself for the larger engine. Oberth had already suggested the solution, film cooling—introducing an alcohol flow not only around the outside of the combustion chamber (regenerative cooling) but down the inside of the wall and the exhaust nozzle to insulate them from the heat of combustion by means of a "film" of fuel. Apparently, others in the propulsion group had forgotten this suggestion, and it is not clear that the idea as applied to the 25-ton engine came from Oberth. Several sources agree that diploma engineer Moritz Pöhlmann, who headed the propulsion design office at Kummersdorf after August 1939, was responsible. Tested on smaller engines, the idea proved its validity, so on the 25-ton engine, there were four rings of small holes drilled into the chamber wall that seeped alcohol along the inside of the motor and nozzle. This film cooling took care of 70 percent of the heat from the burning propellants, the remainder being absorbed into the alcohol flowing in the regenerative cooling jacket on the outside of the chamber. Initially, 10 percent of the fuel flow was used for film cooling, but Pöhlmann refined this by "oozing" rather than injecting the alcohol, without loss of cooling efficiency.[7] Whether this procedure emanated from Oberth or was independently discovered by Pöhlmann, it was an important innovation with at least the technical details worked out by Pöhlmann.

Thiel's group had to come up with a pumping mechanism to transfer the propellants from their tanks to the injectors in the pots above the combustion chamber. The large quantities of propellant that the A-4 would use made it impractical to feed the propellants by nitrogen-gas pressure from a tank (as had been done on the earlier A-2, A-3, and A-5 engines). Such a tank would have had to be too large and heavy to provide sufficient pressure over the 65-second burning time of the engine, creating unnecessary weight for the A-4 to lift. This, in turn, would have reduced its effective performance. In 1937 Thiel had mentioned that there was a the need for pumps to increase the chamber pressure and that some pumps had already been developed. Indeed, von Braun had already begun working in the middle of 1935 with the firm of Klein, Schanzlin & Becker, with factories in southwestern and central Germany, on the development of turbopumps. In 1936 he began discussions with Hellmuth

Walter's engineering office in Kiel about a "steam turbine" to drive the pumps.[8]

In the final design, a turbopump assembly contained separate centrifugal pumps for alcohol and oxygen on a common shaft, driven by the steam turbine. Hydrogen peroxide powered the pumps, converted to steam by a sodium permanganate catalyst. It operated at a rate of more than 3,000 revolutions per minute and delivered some 120 pounds of alcohol and 150 pounds of liquid oxygen per second, creating a combustion-chamber pressure of about 210 pounds per square inch. This placed extreme demands on the pump technology of the day, especially given a differential between the heat of the steam (+725°F) and the boiling point of the liquid oxygen (–297°F).[9]

Moreover, the pumps and turbine had to weigh as little as possible to reduce the load the engine had to lift. Consequently, there were problems with the development and manufacture of both devices. Krafft Ehricke, who worked under Thiel after 1942, said in 1950 that the first pumps "worked unsatisfactorily" so the development "transferred to Peenemünde." He claimed that Peenemünde also developed the steam generator. Schilling suggested this as well, writing that for the steam turbine, "we borrowed heavily from" the Walter firm at Kiel. He said a "first attempt to adapt and improve a torpedo steam generator [from Walter's works] failed because of numerous details (valves, combustion control)." Later, a successful version of the steam turbine emerged, and Heinkel in Bavaria handled the mass production. As for the pumps, there are references in Peenemünde documents as late as January 1943 to problems with them but also to orders for large quantities from Klein, Schanzlin & Becker.[10]

The problems with the pumps included warping of the pump housing because of the temperature difference between the steam and the liquid oxygen; cavitation because of bubbles in the propellants; difficulties with lubrication of the bearings; and problems with seals, gaskets, and choice of alloys (all problems that would recur in later U.S. missiles and rockets). The cavitation problem was especially severe since it could lead to vibrations in the combustion chamber, resulting in explosions. The solution came from redesigning the interior of the pumps and carefully regulating the internal pressure in the propellant tanks to preclude the formation of the bubbles.[11]

Ehricke also reported that development of "control devices for the propulsion system, i.e. valves, valve controls, gages, etc." presented "especially thorny" problems. The items available from commercial firms either weighed too much or could not handle the propellants and pressure differentials. A special laboratory at Peenemünde had to develop them during the period 1937 to 1941, with a pressure-reducing valve having its development period extended until 1942 before it worked satisfactorily.[12]

Technical institutes contributed a small but significant share of the development effort for both the engine and the pumps. A professor named Wewerka of the Technical Institute in Stuttgart provided valuable suggestions for solving design problems in the turbopump. He had written at least two reports on the centrifugal turbopumps in July 1941 and February 1942. In the first, he investigated discharge capacity, cavitation, speed relationships, and discharge and inlet pressures on the alcohol pump, using water instead of alcohol as a liquid to pass experimentally through the pump. Because the oxygen pump had almost identical dimensions to those of the alcohol pump, he merely calculated corrections to give values for the oxygen pump with liquid oxygen flowing through it instead of water through the alcohol pump. In the second report, he studied both units' efficiencies, effects of variations in the pump inlet heads upon pump performance, turbine steam rates, discharge capacities of the pump, and the pumps' impeller design. He performed these tests with water at pump speeds up to 12,000 revolutions per minute.[13]

Schilling pointed to important work that Wewerka and the Technical Institute in Stuttgart had done in the separate area of nozzle design, critical to achieving the highest possible performance from the engine by establishing as optimal an expansion ratio as possible. This issue was complicated by the fact that an ideal expansion ratio at sea level, where the missile was launched, quickly became less than ideal as atmospheric pressure decreased with altitude. Wewerka wrote at least four reports during 1940 studying such things as the divergence of a Laval nozzle and the thrust of the jet discharged by the nozzle. In one report in February, he found that a nozzle divergence of 15 degrees produced maximum thrust. Gerhard Reisig, as well as Schilling, agreed that this was the optimal exit-cone half angle for the A-4. In his account of engine development, Reisig, chief of the measurement group under Steinhoff until 1943, also gives Wewerka, as well as Thiel, credit for shortening the nozzle substantially. In another report, Wewerka found that the nozzle should be designed for a discharge pressure of 0.7 to 0.75 atmosphere, and Reisig says the final A-4 nozzle was designed for 0.8 atmosphere.[14]

Schilling also pointed to other professors, Hase of the Technical Institute of Hannover and Richard Vieweg of the Technical Institute of Darmstadt, for their contributions to the "field of power-plant instrumentation." Other "essential contributions" that Schilling listed included those of Schiller of the University of Leipzig for his investigations of regenerative cooling, and Pauer and Beck of the Technical Institute of Dresden "for clarification of atomization processes and the experimental investigation of exhaust gases and combustion efficiency, respectively." In an immediate postwar interview at Garmisch-Partenkirchen, an engineer named Hans Lindenberg even claimed that the design of the A-4's fuel-injection nozzles "was settled at Dresden." Lindenberg had been doing research on fuel injectors for diesel engines at the Technical Institute of Dresden from 1930 to 1940. Since 1940, partly at Dresden and partly at Peenemünde, he had worked on the combustion chamber of the A-4. His claim may have constituted an exaggeration, but he added that Dresden had a laboratory for "measuring the output and photographing the spray of alcohol jets." Surely it and other technical institutes contributed ideas and technical data important in the design of the propulsion system.[15]

Along similar lines, Konrad Dannenberg, who worked on the combustion chamber and ignition systems at Peenemünde from mid-1940 on, described their development in general terms and then added, "Not only Army employees of many departments participated, but much of the work was supported by universities and contractors, who all participated in the tests and their evaluation. They were always given a strong voice in final decisions."[16]

One final innovation, of undetermined origin, involved the ignition process, which used a pyrotechnic igniter. In the first step of the process, the oxygen valve opened by means of an electrically activated servo system, followed by the alcohol valve. Both opened to about 20 percent of capacity, but since the propellants flowed only as a result of gravity (and slight pressure in the oxygen tank), the flow was only about 10 percent of normal. When lit by the igniter, the burning propellants produced a thrust of about 2.5 tons. When this stage of ignition occurred, the launch team started the turbopump by opening a valve permitting air pressure to flow to the hydrogen peroxide and sodium permanganate tanks. The permanganate solution flowed into a mixing chamber, and as soon as pressure was sufficient, a switch opened the peroxide valve, allowing peroxide to enter the mixing chamber. When pressure was up to 33 atmospheres as a result of decomposing the hydrogen peroxide, the oxygen and alcohol valves opened fully, and the pressure on the turbines in the pumps caused them to operate, feeding the propellants into the combustion chamber. It required only about three-quarters of a second from the time the valve in the peroxide system was electrically triggered until the missile left the ground.[17]

Even after the propulsion system was operational, the propulsion group had by no means solved Schilling's "mysteries of the combustion process." The engine ultimately developed an exhaust velocity of 6,725 feet/second, which translated into a specific impulse of 210 pounds of thrust per pound of propellant burned per second (lbf-sec/lbm), the more usual measure of performance today. Quite low by later standards, this was sufficient to meet the requirements set for the A-4 and constituted a remarkable achievement for the time. As von Braun said after the war, however, "the injector for the A-4 [wa]s unnecessarily complicated and difficult to manufacture." Certainly the 18-pot design of the combustion chamber was inelegant. And despite all the help from an excellent staff at Peenemünde and the technical institutes, Thiel relied on a vast amount of testing. Von Braun said, "Thiel's investigations showed that it required hundreds of test runs to tune a rocket motor to maximize performance," and Dannenberg reported "many burn-throughs and chamber failures," presumably even after he arrived in 1940.[18]

But through a process of trial and error, use of theory where it was available, further research, and testing, the team under von Braun and Thiel had achieved a workable engine that was sufficient to do the job. As late as 1958 in the United States, "The development of almost every liquid-propellant rocket ha[d] been plagued at one time or another by the occurrence of unpredictable high-frequency pressure oscillations in the combustion chamber"—Schilling's "mysteries" still at work. "Today [1958], after some fifteen years of concentrated effort in the United States on liquid-propellant rocket development, there is still no adequate theoretical explanation for combustion instability in liquid-propellant rockets," wrote a notable practitioner in the field of rocketry.[19]

That the propulsion team at Kummersdorf and Peenemünde was able to design a viable rocket engine despite the team's own and later researchers' lack of fundamental understanding of the combustion processes at work shows their skill and perseverance. It also suggests the fundamental engineering nature of their endeavor. Their task was not necessarily to understand all the "mysteries" (although they tried) but to make the rocket work. Their work constituted rocket engineering, not rocket science, because they still did not fully understand *why* what they had done was effective, only *that* it worked.

Even without a full understanding of the combustion process, the propulsion group went on to design engines with better injectors. They did so for both the Wasserfall antiaircraft missile and the A-4, although neither engine went into full production. Both fea-

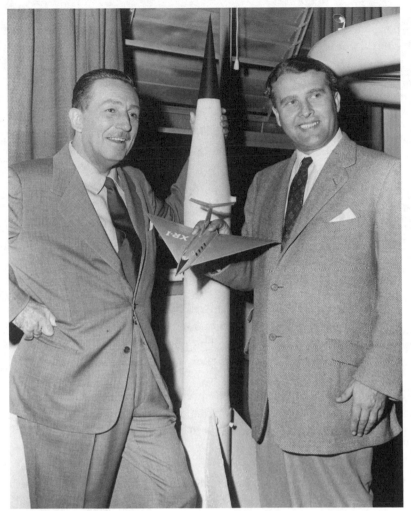

FIG. 3.2
Walt Disney
(*left*), with
his hand on a
model of the
V-2 rocket,
and Wernher
von Braun in
1954 during a
period in which
von Braun
worked with
Disney Studios
to promote
spaceflight on
television, an
example of his
heterogeneous
engineering.
(Photo courtesy
of NASA)

tured an injector plate with orifices so arranged that small streams of propellants impinged upon one another. The streams produced oscillations in the engine (combustion instability), but the developers found the correct angle of impingement that reduced (but never completely eliminated) the oscillations (characterized by chugging and screeching). They also designed a cylindrical rather than a spherical combustion chamber for the A-4, but it had a slightly lower exhaust velocity than the spherical engine.[20]

Under difficult, wartime conditions, in-house contributions and those from technical institutes and industry came together through discussions among the contributors at Kummersdorf and Peenemünde. The pooling of their expertise probably contributed in innumerable ways to the progress of technological development, but the process can only be partially documented. Certainly, technical reports written by both staff at Peenemünde and people at the technical institutes contributed to the fund of engineering knowledge that Peenemünde passed on to the United States. Germans from Peenemünde immigrated to the United States after the war, carrying their knowledge and expertise with them; but in addition, much of the documentation of the engineering work done in Germany was captured by U.S. forces at the end of the war, moved to Fort Eustis, Virginia, and even translated. The full extent of what these documents contributed to postwar rocketry is impossible to know, but the information was available to those engineers who wanted to avail themselves of it. Finally, many actual V-2 missiles, captured and taken to the United States, also provided a basis for postwar developments that went beyond the V-2 but started with its technology.

Propulsion for the MX-774B, Viking, and Vanguard

Meanwhile, several American engines drew upon knowledge of the V-2 but also built upon indigenous American experience from before and during World War II. The engines for the MX-774B test missile, the Viking sounding rocket, and the first stage of the Vanguard launch vehicle are examples. Although none of these engines by themselves contributed in demonstrable ways to later launch-vehicle engine technology, the experience gained in developing them almost certainly informed later developments.

MX-774 B

Reaction Motors, Inc. (RMI) developed both the MX-774B power-plant and the Viking engine. The MX-774B engine (designated XLR-35-RM-1) evolved from the 6000C4 engine the firm had produced during 1945 for the X-1 rocket plane. Both were comparatively small engines, the 6000C4 yielding 6,000 pounds of thrust and the XLR-35-RM-1 having a thrust range of about 7,600 to 8,800 pounds. Like the V-2, both engines used alcohol as fuel and liquid oxygen as the oxidizer. The use of alcohol (95 percent ethanol for the MX-774B) suggested some borrowing from the V-2, but the XLR-35-RM-1 achieved a specific impulse of 227 lbf-sec/lbm, significantly higher than that of the V-2 engine. As in the V-2, the MX-774B engine fed the propellants using two pumps operated by the decomposition of hydrogen peroxide, but the U.S. powerplant employed four separate cylinders as combustion chambers rather than the single, spherical chamber for the V-2. Like the German engine, the XLR-35-RM-1 was regeneratively cooled.

As suggested in chapter 1, the major innovations of the MX-774B that influenced launch vehicles were swiveled (*not* gimballed) engines and light, pressurized propellant tanks that evolved into the "steel balloons" used on the Atlas missile. Both of these innovations were the work of Convair (especially Charlie Bossart), the airframe contractor for MX-774B, not RMI, but the four-cylindered engine was integral to the way swiveling worked, so the engine contractor deserves some of the credit. (Each of the four cylinders could swing back and forth on one axis to provide control in pitch, yaw, and roll; a gimbal, by contrast, could rotate in two axes, not simply a single one.) According to one source, the Germans had tried gimballing on the V-2 but had discarded the idea because of the complexities of rotating the 18-pot engine, and Goddard had patented the idea. But actual gimballing of an engine was apparently first perfected on the Viking. Meanwhile, the air force canceled the MX-774B prematurely, but it did have three test flights in July–December 1948. On the first flight, the engine performed well but an electrical-system failure caused premature cutoff of propellants. On the second flight, the missile broke apart from excessive pressure in the oxygen tank. The third flight was successful.[21]

VIKING

Whereas MX-774B was an army air forces/air force project, the navy sponsored the Viking, with Milton W. Rosen responsible for the development and firing of the rocket. Reaction Motors designed the engine, drawing on its own experience as well as data from the V-2, with the Glenn L. Martin Company designing and building the overall rocket. Viking's pioneering development and use of gimballing were the responsibility of Martin engineers. Like the MX-774B powerplant, Viking drew on the V-2 technology, but Rosen and his engineers designed it specifically for upper-atmospheric research. Rosen's specifications called for a thrust of 20,000 pounds compared with 56,000 for the V-2. Under a contract initiated in September 1946, RMI designed an engine (XLR-10-RM-2) with a single cylindrical thrust chamber.

As with the V-2, the U.S. rocket's propellants were alcohol and liquid oxygen, pumped into the combustion chamber by turbines driven by decomposed hydrogen peroxide. Whereas the V-2 had used alcohol at 75 percent strength and hydrogen peroxide at 82 percent, the Viking used 95 percent ethyl alcohol and 90 percent hydrogen peroxide. Edward A. Neu did the detailed design work on the combustion chamber and injector. Tests caused parts to fail and be replaced. Burnthroughs of the steel combustion-chamber liner (inner wall) led to the substitution of pure nickel, the first known use of this metal for such a purpose. Its superior thermal conductivity and higher melting point solved the cooling problem in conjunction with the regenerative cooling in the original design. One injector caused an explosion, so new designs were necessary. Valves were a problem until M. E. "Bud" Parker borrowed valve designs from the MX-774B engine, which thus did influence at least the Viking design.

After the first launch of a Viking rocket from White Sands, New Mexico, on May 3, 1949, the vehicle experienced component failure, leading to subsequent improvements. As a result, each of the dozen Viking rockets fired through the last launch on February 4, 1955, differed from its predecessor. Rosen thought this was the most important aspect of the program. One example was the growth of the thrust of the various Vikings from 20,450 pounds on the first launch to 21,400 on two others. Even though the engine itself was generally successful, it made no known contributions to engine technology per se other than the experience gained by RMI, Martin, and navy engineers. The real contribution of Viking lay in the gimballing system for steering, not pure propulsion.[22]

VANGUARD FIRST STAGE

For the Vanguard launch vehicle, the prime contractor, the Martin Company, chose General Electric (GE) on October 1, 1955, to develop the first-stage engine. Although GE had earlier developed an A3-B engine that burned alcohol and liquid oxygen, the firm decided to use kerosene and liquid oxygen for the Vanguard (X-405) engine. To achieve the performance needed to launch satellites, the X-405 featured a chamber pressure of 616 pounds per square inch and a 146-second propellant burn. The engine achieved a specific impulse of roughly the 254 lbf-sec/lbm called for in the specifications for the powerplant. The X-405 was regeneratively cooled, the propellants fed by decomposition of hydrogen peroxide to provide the specified chamber pressure. GE was able to deliver the first production engine (P-1) on October 1, 1956. But during static testing, damage occurred to the lining of the combustion chambers in engines P-2 and P-3. When chamber liners also failed in the P-4 engine, the schedule had to be delayed to fix the problem. A redesign entailed adjustments to the cooling system and careful attention to injector specifications to prevent combustion instability and local hot spots. GE had to test 15 injectors and six variations in design between January and April 1956 before the firm's engineers found one that worked. Obviously, the state of the art of injector design did not

FIG. 3.3
A Vanguard
launch vehicle
undergoing a
static test at
Cape Canaveral
in September
1955. (U.S.
Navy photo
courtesy of
NASA)

allow a clear-cut, quick solution, but the overall result of design and testing was a relatively uncomplicated engine with a minimal number of relays and valves. Redesign had worked, the engine never experiencing a burnthrough in flight.[23]

The November 1955 Vanguard schedule specified that six test vehicles would launch between September 1956 and August 1957, with the first satellite-launching vehicle lifting off in October 1957. If the project had remained on schedule, conceivably the navy could have launched a satellite about the same time as the Soviet *Sputnik*. Unfortunately, problems with both the first- and second-stage engines caused delays. On October 23, 1957, a Vanguard test vehicle (without a satellite but with a prototype first-stage engine) did launch successfully almost three weeks after the Soviet satellite began orbiting. Because of the tremendous pressure from the launch of *Sputnik*, the navy decided to launch the next test vehicle with a minimal, 3.4-pound satellite aboard. When the White House announced this test, the press seized upon it as the United States' answer to the Soviets. This test (TV-3) was the first with three "live" stages. The intent was for it to test the three stages and, if all went well, launch the satellite.

On December 6, 1957, the launch began. The first stage ignited, but the vehicle rose slowly, "agonizingly hesitated a moment . . . and . . . began to topple [as] an immense cloud of red flame from burning propellants engulfed the whole area." GE and Martin Company technicians pored over records from ground instrumentation, films of the failed launch, and the two seconds of telemetered data from the toppling inferno. Martin concluded that there had been an "improper engine start" because of low fuel-tank pressure. GE said the start had not been improper and blamed the failed launch on a loose fuel-line connection. As it turned out, Martin was correct in part, but the problem was more extensive than low fuel-tank pressure. Telemetry data indicated that there had been a high-pressure spike on engine start that GE had not noticed on testing because it had used low-response instrumentation. The pressure spike had destroyed a high-pressure fuel line, resulting in the rocket's destruction. To solve the problem, engineers increased the period of oxygen injection into the combustion chamber (ahead of the fuel) from three to six seconds. With this correction and an increase in the minimum pressure in the fuel tank by 30 percent, the first-stage engine worked without problems in 14 static and flight tests following the disaster. Although the engine was largely successful after its first failure, however, it appears to have contributed only experience and data to later launch-vehicle technology. In March 1959, NASA contracted with General Dynamics and GE to adapt the Vanguard first stage as an upper stage (called the Vega) for the Atlas launch vehicle, but in December 1959, the space agency canceled the contracts in favor of the DoD-sponsored Agena B upper stage. Thus ended further use of the GE engine.[24]

Redstone Propulsion

When the von Braun group, relocated to Redstone Arsenal, began developing the Redstone missile, it chose North American Aviation's XLR43-NA-1 liquid-propellant rocket engine, developed for the air force's Navaho missile, as the basis for the Redstone propulsion unit. A letter contract with NAA on March 27, 1951, provided 120 days of research and development to make that engine comply with the ordnance corps' specifications and to deliver a mockup and two prototypes of the engine (then to be designated NAA 75-110, referring to 75,000 pounds of thrust operating for 110 seconds). Supplemental contracts in 1952 and 1953 increased the number of engines to be delivered and called for their improvement. These contracts included 19 engines, with subsequent powerplants purchased by the prime contractor, Chrysler, through subcontracts.[25]

The story of how North American Aviation had initially developed the XLR43-NA-1 illustrates much about the ways launch-vehicle technology developed in the United States. NAA came into existence in 1928 as a holding company for a variety of aviation-related firms. It suffered during the Depression after 1929, and General Motors acquired it in 1934, hiring James H. Kindelberger, nicknamed "Dutch," as its president—a pilot in World War I and an engineer who had worked for Donald Douglas before moving to NAA. Described as "a hard-driving bear of a man with a gruff, earthy sense of humor—mostly scatological [who] ran the kind of flexible operation that smart people loved to work for," he reorganized NAA into a manufacturing firm that built thousands of P-51 Mustangs for the army air forces in World War II, the B-25 Mitchell bomber, and the T-6 Texas trainer. With the more cautious but also visionary John Leland Atwood as his chief engineer, Dutch made NAA one of the principal manufacturers of military aircraft during the conflict, its workforce rising to 90,000 at the height of wartime production before it fell to 5,000 after the end of the war. Atwood became president in 1948, when Dutch rose to chairman of the board and General Motors sold its share of the company. The two managers continued to service the military aircraft market in the much less lucrative postwar climate, when many competitors shifted to commercial airliners.[26]

Despite the drop in business, NAA had money from wartime production, and Kindelberger hired a top-notch individual to head a research laboratory filled with quality engineers in the fields of electronics, automatic control with gyroscopes, jet propulsion, and missiles. He selected William Bollay, a former von Kármán student. Following receipt of his Ph.D. in aeronautical engineering at Caltech, Bollay had joined the navy in 1941 and been assigned to Annapolis where the Bureau of Aeronautics (BuAer) was working on experimental engines, including the JATOs Robert Truax was developing. At war's end, Bollay was chief of the Power Plant Development Branch for BuAer. As such, he was responsible for turbojet engines, and at the time, NAA was developing the FJ-1 Fury, destined to become one of the navy's first jet fighters. Bollay came to work for NAA during the fall of 1945 in a building near the Los Angeles airport, where he would create what became the Aerophysics Laboratory.[27]

On October 31, 1945, the army air forces' Air Technical Service Command released an invitation for leading aircraft firms to bid on studies of guided missiles. NAA proposed a surface-to-surface rocket with a range of 175–500 miles that it designated Navaho (for *N*orth *A*merican *v*ehicle *a*lcohol [plus] *h*ydrogen peroxide and *o*xygen). The proposal resulted in a contract on March 29, 1946, for MX-770, the designation of the experimental missile. Other contracts for the missile followed. The Navaho ultimately evolved into a complicated project before its cancellation in 1958. It included a rocket booster and ramjet engines with a lot of legacies passed on to aerospace technology, but for the Redstone, only the rocket engine that evolved to become NAA 75-10 is relevant.[28]

NAA did not originally intend to manufacture the engine. As an early employee of the firm recalled, the company was "forced into the engine business—we had the prime contract for Navaho and couldn't find a subcontractor who would tackle the engine for it, so we decided to build it for ourselves." NAA's plans for developing the engine began with the German V-2 as a model but soon led to "an entirely new design rated at 75,000 pounds thrust" (as compared with about 56,000 for the V-2). In the spring of 1946, Bollay and his associates had visited Fort Bliss to conduct numerous interviews with many of the Germans who had worked on the V-2, including von Braun, Walter Riedel, and Konrad Dannenberg. By the middle of June 1946, Bollay's team began redesigning the V-2 engine with the aid of drawings and other documents obtained from the Peenemünde files. In September, the firm secured the loan of a complete V-2.[29]

The NAA engineers also conferred with JPL, GE, Bell Aircraft Corp., the National Advisory Committee for Aeronautics' laboratory in Cleveland (later Lewis Research Center), the Naval Ordnance Test Station at Inyokern, and Aerojet about various aspects of rocket technology.[30] Thus, the heritage of the Redstone engine went well beyond what NAA had learned from the V-2.

By October 1947, the Astrophysics Laboratory had grown to more than 500 people. This necessitated a move to a plant in nearby Downey in July 1948. By the following fall, the engineers had taken apart and reconditioned the V-2 engine, examining all of its parts carefully. The team had also built the XLR41-NA-1, a rocket engine like the V-2 but using U.S. manufacturing techniques and design standards, some improved materials, and various replacements of small components. Then, by early 1950, the team had redesigned the engine to a cylindrical shape, replacing the spherical contour of the V-2, which produced efficient propulsion but was hard to form and weld. Bollay's people kept the propellants for the V-2 (75 percent alcohol and liquid oxygen). But in place of the 18-pot design of the V-2, which had avoided combustion instability, NAA engineers developed two types of flat injectors—a doublet version in which the alcohol and liquid oxygen impinged on one another to achieve mixing, and a triplet, wherein two streams of alcohol met one of liquid oxygen. They tested subscale versions of these injectors in small engines fired in the parking lot. Their methodology was purely empirical, showing the undeveloped state of analytical capabilities in this period. They, too, encountered combustion instability. But they found that the triplet type of injector provided slightly higher performance due to improved mixing of the propellants.[31]

Meanwhile, NAA searched for a place where it could test larger engines. It found one in the Santa Susana Mountains northwest of Los Angeles in Ventura County, California. The firm obtained a permit in November 1947 for engine testing there. It leased the land and built rocket-testing facilities in the rugged area where Tom Mix had starred in western movies, using company funds for about a third of the initial costs and air force funding for the rest. By early 1950, the first full-scale static test on XLR43-NA-1 took place.[32]

Full-scale engine tests with the triplet injector revealed severe combustion instability, so engineers reverted to the doublet injector that partly relieved the problem. Although the reduced combustion instability came at a cost of lower performance, the XLR43-NA-1 still outperformed the V-2, enabling use of the simpler and less bulky cylindrical combustion chamber that looked a bit like a farmer's milk container with a bottom that flared out at the nozzle. The engine delivered 75,000 pounds of thrust at a specific impulse 8 percent better than that of the V-2. Further enhancing performance was a 40 percent reduction in weight. The new engine retained the double-wall construction of the V-2 with regenerative and film cooling. Tinkering with the placement of the igniter plus injection of liquid oxygen ahead of the fuel solved the problem with combustion instability. The engine used hydrogen peroxide–powered turbopumps like those on the V-2 except that they were smaller and lighter. It also provided higher combustion pressures.

Like the V-2, the XLR43-NA-1 began ignition with a preliminary stage in which the propellants flowed at only some 10 to 15 percent of full combustion rates. If observation suggested that the engine was burning satisfactorily, technicians allowed it to transition to so-called main stage combustion. To enable the engineers to observe ignition and early combustion, von Braun, who was working with the NAA engineers by this time, suggested rolling a small, surplus army tank to the rear of the nozzle. By looking at the combustion process from inside the tank, engineers could see what was happening while protected from the hot exhaust, enabling them to reduce problems with rough starts by changing sequencing and improving purges of the system in a trial-and-error process. Through such methods, the XLR43-NA-1 became the basis for the Redstone missile's NAA 75-110.[33]

Having supervised the development of this engine and the expansion of the Aerophysics Laboratory to about 2,400 people on staff, Bollay left North American in 1951 to set up his own company, which built army battlefield missiles. In 1949, he had hired Samuel K. Hoffman, who had served as a design engineer for Fairchild Aircraft Company, Lycoming Manufacturing Company, and the Allison Division of General Motors. He then worked his way up from project engineer with the Lycoming Division of the Aviation Corporation to become its chief engineer, responsible for the design, development, and production of aircraft engines. In 1945 he became a professor of aeronautical engineering at his alma mater, Penn State University, the position he left in 1949 to head the Propulsion Section of what became NAA's Aerophysics Laboratory.

As Hoffman later recalled, Bollay had hired him for his practical experience building engines, something the many brilliant but young engineers working in the laboratory did not possess. Hoffman succeeded Bollay in 1951. Meanwhile, he and Bollay had overseen the development of a significantly new rocket engine. Although it had used the V-2 as a starting point and bore considerable resemblance to the cylindrical engine developed at Peenemünde before the end of the war, it had advanced substantially beyond the German technology and provided greater thrust with a smaller weight penalty. Also, it marked the beginnings of another rocket-engine manufacturing organization that went on to become the Rocketdyne Division of NAA in 1955, destined to become the foremost producer of rocket engines in the country.[34]

Development of the NAA 75-110 engine for the Redstone missile did not stop in 1951. Improvements continued through seven engine types, designated A-1 through A-7. Each of these engines had fundamentally the same operational features, designed for identical performance parameters. The engines were interchangeable, requiring only minor modifications in their tubing for them to be installed

TABLE 3.1. *Comparison of Components in Pneumatic Control System for the Redstone A-1 and A-7 Engines*

Components	A-1 Engine	A-7 Engine
Regulators	4	1
Relief valves	2	1
Solenoid valves	12	4
Pressure switches	6	2
Check valves	3	0
Test connections	4	1
Pneumatic filter	0	1
Total	31	10

in the Redstone missile. All of them except A-5 flew on Redstone tests between August 20, 1953, and November 5, 1958, with A-1 being the prototype and A-2, for example, having an inducer added to the liquid-oxygen pump to prevent cavitation (bubbles forming in the oxidizer, causing lower performance of the turbopump and even damage to hardware as the bubbles imploded).[35]

During the course of these improvements, the Chrysler Corporation had become the prime contractor for the Redstone missile, receiving a letter contract in October 1952 and a more formal one on June 19, 1953. Thereafter, it and NAA had undertaken a product-improvement program to increase engine reliability and reproducibility. A comparison of the numbers of components in the pneumatic control system for the A-1 and A-7 engines, used respectively in 1953 and 1958, illustrates the results (see table 3.1).[36]

Obviously, the fewer components needed to operate a complex system like the engine for a large missile, the fewer things there are that can go wrong in its launching and flight. Thus, this threefold reduction in components on a single system for the engine must have contributed significantly to the reliability of its operation. This was especially true since Rocketdyne engineers (as they became after 1955) tested each new component design both in the laboratory and in static firings before qualifying it for production. They also simulated operating conditions at extreme temperatures, levels of humidity, dust, and the like, because the Redstone was scheduled for deployment and use by the army in the field. Static engine tests showed reliability higher than 96 percent for the engines.

This was a remarkably high figure, considering that Rocketdyne purchased about half of Redstone engine components (or parts thereof) from outside suppliers; but the parts had to be built to a higher standard than those used in conventional aircraft. The reason was that the stresses of an operating rocket engine were greater than those for an airplane. All welds for stressed components had to undergo radiographic inspection to ensure reliability. The army then required a minimum of four static engine tests to prove each new model worked satisfactorily before the service would accept the system. Two of these tests had to last for 15 seconds each, and a third was for the full rated duration. This, presumably, was 110 seconds, but according to Chrysler's publication on the Redstone, the engine ultimately produced 78,000 pounds of thrust for a duration of 117 seconds.[37]

Atlas Propulsion

Even though the Viking rocket used alcohol and the Vanguard first stage adopted kerosene as its fuel, the next major advance in alcohol and kerosene propulsion technology came with the Atlas missile. As with the Redstone, North American Aviation designed and built the Atlas engines, which also owed a great deal to NAA's work for the Navaho. Unlike the Redstone, the Atlas engines burned kerosene rather than alcohol. (Both used liquid oxygen as the oxidizer.) Kerosene that would work in rocket engines was another legacy of the protean Navaho program. In January 1953, Lt. Col. Edward Hall and others from Wright-Patterson AFB insisted to Sam Hoffman that he convert from alcohol to a hydrocarbon fuel for a 120,000-pound-thrust Navaho engine. Hoffman protested because the standard kerosene the air force used was JP-4, whose specifications allowed a range of densities. JP-4 clogged a rocket engine's slim cooling lines with residues. The compounds in the fuel that caused these problems did not affect jet engines but would not work easily in rocket powerplants. To resolve these problems, Hoffman initiated the Rocket Engine Advancement Program, resulting in development of the RP-1 kerosene rocket fuel, without JP-4's contaminants and variations in density. This fuel went on to power the Atlas, Thor, and Jupiter engines. The specifications for RP-1 were available in January 1957, before the delivery date of the Atlas engines.[38]

On October 28, 1954, the Western Development Division and Special Aircraft Projects (procurement) Office that Air Force Materiel Command had located next to it issued a letter contract to NAA to continue research and development of liquid-oxygen and kerosene (RP-1) engines for Atlas. The cooperating air force organizations followed this with a contract to NAA for 12 pairs of rocket engines for the series-A flights of Atlas, which tested only two outside booster engines and not the centrally located sustainer engine for the Atlas. The Rocketdyne Division, formed to handle the requirements of Navaho, Atlas, and Redstone, also developed the sustainer engine, which differed from the two boosters in having a nozzle with a higher expansion ratio for optimum performance at higher altitudes once the boosters were discarded.[39]

Using knowledge gained from the Navaho and Redstone engines, the NAA engineers began developing the MA-1 Atlas engine system for Atlases A, B, and C in 1954. (Atlas B added the sustainer engine to the two boosters; Atlas C had the same engines but included improvements to the guidance system and thinner skin on the propellant tanks. Both were test vehicles only.) The MA-1, like its successors the MA-2 and MA-3, was gimballed and used the brazed "spaghetti" tubes forming the inner and outer walls of the regeneratively cooled combustion chamber. NAA had developed the arrangement used in the MA-1 in 1951, perhaps in ignorance of the originator of the concept, Edward Neu at Reaction Motors. NAA/ Rocketdyne began static "hot-fire" tests of the booster engines in 1955 and of all three MA-1 engines in 1956 at Santa Susana. The two booster engines, designated XLR43-NA-3, had a specific impulse of 245 lbf-sec/lbm and a total thrust of 300,000 pounds, much more than the Redstone engine. The sustainer engine, designated XLR43-NA-5, had a lower specific impulse (210 lbf-sec/lbm) and a total thrust of 54,000 pounds.[40]

Produced in 1957 and 1958, these engines ran into failures of systems and components in flight testing that also plagued the Thor and Jupiter engines, which were under simultaneous development and shared many component designs with the Atlas. They used high-pressure turbopumps that transmitted power from the turbines to the propellant pumps via a high-speed gear train. Both Atlas and Thor used the MK-3 turbopump, which failed at high altitude on several flights of both missiles, causing the propulsion system to cease functioning. Investigations showed that lubrication was marginal. Rocketdyne engineers redesigned the lubrication system and a roller bearing, strengthening the gear case and related parts. Turbine blades experienced cracking, attributed to fatigue from vibration and flutter. To solve this problem, the engineers tapered each blade's profile to change the natural frequency and added shroud tips to the blades. These devices extended from one blade to the next, restricting the amount of flutter. There was also an explo-

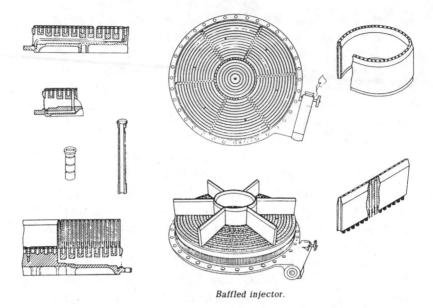

Baffled injector.

FIG. 3.4 Technical drawing of a baffled injector similar to the one used on the Atlas MA-1 engine to prevent combustion instability by containing lateral oscillations in the combustion chamber. (Taken from Dieter K. Huzel and David H. Huang, *Design of Liquid Propellant Rocket Engines* [Washington, D.C.: NASA SP-125, 1967], p. 122)

sion of a sustainer engine caused by rubbing in the oxygen side of the turbopump, solved by increasing clearances in the pump and installing a liner.

Another problem encountered on the MA-1 entailed a high-frequency acoustic form of combustion instability resulting in vibration and increased transfer of heat that could destroy the engine in less than a hundredth of a second. The solution proved to be rectangular pieces of metal called baffles, attached to a circular ring near the center of the injector face and extending from the ring to the chamber walls. Fuel flowed through the baffles and ring for cooling. The baffles and ring served to contain the transverse oscillations in much the way that the 18 pots on the V-2 had done but without the cumbersome plumbing. Together with changing the injection pattern, this innovation made the instability manageable. These improvements came between the flight testing of the MA-1 system and the completion of the MA-3 engine system (1958–63).[41] They showed the need to modify initial designs to resolve problems that appeared in the process of testing and the number of innovations that resulted, although we do not always know who conceived them or precisely how they came about. (But see the account below of Rocketdyne's Experimental Engines Group for some of the explanations.)

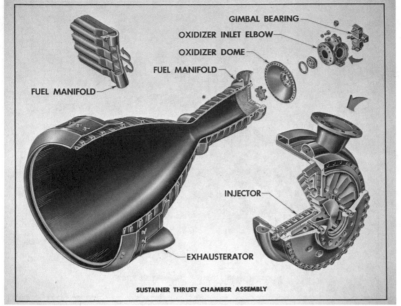

 NASA
C-1983-781

GIMBAL BEARING
OXIDIZER INLET ELBOW
OXIDIZER DOME
FUEL MANIFOLD
FUEL MANIFOLD
INJECTOR
EXHAUSTERATOR
SUSTAINER THRUST CHAMBER ASSEMBLY

National Aeronautics and Space Administration
Lewis Research Center

FIG. 3.5
Technical
drawing
showing
components of
an MA-5
sustainer
engine, used
on the Atlas
space-launch
vehicle, 1983.
(Photo courtesy
of NASA)

The MA-2 "was an uprated and simplified version of the MA-1," used on the Atlas D, which was the first operational Atlas ICBM and later became a launch vehicle under Project Mercury. Both MA-1 and MA-2 systems used a common turbopump feed system in which the turbopumps for fuel and oxidizer operated from a single gas generator and provided propellants to booster and sustainer engines. For the MA-2, the boosters provided a slightly higher specific impulse, with that of the sustainer also increasing slightly. The overall thrust of the boosters rose to 309,000 pounds; that of the sustainer climbed to 57,000 pounds. An MA-5 engine was initially identical to the MA-2 but used on space-launch vehicles rather than missiles. In development during 1961–73, the booster engines went through several upratings, leading to an ultimate total thrust of 378,000 pounds (compared to 363,000 for the MA-2).

The overall MA-3 engine system contained separate subsystems for each of the booster and sustainer engines. Each engine had its own turbopump and gas generator, with the booster engines being identical to one another. The MA-3 exhibited a number of other changes from the MA-2, including greater simplification and better starting reliability resulting from hypergolic thrust-chamber ignition. A single electrical signal caused solid-propellant initiators and gas-gencrator igniters to begin the start sequence. Fuel flow

FIG. 3.6
Technical
drawing of an
injector for an
MA-5 booster
engine, used
on the Atlas
space-launch
vehicle, 1983.
(Photo courtesy
of NASA)

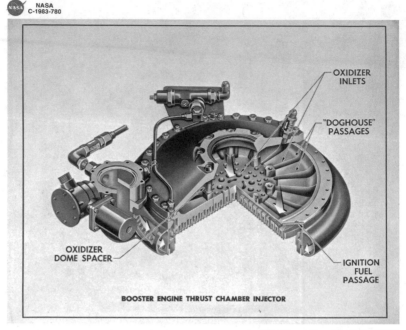

NASA
C-1983-780

OXIDIZER
INLETS

"DOGHOUSE"
PASSAGES

OXIDIZER
DOME SPACER

IGNITION
FUEL
PASSAGE

BOOSTER ENGINE THRUST CHAMBER INJECTOR

National Aeronautics and Space Administration
Lewis Research Center

through an igniter fuel valve burst a diaphragm holding a hypergolic cartridge and pushed it into the thrust chambers. Oxygen flow occurred slightly ahead of the fuel, and the cartridge with its triethyl aluminum and triethyl boron reacted with the oxygen in the thrust chamber and began combustion. Hot gases from combustion operated the turbopump, a much more efficient arrangement than previous turbopumps operated by hydrogen peroxide in rockets like the V-2 and Redstone.

The MA-3 sustainer engine had a slightly higher specific impulse of almost 215 lbf-sec/lbm but the same thrust (57,000 pounds) as the MA-2 sustainer. The total thrust of the boosters, however, went up to 330,000 pounds with a climb in specific impulse to about 250 lbf-sec/lbm. Both specific impulses were at sea level. At altitude the specific impulse of the sustainer rose to almost 310 and that of the boosters to nearly 290 lbf-sec/lbm. The higher value for the sustainer engine at altitude resulted from the nozzles that were designed for the lower pressure outside Earth's atmosphere. The MA-3 appeared on the Atlas E and F missiles, with production running from 1961 to 1964.[42]

Most of the changes from the MA-1 to the MA-3 resulted from a decision in 1957 by Rocketdyne management to create an Experimental Engines Group under the leadership of Paul Castenholz, a design and development engineer who had worked on combustion devices, injectors, and thrust chambers. He "enjoyed a reputation at Rocketdyne as a very innovative thinker, a guy who had a lot of energy, a good leader." The group consisted of about 25 mostly young people, including Dick Schwarz, fresh out of college and later president of Rocketdyne. Bill Ezell, who was the development supervisor, had come to NAA in 1953 and was by 1957 considered an "old-timer" in the company at age 27. Castenholz was about 30. Before starting the experimental program, Ezell had just come back from Cape Canaveral, where there had been constant electrical problems on attempted Thor launches. The Atlas and Thor contracts with the air force each had a clause calling for product improvement, which was undefined, but one such improvement the group sought was to reduce the number of valves, electrical wires, and connections that all had to function in a precise sequence for the missile to operate.

The experimental engineers wanted a system with one wire to start the engine and one to stop it. Buildup of pressure from the turbopump would cause all of the valves to "open automatically by using the . . . propellant as the actuating fluid." This one-wire start arrangement became the solid-propellant mechanism for the MA-3, but the engineers under Castenholz first used it on an X-1 experimental engine on which Cliff Hauenstein, Jim Bates, and Dick Schwarz took out a patent. They used the Thor engine as the starting point and redesigned it to become the X-1. Their approach was mostly empirical, which was different from the way rocket development had evolved by the 1980s, when the emphasis had shifted to more analysis on paper and with a computer, having simulation precede actual hardware development. In the period 1957 to the early 1960s, Castenholz's group started with ideas, built the hardware, and tried it out, learning from their mistakes.

Stan Bell, another engineer in Castenholz's group, noted a further difference from the 1980s: "We were allowed to take risks and to fail and to stumble and to recover from it and go on. Now, everything has got to be constantly successful." Jim Bates added that there were not any "mathematical models of rocket engine combustion processes" in the late 1950s and early 1960s. "There weren't even any computers that could handle them," but, he said, "we had our experience and hindsight."

The reason the engineers in the group moved to a hypergolic igniter was that existing pyrotechnic devices required a delicate balance. It proved difficult to get a system that had sufficient power for a good, assured ignition without going to the point of a hard start that could damage hardware. This led them to the hypergolic cartridge (or slug) used on the MA-3. In the process of developing it, however, the group discovered that a little water in the propellant line ahead of the slug produced combustion in the line but not in the chamber; there the propellants built up and caused a detonation, "blow[ing] hell out of an engine," as Bill Ezell put it. They learned from that experience to be more careful, but Ezell said, "there's probably no degree of analysis that could have prevented that from happening." There were simply a lot of instances in rocket-engine development where the experimenters had to "make the right guess or assumption"; otherwise, there was "no way to analyze it. So you've got to get out and get the hard experience." Ezell also opined that "without the Experimental Engine program going, in my opinion there never would have been a Saturn I," suggesting a line of evolution from their work to later engines.[43]

The experiences and comments of the members of Castenholz's group illuminate the often dimly viewed nature of early rocket engineering. Without the product-improvement clauses in the Atlas and Thor contracts, a common practice of the Non-Rotating Engine Branch of the Power Plant Laboratory at Wright-Patterson AFB, the innovations made by this group probably would not have occurred. They thus would not have benefited Thor and Atlas as well as later projects like Saturn I. Even with the clauses, not every company would have put some 25 bright, young engineers to work on pure experiment or continued their efforts after the first engine explosion. That Rocketdyne did both probably goes a long way toward explaining why it became the preeminent rocket-engine producer in the country.

The changes in the Atlas engines to the MA-3 configuration as a result of the experimental group's work did not resolve all of the problems with the Atlas E and F configurations. The Atlas lifted off with all three engines plus its two verniers (supplementary engines) firing. Once the missile (or later, launch vehicle) reached a predetermined velocity and altitude, it jettisoned the booster engines and structure, with the sustainer engine and verniers then continuing to propel the remaining part of the rocket to its destination. The separation of the booster sections occurred at disconnect valves that closed to prevent the loss of propellant from the feed lines. This system worked through the Atlas D but became a major problem on the E and F models, with their independent pumps for each engine (rather than the previous common turbopump for all of them). Also, the E and F had discarded the use of water in the regenerative cooling tubes because it reacted with the hypergolic slug. The water had ensured a gentle start with previous igniters. With the hypergolic device, testing of the engines by General Dynamics had produced some structural damage in the rear of the missile. Design fixes included no thought of a large pressure pulse when the new models ignited.

On June 7, 1961, the first Atlas E launched from Vandenberg AFB on the California coast at an operational launch site that used a dry flame bucket rather than water to absorb the missile's thrust. The missile lifted off and flew for about 40 seconds before a failure of the propulsion system resulted in destruction of the missile, with its parts landing on the ground and recovered. Rocketdyne specialists analyzed the hardware and data, concluding that a pressure pulse had caused the problem. The pulse had resulted in a sudden upward pressure from the dry flame bucket back onto fire-resistant blankets called boots that stretched from the engines' throat to the missile's firewall to form a protective seal around the gimballing engines. The pressure caused one boot to catch on a drain valve at the bottom of a pressurized oil tank that provided lubrication for the turbopump gearbox. The tank drained, and the gearbox ceased to operate without lubrication. To solve this problem, engineers resorted to a new liquid in the cooling tubes ahead of the propellants to soften ignition and preclude pressure pulses.

Repeated failures of different kinds also occurred during the flight-test program of the E and F models at Cape Canaveral. Control instrumentation showed a small and short-lived pitch upward of the vehicle during launch. Edward J. Hujsak, assistant chief engineer for mechanical and propulsion systems for the Atlas airframe and assembly contractor, General Dynamics, reflected about the evidence and spoke with the firm's director of engineering. Hujsak believed that the problem lay with a change in the geometry of the propellant lines for the E and F models that allowed RP-1 and liquid oxygen (expelled from the booster engines when they were discarded) to mix. Engineers "did not really know what could happen behind the missile's traveling shock front" as it ascended, but possibly the mixed propellants were contained in such a way as to produce an explosion. That could have caused the various failures that were occurring.

The solution entailed additional shutoff valves in the feed lines on the booster side of the feed system, preventing expulsion of the propellants. Engineers and technicians had to retrofit these valves in the operational missiles. However, the air force decided that since there could be no explosion if only one of the propellants were cut off, the shutoff valves would be installed only in the oxygen lines. A subsequent failure on a test flight convinced the service to approve installation in the fuel lines as well, solving the problem.[44] Here

FIG. 3.7
Atlas-Agena
launch on Sep-
tember 11,
1966. (Photo
courtesy of
NASA)

was a further example of engineers not always fully understanding how changes in a design could affect the operation of a rocket. Only failures in flight testing and subsequent analysis pinpointed problem areas and provided solutions.

Propulsion for the Saturn Launch Vehicles

There were other developments relating to kerosene-based engines for Thor and Delta, among other vehicles, but the huge Saturn engines marked the most important step forward in the use of RP-1 for launch-vehicle propulsion. The H-1 engine for the Saturn I's first stage resulted from the work of the Rocketdyne Experimental Engines Group on the X-1. Under a contract to the Army Ballistic

FIG. 3.8
H-1 engines,
which were
used in a
cluster of eight
to power the
first stage
of both the
Saturn I and
the Saturn IB.
(Photo courtesy
of NASA)

Missile Agency (ABMA), let on September 1, 1958, Rocketdyne succeeded in building on its X-1 development to deliver the first production version of the H-1 in a little over half a year. This version had
only 165,000 pounds of thrust, however, less than the Thor MB-3,
Block II, but the H-1 went through versions of 188,000, 200,000,
and 205,000 pounds as the Saturn project evolved, with Saturn I using the first two, and Saturn IB, the final pair.[45]

One problem with the 165,000-pound-thrust H-1 was that it still
used a 20-gallon pressurized oil tank to lubricate the turbopump
gearbox, as had the Thor-Jupiter engine. Later, 188,000-pound versions of the engine eliminated this problem by using RP-1 with
an additive to lubricate the gearbox. This modification required a
blender that mixed fuel from the turbopump with the additive and
supplied it to the gearbox. The H-1 also featured a simplified starting sequence. Instead of auxiliary start tanks under pressure to supply oxygen and RP-1 to begin operation of the turbopump, a solid-
propellant device started the turbines spinning. The engine kept the
hypergolic ignition procedure used in the Atlas MA-3 and the later
Thor-Jupiter engines.[46]

Rocketdyne delivered the first 165,000-pound H-1 engine to
ABMA on April 28, 1959. Von Braun and his engineers conducted
the first static test on this engine 28 days later, with an 8-second,
eight-engine test following on April 29, 1960. On May 17, 1960,
a second static test of eight clustered engines lasted 24 seconds
and generated a thrust of 1.3 million pounds. That fall, the engine

passed its preliminary flight-rating tests, leading to the first flight test on October 27, 1961.[47]

Meanwhile, Rocketdyne had begun uprating the H-1 to 188,000 pounds of thrust, apparently by adjusting the injectors and increasing the fuel and oxidizer flow rates. Although the uprated engine was ready for its preliminary flight-rating tests on September 28, 1962, its uprating created problems with combustion instability that engineers had not solved by that time but did fix without detriment to the schedule. The first launch of a Saturn I with the 188,000-pound engine took place successfully on January 29, 1964.[48]

Development had not been unproblematic. Testing for combustion instability (induced by setting off small bombs in the combustion chamber beginning in 1963) showed that the injectors inherited from the Thor and Atlas could not recover and restore stable combustion once an instability occurred. So Rocketdyne engineers rearranged the injector orifices and added baffles to the injector face. These modifications solved the problem. Cracks in liquid-oxygen domes and splits in regenerative-cooling tubes also required redesign. Embrittlement by sulfur from the RP-1 in the hotter environment of the 188,000-pound engine required a change of materials in the tubular walls of the combustion chamber from nickel alloy to stainless steel. There were other problems, but the Saturn personnel resolved them in the course of the launches of Saturn I and IB from late 1961 to early 1968.[49]

Because the H-1s would be clustered in two groups of four each for the Saturn I first stage, there were two types of engines. H-1Cs used for the four inboard engines were incapable of gimballing to steer the first stage. The four outboard H-1D engines did the gimballing. Both versions used bell-shaped nozzles, but the outboard H-1Ds used a collector or aspirator to channel the turbopump exhaust gases, which were rich in unburned RP-1 fuel, and deposit them in the exhaust plume from the engines to prevent the still-combustible materials from collecting in the first stage's boat tail.[50]

The first successful launch of Saturn I did not mean that developers had solved all problems with the H-1 powerplant. On May 28, 1964, Saturn I flight SA-6 unexpectedly confirmed that the first stage of the launch vehicle could perform its function with an engine out, a capability already demonstrated intentionally on flight SA-4 exactly 14 months earlier. An H-1 engine on SA-6 ceased to function 117.3 seconds into the 149-second stage-one burn. Telemetry showed that the turbopump had ceased to supply propellants. Analysis of the data suggested that the problem was stripped gears in the turbopump gearbox. Previous ground testing had revealed to

FIG. 3.9
Launch of
a Saturn IB
vehicle on
the *Skylab
4* mission
from Launch
Complex 39B
at Kennedy
Space Center
on Novem-
ber 16, 1973.
(Photo courtesy
of NASA)

Rocketdyne and Marshall technicians that there was need for redesign of the gear's teeth to increase their width. Already programmed
to fly on SA-7, the redesigned gearbox did not delay flight testing,
and there were no further problems with H-1 engines in flight.[51]

None of the sources for this history explain exactly how Rocketdyne increased the thrust of each of the eight H-1 engines from
188,000 to 200,000 pounds for the first five Saturn IBs (SA-201
through SA-205) and then to 205,000 pounds for the remaining vehicles. It would appear, as with the uprated Saturn I engines, that
the key lay in the flow rates of the propellants into the combustion
chambers, resulting in increased chamber pressure. After increasing
with the shift from the 165,000- to the 188,000-pound H-1s, these
flow rates increased again for the 200,000-pound and once more for
the 205,000-pound H-1s.[52]

FIG. 3.10 Diagram of the engines used on the Saturn IB and Saturn V. The Saturn IB used eight H-1s on its first stage and a single J-2 on its second stage; the Saturn V relied on five F-1 engines for thrust in its first stage, with five J-2s in the second and one J-2 in the third stage. (Photo courtesy of NASA)

For the Saturn V that launched the astronauts and their spacecraft into their trajectory toward the Moon for the six Apollo Moon landings, the first-stage engines had to provide much more thrust than the eight clustered H-1s could supply. Development of the larger F-1 engine by Rocketdyne originated with an air force request in 1955. NASA inherited the reports and other data from the early development, and when Rocketdyne won the NASA contract to build the engine in 1959, it was, "in effect, a follow-on" effort. Since this agreement preceded a clear conception of the vehicle into which the F-1 would fit and the precise mission it would perform, designers had to operate in a bit of a cognitive vacuum. They had to make early assumptions, followed by reengineering to fit the engines into the actual first stage of the Saturn V, which itself still lacked a firm configuration in December 1961 when NASA selected Boeing to build the S-IC (the Saturn V first stage). Another factor in the design of the F-1 resulted from a decision "made early in the program . . . [to make] the fullest possible use of components and techniques proven in the Saturn I program."

In 1955, the goal had been an engine with a million pounds of thrust, and by 1957 Rocketdyne was well along in developing it. That year and the next, the division of NAA had even test-fired

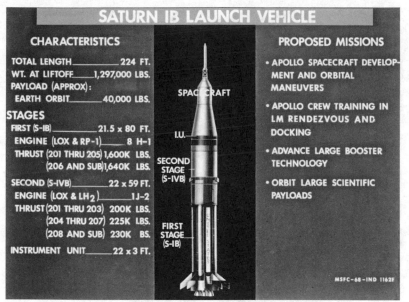

FIG. 3.11 Diagram of the Saturn IB showing its characteristics and proposed mission. (Photo courtesy of NASA)

such an engine, with much of the testing done at Edwards AFB's rocket site, where full-scale testing continued while Rocketdyne did the basic research, development, and production at its plant in Canoga Park. It conducted tests of components at nearby Santa Susana Field Laboratory. At Edwards the future air force Rocket Propulsion Laboratory (so named in 1963) had three test stands (1-A, 1-B, and 2-A) set aside for the huge engine. The 1959 contract with NASA called for 1.5 million pounds of thrust, and by April 6, 1961, Rocketdyne was able to static-fire a prototype engine at Edwards whose thrust peaked at 1.64 million pounds.[53]

Burning RP-1 as its fuel with liquid oxygen as the oxidizer, the F-1 did not break new ground in its basic technology. But its huge thrust level required so much scaling up that, as an MSFC publication said, "An enlargement of this magnitude is in itself an innovation." For instance, the very size of the combustion chamber—40 inches in diameter (20.56 inches for the H-1) with a chamber area almost 4 times that of the H-1 (1,257 to 332 square inches)—required new techniques to braze together the regenerative cooling tubes. Also because of the engine's size, Rocketdyne adopted a gas-cooled, removable nozzle extension to make the F-1 easier to transport.[54]

The engine was bell shaped and had an expansion ratio of 16:1 with the nozzle extension attached. Its turbopump consisted of a single, axial-flow turbine mounted directly on the thrust chamber with separate centrifugal pumps for the oxidizer and fuel that were driven at the same speed by the turbine shaft. This eliminated the

FIG. 3.12
The huge
first stage of
the Saturn V
launch vehicle
being hoisted
by crane from
a barge onto
the B-2 test
stand at the
Mississippi Test
Facility (later
the Stennis
Space Center)
on January 1,
1967. Nozzles
for the F-1
engines show
at the bottom
of the stage.
(Photo courtesy
of NASA)

need for a gearbox, which had been a problematic feature of many earlier engines. A fuel-rich gas generator burning the engine propellants powered the turbine. The initial F-1 had the prescribed 1.5 million pounds of thrust, but starting with vehicle 504, Rocketdyne uprated the engine to 1.522 million pounds. It did so by increasing the chamber pressure through greater output from the turbine, which in turn required strengthening components (at some expense in engine weight). There were five F-1s clustered in the S-IC stage, four outboard and one in the center. All but the center engine gimballed to provide steering. As with the H-1, there was a hypergolic ignition system.[55]

Perhaps the most intricate design feature of the F-1 was the injection system. As two Rocketdyne engineers wrote in 1989, the injector "might well be considered the heart of a rocket engine, since virtually no other single component has such a major impact on overall engine performance." The injector not only inserted the propellants into the combustion chamber but mixed them in a proportion designed to produce optimal thrust and performance. "As is the case with the design of nearly all complex, high technology hardware," the two engineers added, "the design of a liquid rocket injector is not an exact science, although it is becoming more so as analytical tools are continuously improved. This is because the basic physics associated with all of the complex, combustion processes that are affected by the design of the injector are only partly known." A portion of the problem lay with the atomization of the propellants and the distribution of the fine droplets to ensure proper mixing. Even as late as 1989, "the atomization process [wa]s one of the most complex and least understood phenomena, and reliable information [wa]s difficult to obtain." One result of less-than-optimal injector design was combustion instability, whose causes and mechanisms still in 1989 were "at best, only poorly known and understood." Even in 2006, "a clear set of generalized validated design rules for preventing combustion instabilities in new TCs [thrust chambers] ha[d] not yet been identified. Also a good universal mathematical three-dimensional simulation of the complex nonlinear combustion process ha[d] not yet been developed."[56]

This was still more the case in the early 1960s, and it caused huge problems for development of the F-1 injector. Designers at Rocketdyne knew from experience with the H-1 and earlier engines that injector design and combustion instability would be problems. They began with three injector designs, all based essentially on that for the H-1. Water-flow tests provided information on the spacing and shape of orifices in the injector, followed by hot-fire tests in 1960 and early 1961. But as Leonard Bostwick, the F-1 engine manager at Marshall, reported, "None of the F-1 injectors exhibited dynamic stability." Designers tried a variety of flat-faced and baffled injectors without success, leading to the conclusion that it would not be possible simply to scale up the H-1 injector to the size needed for the F-1. Engineers working on the program did borrow from the H-1 effort the use of bombs to initiate combustion instability, saving a lot of testing to await its spontaneous appearance. But on June 28, 1962, during an F-1 hot-engine test in one of the test stands built for the purpose at the rocket site on Edwards AFB, combustion instability caused the engine to melt.[57]

Marshall appointed Jerry Thomson, chief of the MSFC Liquid Fuel Engines Systems Branch, to chair an ad hoc committee to analyze the problem. Thomson had earned a degree in mechanical engineering at Auburn University following service in World War II. Turning over the running of his branch to his deputy, he moved to Canoga Park where respected propulsion engineer Paul Castenholz and a mechanical engineer named Dan Klute, who also "had a special talent for the half-science, half-art of combustion chamber design," joined him on the committee from positions as Rocketdyne managers. Although Marshall's committee was not that large, at Rocketdyne there were some 50 engineers and technicians assigned to a combustion devices team, supplemented by people from universities, NASA, and the air force. Using essentially cut-and-try methods, they initially had little success. The instability showed no consistency and set in "for reasons we never quite understood," as Thomson confessed.[58]

Using high-speed instrumentation and trying perhaps 40–50 design modifications, eventually the engineers found a combination of baffles, enlarged fuel-injection orifices, and changed impingement angles that worked. By late 1964, even following explosions of the bombs, the combustion chamber regained its stability. The engineers (always wondering if the problem would recur) rated the F-1 injector as flight-ready in January 1965. However, there were other problems with the injector. Testing revealed difficulties with fuel and oxidizer rings containing multiple orifices for the propellants. Steel rings called lands held copper rings through which the propellants flowed. Brazed joints held the copper rings in the lands, and these joints were failing. Engineers gold-plated the lands to create a better bonding surface. Developed and tested only in mid-1965, the new injector rings required retrofitting in engines Rocketdyne had already delivered.[59]

Overall, from October 1962 to September 1966, there were 1,332 full-scale tests with 108 injectors during the preliminary, the flight-rating, and flight-qualification testing of the F-1 to qualify the engine for use. According to one expert, this was "probably the most intensive (and expensive) program ever devoted primarily to solving a problem of combustion instabilities."[60]

The resultant injector contained 6,300 holes—3,700 for RP-1 and 2,600 for liquid oxygen. Radial and circumferential baffles divided the flat-faced portion of the injector face into 13 compartments, with the holes or orifices arranged so that most of them were in groups of five. Two of the five injected the RP-1 so that the two streams impinged to produce atomization, while the other three inserted liquid oxygen, which formed a fan-shaped spray that mixed with the RP-1 to combust evenly and smoothly. Driven by the

FIG. 3.13
Fuel tank
assembly for
the Saturn V
S-IC (first)
stage being
prepared for
transportation.
(Photo courtesy
of NASA)

52,900-horsepower turbine, the propellant pumps delivered 15,471 gallons of RP-1 and 24,811 gallons of liquid oxygen per minute to the combustion chamber via the injector.[61]

Despite all the effort that went into the injector design, the turbopump required even more design effort and time. Engineers experienced 11 failures of the system during development. Two of these involved the liquid-oxygen pump's impeller, which required use of stronger components. The other 9 failures involved explosions. Causes varied. The high acceleration of the shaft on the turbopump constituted one problem. Others included friction between moving parts and metal fatigue. All 11 failures necessitated redesign or change in procedures. For instance, Rocketdyne made the turbine manifold out of a nickel-based alloy manufactured by GE, René 41, which had only recently joined the materials used for rocket engines. Unfamiliarity with its welding techniques led to cracking near the welds. It required time-consuming research and training to teach welders proper procedures for using the alloy, which could withstand not only high temperatures but the large temperature differential resulting from burning the cryogenic liquid oxygen. The final version of this turbopump provided the speed and high volumes needed for a 1.5-million-pound-thrust engine and did so with minimal parts and high ultimate reliability.[62]

Once designed and delivered, the F-1 engines required further testing at Marshall and NASA's Mississippi Test Facility. At the latter, contractors had built an S-IC stand after 1961 on the mud of a swamp along the Pearl River near the Louisiana border and the Gulf of Mexico. Mosquito ridden and snake infested, this area served as home to wild pigs, alligators, and panthers. Construction workers faced 110 bites a minute from salt marsh mosquitoes, against which nets, gloves, repellent, and long-sleeved shirts afforded little protection. Spraying special chemicals from two C-123 aircraft did reduce the number of bites to 10 per minute, but working conditions remained challenging. Nevertheless, the stand was ready for use in March 1967, more than a year after the first static test at Marshall. But thereafter, the 410-foot S-IC stand, the tallest structure in Mississippi, became the focus of testing for the first-stage engines.[63]

Despite static testing, the real proof of successful design came only in actual flight. For AS-501, the first Saturn V vehicle, the flight on November 9, 1967, largely succeeded. The giant launch vehicle lifted the instrument unit, command and service modules, and a boilerplate lunar module to a peak altitude of 11,240 miles. The third stage then separated and the service module's propulsion system accelerated the command module to a speed of 36,537 feet per second (about 24,628 miles per hour), comparable to lunar reentry speed. It landed in the Pacific Ocean 9 miles from its aiming point, where the USS *Bennington* recovered it. The first-stage engines did experience longitudinal oscillations (known as the pogo effect), but these were comparatively minor.[64]

Euphoria from this success dissipated, however, on April 4, 1968, when AS-502 (*Apollo 6*) launched. As with AS-501, this vehicle did not carry astronauts onboard, but it was considered "an all-important dress rehearsal for the first manned flight" planned for AS-503. The initial launch went well, but toward the end of the first-stage burn the pogo effect became much more severe than on AS-501, reaching five cycles per second, which exceeded the spacecraft's design specifications. Despite the oscillations, the vehicle continued its upward course. Stage-two separation occurred, and all five of the engines ignited. Two of them subsequently shut down, but the instrument unit compensated with longer-than-planned burns for the remaining three engines and the third-stage propulsion unit, only to have the latter fail to restart in orbit, constituting a technical failure of the mission, although some sources count it a success.[65]

As Apollo Program Director Samuel Phillips told the Senate Aeronautical and Space Sciences Committee on April 22, 1968, 18 days after the flight, pogo was not a new phenomenon, having occurred in the Titan II and come "into general attention in the early days of the Gemini program." Aware of pogo, von Braun's engineers had tested and analyzed the Saturn V before the AS-501 flight and found "an acceptable margin of stability to indicate" it would not develop. The AS-501 flight "tended to confirm these analyses." Each of the five F-1 engines had "small pulsations," but each engine experienced them "at slightly different points in time." Thus, they did not create a problem. But on AS-502, the five 1.5-million-pound engines "came into a phase relationship" so that "the engine pulsation was additive."[66]

All engines developed a simultaneous vibration of 5.5 hertz (cycles per second). The entire vehicle itself developed a bending frequency that increased (as it consumed propellants) to 5.25 hertz about 125 seconds into the flight. The engine vibrations traveled longitudinally up the vehicle structure with their peak occurring at the top where the spacecraft was (and the astronauts would be on a flight carrying them). Alone, the vibrations would not have been a problem, but they coupled with the vehicle's bending frequency, which moved in a lateral direction. When they intersected (with both at about the same frequency), their effects combined and multiplied. In the draft of an article he wrote for the *New York Times,* Phillips characterized the "complicated coupling" as "analogous to the annoying feedback squeal you encounter when the microphone and loud speaker of a public address system . . . coupled." This coupling was significant enough that it might interfere with astronauts' performance of their duties.[67]

NASA formed a pogo task force including people from Marshall, other NASA organizations, contractors, and universities. The task force recommended detuning the five engines, changing the frequencies of at least two so that they would no longer produce vibrations at the same time. Engineers did this by inserting liquid helium into a cavity formed in a liquid-oxygen prevalve with a casting that bulged out and encased an oxidizer feed pipe. The bulging portion was only half filled with the liquid oxygen during engine operation. The helium absorbed pressure surges in oxidizer flow and reduced the frequency of the oscillations to 2 hertz, lower than the frequency of the structural oscillations. Engineers eventually applied the solution to all four outboard engines. Technical people contributing to this solution came from Marshall, Boeing, Martin, TRW, Aerospace Corporation, and North American's Rocketdyne Division.[68] This incidence of pogo showed how difficult it was for

FIG. 3.14
Launch of the
giant Saturn V
on the *Apollo
11* mission
(July 16, 1969)
that carried
Neil Armstrong,
Edwin Aldrin,
and Michael
Collins on a
trajectory to
lunar orbit
from which
Armstrong
and Aldrin
descended
to walk on
the Moon's
surface. (Photo
courtesy of
NASA)

rocket designers to predict when and how such a phenomenon might occur, even while aware of and actively testing for it. The episode also illustrated the cooperation of large numbers of people from a variety of organizations needed to solve such problems.

The redesign worked. On the next Saturn V mission, *Apollo 8* (AS-503, December 21, 1968), the five F-1s performed their mission without pogo (or other) problems. On Christmas Eve the three astronauts aboard the spacecraft went into lunar orbit. They completed 10 circuits around the Moon, followed by a burn on Christmas Day to return to Earth, splashing into the Pacific on December 27. For the first time, humans had escaped the confines of Earth's immediate environs and returned from orbiting the Moon. There were no further significant problems with the F-1s on Apollo missions.[69]

The development of the huge engines had been difficult and unpredictable but ultimately successful.

Analysis and Conclusions

The F-1 engine marked an almost incredible advance beyond the technology of the V-2 engine, which itself had been impressive enough in 1945. In less than 30 years, the sophistication of testing equipment, materials, and understanding had advanced remarkably, although problems with combustion instability and turbopumps remained intractable. An enormous number of engineers and institutions had contributed to the advances, only the most notable of which could be discussed in this chapter. Institutions ranged from laboratories, technical institutes, and outside firms in Germany to American universities, components of the air force and NASA, and contractors in the United States, where engineers in a variety of disciplines shared their expertise and insights.

From 1937, when Thiel wrote down his observations in Germany, to the Apollo Moon landings, increasingly large and sophisticated propulsion units had revealed a variety of problems and mysteries. Even at the end of the period covered by this book, experts did not fully understand all aspects of the complex injection, combustion, and other processes that affected rocket-engine performance. But when problems occurred, engineers could usually locate their sources and develop fixes that worked satisfactorily.

Often, the problems showed up in ground testing, but in many cases, it was not until missiles or launch vehicles actually flew that they revealed design flaws. Many times, solutions yielded only to trial-and-error methodologies, although these were informed by existing theory and increasingly accumulated knowledge. After the period of this chapter, analysis using sophisticated computer technology increasingly added to the arsenal of rocket engineers. But even this did not end use of cut-and-try methodologies. Rocket design and development remained very much an engineering art rather than a mature science capable of predicting (and thus avoiding) all problems.

Development of the engines discussed in this chapter benefited from transfers of engineers from one organization to another. The most notable and famous example of this involved the rocket team under von Braun and its move from Germany to work first for the army and then for NASA. But many other engineers like Paul Castenholz brought expertise from other organizations (not necessarily ones engaged in rocket development) to those involved in designing missiles and launch vehicles. Among factors contributing to the story told here was a production improvement clause in air force contracts that gave rocket firms incentives to experiment, as Rocketdyne did to the benefit of the Atlas and Saturn programs.

Although the V-2 engine provided a (not *the*) starting point for American rocket development, engineers in the United States quickly advanced propulsion technology beyond the stage achieved by von Braun's team in Germany and by early U.S. rocket efforts. There were common threads running from the V-2 to the Saturn V engines, with members of von Braun's team contributing to many of them. But it is too much to say that the A-4 (V-2) constituted "the recognized prototype of all modern booster rocket concepts" or even "the grandfather of all modern guided missiles and space boosters." [70] Rather than a prototype or even an important contributor of genes to later rockets, the V-2 was mostly a point of takeoff for several further American developments. As such, it was important, but most subsequent developments went well beyond its technology. Even the story of alcohol and kerosene rocket engines alone has many more complicating twists and turns than either quotation would suggest. Moreover, other types of propulsion units developed from entirely different roots, as the ensuing chapters will show.

Propulsion with Storable Fuels and Oxidizers, 1942–91

IN THE LAST YEARS OF WORLD WAR II, A substantial part of von Braun's staff at Peenemünde (1,116 people in August 1944) was engaged in development of the antiaircraft missile, Wasserfall, which used hypergolic propellants (nitric acid and vinyl ethyl ether plus additives). These substances could be stored in the propellant tanks because they did not require the special handling and loading just before launch of the cryogenic liquid oxygen, which would boil off if loaded too soon. And they did not require pyrotechnic igniters since they combusted upon contact. Unlike alcohol, however, hypergolics in the United States appear to have developed almost completely without German influence. The evolution began even before the Peenemünders started working on Wasserfall. U.S. development began, in a sense, in December 1939 because of the army air corps' objections to liquid oxygen. In response to these objections, Frank Malina's group at Caltech began working with red fuming nitric acid (RFNA) as an oxidizer and gasoline or benzene as fuel in the development of liquid-propellant JATOs. The group also tried gaseous oxygen and ethylene.[1]

Early Storable Liquid-Propulsion Efforts

It would appear that the Caltech group had not made great progress on liquid propulsion as of July 1940 when it was joined by Malina's roommate, Martin Summerfield, who completed work on his Ph.D. during 1941 in the physics department at Caltech. After joining Malina's group, he went to the Caltech library, consulted the literature on combustion-chamber physics, and found a text with information on the speed of combustion. Using it, he calculated—much in the fashion of Thiel at Kummersdorf—that the combustion chamber being used by the GALCIT team was far too large, resulting in heat transfer that degraded performance. So he constructed a smaller chamber of cylindrical shape that yielded a 20 percent increase in performance. Von Kármán believed that roughly 25 to 30 percent of the heat in the combustion chamber would be lost, based on information about reciprocating engines. The eminent aerodynamicist had therefore concluded that it would be impossible for rocket engines to be self-cooling, restricting both their lightness and length of operation. Summerfield's calculations showed these assumptions about heat transfer to be far too high, indicating that it was possible for a self-cooling engine to operate for a sustained period. Subsequent tests confirmed Summerfield's calculations, and Malina learned about the technique of regenerative cooling from James H. Wyld of Reaction Motors during one of his trips back East.[2]

For the moment, the group worked with uncooled engines burning RFNA and gasoline. Successive engines of 200, 500, and 1,000 pounds of thrust with various numbers of injectors provided some successes but presented problems with throbbing or incomplete initial ignition, which led to explosions. After four months of efforts to improve combustion and ignition, Malina paid a visit to the Naval Engineering Experiment Station in Annapolis in February 1942. There he learned that chemical engineer Ray C. Stiff had discovered in the literature of chemistry that aniline ignited hypergolically with nitric acid. Malina telegrammed Summerfield to replace the gasoline with aniline. He did so, but it took three different injector designs to make the 1,000-pound engine work. The third involved eight sets of injectors each for the two propellants, with the stream of propellants washing against the chamber walls. Summerfield recalled that after 25 seconds of operation, the heavy JATO units glowed cherry red. But they worked on a Douglas A-20A bomber for 44 successive firings in April 1942, the first successful operation of a liquid JATO in the United States. This led to orders by the army air forces (AAF) with the newly formed Aerojet Engineering Corporation, which Malina and von Kármán had helped to found.[3]

Aerojet did considerable business with the AAF and navy for JATO units during the war and had become by 1950 the largest rocket-engine manufacturer in the world, as well as a leader in research and development of rocket technology. Until Aerojet's acquisition by General Tire in 1944–45, the rocket firm and the GALCIT rocket project maintained close technical relations. Although GALCIT/JPL was involved essentially with JATO work from 1939 to 1944, in the summer of 1942 the project began designing pumps to deliver liquid propellants to a combustion chamber instead of feeding the propellants by gas under pressure. By the fall of that year, project engineers were working on using the propellants to cool the combustion chamber of a 200-pound-thrust engine.[4]

Meanwhile, as a result of Stiff's discovery, Truax's group at Annapolis began using 1,500-pound JATOs burning nitric acid and aniline on navy PBY aircraft in 1943. Both Truax and Stiff subsequently got orders to work at Aerojet, where Stiff devoted his efforts to a droppable JATO using storable, hypergolic propellants. Aerojet produced about 100 of these units, and some came to be used by the U.S. Coast Guard. In these ways, Aerojet became familiar with use of storable propellants, and Stiff joined the firm after completing his obligatory service with the navy.[5]

The next important development involving engines with storable propellants was the WAC Corporal sounding rocket (the term WAC standing for Women's Auxiliary Corps or Without Attitude Control, depending upon the source consulted). The Army Ordnance Corps had requested that Malina's project investigate the feasibility of developing a rocket carrying meteorological equipment that could reach a minimum altitude of 100,000 feet. The JPL team redesigned an Aerojet motor that used monoethylene as a fuel and nitric acid mixed with oleum as an oxidizer. The original motor was regeneratively cooled by the monoethylene. JPL adapted the motor to use RFNA containing 6.5 percent nitrogen dioxide as oxidizer and aniline containing 20 percent furfuryl alcohol as a fuel, thereby increasing the exhaust velocity from 5,600 to 6,200 feet per second but leaving the thrust at 1,500 pounds for 45 seconds. According to one source, the specific impulse was 200 lbf-sec/lbm (slightly lower than the V-2).[6]

147
Propulsion
with Storable
Fuels and
Oxidizers,
1942–91

Besides exceeding the requirements of the army, the small, liquid-propellant rocket also functioned as a smaller test version of the Corporal E research vehicle, providing valuable experience in the development of that larger unit. During the testing, the program decided to modify the WAC Corporal to attain higher altitudes. A substantial modification of the engine reduced its weight from 50 to 12 pounds. The WAC A initial version of the rocket had a comparatively thin, cylindrical inner shell of steel for the combustion chamber, with an outer shell that fit tightly around it but was equipped with a joint to permit expansion. Helical coils (ones that spiraled around the outside of the combustion chamber like a screw thread) provided regenerative cooling, with a shower-type injector in which eight fuel streams impinged on eight oxidizer streams. For the modified WAC B engine, designers reduced the combustion chamber in length from 73 to 61 inches and made minor modifications to the injector. It had an inner shell spot-welded to the outer shell, still with helical cooling passages. The injector remained a showerhead with eight pairs of impinging jets.[7]

In a series of flight tests at White Sands Proving Ground, New Mexico, in December 1946, none of the WAC Corporal B vehicles rose more than 175,000 feet in altitude. Apparently the test team suspected cavitation (gas bubbles) in the injector system as the cause of the less-than-optimal performance, since team members constructed three more B-model vehicles with orifice inserts that were screwed in, rather than drilled as before, to achieve cavitation-free injection of the propellants into the combustion chamber. In three February–March 1947 tests, one WAC Corporal B reached an altitude of 240,000 feet. Overall, the WAC Corporal demonstrated that the propulsion system was sound and the nitric acid–aniline–furfuryl alcohol propellant combination was viable.[8]

The WAC Corporal led directly to the successful Aerobee sounding rocket built by Aerojet, which was used by the Applied Physics Laboratory of Johns Hopkins University for research in the upper atmosphere. Then, in the Bumper-WAC project, the WAC Corporal B flew as a second stage on V-2 missiles. The reported altitude of 244 miles and maximum speed of 7,553 feet per second (reached on February 24, 1949) were records. This highly successful launch demonstrated that a rocket's velocity could be increased with a second stage and that ignition of a rocket engine could occur at high altitudes.[9]

In addition, the engine for the WAC Corporal contributed to the Corporal missile's propulsion system. As first conceived, Corporal E was a research vehicle for the study of guidance, aerodynamic, and propulsion problems of long-range rockets. In 1944, von Kármán estimated that a rocket with a range of 30 to 40 miles would be necessary to serve as a prototype for a later missile. He thought such a vehicle would need an engine with 20,000 pounds of thrust and 60 seconds of burning time. Experience at JPL to that point had indicated that the only already-developed rocket type meeting von Kármán's specifications would be a liquid-propellant vehicle burning red fuming nitric acid and aniline. Early plans called for use of centrifugal, turbine-driven pumps to feed the propellants. Since Aerojet had a turborocket under development, JPL thought it could draw on the nearby rocket firm's experience to provide a pump for the Corporal. This design became the never-completed Corporal F. Corporal E used air pressurization, as had the WAC Corporal.[10]

Scaling the WAC Corporal engine up to a larger size proved challenging. The first major design for a Corporal E engine involved a 650-pound, mild-steel version with helical cooling passages. Such a heavy propulsion device resulted from four unsuccessful attempts to scale up the WAC Corporal B engine to 200 pounds. None of them passed their proof testing. In the 650-pound engine, the cooling passages were machined to a heavy outer shell that formed a sort of hourglass shape around the throat of the nozzle. The injector consisted of 80 pairs of impinging jets that dispersed the oxidizer (fuming nitric acid) onto the fuel. The direction, velocity, and diameter of the streams were similar to those employed in the WAC Corporal A. The injector face was a showerhead type with orifices more or less uniformly distributed over it. It mixed the propellants in a ratio of 2.65 parts of oxidizer to 1 of fuel. The outer shell of the combustion chamber was attached to an inner shell by silver solder. When several of these heavyweight engines underwent proof testing, they cracked and nozzle throats eroded as the burning propellant exhausted out the rear of the engine. But three engines with the inner and outer shells welded together proved suitable for flight testing.[11]

On May 22, 1947, the first Corporal E with this heavyweight engine launched from the army's White Sands Proving Ground. Its intended range was 60 miles, and it actually achieved a range of 62.5 (in one account, 64.25) miles. The second launch occurred on July 17, 1947, but the rocket failed to achieve enough thrust to rise significantly until 90 seconds of burning reduced the weight to the point that it flew a very short distance. On November 4, 1947, the third launch was more successful, but its propellants burned for only 43 (instead of 60) seconds before the engine quit. This reduced its range to just over 14 miles. Both it and the "rabbit killer" (the second vehicle, so-called because it flew along the ground) experienced burnthroughs in the throat area, the helical cooling coils proving inadequate for their purpose.[12]

Deciding that in addition to these flaws, the engine was too heavy, the Corporal team determined to design a much lighter-weight engine. Several engines combining features of the WAC Corporal B and 650-pound Corporal E combustion chambers all suffered burnouts of the throat area during static tests. Finally, a redesigned engine weighing about 125 pounds stemmed in part from an examination of the V-2, revealing that its cooling passages were axial (with no helix angle, i.e., they took the shortest distance around the combustion chamber's circumference). Analysis showed the advantage of that arrangement, so JPL adopted it. The inner shell of the new engine was corrugated, and the outer shell, smooth. The shape of the combustion chamber changed from semispherical to essentially cylindrical, with the inside diameter reduced from 23 to 11 inches and the length shortened slightly, contributing to the much lighter weight.

It took two designs to achieve a satisfactory injector, the first having burned through on its initial static test. The second injector had 52 pairs of impinging jets angled about 2.5 degrees in the direction of (but located well away from) the chamber wall. Initially, the Corporal team retained the mixture ratio of 2.65:1. But static tests of the axially cooled engine in November 1948 at the Ordnance–California Institute of Technology (ORDCIT) Test Station in Muroc, California (in the Mojave Desert above the San Gabriel Mountains and well north of JPL), showed that lower mixture ratios yielded higher characteristic velocities and specific impulses, as well as smoother operation. Thus, the mixture ratio was first reduced to 2.45 and then 2.2. Later still, the propellant was changed to stabilized fuming nitric acid (including a very small amount of hydrogen fluoride) as the oxidizer and aniline–furfuryl alcohol–hydrazine (in the percentages of 46.5, 46.5, and 7.0, respectively) as the fuel. With this propellant, the mixture ratio shifted further downward to 2.13 because of changes in the densities of the propellants. The resultant engine, made of mild steel, provided high reliability. Its success rested primarily upon its "unique configuration, wherein the cool, uncorrugated outer shell carrie[d] the chamber pressure loads, and the thin inner shell, corrugated to form forty-four axial cooling passages, [wa]s copper-brazed to the outer shell." Finally, the inside of the inner shell (the combustion chamber inside face) was plated with chrome to resist corrosion from the propellants.[13]

The sixth Corporal E launch took place on November 2, 1950. The missile experienced multiple failures. It landed 35.9 miles downrange, about 35 miles short of projections. Later static tests revealed problems with a propellant regulator that had caused over-rich mixture ratios on both the fifth and sixth launches. Failure of a coupling had resulted in loss of air pressure. The radar beacon to provide overriding guidance in azimuth operated satisfactorily until failure of a flight-beacon transmitter some 36 seconds into the flight. The Doppler beacon never went into operation to cut off propellant flow at the proper moment because the missile failed to achieve the velocity prescribed, but also because the Doppler beacon itself failed at 24 seconds after liftoff. As a final blow, all electronic equipment failed, apparently from extreme vibration.[14]

On launch seven of the Corporal E in January 1951, the vehicle landed downrange at 63.85 miles, 5 miles short of the targeted impact point. This was the first flight to demonstrate propellant shutoff and also the first to use a new multicell air tank and a new air-disconnect coupling. These two design changes to fix some of the problems on launch six increased the reliability of the propulsion system significantly. However, although the Corporal performed even better on launch eight (March 22, 1951), hitting about 4 miles short of the target, on launch nine (July 12, 1951) the missile landed 20 miles beyond the target because of failure of the Doppler transponder and the propellant cutoff system. The final "round" of Corporal E never flew. But the Corporal team had learned from the first nine rounds how little it understood about the flight environment of the vehicle, especially vibrations that occurred when it was operating. The team began to use vibration test tables to make the design better able to function and to test individual components before installation. This testing resulted in changes of suppliers and individual parts as well as to repairs before launch (or redesigns in the case of multiple failures of a given component.)[15]

The next 20 Corporals, with the airframes built by Douglas Aircraft (like the Corporal Es), received the designation Corporal I. Its first flight occurred on October 10, 1951. But the frequency regulator for the central power supply failed on takeoff, causing the missile to follow nearly a vertical trajectory. Range safety cut its flight short so that it would impact between White Sands and the city of Las Cruces, New Mexico. Flight 11 (referred to as round 12, counting the last Corporal E, which never launched) occurred on December 6, 1951. Before the launch, the army invited several companies to bid on production contracts as prime contractors. Ryan Aeronautical Company of San Diego manufactured the engines for both the airframes built by Douglas and those from the new prime contractor, Firestone Tire and Rubber Company of Los Angeles. JPL received the Firestone missiles and disassembled them for inspection. It then rebuilt them and performed preflight testing before sending them to White Sands for the actual flight tests. Then it sent comments to the manufacturer to help improve factory production. According to Clayton Koppes, however, the two major contractors and JPL failed to work together effectively. Meanwhile, between January and December 1952, JPL launched 26 Corporals, including the first 10 of the Firestone lot as well as 16 produced by Douglas.[16]

Because of problems with the missile's guidance system and engineering changes to correct them, a second production order to Firestone for Corporal missiles in late 1954 resulted in a redesignation of the missile as Corporal II. JPL retained technical control of the Corporal program throughout 1955, relinquishing it in 1956 while continuing to provide technical assistance to the army's contractors, including Firestone. Corporal II continued to have problems with its guidance/control system but also with propellant shutoff during firings of the missile by army field forces. Fact-finding investigations and informal discussions on the parts of contractors, the field forces, Army Ordnance Corps, and JPL led to greater care by field forces personnel in following operational procedures. These eliminated shutoff problems when not violated. The army declared the Corporal to be operational in 1954, and in January 1955 the Corporal I deployed to Europe. Eight Corporal II battalions replaced it during 1956 and the first half of 1957.[17]

Although the Corporal was less powerful and had a shorter range than the V-2, the U.S. missile's propulsion system had a higher specific impulse (about 220 lbf-sec/lbm as compared with 210 for the V-2). In some respects, such as the axial nature of the cooling system and the use of Doppler radar for propellant cutoff, the Corporal had borrowed from the V-2. In most respects, however, the American missile was an independent development, in some cases one that separately adopted features developed at Peenemünde after it was too late to incorporate them into the V-2. These included a showerhead injector and the use of hypergolic propellants. Both had been developed for the Wasserfall antiaircraft rocket, and a single injector plate later became a standard element in the construction of the rockets designed in Huntsville.[18]

Among the achievements of the Corporal was testing the effects of vibration on electronic equipment. The vibration tables used for this purpose may have been the first effective simulators of the flight environment in that area. Subsequently, both testing for the effects of vibrations and analysis of components and systems for reliability became standard practice in missile development.[19]

The engine itself was also a notable achievement. Although the idea for the axial direction of cooling flow came from the V-2, the overall engine was certainly original. It was both light and efficient, and even though there seems to be no evidence that its design influenced subsequent engines, it seems likely that propulsion engineers learned something of their art from it. Moreover, the early work of JPL in hypergolics transferred to Aerojet, later the contractor for the Titan II, which used storable liquid propellants that ignited on contact. This technology was also used in the Titan III and Titan IV liquid rockets, which employed direct descendants of the early hypergolic propellants Malina learned about in part from the navy in Annapolis. This was a significant contribution from both indigenous U.S. research efforts during World War II. It illustrates one of the ways that technology transferred from one program to another in American rocketry. The borrowings from the V-2 exemplify a different pattern of information flow.

Vanguard Stage Two

Soon after the army deployed Corporal I, Aerojet had occasion to develop its storable-propellant technology further with stage two of the Vanguard launch vehicle for the navy. The firm's Aerobee sounding rockets, building on the WAC Corporal engine technology, had led to the Aerobee-Hi sounding rocket that provided the basis for the projected stage two. As requirements for that stage became more stringent, though, Aerobee-Hi proved deficient, and Aerojet had to return to the drawing board. The firm charged with designing Vanguard, the Martin Company, contracted with Aerojet on November 14, 1955, to develop the second-stage engine. Martin had determined that the second stage needed a thrust of 7,500 pounds and a specific impulse at altitude of 278 lbf-sec/lbm to provide the required velocity to lift the estimated weight of the Vanguard satellite.[20]

The development of an engine to meet these specifications proved to be difficult. Martin's calculated thrust and specific impulse would not meet the vehicle's velocity requirements without severe weight limitations. Aerojet engineers selected unsymmetrical dimethyl hydrazine (UDMH) and inhibited white fuming nitric acid (IWFNA) as the propellants because they were hypergolic (eliminating problems with ignition), had a high loading density (reducing the size, hence weight, of propellant tanks), and delivered the requisite performance. Another advantage of hydrazine and acid was a comparative lack of problems with combustion instability in experimental research.[21]

153

Propulsion with Storable Fuels and Oxidizers, 1942–91

The history of the evolution from the aniline–nitric acid propellants used in the WAC Corporal (specifically, red fuming nitric acid with 6.5 percent nitrogen dioxide plus aniline with the addition of 20 percent furfuryl alcohol) and in the first Aerobee sounding rocket (35 instead of 20 percent furfuryl alcohol) to the UDMH and IWFNA used in Vanguard is complicated. But it illustrates much about propellant chemistry and the number of institutions contributing to it. The basic aniline-RFNA combination worked as a self-igniting propellant combination. But it had numerous disadvantages. Aniline is highly toxic and rapidly absorbed via the skin. A person who came into contact with a significant amount of it was likely to die rapidly from cyanosis. Moreover, aniline has a high freezing point, so it can be used only in moderate temperatures. RFNA is highly corrosive to propellant tanks, so it has to be loaded into a missile or rocket just before firing, and when poured, it gives off dense concentrations of nitrogen dioxide, which is also poisonous. The acid itself burns the skin, as well. Two chemists at JPL had discovered as early as 1946 that white fuming nitric acid (WFNA) and furfuryl alcohol with aniline were just as poisonous and corrosive but did not produce nitrogen dioxide.

But WFNA turned out to be inherently unstable over time. A complicated substance, it was hard for propellant chemists to analyze in the early 1950s. By 1954, however, researchers at the Naval Ordnance Test Station and at JPL had thoroughly investigated nitrogen tetroxide and nitric acid and come up with conclusions that were to be used in the Titan II. Meanwhile, chemists at the Naval Air Rocket Test Station, Lake Denmark, New Jersey; JPL; the NACA's Lewis Flight Propulsion Laboratory; the air force's Wright Air Development Center in Dayton, Ohio; and Ohio State University, among other places, had reached a fundamental understanding of nitric acid by 1951 and published the information by 1955. In the process, the Naval Air Rocket Test Station was apparently the first to discover that small percentages of hydrofluoric acid both reduced the freezing point of RFNA/WFNA and inhibited corrosion with many metals. Thus were born inhibited RFNA and WFNA, for which the services and industrial representatives under air force sponsorship drew up military specifications in 1954. In this way, the services, the NACA, one university, and the competing industries cooperated to solve a common problem.

During the same period, chemists sought either replacements for aniline or chemicals to mix with it and make it less problematic. Hydrazine seemed a promising candidate, and in 1951 the Rocket Branch of the navy's Bureau of Aeronautics, issued contracts to

Metallectro Company and Aerojet to see if any hydrazine derivatives were suitable as rocket propellants. They found that UDMH rapidly self-ignited with nitric acid, leading to a military specification for UDMH in 1955.[22]

Despite the severe weight limitations on the second-stage engine, the Vanguard project engineers had decided to use a pressure-fed (rather than a pump-fed) propellant-delivery system. The pumps produced angular momentum as they rotated, and for stage two, this would be hard for the roll-control system to overcome, especially after engine cutoff. Concerns about reliability led to a decision to use heated helium gas as the pressurant in the feed system. Aerojet convinced the Martin Company and the navy to use stainless-steel instead of aluminum propellant tanks. Because steel had a better strength-to-weight ratio than aluminum, Aerojet argued that the lighter metal would, paradoxically, have had to weigh 30 pounds more than the steel to handle the pressure.

Moreover, a "unique design for the tankage" placed the sphere containing the helium pressure tank between the two propellant tanks, serving as a dividing bulkhead and saving the weight of a separate bulkhead. A solid-propellant gas generator augmented the pressure of the helium and added its own chemical energy to the system at a low cost in weight. Initially, Aerojet had built the combustion chamber of steel. It accumulated 600 seconds of burning without corrosion, but it was too heavy. So engineers developed a lightweight chamber made up of aluminum regenerative-cooling, spaghetti-type tubes wrapped in stainless steel. It weighed 20 pounds less than the steel version, apparently the first such chamber built of aluminum tubes for use with nitric acid and UDMH.[23]

During 1956 there were problems with welding the stainless-steel tanks despite Aerojet's experience in this area. Martin recommended a different method of inspection and improvements in tooling, which resolved these problems. The California firm also had to try several types of injector before finding the right combination of features. One with 72 pairs of impinging jets did not deliver sufficient exhaust velocity, so Aerojet engineers added 24 nonimpinging orifices for fuel in the center portion of the injector. This raised the exhaust velocity above the specifications but suggested the empirical nature of the design process, with engineers having to test one design before discovering that it would not deliver the desired performance. They then had to use their accumulated knowledge and insights to figure out what modification might work.[24]

The development of the combustion chamber and related equipment illustrated the same process. Despite the use of inhibited white fuming nitric acid, the lightweight aluminum combustion chamber—which could be lifted with one hand—gradually eroded. It took engineers "weeks of experimenting" to find out that a coating of tungsten carbide substantially improved the life of the combustion chamber. There also were problems with the design of valves for flow control, requiring significant modifications.[25]

A final problem lay in testing an engine for start at altitude. At the beginning of the project, there was no vacuum chamber large enough to test the engine, but according to NRL propulsion engineer Kurt Stehling, "Several tests were [eventually?] made at Aerojet with engine starts in a vacuum chamber." In any event, to preclude problems with near-vacuum pressure at altitude, the engineers sealed the chamber with a "nozzle closure" that kept pressure in the chamber until exhaust from ignition blew it out.[26]

The original Vanguard schedule as of November 1955 called for six test vehicles to be launched between September 1956 and August 1957, with the first satellite-launching vehicle to lift off in October 1957.[27] It was not until March 1958, however, that the second stage could be fired in an actual launch—that of Test Vehicle (TV) 4. TV-4 contained modifications introduced into the stage-one engine following the failure of TV-3 (when stage one exploded), but it did not yet incorporate the tungsten-carbide coating in the aluminum combustion chamber of the stage-two engine. And it was still a test vehicle. On March 17, 1958, the slender Vanguard launch vehicle lifted off. It performed well enough (despite a rough start) to place the small 3.4-pound *Vanguard I* satellite in an orbit originally estimated to last for 2,000 (but later revised to 240) years.[28]

On TV-5, launched April 28, 1958, the second stage provided less-than-normal thrust, but the first stage had performed better than normal, compensating in advance for the subpar second stage. Then an electrical problem prevented ignition of the third stage, precluding orbit. On the first nontest Vanguard, Space Launch Vehicle (SLV) 1, apparent malfunction of a pressure switch also prevented orbiting a 21.5-pound satellite on May 27, 1958. Here, the second stage performed normally through cutoff of ignition. On SLV-2, June 26, 1958, the second-stage engine cut off after eight seconds, probably due to clogged filters in the inhibited white fuming nitric acid lines from corrosion of the oxidizer tank. The Vanguard team flushed the oxidizer tanks and launched SLV-3 on September 26, 1958, with a 23.3-pound satellite. Despite the flushing, second-stage performance was below normal, causing the satellite to miss orbital speed by a narrow margin. This time, the problem seemed to be a clogged fuel (rather than oxidizer) filter.

On February 17, 1959, however, all systems worked, and SLV-4 placed the 23.3-pound *Vanguard II* satellite in a precise orbit expected to last for 200 years or more. This did not mean that Aerojet had gotten all of the kinks out of the troublesome second stage. SLV-5 on April 13, 1959, experienced a flame oscillation during second-stage ignition, apparently producing a violent yaw that caused the second and third stages with the satellite to tumble and fall into the ocean. Engineers made changes in the second-stage engine's hydraulic system and programmed an earlier separation of the stage, but on SLV-6 (June 22, 1959), a previously reliable regulating valve ceased to function after second-stage ignition. This caused helium pressure to mount (since it could not vent), resulting in an explosion that sent the vehicle into the Atlantic about 300 miles downrange. At least the problem-plagued Vanguard program ended on a happy note. On September 18, 1959, a test vehicle backup (TV-4BU) version of the launch vehicle placed a 52.25-pound X-ray and environmental satellite into orbit.[29]

Able and Able-Star Upper Stages

Despite the problems with the second stage of Vanguard, the air force used a modified version on its Thor-Able launch vehicle, showing the transfer of technology from the navy to the air service. The Able was more successful than the Vanguard prototype for two reasons. One was special cleaning and handling techniques for the propellant tanks that came into being after Vanguard had taken delivery of many of its tanks. Also, Thor-Able did not need to extract maximum performance from the second stage as Vanguard did, so it did not have to burn the very last dregs of propellant in the tanks. The residue that the air force did not need to burn contained more of the scale from the tanks than did the rest of the propellant. Consequently, the valves could close before most of the scale entered the fuel lines, the evident cause of many of Vanguard's problems.[30]

Designated AJ10-40 (in contrast to the Vanguard second stage's AJ10-37), the Able was a modified Vanguard stage that still used a regeneratively cooled combustion chamber with aluminum-tubular construction. Able kept the propellants (IWFNA and UDMH), tanks, helium pressurization system, and propellant valves from the Vanguard. The engine produced a thrust of about 7,500 pounds for roughly 120 seconds.[31]

First used in 1958, the Able upper stage remained in operation until January 1960, when Aerojet's much more capable Able-Star replaced it. The newer stage resulted from an Advanced Research

Projects Agency directive of July 1, 1959. Aerojet could develop the Able-Star engine (AJ10-104) in a matter of months because it was derived from the Able engines and because it was simple. Directed to make the system rugged, with only those subsystems and components needed to meet requirements for restart, attitude control during coasting periods, and longer burning time than the Able could provide, Aerojet engineers sought "to achieve maximum flight capability through limited redesign, overall simplification and optimum utilization of flight-proven components."[32]

Aerojet designed and built the combustion chamber to be "practically identical" to the one used on the Able upper stages, so it remained an aluminum, regeneratively cooled, pressure-fed device. For unstated reasons that may have involved the air force's desire to have the same propellants for Agena and Able-Star, the latter stage switched from the IWFNA used in Able to IRFNA (inhibited red fuming nitric acid) as the oxidizer, keeping UDMH as the fuel. Helium under pressure continued to feed the propellants to the combustion chamber, where the injector had concentric rings of orifices that mixed the hypergolic IRFNA and UDMH in an impinging-stream pattern. There were three helium containers, made of titanium, to supply the pressurizing gas. Experience had suggested no need for a nozzle closure diaphragm previously used to ensure high-altitude starts. Another change from Able was an optional nozzle extension that allowed an expansion ratio of either 20:1 without it or 40:1 with it. Rated thrust rose from 7,575 to 7,890 pounds with the nozzle extended; rated specific impulse climbed proportionally.[33]

Although Aerojet's design and development of Able-Star were quick, they were not problem-free. The virtually identical combustion chambers for the Able engines required test firings of only 115 seconds in duration. Able-Star's had to undergo five static test firings of 300 seconds in duration because of the longer tanks and the increased burning time of the newer upper stage. With a new design for the injector manifold apparently resulting from the conversion to IRFNA as the oxidizer and coolant, during November 1959 Aerojet experienced a burnthrough of the injector plate and the cooling tubes in its vicinity. In a further piece of apparent cut-and-try engineering, Aerojet made appropriate (but unspecified) adjustments to the designs, and two combustion chambers operated successfully for the full 300 seconds later that month.[34]

The *Transit 1B* launch by a Thor/Able-Star on April 13, 1960, marked the first programmed restart of a rocket engine in flight. For *Transit 2A*—launched on June 22, 1960—there was a problem with sloshing of the propellants in the stage-two tanks, which produced roll forces. This resulted in an imperfect but usable orbit. To limit the sloshing, engineers added anti-slosh baffles to both Able-Star propellant tanks.[35]

In a successful launch of the *Courier 1B* satellite (on October 4, 1960), the anti-slosh baffles apparently had worked. The purpose of the satellite was to test the ability of a spacecraft to relieve crowded communications lines via delayed relay of information. The experiment was successful, with large amounts of data transmitted between Puerto Rico and New Jersey. However, the delay of up to two hours before the message was repeated (after the satellite completed its orbit) was unsatisfactory for military purposes and telephone transmission, so the future lay with much higher, geosynchronous orbits. There, the satellite remained in a fixed position relative to a given location on the rotating Earth, allowing nearly instantaneous relay of messages. Overall, there were 20 Thor/Able-Star launches, of which 5 were failures, for a 75 percent success rate.[36]

Titan II Engines

Although there were other important upper-stage engines using storable propellants, such as the Bell Agena engine (starting with the 8048 model), the most significant engines with hypergolic propellants were those used in the Titans II, III, and IV, designed and built by Aerojet. Here, the previous experience with Vanguard, Able, and Able-Star undoubtedly were extraordinarily valuable, as was Aerojet's involvement with the development of UDMH. In the latter development, Aerojet propellant chemist Karl Klager had been an important contributor. Klager held a Ph.D. in chemistry from the University of Vienna (1934) and had come to this country as part of Project Paperclip quite independently of the von Braun group. He worked for the Office of Naval Research in Pasadena during 1949 and started with Aerojet in 1950. The following year, Aerojet received a contract to develop an in-flight thrust-augmentation rocket for the F-86 fighter. The device never went into production, but in developing it, Aerojet engineers conducted a literature search for candidate propellants, did theoretical performance calculations, and measured physical and chemical properties in the laboratory. Together with RFNA, UDMH seemed highly promising but was not available in sufficient quantities to be used. Klager devised (and patented) production processes that yielded large quantities at reasonable prices, but workers began to get violently ill from the toxic substance. All did recover, and Aerojet learned how to control exposure to the vapors.[37]

FIG. 4.1
Technical
drawing with
description
of the Agena
upper stage
as of 1968.
(Photo courtesy
of NASA)

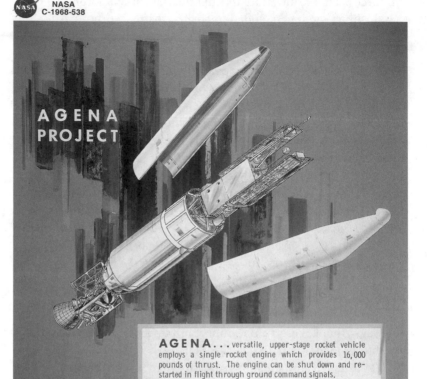

NASA
C-1968-538

AGENA
PROJECT

AGENA...versatile, upper-stage rocket vehicle
employs a single rocket engine which provides 16,000
pounds of thrust. The engine can be shut down and restarted in flight through ground command signals.

Agena and its payload ride into space aboard a large booster
rocket. Following staging, the Agena engine "first-burn"
maneuvers the vehicle and its payload into an earth-
oriented parking orbit. The Agena "second-burn" is
geared to each particular mission - for example, an elliptical earth orbit or the ejection of a payload on a trajectory
to the moon or planets.

This photographic exhibit presents the Agena missions . . .
managed by the Lewis Research Center since January 1963.

National Aeronautics and Space Administration
Lewis Research Center

When the time came in 1960 to begin designing engines for the
Titan II, UDMH had a lower specific impulse than the new missile
required. Hydrazine had better performance but could detonate if
used as a regenerative coolant. Aerojet was the first firm to come
up with an equal mixture of hydrazine and UDMH, Aerozine 50.
This fuel combination ignited hypergolically with nitrogen tetroxide as the oxidizer. Neither was cryogenic. And both could be stored
in propellant tanks for extended periods, offering a much quicker
response time than Titan I's 15 minutes for a propulsion system
burning liquid oxygen and kerosene. Both Aerojet and Martin, the

overall contractor for Titan I, urged a switch to the new propellants, but it was apparently Robert Demaret, chief designer of the Titan, and others from Martin who proposed the idea to the air force's Ballistic Missile Division in early 1958.[38]

In May 1960, the air force signed a letter contract with the Martin Company to develop, produce, and test the Titan II. On October 9, 1959, Aerojet had already won approval to convert the Titan I engines to burn storable propellants. Research and development to that end began in January 1960. The Aerojet engineers also worked to achieve the improved performance called for in the April 30, 1960, plan for Titan II. Although the Titan II engines were based on those for Titan I, the new propellants and the requirements in the April 30 plan necessitated considerable redesign. Because the modifications did not always work as anticipated, the engineers had to resort to empirical solutions until they found the combinations that worked correctly and provided the necessary performance. Since the propellants were hypergolic, there was no need for an igniter in the Titan II engines (called XLR87-AJ-5 for the two engines in stage one and XLR91-AJ-5 for the single stage-two engine). The injectors for the Titan I engines had used alternating fuel and oxidizer passages with oxidizer impinging on oxidizer and fuel on fuel (called like-on-like) to obtain the necessary mixing of the two propellants. For the Titan II, Aerojet engineers tried fuel-on-oxidizer impingement. This evidently mixed the droplets of propellant better because higher performance resulted. But the improvement led to erosion of the injector face, necessitating a return to the like-on-like pattern.

This older arrangement caused combustion instability in the stage-two engines, and engineers tried several configurations of baffles to solve the problem before they came up with one that worked. One potential solution, uncooled stainless-steel baffles, did not last through a full-duration engine test. Copper baffles with both propellants running through them for cooling resulted in corrosion of the copper from the nitrogen tetroxide. An eight-bladed configuration cooled by the oxidizer (evidently using another type of metal) yielded poor performance. The final configuration was a six-bladed, wagon-wheel design (with the baffles radiating outward from a central hub), again cooled by the oxidizer. This solved the problem, at least at for the time being.[39]

The turbopumps for Titan II were similar to those for Titan I, but differences in the densities of the propellants necessitated greater power and lower shaft speed for the Titan II pumps. This resulted in increased propellant flow rates. But Aerojet engineers had to redesign the gears for the turbopumps, making them wider and thus able

FIG. 4.2
Generic
technical
drawing
of a liquid-
propellant
rocket showing
some of its
components,
such as a
turbine gas
generator and
a turbopump.
(Photo courtesy
of NASA)

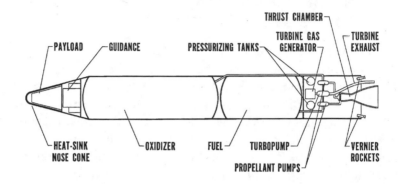

CHEMICAL ROCKET
LIQUID PROPELLANT

National Aeronautics and Space Administration
Lewis Research Center

to withstand greater "tooth pressures" caused by the higher power. From two blades in the inducer for Titan I, the design went to three blades. Engineers also had to redesign the impeller and housing passages to accept the higher flow rates, and there had to be new materials that would not be degraded by the storable propellants.[40]

A significant innovation for the Titan II replaced the use of pressurized nitrogen (in stage one of Titan I) or helium (in stage two) to initiate propellant flow with a so-called autogenous (self-generating) system. Solid-propellant start cartridges initiated the process by spinning the turbines, whereupon gas generators kept the turbines spinning to pressurize the fuel tanks in both stages and to pump the Aerozine 50 into the thrust chamber. The second-stage oxidizer tank did not need pressurization because acceleration was sufficient to keep the nitrogen tetroxide flowing. In the first-stage propulsion system, though, oxidizer from the pump discharge served to pressurize the tank. The result was a simplified system saving the weight from the pressurized-gas storage tanks in Titan I and requiring no potentially unreliable pressure regulators. A similar increase in reliability and saving in weight came from using the exhaust stream from the turbopump in stage two to provide roll control in place of an auxiliary power-drive assembly used in Titan I for the vernier thrusters. Gimbals (used in Titan I) continued to provide pitch, roll, and yaw control in the first stage plus pitch and yaw control in the second stage.[41]

The Titan II propulsion system had significantly fewer parts than its Titan I predecessor. The number of active control components fell from 125 to 30; valves and regulators declined from 91 to 16. The engines had higher thrust and performance, as planned. The Titan II first-stage engines had a combined thrust of 430,000 pounds at sea level, compared to 300,000 for Titan I. Second-stage thrust rose from 80,000 pounds for Titan I to 100,850 pounds for Titan II. Specific impulses rose less dramatically, from slightly above 250 to almost 260 lbf-sec/lbm at sea level for stage one and remained slightly above 310 at altitude (vacuum) for stage two.[42]

A 1965 Aerojet news release on Titan II propulsion credited it to "the efforts of hundreds of men and women" but singled out four of them as leaders of the effort. Three of their biographies illustrate the way that engineers in aerospace migrated from one firm to another or from government work to the private sector, carrying their knowledge of various technologies with them. Robert B. Young was the overall manager of the design, development, and production effort for both Titan I and Titan II. He was a chemical engineering graduate of Caltech, where Theodore von Kármán had encouraged him to devote his knowledge to rocketry. He had worked for a year as director of industrial liaison on the Saturn program at NASA's Marshall Space Flight Center, during part of the Titan years, and had risen within Aerojet's own structure from a project engineer to a vice president and manager of the Sacramento, California, plant. Another leader was Ray C. Stiff Jr., who had discovered aniline as a hypergolic propellant while working at the navy Engineering Experiment Station in Annapolis. His role in the use of self-igniting propellants in JATOs to assist a PBY into the air while carrying heavy loads proved a forerunner "of the storable, self-igniting propellants used to such advantage in the Titan II engine systems." Stiff served as Aerojet's manager of Liquid Rocket Operations near Sacramento and was also a vice president.

A third manager Aerojet mentioned in the release was A. L. Feldman, a rocket engineer educated at Cornell University. While working at Convair, he had been "in on the initial design and development effort for the Atlas engines." After moving to Aerojet, he served as manager for both the Titan I and Titan II engines and assistant manager of Aerojet's Liquid Rocket Operations. A fourth key manager was L. D. Wilson, who earned a degree in engineering at Kansas State University. "At 28, he managed the painstaking design, development, test and production of the 'space start' second-stage engine for Titan I." Wilson then managed the entire propulsion system for the Titan II.[43] Alone among the four managers, he appeared not to have worked for another rocket effort.

Between March 16, 1962, and April 9, 1963, there were 33 research-and-development test flights of Titan II missiles—23 from Cape Canaveral and 10 from Vandenberg AFB. Depending on who was counting, there were variously 8, 9, or 10 failures and partial successes (none of which occurred during the last 13 flights), for a success rate of anywhere from 70 to 76 percent. The problems ranged from failure of electrical umbilicals to disconnect properly on the first, otherwise-successful, Titan II silo launch (from Vandenberg) on February 16, 1963 (pulling missile-guidance cabling with them and causing an uncontrollable roll), to premature engine shutdown, an oxidizer leak, a fuel-valve failure, a leak in a fuel pump, and gas-generator failure. But the most serious problem was initially a mystery whose cause was unclear to the engineers involved. On the launch of the first Titan II on March 16, 1962, about a minute and a half after liftoff from Cape Canaveral, longitudinal oscillations occurred in the first-stage combustion chambers. They arose about 11 times per second for about 30 seconds. They did not prevent the missile (designated N-2) from traveling 5,000 nautical miles and impacting in the target area, but they were nonetheless disquieting.[44]

The reason for concern was that in late 1961 NASA had reached an agreement with the Department of Defense to acquire Titan IIs for launching astronauts into space as part of what soon became Project Gemini. Its mission, as a follow-on to Project Mercury and a predecessor to Project Apollo's Moon flights, was to determine if one spacecraft could rendezvous and dock with another, whether astronauts could work outside a spacecraft in the near weightlessness of space, and what physiological effects humans would experience during extended flight in space. Pogo (as the longitudinal oscillations came to be called) was not particularly problematic for the missile, but it posed potentially significant problems for an astronaut who was already experiencing acceleration of about 2.5 times the force of gravity from the launch vehicle. The pogo effect on the first Titan II launch added another ±2.5 Gs, which perhaps could have incapacitated the pilot of the spacecraft from responding to an emergency if one occurred.

Fixing the problem for Project Gemini, however, was complicated by an air force reorganization on April 1, 1961, creating Ballistic Systems Division (BSD) and Space Systems Division (SSD). The problem for NASA lay in the fact that while BSD was intent on developing Titan II as a missile, SSD would be responsible for simultaneously adapting Titan II as a launch vehicle for the astronauts.[45] A conflict between the two air force interests would soon develop and be adjudicated by General Schriever, then commanding the parent Air Force Systems Command.

Meanwhile, there were further organizational complications for Project Gcmini. SSD assigned development of the Gemini-Titan II launch vehicle to Martin's plant in Baltimore, whereas the Denver plant was working on the Titan II missile. Assisting SSD in managing its responsibilities was the nonprofit Aerospace Corporation. For Gemini, Aerospace assigned James A. Marsh as manager of its efforts to develop the Titan II as a launch vehicle. BSD established its own committee to investigate the pogo oscillations, headed by Abner Rasumoff of Space Technology Laboratories (STL). For the missile, it found a solution in higher pressure for the stage-one fuel tank, which reduced the oscillations and resultant gravitational forces in half on the fourth launch on July 25, 1962, without STL engineers' understanding why. Martin engineers correctly thought the problem might lie in pressure oscillations in the propellant feed lines. They suggested installation of a standpipe to suppress surges in the oxidizer lines of future test missiles. BSD and NASA's Manned Spacecraft Center, which was managing Gemini, agreed.[46]

Although the standpipe later proved to be part of the solution to the pogo problem, initially it seemed to make matters worse. Installed on missile N-11, flying on December 6, 1962, it failed to suppress severe oscillations that raised the gravitational effect from pogo alone to ±5 Gs. This lowered the chamber pressure to the point that instrumentation shut down the first-stage engine prematurely. The following mission, N-13, on December 19, 1962, did not include the standpipe but did have increased pressure in the fuel tank, which had seemed to be effective against the pogo effect on earlier flights. Another new feature consisted of aluminum oxidizer feed lines in place of steel ones used previously. For reasons not fully understood, the pogo level dropped and the flight was successful.

Missile N-15, evidently with the same configuration as N-13, launched on January 10, 1963. The pogo level dropped to a new low, ±0.6 G, although problems with the gas generator in stage two severely restricted the vehicle's range. This was still not a low enough oscillation level for NASA, which wanted it reduced to ±0.25 G, but it satisfied BSD, which "froze" the missile's design with regard to further changes to reduce oscillations. Higher pressure in the first-stage fuel tanks plus use of aluminum for the oxidizer lines had reduced the pogo effect below specifications for the missile, and BSD believed it could not afford the risks and costs of further experimentation to bring the pogo effect down to the level NASA wanted.[47]

NASA essentially appealed to Schriever, with NASA's Brainerd Holmes, deputy associate administrator for manned space flight, complaining that no one understood what caused either the pogo oscillations or unstable combustion, another problem affecting Titan II. So Holmes said it was impossible to "man-rate" the missile as a launch vehicle. The result, on April 1, 1963, was the formation of a coordinating committee to address both problems, headed by BSD's Titan II director and including people from Aerospace Corporation and STL.

After engineers from Aerojet, Martin, STL, and Aerospace studied the problems, Sheldon Rubin of Aerospace looked at data from static tests and concluded that as the *fuel* pumped, a partial vacuum formed in the fuel line, causing resonance. This explained why the *oxidizer* standpipes had failed to suppress the pogo effect. The solution was to restore the standpipe, keep the increase in tank pressure and the aluminum oxidizer feed lines, and add a fuel surge chamber (also called a piston accumulator) to the fuel lines. Nitrogen gas pressurized the standpipe after the nitrogen tetroxide had filled the oxidizer feed lines. An entrapped gas bubble at the end of the standpipe absorbed pressure pulsations in the oxidizer lines. The surge chamber included a spring-loaded piston. Installed perpendicular to the fuel feed line, it operated like the standpipe to absorb pressure pulses. Finally, on November 1, 1963, missile N-25 carried both of these devices. The successful flight recorded pogo levels of only ±0.11 G, well below NASA's maximum of ±0.25 G. Subsequent tests on December 12, 1963, and January 15, 1964, included the suppression devices and met NASA standards, the January 15 mission doing so even with lower pressures in the fuel tank. This seemed to confirm that the two devices on the propellant lines had fixed the pogo problem.[48]

Meanwhile, the combustion instability Holmes had mentioned at the same time as the pogo problem, turned out to be another major issue. It never occurred in flight, but it appeared in a severe form during static testing of second-stage engines. Several engines experienced such "hard starts" that the combustion chambers fell from the injector domes as if somebody had cut them away with a laser beam. Engineers examined the test data and concluded that combustion instability at the frequency of 25,000 cycles per second had sliced through the upper combustion chamber near the face of the injector with a force of ±200 pounds per square inch. This occurred on only 2 percent of the ground tests of second-stage engines, but for Gemini, even this was too high.

Aerojet instituted the Gemini Stability Improvement Program (GEMSIP) in September 1963 to resolve the problem with combustion instability. Apparently, the instability occurred only when second-stage engines were tested in an Aerojet facility that simulated the air pressure at 70,000 feet, because there was no combustion instability in the first-stage engines at this stage of their development. The reason was that air pressure at sea level slowed the flow of propellants through the injectors. Aerojet engineers could solve the problem for the second stage by filling the regenerative-cooling tubes that constituted the wall of the combustion chamber with a very expensive fluid that afforded resistance to the rapid flow of propellants similar to that of air pressure at sea level.

Aerojet and the air force finally agreed on a more satisfactory solution, however. This involved a change in injector design with fewer but larger orifices and a modification of the six-bladed baffles radiating out from a hub that Aerojet thought had already solved the combustion-instability problem in the Titan II missile. Aerojet engineers increased the number of baffles to seven and removed the hub for the Gemini configuration. Testing in the altitude chamber at the air force's Arnold Engineering Development Center proved that the new arrangement worked.[49]

A final problem that occurred in flight testing and required re-engineering involved the gas generator in the stage-two engine. This issue was a matter of concern to the Titan II Program Office at BSD, not just to SSD and NASA. Engineers and managers first became aware there was a problem on the second Titan II test flight (June 7, 1962) when telemetry showed that the second-stage engine had achieved only half of its normal thrust soon after engine start. When the tracking system lost its signal from the vehicle, the range safety officer caused cutoff of the fuel flow, making the reentry vehicle splash down well short of its target area. The data from telemetry on this flight were inadequate for the engineers to diagnose the problem. It took two more occurrences of gas-generator problems to provide enough data to understand what was happening. Particles were partially clogging the small openings in the gas generator's injectors. This restricted propellant flow and resulted in loss of thrust. Technicians very thoroughly removed all foreign matter from components of the generators in a clean room before assembly, separated the generators from the engines in transport, and subjected the assemblies to blowdown by nitrogen before each test flight to ensure no foreign particles were present.

These methods did not solve the problem but did narrow the list of sources for the particles. It became apparent that there was no problem with stage-one gas generators because sea-level air pressure did not allow particles from the solid-propellant start cartridges to reach the injector plates for the generators. Aerojet had tested the system for stage two in its altitude chamber, but it could simulate only 70,000 feet of altitude, which engineers assumed was high enough. There had been no problems with gas generators during the tests. It turned out, however, that even at 70,000 feet, enough atmosphere was present to cushion the injectors from the particles. At 250,000 feet, where the stage-two engine ignited, the atmosphere was so thin that particles from the start cartridge flowed into the gas generator, sometimes in sufficient quantity to cause difficulties. To rectify the problem, engineers added a rupture disk to the exhaust of the gas generator. This kept enough pressure in the system to cushion the flow of particles until ignition start, when the disk ruptured. Gas-generator failure was not a problem after this design change.[50]

The engines for Titan II went on to form the core of the Titan III and IV space-launch vehicles. Titan IIs also became launch vehicles in their own right, making their engines key propulsion elements in three different series of launch vehicles. Their use through the end of the period covered by this book suggested the importance of storable propellants for the history of space flight. But development of hypergolic propulsion did not end with these rockets.

Transstage

An important step forward occurred with the third liquid-propellant stage for the Titan III, known as Transstage, for which the air force decided on a pressure-fed engine that would use the same nitrogen tetroxide as oxidizer and Aerozine 50 for fuel as stages one and two. As planned, it would have two gimballed thrust chambers, each producing 8,000 pounds of thrust, and a capability of up to three starts over a six-hour period. Aerojet won this contract, with a Phase I agreement signed in early 1962 and a Phase II (development) award issued on January 14, 1963.[51]

Aerojet designed the Transstage engine (designated AJ10-138) at about the same time as a larger propulsion unit for the Apollo service module. The two engines used basically the same design, featuring the same propellants, ablatively cooled thrust chambers, and a radiatively cooled nozzle assembly. Since the Apollo service module's engine bore the designation AJ10-137, its development apparently began earlier in 1962, but it also lasted longer. Although

Aerojet designed and built them both, and more information is available about the development of the spacecraft engine, it is not clear that any of the latter's problems and solutions are relevant to the Transtage engine, which was less than half as powerful and roughly half the length and diameter of its sibling.[52]

Apparently, these two engines were not the only ones with ablatively cooled combustion chambers in this period, because an important NASA publication on liquid-propellant rocket engines issued in 1967 stated that such "thrust chambers have many advantages for upper-stage applications. They are designed to meet accumulated duration requirements varying from a few seconds to many minutes." Although construction could vary, in one example (unspecified), the ablative liner used a high-silica fabric impregnated with phenolic resin and then tape-wrapped on a mandrel. Asbestos impregnated with phenolic served as an insulator on the outer surface of the liner. A strong outer shell consisted of layers of one-directional glass cloth to provide longitudinal strength. Circumferential glass filaments "bonded with epoxy resin" provided "hoop strength."[53] This appears to have described the Transtage combustion chamber (as well as others?).[54]

On July 23, 1963, Aerojet had successfully operated a Transtage engine for 4 minutes, 44 seconds, considered "a long duration firing." During that static test, the engine started and stopped three times, demonstrating the restart capability. However, a more critical test of this crucial capability (which would allow it to place multiple satellites into different orbits on a single launch or to position a single satellite in a final orbit, such as a geostationary orbit, without a need for a separate kick motor) would occur in the simulated-altitude test chamber at Arnold Engineering Development Center in Tullahoma, Tennessee. In August 1963, tests at that center confirmed suspicions from the July 23 test that the combustion chamber would burn through before completing a full-duration firing (undefined). In addition, gimballing of the engine in a cold environment revealed a malfunction of a bipropellant valve (that fed propellants to the combustion chamber) and a weakness in the nozzle extension, made of aluminide-coated columbium and radiation cooled with an expansion ratio of 40:1. Information about how Aerojet solved these problems is not available in any of the sources for this book, with the official history of the Titan III merely stating that "by the close of 1963, an extensive redesign and testing program was underway to eliminate these difficulties so the contractor could make his first delivery of flight engine hardware—due in mid December 1963."[55]

169

*Propulsion
with Storable
Fuels and
Oxidizers,
1942–91*

One Aerojet source does not comment on these particular difficulties but does refer to "the error of trying to develop in a production atmosphere." The source explained in this connection that development of this small engine occurred while Titan I was starting into production, causing management and engineers/technicians to pay less attention to it. But presumably, the speed required in Transtage's development was also a factor in these particular problems. Obviously, engineers had not expected them and had to adjust designs to correct the difficulties. In any event, engine deliveries did not occur in mid-December, as initially planned, but started in April 1964.

Aerojet engineer and manager Ray Stiff recalled that after engine deliveries began, the air force started to impose new requirements. Because Transtage needed to perform a 6.5-hour coast while in orbit and then be capable of "a variety of firing, coast, and refire combinations," there had to be "unique insulation requirements," to protect propellants from freezing in the extreme cold of orbit in space, especially when shaded from the sun. But this insulation retained the heat from combustion, which built up around the injector with presumed dire consequences for continued performance. Stiff does not reveal how Aerojet solved this problem, stating only that the engine's injector was "baffled for assurance of stable combustion."[56]

Other sources reveal that the injector used an "all-aluminum flat faced design" with a "concave spherical face, [and] multiple-orifice impinging patterns." The baffle was fuel cooled, so perhaps an adjustment in this feature solved the heating problem. According to an Aerojet history written by former employees and managers, "The injector design has undergone two performance upgrade programs which resulted in the very high specific impulse value of 320 lbf-sec/lbm, and the design has been carried over into later versions of the Delta."[57] (Most sources do not rate the specific impulse this high.)

In any event, the two initial Transtage engines each yielded 8,000 pounds (lbf) of thrust with a specific impulse of more than 300 lbf-sec/lbm. Pressurized by cold helium gas, each of the hypergolic propellants was stored in tanks of a titanium alloy that the prime contractor, Martin, machined in its Baltimore Division. The titanium forgings came from the Ladish Company of Cudahy, Wisconsin. Although titanium was difficult to machine, it was gaining increasing use for liquid-propellant tanks. With a fuel tank about 4 feet in diameter by 13.5 feet in length and an oxidizer tank measuring about 5 by 11 feet, Transtage's propellant containers were hardly huge but were reportedly some of the largest yet produced from titanium. Each overall engine was 6.8 feet long with its diameter ranging from 25.2 to 48.2 inches. Its rated burning time was a robust 500 seconds, and its total weight was only 238 pounds.[58]

Transtage advanced storable-propellant technology but also represented a further example of trial-and-error engineering. Other upper stages used the technology developed for Transtage and for the Apollo service module's engine.

Delta Upper Stages

One example of this influence was a second stage used on the Delta launch vehicle featuring an Aerojet engine designated AJ10-118F. This was the F model in a series of engines originally derived from the Vanguard second stage. This particular engine was similar to the Transtage propulsion unit (AJ10-138), but the two were not identical. Both used a fiberglass combustion chamber impregnated with resin and an ablative lining for cooling. Like the Titan II engines, both used a mixture of 50 percent hydrazine and 50 percent UDMH as the fuel, igniting hypergolically with a nitrogen-tetroxide oxidizer. This replaced the IRFNA used on earlier versions of the AJ10-118 and increased the specific impulse from more than 265 to upward of 290 lbf-sec/lbm. The F version of the engine had a thrust of between 9,235 and 9,606 pounds, well above the roughly 7,575 pounds of the earlier versions, and it was capable of up to 10 starts in orbit. The new engine completed its preliminary design in 1970 but did not fly until July 23, 1972.[59]

Another Delta upper stage that used storable propellants was TRW's TR-201 second-stage engine. Design of this engine began in October 1972, its combustion chamber made of quartz phenolic, with cooling by ablation as had been true of the AJ10-118F, but the TR-201 weighed only 298 pounds in contrast to the Aerojet engine's reported dry weight of 1,204 pounds. Both engines burned nitrogen tetroxide with a 50/50 mixture of hydrazine and UDMH, igniting hypergolically, but the TRW propulsion unit yielded 9,900 pounds of thrust, whereas the Aerojet unit yielded a maximum of 9,606 pounds. The newer system did provide only 5 instead of 10 restarts.[60]

Analysis and Conclusions

Launch-vehicle engines with storable propellants represented an almost totally indigenous development only partly affected by known foreign influences. They evolved from the early JATOs through the WAC Corporal and the Corporal, the Vanguard second stage, and the Able and Able-Star upper stages, to the core engines for the Titan launch vehicles. Thereafter, the Titan Transtage, the Aerojet second stage for the later Delta launch vehicles, and the TR-201 built by TRW continued the evolution. Along the way, the later Agena engines also used storables but appear not to have directly influenced other (mostly Aerojet) propulsion units.

Like other propulsion systems, engines burning storables experienced their share of developmental problems. A great many organizations contributed to the solution of such problems, ranging from the armed services, the NACA and NASA, and industry, to universities. In many cases, engineers did not anticipate or even understand the problems immediately when they occurred, and it took trial and error or gathering of further data to arrive at solutions, not all of which worked as planned. This suggested that rocketry was not a fully mature science in the sense of a body of knowledge that allowed designers to anticipate potential problems and solve them before testing occurred. It was much more an experimental process in which only testing revealed what did and did not work. Nevertheless, engineers resolved the problems and developed a series of engines that worked satisfactorily.

Propulsion with Liquid Hydrogen and Oxygen, 1954–91

ALTHOUGH ROCKET DEVELOPERS HAD USED the cryogenic liquid oxygen as a propellant for a long time, the first operational rocket to use the even colder liquid hydrogen as a fuel was the Centaur upper stage. Although Centaur posed great difficulties in its development (initially as a second stage for the Atlas launch vehicle), it drew upon a great deal of previous theoretical and practical effort by a large number of people. Both Goddard and Oberth had written about the advantages of hydrogen as a rocket fuel, and as part of von Braun's team in Germany, Walter Thiel recognized its potential. However, he had experienced leaks and problems in trying to use the fuel, writing in 1937 that "the extremely low temperature of the liquid hydrogen . . . ; the high boil-off rate . . . ; the danger of explosion; the large tank volume required as a result of the low specific weight . . . ; and the need to use insulated tanks and ducts, create . . . difficulties which will pose strong obstacles to . . . experimental and development activities."[1]

The "extremely low temperature" to which Thiel referred equated to −423°F, above which liquid hydrogen boiled and became a gas, requiring much more space to contain it. This compared with the

−293°F at which liquid oxygen boiled, still a very low temperature. Despite this and the other difficulties to which Thiel referred, hydrogen provided more thrust per pound of fuel burned per second than any other chemical propellant then available—about 35 to 40 percent more than RP-1 when burned with liquid oxygen. No doubt because of this high performance, Herrick L. Johnston created a cryogenics laboratory at Ohio State University during World War II, where by 1943 he had produced liquid hydrogen. The university experimented with a rocket that burned hydrogen and oxygen from 1947 to 1950, and Aerojet performed similar tests from 1945 to 1949. Both programs developed pumps for liquid hydrogen and operated thrust chambers. JPL also tested a liquid-hydrogen engine in 1948. There was, however, no immediate use of the valuable data from these programs.[2]

In 1954, a small group of researchers at the NACA Lewis Flight Propulsion Laboratory began experimenting with liquid-hydrogen rocket engines. Lewis engineers tested tanks, pumps, heat exchangers, and turbojet engines. The efforts culminated in a joint flight-research project with the air force in late 1956 and early 1957 in which one engine of a B-57 bomber actually operated with gaseous hydrogen as its fuel. The laboratory developed a predilection for liquid hydrogen, and Lewis associate director Abe Silverstein supported its development. Since he was later a key manager at NASA Headquarters and then director of the Lewis Research Center (as the laboratory became in 1958), these efforts provided an important background to the development of Centaur.[3]

Meanwhile, a more immediately important step in the use of hydrogen as a fuel came in 1956–58 with the air force's highly secret Project Suntan—an attempt to produce an airplane fueled with hydrogen to outperform the U-2 reconnaissance aircraft. The project involved contracts with Lockheed Aircraft for two CL-400 aircraft and with Pratt & Whitney Division of United Aircraft to study an engine powered by hydrogen, then to develop it if that proved feasible. At Wright Air Development Center in Ohio, the air force put Lt. Col. John D. Seaberg, an aeronautical engineer, in charge of overseeing work on the airframe, airplane systems, and liquid-hydrogen fuel tanks. The military canceled the Suntan project before its completion but not before Pratt & Whitney had designed a new engine, model 304, and a centrifugal pump to feed its liquid hydrogen. The air force also funded two liquid-hydrogen plants near Pratt & Whitney's isolated test center in West Palm Beach, Florida, where engineers could do research on hydrogen in an area distant from population centers. By the effective cancellation of Suntan in

June 1958, the project had laid some of the technological ground-work for Centaur's RL10 engine.[4]

Centaur, in turn, prepared the way for the technology surrounding the J-2 engine in the Saturn launch vehicles, much larger than the RL10 used on Centaur. The next step in the evolution of liquid-hydrogen propulsion was the space shuttle main engine, which was much more demanding of its developers than even the RL10 and J-2. But Centaur itself posed significant problems.

Centaur Propulsion

Before the defense establishment transferred the technology from Project Suntan to rocketry, it had to be nudged by a proposal from Convair's Krafft Ehricke. Called to service in a Panzer division on the western and then eastern fronts during World War II, the young German was still able to earn a degree in aeronautical engineering at the Berlin Technical Institute. He was fortunate enough to be assigned to Peenemünde in June 1942, where he worked closely with Thiel. Although he came to the United States as part of von Braun's group and moved with it to Huntsville, Ehricke was a much less conservative engineer than von Braun. Whether for that reason or others, he transferred to Bell Aircraft in 1952 when it was working on the Agena upper stage and other projects. Not happy there either by the time he left (when he believed interest had shifted away from space-related projects), he heeded a call from Karel Bossart to work at Convair in 1954.[5]

At the San Diego firm, Ehricke initially served as a design specialist on Atlas and was involved with Project Score. By 1956, he was beginning to study possible boosters for orbiting satellites but could find no support for such efforts until after *Sputnik I*. Then, General Dynamics managers asked him to design an upper stage for Atlas. (Consolidated Vultee Aircraft Corporation merged into General Dynamics Corporation on April 29, 1954, to become the Convair Division of the larger firm.) Ehricke and other engineers, including Bossart, decided that liquid hydrogen and liquid oxygen were the propellants needed. Ehricke worked with Rocketdyne to develop a proposal titled "A Satellite and Space Development Plan." This featured a four-engine stage with pressure feeding of the propellants, neither Rocketdyne nor Ehricke being aware of Pratt & Whitney's pumps. In December 1957, James Dempsey, vice president of the Convair Division, sent Ehricke and another engineer off to Washington, D.C., to pitch the design to the air force.[6]

175

*Propulsion
with Liquid
Hydrogen
and Oxygen,
1954–91*

The air service did not act on the proposal, but on February 7, 1958, Ehricke presented it to the new Advanced Research Projects Agency, created by the Department of Defense. For a time, ARPA exercised control over all military and civilian space projects before relinquishing the civilian responsibility to NASA in October 1958. Thereafter, for a year, ARPA remained responsible for all military space projects, including budgets. The new agency made Ehricke aware of Pratt & Whitney's hydrogen pumps and encouraged Convair to submit a proposal using two 15,000-pound-thrust, pump-fed engines, which it did in August 1958. That same month, ARPA issued order number 19-59 for a high-energy, liquid-propellant upper stage to be developed by Convair–Astronautics Division of General Dynamics Corporation, with liquid-oxygen/liquid-hydrogen engines to be developed by Pratt & Whitney.[7]

In October and November 1958, at ARPA's direction the air force followed up with contracts to Pratt & Whitney and Convair for the development of Centaur, but NASA's first administrator, Keith Glennan, requested that the project transfer to his agency. Deputy Secretary of Defense Donald Quarles agreed to this arrangement in principle, but ARPA and the air force resisted the transfer until June 10, 1959, when NASA associate administrator Richard E. Horner proposed that the air force establish a Centaur project director, locate him at the Ballistic Missile Division in California, but have him report to a Centaur project manager at NASA Headquarters. NASA would furnish technical assistance, with the air force providing administrative services. The DoD agreed, and the project transferred to NASA on July 1, 1959. Lieutenant Colonel Seaberg from the Suntan project became the Air Research and Development Command project manager for Centaur in November 1958, located initially at command headquarters on the East Coast. Seaberg remained in that position with the transfer to NASA but moved his location to BMD. Milton Rosen became the NASA project manager. In November 1958, Ehricke became Convair's project director for Centaur.[8]

Complicating Centaur's development, in the fall of 1958 NASA engineers had conceived of using the first-stage engine of Vanguard as an upper stage for Atlas, known as Vega. NASA intended that it serve as an interim vehicle until Atlas-Centaur was developed. Under protest from Dempsey that Convair already had its hands full with Atlas and Centaur, on March 18, 1959, NASA contracted with General Dynamics to develop Atlas-Vega. With the first flight of the interim vehicle set for August 1960, Vega at first became a higher priority for NASA than Centaur. As such, it constituted an impediment to Centaur development until NASA canceled Vega on

December 11, 1959, in favor of the DoD-sponsored Agena B, which had a development schedule and payload capability similar to Vega's but a different manufacturer (Bell).[9]

Besides Vega's competition for resources until this point, another hindrance to development of Centaur came from liquid hydrogen's physical characteristics. Its very low density, extremely cold boiling point, low surface tension, and wide range of flammability made it extremely difficult to work with. Ehricke had some knowledge of this from working with Thiel, but the circumstances of the contract with the air force limited the amount of testing he could perform to overcome hydrogen's peculiarities.[10]

One limitation was funding. When ARPA accepted the initial proposal and assigned the air force to handle its direction, the stipulations were that there be no more than $36 million charged by Convair-Astronautics for its work, that a first launch attempt occur by January 1961, and that the project not interfere with Atlas development. At the same time, Convair was to use off-the-shelf equipment as well as Atlas tooling and technology as much as possible. Funding for the Pratt & Whitney contract was $23 million, bringing the total initial funding to $59 million for the first six launches the contract required, not including the costs of a guidance/control system, Atlas boosters, and a launch complex. Ehricke believed that, until it was too late, the limited funding restricted the necessary ground testing his project engineers could do. Also restrictive was the absence of the DoD's highest priority (known as DX), which meant that subcontractors who were also working on projects with the DX priority could not give the same level of service to Centaur as they provided to higher-priority projects.[11]

Under these circumstances, Convair and Pratt & Whitney proceeded with designs for the Centaur structure and engines. The Centaur stage used the steel-balloon structure of Atlas, with the same 10-foot diameter. The lightness of the resulting airframe seemed necessary for Centaur because of liquid hydrogen's low density, which made the hydrogen tank much larger than the oxygen tank. Conventional designs with longerons and ring frames would have created a less satisfactory mass fraction than did the pressurized tanks with thin skins (initially only 0.01 inch thick). The elliptical liquid oxygen tank was on the bottom of the stage. To create the shortest possible length and the lowest weight, the engineers on Ehricke's project team made the bottom of the liquid-hydrogen tank concave so that it fit over the convex top of the oxygen tank.

This arrangement solved space and weight problems (saving about 4 feet of length and roughly 1,000 pounds of weight) but created others in the process. One resulted from the smallness of the hydrogen molecules and their extreme coldness. The skin of the oxygen tank had a temperature of about −299°F, which was so much "warmer" than the liquid hydrogen at −423°F that the hydrogen would gasify from the relative heat and boil off. To prevent that, the engineers devised a bulkhead between the two tanks that contained a fiberglass-covered Styrofoam material about 0.2 inch thick in a cavity between two walls. Technicians evacuated the air from the pores in the Styrofoam and refilled the spaces with gaseous nitrogen. They then welded the opening. When they filled the upper tank with liquid hydrogen, the upper surface of the bulkhead became so cold that it froze the nitrogen in the cavity, thus creating a vacuum as the nitrogen contracted into the denser solid state, a process called cryopumping.[12]

Because of the limited testing, it was not until the summer and early fall of 1961 that the Centaur engineers and managers learned of heat transfer across the bulkhead that was more than 50 times the amount expected. It turned out that there were very small cracks in the bulkhead through which the hydrogen was leaking and destroying the vacuum, causing the heat transfer and resultant boil-off of the fuel. This necessitated venting to avoid excessive pressure and explosion in the hydrogen tank. But the venting depleted the fuel, leaving an insufficient quantity for the second engine burn required of Centaur for coasting in orbit and then propelling a satellite into a higher orbit.

General Dynamics had used Atlas manufacturing techniques for the materials on the bulkhead. Atlas's quality-control procedures permitted detection of leaks in bulkheads down to about 1/10,000 inch. Inspections revealed no such leaks, but the engineers learned in the 1961 testing that hydrogen could escape through even finer openings. Very small cracks that would not be a problem in a liquid-oxygen tank caused major leakage in a liquid-hydrogen tank.[13]

By the time Convair-Astronautics had discovered this problem, NASA had assigned responsibility for the Centaur project to the Marshall Space Flight Center (on July 1, 1960), with Seaberg's Centaur Project Office remaining at BMD in California. Hans Hueter became director of Marshall's Light and Medium Vehicles Office in July, with responsibility for managing the Centaur and Agena upper stages. During the winter of 1959–60, NASA also established a Centaur technical team following the cancellation of the Vega project. This team consisted of experts at various NASA locations to recommend ways the upper stage could be improved. In January 1960, navy commander W. Schubert became the Centaur project chief at NASA Headquarters.[14]

From December 11 to 14, 1961, John L. Sloop visited General Dynamics/ Astronautics (GD/A) to look into Centaur problems, particularly the one with heat transfer across the bulkhead. Sloop had been head of Lewis Laboratory's rocket research program from 1949 until 1960, when he moved to NASA Headquarters. There in 1961 he became deputy director of the group managing NASA's small and medium-sized launch vehicles. Following his visit, he wrote, "GD/A has studied the problem and concluded that it is not practical to build bulkheads where such a vacuum [as the one Ehricke's team had designed] could be maintained." The firm also believed "that the only safe way to meet all Centaur missions is to drop the integral tank design and go to separate fuel and oxidizer tanks." Sloop disagreed: "If a decision must be made now, I recommend we stick to the integral tank design, make insulation improvements, and lengthen the tanks to increase propellant capacity."[15]

Sloop's optimism was justified. After the Centaur team began "a program of designing and testing a number of alternate designs," tests revealed that adding nickel to the welding of the double bulkhead (and elsewhere), significantly increased the single-spot shear strength of the metal at $-423°F$.[16]

Centaur development experienced many other problems. Several of them involved the engines. After enduring "inadequate facilities, slick unpaved roads, mosquitoes, alligators, and 66 inches of rain in a single season" while developing the 304 engine for Suntan at West Palm Beach, Pratt & Whitney engineers also "discovered the slippery nature of hydrogen." The extreme cold of liquid hydrogen precluded using rubber gaskets to seal pipe joints, designers having to resort to aluminum coated with Teflon and then forced into flanges that mated with them. There had to be new techniques for seals on rotating surfaces, where carbon impregnated with silver found wide use. Another concern with the cryogenic hydrogen was that the liquid not turn to gas before reaching the turbopumps. The engineers initially solved that problem by flowing propellants to the pumps before engine start, precooling the system.[17]

The turbopump for the 304 engine used oil to lubricate its bearings. This had to be heated to keep it from freezing in proximity to the cold pump, creating a temperature gradient. To solve this problem for the RL10, the Pratt & Whitney engineers coated the cages holding the bearings with fluorocarbons similar to Teflon and arranged to keep the bearings cold with minute amounts of liquid hydrogen. This produced the same effect as lubrication, because it turned out that the main function of oil was to keep the bearings from overheating. The substance from which Pratt & Whitney nor-

179

Propulsion
with Liquid
Hydrogen
and Oxygen,
1954–91

mally made its gears, called Waspalloy, bonded in the hydrogen environment. Engineers replaced it with carbonized steel coated with molybdenum disulfide for dry lubrication. This solved the bonding problem but subjected some unlucky engineers to observing tests of the new arrangement by using binoculars from an observation post with only a screen door. Late at night, alligator croakings and other noises created uneasiness for many young observers unused to swamp sounds.[18]

The first component tests of the combustion chamber for the RL10, including stainless-steel regenerative-cooling tubes brazed with silver, took place in May 1959. As with many other initial tests of combustion chambers, there were signs of burnthrough, so the engineers changed the angle at which the hydrogen entered the tubes and aligned the tubes more carefully so they did not protrude into the exhaust stream. Engine firings two months after this showed that the changes had solved the burnthrough problem, but the chamber's conical shape produced inefficient burning. Engineers changed the design to a bell shape and conducted a successful engine run in September 1959, less than a year from the date of the initial contract.[19]

A major innovation in the design of the RL10 took advantage of the cold temperature of liquid hydrogen in order to dispense with a gas generator to drive the turbopump. The cryogenic fuel passed from the tank into the tubes of the combustion chamber for cooling. As it did so, it absorbed heat, which caused the fuel to vaporize and expand. This provided enough kinetic energy to drive the turbine that operated both the liquid-hydrogen and liquid-oxygen pumps. It also provided the power for the hydraulic actuators that gimballed the engine. This process, called the "bootstrap" cycle, still used hydrogen-peroxide boost pumps to start the process. Hydrogen peroxide also powered attitude-control rockets and ullage-control jets that propelled the Centaur forward in a parking orbit and thereby forced the liquid hydrogen to the rear of the tanks. There it could be pumped into the engines for ignition.[20]

Before the RL10 underwent its first test in an upright position on a test stand in its two-engine configuration for the Centaur, it underwent 230 successful horizontal firings. It produced 15,000 pounds of thrust and achieved a specific impulse of about 420 lbf-sec/lbm at an expansion ratio of 40:1 through its exhaust nozzle. As required by its missions in space, it reliably started, stopped, and restarted so that it could coast in a parking orbit until it reached the optimum point for injection into an intended orbit (or trajectory for interplanetary voyages). On November 6, 1960, two RL10s, upright for the first time on a test stand at the Pratt & Whitney facility in Florida, fired at the same time and did so successfully—for a short time until a problem occurred with the timer on the test stand. When engineers repeated the test the next day, only one engine fired. The other filled with hydrogen and oxygen until the flame from the first engine caused an explosion that damaged the entire propulsion system beyond repair.

A tape recording of the countdown suggested that the problem had stemmed from the faulty operation of a test-stand sequencer, so engineers did not suspect difficulties with the engine itself. By January 12, 1961, they repaired the test stand and tested another pair of engines. This time, they put a blast wall between the two engines and installed a shutoff valve on the hydrogen tank. They also separated the exhaust systems for the two engines by a greater distance. During this test, there was no problem with the sequencing, but the explosion recurred. In the vertical position, engineers learned, gravity was affecting the mixing of the oxygen with the hydrogen differently than it had in the horizontal position. So in a further instance of cut-and-try engineering, designers had to adjust the method of hydrogen feed. They also designed a method of measuring the density of the mixture to ensure the presence of enough oxygen for ignition. With these adjustments, the two engines fired simultaneously in the vertical test stand on April 24, 1961. Following this success, the engines completed 27 successful dual firings at Pratt & Whitney and 5 more at the rocket site on Edwards AFB in California. They then passed the flight-rating test from October 30 to November 4, 1961, in which they completed 20 firings equivalent in duration to six Centaur missions.[21]

To protect the liquid hydrogen in its tank from boiling off while the vehicle was on the launching pad and during ascent through the atmosphere, engineers had designed four jettisonable insulation panels made of foam-filled fiberglass. These were about a centimeter (0.39 inch) thick, held on the tank by circumferential straps. To keep air from freezing between the tank and the insulating foam, thereby bonding the panels to the tank, engineers designed a helium system to purge the air. To limit the weight penalty imposed by the panels (1,350 pounds), they had to be jettisoned as soon after launch as the atmosphere thinned and the ambient temperature dropped.[22]

Because of delays resulting from the engine ignition problem, difficulties with elaborate test instrumentation (such as a television camera and sensors inside the liquid-hydrogen tank), and other issues, an Atlas LV-3 with a Centaur upper stage did not launch for the first time until May 8, 1962, 15 months later than planned. The

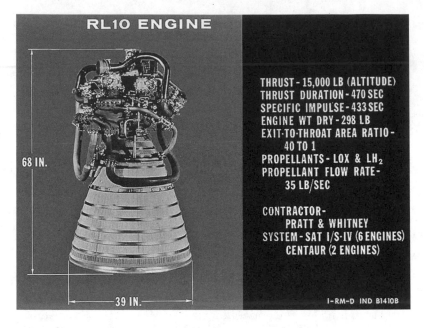

goals of the test flight were to proceed through the boost phase with jettison of the insulation and a nose fairing, followed by Centaur's separation from the Atlas. With only a partial load of fuel, the Centaur was to coast for 8 minutes, reignite, and burn for 25 seconds.[23]

On the launch, the two stages rose normally until they approached maximum dynamic pressure (with resultant aerodynamic buffeting) as the vehicle got close to the speed of sound 54.7 seconds into the launch. Then, an explosion occurred as the liquid-hydrogen tank split open. Initially, engineers decided that aerodynamic forces had destroyed the insulation and ruptured the tank. About five years later, tests suggested that the real culprit was differential thermal expansion between a fiberglass nose fairing and the steel tank, causing a forward ring to peel off the tank.[24]

Even before this launch, the difficulties with engine development, resultant schedule delays, and problems such as the one with the bulkhead between the hydrogen and oxygen tanks had led to close scrutiny of the Centaur project and danger of its cancellation. Following John Sloop's visit to General Dynamics to look into such problems, he had expressed concerns about the firm's organization. Krafft Ehricke, the program director, had only five men reporting directly to him, and Deane Davis, the project engineer, had direct charge of only two people. Many other people worked on Centaur (27 of them full-time), but most of them were assigned to six operating divisions not directly under project control. Sloop wrote, "As far as I could tell in three days of discussion, the only people who have direct and up-to-date knowledge of all Centaur systems are Mr. Ehricke and Mr. Davis." Marshall Space Flight Center had "a very competent team of four men stationed at GD/A," and they were well aware of the "management deficiencies" emphasized in Sloop's comments.[25]

Hans Hueter wrote on January 4, 1962, to GD/A president James Dempsey stating his concern about the way the Centaur Program Office was organized in "relation to the line divisions." He mentioned that the two of them had discussed this issue "several times" and reiterated his and other NASA employees' "impression that the systems engineering is carried on singlehandedly by your excellent associates, Krafft Ehricke and Dean [sic] Davis." He added, "The individual fields such as propulsion, thermal and liquid behavior, guidance and control, and structures are covered in depth in the various engineering departments but coordination is sorely lacking."[26]

In response to NASA's concerns about this matrix organization, Dempsey shifted to a "projectized" arrangement in which roughly 1,100 employees at Astronautics were placed under the direct authority of the Centaur program director. Ehricke was reassigned as the director of advanced systems and Grant L. Hansen became Centaur program director and Astronautics vice president on February 1, 1962. Trained as an electrical engineer at Illinois Institute of Technology, Hansen had worked for Douglas Aircraft from 1948 to 1960 on missile and space systems, including the Thor, with experience in analysis, research and development, design, and testing. He came to GD/A in 1960 to direct the work of more than 2,000 people on Atlas and Centaur. After February 1962, Ehricke continued to offer Hansen advice. Although he was imaginative and creative, the company had decided Ehricke "wasn't enough of a[n] S.O.B. to manage a program like this." Hansen proved to be effective, although it is only fair to note that he was given authority and an organization Ehricke had lacked.[27] S.O.B. or not, had Ehricke started with Hansen's organization and adequate funding, Centaur development could have been smoother from the beginning. In any event, this sequence of events showed how management arrangements and technical problems interacted.

Several other programmatic changes occurred around this time. On January 1, 1962, for example, NASA (in agreement with the DoD) transferred the Centaur Project Office from Los Angeles to Huntsville, Alabama, and converted existing air force contracts to

NASA covenants. Lieutenant Colonel Seaberg ceased being project manager, and Francis Evans at Marshall Space Flight Center assumed those duties under Hueter's direction. By this time, funding had grown from the original $59 million to $269 million, and the number of Centaur vehicles to be delivered had risen from 6 to 10.[28]

Meanwhile, following the May 8, 1962, explosion, a congressional Subcommittee on Space Sciences, chaired by Rep. Joseph E. Karth (D-Minnesota), began hearings on the mishap. In a report issued on July 2, 1962, the parent Committee on Science and Astronautics in the U.S. House of Representatives stated that "management of the Centaur development program has been weak and ineffective both at NASA headquarters and in the field."[29] NASA did not immediately make further changes, but Marshall management of Centaur posed problems. These came out in the hearings, prompting unfavorable comment in the committee report. Von Braun had remarked about GD/A's "somewhat bold approach. In order to save a few pounds, they have elected to use some rather, shall we say, marginal solutions where you are bound to buy a few headaches before you get it over with." Hansen agreed that his firm was inclined "to take a little bit more of a design gamble to achieve a significant improvement, whereas I think they [Marshall engineers] build somewhat more conservatively." The congressional report noted, "Such a difference in design philosophy can have serious consequences."[30]

Ehricke characterized the design approach of the von Braun team as "Brooklyn Bridge" construction. The contrast between that and the approach of General Dynamics appears in an account of a Marshall visit to GD/A that Deane Davis wrote at an unspecified date soon after Marshall took over responsibility for Centaur in July 1960. A group led by von Braun and including Hueter and structures chief William Mrazek had come to GD/A for a tour and briefings on Atlas and Centaur. Mrazek and Bossart had gotten into a discussion of the structure of the steel-balloon tanks, with Mrazek (according to Davis's account) unwilling to admit that they could have any structural strength without ribs. Bossart took him out to a tank and handed him a fiberglass mallet containing lead to give it a weight of 7 pounds. It had a rubber cover and a 2-foot handle. Bossart invited Mrazek to hit the tank with it. After a tap and then a harder whack, he could not find a dent. Bossart urged him to "stop fiddling around. Hit the damned thing!" When Mrazek gave it a "smart crack," the mallet bounced back so hard it flew about 15 feet, knocking off the German's glasses on the way and leaving only a black smear (no dent) on the tank. Davis wrote that Hueter was as amazed as Mrazek by the strength of the tank.[31]

This account is difficult to accept entirely at face value because Mrazek had already designed the Redstone with an integral-tank structure that was hardly as light as Bossart's steel balloon but was also not quite bridgelike. Nevertheless, even in 1962 von Braun was clearly uncomfortable with Bossart's "pressure-stabilized tanks," which he called "a great weightsaver, but . . . also a continuous pain in the neck" that "other contractors, for example the Martin Co., for this very reason have elected not to use." No doubt because of such concerns, von Braun sought quietly to have the Centaur canceled in favor of a Saturn-Agena combination.[32]

Faced with this situation, on October 8, 1962, NASA Headquarters transferred management of the Centaur program to the Lewis Research Center, to which Silverstein had returned as center director in 1961 from his position at NASA Headquarters. A "sharp, aggressive, imaginative, and decisive leader," Silverstein could be "charming or abrasive," in the words of John Sloop. Deane Davis, who worked with him on Centaur, called him a "giant among giants" and a man he "admired, adored, hated, wondered about—and mostly always agreed with even when I fought him. Which was often." Under Silverstein's direction, the Lewis center required much more testing than even the Marshall group had done. Lewis tested everything that could "possibly be proven by ground test." Yet despite such aggressive oversight, Grant Hansen expressed admiration for Lewis and its relationship with his own engineers.[33]

Because the RL10 had been planned for use on Saturn as well as Centaur, its management remained at Marshall. The reason given for Centaur's transfer was that it would allow the Huntsville engineers to concentrate on the Saturn program. A NASA news release quoted NASA administrator James Webb, "This, I feel, is necessary to achieve our objectives in the time frame that we have planned. It will permit the Lewis Center to use its experience in liquid hydrogen to further the work already done on one of the most promising high energy rocket fuels and its application to Centaur. . . ."[34]

Long before this transfer, engineers from the Cleveland facility had been actively involved in helping solve both engine and structural problems with the vehicle. Their involvement included use of an altitude chamber at their center. Other facilities, including a rocket sled track at Holloman AFB, New Mexico, had also been involved in Centaur development. For example, in 1959 GD/A had done some zero-G testing in an air force C-131D aircraft at Wright-Patterson AFB (and also, at some point, in a KC-135). The same year, the firm had acquired a vacuum chamber for testing gas expansion and components. With additional funding (to a total of about $63 million) in 1960, GD/A extended testing to include use of the vacuum test facility at the air force's Arnold Engineering Development Center in Tullahoma, Tennessee, zero-G test flights using Aerobee rockets, and additional static ground testing, including modifying test stand 1-1 at the rocket site on Edwards AFB for Centaur's static tests. In 1961, when GD/A's funding rose to $100 million, there were wind-tunnel tests of the Centaur's insulation panels at NASA's Langley Research Center, additional zero-G testing, and construction of a coast-phase test stand to evaluate the attitude-control system.[35]

At Lewis, Silverstein decided to direct the Centaur project himself, assisted by two managers under his personal direction and some 41 people involved with technical direction. Some 40 Marshall engineers helped briefly with the program's transition. By January 1963, the changeover was mostly complete and Centaur had acquired a DX priority. Then, costs for Centaur were estimated at $350 million, and containing them became an issue. Despite this, Silverstein decided that the first eight Centaurs after the transfer would constitute test vehicles. By this time, Surveyor spacecraft had been assigned as Centaur payloads, and Silverstein determined that none of them would be launched until the test vehicles had demonstrated Centaur's reliability.[36]

By February 1963, Silverstein had appointed David Gabriel as Centaur manager but placed the project office in the basement of his own administrative building so he could continue to keep tabs on the project. Some continuity with the period of Marshall management came in the retention of Ronald Rovenger as chief of the NASA field office at GD/A. Instead of 4, his office rose to a complement of 40 NASA engineers. It took until April 1964, but Lewis renegotiated the existing contracts with GD/A into a single cost-plus-fixed-fee document for 14 Centaur upper stages plus 21 test articles. The estimated cost of the agreement was roughly $321 million plus a fixed fee of $31 million, very close to the estimate of $350 million at the beginning of 1963. However, Silverstein felt the need for a second contract to cover further modifications resulting from Lewis's technical direction. Soon the Lewis staff working on Centaur grew to 150 people. Silverstein continued to give the project his personal attention and made a major decision to abandon temporarily the use of a parking orbit and restart for Surveyor. This required a direct ascent to the Moon, considerably narrowing the "window" for each launch.[37]

These and other changes under Lewis direction did not immediately solve all of Centaur's problems. Test flights and resultant

TABLE 5.1. *Atlas-Centaur Test Flights*

Flight	Date	Mission	Objective	Outcome
AC-2	Nov. 27, 1963	R&D, single-burn	Achieve separation of Centaur, Earth orbit, data on nose cone, insulation panels	Successful, achieved orbit close to that planned, gathered data
AC-3	June 30, 1964	R&D, single-burn, restart boost pumps	Test jettison of redesigned insulation panels and nose cone, gather data from restart	Jettison successful but failure of driveshaft in hydraulic pump prevented gimballing
AC-4	Dec. 11, 1964	R&D, two-burn	Restart engines, carry Surveyor model	Partial success; first burn successful but ullage motors not powerful enough to keep LH_2 at bottom of tank;[a] weak restart
AC-5	Mar. 2, 1965	R&D, single-burn, separable Surveyor model	Simulate Surveyor launch	Failed; Atlas fuel valve closed, causing an explosion
AC-6	Aug. 11, 1965	R&D, single-burn, separable Surveyor model	Demonstrate capability of launching Surveyor model similar to actual spacecraft	Successful in separating model and sending on planned course
AC-8	Apr. 7, 1966	R&D, two-burn, separable Surveyor model	Perform 25-minute coast in parking orbit, re-ignite Centaur engine, and send Surveyor model to a target location simulating the Moon	Partial failure; in parking orbit there was a hydrogen peroxide leak and too little remained to power tank boost pumps

(continued)

TABLE 5.1. *Continued*

Flight	Date	Mission	Objective	Outcome
AC-9	Oct. 26, 1966	R&D, two-burn, separable Surveyor model	Demonstrate restart capability, send Surveyor model on simulated trajectory to Moon	Successful

ᵃLH₂ is liquid hydrogen.

difficulties are summarized in table 5.1, beginning with Atlas-Centaur 2 (AC-2).[38]

Data from instrumentation on the insulation panels over the liquid-hydrogen tank on AC-2 showed conclusively that the design for the panels used on AC-1 was not adequate. Engineers designed thicker panels with heavier reinforcement, increasing their weight by almost 800 pounds. This made it all the more important to jettison them at about 180 seconds after launch to get rid of the unwanted weight. A minor redesign fixed the problem with the driveshaft that failed on AC-3. To fix the problem on AC-4 with liquid hydrogen moving away from the bottom of the tank where the fuel had to exit, however, required investigation and multiple modifications. A slosh baffle in the liquid-hydrogen tank helped limit movement of the fuel away from the tank bottom. Screens in the ducts bringing bleed-off hydrogen gas back to the tank reduced energy that could disturb the liquid. On the coasting portion of AC-4's orbit, liquid hydrogen had gotten into a vent intended to exhaust gaseous hydrogen, thereby releasing pressure from boil-off. The liquid exiting into the vacuum of space created a sideward thrust that tumbled the Centaur and Surveyor models. Fixing this problem required a complete redesign of the venting system.

A further change increased thrust in both the yaw- and pitch-control engines as well as those that settled liquid hydrogen in the bottom of the tank during coast. The added thrust in both types of engines helped keep the Centaur on course and hold the easily displaced liquid hydrogen in the bottom of its tank. Fortunately, these changes were unnecessary before the launch of AC-5 but were implemented for AC-8, which also incorporated the uprated RL10A-3-3 engine with slightly greater specific impulse from a larger expansion ratio for the exhaust nozzle and an increased chamber pressure.[39]

Meanwhile, in response to the explosion on AC-5, engineers locked the Atlas valves in the open position. AC-6 amounted to a semioperational flight. The Surveyor model went to the coordinates in space it was intended to reach (simulating travel to the Moon) even without a trajectory correction in midcourse. With AC-7 shifted to a later launch and AC-8 having problems with hydrogen peroxide rather than liquid hydrogen, the Atlas-Centaur combination was ready for operational use, although there would be one more research-and-development flight sandwiched between launches of operational spacecraft (AC-9; see table 5.1). Atlas-Centaur performed satisfactorily on all of the Surveyor launches, although two of the spacecraft had problems. But five of the seven missions were successful, providing more than 87,000 photographs and much scientific information for Apollo landings and lunar studies. *Surveyors 1, 2,* and *4* all used single-burn operations by Centaur, but *Surveyors 3* and *5–7* employed dual-burn trajectories. On *Surveyors 5–7* the Atlases were all SLV-3Cs with longer tanks, hence greater propellant volumes. The SLV-3C flew only 17 missions but was successful on all of them before being replaced by the SLV-3D, used with the advanced Centaur D-1A.[40]

The D-1A resulted from a NASA decision to upgrade the Centaur, with the Lewis Research Center responsible for overseeing the $40 million improvement program, the central feature of which was a new guidance/control computer, developed at a cost of about $8 million. Among payloads for the Centaur D-1A were Intelsat communications satellites. With the first launch of *Intelsat V*, having more relay capacity (and weight), on December 6, 1980, the Centaur began to use engines that were adjusted to increase their thrust (per engine) from the original 15,000 to about 16,500 pounds. The 93.75 percent success rate for the 32 SLV-3D/D-1A (and D-1AR) launches showed that Silverstein's insistence on extended testing and detailed oversight had paid off.[41]

During the early 1980s, General Dynamics converted to new versions of Atlas and Centaur. The Atlas G added 81 inches to the length of the propellant tanks, and Pratt & Whitney made several changes to the Centaur engines, including removal of the boost pump, for a significant weight savings. There was no change in the RL10's thrust, but further modification shifted from hydrogen peroxide to the more stable hydrazine for the attitude-control and propellant-settling engines. This made the RL10A-3-3A a substantially different machine than its predecessor, the RL10A-3-3.[42]

As of early 1991, the Centaur had had a 95 percent success rate on 76 flights. This included 42 successes in a row for Centaur D-1 and D-1A between 1971 and 1984. The vehicle, as well as its Atlas booster, would continue to evolve into the 21st century, with the successful launch of an Atlas V featuring a Russian RD-180 engine and a Centaur with a single RL10 engine, signifying both the end of the cold war and the continuing evolution of the technology. Meanwhile, development of the Centaur had led to the use of liquid-hydrogen technology both on upper stages of the Saturn launch vehicle and on the Space Shuttle. Despite a difficult start and continuing challenges, the Centaur had made major contributions to U.S. launch-vehicle technology.[43]

Propulsion for the Saturn Upper Stages

The initial decision to use liquid-hydrogen technology in the upper stages of the Saturn launch vehicles came from a Saturn Vehicle Team, chaired by Abe Silverstein and including other representatives from NASA Headquarters, the air force, the Office of Defense Research and Engineering, and the Army Ballistic Missile Agency (von Braun, himself). Meeting in December 1959, this group, influenced by Silverstein's convictions about the performance capabilities of liquid hydrogen, agreed to employ it in the Saturn upper stages. Silverstein managed to convince even von Braun, despite reservations, to take this step. But von Braun later told William Mrazek he was not greatly concerned about the difficulties of the new fuel because many Centaur launches were scheduled before the first Saturn launch with upper stages. His group could profit from what these launches revealed to solve any problems with the Saturn I upper stages.[44]

THE S-IV STAGE

On April 26, 1960, NASA awarded a contract to the Douglas Aircraft Company to develop the Saturn I second stage, the S-IV. Between January and March 1961, NASA decided to use Pratt & Whitney RL10 engines in this stage. But instead of the two RL10s in Centaur, the S-IV held six such engines. Benefiting from consultations NASA arranged with Convair and Pratt & Whitney, Douglas did use a tank design similar to Convair's, with a common bulkhead between the liquid oxygen and the liquid hydrogen. But Douglas also relied on its own experience in its use of materials and methods of manufacture. So the honeycomb material in the common bulkhead of the propellant tank was different from Convair's design, drawing upon Douglas's work with panels in aircraft wings and some earlier missile designs. Douglas succeeded in making the larger tanks and S-IV stage in time for the first launch (SA-5) of a Saturn I featuring a live second stage on January 29, 1964.[45]

Remarkably, this launch was successful despite a major accident only five days earlier. Douglas engineers and technicians knew that they had to take special precautions with liquid oxygen and liquid hydrogen. The latter was especially insidious because if it leaked and caught fire in the daylight, the flames were virtually invisible. Infrared TV cameras did not totally solve the problem because of the difficulty of positioning enough of them to cover every cranny where hydrogen gas might hide. So crews with protective clothes carried brooms in front of them. If a broom caught fire, hydrogen was leaking and burning.

Despite such precautions, on January 24, 1964, at a countdown to a static test of the S-IV, the stage exploded. Fortunately, the resultant hydrogen fire was short-lived, and a NASA committee with Douglas Aircraft membership determined that the cause was a rupture of a liquid-oxygen tank resulting from the failure of two vent valves to relieve pressure that built up. The relief valves were incapacitated by solid oxygen, which had frozen because helium gas to pressurize the oxygen tank had come from a sphere submerged in the liquid hydrogen portion of the tank. This helium was colder than the freezing point of oxygen. The pressure got so high because the primary shutoff valve for the helium failed to close when normal operating pressure had developed in the oxygen tank. Testing of the shutoff valve showed that it did not work satisfactorily in cold conditions. Because this valve had previously malfunctioned, it should have been replaced by this time. In any event, Saturn project personnel did apparently change it to another design before the launch five days later. The committee "found that no single person, judgment, malfunction or event could be directly blamed for this incident," but if "test operations personnel had the proper sensitivity to the situation the operation could have been safely secured" before the accident got out of hand.[46]

On the six test flights with the S-IV stage (SA-5 through SA-10, the last occurring July 30, 1965), it and the already tested RL10 engines worked satisfactorily. They provided 90,000 pounds of thrust and demonstrated, among other things, that liquid-hydrogen technology had matured significantly, at least when using RL10 engines.[47]

THE S-IVB STAGE

For the intermediate version of the Saturn launch vehicle, the Saturn IB, engineers for the S-IVB second stage further added to the payload capacity of the overall vehicle through reducing the weight of the stage by some 19,800 pounds. Part of the reduction came from redesigned and smaller aerodynamic fins. Flight experience with the Saturn I also revealed that the initial design of the stage had been excessively conservative, and engineers were able to trim propellant tanks, a "spider [structural] beam," and other components as well as to remove "various tubes and brackets no longer required." But production techniques and most tooling did not change significantly.[48]

The S-IVB featured a totally new and much larger engine, the J-2, with more thrust than the six RL10s used on the Saturn I. This was the liquid-hydrogen/liquid-oxygen engine the Silverstein committee had recommended for the Saturn upper stages on December 15, 1959, following which NASA requested proposals from industry to design and build it. There were five companies competing for the contract, with the three top candidates being North American Aviation's Rocketdyne Division, Aerojet, and Pratt & Whitney. Having built the RL10, Pratt & Whitney might seem to have been the logical choice, but even though NASA's source evaluation board had judged all three firms as capable of providing a satisfactory engine, Pratt & Whitney's proposal cost more than twice those of Aerojet and Rocketdyne. Rocketdyne's bid was lower than Aerojet's, based on an assumption of less testing time, but even if the testing times were equalized, it appeared that Rocketdyne's cost was still lower. Thus, on May 31, 1960, Glennan decided to negotiate with Rocketdyne for a contract to design and build the engine. The von Braun group and Rocketdyne then worked together on the design of the engine. A final contract signed on September 10, 1960, stated that the engine would ensure "maximum safety for manned flight" while using a conservative design to speed up development.[49]

Rocketdyne began the development of the J-2 on September 1, 1960, with a computer simulation to assist with the configuration. Most of the work took place at the division's main facility at Canoga Park in northwestern Los Angeles, with firing and other tests at the Santa Susana Field Laboratory in the nearby mountains. By early November, the Rocketdyne engineers had designed a full-scale injector and by November 11 had conducted static tests of it in an experimental engine. Rocketdyne also built a large vacuum chamber to simulate engine firings in space. By the end of 1961, it was evident that the J-2 would provide power for not only the second stage of Saturn IB but the second and third stages of the Saturn V (then known as the Saturn C-5). In the second stage of Saturn V, there would be a cluster of five J-2s; on the S-IVB second stage of

Saturn IB and the S-IVB third stage of Saturn V, there would be a single J-2.[50]

Rocketdyne's engineers borrowed technology from Pratt & Whitney's RL10, but since the J-2 (with its initial design goal of 200,000 pounds of thrust at altitude) was so much larger than the 15,000-pound RL10, designers first tried flat-faced copper injectors similar to designs Rocketdyne was used to in its liquid-oxygen/RP-1 engines. Heating patterns for liquid hydrogen turned out to be quite different from those for RP-1, and injectors got so hot the copper burned out. The RL10 had used a porous, concave injector of a mesh design, cooled by a flow of gaseous hydrogen, but Rocketdyne would not adopt that approach until 1962, when Marshall engineers insisted designers visit Lewis Research Center to look at examples. Under pressure, the California engineers adopted the RL10 injector design, and problems with burnout ceased. In this instance, a contractor benefited from an established design from another firm, even if only under pressure from the customer, illustrating the sometimes difficult process of technology transfer. Thus, Rocketdyne avoided further need for injector design, which, in NASA's assistant director for propulsion A. O. Tischler's words, was still "more a black art than a science."[51]

Rocketdyne expertise seems to have been more effective in designing the combustion chamber, consisting of intricately fashioned stainless-steel cooling tubes with a chamber jacket made of Inconel, a nickel-chromium alloy capable of withstanding high levels of heating. Using a computer to solve a variety of equations having to do with energy, momentum, heat balance, and other factors, designers used liquid hydrogen to absorb the heat from combustion before it entered the injector, "heating" the fuel in the process from $-423°F$ to a gaseous temperature of $-260°F$. The speed of passage through the cooling tubes varied, with adjustments to match computer calculations of the needs of different locations for cooling.[52]

Because of the low density of hydrogen and the consequent need for a higher-volume flow rate for it vis-à-vis the liquid oxygen (although by weight, the oxygen flowed more quickly), Rocketdyne decided to use two different types of turbopumps, each mounted on opposite sides of the thrust chamber. For the liquid oxygen, the firm used a conventional centrifugal pump of the type used for both fuel and oxidizer in the RL10. This featured a blade that forced the propellant in a direction perpendicular to the shaft of the pump. It operated at a speed of 7,902 revolutions per minute and achieved a flow rate of 2,969 gallons per minute. For the liquid hydrogen, an axial-type pump used blades operating like airplane propellers to force the propellant in the direction of the pump's shaft. Operating in seven stages (to one for the liquid-oxygen pump), the fuel pump ran at 26,032 revolutions per minute and sent 8,070 gallons of liquid hydrogen per minute to the combustion chamber. (By contrast, in terms of weight, 468 pounds of liquid oxygen to 79 pounds of liquid hydrogen per second flowed from the pumps.) A gas generator provided fuel-rich gas to drive the separate turbines for the two pumps, with the flow first to the hydrogen and then to the oxygen pump. The turbine exhaust gas flowed into the main rocket nozzle for disposal and a slight addition to thrust.[53]

In testing the J-2, engineers experienced problems with such issues as insulation of the cryogenic liquid hydrogen, sealing it to avoid leaks that could produce explosions, and a phenomenon known as hydrogen embrittlement in which the hydrogen in gaseous form caused metals to become brittle and break. To prevent this, technicians had to coat high-strength super alloys with copper or gold. Solving problems that occurred in testing often involved trial-and-error methods. Engineers and technicians never knew, until after further testing, whether a given "fix" actually solved a problem (or instead created a new one). Even exhaustive testing did not always discover potential problems before flights, but engineers always hoped to find problems in ground testing rather than flight.[54]

Rocketdyne completed the preliminary design for the 200,000-pound-thrust J-2 in April 1961, with the preflight readiness testing finished in 1964 and engine qualification, in 1965. The engine was gimballed for steering, and it had a restart capability, using helium stored in a separate tank within the liquid-hydrogen tank to operate the pneumatic system. Soon after the 200,000-pound J-2 was qualified, Rocketdyne uprated the engine successively to 205,000, 225,000, and then 230,000 pounds of thrust at altitude. Engineers did this partly by increasing the chamber pressure. They also adjusted the ratio of oxidizer to fuel. The 200,000-pound-thrust engine used a mixture ratio of 5:1, but the more powerful versions could adjust the mixture ratio in flight up to 5.5:1 for maximum thrust and as low as 4.5:1 for a lower thrust level. During the last portion of a flight, the valve position shifted to ensure the simultaneous emptying of the liquid oxygen and the liquid hydrogen from the propellant tanks (technically, a single tank with a common bulkhead, but referred to in the plural as if there were separate tanks). The 225,000-pound-thrust engine had replaced the 200,000-pound version on the production line by October 1966, with the 230,000-pound engine available by about September 1967. As the uprated versions became available, Rocketdyne gradually ceased producing the lower-rated ones.[55]

Even with six RL10s, the S-IV stage had been only about 39.7 feet tall by 18.5 feet in diameter. To contain the single J-2 and its propellant tank, the S-IVB had to be 58.4 feet tall by 21.7 feet in diameter. NASA selected Douglas to modify its S-IV to accommodate the J-2 on December 21, 1961. Douglas had already designed the S-IV to have a different structure from that of the Centaur, with the latter's steel-balloon design (to provide structural support) being replaced by a self-supporting structure more in keeping with the "man-rating" that had initially been planned for Saturn I and transferred to Saturn IB, which actually would launch astronauts into orbit. This structure was made of aluminum and consisted of "skin-and-stringer" type construction.

The propellant tank borrowed a wafflelike structure with ribs from the Thor tanks Douglas had designed. The common bulkhead between the liquid hydrogen and the liquid oxygen required only minor changes from the smaller one in the S-IV. After conferring with Convair about the external insulation used to keep the liquid hydrogen from boiling away rapidly in the Centaur, Douglas engineers had decided on internal insulation for the fuel tank in the S-IV. They chose woven fiberglass threads cured with polyurethane foam to form a tile that technicians shaped and installed inside the tank. This became the insulation for the S-IVB as well.[56] Thus, in this case technology did not transfer between firms, but shared information helped with a technical decision.

195
Propulsion
with Liquid
Hydrogen
and Oxygen,
1954–91

For steering the S-IVB during the firing of the J-2, Douglas had initially designed a slender actuator unit to gimbal the engine, similar to devices on the firm's aircraft landing gear. Marshall engineers said the mission required stubbier actuators. This proved to be true, leading Douglas to subcontract the work to Moog Servo Controls, Inc., of Aurora, New York, which used Marshall specifications to build the actuators. The gimballed engine could adjust the stage's direction in pitch and yaw. For roll control during the firing of the J-2, and for attitude control in all three axes during orbital coast, an auxiliary propulsion system provided the necessary thrust.[57]

Although they had the same designation, the S-IVB used on the Saturn V was heavier and different in several respects from the one on the Saturn IB. As the third stage on the Saturn V, the S-IVB profited greatly from the development and testing for the Saturn IB second stage. But unlike the latter, it required an aft interstage that flared out to the greater diameter of the Saturn V plus control mechanisms to restart the engine in orbit for the burn that would send the Apollo spacecraft on its trajectory to lunar orbit. To match with the greater girth of the S-II, the aft skirt for the third stage was heavier than the one for the S-IVB second stage. The forward skirt was heavier as well to permit a heavier payload. The auxiliary propulsion and ullage system weighed more for the third stage of the Saturn V than the comparable second stage on the IB because of increased attitude control and venting needed for the lunar missions. Finally, the propulsion system was heavier for the Saturn V third stage because of the need to restart. The total additions came to some 11,000 pounds of dry weight. Whereas the first burn of the single J-2 engine would last only about 2.75 minutes to get the third stage and payload to orbital speed at about 17,500 miles per hour, the second burn would last about 5.2 minutes and would accelerate the stage and spacecraft to 24,500 miles per hour, the typical escape velocity for a lunar mission.[58]

On the aft skirt assembly, mounted 180 degrees apart, were two auxiliary propulsion modules. Each contained three 150-pound-thrust attitude-control engines and one 70-pound-thrust ullage-control engine. Built by TRW, the attitude-control engines burned a hypergolic combination of nitrogen tetroxide and monomethyl hydrazine. They used ablative cooling and provided roll control during J-2 firing and control in pitch, yaw, and roll during coast periods. The ullage-control engines, similar to those for attitude control, fired before the coast phase to ensure propellants concentrated near the aft end of their tanks. They fired again before engine restart to position propellants next to feed lines. There were also two ullage-control motors 180 degrees apart between the auxiliary propulsion modules. These motors fired after separation from the S-II stage to ensure that the propellants in the engine's tanks were forced to the rear of the tanks before ignition of the third-stage J-2. The two motors were Thiokol TX-280s burning solid propellants to deliver about 3,390 pounds of thrust.[59]

Despite the relatively modest changes in the S-IVB for Saturn V, development was not problem-free. In acceptance testing of the third stage at Douglas's Sacramento test area on January 20, 1967, the entire stage exploded. Investigation finally revealed that a helium storage sphere had been welded with pure titanium rather than an alloy. When it exploded, it cut propellant lines and allowed the propellants to mix, ignite, and explode, destroying the stage and adjacent structures. The human error led to revised welding specifications and procedures. Despite the late date of this mishap, the S-IVB was ready for the first Saturn V mission on November 9,

1967, when it performed its demanding mission, including restart, without notable problems.[60]

THE S-II STAGE

The S-II second stage for the Saturn V proved to be far more problematic than the S-IVB third stage. On September 11, 1961, NASA had selected North American Aviation to build the S-II. The division of North American that won the S-II contract was the Space and Information Systems Division (previously the Missile Division), headed by Harrison A. Storms Jr., who had managed the X-15 project. An able, articulate engineer, Storms was charismatic but mercurial. His nickname, "Stormy," reflected his personality as well as his last name. (People said that "while other men fiddle, Harrison storms.") His subordinates proudly assumed the title of Storm Troopers, but he could be abrasive, embodying what X-15 test pilot and engineer Scott Crossfield called "the wire brush school of management."[61]

When Storms's division began bidding on the S-II contract, the configuration of the stage was in flux. Early in 1961 when NASA administrator James Webb authorized Marshall to initiate contractor selection, 30 aerospace firms attended a preproposal conference. There, NASA announced that the stage would contain only four J-2 engines (instead of the later five), and it would be only about 74 feet tall (compared with the later figure of 81 feet, 7 inches for the actual S-II). The projected width was 21 feet, 6 inches (rather than the later 33 feet). It still seemed imposingly large, but it was "the precision it would require [that] gave everybody the jitters—like building a locomotive to the tolerance of a Swiss watch," as Storms's biographer put it. This sort of concern whittled the number of interested firms down to seven. A source evaluation board eliminated three, leaving Aerojet, Convair, Douglas, and North American to learn that they were now bidding on a stage enlarged to at least a diameter of 26 feet, 9 inches—still well short of the final diameter. Also still missing was precise information about configuration of the stages above the S-II. The Marshall procurement officer did emphasize that an important ingredient in NASA's selection would be "efficient management."[62]

Once Storms's division won the contract for the stage, it did not take long for NASA to arrive at the decision, announced January 10, 1962, that the S-II would hold five J-2 engines. Designers decided to go with a single tank for the liquid hydrogen and liquid oxygen with a common bulkhead between them, like the design for Douglas's much smaller common tank for the S-IVB. (The S-II contained 260,000 gallons of liquid hydrogen and 83,000 gallons of liquid oxygen to 63,000 and 20,000 gallons, respectively, in the S-IVB.) As with the Douglas stage, common parlance referred to each segment as if it were a separate tank. Obviously, the common bulkhead was much larger in the second than the third stage (with a diameter of 33 rather than 21.75 feet), requiring unusual precision in the welding to preclude leakage. The bulkhead consisted of the top of the liquid-oxygen tank, a sheet of honeycombed phenolic insulation bonded to the metal beneath it, and the bottom of the liquid-hydrogen tank. Careful fitting, verified by ultrasonography, ensured complete bonding and the absence of gaps. Not only did fit have to be perfect but there were complex curvatures and a change in thickness from a maximum of about 5 inches in the center to somewhat less at the periphery.[63]

Unlike Douglas but like Convair (in the Centaur), North American decided to use external insulation, which (it argued) increased the strength of the tank because of the extreme cold inside the tank, which was imparted to the tank walls. Initially, Storms's engineers tried insulation panels, but the bonding failed repeatedly during testing. Using trial-and-error engineering, designers turned to spraying insulation directly onto the tank, allowing it to cure, and then adjusting it to the proper dimensions. Once the tanks were formed and cleaned, North American installed slosh baffles inside the tanks.[64]

The reason that insulation on the outside of the liquid-hydrogen tank increased its strength was the use of an aluminum alloy designated 2014 T6 as the material for the S-II tanks. Employed long before on the Ford Trimotor, it had the unusual characteristic of getting stronger as it got colder. At –400°F, it was 50 percent stronger than at room temperature. With the insulation on the outside, this material provided a real advantage with the –423°F liquid hydrogen inside. Both the oxidizer and fuel tank walls could be 30 percent thinner than with another material.

Unfortunately, aluminum 2014 T6 was difficult to weld with almost 104 feet of circumference. On the first try at attaching two cylinders to one another, welders got about four-fifths around the circle when the remaining portion of the metal "ballooned out of shape from the heat buildup." The Storm Troopers had to resort to powerful automated welding equipment to do the job. Each ring to be welded had to be held in place by a huge precision jig with about 15,000 adjustment screws around the circumference, each less than an inch from the next. A mammoth turntable rotated the seam through fixed weld heads with microscopic precision. A huge clean room allowed the humidity to be kept at 30 percent. In all of this, Marshall's experience with welding, including that for the S-IC stage, helped Storms's people solve their problems.[65]

Despite such help, there was considerable friction between Storms's division, on the one hand, and Marshall on the other, especially with Eberhard Rees, von Braun's deputy director for technical matters. North American fell behind schedule and had increasing technical and other problems. Marshall officials began to complain about management problems with the contractor, including a failure to integrate engineering, budgeting, manufacturing, testing, and quality control. At the same time, Storms's division was the victim of its own delays on the Apollo spacecraft it was also building. The weight of Apollo payloads kept increasing. This required lightening the launch-vehicle stages to compensate. The logical place to do so was the S-IVB stage, because a pound reduced there had the same effect as 4 or 5 pounds taken off the S-II (or 14 pounds from the S-IB). This resulted from the lower stages having to lift the upper ones plus themselves. But the S-IVB, used on the Saturn IB, was already in production, so designers had to make reductions in the thickness and strength of the structural members in the S-II.[66]

By mid-1964, the S-II insulation was still a problem. Then in October 1964, burst tests showed that weld strength was lower than expected. On October 28, a rupture of the aft bulkhead for an S-II occurred during hydrostatic testing. As the date for launch of the first Saturn V (1967) approached, von Braun proposed eliminating a test vehicle to get the program back on schedule. Sam Phillips agreed. Instead of a dynamic as well as a structural test vehicle, the structural stage would do double duty.

But on September 29, 1965, the combined structural and dynamic test vehicle underwent hydraulic testing at Seal Beach. While the tanks filled with water, the vehicle was simultaneously subjected to vibration, twisting, and bending to simulate flight loads. Even though the thinned structure was substantially less strong than it would have been at the colder temperatures that would have prevailed with liquid hydrogen in the tanks, Marshall had insisted on testing to 1.5 times the expected flight loads. At what was subsequently determined to be 1.44 times the load limit, the welds failed and the stage broke apart with a thunderous roar as 50 tons of water cascaded through the test site. The program was short another test vehicle. Storms's people looked at the effect on the cost of the program and concluded that to complete the program after the failure would raise the cost of the contract from the initial $581 million to roughly $1 billion.[67]

199

Propulsion
with Liquid
Hydrogen
and Oxygen,
1954–91

When Lee Atwood, president of North American, flew to Huntsville on October 14, Brig. Gen. Edmund O'Connor of the air force, director of Marshall's Industrial Operations, told von Braun, "The S-II program is out of control. . . . [M]anagement of the project at both the program level and the division level . . . has not been effective." Von Braun told Atwood the S-II needed a more forceful manager than William F. Parker, quiet but technically knowledgeable, whom Storms had appointed to head the program in 1961. Von Braun apparently got Atwood's agreement to replace Parker and put a senior manager in charge of monitoring the program.[68]

The day after Atwood's visit to Huntsville, Rees flew to Houston, where he met with other Apollo managers, including Phillips. The Manned Spacecraft Center was managing Storms's programs for the Apollo spacecraft, and Houston manager Joseph Shea had complaints similar to those of Rees about Storms's control of costs and schedules. Phillips decided to head an ad hoc fact-finding ("tiger") team with people from Marshall and Houston to visit North American and investigate.[69]

The team descended upon North American on November 22, and on December 19, 1965, Phillips presented the findings. George Mueller had already expressed concerns to Lee Atwood about the S-II and spacecraft programs at Storms's Space and Information Systems Division. In a letter to Atwood dated December 19 he reiterated, "Phillips' report has not only corroborated my concern, but has convinced me beyond doubt that the situation at S&ID requires positive and substantive actions immediately in order to meet the national objectives of the Apollo Program." After pointing to numerous delays and cost overruns on both the S-II and the spacecraft, Mueller wrote, "It is hard for me to understand how a company with the background and demonstrated competence of NAA could have spent 4 1/2 years and more than half a billion dollars on the S-II project and not yet have fired a stage with flight systems in operation." He said Sam Phillips was convinced the division could do a better job with fewer people and suggested transferring to another division groups like Information Systems that did not contribute directly to the spacecraft and S-II projects.[70]

A memorandum from Phillips to Mueller the day before had been even more scathing: "My people and I have completely lost confidence in NAA's competence as an organization to do the job we have given them." He made specific recommendations for management changes, including "that Harrison Storms be removed as President of S&ID. . . . [H]is leadership has failed to produce results which could have and should have been produced." After assuring Phillips and Mueller he would do what he could to correct problems, Atwood visited Downey and was reportedly impressed by the design work. He did not replace Storms, but Stormy himself had already placed retired air force Maj. Gen. Robert E. Greer in a position to oversee the S-II. In January 1966, Greer added the titles of vice president and program manager for the program, keeping Bill Parker as his deputy. Greer agreed in a later interview that there were serious problems with S-II management. He revamped the management control center to ensure more oversight and incorporated additional meetings the Storm Troopers called "Black Saturdays," implicitly comparing them with Schriever's meetings at the Western Development Division. However, Greer, who had served at the (renamed) Ballistic Missile Division, held them daily at first, then several times a week, not monthly. With Greer's systems management and Parker's knowledge of the S-II, there seemed to be hope for success.[71]

But setbacks continued. On May 28, 1966, in a pressure test at the Mississippi Test Facility, another S-II stage exploded. Human error was to blame for a failure to reconnect pressure-relief switches after previous tests, but inspection revealed tiny cracks in the liquid-hydrogen cylinders that also turned up on other cylinders already fabricated or in production. Modification and repair occasioned more delays. But it took the Apollo fire in the command module during January 1967 and extreme pressure from Webb to cause Atwood to separate Information Systems from the Space Division (as it became), to move Storms to a staff position, and to appoint recent president of Martin Marietta William B. Bergen as head of Space Division, actually a demotion for which he volunteered from a position in which he had been Storms's boss. Bergen's appointment may have been more important for the redesign of the command module than for the S-II, and certainly Storms and North American were not solely to blame for the problems with either the stage or the spacecraft. But by late 1967, engineers had largely solved problems with both or had them on the way to solution.[72]

FLIGHT TESTING

Although flight testing the Saturn launch vehicles went remarkably well, there were problems, some of which involved the upper stages. For example, on April 4, 1968, during the launch of AS-502 (*Apollo 6*), there was "an all-important dress rehearsal for the first manned flight" planned for AS-503. Stage-two separation occurred, and all five J-2 engines ignited. Then, at 319 seconds after launch, there was a sudden 5,000-pound decrease in thrust, followed by a

cutoff signal to the number two J-2 engine. This signal shut down not only engine number two but number three as well (about a second apart). It turned out that signal wires to the two engines had been interchanged. This loss of the power from two engines was a severe and unexpected test for the instrument unit (IU), but it adjusted the trajectory and the time of firing (by about a minute) for the remaining three engines to achieve (in fact, exceed) the planned altitude for separation of the third stage.[73]

When the IU shut down the three functioning engines in the S-II and separated it from the S-IVB, that stage's lone J-2 ignited and placed itself, the instrument unit, and the payload in an elongated parking orbit. To do this, the IU directed it to burn 29.2 seconds longer than planned to further compensate for the two J-2s that had cut off in stage two. The achievement of this orbit demonstrated "the unusual flexibility designed into the Saturn V." However, although the vehicle performed adequately during orbital coast, the J-2 failed to restart and propel the spacecraft into a simulated translunar trajectory. After repeated failures to get the J-2 to restart, mission controllers separated the command and service modules from the S-IVB, used burns of the service module's propulsion system to position the command module for reentry tests, and performed these tests to verify the design of the heat shield, with reentry occurring "a little short of lunar space velocity," followed by recovery. Although this is sometimes counted a successful mission (in which Phillips and von Braun both said a crew could have returned safely), von Braun also said, "With three engines out, we just cannot go to the Moon." And in fact, restart of the S-IVB's J-2 was a primary objective of the mission, making it technically a failure.[74]

A team of engineers from Marshall and Rocketdyne attacked the unknown problem that had caused the J-2 engine failures. (It turned out to be a single problem for two engines that had failed, one in stage two and the one in stage three that would not restart.) The team, which included Jerry Thomson from the F-1 combustion-instability effort, examined the telemetry data from the flight and concluded that the problem had to be a rupture in a fuel line. But why had it broken?

203
*Propulsion
with Liquid
Hydrogen
and Oxygen,
1954–91*

Increasing pressures, vibrations, and flow rates on test stands, computer analyses, and other tests led engineers to suspect a bellows section in the fuel line. To allow the line to bend around various obstructions, this area had a wire-braid shielding. On the test stand it did not break from the abnormal strains to which it was subjected. (Artificially severing the line did produce measurements that duplicated those from the flight, however.) Finally, Rocketdyne test personnel tried it in a vacuum chamber simulating actual conditions in space. Eight lines tested there at rates of flow and pressures no greater than during normal operations led to failures in the bellows section of all eight lines within 100 seconds. Motion pictures of the tests quickly revealed that in the absence of atmospheric moisture in the vacuum chamber (and in space), frost did not form inside the wire braiding as it had in regular ground tests during cryogenic liquid-hydrogen flow. The frost had kept the bellows from vibrating to the point of failure, but in its absence, a destructive resonance occurred. Engineers eliminated the bellows and replaced them with a stronger design that still allowed the necessary bends. Testing of the fuel-line redesign on the J-2 at the Mississippi Test Facility in August 1968 showed that this change had solved the problem.[75]

The successful *Apollo 8* mission around the Moon verified the success of all the modifications to the launch vehicle since AS-502, with all launch-vehicle objectives for the mission achieved. AS-504 for *Apollo 9* was the first Saturn V to use five 1.522-pound-thrust engines in stage one and six 230,000-pound-thrust J-2 engines in the upper stages. It had minor problems with rough combustion but was successful. The Saturn V for AS-505 (*Apollo 10*) and all subsequent Apollo missions through *Apollo 17* (the final lunar landing) used F-1 and J-2 engines with the same thrust ratings as AS-504. There were comparatively minor adjustments in the launch vehicles that followed AS-505—"in timing, sequences, propellant flow rates, mission parameters, trajectories." On all missions there were malfunctions and anomalies that required fine-tuning. For example, evaluations of the nearly catastrophic *Apollo 13* flight showed that oscillations in the S-II's feed system for liquid oxygen had resulted in a drop in pressure in the center engine's plumbing to below what was necessary to prevent cavitation in the liquid-oxygen pump. Bubbles formed in the liquid oxygen, reducing pump efficiency, hence thrust from the engine. This led to automatic engine shutdown.

Although the oscillations remained local, and even engine shutdown did not hamper the mission, engineers at the Space Division of North American Rockwell (as the firm had become following a merger with Rockwell Standard) nevertheless developed two modifications to correct the problem. One was an accumulator. It served as a shock absorber, consisting of a "compartment or cavity located in the liquid oxygen line feeding the center engine." Filled with gaseous helium, it served to dampen or cushion the pressures in the liquid-oxygen line. This changed the frequency of any oscillation in the line so that it differed from that of the engines as a whole and the thrust structure, thus prevented coupling, which had caused the problem in *Apollo 13*. As a backup to the accumulator, engineers installed a "G" switch on the center engine's mounting beam consisting of three acceleration switches that tripped in the presence of excessive low-frequency vibration and shut off the center engine. With these modifications, the J-2 and Saturn V were remarkably successful on *Apollo 14* through *17*.[76]

The Space Shuttle Main Engines

Despite the experience with Centaur and the Saturn upper-stage engines, the main engines for the Space Shuttle presented a formidable challenge, mainly because of the extreme demands placed upon the engines in a system that also used solid-propellant rocket boosters but still required a great deal of thrust from the main engines. In a partly reusable system, NASA's requirements for staged combustion and extremely high chamber pressure made development of the space shuttle main engines (SSMEs) extraordinarily difficult.

The story of this development began in one sense on June 10, 1971, when—with the general configuration of the Space Shuttle still in flux—Dale D. Myers, NASA's associate administrator for Manned Space Flight, communicated to the directors of the Manned Spacecraft Center (MSC), the Marshall Space Flight Center (MSFC), and the Kennedy Space Center (KSC) the management plan for the Space Shuttle. This gave lead-center responsibilities to MSC but retained general direction of the program at NASA Headquarters in Washington, D.C. MSC would have responsibility for system engineering and integrating the components, with selected personnel from MSFC and KSC collocated in Houston to support this effort. Marshall would have responsibility for the main propulsion elements, while Kennedy would manage the design of launch and recovery infrastructure and launch operations.[77]

Myers had managed the Navaho missile effort for North American and had become vice president of the Space Division, where he had been the general manager for the Apollo spacecraft. He had also overseen North American Rockwell's studies for the Space Shuttle. In addition, he had experience with aircraft projects. Thus, he came to his new job with a strong background in all aspects of the shuttle (as launch vehicle, spacecraft, and airplane). At Marshall, von Braun had moved on in 1970 to become deputy associate administrator for planning at NASA Headquarters.

His deputy director for scientific and technical matters, Eberhard Rees, had succeeded him as Marshall center director until Rees retired in 1973, to be succeeded by Rocco A. Petrone, who had earned a doctorate in mechanical engineering from MIT. Petrone had come from NASA Headquarters and returned there in 1974. He was succeeded by William R. Lucas, a chemist and metallurgist with a doctorate from Vanderbilt University who had worked at Redstone Arsenal and then Marshall since 1952 and become deputy director in 1971. Petrone reorganized Marshall, deemphasizing in-house capabilities to oversee and test large project components and giving more authority to project officers, less to lab directors, a change Myers approved. As Rees put it, Myers was "somewhat allergic to 'too much' government interference" with contractors, preferring less stringent oversight than Marshall had provided in the past.[78]

In February 1970, Marshall had released a request for proposals for the Phase B (project definition) study of the space shuttle main engine. Contracts went to Rocketdyne, Pratt & Whitney, and Aero-jet General. The engine was to burn liquid hydrogen and liquid oxygen in a 6:1 ratio at a combustion-chamber pressure of 3,000 pounds per square inch, well above that of any production engine, including the Saturn J-2, which had featured a pressure of about 787 pounds at the injector end of the 230,000-pound-thrust version. The shuttle engine was to produce a thrust of 415,000 pounds of force at sea level or 477,000 pounds at altitude. Although Rocketdyne had built the J-2 and a development version, the J-2S, with a thrust of 265,000 pounds and chamber pressure of 1,246 pounds per square inch, Pratt & Whitney had been developing an XLR129 engine for the Air Force Rocket Propulsion Laboratory. The engine actually delivered 350,000 pounds of thrust and operated at a chamber pressure of 3,000 pounds per square inch during 1970.[79] Pratt & Whitney thus seemed to have an advantage in the competition.

At Rocketdyne, seasoned rocket engineer Paul Castenholz, who had helped troubleshoot the F-1 combustion-instability and injector problems and had been project manager for the J-2, headed the SSME effort as its first project manager, even though he was a corporate vice president. He saw that there was not time to build sophisticated turbopumps, so he decided to build a complete combustion chamber fed by high-pressure tanks. The NASA study contract did not provide funds for such an effort, so Castenholz convinced North American Rockwell to approve up to $3 million in company funds for the effort. By 1971, testing the engine at Nevada Field Laboratory near Reno, Rocketdyne had a cooled thrust chamber that achieved full thrust for 0.45 second. The thrust was 505,700 pounds at a chamber pressure of 3,172 pounds per square inch, exceeding the performance of Pratt & Whitney's XLR129 by a considerable margin.[80]

Funding constraints led to combining Phase C and D contracts (to include actual vehicle design, production, and operations), so on March 1, 1971, Marshall released to the three contractors a request for proposals to design, develop, and deliver 36 engines. In July NASA selected Rocketdyne as winner of the competition, but Pratt & Whitney protested the choice to the General Accounting Office (GAO) as "manifestly illegal, arbitrary and capricious, and based upon unsound, imprudent procurement decisions." On March 31, 1972, the GAO finally decided the case in favor of Rocketdyne, with the contract signed August 14, 1972. This protest delayed development, although Rocketdyne worked under interim and letter contracts until the final contract signature.[81]

It was not until May 1972 that Rocketdyne could begin significant work on the space shuttle main engine in something close to its final configuration, although some design parameters would change even after that. By then, however, NASA had decided on a "parallel burn" concept in which the main engines and the solid-rocket boosters would both ignite at ground level. The space agency had already determined in 1969 that the engine would employ staged combustion, in which the hydrogen-rich turbine exhaust contributed to combustion in the thrust chamber. It was the combination of high chamber pressure and staged combustion that made the SSMEs a huge step forward in combustion technology. In the meantime, they created great problems for the shuttle, but one of them was *not* combustion instability, the usual plague for engine development. Castenholz and his engineers had started development of the engine with an injector based on the J-2, which had shown good stability. For the shuttle, according to Robert E. Biggs, a member of the SSME management team at Rocketdyne since 1970, the firm had added "two big preventors [of instability] on an injector that was basically stable to begin with." He evidently referred to coaxial baffles, and they seem to have worked.[82]

The XLR129 had been a staged-combustion engine, and its success had given NASA and industry the confidence to use the same concept on the shuttle. But timing for such an engine's ignition was both intricate and sensitive, as Rocketdyne and Marshall would learn. Rocketdyne's design used two preburners with low- and high-pressure turbopumps to feed each of the propellants to the combustion chamber and provide the required high pressure. The XLR129 had used only a single preburner, but two of them provided finer control for the shuttle in conjunction with an engine-mounted computer, subcontracted to Honeywell for development. This computer monitored and regulated the propulsion system during start, automatically shut it down if it sensed a problem, throttled the thrust during operation, and turned off the engine at mission completion.[83]

By the winter and spring of 1974, development of the Honeywell controller had experienced difficulties relating to its power supply and interconnect circuits. These problems attracted the attention of NASA administrator James C. Fletcher and his deputy, George M. Low. The latter commented that Rocketdyne had done a "poor job" of controlling Honeywell, which itself had done a "lousy job" and was in "major cost, schedule, and weight difficulty." Rocketdyne had fallen behind in converting test stands at Santa Susana for testing components of the engine, including turbopumps. A cost overrun of about $4 million required congressional reprogramming. In a program that was underfunded to begin with, this was intolerable, so pressured by Fletcher and Low, Rockwell International, as the firm became in 1973, shifted Castenholz to another position, replacing him ultimately with Dominick Sanchini, a tough veteran who had led development of the main-engine proposal in 1971. Despite 27 successful years devoted to the rocket business, with important achievements to his credit, Castenholz would no longer contribute directly to launch-vehicle development.

Meanwhile, about the same time, Marshall made J. R. Thompson its project manager for the space shuttle main engine. Trained as an aeronautical engineer at Georgia Institute of Technology, where he graduated in 1958, Thompson had worked for Pratt & Whitney before becoming a liquid-propulsion engineer at Marshall on the Saturn project in 1963, the year he earned his master's degree in mechanical engineering at the University of Florida. He became the space engine section chief in 1966, chief of the man/systems integration branch in 1969, and main-engine project manager in 1974.[84]

In May 1975, both component testing (at Santa Susana) and prototype engine testing began, the latter at NASA's National Space Technology Laboratories (the former Mississippi Test Facility). Typically, there was about a month between testing of a component at Santa Susana and a whole engine in Mississippi. But test personnel soon learned that the highly complicated test hardware at Santa Susana was inadequate. As Robert Frosch, NASA administrator, said in 1978, "We have found that the best and truest test bed for all major components, and especially turbopumps, is the engine itself." Consequently, because of insufficient equipment to test components as well as engines, the program gradually ceased testing at Santa Susana between November 1976 and September 1977.[85]

There were many problems during testing, especially with turbopumps and timing. The timing problems involved "how to safely start and shut down the engine." After five years of analysis, as Biggs explained, Rocketdyne engineers had "sophisticated computer models that attempted to predict the transient behavior of the propellants and engine hardware during start and shutdown." Test personnel expected that the engine would be highly sensitive to minute shifts in propellant amounts, with the opening of valves being time-critical. Proceeding very cautiously, testers took 23 weeks and 19 tests, with replacement of eight turbopumps, to reach two seconds into a five-second start process. It took another 12 weeks, 18 tests, and eight more turbopump changes to momentarily reach the minimum power level, which at that time was 50 percent of rated thrust. Eventually Biggs's people developed a "safe and repeatable start sequence" by using the engine-mounted computer, also called the main-engine controller. "Without the precise timing and positioning" it afforded, probably they could not have developed even a satisfactory start process for the engine, so sensitive was it.

Following purging of the propulsion system with dry nitrogen and helium to eliminate moisture (which the propellants could freeze if left in the system), then a slow cooldown using the cryogenic propellants, full opening of the main fuel valve started the fuel flow that initially occurred from the latent heating and expansion that the hardware (still warmer than the liquid hydrogen) imparted to the cryogenic propellant. However, the flow was pulsating with a pressure oscillation of about two cycles per second (hertz) until chamber pressure in the main thrust chamber stabilized after 1.5 seconds. Then oxidizer flowed to the fuel and oxidizer preburners and the main combustion chamber in carefully timed sequence such that liquid oxygen arrived at the fuel preburner 1.4 seconds after the full opening of the main fuel valve, at the main combustion chamber at 1.5 seconds, and at the oxidizer preburner at 1.6 seconds. Test experience revealed that a key time was 1.25 seconds into the priming sequence. If the speed of turbine revolution in the high-pressure fuel turbopump at that precise moment was not at least 4,600 revolutions per minute, the engine could not start safely. So, 1.25 seconds became a safety checkpoint.

209
Propulsion
with Liquid
Hydrogen
and Oxygen,
1954–91

If any "combustor prime" coincided with a downward oscillation (dip) in the fuel flow, excessively high temperatures could result. Other effects of inaccurate timing could be destruction of the high-pressure oxidizer turbopump. Also, a 1 to 2 percent error in valve position or a timing error of as little as a tenth of a second could seriously damage the engine. Because of these problems, the first test to achieve 50 percent of rated thrust occurred at the end of January 1976. The first test to reach the rated power level was in January 1977. Not until the end of 1978 did the engineers achieve a final version of the start sequence that precluded the problems they encountered over more than three years of testing. There were also issues with shutdown sequencing, but they were less severe than those with safe engine start, especially critical because astronauts would be aboard the shuttle when it started.[86]

One major instance of problems with the high-pressure turbopumps occurred on March 12, 1976. Earlier tests of the high-pressure liquid-hydrogen pump, both at Santa Susana and in Mississippi, had revealed significant vibration levels, but not until the March 12 test had engineers recognized this as a major problem. The prototype-engine test on that day was supposed to last 65 seconds to demonstrate a 50 percent power level, rising to 65 percent for a single second. The test did demonstrate 65 percent power for the first time, but engineers had to halt the test at 45.2 seconds because the high-pressure fuel turbopump was losing thrust. After the test, the pump could not be rotated with a tool used to test its torque. Investigation showed that there had been a failure of the turbine-end bearings supporting the shaft. Test data showed a major loss in the efficiency of the turbines plus a large vibration with a frequency about half the speed of the pump's rotation. Experts immediately recognized this as characteristic of subsynchronous whirl, an instability in the dynamics of the rotors.

Although recognizing the problem, test personnel evidently did not know what to do about it in a system whose turbine-blade stresses and tip speeds were still close to the limits of technology in 1991 and must have been at the outskirts of the state of the engineering art 15 years earlier. In any event, to speed up a solution, the program assembled a team that ultimately included the premier rotordynamics experts in government, industry, and academia, from the United States and Great Britain. The pump was centrifugal, driven by a two-stage turbine 11 inches in diameter that was designed to deliver 75,000 horsepower at a ratio of 100 horsepower per pound, an order-of-magnitude improvement over previous turbopumps. The team studied previous liquid-hydrogen turbopumps like that on the J-2, which had exhibited subsynchronous whirl. Following a test program involving engine and laboratory tests, as well as those on components and subsystems, the investigators found 22 possible causes; the most likely appeared to be hydrodynamic problems involving seals that had a coupling effect with the natural frequency of the rotating turbines. Efforts to decrease the coupling effect included damping of the seals and stiffening the shaft. The fixes did not totally end the whirl but did delay its inception from 18,000 revolutions per minute, which was below the minimum power level, to 36,000 revolutions per minute, above the rated power level.

As these design improvements increased operating speeds, investigators learned that a mechanism unrelated to subsynchronous whirl was still overheating the turbine bearings, which had no lubrication but were cooled by liquid hydrogen. The team's extensive analysis of the cooling revealed that a free vortex was forming at the bottom of the pump's shaft where coolant flowed. This vortex reduced the pressure, hence the flow of coolant. In a piece of cut-and-try engineering, designers introduced a quarter-sized baffle that changed the nature of the vortex and allowed more coolant to flow. This fix and the elevation of the whirl problem to above the rated power level permitted long-duration tests of the engine for the first time by early 1977.[87]

This problem with the fuel pump had delayed the program, but it was not as diabolical as explosions in the high-pressure liquid-oxygen turbopump. If a fire started in the presence of liquid oxygen under high pressure, it incinerated the metal parts, usually removing all evidence that could lead to a solution. After solution of the fuel-pump-whirl problem, there were four fires in the high-pressure oxygen turbopump between March 1977 and the end of July 1980. This turbopump was on the same shaft as the low-pressure oxygen turbopump that supplied liquid oxygen to the preburners. The common shaft rotated at a speed of nearly 30,000 revolutions per minute. The high-pressure pump was centrifugal and provided as much as 7,500 gallons of liquid oxygen at a pressure higher than 4,500 pounds per square inch. An essential feature of the pump's design was to keep the liquid oxygen fully separated from the hydrogen-rich gas that drove its turbines. To ensure separation, engineers and technicians had used various seals, drains, and purges.

Despite such precautions, on March 24, 1977, an engine caught fire and burned so severely it removed most physical evidence of its cause. Fortunately, investigators used data from instrumentation to determine that the fire started near a complex liquid-oxygen seal. Since it was not evident what a redesign should involve, testing on other engines resumed, indicating that one of the purges did not prevent the mixing of liquid oxygen and fluids draining from hot gas. On July 25, 1977, engineers tried out a new seal intended as an interim fix. But it worked so well it became the permanent solution, together with increasing the flow rate of the helium purge and other measures.[88]

On September 8, 1977, there was another disastrous fire originating in the high-pressure oxygen turbopump. Data made it clear that the problem involved gradual breakdown of bearings on each end of the turbopump's shaft, but there was no clear indication of the cause. Fixes included enhanced coolant flow, better balance in the rotors, heavier-duty bearings, and new bearing supports. The other two fires did not involve design flaws but did entail delays. In 1972, the shuttle program had expected to launch a flight to orbit by early March 1978. The engine and turbopump problems and many others involving the propulsion system were but some of the causes for not making that deadline, but engines would have kept the shuttle from flying that early if everything else had gone as planned.

By March 1978, the expected first-flight date had slipped to March 1979, but an engine fire and other problems caused even a Septem-

FIG. 5.3
Space Shuttle
Columbia
launching from
Pad 39A at
Cape Canaveral
on the first
shuttle mission,
April 12, 1981.
(Photo courtesy
of NASA)

ber 1979 launch to be postponed. By early 1979, turbopumps were demonstrating longer periods between failures. By 1980, engines were expected to reach 10,000 seconds of testing *apiece*, a figure it had taken the entire program until 1977 to reach for all engines *combined*. But there continued to be failures in July and November 1980. Thus, not until early 1981 was the space shuttle main engine fully qualified for flight. Problems had included turbine-blade failures in the high-pressure fuel turbopump, a fire involving the main oxidizer valve, failures of nozzle feed lines, a burnthrough of the fuel preburner, and a rupture in the main-fuel-valve housing. But finally on April 12, 1981, the first Space Shuttle lifted off. After much troubleshooting and empirical redesign, the main engines finally worked.[89]

The large number of problems encountered in the development of the space shuttle main engines resulted from its advanced design. The high chamber and pump pressures as well as an operating life of 7.5 hours greatly exceeded those of any previous engine. Each shuttle had three main engines, which could be gimballed 10.5 degrees in each direction in pitch and 8.5 degrees in yaw. The engines could be throttled over a range from 65 to 109 percent of their rated power level (although there had been so many problems trying to demonstrate the 109 percent level in testing that it was not available on a routine basis until 2001). Moreover, the 65 percent minimum power level (changed from the original 50 percent level) was unavailable at sea level because of flow separation. During launch, the three main engines ignited before the solid-rocket boosters. When computers and sensors verified that they were providing the proper thrust level, the SRBs ignited. To reduce vehicle loads during the period of maximum dynamic pressure (reached at about 33,600 feet some 60 seconds after liftoff) and to keep vehicle acceleration at a maximum of 3 Gs, the flight-control system throttled back the engines during this phase of the flight. Throttling also made it feasible to abort the mission either with all engines functioning or with one of them out.[90]

At 100 percent of the rated power level, each main engine provided 375,000 pounds of thrust at sea level and 470,000 pounds at altitude. The minimum specific impulse was more than 360 lbf-

FIG. 5.4
The space shuttle main engine firing during a test at the National Space Technologies Laboratories (later the Stennis Space Center), January 1, 1981, showing the regenerative cooling tubes around the circumference of the combustion chamber. (Photo courtesy of NASA)

sec/lbm at sea level and 450 lbf-sec/lbm at altitude. This was substantially higher than the J-2 Saturn engine, which had a sea-level specific impulse of more than 290 lbf-sec/lbm and one at altitude of more than 420 lbf-sec/lbm. The J-2's thrust levels were also substantially lower at 230,000 pounds at altitude. Not only were the SSMEs much more powerful than the earlier engines using liquid-hydrogen technology but they were also vastly more sophisticated.[91]

External Tank

Another major part of the shuttle propulsion system was the external tank (ET), the only major nonreusable portion of the launch vehicle. It was the largest (and, when loaded, the heaviest part of the Space Shuttle), at about 154 feet in length and 27.5 feet in diameter. NASA issued a request for proposals for design and construction to Chrysler, McDonnell Douglas, Boeing, and Martin Marietta on April 2, 1973. All four bidders submitted their proposals on May 17. The source selection board gave the highest technical ratings to Martin Marietta and McDonnell Douglas. Martin argued that it alone among the bidders had relevant experience, with the Titan III core vehicle being situated between two large solid-rocket motors. Martin's costs were by far the lowest of the four, although the board recognized that it was bidding below true expected costs—"buying in" as it was called. But as NASA deputy administrator George Low said, "We nevertheless strongly felt that in the end Martin Marietta costs would, indeed, be lower than those of any of the other contenders." Consequently, on August 16, 1973, NASA selected Martin Marietta (Denver Division) to negotiate a contract for the design, development, and testing of the external tank, a selection that, this time, the other competitors did not protest. NASA required assembly of the structure at the Marshall-managed Michoud facility near New Orleans.[92]

The external tank seemed to some to pose few technological demands. James Kingsbury, head of Marshall's Science and Engineering Directorate, stated, "There was nothing really challenging technologically in the Tank. . . . The challenge was to drive down the cost." Similarly, Larry Mulloy, who was Marshall's project manager for the solid-rocket booster but also worked on the tank, stated, "There was no technological challenge in the building of the External Tank. The only challenge was building it to sustain the very large loads that it has to carry, and the thermal environment that it is exposed to during ascent" and do so within a weight limit of about 75,000 pounds. As it turned out, however, there was in fact a major challenge, only fully appreciated after loss of Space Shuttle *Columbia* on February 1, 2003, to a "breach in the Thermal Protection System on the leading edge of the left wing" resulting from its being struck by "a piece of insulating foam" from an area of the external tank known as the bipod ramp. During reentry into the atmosphere, this breach allowed aerodynamic superheating of the wing's aluminum structure, melting, and the subsequent breakup of the orbiter under increasing aerodynamic forces.[93]

The external tank had to carry the cryogenic liquid-hydrogen and liquid-oxygen propellants for the three shuttle main engines. It also served as the "structural backbone" for the shuttle stack and had to withstand substantial heating as the shuttle accelerated to supersonic speeds through the lower atmosphere, where dynamic pressures were high. This heating was much more complex than on a launch vehicle like the Saturn V. At the top, the tank needed only to withstand the effects of high-speed airflow. But further down, the tank's insulation had to encounter complex shock waves as it passed through the transonic speed range (roughly Mach 0.8 to 1.2). As the airflow became supersonic, shock waves came from the nose of the orbiter, the boosters, and the structural attachments connecting the tank, boosters, and orbiter. As the waves impinged on the sides of the external tank, they created heating rates up to 40 British thermal units per square foot per second. This was much smaller than the heating of a nose cone reentering the atmosphere, but it was substantial for the thin aluminum sheeting of which the external tank was formed to reduce weight.[94]

As designers examined the requirements for the external tank, they found that not even the arrangement of the hydrogen and oxygen tanks involved a simple application of lessons from the Centaur and Saturn. In both, the liquid-hydrogen tank was above the liquid-oxygen tank. Since liquid oxygen was 6 times as heavy as liquid hydrogen, this arrangement made it unnecessary to strengthen the hydrogen tank to support the heavier oxygen during liftoff. Also, with the lighter hydrogen on top, the inertial forces necessary to change the attitude of the vehicle were lower than would have been the case had the reverse arrangement prevailed. For the shuttle, however, the engines were not directly under the tanks, as was the case for the Saturn upper stages and Centaur. Instead, they were off to one side. With the heavy oxygen tank on the bottom of the external tank, its weight would have created an inertial force difficult to overcome by gimballing of the SSMEs and the SRB nozzles. Especially after the separation of the solid boosters, the weight of the oxygen tank would have tended to cause the orbiter to spin around

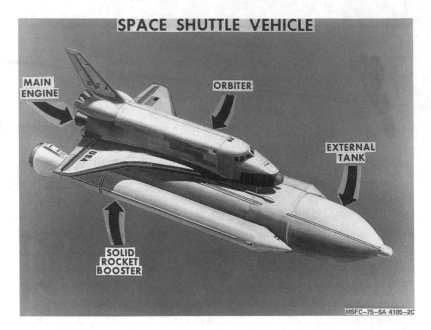

the tank's center of gravity. Placing the oxygen tank on top moved the shuttle stack's center of gravity well forward, making steering much more feasible. But it also forced designers to make the liquid-hydrogen tank (and also an intertank structure between it and the oxygen tank) much sturdier than had been necessary on the Saturn upper stages.[95]

This, in turn, compounded a problem with the ET's weight. The initial empty weight allowance had been 78,000 pounds, but in 1974, the Johnson Space Center in Houston (renamed from the Manned Spacecraft Center in 1973) reduced the goal to 75,000 pounds. Moreover, NASA asked Martin Marietta if it could not only reduce the weight but do so at no additional cost. In fact, the space agency suggested that it would be helpful actually to reduce the cost. Even though Marshall lowered the safety factor for the ET, the initial tank used on shuttle flights 1–5 and 7 weighed some 77,100 pounds. But through concerted efforts, Martin Marietta was able to achieve a 10,300-pound weight reduction for the lightweight tanks first used on flight 6 of the shuttle. The firm attained the weight reduction through a variety of design changes, including eliminating some portions of longitudinal structural stiffeners in the hydrogen tank, using fewer circumferential stiffeners, milling some portions of the tank to a lower thickness, using a different type of aluminum that was stronger and thus allowed thinner sections, and redesigning anti-slosh baffling.[96]

The resultant external tank included a liquid-hydrogen tank that constituted 96.66 feet of the ET's roughly 154 feet in length. It had semi-monocoque design with fusion-welded barrel sections, forward and aft domes, and five ring frames. It operated at a pressure range of 32 to 34 pounds per square inch and contained an anti-vortex baffle but no elaborate anti-slosh baffles, because the lightness of the liquid hydrogen made its sloshing less significant than that of liquid oxygen. The feed line from the tank allowed a maximum flow rate of 48,724 gallons per minute from its 385,265-gallon (237,641-pound) capacity. The intertank structure was much shorter at 22.5 feet. Made of both steel and aluminum, it, too, was semi-monocoque in structure with a thrust beam, skin, stringers, and panels. It contained instrumentation and a device called an umbilical plate for supply of purge gas, detection of hazardous gas escaping from the tanks, and boil-off of hydrogen gas while on the ground. The intertank also had a purge system that removed the highly combustible propellants if they escaped from their tanks or plumbing fixtures.

Above the intertank was the liquid-oxygen tank. Its 49.33 feet of length, combined with those of the intertank and the liquid-hydrogen tank, exceeded the total length of the ET because it and its liquid-hydrogen counterpart extended into the intertank. The liquid-oxygen tank was an aluminum monocoque structure operating with a pressure range of 20–22 pounds per square inch. It allowed a maximum of 2,787 pounds (19,017 gallons) of liquid oxygen to flow to the main engines when they were operating at 104 percent of their rated thrust. Containing both anti-slosh and anti-vortex mechanisms, the tank had a capacity of 143,351 gallons, or 1,391,936 pounds, of oxidizer.[97]

217

Propulsion
with Liquid
Hydrogen
and Oxygen,
1954–91

The thermal-protection system for the external tank had to withstand the complex aerodynamic heating generated by the shuttle structure and keep the cryogenic propellants from boiling. The tank was coated with an inch of foam similar to that used on the Saturn S-II. Unlike the S-II insulation, however, which had to protect only against boil-off and not against the formation of ice on the foam from the liquid hydrogen and the liquid oxygen, that on the ET could not permit ice formation, because if ice came off the tank during launch, it could easily damage the critical and delicate thermal-protection system on the orbiter. Thus, the external tank's insulation had to be thicker than that on the S-II. It was in fact so effective that despite the extreme temperatures inside the tanks, the surface of the insulation felt "only slightly cool to the touch." For the first two shuttle flights, there was a white, fire-retardant latex coating on top of the foam, but thereafter, following testing to determine that the foam alone provided sufficient protection during ascent, the shuttle team dispensed with this coating, saving 595 pounds and leaving the orange foam to add its distinctive color to the white of the orbiter and solid-rocket boosters at launch.[98]

Like the main engines, the external tank underwent extensive testing before the first shuttle launch. The entire propulsion system was, of course, designed under Marshall oversight, with Center Director Lucas continuing von Braun's practice of using weekly notes for overall communication and systems engineering. In view of this, the Columbia Accident Investigation Board was perhaps unfairly critical in 2003 when it wrote:

> In the 1970s, engineers often developed particular facets of a design (structural, thermal, and so on) one after another and in relative isolation from other engineers working on different facets. Today, engineers usually work together on all aspects of a design as an integrated team. The bipod fitting [in the area where foam separated on *Columbia*'s last flight] was designed from a structural standpoint, and the application process for foam (to prevent ice formation) and Super Lightweight Ablator (to protect from high heating) were developed separately.

However, the board went on to note in all fairness:

> It was—and still is—impossible to conduct a ground-based, simultaneous, full-scale simulation of the combination of loads, airflows, temperatures, pressures, vibration, and acoustics the External Tank experiences during launch and ascent. Therefore, the qualification testing did not truly reflect the combination of factors the bipod would experience during flight. Engineers and designers used the best methods available at the time: test the bipod and foam under as many severe combinations as could be simulated and then interpolate the results. Various analyses determined stresses, thermal gradients, air loads, and other conditions that could not be obtained through testing.[99]

Design requirements specified that the Space Shuttle system not shed any debris, but on the first shuttle flight, the external tank produced a shower of particles, causing engineers to say they would have been hard-pressed to clear *Columbia* for flight if they had known this would happen. When the bipod ramp lost foam on shuttle flight 7, wind-tunnel testing showed that the ramp area was designed with an aerodynamically too steep angle, and designers changed the ramp angle from 45 degrees to a shallower 22 to 30 degrees. However, this and a later "slight modification to the ramp impingement profile" failed to prevent the destruction of Space Shuttle *Columbia* on February 1, 2003. It is beyond the scope of this history to discuss the *Columbia* accident further, but despite advances in analytical capabilities until 2003, the board was unable to pinpoint the "precise reasons why the left bipod foam ramp was lost."[100]

This was so even though the board included a staff of more than 120 people aided by about 400 NASA engineers in a lengthy and extensive investigation lasting months. The reasons a definitive explanation was impossible included the fact that foam did not "have the same properties in all directions" or the "same composition at every point." It was "extremely difficult to model analytically or to characterize physically . . . in even relatively static conditions, much less during the launch and ascent of the Shuttle." Factors that may have caused the foam to separate and damage the wing included "aerodynamic loads, thermal and vacuum effects, vibrations, stress in the External Tank structure, and myriad other conditions" including "wind shear, associated Solid Rocket Booster and Space Shuttle Main Engine responses, and liquid oxygen sloshing in the External Tank." Even in 2003, "Non-destructive evaluation techniques for determining External Tank foam strength have not been perfected or qualified."[101]

219
*Propulsion
with Liquid
Hydrogen
and Oxygen,
1954–91*

With statements such as, "In our view, the NASA organizational culture had as much to do with this accident as the foam," the accident investigation board clearly implicated more than technology in the causes of the *Columbia* accident. But a major cause was NASA and contractor engineers' failure to understand the reasons for and full implications of foam shedding from the external tank. As well-known space commentator John Pike said, "The more they study the foam, the less they understand it." And as a newspaper article stated, "Getting every ounce of the foam to stick to the external tank has bedeviled NASA engineers for 22 years. . . . Why foam falls off any area of the tank remains a scientific mystery." In the more sober language of the CAIB report, "Although engineers have made numerous changes in foam design and application in the 25 years the External Tank has been in production, the problem of foam-shedding has not been solved."[102]

Whatever the larger causes of the accident, from the perspective of this book, this was but one more instance in which engineers did not have the design, development, and operation of rockets "down to a science." Despite countless billions of dollars spent on researching, developing, and operating a large number of missiles and rockets; despite a great deal of effort on NASA's and contractors' parts to understand and correct this particular problem, there were aspects of rocketry (including this one) that eluded the understanding of engineers and even scientists such as investigation board member Douglas D. Osheroff, a Nobel Prize–winning physicist from Stanford University. Osheroff had conducted some simple experiments with foam that helped him understand the "basic physical properties of the foam itself" but also demonstrated "the difficulty of understanding why foam falls off the external tank." As he said, "Attempts to understand [the] complex behavior and failure modes" of the components of the shuttle stack were "hampered by their strong interactions with other systems in the stack."[103]

Analysis and Conclusions

Despite the known power of hydrogen as a rocket propellant, its use on Centaur came fairly late in the history of launch-vehicle technology. This resulted from the known difficulties of harnessing the thrust hydrogen could provide. Once Krafft Ehricke and Convair decided to use liquid hydrogen, they encountered both predicted and unexpected problems that also plagued Pratt & Whitney's development of the RL10 engine. Further complications afflicted the J-2 and the Saturn stages on which it flew.

Even after engineers' considerable experience with liquid-hydrogen technology, the space shuttle main engine also tested their ingenuity. Because of requirements for high pressure, throttleability, and higher thrust levels than earlier hydrogen-fueled engines, the SSME defied the abilities of rocket engineers to predict and solve problems on the drawing board. Only extensive testing and redesign allowed the SSME to function, and then only with limitations and careful monitoring. Although it was a powerful testament to the achievements of its engineers and those who had gone before, it demonstrated the difficult conditions under which rocket engineers still labored more than half a century after Goddard first began to develop liquid-propellant rockets. The tragic *Columbia* accident further accentuated the unknowns that plagued rocket engineers.

In addition to the themes discussed in the introduction to this history and its early chapters, development of liquid-hydrogen engines illustrated in extreme form the ways in which materials technology was important in rocketry. Additionally, liquid-hydrogen engines

demonstrated some of the many uses of computers for simulation, analysis, modeling, solution of complex equations, monitoring, and control—among other functions. Although propulsion and other aspects of rocketry continued to exhibit numerous mysteries, the tools available for at least penetrating (if not solving) them and for making engines work to a high degree of reliability were becoming increasingly sophisticated as time went on.

CHAPTER 6

Solid Propulsion: JATOs to Minuteman III, 1939–70

SOLID-PROPELLANT ROCKETRY HAS A MUCH LONGer history than its liquid counterpart, but the long-existing "powder" rockets used for fireworks and other purposes had such low specific impulses that they could not serve to propel launch vehicles. Development of more powerful solid propellants began in the United States around 1939. With the impetus of World War II, solid-propellant rocketry made important strides, with several different organizations contributing to these developments. GALCIT/JPL made important contributions to solid-propellant development with its castable composite propellants (consisting of solid ingredients with a binder that held them together and assumed the shape of a mold or casing). Caltech operations at Eaton Canyon, California, did important work with double-base propellants (consisting usually of nitrocellulose and nitroglycerin), while on the East Coast, what became the Allegany Ballistics Laboratory (ABL) also contributed significantly to double-base technology. Other contributors to solid-propellant technology soon joined in the effort.

Early Castable Composite Propellants

Castable composite propellants grew out of a grant Theodore von Kármán and Frank Malina arranged with the National Academy of Sciences (NAS) Committee on Army Air Corps Research in January 1939. With the $1,000 allotment, Malina and his associates at GALCIT studied jet-assisted takeoff (JATO) of aircraft and prepared a proposal for research on the subject. This led to an NAS contract for $10,000, effective July 1, 1939, and to subsequent contracts with the army air corps and the navy for JATO units (with both liquid and solid propellants). JATOs actually used rocket (rather than jet) thrust to help heavily loaded aircraft take off on a short runway.[1]

The key individual in the development of the first castable composite propellant was John W. Parsons, a propellant chemist on Malina's team. Parsons, largely self-taught, had taken some chemistry courses from the University of Southern California in 1935–36 but did not graduate. He worked as a chemist for Hercules Powder Company in Los Angeles from 1932 to 1934 and then was chief chemist for Halifax Explosives Company in Saugas, California, from 1934 to 1938. In 1939–40, Parsons sought a solution to the problem of controlled burning for many seconds in a solid-propellant rocket motor. This was critical to the development of a JATO unit. It was he, apparently, who conceived the concept of "cigarette-burning" at only one end of the propellant. But repeated tests of powder, compressed into a chamber and coated with a variety of substances to form a seal with the chamber wall, resulted in explosions. Authorities von Kármán consulted advised that a powder rocket could burn for only two or three seconds.

Not satisfied with this expert opinion, von Kármán characteristically turned to theory for a solution. He devised four differential equations describing the operation of the rocket motor and handed them to Malina for solution. In solving them, Malina discovered that, theoretically, if the combustion chamber were completely filled by the propellant charge, if the physical properties of the propellant and the ratio of the area of burning propellant to the throat area of the chamber's nozzle remained constant, thrust also would do likewise and there would be no explosions. Encouraged by these findings, Parsons and others came up with a compressed powder design that worked effectively (after one initial explosion) for 152 successive motors used in successful flight tests of JATO units on an Ercoupe aircraft in August 1941, convincing the navy to contract for a variety of assisted takeoff motors.

After storage under varying temperatures, however, the motors usually exploded. Parsons then found a solution to that problem. Apparently watching a roofing operation about June 1942, he concluded that asphalt as a binder and fuel mixed with potassium perchlorate as an oxidizer would yield a stable propellant. This proved to be true. Thus the theory of von Kármán and Malina combined with

FIG. 6.1 An Ercoupe aircraft, piloted by Capt. Homer A. Boushey Jr., taking off with the assistance of a solid-propellant jet-assisted takeoff (JATO) unit developed by the Guggenheim Aeronautical Laboratory California Institute of Technology (GALCIT, which later became the Jet Propulsion Laboratory) in the first use of an American JATO, August 12, 1941. (Photo courtesy of NASA/JPL-Caltech)

the practical knowledge and imagination of Parsons to produce a castable, composite solid propellant that, with later improvements, made large solid-propellant rockets possible. A fundamental technological breakthrough, this formed the basis of many later castable propellants with much higher performance than asphalt–potassium perchlorate.[2]

Meanwhile, to produce its JATOs (both solid and liquid), five members of the GALCIT project (Malina, von Kármán, Martin Summerfield, Parsons, and Edward S. Forman), plus von Kármán's lawyer, Andrew G. Haley, formed the Aerojet Engineering Corporation in March 1942 (Aerojet General Corporation after its acquisition by General Tire and Rubber Company in 1944–45). Aerojet did much business with the army air forces and navy for JATO units during the war and became by 1950 the largest rocket engine manufacturer in the world and a leader in research and development of rocket technology. Until the acquisition by General Tire, Aerojet and the GALCIT project maintained close technical relations.[3]

The initial asphalt–potassium perchlorate propellant—known as GALCIT 53—did not have a particularly impressive performance compared, for example, with ballistite (a double-base composition). But it operated effectively at temperatures down to 40°F. At even lower temperatures, however, GALCIT 53 cracked. It also melted in the tropical sun and was very smoky when burning. This last characteristic restricted visibility for the takeoff of second and follow-on aircraft using JATO units on a single runway. Consequently, researchers at GALCIT and its successor, JPL, began searching for an elastic binder with storage limits beyond GALCIT 53's extremes of –9°F to 120°F. In particular, a young engineer named Charles Bartley, who was employed at JPL from June 1944 to August 1951, began examining synthetic rubbers and polymers, eventually hitting upon a liquid polysulfide compound designated LP-2 as a solid-propellant binder. The Thiokol Chemical Corporation made it for sealing aircraft tanks and other applications.[4]

225
Solid
Propulsion:
JATOs to
Minuteman III,
1939–70

Like many innovations, LP-2 had resulted from an initial, inadvertent discovery. In 1926, Joseph C. Patrick, a physician who found chemistry more interesting than medicine, sought an inexpensive way to produce antifreeze from ethylene using sodium polysulfide as a hydrolyzing agent. His procedure yielded a synthetic rubber instead of antifreeze. It led him to cofound Thiokol, which marketed the material in the form of gaskets, sealants, adhesives, and coatings (the polysulfide polymer being resistant to weather, solvents, and electrical arcing). Then in 1942, Patrick and an employee, H. L. Ferguson, found a way to make the first liquid polymer that included no volatile solvent yet could be cured to form a rubberlike solid. During World War II it was used to seal fuel tanks in aircraft, gun turrets, fuselages, air ducts, and the like.[5]

Before learning of LP-2, Bartley and his associates at JPL had tried a variety of moldable synthetic rubbers as both binders and fuels, including Buna-S, Buna-N, and neoprene. Neoprene had the best properties for use as a binder and burned the best of the lot, but molding it required high pressures. Like the extrusion process used with double-base propellants (forcing them through a die), this made the production of large propellant grains (masses of propellant) impractical. Meanwhile, Thiokol chemists had begun to release data about LP-2. At a meeting of the American Chemical Society, Bartley asked about a liquid that would polymerize to a solid elastomer (rubberlike substance). Frank M. McMillan, who represented Shell Oil in the San Francisco area, knew about Thiokol's product and shared the information with Bartley, who acquired small quantities from Walt Boswell, Thiokol's representative for the western United States.[6]

With encouragement from Army Ordnance and the navy, Bartley—joined by John I. Shafer, a JPL design engineer, and

H. Lawrence Thackwell Jr., a specialist in aircraft structures—began in 1947 to develop a small rocket designated Thunderbird, with a 6-inch diameter. They used it for testing whether polysulfide propellants could withstand the forces of high acceleration that a potential large launch vehicle might encounter. Bartley had already found that an end-burning grain of polysulfide propellant did not produce steady thrust but burned faster at first and then leveled off. He attributed this to accelerated burning along the case to form a convex cone, a hypothesis he confirmed by quenching the flame partway through the burn.

To solve the problem of unsteady thrust, the three JPL engineers adopted a grain design that had been developed in Great Britain in the late 1930s but was similar to one developed independently in 1946 for double-base propellants by an American, Edward W. Price. It featured an internal-burning, star-shaped cavity. This design protected the case from excess heat because the burning was in the middle of the propellant grain. It also provided a constant level of thrust because as the star points burned away, the internal cavity became a cylinder with roughly the same surface area as the initial star. Bartley had read about the star design from a British report he did not specify and had instructed Shafer to investigate it. Shafer found that the government-owned, contractor-operated Allegany Ballistics Laboratory had used the British design in the uncompleted Vicar rocket and a scaled-down version named the Curate. Using equations from the ABL report on the projects, Shafer began developing a number of star designs in 1947. Combining a polysulfide propellant with the star design and casting it in the case so that it bonded thereto, the team under Bartley produced the successful Thunderbird rocket that passed its flight tests in 1947–48.[7]

Another significant development was the replacement of potassium perchlorate as an oxidizer by ammonium perchlorate, which offered higher performance (specific impulse) and less smoke. Apparently, the Thunderbird used a propellant designated JPL 100, which contained a mixture of ammonium perchlorate and potassium perchlorate in a polysulfide binder. In 1947, however, JPL had developed a JPL 118 propellant that used only ammonium perchlorate as an oxidizer together with polysulfide as the binder and a couple of curing agents. Although this propellant had yet to be fully investigated in 1947, by mid-1948 JPL had tested it and showed that it had a specific impulse of at least 198 lbf-sec/lbm at sea level, using an expansion ratio of 10 for the rocket nozzle. This was still relatively low compared with a typical performance of double-base

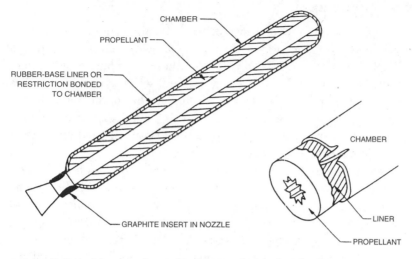

CHAMBER

PROPELLANT

RUBBER-BASE LINER OR
RESTRICTION BONDED
TO CHAMBER

CHAMBER

GRAPHITE INSERT IN NOZZLE

LINER

PROPELLANT

227

*Solid
Propulsion:
JATOs to
Minuteman III,
1939–70*

FIG. 6.2 Technical drawing of an early solid-propellant rocket, featuring a star-shaped, internal-burning cavity; a graphite insert in the nozzle to protect it from hot exhaust gases; a liner for the chamber wall; and case bonding. (Courtesy of NASA/JPL-Caltech, taken from H. L. Thackwell Jr. and J. I. Shafer, "The Applicability of Solid Propellants to Rocket Vehicles of V-2 Size and Performance," JPL ORDCIT Project Memorandum No. 4-25, July 21, 1948, p. 12 in a portion of the memorandum released to the author by JPL and its NASA Management Office)

propellants (about 230 lbf-sec/lbm) but higher than the 185 lbf-sec/lbm for the asphalt–potassium perchlorate propellant and 190 lbf-sec/lbm for JPL 100.[8]

Aerojet also began using ammonium perchlorate in its aeroplex (polyester polymer) propellants in 1948 to increase specific impulse and reduce smoke. Funded by the navy's Bureau of Aeronautics to develop a basic understanding of the production and employment of solid propellants, Aerojet increased the specific impulse of its ammonium perchlorate propellants to 235 lbf-sec/lbm, but aeroplex was not case bondable, leading the firm to switch in 1954 to a polyurethane propellant that was.[9]

In the interim, Thiokol sought to sell its polymer to Aerojet and another manufacturer of rockets, the Hercules Powder Company, but both rejected Thiokol's polymer because its 32 percent sulfur content made it a poor fuel. Army Ordnance then encouraged Thiokol to go into the rocket business itself. In early 1948, the firm set up rocket operations in a former ordnance plant in Elkton, Maryland. It moved some operations in April 1949 to the army's new Rocket Research and Development Center at Redstone Arsenal in Huntsville, Alabama.[10]

About this time, under contract to the army, Thiokol produced a T-40 motor intended for use as a JATO unit. As a propellant, it used JPL 100 (rechristened T-10 by Thiokol) in a case-bonded motor design. Also in 1949, Thiokol designed the T-41 motor for the Hughes Aircraft Company's Falcon missile under development for the air force. This was a shorter version of JPL's Thunderbird motor. It began production at Elkton, then moved to Huntsville, where a larger version called the T-42 evolved from it.[11]

According to Edward N. Hall, later an air force colonel who was important in promoting the development of solid propellants, the Falcon tactical (air-to-air) missile contributed "quality control techniques for rubber-base propellants, design data for case-bonded grains, [and] aging characteristics of rubber-based propellants" to the evolving store of knowledge about solid-propellant technology. It appears that Thiokol did not make these contributions on its own. JPL provided considerable assistance in an early example of technology transfer. In October 1947, Charles Bartley of JPL was present at a meeting of Thiokol personnel, representatives of Army Ordnance, and the navy's Bureau of Aeronautics to discuss the kind of work Thiokol was expected to do in the further development of polysulfide propellants. The next day, Bartley met again with Thiokol personnel to relate JPL's experience with polysulfide-perchlorate propellants.[12]

In about January or February 1949, a trip report by a Thiokol employee discussed a visit to JPL's Solid Rocket Section, of which Bartley was the chief. The report covered such matters as the grease used for extracting the mandrel to create the internal cavity in the grain once it cured and igniters that employed black or a special igniter powder. Also discussed were grinding ammonium and potassium perchlorate, combining them with the liquid polymer in a vertical mixer, pouring the propellant, preparing the liner for the combustion chamber, and testing. Also reported was a visit to Western Electrochemical Company, which supplied the perchlorate. The document concluded with some recommended changes in Thiokol's operating procedures at Elkton.[13]

As helpful as JPL's assistance was, however, the contributions Hall mentions seem to have come also from work done independently at Thiokol's Elkton and Huntsville plants. For example, Thiokol discovered that the size of perchlorate particles was important in motor operation and propellant castability, so it introduced a micromerograph to measure particle size. To reduce the deleterious absorption of moisture by the perchlorates, Thiokol installed air conditioning in the grinding rooms. The firm determined the optimal mixing time for the propellant and replaced a barium grease JPL had used to extract the mandrel from the middle of the cast propellant after curing with a Teflon coating. This latter step was necessary not only because the grease-affected part of the propellant had to be sanded after extraction but also because the grease had enfolded into the propellant, causing weak areas. Thiokol also introduced a "temperature-programmed cure cycle," pressurized curing, and a method of casting that eliminated propellant voids resulting from shrinkage and air bubbles.[14] These details provide early examples of information—rare in the literature about rocketry—about which firms introduced specific innovations, illustrating the ways technology sometimes transferred.

THE SERGEANT TEST VEHICLE

While these developments were occurring at Thiokol, JPL worked with a test vehicle named the Sergeant, not to be confused with the later missile of that name. Army Ordnance had authorized the development of this test vehicle, a sounding rocket with a diameter of 15 inches, which was quite large for the day (although only an inch larger than an aircraft rocket developed at the Naval Ordnance Test Station, Inyokern, California, in 1945 and called the "Big Richard"). Designed with an extremely thin steel case of 0.065 inch and a star-shaped perforation, the Sergeant test vehicle was expected to attain an altitude of up to 700,000 feet while carrying a 50-pound payload. Static tests with a thicker case in February 1949 showed that a polysulfide grain of that diameter could function without deformation.

But when the JPL researchers (including Bartley, Shafer, and Thackwell) shifted to the thinner case, the result was 12 successive explosions through April 27, 1950. At this point, JPL director Louis G. Dunn canceled the project for the sounding rocket and reduced all solid-propellant work at the laboratory to basic research. The researchers soon determined that the causes of the explosions included a chamber pressure that was too high for the thin case and points on the star configuration that were too sharp, causing cracks as pressure built up. An easy solution would have been a thicker case and rounded points on the star. When Dunn canceled the project, Thackwell took his knowledge of solid-propellant rocketry to Thiokol's Redstone Division in Huntsville.[15]

THE RV-A-10 MISSILE

In the meantime, Thiokol had teamed up with General Electric in the Hermes project to produce a solid-propellant missile (initially known as the A-2) that was much larger than the Sergeant sounding rocket. It operated on a shoestring budget until canceled, but it still made significant progress in solid-propellant technology.[16]

The original requirements for the A-2 were to carry a 500-pound warhead to a range as far as 75 nautical miles, but these changed to a payload weighing 1,500 pounds, necessitating a motor with a diameter of 31 inches. Thiokol started developing the motor in May 1950, a point in time that allowed the project to take advantage of work on the Sergeant sounding rocket and of Larry Thackwell's experience with it. By December 1951, the program had successfully completed a static test of the 31-inch motor. From January 1952 through March 1953, there were 20 more static tests at Redstone Arsenal and four flight tests of the missile at Patrick AFB, Florida. In the process, the missile came to be designated the RV-A-10. The project encountered unanticipated problems with nozzle erosion and combustion instability that engineers were able to solve.[17]

The four flight tests achieved a maximum range of 52 miles (on flight one) and a maximum altitude of 195,000 feet (flight two) using a motor case 0.20 inch thick and a propellant grain featuring a star-shaped perforation with broad tips on the star. The propellant was designated TRX-110A. It included 63 percent ammonium perchlorate by weight as the oxidizer. The propellant took advantage of an air force–sponsored project (MX-105) titled "Improvement of Polysulfide-Perchlorate Propellants" that had begun in 1950 and issued a final report (written by Thiokol employees) in May 1951. On test motor number two a propellant designated T13, which contained polysulfide LP-33 and ammonium perchlorate, achieved a specific impulse at sea level of more than 195 lbf-sec/lbm at 80°F but also experienced combustion instability. This led to the shift to TRX-110, which had a slightly lower specific impulse but no combustion instability.[18]

Thiokol had arrived at the blunter-tipped star perforation as a result of Thackwell's experience (at JPL) with the Sergeant test vehicle and of photoelastic studies of grains performed at the company's request by the Armour Institute (later renamed the Illinois Institute of Technology). This, together with a thicker case wall than JPL had used with the Sergeant sounding rocket, eliminated JPL's problems with cracks and explosions. However, TRX-110 proved not to have enough initial thrust. The solution was to shift the size of the ammonium perchlorate particles from a mixture of coarse and fine pieces to one of consistently fine particles, which yielded not only higher initial thrust but also a more consistent thrust over time—a desirable trait. Meanwhile, the Thiokol-GE team gradually learned about the thermal environment to which the RV-A-10 nozzles were exposed. Design of the nozzles evolved through subscale and full-scale motor tests employing various materials and techniques for fabrication. The best materials proved to be SAE 1020 steel with carbon inserts, and a roll weld proved superior to casting or forging for producing the nozzle itself.[19]

Another problem encountered in fabricating the large grain for the RV-A-10 was the appearance of cracks and voids when it was cured at atmospheric pressure, probably the cause of a burnout of the liner on motor number two. The solution proved to be twofold: (1) Thiokol poured the first two mixes of propellant into the motor chamber at a temperature 10°F hotter than normal, with the last mix 10°F cooler than normal; then, (2) Thiokol personnel cured the propellant under 20 pounds per square inch of pressure with a layer of liner material laid over it to prevent air from contacting the grain. Together, these two procedures eliminated the voids and cracks.[20]

With these advances in the art of producing solid-propellant motors, the RV-A-10 became the first known solid-propellant rocket motor of such a large size—31 inches in diameter and 14 feet, 4 inches long—to be flight tested as of February–March 1953. Among its other firsts were scaling up the mixing and casting of polysulfide propellants to the extent that more than 5,000 pounds of it could be processed in a single day; the routine use of many mixes in a single motor; the use of a tubular igniter rolled into coiled plastic tubing (called a jelly roll) to avoid the requirement for a heavy closure at the nozzle end to aid in ignition; and one of the early uses of jet vanes inserted in the exhaust stream of a large solid-propellant rocket to provide thrust vector control.

As recently as December 1945, the head of the Office of Scientific Research and Development during World War II, Vannevar Bush, had stated, "I don't think anybody in the world knows how [to build an accurate intercontinental ballistic missile] and I feel confident it will not be done for a long time to come." Many people, even in the rocket field, did not believe that solid-propellant rockets could be efficient enough or of long enough duration to serve as long-range missiles. The RV-A-10 was the first rocket to remove such doubts from at least some people's minds.[21] Arguably, it provided a significant part of the technological basis for the entire next generation of missiles, from Polaris and Minuteman to the large solid boosters for the Titan IIIs and IVs and the Space Shuttle, although many further technological developments would be necessary before they became possible (including significant improvements in propellant performance).

At the beginning of recent solid-propellant development during World War II, the vast majority of rockets produced for use in combat employed extruded double-base propellants. These were limited in size by the nature of the extrusion process used at that time to produce them. In extrusion using a solvent, nitrocellulose was suspended in the solvent, which caused the nitrocellulose to swell. It was formed into a doughlike composition and then extruded (forced) through dies to form it into grains. This process of production limited the size of the grains to thin sections so the solvent could evaporate, and the elasticity of the grain was too low for bonding large charges to the motor case. With a solventless (or dry) process, there were also limitations on the size of the grain and greater hazards of explosion than with extrusion using a solvent.

These factors created the need for castable double-base propellants. But before a truly viable process for producing large castable propellants could be developed, the United States, because it was at war, needed a variety of rockets to attack such targets as ships (including submarines), enemy fortifications, gun emplacements, aircraft, tanks, and logistical systems. The development of these weapons did not lead directly to any launch-vehicle technology, but the organizations that developed them later played a role in furthering that technology. Two individuals provided the leadership in producing the comparatively small wartime rockets with extruded grains. One was Clarence Hickman, who had worked with Goddard on rockets intended for military applications during World War I. He then earned a Ph.D. at Clark University and went to work at Bell Telephone Laboratories. After consulting with Goddard, in June 1940 Hickman submitted a series of rocket proposals to Frank B. Jewett, president of Bell Labs and chairman of a division in the recently created National Defense Research Committee (NDRC). The upshot was the creation of Section H (for Hickman) of the NDRC's Division of Armor and Ordnance. Hickman's section had responsibility for researching and developing rocket ordnance. Although Section H was initially located at the Naval Proving Ground at Dahlgren, Virginia, it worked largely for the army.

Hickman chose to use wet-extruded, double-base propellants (employing a solvent) because he favored the shorter burning times they afforded compared with dry-extruded ones. He and his associates worked with this propellant at Dahlgren, moved to the Navy Powder Factory at Indian Head, Maryland, and finally to Allegany Ordnance Plant, Pinto Branch, on the West Virginia side of the Potomac

River west of Cumberland, Maryland. There at the end of 1943 they set up Allegany Ballistics Laboratory, a rocket-development facility operated for Section H by George Washington University. By using traps, cages, and other devices to hold the solvent-extruded, double-base propellant, they helped develop the bazooka antitank weapon, a 4.5-inch aircraft rocket, JATO devices with less smoke than those produced by Aerojet using Parson's asphalt-based propellant, and a recoilless gun.[22] Under different management, ABL later became an important producer of upper stages for missiles and rockets.

Hickman's counterpart on the West Coast was physics professor Charles Lauritsen of Caltech. Lauritsen was vice chairman of the Division of Armor and Ordnance (Division A), and in that capacity he had made an extended trip to England to observe rocket developments there. The English had developed a way to make solvent-less, double-base propellant by dry extrusion. This yielded a thicker grain that would burn longer than the wet-extruded propellant but required extremely heavy presses for the extrusion. However, the benefits were higher propellant loading and the longer burning time that Lauritsen preferred.

Convinced of the superiority of this kind of extrusion and believing that the United States needed a larger rocket program than Section H could provide with its limited facilities, Lauritsen argued successfully for a West Coast program. Caltech then set up operations in Eaton Canyon in the foothills of the San Gabriel Mountains northeast of the campus in Pasadena. It operated from 1942 to 1945 and expanded to a 3,000-person effort involving research, development, and pilot production of rocket motors; development of fuses and warheads; and static and flight testing. The group produced an antisubmarine rocket 7.2 inches in diameter, a 4.5-inch barrage rocket, several retro-rockets (fired from the rear of airplanes at submarines), 3.5- and 5-inch forward-firing aircraft rockets, and the 11.75-inch "Tiny Tim" rocket that produced 30,000 pounds of thrust and weighed 1,385 pounds. (This last item later served as a booster for the WAC Corporal.)

By contrast with Section H, Section L (for Lauritsen) served mainly the navy's requirements. In need of a place to test and evaluate the rockets being developed at Eaton Canyon, in November 1943 the navy established the Naval Ordnance Test Station (NOTS) in the sparsely populated desert region around Inyokern well north of the San Gabriel Mountains. Like the Allegany Ballistics Laboratory, NOTS was destined to play a significant role in the history of U.S. rocketry, mostly with tactical rockets but also with contributions to ballistic missiles and launch vehicles.

One early contribution was the "White Whizzer" 5.0-inch rocket developed by members of the Caltech team who had already moved to NOTS but were still under direction of the university rather than the navy. By about January 1944, combustion instability had become a problem with the 2.25-inch motors for some of the tactical rockets. These rockets used tubular, partially internal-burning charges of double-base propellant. Radial holes in the grain helped solve severe pressure excursions—it was thought, by allowing the gas from the burning propellant to escape from the internal cavity. Edward W. Price, who had not yet received his bachelor's degree but would later become one of the nation's leading experts in combustion instability, suggested creating a star-shaped perforation in the grain for internal burning. He thought this might do a better job than the radial holes in preventing oscillatory gas flow that was causing the charges of propellant to split. He tested the star perforation, and it did produce stable burning.

In 1946, Price applied this technique to the White Whizzer, which featured a star-perforated, internal-burning grain with the outside of the charge wrapped in plastic to inhibit burning there. This geometry allowed higher loading of propellant (the previous design having channels for gas flow both inside and outside the grain). And since the grain itself protected the case from the heat in the internal cavity, the case could be made of lightweight aluminum, providing better performance than heavier cases that were slower to accelerate because of the additional weight. Ground-launched about May 1946, the White Whizzer yielded a speed of 3,200 feet per second, then a record for solid rockets. The internal-burning, aluminum-cased design features later appeared in the 5.0-inch Zuni and Sidewinder tactical missiles. The internal-burning feature of the design also came to be applied to a great many other solid rockets, including ballistic missiles and stages for launch vehicles. This apparently was the first flight of a rocket using such a grain design in the United States, preceding JPL's use of a similar design, known as the Deacon, and also flight testing of the first member of the Vicar family to be flown.[23]

CASTABLE DOUBLE-BASE PROPELLANT

The next major development in double-base propellants was a method for casting (rather than extruding) the grain. The company that produced the first known rocket motor using this procedure was the Hercules Powder Company, which had operated the government-owned Allegany Ballistics Laboratory since the end of World War II. The firm came into existence in 1912 when an antitrust suit against its parent company, E. I. du Pont de Nemours & Company, forced du Pont to divest some of its holdings. Hercules began as an explosives firm that produced more than 50,000 tons of smokeless powder during World War I. It then began to diversify into other uses of nitrocellulose. During World War II, the firm supplied large quantities of extruded double-base propellants for tactical rockets. After the war, it began casting double-based propellants by beginning with a casting powder consisting of nitrocellulose, nitroglycerin, and a stabilizer. Chemists poured this into a mold and added a casting solvent of nitroglycerin plus a diluent and the stabilizer. With heat and the passage of time, this yielded a much larger grain than could be produced by extrusion alone.

Wartime research by John F. Kincaid and Henry M. Shuey at the National Defense Research Committee's Explosives Research Laboratory at Bruceton, Pennsylvania (operated by the Bureau of Mines and the Carnegie Institute of Technology), had yielded this process. Kincaid and Shuey, as well as other propellant chemists, had developed it further after transferring to ABL, and under Hercules management, ABL continued work on cast double-base propellants. This led to the flight testing of a JATO using this propellant in 1947. The process allowed Hercules to produce a propellant grain that was as large as the castable, composite propellants that Aerojet, Thiokol, and Grand Central were developing in this period but with a slightly higher specific impulse (also with a greater danger of exploding rather than burning and releasing the exhaust gases at a controlled rate).[24]

The navy had contracted with Hercules for a motor to be used as an alternative third stage on Vanguard (designated JATO X241 A1). The propellant that Hercules' ABL initially used for the motor was a cast double-base formulation with insulation material between it and the case. This yielded a specific impulse of about 250 lbf-sec/lbm, higher both than Grand Central's propellant for its Vanguard third-stage motor and the specification of 245 lbf-sec/lbm for both motors. A key feature of the motor was its case and nozzle, made of laminated fiberglass. ABL had subcontracted work on the case and nozzle to Young Development Laboratories, which developed a method during 1956 of wrapping threads of fiberglass soaked in epoxy resin around a liner made of phenolic asbestos. (A phenol is a compound used in making resins to provide laminated coatings or form adhesives.) Following curing, this process yielded a strong, rigid Spiralloy (fiberglass) shell with a strength-to-weight ratio 20 percent higher than the stainless steel Aerojet was using for its propellant tanks on stage two of Vanguard.[25]

In 1958, while its third-stage motor was still under development, Hercules acquired this fiberglass-winding firm. Richard E. Young, a test pilot who had worked for the M. W. Kellogg Company on the Manhattan Project, had founded it. In 1947, Kellogg had designed a winding machine under navy contract, leading to a laboratory in New Jersey that built a fiberglass nozzle. It moved to Rocky Hill, New Jersey, in 1948. There, Young set up the development laboratories under his own name and sought to develop lighter materials for rocket motors. He and the firm evolved from nozzles to cases, seeking to improve a rocket's mass fraction (the mass of the propellant divided by the total mass of a stage or rocket), which was as important as specific impulse in achieving high velocities. In the mid-1950s, ABL succeeded in testing small rockets and missiles using cases made with Young's Spiralloy material.[26]

This combination of a cast double-base propellant and the fiberglass case and nozzle created a lot of problems for Hercules engineers. By February 1957, ABL had performed static tests on about 20 motors, 15 of which resulted in failures of insulation or joints. Combustion instability became a problem on about a third of the tests. Attempting to reduce the instability, Hercules installed a plastic paddle in the combustion zone to interrupt the acoustic patterns (resonance) that caused the problem. This did not work as well as hoped, so the engineers developed a suppressor of thicker plastic. They also improved the bond between insulator and case, then cast the propellant in the case instead of just sliding it in as a single piece. Nine cases still failed during hydrostatic tests or static firings. The culprits were high stress at joints and "severe combustion instability."[27]

In February 1958, ABL began developing a follow-on third-stage motor designated X248 A2 in addition to X241. Perhaps it did so in part to reduce combustion instability, because 3 percent of the propellant in the new motor consisted of aluminum, which burned in the motor and produced particles in the combustion gases that suppressed (damped) high-frequency instabilities. But another motivation was increased thrust. The new motor was the one that actually flew on the final Vanguard mission, September 18, 1959. As of August 1958, ABL had developed a modification of this motor, X248 A3, for use as the upper stage in a Thor-Able lunar probe. By this time, ABL was testing the motors in an altitude chamber at the air force's Arnold Engineering Development Center and was experiencing problems with ignition and with burnthroughs of the case the last few seconds of the static tests.[28]

The X248 solid-rocket motor consisted of an epoxy-fiberglass case filled with the case-bonded propellant. The nozzle was still made of epoxy fiberglass, but with a coating of "ceramo-asbestos." By November 11, 1958, wind-tunnel static tests had shown that the X248 A2 filament-wound exit cone was adequate. By this time also, the motor had a sea-level theoretical specific impulse of about 235, which extrapolated to an impulse at altitude of some 255 lbf-sec/lbm, and designers had overcome the other problems with the motor. The X248 offered a "considerable improvement in reliability and performance over the X241 contracted for originally," according to Kurt Stehling. He also said the ABL version of the third stage successfully launched the *Vanguard III* satellite weighing 50 pounds, whereas Grand Central Rocket's third stage could orbit only about 30 pounds.[29]

The Sergeant Missile Powerplant

Meanwhile, the first major application of the technologies developed for the RV-A-10 was the Sergeant missile, for which JPL began planning in 1953 under its ORDCIT contract with Army Ordnance. JPL submitted a proposal for a Sergeant missile in April 1954, and on June 11, 1954, the army's chief of ordnance programmed $100,000 for it. At the same time, he transferred control of the effort to the commanding general of Redstone Arsenal. Using lessons learned from the liquid-propellant Corporal missile, JPL proposed a co-contractor for the development and ultimate manufacture of the missile. In February 1956, a Sergeant Contractor Selection Committee unanimously chose Sperry Gyroscope Company for this role, based on JPL's recommendation and Sperry's capabilities and experience with other missiles, including the Sparrow I air-to-air missile system for the navy. In April 1954, the Redstone Arsenal had reached an agreement with the Redstone Division of Thiokol to work on the solid-propellant motor for the Sergeant, with the overall program to develop Sergeant beginning in 1955.[30]

There is no need to provide a detailed history of the Sergeant missile here. It took longer to develop than originally planned and was not operational until 1962. By then the navy had completed the far more significant Polaris A1, and the air force was close to fielding the much more important Minuteman I. The Sergeant did meet a slipped ordnance support readiness date of June 1962 and became a limited-production weapons system until June 1968. It did equal its predecessor, Corporal, in range and firepower in a package only

237

Solid
Propulsion:
JATOs to
Minuteman III,
1939–70

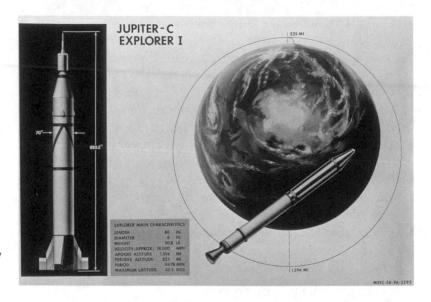

JUPITER-C
EXPLORER I

EXPLORER MAIN CHARACTERISTICS
LENGTH	80	IN.
DIAMETER	6	IN.
WEIGHT	30.8	LB
VELOCITY (APPROX.)	18,000	MPH
APOGEE ALTITUDE	1,594	MI
PERIGEE ALTITUDE	225	MI
PERIOD	114.8	MIN
MAXIMUM LATITUDE	33.3	DEG

MSFC-5B-PA-3292

half as large and requiring less than a third as much ground-support equipment. Its solid-propellant motor could also be readied for firing much more quickly than the liquid-propellant Corporal.[31]

The Sergeant motor was a modification or direct descendant of the RV-A-10's motor. The latter (using the TRX-110A propulsion formulation) employed 63 percent ammonium perchlorate as an oxidizer, whereas the TP-E8057 propellant for the Sergeant motor (designated JPL 500) had 63.3 percent of that oxidizer and 33.2 percent LP-33 liquid polymer in addition to small percentages of a curing agent, two reinforcing agents, and a curing accelerator. At a nozzle expansion ratio of 5.39, its specific impulse was about 185 lbf-sec/lbm, considerably lower than the performance of Polaris A1. It employed a five-point-star grain configuration, used a case of 4130 steel at a nominal thickness of 0.109 inch (almost half that of the RV-A-10 case), and a nozzle (like that of the RV-A-10) using 1020 steel with a graphite nozzle-throat insert.[32] Ironically, perhaps, the main contributions the Sergeant made to launch-vehicle technology were through a scaled-down version of the missile used for testing. These smaller versions became the basis for upper stages in reentry test vehicles for the Jupiter missile and in the launch vehicles for Explorer and Pioneer satellites.[33]

Polaris Propulsion

Meanwhile, the navy's Polaris missile had made more far-reaching contributions. Until Polaris A1 became operational in 1960, all U.S.

long-range missiles had used liquid propellants. These had obvious advantages in their performance, but their extensive plumbing and large propellant tanks made protecting them in silos difficult and costly. Such factors also made them impractical for use on ships. After the operational date of Minuteman I in 1962, the Department of Defense began phasing out liquid-propellant strategic missiles.[34]

Meanwhile, given the advantages that liquid propellants enjoyed in terms of performance, their head start within the defense establishment, and the disinclination of most defenders of liquids to entertain the possibility that solid propellants could satisfy the demanding requirements of the strategic mission, how did this solid-propellant breakthrough occur? The answer is complicated and technical. But fundamentally, it happened because a number of heterogeneous engineers promoted solids; a variety of partners in their development brought about significant technical innovations; and although interservice rivalries encouraged the three services to development separate missiles, interservice cooperation ironically helped them do so. Despite such cooperation and the accumulating knowledge about rocket technology, however, missile designers still could not foresee all the problems that their vehicles would develop during ground and flight testing. Thus, when problems did occur, rocket engineers still had to gather information about what had caused problems and exercise their ingenuity to develop solutions that would cope with the unexpected.

By the time that Polaris got under way in 1956 and Minuteman in 1958, solid-propellant rocketry had already made the tremendous strides forward discussed previously. But there were still enormous technical hurdles to overcome. The problems remaining to be solved included higher performance; unstable combustion; the inadequate durability of existing nozzle materials under conditions of heat and exposure to corrosive chemicals from the exhaust of the burning propellants; a lack of materials and technology to provide light but large combustion chambers so the burning propellants had to overcome less mass during launch; and ways to terminate combustion of the propellant immediately after the desired velocity had been achieved (for purposes of accuracy) and to control the direction of the thrust (for steering).[35]

Once the navy had overcome the bureaucratic obstacles to developing its own, solid-propellant missile, the Special Project Office (SPO) under Adm. William F. Raborn and Capt. Levering Smith achieved breakthroughs in a number of these technical areas. In early January 1956, the navy had sought the assistance of the Lockheed Missile and Space Division and the Aerojet General Corporation in developing a solid-propellant ballistic missile. The initial missile the two contractors and the SPO conceived was the Jupiter S (for "solid"). It had enough thrust to carry an atomic warhead the required distance, a feat it would achieve by clustering six solid rockets in a first stage and adding one for the second stage. The problem was that Jupiter S would be about 44 feet long and 10 feet in diameter. An 8,500-ton vessel could carry only 4 of them but could carry 16 of the later Polaris missiles. With Polaris not yet developed, the navy and contractors still were dissatisfied with Jupiter S and continued to seek an alternative.[36]

One contribution to a better solution came from Atlantic Research Corporation (ARC). Keith Rumbel and Charles B. Henderson, chemical engineers with degrees from MIT who were working for ARC, had begun theoretical studies in 1954 of how to increase solid-propellant performance. They learned that other engineers, including some from Aerojet, had calculated an increase in specific impulse from adding aluminum powder to existing ingredients. But these calculations had indicated that once aluminum exceeded 5 percent of propellant mass, performance would again decline. Hence, basing their calculations on contemporary theory and doing the cumbersome mathematics without the aid of computers, the other researchers abandoned aluminum as an additive except for damping combustion instability. Refusing to be deterred by theory, Rumbel and Henderson tested polyvinyl chloride with much more aluminum in it. They found that with additional oxygen in the propellant and a flame temperature of at least 2,310 kelvin, a large percentage of aluminum by weight yielded a specific impulse significantly higher than that of previous composite propellants.[37]

ARC's polyvinyl chloride, however, did not serve as the binder for Polaris. Instead, the binder used was a polyurethane material developed by Aerojet in conjunction with a small nitropolymer program funded by the Office of Naval Research about 1947 to seek high-energy binders for solid propellants. A few Aerojet chemists synthesized a number of high-energy compounds, but the process required levels of heating that were unsafe with potentially explosive compounds. Then one of the chemists, Rodney Fischer, found "an obscure reference in a German patent" suggesting "that iron chelate compounds would catalyze the reaction of alcohols and isocyanates to make urethanes at essentially room temperature." This discovery started the development of polyurethane propellants in many places besides Aerojet.

In the meantime, in 1949 Karl Klager, then working for the Office of Naval Research in Pasadena, suggested to Aerojet's parent firm, General Tire, that it begin work on foamed polyurethane, leading to two patents held by Klager, along with Dick Geckler and R. Parette of Aerojet. In 1950, Klager began working for Aerojet. By 1954, he headed the rocket firm's solid-propellant development group. Once the Polaris program began in December 1956, Klager's group decided to reduce the percentage of solid oxidizer as a component of the propellant by including oxidizing capacity in the binder, using a nitromonomer as a reagent to produce the polyurethane plus some inert polynitro compounds as softening agents. In April 1955, the Aerojet group found out about the work of Rumbel and Henderson. Overcoming explosions due to cracks in the grain and profiting from other developments from multiple contributors, they discovered successful propellants for both stages of Polaris A1.

These consisted of a cast, case-bonded polyurethane composition including different percentages of ammonium perchlorate and aluminum for stages one and two, both of them featuring a six-point, internal-burning, star configuration. With four nozzles for each stage, this propellant yielded a specific impulse of almost 230 lbf-sec/lbm for stage one and nearly 255 lbf-sec/lbm for stage two. The latter specific impulse was higher in part because of the reduced atmospheric pressure at the high altitudes where it was fired, compared with stage one, which was fired at sea level.[38]

241

*Solid
Propulsion:
JATOs to
Minuteman III,
1939–70*

The addition of aluminum to Aerojet's binder essentially solved the problem of performance for Polaris. Other innovations in the areas of warhead size plus guidance and control were necessary to make Polaris possible, but taken together with those for the propellants, they enabled Polaris A1 to be only 28.6 feet long and 4.5 feet in diameter (as compared with Jupiter S's 44 feet and 10 feet, respectively). The weight reduction was from 162,000 pounds for Jupiter S to less than 29,000 pounds for Polaris. The cases for both stages of Polaris A1 consisted of rolled and welded steel. This had been modified according to Aerojet specifications resulting from extensive metallurgical investigations.

Each of the four nozzles for stage one (and evidently, stage two as well) consisted of a steel shell, a single-piece throat of molybdenum, and an exit-cone liner made of "molded silica phenolic between steel and molybdenum." A zirconium oxide coating protected the steel portion. The missile's steering came from jetavators designed by Willy Fiedler of Lockheed, a German who had worked on the V-1 program during World War II and had developed the concept for the device while employed by the U.S. Navy at Point Mugu Naval Air Missile Test Center, California. He had patented the idea and then adapted it for Polaris. Jetavators for stage one were molybdenum

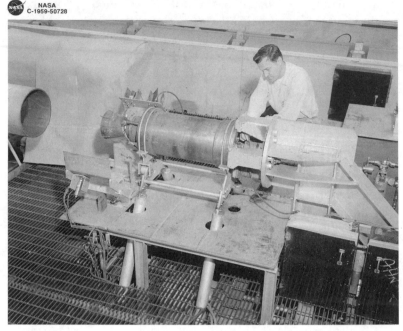

rings with spherical inside surfaces that rotated into the exhaust stream of the four nozzles and deflected the flow to provide pitch, yaw, and roll control. The jetavators for stage two were similar.[39]

Besides requiring steering, the missile needed precise thrust termination when it reached the correct point in its trajectory. This could be achieved on liquid-propellant missiles simply by stopping the flow of propellants. For solids, the task was more difficult. The Polaris team used pyrotechnics to blow out plugs in six ports in front of the second stage at the proper moment in the trajectory. This permitted exhaust gases to escape and halt the acceleration so that the warhead would travel on a ballistic path to the target area.[40]

Flight testing of Polaris revealed, among other problems, a loss of control due to electrical-wiring failure at the base of stage one. This resulted from aerodynamic heating and a backflow of hot exhaust gases. To diagnose and solve the problem, engineers in the program obtained the help of "every laboratory and expert," using data from four flights, wind tunnels, sled tests, static firings, "and a tremendous analytic effort by numerous laboratories." The solution placed fiberglass flame shielding supplemented by silicone rubber over the affected area to shield it from hot gases and flame.[41]

Another problem for Polaris to overcome was combustion instability. Although this phenomenon is still not fully understood, gradually it has yielded to research in a huge number of institutions, including universities and government labs, supported by funding by the three services, the Advanced Research Projects Agency, and NASA. Levering Smith credited Edward W. Price in the Research Department at NOTS with helping to understand the phenomenon. By this time, Price had earned a B.S. in physics and math at UCLA. In February 1960, he completed a major (then-classified) paper on combustion instability, which stated, "This phenomenon results from a self-amplifying oscillatory interaction between combustion of the propellant and disturbances of the gas flow in the combustion chamber." It could cause erratic performance, even destruction of motor components. Short of this, it could produce vibrations that would interfere with the guidance/control system. To date, "only marginal success" had been achieved in understanding the phenomenon, and "trial-and-error development continues to be necessary." But empirical methods gradually were yielding information, for example, that energy fluxes could amplify pressure disturbances, which had caused them in the first place.[42] The subsequent success of Polaris showed that enough progress had been made by this time that unstable combustion would not be a major problem for the missile.

243
Solid
Propulsion:
JATOs to
Minuteman III,
1939–70

Long before Polaris A1 was operational, in April 1958 the DoD had begun efforts to expand the missile's range from the 1,200-nautical-mile reach of the actual A1 to the 1,500 nautical miles originally planned for it. The longer-range missile, called Polaris A2, was originally slated to achieve the goal through higher-performance propellants and lighter cases and nozzles in both stages. But the navy Special Projects Office decided to confine these improvements to the second stage, where they would have greater effect. (With the second stage already at a high speed and altitude when it began firing, it did not have to overcome the weight of the entire missile and the full effects of the Earth's gravity at sea level.) Also, in the second stage, risk of detonation of a high-energy propellant after ignition would not endanger the submarine. Hence, the SPO invited the Hercules Powder Company to propose a higher-performance second stage.[43]

As a result, Aerojet provided the first stage for Polaris A2, and Hercules, the second. Aerojet's motor was 157 inches long (compared with 126 inches for Polaris A1; the additional length could be accommodated by the submarines' launch tubes because the navy had them designed with room to spare). It contained basically the same propellant used in both stages of Polaris A1 with the same grain configuration. Hercules' second stage had a filament-wound case and a cast, double-base grain that contained ammonium perchlorate, nitrocellulose, nitroglycerin, and aluminum, among other ingredients. The grain configuration consisted of a 12-point, internal-burning star. It yielded a specific impulse of more than 260 lbf-sec/lbm under firing conditions. The motor was 84 inches long and 54 inches in diameter, featuring four swiveling nozzles with exit cones made of steel, asbestos phenolic, and Teflon plus a graphite insert.[44]

This second stage motor resulted from an innovation that increased performance by adding ammonium perchlorate to the cast, double-base process used in Hercules' third stage for the Vanguard launch vehicle. Hercules' ABL developed this new kind of propellant, known as composite-modified double base (CMDB), by 1958, evidently with the involvement of John Kincaid and Henry Shuey, developers of the earlier cast, double-base process.[45]

Even before 1958, however, Atlantic Research Corporation had developed a laboratory process for preparing CMDB. In its manufactured state, nitrocellulose is fibrous and unsuitable for use as an unmodified additive to other ingredients being mixed to create a propellant. Arthur Sloan and D. Mann of ARC, however, developed a process that dissolved the nitrocellulose in nitrobenzene and then separated out the nitrocellulose by mixing it with water under high shear (a process known as elutriation). The result was a series of compact, spherical particles of nitrocellulose with small diameters (about 1 to 20 microns). Such particles combined readily with liquid nitroplasticizers and crystalline additives in propellant mixers. The result could be cast into cartridge-loaded grains or case-bonded rocket cases and then converted to a solid with the application of moderate heat. Sloan and Mann patented the process and assigned it to ARC. Then, in 1955, Keith Rumbel and Charles Henderson at ARC began scaling the process up to larger grain sizes and developing propellants. They developed two CMDB formulations beginning in 1956. When ARC's pilot plant became too small to support the firm's needs, production shifted to Indian Head, Maryland. Because the plastisol process they had developed was simpler, safer, and cheaper than other processes then in existence, Henderson said that Hercules and other producers of double-base propellants eventually adopted his firm's basic method of production.

Engineers did not use it for upper stages of missiles and launch vehicles until quite a bit later, however, and then only after chemists at several different laboratories had learned to make the propellant more rubberlike by extending the chains and cross-linking the molecules to increase the elasticity. Hercules' John Allabashi at ABL began in the early 1960s to work on chain extenders and cross-linking, with Ronald L. Simmons at Hercules' Kenvil, New Jersey, plant continuing this work. By about the late 1960s, chemists had mostly abandoned use of plastisol nitrocellulose in favor of dissolving nitrocellulose and polyglycol adipate together, followed by a cross-linking agent such as isocyanate. The result was the type of highly flexible CMDB propellant used on the Trident submarine-launched ballistics missiles beginning in the late 1970s.[46]

Meanwhile, the rotatable nozzles on the second stage of Polaris A2, which were hydraulically operated, were similar in design to those already being used on the air force's Minuteman I, and award of the second-stage contract to Hercules reportedly resulted from the performance of the third-stage motor Hercules was developing for Minuteman I, once again illustrating technology transfer between services. (Stage one of the A2 retained the jetavators from A1.) The A2 kept the same basic shape and guidance/control system as the A1, the principal change being more reliable electronics for the guidance/control system. By the time Polaris A2 became operational in June 1962, now–Vice Admiral Raborn had become deputy chief of naval operations for research and development. In February 1962, Rear Adm. I. J. "Pete" Gallantin became director of the Special Projects Office with Rear Adm. Levering Smith remaining as technical director.[47]

As a follow-on to Polaris A2, in September 1960, Secretary of Defense Robert McNamara approved development of a 2,500-nautical-mile version of Polaris that became the A3. To create a missile that would travel an additional 1,000 nautical miles while being launched from the same tubes on the submarine as the A1 required new propellants and a higher mass fraction. The new requirement also resulted in a change from the "bottle shape" of the A1 and A2 to a shape resembling a bullet. In the attempt to help increase the mass fraction, Aerojet, the first-stage manufacturer, acquired the Houze Glass Corporation at Point Marion, Pennsylvania, and moved that firm's furnaces, patents, technical data, and personnel to the Aerojet Structural Materials Division in Azusa, California, in early 1963. This acquisition gave Aerojet the capability to make filament-wound cases like those used by Hercules on stage two of Polaris A2. The new propellant Aerojet used was a nitroplasticized polyurethane containing ammonium perchlorate and aluminum, configured with an internal-burning, six-point star. This combination raised the specific impulse less than 10 lbf-sec/lbm.[48]

Unfortunately, the flame temperature of the new propellant was so high that it destroyed the nozzles on the first stage. Aerojet had to reduce the flame temperature from a reported 6,300°F to slightly less than 6,000°F and to make the nozzles more substantial, using silver-infiltrated tungsten throat inserts to withstand the high temperature and chamber pressure. As a result, the weight saving from using the filament-wound case was lost in the additional weight of the nozzle. Hence, the mass fraction for the A3's first stage was actually slightly lower than that for the A2, meaning that the same quantity of propellant in stage one of the A3 had to lift slightly more weight than did the lower-performing propellant for stage one of the A2.[49]

For stage two of the A3, Hercules used a propellant containing an energetic high explosive named HMX, a smaller amount of ammonium perchlorate, nitrocellulose, nitroglycerin, and aluminum, among other ingredients. It configured this propellant into an internal-burning cylindrical configuration with many major and minor slots in the aft end of the stage, creating a cross section that resembled a Christmas-tree ornament. This propellant offered a significantly higher specific impulse than stage two of Polaris A2. Also, the new stage two used a different method of achieving thrust vector control (steering). It injected Freon into the exhaust, creating a shock pattern to deflect the stream and achieve the same results as movable nozzles at a much smaller weight penalty.

A further advantage of this system was its lack of sensitivity to the temperature of the propellant flame. The Naval Ordnance Test Station performed the early experimental work on this use of a liquid for thrust vector control. Aerojet, Allegany Ballistics Laboratory, and Lockheed did analytical work, determined the ideal locations for the injectors, selected the fluid to be used, and developed the injectors as well as a system for expelling excess fluid. The Polaris A3 team first successfully tested the new technology on the second stage of flight A1X-50 on September 29, 1961. This and other changes increased the mass fraction for stage two of Polaris A3 to 0.935 (from 0.871 for stage two of the A2), a major improvement that together with the increased performance of the new propellant, contributed substantially to the greater range of the new missile.[50]

Minuteman Propulsion

Development of the propellant for Minuteman began at Wright-Patterson AFB and continued after Lt. Col. Edward N. Hall transferred to the Western Development Division as chief for propulsion development in the liquid-propellant Atlas, Titan, and Thor programs. In December 1954, he invited major manufacturers in the solid-propellant industry (Aerojet, Thiokol, Atlantic Research, Phillips Petroleum Company, Grand Central, and Hercules) to discuss prospects for solids. The result apparently was the Air Force Large [Solid] Rocket Feasibility Program (AFLRP), which involved a competition starting in September 1955 with specific companies looking at different technologies. It appears that the propellant for Polaris benefited from Aerojet's participation in this air force program.[51]

MINUTEMAN I

Despite this preparatory work for Minuteman, the missile did not begin formal development until the air force secured final DoD approval in February 1958. Meanwhile, civilian engineers employed by the air force at the Non-Rotating Engine Branch at Wright-Patterson AFB had continued efforts to develop large, solid-propellant motors. Perhaps from sources at Aerojet, they learned about adding large quantities of aluminum to a solid propellant to increase its performance. They combined this with other information they had been gathering on solid propellants while Hall was still with the branch. Bill Fagan from the branch carried this information to Hall at the Ballistic Missile Division (as the WDD had become).[52]

247

Solid
Propulsion:
JATOs to
Minuteman III,
1939–70

The specifics of Minuteman technology continued to evolve, but its basic concept took advantage of the reduced complexity of solids over liquids. This cut the number of people needed to launch it. Each missile could be remotely launched from a control center using communications cables, without a crew of missileers in attendance. The air force initially considered using mobile Minutemen but ultimately decided to launch them from silos. Because solids were more compact than liquids, Minuteman IA (by one account) was only 53.8 feet long to Atlas's 82.5, Titan I's 98, and Titan II's 108 feet in length. Its diameter was slightly over half that of the other three missiles (5.5 feet to the others' 10), and its weight was only 65,000 pounds to Atlas's 267,136, Titan I's 220,000, and Titan II's 330,000 pounds. All of this made the costs of silos much lower and substantially reduced the thrust needed to launch the missile. Consequently, the initial costs of Minuteman were a fifth and the annual maintenance costs a tenth those of Titan I. Moreover, a crew of *two* could launch *10* Minutemen, whereas it took *six* people to launch *each* Titan I—a 30-fold advantage in favor of Minuteman.[53]

Minuteman development used multiple approaches to arrive at individual technologies, as had been true with Atlas. Ballistic Missile Division (BMD) contracted separately with Aerojet and Thiokol to work on all three stages of the missile. A later contract with Hercules assigned it to work on the third stage, too. As firms developed technologies, parallel development gave way to specific responsibilities, with Thiokol building the first stage, Aerojet the second, and Hercules the third. Space Technology Laboratories retained its role in systems engineering and technical direction at BMD. These and other companies and organizations all sent representatives to frequent program-review meetings and quarterly gatherings of top officials. They examined progress and identified problems requiring solution. Then, the relevant organizations found solutions to keep the program on track.[54]

One major technical challenge involved materials for the nozzle throats and exit cones. The addition of aluminum to the propellant provided a high enough specific impulse to make Minuteman feasible, as it had done for Polaris, and its combustion produced aluminum oxide particles that damped instabilities in the combustion chamber. But the hot product flow degraded the nozzle throats and other exposed structures. It seemed that it might not be possible to design a vectorable nozzle that would last the 60 seconds needed for the missile to reach its ballistic trajectory so it could arrive accurately on target. Solving this problem required "many months and many dollars . . . spent in a frustrating cycle of design, test, failure, redesign, retest, and failure." The Minuteman team used many different grades and exotic compounds of graphite, which seemed the most capable material, but all of them experienced blowouts or performance-degrading erosion. One solution was a tungsten throat insert, a compromise in view of its high weight and cost. For the exit cones, the team tried Fiberite molded at high pressure and loaded with silica and graphite cloth. It provided better resistance to erosion than graphite but still experienced random failures.[55]

Another significant problem concerned the vectorable feature of the nozzles. Polaris had solved its steering problem with jetavators, but flight-control studies for Minuteman showed a need for the stage-one nozzles to vector the thrust eight degrees, more than Minuteman engineers thought jetavators could deliver. Thiokol's test of the motor in 1959—the largest solid-propellant powerplant yet built—resulted in the ejection of all four nozzles after 30 milliseconds of firing, well before the full stage had ignited. Five successive explosions of the motors and their test stands occurred in October 1959, each having a different failure mode. BMD halted first-stage testing in January 1960. Discussion among BMD, STL, and Thiokol personnel revealed two problem areas, internal insulation and the nozzles themselves, as masking other potential problems.

There followed two concurrent programs of testing. Firings with battleship-steel cases tested movable nozzles, while participants used flight-weight cases to test a single, fixed nozzle massive enough to sustain a full-duration firing. Thiokol solved the problem with insulation by summer but did not resolve the nozzle issue until fall. This was close to the date set for all-up testing of the entire missile. However, General Phillips had ordered Thiokol to begin manufacturing the first stage except the nozzles, permitting installation of the nozzles as soon as their problem was solved.[56]

Among many other difficulties, a major concern was launching from a silo. The first successful launch of the missile occurred in early February 1961, which Phillips referred to as "December 63rd" since the planned date had been in December 1960. It and two succeeding launches took place from a surface pad and were so successful that the team advanced the first silo launch to August 1961. The missile blew up in the silo, giving credence to critics in STL who had argued that firing a missile from a silo was impossible. As Phillips said, the missile "really came out of there like a Roman candle."[57]

Fortunately, team members recovered enough of the guidance system from the wreckage to find that the problem was not the silo launch itself but quality control. Solder tabs containing connections had vibrated together, causing all of the stages to ignite simultaneously. Knowing this, the team was able to prepare the fifth missile for flight with the problem solved by mid-November, when it had a successful flight from the silo. Previous testing of silo launches aided this quick recovery. In early 1958, BMD and STL engineers had arranged for development of underground silos. They divided the effort into three phases, with the first two using only subscale models of Minuteman. The third tested full-scale models. Most testing occurred at the air force's rocket site on Edwards AFB in the remote Mojave Desert, but Boeing (contractor for missile assembly and test) tested subscale models in Seattle.

At the rocket site on Leuhman Ridge at Edwards, subscale silos investigated heat transfer and turbulence in some 56 tests by November 1958. Meanwhile, Boeing modeled the pressures that the rocket's exhaust gases imparted to the missile and silo. It also examined acoustic effects of the noise levels generated by the rocket motor in the silo on delicate systems such as guidance. Armed with such data, engineers at Edwards began one-third–scale tests in February 1959. Full-scale tests initially used a mock-up made of steel plate with ballast to match the weight and shape of the actual missile and only enough propellant (in the first-stage motor) to provide about three seconds of full thrust—enough to move the missile, on a tether, out of the silo and to check the effects of the thrust on the silo and missile. They configured the tether so that the missile

249

Solid
Propulsion:
JATOs to
Minuteman III,
1939–70

would not drop back on the silo and damage it. These tests ensured that the second silo launch at Cape Canaveral on November 17, 1961, was fully successful.[58]

The all-up testing on Minuteman was itself a significant innovation later used on other programs, including the Saturn launch vehicle for the Apollo program. It differed from the usual practice for liquid-propellant missiles—gradually testing a missile's different capabilities over a series of ranges and tests (for first-stage or booster propulsion, for second-stage or sustainer-engine propulsion, for guidance/control, and so forth). For the first time, it tested all of the missile's functions at once over the full operational range. Although the practice accorded well with general procedures at BMD, such as concurrency, its use came about in an odd way. According to Otto Glasser, he was briefing Secretary of the Air Force James H. Douglas on Minuteman, with Gen. Curtis LeMay, vice chief of staff of the air force, sitting next to Douglas. Douglas insisted Glasser had moved the first flight of the missile to a year later than the original schedule. Glasser protested (to no avail) that this was not the case, and the only way he could conceive to cut a year out of the development process was all-up testing. "Boy, the Ramo-Wooldridge crowd came right out of the chair on that," Glasser said. They protested "a test program . . . with that sort of lack of attention to all normal, sensible standards." But all-up testing "worked all the way."[59]

Overcoming these and other problems, BMD delivered the first Minuteman I to the Strategic Air Command in October 1962, almost exactly four years after the first contracts had been signed with contractors to begin the missile's development. This was a year earlier than initially planned because of the speeded-up schedule. The missile in question was the A model of Minuteman I, later to be succeeded by a B model. The former was 53.7 feet long and consisted of three stages plus the reentry vehicle. Thiokol's first stage included a new propellant binder developed by the company's chemists from 1952 to 1954. Thiokol first tried a binder called polybutadiene–acrylic acid, or PBAA, an elastomeric (rubberlike) copolymer of butadiene and acrylic acid that allowed higher concentrations of solid ingredients and greater fuel content than previous propellants. It had a higher hydrogen content than earlier Thiokol polysulfide polymers. With PBAA, a favorable reaction of oxygen with the aluminum generated significant amounts of hydrogen in the exhaust gases, reducing the average molecular weights of the combustion products (since hydrogen is the lightest of elements). This added to the performance, with Minuteman being the first rocket to use the new binder.[60]

But testing showed PBAA had a lower tear strength than poly-sulfide, so Thiokol added 10 percent acrylonitrile, creating poly-butadiene–acrylic acid–acrylonitrile (PBAN). The binder and curing agent constituted only 14 percent of the propellant, with ammonium perchlorate (oxidizer) and aluminum (fuel) the two other major in-gredients. The combination yielded a theoretical specific impulse of more than 260 lb-sec/lb, with the actual specific impulse at sea level at 70°F somewhat lower than 230.[61]

For stage two of Minuteman I, Aerojet used the polyurethane binder employed in Polaris, with ammonium perchlorate as the oxidizer and aluminum powder the major fuel. It used two slightly different propellant grains, with a faster-burning inner grain and a slower-burning outer one. The combination resulted in a conversion of the four-point, star-shaped, internal-burning cavity to a cylindri-cal one as the propellant burned, avoiding slivers of propellant that did not burn. The propellant yielded a vacuum specific impulse of nearly 275 lbf-sec/lbm at temperatures ranging from 60°F to 80°F.[62]

251

Solid
Propulsion:
JATOs to
Minuteman III,
1939–70

For stage three, the Hercules Powder Company used a glass-filament–wound case instead of the steel employed on stages one and two, plus a very different propellant than for the first two stages. The third stage featured four phenolic-coated aluminum tubes for thrust termination and a grain consisting of two separate composi-tions. The one used for the largest percentage of the grain included the high-explosive HMX, combined with ammonium perchlorate, nitroglycerin, nitrocellulose, aluminum, a plasticizer, and a stabi-lizer. The second composition had the same basic ingredients mi-nus the HMX and formed a horizontal segment at the front of the motor. A hollow core ran from the back of the motor almost to the segment containing the non-HMX composition. It was roughly cone shaped before tapering off to a cylinder. This motor yielded a specific impulse of more than 275 lbf-sec/lbm at temperatures ranging from 60°F to 80°F. The four nozzles for stage three of Min-uteman I rotated in pairs up to four degrees in one plane to provide pitch, yaw, and roll control.[63] Minuteman I, Wing I became opera-tional at Malmstrom AFB, Montana, in October 1962.[64]

It would be tedious to follow the evolution of Minuteman through all the improvements in its later versions, but some discussion of the major changes is appropriate. Wings II through V of Minuteman I (each located at a different base) featured several changes to increase the missile's range. This had been shorter than initially planned be-cause of the acceleration of the Minuteman I schedule. The shorter range was not a problem at Malmstrom because it was so far north (hence closer to the Soviet Union), but range became a problem starting with Wing II. Consequently, for it and subsequent missiles, more propellant was added to the aft dome of stage one, and the exit cone included contouring that made the nozzle more efficient. In stage two, the material for the motor case was changed from steel to titanium. Titanium is considerably lighter than steel but more expensive. Since each pound of reduced weight yielded an extra mile of range, use of titanium seemed worth the extra cost. The nozzles also were lighter. Overall, the reduction in weight totaled slightly less than 300 pounds despite an increase in propellant weight. The increase in propellant mass plus the decrease in weight yielded a range increase of 315 miles to a figure usually given as 6,300 nautical miles. There were no significant changes to stage three.[65]

MINUTEMAN II

For Minuteman II, the major improvements occurred in Aerojet's stage two. There had been problems with cracking and ejection of graphite from the nozzles and aft closure of stage one. An air force reliability improvement program solved these difficulties. There had also been problems with insulation burning through in the aft dome area of stage three. Unspecified design changes inhibited the flow of hot gases in that region. Stage two, however, featured an entirely new rocket motor with a new propellant, a slightly greater length, a substantially larger diameter, and a single fixed nozzle that used a liquid-injection thrust-vector-control system for directional control.[66]

The new propellant was carboxy-terminated polybutadiene (CTPB), which propellant companies other than Aerojet had developed. Some accounts attribute its development to Thiokol, which first made the propellant in the late 1950s and converted it into a useful propellant in the early 1960s. Initially, Thiokol chemists used an imine known as MAPO and an epoxide in curing the CTPB. It turned out that the phosphorous-nitrogen bond in the imine was susceptible to hydrolysis, causing degradation and softening of the propellant. According to Thiokol historian E. S. Sutton, "The post-curing problem was finally solved by the discovery that a small amount of chromium octoate (0.02%) could be used to catalyze the epoxide-carboxyl reaction and eliminate this change in properties with time." A history of Atlantic Research Corporation agrees that Thiokol produced the CTPB but attributes the solution of the curing problem to ARC, which is not incompatible with Sutton's account. According to the ARC history, "ARC used a complex chromium compound, which would accelerate the polymer/epoxy reaction, paving the way for an all epoxy cure system for CTPB polymer." The result was "an extremely stable binder system."[67]

It frequently happens in the history of technology that innovations occur to different people at about the same time. This appears to have been the case with CTPB, which Aerojet historians attribute to Phillips Petroleum and Rocketdyne without providing details. These two companies may have been the source for information about the CTPB that Aerojet used in Minuteman II, stage two. Like Thiokol, in any event, Aerojet proposed to use MAPO as a cross-linking agent. TRW historians state that their firm's laboratory investigations revealed the hydrolysis problem. They state that "working with Aerojet's research and development staff," they developed "a formulation that eliminated MAPO. . . ." The CTPB that resulted from what apparently was a multicompany development effort had better fuel values than previous propellants, good mechanical properties such as the long shelf life required for silo-based missiles, and a higher solids content than previous binders. The propellant consisted primarily of CTPB, ammonium perchlorate, and aluminum. It yielded a vacuum specific impulse more than 15 lbf-sec/lbm higher than the propellant used in stage two of Minuteman I, Wing II.[68]

Although CTPB marked a significant step forward in binder technology, it was not as widely used as it might have been because of its higher cost compared with PBAN. Another factor was the emergence in the late 1960s of an even better polymer with lower viscosity and lower cost, hydroxy-terminated polybutadiene (HTPB). It became the industry standard for newer tactical rockets. HTPB had many uses as an adhesive, sealant, and coating, but to employ it in a propellant required, among other things, the development of suitable bonding agents. These tightly linked the polymer to such solid ingredients as ammonium perchlorate and aluminum. Without such links, the propellant could not withstand the temperature cycling, ignition pressure, and other forces that could cause the solid particles to separate from the binder network. This would produce voids in the grain that could result in cracks and structural failure.

A key figure in the development of HTPB for use as a binder was Robert C. Corley, who served as a research chemist and project manager at the Air Force Rocket Propulsion Laboratory at Edwards AFB from 1966 to 1978 and rose through other positions to become the lab's chief scientist from 1991 to 1997. But many other people from Thiokol, Aerojet, the army at Redstone Arsenal, Atlantic Research, Hercules, and the navy were also involved. Even HTPB did

253
Solid
Propulsion:
JATOs to
Minuteman III,
1939–70

not replace PBAN for all uses, including the Titan III, Titan IVA, and Space Shuttle solid-rocket motors, because PBAN could be produced for the comparatively low cost of $2.50 per pound at a rate in the 1980s of 4 million pounds per year, much higher than for any other propellant.[69]

To return to Minuteman II, however, the second major change in the stage-two motor was the shift to a single nozzle with liquid thrust vector control replacing movable nozzles for control in pitch and yaw. Static firings had shown that the same propellants produced seven to eight points less specific impulse when fired from four nozzles than from a single one. With the four nozzles, liquid particles agglomerated in their approach sections and produced exit-cone erosion, changing the configuration of the exit cone in an unfavorable way. The solution was not only a single nozzle on Minuteman II's second stage but also the change in thrust vector control. The navy had begun testing a Freon system for thrust vector control in the second stage of Polaris A3 in September 1961, well before the Minuteman II, stage-two program began in February 1962. The system was low in weight, was insensitive to propellant flame temperature, and posed negligible constraints on the design of the nozzle. The Minuteman engineers adopted it—but one more example of borrowings back and forth between the Polaris and Minuteman projects despite the air force's view of Polaris as a threat to its roles and missions.

Despite this pioneering work by the navy and its contractors, according to TRW historians, their firm still had to determine how much "vector capability" stage two of Minuteman II would require. TRW analyzed the amount of injectant that could be used before sloshing in the tank permitted the ingestion of air, and it determined the system performance requirements. Since Aerojet was involved in the development of the system for Polaris, probably its participation in this process was also important. In any event, the Minuteman team, like the navy, used Freon as the injectant, confining it in a rubber bladder inside a metal pressure vessel. Both TRW and Aerojet studied the propensity of the Freon to "migrate" through the bladder wall and become unavailable for its intended purpose. They found that only 25 of 262 pounds of Freon would escape, leaving enough to provide the necessary control in pitch and yaw. A separate solid-propellant gas generator provided roll control. In addition to these changes, stage two of Minuteman II increased in length from 159.2 inches for Minuteman I to 162.32 inches. The diameter increased from 44.3 to 52.17 inches, resulting in an overall weight increase from 11,558.9 to 15,506 pounds. Some 3,382.2 of this additional 3,947.1 pounds consisted of propellant weight. Even so, the propellant mass fraction decreased slightly from 0.897 to 0.887.[70]

The Strategic Air Command put the first Minuteman II squadron on operational alert in May 1966, with initial operational capability declared as of December 1966. In the next few years, the air force began replacing Minuteman Is with Minuteman IIs.[71]

MINUTEMAN III

Minuteman III featured multiple, independently targetable reentry vehicles with a liquid fourth stage for deployment of this payload. This last feature was not particularly relevant to launch-vehicle development except that the added weight required for it necessitated higher booster performance. Stages one and two did not change from Minuteman II, but stage three became larger. Hercules lost the contract for the larger motor to Aerojet. Subsequently, Thiokol and a new organization, the Chemical Systems Division of United Technologies Corporation, won contracts to build replacement motors. Stage three featured a fiberglass motor case, the same basic propellant Aerojet had used in stage two only in slightly different proportions, a single nozzle that was fixed in place and partially submerged into the case, a liquid-injection thrust-vector-control system for control in pitch and yaw, a separate roll-control system, and a thrust-termination system.

Aerojet had moved its filament-wound case production to Sacramento. It produced most of the Minuteman fiberglass combustion chambers there but ceased winding filament in 1965. Meanwhile, Young had licensed his Spiralloy technology to Black, Sivalls, and Bryson in Oklahoma City, which became a second source for the Minuteman third-stage motor case. This instance and the three firms involved in producing the third stage illustrate the extent to which technology transferred among the contractors and subcontractors for government missiles and rockets.

The issue of technology transfer among competing contractors and the armed services, which were also competing over funds and missions, is a complex one about which a whole chapter—even a book—could be written. To address the subject briefly, there had been a degree of effort to exchange knowledge about rocket propulsion technology beginning in 1946 when the navy provided funding for a Rocket Propellant Information Agency (RPIA) within the Johns Hopkins University's Applied Physics Laboratory. The army added support in 1948, and the RPIA became the Solid Propellant Information Agency (SPIA). The air force joined the other services in 1951. After the *Sputnik* launch, the newly created NASA began participating in SPIA activities in 1959. Meanwhile, the navy created the Liquid Propellant Information Agency (LIPA) in 1958. The SPIA and LPIA combined on December 1, 1962, to create the Chemical Propulsion Information Agency (CPIA).

With the further development of rockets and missiles, the need had become obvious by 1962 for a better exchange of information. So the DoD created an Interagency Chemical Rocket Propulsion Group in November 1962, the name later changing to the Joint Army/Navy/NASA/Air Force (JANNAF) Interagency Propulsion Committee. Together with CPIA, JANNAF effectively promoted sharing of technology. In addition, "joint-venture" contracts, pioneered by Levering Smith of the navy, often mandated the sharing of manufacturing technology among companies. These contracts served to eliminate the services' dependence for a given technology on sole sources that could be destroyed by fire or possible enemy targeting. It also provided for competitive bidding on future contracts. The air force had a similar policy.[72]

Meanwhile, the propellant for Aerojet's third stage of Minuteman had less CTPB and more aluminum than the second stage. The grain configuration consisted of an internal-burning cylindrical bore with six "fins" radiating out in the forward end. The igniter used black-powder squibs to start some of the CTPB propellant, which in turn spread the burning to the grain itself. The 50 percent submerged nozzle had a graphite phenolic entrance section, a forged tungsten throat insert, and a carbon-phenolic exit cone. As compared with the 85.25-inch-long, 37.88-inch-diameter third stage of Minuteman II, that for Minuteman III was 91.4 inches long and 52 inches in diameter. The mass fraction improved from 0.864 to 0.910, and with a nearly 10-lbf-sec/lbm greater specific impulse, the new third stage had more than twice the total impulse of its predecessor—2,074,774 as compared with 1,006,000 pounds force per second.[73]

The thrust-vector-control system for the new stage three was similar to that for stage two except that strontium perchlorate was used instead of Freon as the injectant into the thrust stream to provide control in the pitch and yaw axes. Helium gas provided the pressure to insert the strontium perchlorate instead of the solid-propellant gas generator used in the second stage. Roll control again came from a gas generator supplying gas to nozzles pointing in opposite directions. When both were operating, there was neutral torque in the roll axis. When roll torque was required, the flight-control system closed a flapper on one of the nozzles, providing unbalanced thrust to stop any incipient roll.

To ensure accuracy for the delivery of the warheads, Minuteman had always required precise thrust termination for stage three, determined by the flight-control computer. On Minuteman I, the thrust-termination system consisted of four thick carbon-phenolic tubes integrally wound in the sidewall of the third-stage case and sealed with snap-ring closures to form side ports. Detonation of explosive ordnance released a frangible section of the snap ring, thereby venting the combustion chamber and causing a momentary negative thrust that resulted in the third stage dropping away from the postboost vehicle.

The system for Minuteman III involved six circular-shaped charges on the forward dome. Using data from high-speed films and strain gauges, the Minuteman team learned that this arrangement worked within 20 microseconds, cutting holes that resulted in a rupture of the pressure vessel within 2 additional milliseconds. But the case developed cracks radiating from the edge of the holes. TRW used a NASTRAN computer code to define propagation of the cracks. It then determined the dome thickness needed to eliminate the failure of the fiberglass. Aerojet wound "doilies" integrally into the dome of the motor case under each of the circular charges. This eliminated the rupturing, allowing the system to vent the pressure in the chamber and produce momentary negative thrust.[74]

Minuteman IIIs achieved their initial operational capability in June 1970, the first squadron of the upgraded missiles turned over to an operational wing at Minot AFB, North Dakota, in January 1971. By July 1975, there were 450 Minuteman IIs and 550 Minuteman IIIs deployed at Strategic Air Command bases.[75]

Analysis and Conclusions

The deployment of Minuteman I in 1961 marked the completion of a solid-propellant breakthrough in terms of its basic technology, though innovations and improvements continued to occur. But the gradual phase-out of liquid-propellant missiles followed inexorably from the appearance of the first Minuteman. The breakthrough in solid-rocket technology required the extensive cooperation of a great many firms, government laboratories, and universities, only some of which could be mentioned in this chapter. It occurred on many fronts ranging from materials science and metallurgy through chemistry to the physics of internal ballistics and the mathematics and physics of guidance and control, among many other disciplines. It was partially spurred by interservice rivalries for roles and missions. Less well known, however, was the contribution of interservice cooperation. Necessary funding for advances in and sharing of technology came from all three services, the Advanced Research Projects Agency, and NASA. Technologies such as aluminum fuel, methods of thrust vector control, and improved guidance and control transferred from one service's missiles to another. Also crucial were the roles of heterogeneous engineers like Raborn, Schriever, and Ed Hall. But a great many people with more purely technical skills, such as Levering Smith, Sam Phillips, Ed Price, Karl Klager, Robert Corley, Keith Rumbel, and Charles Henderson made vital contributions. Without all of these factors and contributors, the breakthrough would not have been possible.

Titan and Shuttle Boosters, Other Solid Propulsion, 1958–91

IN SOLID-PROPELLANT TECHNOLOGY FOL-lowing the Polaris and Minuteman breakthroughs, the most notable developments were the huge solid-rocket motors on the Titan launch vehicles and the still larger solid-rocket boosters on the shuttle. Both derived significantly from Polaris and Minuteman. But there were also important uses of innovations from the two solid-propellant missiles for stages and boosters in the Scout and Delta launchers and for upper stages on other launch vehicles, including Atlas and the Titans. Not all of the solid-propellant innovations for launch vehicles stemmed from the two missile programs, but the solid-propellant revolution in missilery was an important precursor for what followed in launch-vehicle development.

Titan Solid-Rocket Motors

After Polaris and Minuteman the next major step in solid-propellant technology came with the huge solid-rocket motors for the Titan III and IV. Although Aerojet General, Thiokol, Lockheed Propulsion Company, Hercules Powder Company, the Atlantic Research Corporation, and Rocketdyne Division of North American Aviation had all responded to the air force request for proposals on the boosters, a new firm named United Technology Corporation (UTC) won the bid on May 9, 1962.[1]

How did a recently founded corporation win a major contract against six established and experienced rocket firms? The entire answer to this question lies in unavailable (maybe no longer existent) source selection board documents, but part of the answer involved the individual experience and connections of UTC's managers and engineers.

FIG. 7.1 Launch of a Delta E rocket from Cape Kennedy on December 5, 1968, showing the thrust from the solid-rocket boosters and the first stage. Also shown is the lack of a constant diameter for the different core stages, unlike the later Deltas, which had a consistent 8-foot diameter. (Photo Courtesy of NASA)

The president of the new firm—which had first located in Los Angeles and then moved to new facilities at Morgan Hill in Sunnyvale, California (near Palo Alto)—was Donald L. Putt. He had retired from the air force as a lieutenant general serving as the deputy chief of staff for development. Having played a major role in assembling the team for Minuteman, he also had ties to the Jet Propulsion Laboratory through Caltech, where he had earned a master's degree in aeronautical engineering under Theodore von Kármán. Another executive at the firm (initially called United Research Corporation in 1958) was Barnet R. Adelman. With even stronger ties to JPL and Minuteman, Adelman had played a major role in founding UTC and was its vice president, general manager, and director of operations.

During 1962, he succeeded Putt as president of UTC (later renamed United Technology Center).

Putt and Adelman recruited a large number of key solid-propellant rocket engineers from industry and government. One was David Altman, who had done important work in propellants and combustion at JPL before transferring to Ford Motor Company's Aeroneutronic Systems. He became director of UTC's research division. Altman recalled that in the mid-1950s, he and Adelman had discussed segmenting, as featured in Titan III's large solid-rocket motors. Other major figures on UTC's team of engineers had worked for Aerojet, Atlantic Research, Thiokol, the Naval Ordnance Test Station, and Ramo-Wooldridge's Space Technology Laboratories. In March 1960, the slender, mustachioed Adelman said that UTC had recruited 10 of the 40 or so "really top-grade men" in solid-propellant technology in the United States.

Not long after the founding of UTC, United Aircraft Corporation purchased one-third interest in the rocket firm, later becoming its sole owner. When United Aircraft changed its name to United Technologies Corporation in 1975, its solid-propellant division became Chemical Systems Division (CSD). To avoid confusion between United Technology Corporation and United Technologies Corporation (the parent firm), UTC will henceforth refer to the solid-propellant division until it became CSD.[2]

Although Adelman was an early proponent of segmented motors, Aerojet got a head start in testing them. In 1957—before the founding of UTC—the older rocket firm responded to indications that the air force might soon need huge solid-propellant motors by slicing a Regulus II booster (with a 20-inch diameter) into three portions. It relinked them with bolted flange joints and successfully fired them using the original Regulus propellant and nozzle. Performance matched that of the Regulus's unsegmented motor.

The reason for this test was the perception that large solid motors would soon become too huge for transport on anything but barges. Probably encouraged by Aerojet's initial success, about April 1959 the Powerplant Laboratory of the air force's Wright Air Development Center in Dayton, Ohio, sent out requests for proposals for a contract later worth $495,000 to test segmented motors. Aerojet won the bid, which it implemented after the Powerplant Laboratory's move to the rocket site at Edwards AFB, California, in July 1959. The firm tested 100-inch-diameter motors in the ultimately successful attempt to achieve 20 million pound-seconds of total impulse, although the initial goal was a more modest 230,000 pounds for 80 seconds (the equivalent of 18.4 million pound-seconds of total impulse). Aerojet first fired a Minuteman first stage (65 inches in diameter), cut in half and reconnected with a lock-ring (or lock-strip) joint configured in similar fashion to subsequent joints used in these tests. It featured inner and outer lock strips held together by a lock-strip key in the center and an O-ring inside of that. The key and the O-ring held parts of the joint together and precluded leaking. On May 5, 1961, this motor provided 160,000 pounds-force (lbf) for 60 seconds.[3]

Aerojet next tested a variety of 100-inch segmented motors, beginning with one designated TW-1 on June 3, 1961, and concluding with an FW-4 motor on October 13, 1962. Besides segmentation, the motors also tested nozzle materials and thrust-vector-control systems using fluids that reacted with the rocket's exhaust gases to change the direction of the thrust. With five center segments, a length of 77 feet, and a weight of 876,000 pounds, the intermediate FW-3 (tested on June 9, 1962) was the largest solid-rocket motor yet built. There were various problems with the Aerojet tests, including spalling (breaking off of fragments) and even ejection of the nozzle throat. Although not all aspects of the tests of these 100-inch-diameter motors were successful, they demonstrated that a large, segmented design was feasible, easing transportation of such huge rocket motors. The lock-strip joint had also been successful. However, failures of the nozzle-throat inserts and the thrust-vector-control systems showed the need for further development in those areas. Other tests of segmented motors by Lockheed and UTC also revealed problems with nozzles.[4]

Despite Aerojet's priority in actually testing segmented motors, Adelman had obtained a patent for a segmented-joint design for such large solid motors. Assisted by Tom Polter from the nearby Stanford Research Institute in Palo Alto, UTC began development of a specific propellant for large, segmented boosters, starting with the proven PBAN used in stage one of Minuteman, with which Adelman would have been familiar from his own work on that missile. Using its own funds, UTC successfully tested a P-1 solid-propellant motor on December 15, 1960. The motor, with a diameter of 87 inches, yielded more than 200,000 pounds-force for about 75 seconds, followed by P-1-2 on February 9, 1961. The latter motor had two middle segments plus a forward and aft closure. With a case composed of low-carbon steel plate and a fixed nozzle using nitrogen tetroxide to provide thrust vector control, it yielded 79 seconds of thrust at 399,000 pounds-force and demonstrated the basic type of thrust vector control used on the Titan IIIC, which also used nitrogen tetroxide. It was followed by a P-2 motor with only one center segment. The P-2 yielded roughly 500,000 pounds-force over a period of 75 seconds.

Initially, UTC employed cases with a taper of 1.22 degrees, believing that this prevented erosive burning of the grain in the long internal cavities of the propellant by providing a larger area as the rapidly expanding gases passed toward the expanded rear of the motor. Later, however, UTC's engineers abandoned this design for zero taper in their cases. This had the advantage of interchangeability of segments, and apparently erosive burning proved to be preventable through tapering only the internal-burning cavity.[5]

263

Titan and
Shuttle
Boosters,
Other Solid
Propulsion,
1958–91

All of the design and testing done by UTC to this point had preceded its May 1962 contract with the air force for Titan III solid-rocket motors. But much remained to be done, with many problems to be solved. Developmental testing of 120-inch-diameter motors—the size that would actually be used on the Titan IIIC—began on February 23, 1963, at UTC's Coyote Canyon test site in the Diablo Mountain Range southeast of Sunnyvale. The initial test motor contained only one center segment and was the first of four "subscale" tests of 120-inch motors. The February 23 test achieved a peak thrust of a million pounds. This came from a motor about the same size as the contemporary liquid-propellant Atlas booster but with about two and a half times as much thrust as the Atlas.[6]

The advantages of solid motors over liquid rockets involved several factors. Although liquid propellants had higher specific impulses, solids had densities 50 to 70 percent greater than most liquids. They also required no pumping or other complicated plumbing, which added to the weight of liquid engines and thus reduced their thrust-to-weight ratios. Finally, because of the ability to adjust the sizes and shapes of internal-burning cavities in solid-propellant rockets to provide huge, instantaneous increments of thrust (because the burning area was so large), solid-rocket motors were much better able to lift launch vehicles quickly through the area of high gravity near the Earth than were liquid rockets with their greater weight in relation to the thrust they delivered.[7]

Three tests with subscale 120-inch rockets following the one on February 23 included a sled test at the Naval Ordnance Test Station, China Lake, California, in June 1964 to see if there was significant hazard in using the 120-inch segments. A single-segment motor was ignited and sent down the sled track, where it smashed into a concrete abutment at 435 miles per hour. One of a series of hazard classification tests, it showed that the propellant would not detonate on impact. Other subscale testing included four motors subjected to altitude testing at the Arnold Engineering Development Center in Tennessee to obtain data on liquid thrust vector control.[8]

In the midst of these subscale tests, on July 20, 1963, UTC had statically fired the first full-scale, 5-segment motor at Coyote Canyon. Brig. Gen. Joseph S. Bleymaier, system program director within Space Systems Division, wrote to Putt that this was "truly an outstanding and significant event in the life of the Titan III Program." The motor yielded 1.2 million pounds of thrust over a burning time of roughly 112 seconds. The nitrogen-tetroxide thrust-vector-control system worked effectively, yielding an adequate five degrees of thrust deflection. The system used 24 injectant valves in four groups of six. Electrical commands from the guidance/control system caused the valves to spray the fluid into the 5,000-degree exhaust gases, creating a shock wave that deflected the hot gases and thereby would have changed the Titan IIIC's course in a flight test. This was not an operationally configured motor, so testing of such motors would be needed to evaluate the more difficult environment they would experience in actual flight.[9]

The PBAN propellant UTC developed for the solid-rocket motors of Titan IIIC—the so-called zero stage—was tougher than other PBAN propellants because it contained methyl nadic anhydride. It had a mass fraction of 85.3 percent and a configuration in which an eight-point star in the forward closure transitioned into a tapered, near-cylindrical opening through the five segments and aft closure. This yielded a propellant specific impulse of more than 260 lbf-sec/lbm.[10]

As the earlier testing of large, segmented motors by Aerojet had suggested might be the case, how to ensure that uncooled nozzles could withstand 5,000-degree exhaust gases flowing supersonically through them for extended periods (up to 120 seconds) became a major concern for UTC engineers. The nonrotating nozzle canted six degrees from the axis of the motor to direct the undeflected thrust toward the Titan III's center of gravity. Inside the nozzle, engineers had designed a throat section consisting of three bulk graphite rings. They apparently worked for the subscale motors, but when tried in full-scale tests, the graphite cracked under thermal stresses. This resulted in the loss of a nozzle during a static test in August 1964, so engineers changed the design to a graphite cloth bonded with a phenolic resin. The new design necessitated new materials, new tooling and parts, and new procedures, but UTC made the change in six weeks. It successfully tested the new design in September 1964. A major gamble for UTC, the tape-wrapped carbon-phenolic throat marked a big advance in large, solid-rocket technology. It worked flawlessly on the Titans and paved the way for the giant solid-rocket boosters on the Space Shuttle, which used the same technology for its nozzle throats.[11]

Another major challenge for UTC engineers was how to connect the segments of the solid-rocket motors so that they were able to withstand pressures of 850 pounds per square inch as they launched through the atmosphere. Aerojet's lock-strip joint offered a possible solution, but in cooperation with sister Pratt & Whitney Aircraft Division of United Aircraft Corporation, UTC engineers developed a different type called a clevis joint, tested as early as 1960. It featured circumferential "male" and "female" segments that projected from the ends of each segment of the motor, with the male clevis joint facing upward (when the vehicle was on the launch pad) and the female joint projecting a slot downward, into which the male joint fit in a "tongue-and-groove" arrangement. Some 237 hand-placed and 3 fixed pins held both segments together.

An O-ring in a slot between the inside of the female segment and the male segment kept hot gases from escaping. In addition, insulation between the propellant and the case protected the O-rings from heating. Such heating could occur only if there was a debonding of the propellant and the insulation from the case, allowing a high-pressure gas blow-by to reach the O-ring. Improper sealing of the O-ring could occur due to low external temperatures at launch, making the flexible material rigid. So UTC engineers added heating strips to prevent this and improve reliability.[12]

Testing of these and other design features of the solid-rocket motors involved nine full-scale, 120-inch developmental tests plus five full-scale preflight readiness tests. In these tests, engineers demonstrated the interchangeability of segments using the clevis joint. Also tested was the motor case, which itself presented some problems. The cases initially consisted of a rolled and welded, low-alloy, high-strength steel known as Ladish D6AC. UTC had chosen two subcontractors, Curtis-Wright and Westinghouse, to provide them. Experience with earlier missiles, including Minuteman, yielded a large database on welding and processing this material. But the Titan 120-inch cases posed new problems because of greater thickness of the metal and size of the segments. As a result, both contractors experienced significant problems in their welding operations. Despite them, the motor cases remained on schedule. Subsequently, assisted by Westinghouse and UTC, the Ladish Company eliminated the need for welding by developing a new process called roll-ring forging (also known as roll extrusion case forging), which offered an additional savings in weight as well as improved reliability of the motor cases.[13]

These developments culminated on June 18, 1965, when two solid-rocket motors, both 84.65 feet long, provided a peak thrust of 2,647,000 pounds before being jettisoned about two minutes after liftoff of the first Titan III-C, turning over lifting duties to the liquid-propellant center-core section of the first large air force launch vehicle specifically designed as a space booster. The launch occurred a month and 20 days after the fifth preflight readiness test and only a little over three years after UTC had won the Phase I contract for the solid-rocket boosters from the air force.[14]

Subsequently, CSD developed and tested a 7-segment version of the solid-rocket motors for the abortive Titan IIIM in 1969 and 1970. Until the Titan IV came along, the company did not get the chance to use the longer motors in an actual launch vehicle, but presumably the opportunity to test them made development of a 5.5-segment motor for the Titan 34D a comparatively easy task. The firm tested the 34D motors on August 25, 1979, at its Coyote Test Facility near San Jose for the first time with complete success.[15]

With the exception of the extra half segment, which increased the length of the solid-rocket motors from 84.65 to 90.33 feet, the zero stage for the Titan 34D was not significantly different from that for the Titan IIIC. The motors retained their 10-foot diameter, and the theoretical specific impulse for the ammonium perchlorate–PBAN–aluminum binder remained above 260 lbf-sec/lbm. The grain configuration stayed the same, with the conical internal cavity extended through the extra half segment into the aft closure. The case and nozzle remained basically unchanged as well. With little difference in the average thrust, the total impulse went up (from 1.13 million to 1.23 million pounds of force) because of the added propellant in the extra half segment.[16]

With the Titan IV, the 7-segment motors originally developed for the Titan IIIM found a use. The initial version of the new booster (later called Titan IVA) had twin, 7-segment solid-rocket motors produced by CSD under subcontract to Martin Marietta. These motors contained essentially the same PBAN propellant and grain configuration as the Titan 34D but with the additional 1.5 segments, bringing the length to about 122 feet and the motor thrust to 1.39 million pounds per motor. It still used liquid injection of nitrogen tetroxide for thrust vector control in a fixed, canted nozzle, as had the earlier Titan solid-rocket motors. But in the Titan IVA the initial expansion ratio increased from 8:1 to 10:1, with the addition of an exit-cone extension. The cases continued to be made of steel

NASA
C-1977-178

FIG. 7.2
Example of
a filament-
wound case
for a solid-
propellant
stage. (Photo
courtesy of
NASA)

National Aeronautics and Space Administration
Lewis Research Center

with field joints and a single O-ring. As originally proposed for the
Titan IIIM, the first version of the 7-segment motors went through
a development period from 1965 to 1970, with four static tests in
1969 and 1970. CSD revived the 7-segment design for the Titan IV
but added reliability measures adopted for the 34D following an
April 1986 solid-rocket-motor failure as well as the January 1986
Challenger accident of the Space Shuttle. Two successful static
tests in December 1987 and February 1988 completed qualification
of the 7-segment motors.[17]

Concern on the part of the air force that CSD would be unable to produce enough solid-rocket motors led Martin Marietta to subcontract in 1987 with a second source, Hercules Aerospace Company (formerly, Hercules Powder Company), to provide 15 sets of motors, known as the solid-rocket motor upgrade (SRMU), with higher performance than the CSD motors. The new motors used an HTPB-based propellant, a filament-wound, graphite-epoxy composite case with a movable nozzle, and only three segments, yielding a 25 percent increase in lift capacity compared with the Titan IVA zero stage. But the motors on what became the Titan IVB were delayed in their development. An initial test at the rocket site on Edwards AFB (known at the time as Phillips Laboratory) in 1990 had to be halted when a crane moving one of the segments collapsed. The segment fell to the ground and ignited, resulting in a fatality. On April 1, 1991, the motor undergoing the delayed test produced more internal pressure than predicted because of a propellant grain deformation, causing the case to rupture after two seconds of firing. Ultimately, the first Titan IVB with SRMUs did launch on February 23, 1997, after the end of the period covered by this book.[18]

Shuttle Solid-Rocket Boosters

The solid-rocket motors for the Titans III and IV carried the evolution of solid-propellant technology from the significant achievements of the Polaris and Minuteman to a new level. The next step yielded the still larger solid-rocket boosters (SRBs) on the Space Shuttles. After UTC had developed the 7-segment solid-rocket motors for the Titan, NASA decided in March 1972 to use SRBs on the shuttle. Even before this decision, the Marshall Space Flight Center had provided contracts of $150,000 each to the Lockheed Propulsion Company, Thiokol, UTC, and Aerojet General to study configurations of such motors. Using information from these studies, NASA issued a request for proposals (RFPs) on July 16, 1973, to which all four companies responded with initial technical and cost proposals in late August 1973, followed by final versions on October 15.

Because the booster cases would be recoverable, unlike those for the Titan III, and because they had to be rated to carry astronauts, they needed to be sturdier than their predecessors. Lockheed, UTC, and Thiokol all proposed segmented cases without welding. Although Aerojet had been an early developer of such cases, it ignored a requirement in the RFP and proposed a welded case without segmentation, arguing that such a case would be lighter, less costly, and safer, with transportation by barge to launch sites from Aero-

FIG. 7.3
Space Shuttle
solid-rocket
booster in a
test stand at a
Thiokol test site
in 1979. (Photo
courtesy of
NASA)

jet's production site. Had Aerojet won the contract, it is possible that the *Challenger* disaster never would have occurred. However, the source evaluation board with representatives from five NASA centers and the three military services ranked Aerojet last, with a score of 655 for mission suitability. By contrast, respective scores for Lockheed, Thiokol, and UTC were 714, 710, and 710. The board selected Thiokol as winner of the competition, based on its cost, the lowest of the three, and also its perceived managerial strengths. NASA announced the selection on November 20, 1973.[19]

Since Thiokol had plants in Utah, NASA administrator James C. Fletcher's home state, the decision was controversial. Lockheed protested, but the General Accounting Office decided on June 24, 1974, that "no reasonable basis" existed to question the validity of NASA's decision. Thiokol, meanwhile, proceeded with design and development based on interim contracts, the final one for design awarded on June 26, 1974, followed by one for development, testing, and production on May 15, 1975.[20]

Part of the legacy from which Thiokol developed the technology for its SRBs came from the air force's Large Segmented Solid Rocket Motor Program (designated 623A), of which Aerojet's testing of 100-inch-diameter solids in the early 1960s had been an early part. In late 1962 the Air Force Rocket Propulsion Laboratory at Edwards AFB inaugurated a successor program. Its purpose was to develop large solid motors that the DoD and NASA could use for space-launch vehicles. The air force provided funding for 120- and 156-inch-diameter segmented motors and for continuation of work on thrust-vector-control systems. NASA then paid for part of the 156-inch and all of a 260-inch program. In the course of testing thrust-vector-control systems, Lockheed had developed a Lock-seal mounting structure that allowed the nozzle to gimbal, and Thiokol later scaled it up to the size required for large motors, call-

ing it Flexseal.

Lockheed tested both 120- and 156-inch motors in the program, and Thiokol tested 156-inch motors with both gimballed (Flexseal) and fixed nozzles. These tests concluded in 1967, as did those for 260-inch-diameter motors by Aerojet and Thiokol. There were no direct applications of the 260-inch technologies, but participation in the 120- and 156-inch portions of the Large Segmented Solid Rocket Motor Program gave Thiokol experience and access to designs, materials, fabrication methods, and test results that contributed to development of the solid-rocket boosters for the Space Shuttle. The firm also drew upon its experience with Minuteman.[21]

The design for the solid-rocket booster was intentionally conservative, using a steel case of the same type (D6AC) used on Minuteman and the Titan IIIC. The Ladish Company of Cudahy, Wisconsin, made the cases for each segment without welding, using the rolled-ring forging process that it had helped develop for the Titan IIIC. In this process, technicians punched a hole in a hot piece of metal and then rolled it to the correct diameter. For the shuttle, the diameter turned out to be 12.17 feet (146 inches), with the overall length of the booster being 149 feet. Each booster consisted of four segments plus fore and aft sections. The propellant consisted of the same three principal ingredients used in the first stage of the Minuteman missile, ammonium perchlorate, aluminum, and PBAN polymer. Its grain configuration was an 11-point star in the forward end converging into a large, smooth, tapered cylindrical shape. This combination yielded a theoretical specific impulse of more than 260 lbf-sec/lbm.[22]

Marshall Space Flight Center sought "to avoid inventing anything new" in the booster's design, according to George Hardy, project manager for the solid-rocket booster at Marshall from 1974 to 1982. The best example of this approach was the PBAN propellant. Other propellants offered higher performance, but with cost and human-rating being prime considerations, Thiokol employed a tried-and-true propellant used on the first stage of Minuteman and in the navy's Poseidon missile. As Thiokol deputy director for the booster,

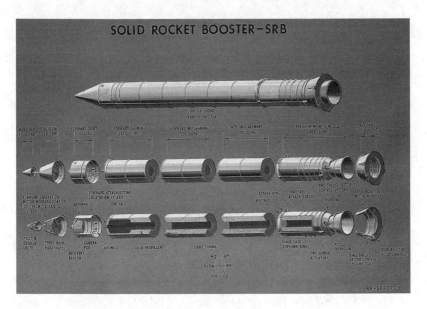

FIG. 7.4 Technical drawing of the Space Shuttle solid-rocket booster showing its segments and internal-burning core with other components, including its nozzle with gimbal actuators for directional (vector) control of the thrust. (Photo courtesy of NASA)

John Thirkill, said in 1973, "Over the last fifteen years, we've loaded more than 2,500 first stage Minuteman motors and around 500 Poseidon motors with this propellant."[23]

The configuration of the propellant grain caused the thrust to vary, providing the boost required for the planned trajectory but keeping the acceleration to 3 Gs for the astronauts. For the first six shuttle missions, the initial thrust was 3.15 million pounds per booster. The 11-point star in the forward section of the SRB had long, narrow points, providing an extensive burning surface. As the points burned away, the surface declined, reducing the thrust as the point of maximum dynamic pressure approached at about 60 seconds into the launch. At 52 seconds after liftoff, the star points had burned away to provide a cylindrical perforation in both the forward and rear segments of the booster. As this burned, expanding its diameter, the thrust increased slightly from the 52nd to about the 80th second. Thereafter, it tapered to zero as the burning consumed the propellant at about the 120th second, when the SRBs separated from the rest of the shuttle. The separated boosters, slowed by parachutes, soon fell into the ocean.[24]

A major drawback of the PBAN propellant was that about 20 percent of its exhaust's weight consisted of hydrogen chloride, which not only was toxic and corrosive but could damage the ozone layer that protected Earth from excessive ultraviolet radiation. NASA studies of the possible ozone depletion showed, however, that it would be slight, so there was no need to shift to a less powerful propellant.[25]

Once the Ladish Company had forged the motor cases in Wisconsin, the segments traveled by railroad to a firm named Cal Doran near Los Angeles. There, heat treatment imparted greater strength and toughness to the D6AC steel. Then the segments went further south to Rohr Industries in Chula Vista, near San Diego, for the addition of tang-and-clevis joints to the ends of the segments. On these joints, shuttle designers had departed from the Marshall advice "to avoid inventing anything new." Although the shuttle field joints resembled those for Titan IIIC, in many respects they differed. One key change lay in orientation. For the Titan solid-rocket motor, the single tang pointed upward from a lower segment of the case and fit into the two-pronged clevis, which encased it. This protected the joint from rain or dew dripping down the case and entering the joint. In the shuttle, the direction was reversed.

A second major difference lay in the Titan joint's having used only one O-ring, whereas the shuttle employed two. Insulation on the inside of the Titan motor case protected the case, and with it, the O-ring, from excessive heating. To keep the protective mechanisms from shrinking in cold temperatures and then possibly allowing a gas blow-by when the motor was firing, there were heating strips on the Titan. Both the Titan and the shuttle used putty to improve the seal provided by the O-ring(s), but the shuttle added the second O-ring for supposed further insurance. It did not include heating strips, however. One further difference in the joints was in the number of pins holding the tang and clevis together. Whereas the Titan motor had used 240 such pins fitting into holes in the tang and clevis and linking them, the shuttle had only 177, despite its larger diameter.[26] There is no certainty in counterfactual history, but perhaps if the shuttle designers had simply accepted the basic design of the Titan tang-and-clevis joints, the *Challenger* accident would not have occurred because of leaking hot gases through a field joint that ignited the external tank.

Unlike the field joint, the nozzle for the solid-rocket boosters did follow the precedents of the Titan solid-rocket motors and the Large Segmented Solid Rocket Motor Program. The shuttle employed carbon-phenolic throats to ablate under the extreme heating from the flow and expansion of the hot gases from the burning propellant in the motor itself. In the case of the shuttle, the propellants burned at a temperature of 5,700°F, so ablation was needed to vaporize and thereby prevent thermal-stress cracking followed by probable ejection of portions of the nozzle. As of June 1979, the expansion ratio of the nozzle was 7.16:1, used for the first seven missions. Starting with the eighth mission, modifications of the nozzle increased the initial thrust of each motor from 3.15 million to 3.3 million pounds. These changes extended the length of the nozzle exit cone by 10 inches and decreased the diameter of the nozzle throat by 4 inches. The latter change increased the expansion ratio to 7.72:1, thereby adding to the booster's thrust.[27]

The nozzle was partially submerged, and for gimballing, it used the Flexseal design Thiokol had scaled up in the 156-inch motor testing from the Lockheed's Lockseal design. It was capable of eight degrees of deflection, necessitated among other reasons by the shuttle's now-familiar roll soon after liftoff to achieve its proper trajectory. Having less thrust, the space shuttle main engines were incapable of achieving the necessary amount of roll, and the liquid-injection thrust-vector-control system used on the Titan solid-rocket motors would not have met the more demanding requirements of the shuttle. Hence the importance of the Lockseal-Flexseal development during the Large Segmented Solid Rocket Motor Program supported by both NASA and the air force.[28]

Although there were only four segments of the solid-rocket boosters that were joined by field joints, there were actually 11 sections joined by tang-and-clevis joints. Once they had been through machining and fitting processes, they were assembled at the factory into four segments. The joints put together at the factory were called factory joints as distinguished from the field joints, which technicians assembled at Kennedy Space Center. Thiokol poured and cast the propellant into the four segments at its factory in Brigham City, Utah, usually doing so in matched pairs from the same batches of propellant to reduce thrust imbalances. At various times, the solid-rocket motors used four different D6AC-steel cases, with slight variations in thickness.[29]

In part because of its simplicity compared with the space shuttle main engine, the solid-rocket booster required far less testing than the liquid-propellant engine. Certification for the SSMEs had required 726 hot-fire tests and 110,000 seconds of operation, but the solid-rocket boosters needed only four developmental and three qualification tests with operation of less than 1,000 seconds total—0.9 percent of that for the SSMEs. There were, however, other tests. One was a hydroburst test on September 30, 1977, at Thiokol's Wasatch Division in Utah. This demonstrated that, without cracking, a case could withstand the pressures to which it would be subjected during launch. A second hydroburst test on September 19, 1980 (with only the aft dome, two segments, and the forward dome), was also successful. There were other tests of the tang-and-clevis joints that put them under pressure until they burst. They withstood pressures between 1.72 and 2.27 times the maximum expected from liftoff through separation.[30]

The first developmental static test, DM-1 on July 18, 1977, at Thiokol's Wasatch Division was successful, but the motor delivered only 2.9 million pounds of maximum thrust compared with an expected 3.1 million. There were other anomalies, including excessive erosion in parts of the nozzle. Modification included additional ammonium perchlorate in the propellant and changed nozzle coatings. DM-2 on January 18, 1978, was another success but led to further adjustments in the design. It turned out that the rubber insulation and polymer liner protecting the case were thicker than necessary, leading to reduction in their thickness. This lowered their weight from 23,900 to 19,000 pounds. There were also modifications in the igniter, grain design, and nozzle coating to reduce the flame intensity of the igniter, the rate of thrust increase for the motor, and erosion of portions of the nozzle. As the motor for DM-3 was being assembled, a study of the DM-2 casing revealed that there had been an area with propellant burning between segments. This required disassembling the motor and increasing the thickness of a noncombustible inhibitor on the end of each segment. Designers also extended the rubber insulation to protect the case at the joints. This delayed the DM-3 test from July to October 19, 1978.

Again, the test was satisfactory; but although the thermal protection on the nozzle had been effective, the igniter once more caused the thrust to rise too quickly. Designers could see no evident solution to the rapid rate of thrust increase, an apparent tacit admission that engineers did not fully understand the complex combustion process. It did seem evident, though, that the rate had to rise quickly to preclude thrust imbalances between the two motors, so the engineers went back to an igniter design closer to that used in the DM-1 test and simply accepted the rapid thrust rise (for the moment, at least). On February 17, 1979, DM-4 ended the four developmental tests with a successful firing. The qualification tests, QM-1 through -3 from June 13, 1979, to February 13, 1980, were all successful. These seven tests furnished the data needed to qualify the solid-rocket motor for launch—excluding the electronics, hydraulics, and other components not Thiokol's responsibility. Other tests on booster recovery mechanisms, complete booster assemblies, loads on the launch pad and in flight, and internal pressure

FIG. 7.5
Testing of a
developmental
motor
following the
Challenger
accident.
(Photo courtesy
of NASA)

took place at Marshall and at the National Parachute Test Range, El
Centro, California. The program completed all of these tests by late
May 1980, well before the first shuttle flight.[31] Of course, this was
after the first planned flight, so if the main-engine development had
not delayed the flights, presumably the booster development would
have done so to some degree.

Smaller Solid-Propellant Stages and Boosters

Even early in launch-vehicle history, some missile programs had already begun to influence solid-propellant developments. In 1956, a creative group of engineers at Langley's Pilotless Aircraft Research Division (PARD) began formulating ideas that led to the Scout launch vehicles. This group included Maxime A. Faget, later famous for designing spacecraft; Joseph G. Thibodaux Jr., who promoted the spherical design of some rocket and spacecraft motors beginning in 1955; Robert O. Piland, who put together the first multistage rocket to reach the speed of Mach 10; and William E. Stoney Jr., who became the first head of the group responsible for developing the Scout, which he also christened. Wallops, established as a test base for the National Advisory Committee for Aeronautics' (NACA) Langley Memorial Aeronautical Laboratory in 1945, had a history of using rockets, individually or in stages, to gather data at high speeds on both aircraft models and rocket nose cones. These data made it possible to design supersonic aircraft and hypersonic missiles at a time when ground facilities were not yet capable of providing comparable information. It was a natural step for engineers working in such a program to conceive a multistage, hypersonic, solid-propellant rocket that could reach orbital speeds of Mach 18.[32]

SCOUT

In 1957, after a five-stage rocket vehicle at Wallops had reached speeds of Mach 15, PARD engineers began to study in earnest how to increase the speed of solid-propellant combinations even further. The group learned that Aerojet had developed the largest solid-propellant motor then in existence as part of its effort to convert the Jupiter to a solid-propellant missile for use aboard ship. Called the Jupiter Senior, the motor was 30 feet long and 40 inches in diameter, and it weighed 22,650 pounds, more than 3 times as much as the contemporary Sergeant missile's motor. Using a propellant of polyurethane, ammonium perchlorate, and aluminum, the Jupiter Senior motor provided a thrust of up to about 100,000 pounds for 40 seconds in two successful static firings in March–April 1957. It eventually amassed a record of 13 static tests and 32 flights without a failure, and it prepared the way for the Aerojet motors used in Polaris and Minuteman.

About the time that the PARD engineers learned about Jupiter Senior, they found out Thiokol had discovered a way to improve the Sergeant motor by shifting from the polysulfide binder used on the missile to a polybutadiene–acrylic acid binder with metallic additives. This offered a possible 20 percent increase in specific impulse. These developments led Stoney to analyze a four-stage vehicle with the Jupiter Senior as stage one, the improved Sergeant as stage two, and two Vanguard X248 motors as the third and fourth stages. Even after *Sputnik*, in early 1958 NACA Headquarters told the PARD team that it would not be receptive to developing a fourth launch vehicle when Vanguard, Jupiter C, and Thor-Able were well along in development or already available.[33]

However, with plans moving forward for what became NASA, in March 1958 NACA Headquarters asked Langley Aeronautical Laboratory to prepare a program of space technology. As a necessary part of this program, Langley included Scout—only later an acronym meaning Solid Controlled Orbital Utility Test system—to investigate human space flight and problems of reentry. The program called for $4 million to fund five vehicles for these purposes. By May 6, 1958, when Scout had become part of the space program, further analysis suggested that the third stage needed to be larger than the X248. But by then, plans for America's space efforts were becoming so extensive that the extra costs for such development were hardly significant. By that time Langley had also arranged a contract with Thiokol for four improved Sergeant motors.[34]

Langley assigned Stoney as project officer but gave Thibodaux's Rocket Section at PARD the responsibility for the initial five contracts needed to develop the Scout. A contract with Aerojet for the first stage became effective on December 1, 1958. The name of the Aerojet first stage changed from Jupiter Senior to Aerojet Senior, also called Algol I. As developed by December 1959, the motor was 29.8 feet long and 40 inches in diameter. With a steel case and polyurethane–aluminum–ammonium perchlorate propellant configured in an eight-point gear (a cylinder with eight gear-shaped, squared-off "points" radiating from it), it yielded a specific impulse of only about 215 lbf-sec/lbm and a low mass fraction of 0.838 but an average thrust of upward of 100,000 pounds depending upon the ambient temperature.[35]

This was a far cry from the huge boosters for the Titans and Space Shuttle, but it became the first stage of the successful Scout program. Thiokol's second stage presented some problems. The firm was finding it difficult to adapt a new propellant for what came to be called the Castor I (or TX-33-35) second-stage motor. Initial static firings had been successful, but then Thiokol encountered unspecified difficulties that had to be overcome. Although the grain design was the same as for the Sergeant, the Castor used a polybutadiene acrylic acid–aluminum–ammonium perchlorate propellant (also employed as an interim propellant on Minuteman I) and was 20.5 feet long to Sergeant's 16.3 feet, with an identical 31-inch diameter. Once Thiokol engineers overcame developmental problems with the propellant, the Castor yielded a specific impulse of almost 275 lbf-sec/lbm to only 186 for Sergeant (although the two figures were not comparable because for Scout, the Castor was used at altitude with a larger expansion angle than for Sergeant, which launched on the ground). According to figures supplied by Thiokol, Castor's average thrust was 64,340 pounds compared to Sergeant's 41,200.[36]

The initial four-stage Scout with all stages live flew on July 1, 1960, in the first of nine developmental flights labeled ST-1 through ST-9 (for Scout Tests 1–9), all launched from Wallops. NASA treated them as operational missions, having them carry Explorer spacecraft, ionospheric probes, and one reentry payload. The December 4, 1960, launch of ST-3 was the first attempted orbital mission with the Scout. The Algol IA first stage performed properly, but the Castor IA second stage did not ignite because of human failure to detect a defect in the ignition system. ST-4 on February 16, 1961, thus became the first entirely solid-propellant launch vehicle to achieve orbit.[37]

From these (by later standards) somewhat primitive beginnings, the Scout went on to incorporate more sophisticated technologies. For instance, the Antares IIA, designed by Allegany Ballistics Laboratory and produced by Hercules at its Bacchus Works in Magna, Utah, marked a considerable improvement over the first stage-three motor for the Scout, also a Hercules product. The Antares IIA featured a composite, modified, double-base propellant including ammonium perchlorate, HMX, nitrocellulose, nitroglycerin, and aluminum. Even with a smaller nozzle expansion ratio, this yielded an increase in average thrust from about 13,000 pounds for the older motor to about 21,000 for X259 Antares IIA. This stage first launched on March 29, 1962, in an early (A1) version. The A2 completed its development in June of that year, almost simultaneously with Hercules' second stage for Polaris A2, which also used a composite-modified double-base propellant, although one without HMX and with a lower level of performance (probably reflecting the fact that the Polaris motor had an earlier date of development completion by about six months). For Polaris, HMX usage awaited the A3 version, with the Antares IIA actually using it before the missile, reversing the usual practice for launch vehicles to borrow technology from missiles.[38]

About this time, some earlier Scout technologies found use in other programs. For example, the thrust-augmented Thor (TAT), which entered the launch-vehicle inventory in 1963, incorporated three Thiokol TX-33-52 (Castor I) solid-propellant rocket boosters to supplement the power of the liquid-propellant first stage. The TAT consisted of a Thor with about 170,000 pounds of thrust and three Castor I solid-propellant rocket boosters, which increased liftoff thrust to 331,550 pounds.[39]

The TAT soon gave way to a further improved vehicle with a replacement for the Castor I. The air force's Space Systems Division had announced contracts for a long-tank Thor (called Thorad) to replace the thrust-augmented Thor in January 1966. Douglas would provide the new Thor, with thrust augmentation continuing to be provided by Thiokol; only for the Thorad, the three solid motors would be Castor IIs. The Thorad was more than 70 feet long, as compared with 56 feet for the TAT. The added length came mainly in the form of the extended tanks that increased the burning time of the first stage. For the Castor II (TX-354-5), basically developed (as the TX-354-3) in 1964 for the Scout second stage, among other applications, Thiokol kept the steel case used on Castor I but substituted carboxy-terminated polybutadiene for the polybutadiene–acrylic acid used as the binder for the earlier version, keeping aluminum and ammonium perchlorate as fuel and oxidizer. This increased the specific impulse from under 225 for the Castor I to more than 235 lbf-sec/lbm for Castor II and the total impulse from 1.63 million to 1.95 million pounds, improving the payload capacity for the Thorad by 20 percent over the TAT.[40]

A further major advance in propulsion technology for the Scout came in 1977–79 when, under contract to the Vought Corporation, Thiokol produced a new third-stage motor at its Elkton Division in Maryland. This was the Antares IIIA (TE-M-762, Star 31), employing a HTPB-based binder combined with ammonium perchlorate and aluminum. This propellant increased the specific impulse from about 285 for the composite-modified double-base propellant used by Hercules in the Antares IIB to more than 295 lbf-sec/lbm. In addition to the higher-performance propellant, Thiokol used a composite case made of Kevlar 49 and epoxy. Introduced commercially in 1972, Kevlar 49 was DuPont's registered trademark for an aramid (essentially nylon) fiber that combined light weight, high strength, and toughness. Lighter than fiberglass, it yielded a mass fraction of

FIG. 7.6
Scout S-131R
on August 10,
1965, with a
new Castor II
second stage.
(Photo courtesy
of NASA)

1965-L-06138   Langley Research Center
                               Hampton, Virginia 23681-0001

0.923 compared with Antares IIB's already high 0.916. Burning much
longer than the propellant in the Antares IIB, the one in the Antares
IIIA produced a lower average thrust, but its total impulse at the
high altitudes in which it operated was 840,000 pounds compared
with 731,000 pounds for the Antares IIB. No doubt because of the
higher erosive propensities of the Antares IIIA motor, which had a
higher chamber pressure than the Antares IIB, the newer motor used
4-D carbon-carbon (pyrolitic graphite) for the nozzle-throat insert.[41]

Launched initially at the end of October 1979, the Scout version
G1 with the Antares IIIA as its third stage appears to have been the
first *launch vehicle* to use an HTPB propellant, but the *first use* of
the substance may have been on an improved Maverick tactical (air-

to-surface) missile. Thiokol provided the Maverick's initial motor, with development starting in 1968, but under contract to the Air Force Rocket Propulsion Laboratory at Edwards AFB, Aerojet had begun in August 1975 to develop the improved motor with HTPB propellant. By October 1976, Aerojet had produced 12 demonstration verification motors. Aerojet did get production orders for some version of an improved Maverick motor. But interestingly, an organization called the ATK Tactical Systems Company, producer of the Maverick heavy warheads, later claimed to be under contract to provide a rocket motor very similar to the Aerojet design with an HTPB propellant, an HTPB liner, an aluminum case, an 11-inch diameter, and a glass phenolic exit cone, all features of Aerojet's motor.[42]

281
Titan and
Shuttle
Boosters,
Other Solid
Propulsion,
1958–91

Another motor that used HTPB was Thiokol's Star 48, used on the Payload Assist Module (PAM)—a third stage on the Delta and an upper-stage motor used from the Space Shuttle. Thiokol began developing the motor in 1976. The firm made the Star 48 motor case with titanium and used the recently developed advanced composite, carbon-carbon, for the nozzle's exit cone. The PAM was an offshoot of Minuteman, stage three, which Thiokol began producing in 1970 essentially using the original Aerojet design. The purpose of the PAM on the shuttle was to propel satellites from a low parking orbit (about 160 miles above Earth) to a higher final orbit, including a geosynchronous transfer orbit. It used the same basic HTPB–aluminum–ammonium perchlorate propellant as Thiokol's Antares IIIA rocket motor.[43]

The Inertial Upper Stage (IUS) featured a much more problematic set of motors using HTPB propellant. Designed under management of the Space and Missile Systems Organization (SAMSO—a recombination of the air force's Ballistic and Space Systems Divisions) primarily for use with the Space Shuttle (for when orbiter payloads needed to be placed in geosynchronous orbit), IUS became a difficult stage to develop for a variety of complicated reasons. Many of them were technical, but the major ones involved management. Some, but far from all, of the management problems resulted from the fact that the IUS, which initially stood for *Interim* Upper Stage, was conceived as a temporary expedient until a more capable Space Tug could fly with the shuttle. When the Space Tug was not terminated but "just slid out year-by-year under budget pressure," as one air force general expressed it, the IUS shifted from being a minimal modification of an existing upper stage such as Transtage or Agena to become, starting about 1978, a projected "first line vehicle in the Space Transportation System." Yet "considerable cost reduction pressure [remained] as an outgrowth of the *interim* stage thinking."

Moreover, the air force was developing the vehicle under "a contract structure which strongly incentivized performance, but only provided limited cost incentives."[44]

The IUS ultimately overcame its birth pangs to become "an integral part of America's access to space for both military and civilian sectors." It had its beginnings in 1969 when presidential direction gave impetus to studies leading to the Space Shuttle. Since the shuttle would be incapable of reaching geosynchronous and other high orbits, the IUS ultimately became the solution. The DoD agreed to develop it, proposing in 1975 that it use solid propellants to hold down costs.

In August 1976, the air force selected Boeing Aerospace Company as the prime IUS contractor. The contract provided incentives for meeting performance and cost targets, but Boeing was liable for only 10 percent of cost overruns. Moreover, cost projections for IUS had been based on assumptions, according to Maj. Gen. William Yost of the air force, that "the M-X and Trident missile programs would develop most of the solid rocket motor technology . . . needed by the IUS. Unfortunately, the schedules for those programs slipped far enough that the IUS program became the leader in developing the solid rocket motor technology necessary to meet our performance requirements." This led the contractor to increase "spending to insure that he will achieve his performance goals and earn the performance fees." As a condition of revising the contract with Boeing in 1979, the air force insisted that the firm's apparent "management deficiencies be resolved," and Boeing appointed a new program manager, assigned senior managers to oversee major subcontractors, and instituted formal review to correct the problems.[45]

Boeing had begun a planned 18-month preliminary design phase in August 1976 when it won the contract, to be followed by a 28-month development phase. This would have made the IUS available by June 1980. Soon after winning the basic contract, Boeing subcontracted with CSD to design and test the solid motors to be used in the IUS. CSD chose to use a hydroxy-terminated polybutadiene propellant, as had Thiokol in the Antares IIIA motor for Scout. CSD selected a carbon-carbon material for the nozzle, which would be manufactured using a new process that held costs to a low level. It was making the case out of Kevlar. Thiokol was also using the same or similar materials on the contemporary Antares motor, raising questions about the extent to which CSD was taking the lead "in developing the solid rocket motor technology" needed for the IUS (as Yost claimed), but it appears that CSD and Thiokol were, in effect, competing for that lead from 1977 to 1979, with Thiokol winning the contest.[46]

At first things seemed to be going well with motor development. CSD conducted a series of tests in 1977 to prove the adequacy of the nozzle and motor. It subjected the nozzles to successful 85-second tests at the Air Force Rocket Propulsion Laboratory on June 10 and July 15. A follow-on 145-second test of the nozzle at the laboratory on October 7 was again successful. Moving to the Arnold Engineering Development Center (AEDC), CSD subjected a full-scale motor with 21,000 pounds of propellant to a 154-second test, which it completed successfully. On May 26, 1978, a further test of the nozzle material using the carbon-carbon made with the new, cost-saving technique again occurred without problems in a 140-second test firing at the Rocket Propulsion Laboratory.

283

Titan and

Shuttle

Boosters,

Other Solid

Propulsion,

1958–91

But on October 19, 1978, a test of the Kevlar case at AEDC resulted in its bursting at only 750 pounds per square inch of water pressure instead of CSD's prediction of 1,050 pounds. The firm decided that defective manufacturing equipment caused the failure. After redesigning the equipment and strengthening the structure of the case, AEDC conducted six more tests between January and September 1979. Five of them were successful, with the cases withstanding higher pressures than specified. By this time, the design of the IUS had evolved into two stages with similar larger and smaller motors. A test firing of the large motor was scheduled on October 17, 1978. Inspection of the motor revealed some propellant that was improperly cured, resulting in softness and blistering, delaying the test. With the propellant recast, the test occurred on March 16, 1979, with a 145-second firing that generated more than 50,000 pounds of thrust. Engineers vectored the nozzle several times, demonstrating its ability to direct the thrust for course corrections. A follow-on test of the small motor occurred on June 25, again with the nozzle moving. Both tests were successful.[47]

Most other tests in 1979 went well in most respects, but cracks had appeared in the nozzle of the small motor. Moreover, a special feature of the nozzle for the smaller motor was an extendable exit cone, which was added to the design in 1978. This was a series of conical pieces that in the final design (as of 1983) telescoped out (extended) and fit over one another to increase the nozzle expansion ratio from 49.3:1 without the extension to 181.1:1 with the pieces extended. Although the design, which would be used only on some missions, increased the weight of the motor, it added about 15 lbf-sec/lbm to the specific impulse. Unfortunately, about half the exit cones for the small motors were defective. Finally, five motors proved to have more "bad" propellant. Boeing and CSD said they could still be tested, but Aerospace Corporation, advising SAMSO, disagreed.

On October 1, 1979, SAMSO formed a tiger team of experts from several organizations (including NASA, the Rocket Propulsion Laboratory, and Aerospace Corporation) to investigate technical concerns and management. This resulted in the management changes at Boeing already mentioned and a change in one supplier. CSD had been making the large Kevlar motor cases, and Brunswick Corporation made the small one, which the team found to be superior. As a result, Brunswick became the supplier of both sets of cases.

During 1980, the production team solved the other problems. For example, the cracks in the nozzle of the smaller motor proved to result from unequal expansion of two materials. A silica-phenolic insulation material expanded faster than the carbon-carbon next to it. The solution was to wrap the silica phenolic with graphite to limit expansion. The problem with the exit cones resulted from the methods of the supplier, Kaiser, still learning about the properties of carbon-carbon. A change in tooling and ply patterns plus improved quality-control procedures provided the solution. The degraded propellant had all come from a single batch and was usable in tests. As a result, three rocket motor tests of each motor (small and large) during 1980 at the AEDC were successful. (All of these development tests at AEDC simulated conditions the motors would actually face in flight at altitude.) There were further problems with propellant cracks, delamination of the carbon material in the extendable exit cones, and the mechanism for extending the exit cones, but engineers solved them, too.[48]

The various technical and managerial problems had led to more than two years of delay and to cost overruns that basically doubled the originally projected cost of the IUS. Although many of the problems resulted from contractual arrangements and the initial, interim character of the upper stage, many of them involved fabrication methods and quality control. They showed that despite more than two and a half decades of continuous rocket development, rocket engineering in the United States still required constant attention to small details and, where new technology was involved, a certain amount of trial and error, although Thiokol's success with Antares IIIA showed that sometimes the process of innovation could go more smoothly. (But not always, as Thiokol's later problems with the shuttle solid-rocket boosters showed.) Because the IUS was designed principally for use on the Space Shuttle, NASA's delays with that program made the stretch-out of the IUS schedule less problematic than it could have been.[49]

On October 30, 1982, the first Titan 34D and the first IUS together successfully launched a Defense Satellite Communications Satellite II and the first DSCS III into geosynchronous orbit from Cape Canaveral. As planned, the second-stage burn achieved low-Earth orbit, with the first IUS motor carrying the third stage and the satellites into transfer orbit. The second IUS motor placed the payloads in geostationary orbit, with hydrazine thrusters making final adjustments in the placement of each satellite. During launch the telemetry failed, attributed to a leak in the seal of a switch. But the guidance/control system, flying "blind" (without telemetry) or external control from Earth autonomously carried out the provisions of the flight plan, as designed.[50]

As completely designed, the IUS was roughly 17 feet long and had a maximum diameter of 9.25 feet. Fully loaded, the large, first-stage motor (SRM-1) carried 21,400 pounds of ammonium perchlorate–HTPB–aluminum propellant, but the propellant load could be reduced as required for specific missions (as was done with the first launch). The smaller, second-stage motor (SRM-2) could carry up to 6,000 pounds of the same propellant. The propellant-delivered specific impulse of SRM-1 was upward of 295, that for SRM-2 about 290, increased to more than 300 lbf-sec/lbm with the extendable exit cone.[51]

To mention just one other use of an HTPB propellant, this technology came to the Delta with the Castor IVA strap-ons. A Castor IV (TX-526) had actually replaced the Castor II strap-ons in December 1975 for the Delta model 3914, but it was a reversion from the carboxy-terminated polybutadiene used in the older strap-on to polybutadiene–acrylic acid (PBAA) as the binder. The reason for the shift may have been cost, since the Castor IV at 29.8 feet long and 40 inches in diameter contained much more propellant than the 19.8-foot by 31-inch Castor II, and CTPB was more expensive than PBAA. But in the early 1980s, Goddard Space Flight Center (manager of the Delta program) shifted to an uprating with the Castor IVA. Tested and qualified in 1983, the new motors were not introduced then because of the impending phaseout of the Delta in favor of the Space Shuttle. With the post-*Challenger* resurrection of expendable launch vehicles, McDonnell Douglas proposed incorporating the Castor IVAs on Delta II as a low-risk improvement. The new strap-ons kept the steel case and graphite nozzle throat material. But they used the HTPB-aluminum binder with a higher loading of

solids. This increased the average thrust for the same-sized motor from 85,105 to 98,187 pounds.[52]

Analysis and Conclusions

Although the solid-propellant breakthrough achieved by the Polaris and Minuteman programs provided many technologies to launch vehicles, others followed. These included the carbon-phenolic throat, segmenting, and the tang-and-clevis joints for the Titan SRM; Flexseal nozzles used on the Space Shuttle's huge solid-rocket boosters; and the use of HMX in the propellant for the Antares IIA stage of the Scout launch vehicle. Although it apparently found its first use on an improved motor for the Maverick tactical missile, HTPB propellant seems to have first appeared on a launch vehicle in the Scout G1.

Although sometimes innovations occurred without many apparent problems, as in Thiokol's use of HTPB in the Scout's Antares IIIA, the IUS, employing many similar technologies, faced a whole host of difficulties, many of them technical. The field joints for the shuttle caused the *Challenger* tragedy, and when Hercules developed the solid-rocket motor upgrade for the Titan IVB, technical problems delayed launch of the first uprated launch vehicle until well beyond the period covered by this history. Rocket engineers continued to advance the state of their art, but often they could do so only by trial and error. There was no such thing as a mature rocket science that could guide them effortlessly through the design of new technologies, but accumulated experience, data, computers, instrumentation, and telemetry allowed practitioners to solve most problems.

CHAPTER 8

Conclusions and Epilogue

DURING THE LAST 45 YEARS, LAUNCH VEHI-cles have propelled countless spacecraft and satellites into space, in the process revolutionizing life on planet Earth. Americans have become dependent upon satellites for everything from what they watch on television to how they wage war. Space telescopes and other spacecraft have greatly expanded our knowledge of the universe. What enabled the United States to develop the technology for access to space so quickly? One major contributor was the cold war, whose terminus is the end point for this book. Had it not been for the Soviet threat, symbolized by *Sputnik*, the enormous expenditures needed to develop U.S. missiles, launch vehicles, and satellites would have been lacking.[1]

There seems to be no accurate compilation of total expenditures on missiles and launch vehicles during the cold war. Obviously, however, the outlays were enormous and constituted a virtual sine qua non for the speedy development of the technology. An early (1965) estimate of the total costs for ballistic missiles to that point in time suggested a figure of $17 billion, equal to some $106 billion in 2005 dollars. Including missile sites, which were irrelevant to launch vehicles, this figure also covered factories for producing propellants, engines, airframes, and guidance/control systems; test facilities; ranges with their testing, tracking, and control equipment; laboratories; and much else.[2] A further indicator of the huge costs of missiles and launch vehicles was the $9.3 billion (nearly $55 billion in 2005 dollars) spent on the Saturn launch-vehicle family.[3]

Fears of Soviet missile attacks and the spending they stimulated were one factor in the development of launch-vehicle technology. They also provided the context for a second major contributor, the work of heterogeneous engineers in stimulating Congress, several presidential administrations, and the American people to invest the money needed

FIG. 8.1
Monkey Baker posing with a model of a Jupiter vehicle, one of which launched it into space in an early example of the use of a missile as a launch vehicle, part of the space race inaugurated by the Soviets' launch of *Sputnik*. (Photo courtesy of NASA)

for rapid development. Without individuals like Trevor Gardner, John von Neumann, Bernard Schriever, Theodore von Kármán, Wernher von Braun, and William F. "Red" Raborn, funding for missiles and rockets (with their frequent failures in the early years) would not have been forthcoming.

As missiles and launch vehicles increased in size and complexity, it is not surprising that many of them experienced failure. Americans recognized the arcane nature of the technology by their use of the term "rocket science" to describe it. Ironically, the rocket "scientists" could not always predict the problems the technology encountered in operation. Methods of testing rockets and missiles, technical reports, computer tools, and other supporting infrastructure continued to grow. But as recently as 2003, when the *Columbia* disaster occurred, NASA discovered once again that it did not fully understand all aspects of rocket behavior despite extensive experience. Hardly an isolated case, this major accident simply reemphasized that predictability of rocket behavior had been problematic from Robert Goddard's inability to reach the altitudes he had forecast until very near the present. If we define rocket science as a body of knowledge complete and mature enough to allow accurate predictions of problems, then clearly, such a science does not exist. Maybe it will someday, but what we currently have is rocket engineering.

Of course, there are other ways of defining science. And recent science has hardly been immune from uncertainties, such as those regarding the big bang theory about how the universe arose. Moreover, the success of rocket developers in resolving unanticipated problems and getting their creations to work certainly compares favorably with scientists' accommodations of unexpected data by adjustment of theories. The difference lies in science's basic quest to understand the universe as compared with rocket engineers' effort to make their vehicles meet design goals. These engineers used any available resources to reach that end, including science. Certainly the engineers, especially those engaged in developing engineering theory (often called engineering science), wanted to understand how rockets worked. But often they had to "fix" problems in the absence of such fundamental understanding. In such cases, they had to resort to trial and error, finding a solution that worked without necessarily understanding *why* it worked. Accumulated knowledge, engineering theory, and intuition helped in correcting problems, but the solution did not always work when a particular technology had to be scaled up to a larger size. Sometimes, in fact, innovative solutions ran counter to existing theory.

This reality shows that the basic process of developing rockets constituted engineering, not science. Such an argument tallies with the general theses of Edwin Layton, Walter Vincenti, and Eugene S. Ferguson about engineering in general as different from science—especially their points about engineers' focus on *doing* as opposed to scientists' *knowing*, on the importance of design for engineers, and on the role of art in that design. Vincenti, especially, proposed more historical analysis of the ways engineers sometimes must make decisions in the absence of complete or certain knowledge.[4]

Research for this book did not start with the thought of applying Vincenti, Layton, and Ferguson's arguments to rocket technology. Instead, as I gathered information about the process of missile and launch-vehicle development, I became increasingly convinced that it fit the mold of engineering, not science. This is particularly true in the areas of injection, ignition, and propulsion of liquid propellants and of combustion instability in solids. Problems in these areas occurred in the design of the V-2, the H-1, F-1, and space shuttle main engines as well as many solid-propellant motors. A. O. Tischler, NASA assistant director for propulsion, in 1962 called injector design "more a black art than a science."[5] With the passage of time, the art became less "black," but art it remained.

Problems with rocket design were not exclusive to propulsion. As early designs had to be scaled up or modified with new and better materials to improve performance, unanticipated problems continued to occur through the end of the period of this book and beyond. Failure to understand the behavior of foam covering the Space Shuttle's external tank as it rose through the atmosphere continued beyond the *Columbia* disaster. Problems in developing the solid-rocket motor upgrade for the Titan IVB persisted beyond the end of the cold war. These and other instances demonstrate the continuing uncertainties accompanying rocket engineering, especially in an environment where speed and cost control limited basic research.

In the face of this unpredictability, it is noteworthy that missile and launch-vehicle technology evolved as quickly as it did. Design and development engineers did exceptionally well to find innovative solutions to problems and allow the technology to advance as successfully as it did.

Another key to the speedy development of rocket technology was the process of innovation. Sadly, known sources often shine little light on the individuals or processes involved. Interviews and correspondence with rocket engineers sometimes yield information.[6] But even the principals in a particular development frequently cannot remember who came up with a discovery or how it came about. Engineers typically worked in large teams to design rocket systems or components. And many innovations involved more than one firm. Otto Glasser at the Western Development Division offered an interesting analogy for the difficulty of finding out who contributed significantly to innovation under such circumstances: "If you were to back into a buzz saw could you tell me which tooth it is that cut you?"[7]

Many innovations did not arise from initial design but occurred in response to problems during testing. Examples of these that seem to fit Glasser's "which tooth?" analogy include the process of roll-ring forging developed by UTC, Westinghouse, and the Ladish Company and UTC's tape-wrapped, carbon-phenolic nozzle throat for the Titan solid-rocket motors. The companies doing the innovating are clear, but we do not know which individuals were the principal innovators. How Aerojet engineers fixed problems with the Transtage (ranging from a weakness in a nozzle extension to malfunctioning bipropellant valves) likewise remains somewhat mysterious. Regardless, all of these technologies appear to exemplify trial-and-error engineering.

What we do know about innovations in rocket development suggests that they did not follow a single pattern. Hugh Aitken provided a felicitous description in his book about radio technology, saying that it involved "a process extending over time in which information from several sources came to be combined in new ways."[8] In the case of missiles and launch vehicles, large numbers of firms, institutions, and organizations helped provide the requisite information. Among those that contributed were firms such as Aerojet, Rocketdyne, Pratt & Whitney, Douglas, the Martin Company, UTC/CSD, and Thiokol; and other organizations like the air force's Western Development Division and its successors, the army's counterparts at Redstone Arsenal, the navy's special projects office and its successors, NASA Headquarters and various centers (notably JPL, Langley, Lewis, and Marshall for rocketry), the Naval Ordnance Test Station and its successors, the Air Force Rocket Propulsion Laboratory (under various names), the Arnold Engineering Development Center, the Chemical Propulsion Information Agency (CPIA) and its predecessors, and the Armour Institute (later Illinois Institute of Technology).

During developmental planning, representatives from entities like these met to exchange ideas and information. Then, if problems arose for which there were no known explanations and/or no evident solutions, as often happened, engineers and other experts from perhaps different organizations met to brainstorm and troubleshoot. With the enduring problem of combustion instability, for instance, numerous university researchers, as well as other engineers, have long been seeking both understanding and solutions.[9] Surviving sources indicate that the general process was often complex, with no record of specific contributors except the authors of technical reports. But the authors themselves often wrote in the passive voice, masking individual participants beyond the authors themselves, who presumably were involved. Engineers sometimes remembered (but how accurately?) some details of solutions but not always the precise process.

Among the factors that conditioned rapid development of missile technology, the existing literature points to interservice competition, often as a problem but also as a spur to innovation.[10] Virtually unnoticed in the literature but probably more important was interservice and interagency cooperation. The CPIA was a key promoter of cooperative exchange of information, but not the only one. For instance, the air force saw the navy's Polaris program as a competitor for roles, missions, and funding. The Polaris competition encouraged the air force's development of its own solid-propellant missile, Minuteman. Yet ironically, Polaris itself might not have been possible without technologies the air force developed. Minuteman, in turn, borrowed the use of aluminum as a fuel from the navy. Likewise, the air force reluctantly accepted NASA as a developer of rocket technology, and the army was not happy to lose the von Braun team and JPL to the civilian space agency. Both services, however, cooperated with NASA (and vice versa), with the air force

FIG. 8.2
A static test of
a Space Shuttle
solid-rocket
booster at the
Morton Thiokol
test site in
Wasatch, Utah,
on January 20,
1989. (Photo
courtesy of
NASA)

loaning important managers like Samuel Phillips to help NASA with its programs. Moreover, many astronauts came to NASA from the U.S. Marine Corps, the navy, and the air force.[11]

Technology transfer also contributed to rapid rocket development, but its details remained almost as elusive as those involving innovation. Federal contracting agencies often precluded contractors from treating innovations developed under government contract as trade secrets or company property. Lockheed, for example, was unable to protect its Lockseal technology, permitting Thiokol to increase its size and use it to vector the exhaust from the shuttle solid-rocket boosters under the name Flexseal.

Engineers frequently learned about the rocket technology of one firm or organization, established their credentials, and moved to another organization, carrying their knowledge with them. This helped transfer technology and promote overall rocket development. For instance, after Charles Bartley developed early rubberized, composite solid propellants at JPL, he founded the Grand Central Rocket Company, which participated in solid-rocket development and then became part of Lockheed Propulsion Company in 1960–61.[12] Bartley also transferred JPL technologies to Thiokol when it entered the rocket business. Barnet R. Adelman had worked with both liquid and solid propellants at JPL. He then became technical director of the Rocket Fuel Division at Phillips Petroleum and then director of vehicle engineering for the Ramo-Wooldridge Corporation. At Ramo-Wooldridge, he became a major supporter of the Minuteman missile, along with Col. Edward N. Hall. Next, he helped found United Research Corporation (later UTC/CSD). The knowledge he carried with him undoubtedly helped UTC develop the solid-rocket motors for the Titan III and IVA.[13] Adelman and other UTC executives' knowledge of people in the solid-propellant field also enabled them to hire other experienced engineers who furthered the success of the firm.

The previous chapters have covered many other examples of technology transfer through people moving from one organization to another. A well-known example was the von Braun team, including Krafft Ehricke, who brought German V-2 technology to the United States. Importantly, though, the technology they transferred was only part of the story. Americans, notably Rocketdyne engineers, learned much from the V-2 and its German developers, but they went on to create major innovations of their own in developing successor engines, extending from the Redstone to the space shuttle main engine. This synergism contributed in complex ways to American rocket development.

Management systems constituted another factor in the rapid development of missile and launch-vehicle technology. Without such systems (and the systems engineering they fostered), the various components of rockets would not have worked together with increasing reliability to launch their payloads as time passed. Such systems (and the individual management skills that complemented and implemented them) were especially necessary as the numbers of people from industry, government, and universities increased and became interdependent. Growth was rapid. The Atlas missile had only 56 major contractors in 1955. By decade's end, the number had escalated to roughly 2,000. To keep this many organizations on schedule and to ensure quality control, Gen. Bernard Schriever availed himself of a systems engineering–technical direction contractor (Ramo-Wooldridge). Beyond that problematic arrangement, the Western Development Division instituted a management-control system to keep track of schedules and to deal with problems as they arose. Graphs, charts, and computer tracking permitted Schriever and his successors to keep their projects more or less on schedule.

The enormously complex Polaris system, likewise, led Adm. "Red" Raborn of the navy to oversee development of the Program Evaluation and Review Technique, analogous to Schriever's system. Critics complained about both systems, but without some such arrangements, early missile development could hardly have been as successful and rapid as it was.

George Mueller and Sam Phillips brought these kinds of systems to NASA, enabling it to land astronauts on the Moon in less than a decade from President Kennedy's 1961 exhortation to do so. These systems allowed Apollo to stay on schedule and within budget while still achieving configuration control. The overall success of missile and launch-vehicle development owed much to such arrangements.

The basic processes of rocket engineering did not change abruptly with the end of the cold war about 1991. But the context in which research and development had to occur suffered a drastic shift. It became less urgent for new technologies to appear, while Congress exercised stringent oversight over costs and schedules. Basing itself on studies in the late 1980s and early 1990s, the air force responded to the new environment with the Evolved Expendable Launch Vehicle (EELV) program. This replaced Titan II, Delta II, Atlas II, and Titan IV with a new series of boosters capable of launching 2,500 to 45,000 pounds into low-Earth orbit with a 98 percent reliability rate. This exceeded capabilities of previous launch vehicles at costs 25 to 50 percent below earlier figures.

The air force provided four $30 million contracts in August 1995 to Lockheed Martin, Alliant Techsystems (which acquired Hercules Aerospace Company, the former Hercules Powder Company, in March 1995), Boeing, and McDonnell Douglas to develop proposals for the EELV vehicles. Out of this process, McDonnell Douglas (later acquired by Boeing) and Lockheed Martin won contracts for actual development.[14] The further development of this program is beyond the scope of this book, but the Lockheed Martin Atlas V's successful launch on August 21, 2002, and that of Boeing's Delta IV on November 20, 2002, suggested that the EELV launchers would capture most of the military market. The use of a Russian RD-180 engine on the Atlas V symbolized the radical change that had occurred since the end of the cold war. The air force reportedly believed as of August 2002 "that through 2020 the two new EELV families w[ould] reduce the cost per pound to orbit to $7,000 compared with $20,000 for the old booster fleet," saving "$10 billion in launch costs"—a 50 percent reduction "compared with launching the same military payloads on old Delta, Atlas and Titan boosters."[15]

Similar concerns about cost affected NASA's efforts to develop new launch vehicles.[16] NASA also had to contend with concerns about safety after the *Columbia* disaster. In 2005–2006, the agency developed a concept for a safer pair of launch vehicles that would use technologies from the Space Shuttle or other existing hardware without the problems of an orbiter with wings that could be struck by debris from an external tank. A crew launch vehicle (named Ares I) would consist of one enlarged solid-rocket booster derived from the shuttle, a stage powered by a Rocketdyne J-2X engine (evolved from the J-2 used on the Saturn V), and a crew capsule at the top of the stack, equipped with an escape rocket to separate the crew from the launch vehicle in the event of problems. In this Apollo-like capsule, the crew would face little danger from debris separating from the shuttle on launch, as happened with tragic consequences during the *Columbia* launch in 2003 and again (without significant damage) during the launch of Space Shuttle *Discovery* in 2005 and subsequent shuttle launches in 2006.

For future space exploration, NASA also planned a heavy-lift launch vehicle named Ares V with two solid-rocket boosters, a central element derived from the shuttle's external tank, five RS-68 engines modified from the Delta IV, and an earth-departure stage propelled by a J-2X engine. Like Ares I, this vehicle would be configured in stages, but the first-stage solid-rocket boosters would flank the central booster tank, with the liquid engines above the tank. Ares V thus resembled a Titan IV in its general configuration. NASA calculated that these two future vehicles would be 10 times as safe as the shuttle and would not cost as much as a completely new vehicle because of the use of proven technologies.[17] However, both vehicles were in a state of development and could easily change as further possibilities came under study.

It would be foolhardy to predict how the struggle for cheaper access to space will play out in the new environment ushered in by the fall of the Soviet Union. However, maybe this history of the uncertainties and difficulties of developing launch vehicles in a different environment will highlight the kinds of problems rocket engineers can expect to encounter in a more cost-constrained atmosphere. Rocket reliability improved significantly in the 50 years or so following the serious beginnings of U.S. missile and rocket development. Recently, launch vehicles have experienced only a 2–5 percent failure rate. By comparison, the first 227 Atlas launches failed 30 percent of the time. Nevertheless, in 2003 the Columbia Accident Investigation Board stated, "Building and launching rockets is still a very dangerous business and will continue to be so for the foreseeable future while we gain experience at it. It is unlikely that launching a space vehicle will ever be as routine an undertaking as commercial air travel."[18] Knowledge of this reality, coupled with the historical experiences recounted previously, may help contemporary rocket engineers design both cheaper and better launch vehicles. Perhaps Congress and the American people can also benefit from knowing the kinds of challenges rocket engineers are likely to face.

NOTES

Introduction

1. See Edwin Layton, "Mirror-Image Twins: The Communities of Science and Technology in 19th Century America," *Technology and Culture: The International Quarterly of the Society for the History of Technology* 12 (1971): 562–63, 565, 575–76, 578, 580; Edwin T. Layton Jr., "Technology as Knowledge," *Technology and Culture: The International Quarterly of the Society for the History of Technology* 15 (1974): 40; Edwin Layton, "Presidential Address: Through the Looking Glass, or News from Lake Mirror Image," *Technology and Culture: The International Quarterly of the Society for the History of Technology* 28 (1987): 602, 605; Walter G. Vincenti, *What Engineers Know and How They Know It: Analytic Studies from Aeronautical History* (Baltimore, Md.: Johns Hopkins University Press, 1990), pp. 4, 6–7, 161; Eugene S. Ferguson, *Engineering and the Mind's Eye* (Cambridge, Mass.: MIT Press, 1992), pp. xi, 1, 3, 9, 12, 194. Cf. Bruno Latour, *Science in Action: How to Follow Scientists and Engineers through Society* (Cambridge, Mass.: Harvard University Press, 1987), pp. 107, 130–31, 174, and Layton himself as quoted in *The Social Construction of Technological Systems: New Directions in the Sociology and History of Technology,* ed. Wiebe E. Bijker, Thomas P. Hughes, and Trevor J. Pinch (Cambridge, Mass.: MIT Press, 1987), p. 20.

2. Résumé, Ronald L. Simmons, no date (after 2000), sent to author in the summer of 2002; e-mail messages, Ronald L. Simmons to J. D. Hunley, July 15, 2002 (quotations from e-mails).

3. For a discussion of nuclear propulsion, see Ray A. Williamson and Roger D. Launius, "Rocketry and the Origins of Space Flight," in *To Reach the High Frontier: A History of U.S. Launch Vehicles,* ed. Roger D. Launius and Dennis R. Jenkins (Lexington: University Press of Kentucky, 2002), pp. 60–63.

4. Cf. NASA Education Division, *Rockets: Physical Science Teacher's Guide with Activities* (Washington, D.C.: NASA EP-291, 1993), pp. 12–18.

5. Donald MacKenzie, *Inventing Accuracy: A Historical Sociology of Nuclear Missile Guidance* (Cambridge, Mass.: MIT Press, 1990), p. 28 (and more generally, pp. 410–13); John Law, "Technology and Heterogeneous Engineering: The Case of the Portuguese Expansion," in *The Social Construction of Technological Systems: New Directions in the Sociology and History of Technology,* ed. Wiebe E. Bijker, Thomas P. Hughes, and Trevor Pinch (Cambridge, Mass.: MIT Press, 1987), pp. 111–34.

Chapter 1

1. This chapter severely condenses numerous chapters in a much longer and differently organized manuscript. Consequently, there is room to cite only the most important sources. For most of the information about Goddard, see J. D. Hunley, "The Enigma of Robert H. Goddard," *Technology and Culture: The International Quarterly of the Society for the History of Technology* 36 (Apr. 1995): 327–50. The Goddard portion of this chapter borrows extensively from this last source, published at the time by the University of Chicago Press, but now by the Johns Hopkins University Press, which has kindly allowed me to use material from the article. See also George P. Sutton, *History of Liquid Propellant*

Rocket Engines (Reston, Va.: American Institute of Aeronautics and Astronautics, 2006), esp. pp. 75, 139, 224, 257–69.

2. Esther C. Goddard and G. Edward Pendray, eds., *The Papers of Robert H. Goddard* (hereafter cited as *Goddard Papers*), 3 vols. (New York: McGraw-Hill, 1970), pp. 176, 177, 190, 224, 233, 277, 322–23, 451, 469, 470–71, 472–73, 524, 528, 531, 663, 680, 726, 744, 832, 838, 851, 874, 930, 1028, 1061, 1168, 1264, 1352, 1423, 1433, 1443, 1466, 1502, esp. 1557.

3. Frank H. Winter, *Rockets into Space* (Cambridge, Mass.: Harvard University Press, 1990), p. 18, and his *Prelude to the Space Age: The Rocket Societies* (Washington, D.C.: Smithsonian Institution Press, 1983), p. 14, respectively.

4. "A Method of Reaching Extreme Altitudes," *Goddard Papers*, pp. 337–38, 397.

5. Winter, *Rockets into Space*, p. 29; diary entries, photo captions, and report, *Goddard Papers*, pp. 580–82, 587–90, 769; Milton Lehman, *Robert H. Goddard: Pioneer of Space Research* (New York: Da Capo Press, 1988), p. 130; Robert H. Goddard, *Rocket Development: Liquid-Fuel Rocket Research, 1929–1941*, ed. Esther C. Goddard and G. Edward Pendray (New York: Prentice-Hall, 1948), pp. xix, 107; *Goddard Papers*, pp. 786, 911, 917, 983, 1053, 1185, 1200, 1207, 1663–66.

6. Theodore von Kármán with Lee Edson, *The Wind and Beyond: Theodore von Kármán, Pioneer in Aviation and Pathfinder in Space* (Boston: Little, Brown, 1967), p. 242; Hunley, "Enigma of Robert H. Goddard," pp. 345–46; Goddard, *Rocket Development*, pp. 17–18, 20–31, 44, 90–91, 101, 104, 107, 108, 125; Goddard's notes from "Test of September 29, 1931," pp. 102–14, esp. p. 113, box 18, Goddard Papers at Clark University, Worcester, Mass.; "Report on Rocket Work at Roswell, New Mexico," Dec. 15, 1931, *Goddard Papers*, p. 815; Esther Goddard, "Excerpts from Diary of Robert H. Goddard 1898–1945," p. 527 of typescript at Clark University, entry for Sept. 29, 1931.

7. "Liquid-Propellant Rocket Development," *Goddard Papers*, pp. 968–84; letter, Goddard to Abbot, Sept. 28, 1935, ibid., p. 937.

8. Hans Barth, *Hermann Oberth: "Vater der Raumfahrt"* (Munich: Bechtle, 1991), pp. 15, 25, 67–72, 367n1; Oberth's contribution to *Männer der Rakete*, ed. Werner Brügel (Leipzig: Verlag Hachmeister & Thal, 1933), p. 43.

9. Lehman, *Goddard*, p. 133; cf. *Goddard Papers*, pp. 522, 736.

10. Hermann Oberth, *Die Rakete zu den Planetenräumen* (1923; repr., Nuremberg: Uni-Verlag, 1960), passim, esp. pp. 90–92.

11. Michael J. Neufeld, "Weimar Culture and Futuristic Technology: The Rocketry and Spaceflight Fad in Germany, 1923–1933," *Technology and Culture* 31 (1990): 731–32; Barth, *Oberth*, pp. 94–98; I[lse] Essers, *Max Valier: Ein Vorkämpfer der Weltraumfahrt* (Düsseldorf: VDI-Verlag, 1968), pp. 82–117, 166, 181–82, 308–309; Hermann Oberth, *Ways to Spaceflight*, trans. Agence Tunisienne de Public-Relations (Washington, D.C.: NASA TT F-622, 1972), pp. 378–79.

12. Erik Bergaust, *Wernher von Braun* (Washington, D.C.: National Space Institute, 1976), pp. 34–36; Ernst Stuhlinger and Frederick I. Ordway, *Wernher von Braun: Aufbruch in den Weltraum* (Munich: Bechtle, 1992), p. 46; Barth, *Oberth*, p. 194; von Braun's comment in a letter to Oberth in 1948, in *Hermann Oberth: Briefwechsel*, ed. Hans Barth, 2 vols. (Bucharest: Kriterion Verlag, 1979–84), I:139.

13. *Hermann Oberth: Briefwechsel*, ed. Hans Barth, 2 vols. (Bucharest: Kriterion Verlag, 1979–84), II:100; John Elder, "The Experience of Hermann

Oberth," paper presented at the 42nd Congress of the International Astronautical Federation, Oct. 5–11, 1991, Montreal, Canada, pp. 5, 8, published in *History of Rocketry and Astronautics: Proceedings of the Twenty-fifth History Symposium of the International Academy of Astronautics,* vol. ed. J. D. Hunley, AAS History Series (San Diego: Univelt, 1997), 20:12; Michael J. Neufeld, "The Guided Missile and the Third Reich: Peenemünde and the Forging of a Technological Revolution," in *Science, Technology and National Socialism,* ed. Monika Renneberg and Mark Walker (Cambridge: Cambridge University Press, 1994), pp. 51–71, esp. 54–58; Konrad K. Dannenberg, "Hermann Oberth: Half a Century Ahead," http://www.meaus.com/centuryAhead.html (accessed Nov. 13, 2003).

14. *Goddard Papers,* p. v.

15. J. D. Hunley, "The Legacies of Robert H. Goddard and Hermann J. Oberth," *Journal of the British Interplanetary Society* (hereafter *JBIS*) 49 (1996): 43–48.

16. Wernher von Braun, "Reminiscences of German Rocketry," *JBIS* 15, no. 3 (May–June 1956): 128–31, 134; von Braun, "Behind the Scenes of Rocket Development in Germany, 1928 through 1945," pp. 13–14, quotation from p. 11, manuscript available at the U.S. Space and Rocket Center, Huntsville, Ala. (in 1995, part of the von Braun collection in a folder marked "Manuscript: Behind the Scenes . . ."); Walter Dornberger, *V-2,* trans. James Cleugh and Geoffrey Halliday (New York: Viking, 1958), pp. 26, 33, 36, 40–41; Michael J. Neufeld, *The Rocket and the Reich: Peenemünde and the Coming of the Ballistic Missile Era* (New York: Free Press, 1995), pp. 54–55.

17. Neufeld, *Rocket and the Reich,* pp. 68–70, 83–84, 204, 220–22, 264, 273; Dornberger, *V-2,* pp. xvii–xviii, 54–56, 214, 218–23; interview of Fritz Mueller by Michael Neufeld, Huntsville, Ala., Nov. 6, 1989, tape 1, side 2, on file in the Smithsonian National Air and Space Museum (NASM) Space Division, Washington, D.C.; von Braun, "Reminiscences," pp. 129–30, 133, 137; Donald MacKenzie, *Inventing Accuracy: A Historical Sociology of Nuclear Missile Guidance* (Cambridge, Mass.: MIT Press, 1990), pp. 53, 299; Frederick Ordway III and Mitchell R. Sharpe, *The Rocket Team* (New York: Thomas Y. Crowell, 1979), p. 35; Konrad K. Dannenberg, "From Vahrenwald via the Moon to Dresden," in *History of Rocketry and Astronautics: Proceedings of the Twenty-fourth Symposium of the International Academy of Astronautics, Dresden, Germany, 1990,* ed. J. D. Hunley, AAS History Series (San Diego: Univelt, 1997), 19:122–23; Guido De Maeseneer, *Peenemünde: The Extraordinary Story of Hitler's Secret Weapons, V-1 and V-2* (Vancouver: AJ Publishing, 2001), pp. 304–305; H. A. Schulze, "Technical Data on the Development of the A4 (V-2)," prepared by the Historical Office, George C. Marshall Space Flight Center, Feb. 25, 1965, pp. 23–24, seen in the U.S. Space and Rocket Center, Schulze Collection; Henry Friedman, "Summary Report on A-4 Control and Stability," June 1947 (report no. F-SU-2152-ND), prepared at Headquarters Air Materiel Command, Wright Field, Dayton, Ohio, pp. 10, 15, seen in the NASA Historical Reference Collection (hereafter NHRC), filed under V-2 in Lektriever 4; Heinz Dieter Hölsken, *Die V-Waffen: Entstehung-Propaganda-Kriegseinsatz* (Stuttgart: Deutsche Verlags-Anstalt, 1984), pp. 163, 200–201.

18. J. D. Hunley, "Braun, Wernher von" in *Dictionary of American Biography,* Supplement 10, 1976–80 (New York: Charles Scribner's Sons, 1995), pp. 65–68, and "Wernher von Braun, 1912–1977," in *Notable Twentieth-Century Scientists,* ed. Emily J. McMurray (New York: Gale Research, 1995), pp. 2093–96.

19. Neufeld, *Rocket and the Reich,* pp. 5–21, 118–24, 127, 129, 139, 141–43, 144, 161–64, 167–74, 191–95, 201–203, 223, 247, 257, 264, 273.

20. Dieter K. Huzel, *Peenemünde to Canaveral* (Englewood Cliffs, N.J.: Prentice-Hall, 1962), p. 126, for the quotation; numerous reports of meetings scattered throughout the documents that survive from Peenemünde and Kummersdorf, e.g., Niederschrift no. 401/37, 6/8–9/9/37 on roll 6 of microfilm at NASM, FE 74b, and Niederschrift über die Besprechung am 23.4.42 in folder 3 of the Peenemünde Document Collection at NASM.

21. Ernst Stuhlinger et al., "Preface," *From Peenemünde to Outer Space, Commemorating the Fiftieth Birthday of Wernher von Braun, March 23, 1962,* ed. Ernst Stuhlinger et al. (Huntsville, Ala.: NASA Marshall Space Flight Center, 1962), pp. vii–viii, for first two quotations; Ernst Stuhlinger and Frederick L. Ordway III, *Wernher von Braun: A Biographical Memoir* (Malabar, Fla.: Krieger, 1994), p. 37, for third quotation.

22. Frank J. Malina, "The Jet Propulsion Laboratory: Its Origins and First Decade of Work," *Spaceflight* 6 (1964): 160–61; "Biographical Information" compiled by Malina on May 1, 1968, and available in folder 001418, "Malina, Frank J.," in NHRC; FBI file on Parsons, no. 65-59589, p. 8, seen at FBI Headquarters in Washington, D.C.; interview of Frank Malina by R. Cargill Hall, Oct. 29, 1968, p. 1, transcript at the JPL Archives in Pasadena, Calif.; interview of Malina by James H. Wilson, June 8, 1973, p. 17, transcript in JPL Archives in Pasadena.

23. Homer E. Newell Jr., "Guided Missile Kinematics" (Naval Research Laboratory, May 22, 1945), p. 1, seen in the National Archives (NA), Record Group (RG) 218, Joint New Weapons Committee (JNWC), Subj. File May 1942–45.

24. Frank J. Malina, "On the GALCIT Rocket Research Project, 1936–38," in *First Steps toward Space,* Smithsonian Annals of Flight, no. 10, ed. Frederick C. Durant III and George S. James (Washington, D.C.: Smithsonian Institution Press, 1974), pp. 117, 120–21; Frank J. Malina, "America's First Long-Range-Missile and Space Exploration Program: The ORDCIT Project of the Jet Propulsion Laboratory, 1943–1946: A Memoir," in *Essays on the History of Rocketry and Astronautics: Proceedings of the Third through the Sixth History Symposia of the International Academy of Astronautics,* ed. R. Cargill Hall, AAS History Series, vol. 7, pt. 2 (San Diego: Univelt, 1986), p. 358; Frank J. Malina, "Rocketry in California," *Astronautics* 41 (July 1938): 3–6, found in an unnumbered folder in the Frank J. Malina Collection, Library of Congress, Manuscripts Division, box 12; Malina, "Report on Jet Propulsion for the National Academy of Sciences Committee on Air Corps Research," Dec. 21, 1938, Malina Collection, box 9, folder 9.1; and Malina, "Characteristics of the Rocket Motor Unit Based on the Theory of Perfect Gases," *Journal of the Franklin Institute* 230 (Oct. 1940): 433–54.

25. Frank Malina, "The Rocket Pioneers: Memoirs of the Infant Days of Rocketry at Caltech," *Engineering and Science* 31, no. 5 (Feb. 1968): 32; Judith R. Goodstein, *Millikan's School: A History of California Institute of Technology* (New York: W.W. Norton, 1991), esp. pp. 74–75, 163–64; Malina, "GALCIT Rocket Research Project," pp. 120–21; Alan E. Slater, ed., "Research and Development at the Jet Propulsion Laboratory, GALCIT," *JBIS* 6 (Sept. 1946): 41–45, 50–54; Frank Malina, "The U.S. Army Air Corps Jet Propulsion Research Project, GALCIT Project No. 1, 1939–1946: A Memoir," in *History of Rocketry and Astronautics,* ed. Hall, vol. 7, pt. 2, pp. 160–62, 167–68, 179–80, 194–95; J. D. Hunley, interview with Martin Summerfield, Sept. 27, 1994, transcript in author's possession, pp. 3–8; Malina, "ORDCIT Project," pp. 353–54, 356–70; Howard S. Seifert, "History of Ordnance Research at the Jet Propulsion Laboratory, 1945–1953" (Pasadena, Calif.: Jet Propulsion Laboratory, Caltech, July 29,

1953), pp. 18–20, seen in the JPL Archives, History Collection, folder 3-97; F. J. Malina, "Development and Flight Performance of a High Altitude Sounding Rocket the 'WAC Corporal,'" JPL Report no. 4-18, Jan. 24, 1946, pp. 6–8; Clayton R. Koppes, *JPL and the American Space Program: A History of the Jet Propulsion Laboratory* (New Haven, Conn.: Yale University Press, 1982), pp. 30–31.

26. Frank H. Winter and George S. James, "Highlights of 50 Years of Aerojet, a Pioneering American Rocket Company, 1942–1992," paper presented at the 44th IAF Congress, Oct. 16–22, 1993, Graz, Austria, pp. 2–3.

27. Department of the Army, Ordnance Corps, "Report No. 20-100, The Corporal: A Surface-to-Surface Guided Ballistic Missile" (Pasadena, Calif.: Jet Propulsion Laboratory, Caltech, Mar. 17, 1958), pp. 2–4, 7–8, 10–11, 16, 20–26, 53, 55–59, 89, 105–10, 137–38, from the JPL Archives, History Collection, folder 3-355; Seifert, "History of Ordnance Research at the Jet Propulsion Laboratory," pp. 4, 10, 20, 25, 30; James W. Bragg, "Development of the Corporal: The Embryo of the Army Missile Program," Historical Monograph No. 4 (Redstone Arsenal, Ala.: Reports and Historical Branch, Army Ordnance Missile Command, 1961), 1:xv, 44, 108–109, 112, 115–17, 165–67, 170; 2:17-4 to 17-6, 19-1 to 19-3, 19-6 to 19-7, 28-2; Koppes, *JPL*, pp. 31–32, 39, 47, 51–53, 64–65; William H. Pickering with James H. Wilson, "Countdown to Space Exploration: A Memoir of the Jet Propulsion Laboratory, 1944–1958," in *History of Rocketry and Astronautics*, ed. Hall, vol. 9, pt. 2, p. 393; Ted Nicholas and Rita Rossi, *U.S. Missile Data Book, 1994*, 18th ed. (Fountain Valley, Calif.: Data Search Associates, Nov. 1993), pp. 3-2, 3-5; Frederick I. Ordway III and Ronald C. Wakeford, *International Missile and Spacecraft Guide* (New York: McGraw-Hill, 1960), p. 3.

28. [Mary T. Cagle], "History of the Sergeant Weapon System" (Redstone Arsenal, Ala.: U.S. Army Missile Command, [1963]), pp. 23–25, 31, 43–47, 97.

29. Ibid., pp. 64–65, 193–94, 199–200, 202–203; Koppes, *JPL*, pp. 63–66, 71–77.

30. Koppes, *JPL*, pp. 79–93; JPL, "Explorer I," *Astronautics* (Apr. 1958): 22, 83; James M. Grimwood and Frances Strowd, "History of the Jupiter Missile System" (Huntsville, Ala.: Army Ordnance Missile Command, 1962), p. 81; John W. Bullard, "History of the Redstone Missile System," Historical Monograph No. AMC 23 M (Redstone Arsenal, Ala.: Army Missile Command, 1965), pp. 140–46.

31. Hunley, interview with Martin Summerfield, Sept. 27, 1994, p. 25; Malina, "Jet Propulsion Laboratory," pp. 164, 217–18; interview of Homer Joe Stewart by John L. Greenberg, Oct. 13–Nov. 9, 1982, in the Caltech Archives, Pasadena, pp. 5–9, 73–74, 82–85; R. C. Miles, "The History of the ORDCIT Project up to 30 June 1946" (n.d.), pp. 52–56, copy in the JPL Archives.

32. Koppes, *JPL*, pp. 31–32, 47, 64–65; interview of Malina by James H. Wilson, June 8, 1973, pp. 34–35, transcript in JPL Archives, Pasadena, Calif.; interview of Seifert by Wilson, Aug. 5, 1971, pp. 2, 13–15, transcript in JPL Archives; JPL organizational charts from the Jack James Collection, JPL 119, folder 6, Sept. 1, 1950, through Nov. 15, 1955; interview of James D. Burke, JPL, by P. Thomas Carroll and James H. Wilson, Aug. 15, 1972, seen in the JPL Archives, JPL History Collection, HF 3-577.

33. Stephen B. Johnson, "Craft or System?: The Development of Systems Engineering at JPL," *Quest: The History of Spaceflight Quarterly* 6: 2 (1998): esp. 19–20; interview of William H. Pickering by Michael Q. Hooks in Pasadena, Calif., Oct. 20–Dec. 12, 1989, p. 24, JPL Archives.

34. Koppes, *JPL*, esp. pp. 77, 95, 105.

35. Winter, *Prelude to the Space Age*, pp. 73–74, 82, 84; G. Edward Pendray, "Early Rocket Development of the American Rocket Society," in *First Steps to-*

ward Space, ed. Durant and James, pp. 141–51, quotations from pp. 141 and 148; James H. Wyld, "The Liquid-Propellant Rocket Motor," *Mechanical Engineering* 69, no. 6 (June 1947): 461; Hunley, interview with Summerfield, pp. 3–8.

36. Frederick I. Ordway and Frank H. Winter, "Pioneering Commercial Rocketry in the United States of America, Reaction Motors, Inc., 1941–1958, Part 1: Corporate History," *JBIS* 36 (1983): 534–35, 542–43, 545–51; Frank H. Winter and Frederick I. Ordway III, "Pioneering Commercial Rocketry in the United States of America, Reaction Motors, Inc., 1941–1958, Part 2: Projects," *JBIS* 38 (1985): 156–58, 160–64; Robert C. Truax, "Liquid Propellant Rocket Development by the U.S. Navy during World War II: A Memoir," in *History of Rocketry and Astronautics,* ed. John L. Sloop, AAS History Series (San Diego: Univelt, 1991) 12:61, 65–67; Frederick I. Ordway III, "Reaction Motors Division of Thiokol Chemical Corporation: An Operational History, 1958–1972 (Part II)," in *History of Rocketry and Astronautics,* ed. Sloop, p. 137; Frank H. Winter, "Reaction Motors Division of Thiokol Chemical Corporation: A Project History, 1958–1972 (Part III)," in *History of Rocketry and Astronautics,* ed. Sloop, pp. 175–201; J. D. Hunley, "The Evolution of Large Solid Propellant Rocketry in the United States," *Quest: The History of Spaceflight Quarterly* 6, no. 1 (Spring 1998): 22–38.

37. Winter and Ordway, "Reaction Motors . . . Projects," p. 164; pers. comm., Apr. 9, 2002, by Frank Winter correcting the date for Neu's patent from the one in the article to a filing date of Apr. 5, 1950, with the patent granted June 22, 1965.

38. Winter, *Prelude to the Space Age,* p. 84; R. C. Truax, "Annapolis Rocket Motor Development," in *First Steps toward Space,* ed. Durant and James, pp. 295–301; Officer Biographical Files, Robert C. Truax, Naval Historical Center, Navy Yard, Washington, D.C.; biographies of Ray C. Stiff Jr. by Aerojet, 1963 and 1969, in NASM archives folder CS-882500-01, "Stiff, Ray C., Jr.," quotation from 1969 biography; Truax, "Liquid Propellant Rocket Development," pp. 58–61.

39. John R. London III, "Brennschluss over the Desert: V-2 Operations at White Sands Missile Range, 1946–1952," in *History of Rocketry and Astronautics,* ed. Lloyd H. Cornett Jr., AAS History Series (San Diego: Univelt, 1993) 15:350–51; [United States Army Ordnance Corps/General Electric Company], "Ordnance Guided Missile & Rocket Programs," vol. X, "Hermes Guided Missile Systems, Inception through 30 June 1955," technical report, filed as a book in the NASM library, 3–5, 7, 12, 21–24, 29–30, 57–68, 79–80, 89–90, 97–102, 121–23, 158; U.S. Army Ordnance Corps/General Electric Company, "Hermes Guided Missile Research and Development Project, 1944–1954," pp. ii, 5–12, unclassified condensation, Sept. 25, 1959, seen in NHRC, folder 012069, "U.S. Army Hermes Rocket"; Col. H. N. Toftoy, "A Brief History of the Hermes II Project," p. 1, originally from NA RG 156, E. 1039A, box 35, seen in NASM archives folder OH-033005-01, "Hermes II Missile"; Clarence G. Lasby, *Project Paperclip: German Scientists and the Cold War* (New York: Atheneum, 1971), p. 39; interview of Richard Porter by David DeVorkin, Apr. 16, 1984, filed with the Space Division, NASM, pp. 26–30; Stuhlinger and Ordway, *Wernher von Braun,* p. 67; Tom Bower, *The Paperclip Conspiracy: The Hunt for Nazi Scientists* (Boston: Little, Brown, 1987), p. 129; von Kármán, *Wind and Beyond,* pp. 264–65.

40. L. D. White, "Final Report, Project Hermes V-2 Missile Program," General Electric Report R52A0510, Sept. 1952, pp. 9, 16, 31–35, 117, 121–23, 126–28, 144, found in NHRC, folder 012069, "U.S. Army Hermes Rocket"; London,

"Brennschluss," pp. 341, 348; Joel Powell and Keith J. Scala, "Historic White Sands Missile Range," *JBIS* 47 (1994): 88–90; Army Ordnance/GE, "Hermes Guided Missile Research," pp. 1–2; David H. DeVorkin, *Science with a Vengeance: How the Military Created the US Space Sciences after World War II* (New York: Springer-Verlag, 1992), pp. 3–5, 341–46; Homer E. Newell, *Beyond the Atmosphere: Early Years of Space Science* (Washington, D.C.: NASA SP-4211, 1980), p. 37.

41. Bragg, "Development of the Corporal," pp. 76–77, 89; Frank J. Malina, "Origins and First Decade of the Jet Propulsion Laboratory," in *The History of Rocket Technology: Essays on Research, Development, and Utility,* ed. Eugene M. Emme (Detroit: Wayne State University Press, 1964), p. 65; "Bumper 8: 50th Anniversary of the First Launch on Cape Canaveral," group oral history interview by Roger Launius and Lori Walters on July 24, 2000, at the Kennedy Space Center, p. 46, comment by William Pickering.

42. Bragg, "Development of the Corporal," pp. 105–106, 14-1, 14-2, 14-5, 14-7, 14-8; London, "Brennschluss," pp. 353–54; Army Ordnance/GE, "Hermes Guided Missile Research," p. 4; General Electric, "Progress Report on Bumper Vehicle," Feb. 1950, pp. 6–9, seen in JPL Archives, JPL History Collection, item 3-350; S. Starr, "The Launch of Bumper 8 from the Cape, the End of an Era and the Beginning of Another," paper delivered at the 52nd International Astronautical Congress, Oct. 1–5, 2001, Toulouse, France, pp. 4, 7, 9.

43. London, "Brennschluss," p. 355; White, "Final Report," pp. 24, 26, 41, 43; Graham Spinardi, *From Polaris to Trident: The Development of US Fleet Ballistic Missile Technology* (Cambridge: Cambridge University Press, 1994), pp. 20, 202–203n8; Army Ordnance/GE, "Hermes Guided Missile Research," p. 2; "GE Reveals Hermes Missile Milestones," *Aviation Week,* Mar. 8, 1954, pp. 30–31.

44. *Challenge, General Electric Company Missile and Space Division,* 10th Anniversary Issue (Spring 1965): 2, 4, 6–7, quotations from pp. 4 and 7; Constance McLaughlin Green and Milton Lomask, *Vanguard: A History* (Washington, D.C.: Smithsonian Institution Press, 1971), pp. 43, 177; Linda Neuman Ezell, *NASA Historical Data Book,* vol. II: *Programs and Projects, 1958–1968* (Washington, D.C.: NASA SP-4012, 1988), pp. 45, 86; Nicholas and Rossi, *U.S. Missile Data Book, 1994,* pp. 3-2 through 3-3; R. A. Fuhrman, "Fleet Ballistic Missile System: Polaris to Trident," von Kármán Lecture for 1978 at the 14th annual meeting of the AIAA, Feb. 1978, Washington, D.C., p. 8; Spinardi, *Polaris to Trident,* p. 23; Powell and Scala, "White Sands," p. 91; Bullard, "History of the Redstone," p. 10.

45. Cf., e.g., Alan J. Levine, *The Missile and Space Race* (Westport, Conn.: Praeger, 1994), p. 13; London, "Brennschluss," p. 365.

46. Julius H. Braun, "The Legacy of HERMES," paper IAA-90-625 delivered at the 41st Congress of the International Astronautical Federation, Oct. 6–12, 1990, Dresden, GDR, reprinted in *History of Rocketry and Astronautics,* ed. Hunley, quotations in 19:135–37, 141.

47. Technical Report Number 10, Headquarters, Res & Dev Sv Sub-Office (Rocket), Fort Bliss, Texas, "Questions by Dr. Martin Summerfield, Jet Propulsion Laboratory, California Institute of Technology, Answers by Professor W. von Braun with the collaboration of Mr. J. Paul and Professor C[arl] Wagner," ed. T/Sgt. E. Wormser, from notes taken by Summerfield, Apr. 19, 1946, pp. 1, 3–4, U.S. Space and Rocket Center, Schulze Collection; Hunley interview with Summerfield; Koppes, *JPL,* p. 40.

48. Costs of V-2 firings from Bullard, "History of the Redstone," p. 11.

49. Ibid., pp. 12–14, 17–18; U.S. Army Ordnance Missile Command, Public Information Office, "History of Redstone Arsenal," Feb. 20, 1962.

50. Bullard, "History of the Redstone," p. 19; Roger E. Bilstein, *Stages to Saturn: A Technological History of the Apollo/Saturn Launch Vehicles* (Washington, D.C.: NASA SP-4206, 1980), pp. 390–91; Ordway and Sharpe, *Rocket Team*, pp. 363–66; Andrew J. Dunar and Stephen P. Waring, *Power to Explore: A History of Marshall Space Flight Center, 1960–1990* (Washington, D.C.: NASA SP-4313, 1999), pp. 3, 14; Kaylene Hughes, "Two 'Arsenals of Democracy': Huntsville's World War II Army Architectural Legacy," http://www.redstone.army.mil/history/arch/index.htm (accessed Apr. 1, 2002), p. 2.

51. Bullard, "History of the Redstone," pp. 22–25, 27–41, 53–59, 67–68, 95; "Redstone," http://www.redstone.army.mil/history/systems/redstone/welcome .htm (accessed Jan. 16, 2002), p. 2; Wernher von Braun, "The Redstone, Jupiter, and Juno," in *History of Rocket Technology*, ed. Emme, p. 109; Jacob Neufeld, *The Development of Ballistic Missiles in the United States Air Force, 1945–1960* (Washington, D.C.: Office of Air Force History, 1990), pp. 37–38, 66; F[rank] H. Winter, "Rocketdyne—a Giant Pioneer in Rocket Technology: The Earliest Years, 1945–1955," IAA paper 97-IAA.2.2.08, delivered at the 48th International Astronautical Congress, Oct. 6–10, 1997, Turin, Italy, pp. 2–4, 9; Thomas A. Heppenheimer, "The Navaho Program and the Main Line of American Liquid Rocketry," *Air Power History* (Summer 1997), p. 6; Dale D. Myers, "The Navaho Cruise Missile—a Burst of Technology," in *History of Rocketry and Astronautics*, ed. J. D. Hunley, 20:121–32 (hereafter cited as Myers, "Navaho"); John C. Lonnquest and David F. Winkler, *To Defend and Deter: The Legacy of the United States Cold War Missile Program*, USACERL Special Report 97/01 (Rock Island, Ill.: Defense Publishing Service, 1996), pp. 3–4, 24–25; William F. Ezell and J. K. Mitchell, "Engine One," (Rocketdyne), *Threshold: An Engineering Journal of Power Technology*, no. 7 (Summer 1991): 54; F. H. Winter, "The East Parking Lot Rocket Experiments of North American Aviation, Inc., 1946–1949," IAA paper 99-IAA.2.2.07 delivered at the 50th International Astronautical Congress, Oct. 4–8, 1999, Amsterdam, pp. 2, 9–10.

52. Bullard, "History of the Redstone," pp. 70, 92, 100, 162–65; von Braun, "Redstone, Jupiter, and Juno," pp. 110–11; Nicholas and Rossi, *U.S. Missile Data Book, 1994*, pp. 3-5 to 3-9; Ordway and Wakeford, *International Missile and Spacecraft Guide*, p. 15.

53. Von Braun, "Redstone, Jupiter, and Juno," pp. 111, 113–15; John B. Medaris with Arthur Gordon, *Countdown for Decision* (New York: G. P. Putnam's Sons, 1960), pp. 119, 142–43, 202, 222–24; Michael E. Baker and Kaylene Hughes, *Redstone Arsenal Complex Chronology*, part II, *Nerve Center of Army Missilery, 1950–62*, section B, *The ABMA/AOMC Era (1956–62)* (Redstone Arsenal, Ala.: U.S. Army Missile Command Historical Division, 1994), p. 1; Michael H. Armacost, *The Politics of Weapons Innovation: The Thor-Jupiter Controversy* (New York: Columbia University Press, 1969), p. 144; presentation of William R. Lucas, "Redstone, Juno, and Jupiter," in "Rocketry in the 1950's, Transcript of AIAA Panel Discussions," NASA Historical Report No. 36, pp. 46–58, and comments of William H. Pickering, pp. 70–71 of the same report; Allen E. Wolfe and William J. Truscot, "Juno Final Report," vol. I, "Juno I: Re-entry Test Vehicles and Explorer Satellites," JPL Technical Report No. 32-31, Sept. 6, 1960, pp. 4, 43–45, 75, 78, seen in NHRC, folder 012071, "Jupiter C (Juno I)"; Bill B. Greever, "General Description and Design of the Configuration of the Juno I and Juno II Launching Vehicles," *IRE Transactions on Military Electronics* MIL-4, nos.

2–3 (Apr.–July, 1960): 71, published by the Institute of Radio Engineers, seen in NHRC, folder 012072, "Juno Launch Vehicles"; Wernher von Braun, "Rundown on Jupiter-C," *Astronautics*, Oct. 1958, pp. 32, 80, 84; JPL, "Explorer I," pp. 20, 22, 83–84; William H. Pickering, "History of the Cluster System," in *From Pee-nemünde to Outer Space*, ed. Stuhlinger et al., pp. 141–62.

54. Glenn P. Hastedt, "Sputnik and Technological Surprise," in *Reconsidering Sputnik: Forty Years since the Soviet Satellite*, ed. Roger D. Launius, John M. Logsdon, and Robert W. Smith (Amsterdam: Harwood Academic Publishers, 2000), p. 401; NASA Marshall Space Flight Center, Saturn/Apollo Systems Office, "The Mercury-Redstone Project," Dec. 1964, pp. 1-5, 1-9, 3-1, 5-1 to 5-37, 8-5, seen in NHRC, folder 012091, "History of the Redstone"; Joachim P. Kuettner, "Mercury-Redstone Launch-Vehicle Development and Performance," in *Mercury Project Summary including Results of the Fourth Manned Orbital Flight May 15 and 16, 1963*, ed. Kenneth S. Kleinknecht and W. M. Bland Jr. (Washington, D.C.: NASA SP-45, 1963), pp. 69–74, 78–79; NASA Office of Congressional Relations, *Mercury-Redstone III Sub-Orbital Manned Flight* (Washington, D.C.: NASA, 1961), p. 5-1; Mitchell R. Sharpe and Bettye R. Burkhalter, "Mercury-Redstone: The First American Man-Rated Space Launch Vehicle," in *History of Rocketry and Astronautics, Proceedings of the Twenty-second and Twenty-third History Symposia of the International Academy of Astronautics*, ed. John Becklake, AAS History Series (San Diego: Univelt, 1995), 17:369; Loyd S. Swenson Jr., James M. Grimwood, and Charles C. Alexander, *This New Ocean: A History of Project Mercury* (Washington, D.C.: NASA SP-4201, 1998), pp. 91, 92, 96, 99–102, 122, 181, 328–30; Ezell, *NASA Historical Data Book*, 2:143–44.

55. R. Cargill Hall, "Origins and Development of the Vanguard and Explorer Satellite Programs," *The Airpower Historian* 11, no. 1 (Jan. 1964): 101–11, and the sources cited in notes below on Viking and Vanguard.

56. Rosen's official NASA biography, Feb. 6, 1962, seen in NHRC, folder 001835, "Rosen, Milton W. (Misc. Bio)"; interview with Milton William Rosen by David DeVorkin, Washington, D.C., Mar. 25, 1983, pp. 8-31, 44, copy available through the Space History Division, NASM; Milton W. Rosen, *The Viking Rocket Story* (New York: Harper & Brothers, 1955), pp. 18–23, 28, 58–62, 64, 66, 236–37; comments of Rosen on a draft treatment of Viking, May 8, 2002, and in a telephone conversation with author on May 17, 2002; William B. Harwood, *Raise Heaven and Earth: The Story of Martin Marietta People and Their Pioneering Achievements* (New York: Simon & Schuster, 1993), p. 256.

57. Rosen, *Viking Rocket*, p. 26; Rosen interview by DeVorkin, p. 31; Winter and Ordway, "Reaction Motors . . . Projects," pp. 161–63; John P. Hagen, "The Viking and the Vanguard," in *History of Rocket Technology*, ed. Emme, p. 124; The Glenn L. Martin Company, "Design Summary, RTV-N-12 Viking, Rockets 1 to 7," Jan. 1954, pp. 5, 60–68, 210, seen in NASM Archives folder OV-550500-05, "Viking Sounding Rocket"; Harwood, *Raise Heaven and Earth*, p. 254; Rosen's comments on an earlier draft and his explanation by telephone, May 16, 2002.

58. Michael J. Neufeld, "Orbiter, Overflight, and the First Satellite: New Light on the Vanguard Decision," in *Reconsidering Sputnik*, ed. Launius, Logsdon, and Smith, pp. 231–49; "Project Vanguard, a Scientific Earth Satellite Program for the International Geophysical Year," A Report to the Committee on Appropriations, U.S. House of Representatives, by Surveys and Investigations Staff [ca. Feb. 15, 1959], p. 61, found in NASM Archives, folder OV 106120-01, "Vanguard II Launch Vehicle 4"; NASA bio, "John P. Hagen," Feb. 17, 1959, seen in NHRC, folder 006640, "Vanguard II (Feb. 17, 1959)"; Project Vanguard Staff,

"Project Vanguard Report of Progress, Status, and Plans, 1 June 1957," NRL Report 4969 (Washington, D.C.: Naval Research Laboratory, 1957), pp. 2-6 to 2-7, seen in NHRC, folder 006601, "Vanguard Project: Origins and Progress Reports"; Kurt R. Stehling, *Project Vanguard* (Garden City, N.Y.: 1961), p. 301; Green and Lomask, *Vanguard,* pp. 57–90.

59. Hagen, "The Viking and the Vanguard," pp. 127–28; Hall, "Vanguard and Explorer," pp. 109, 111; Harwood, *Raise Heaven and Earth,* pp. 286–87; Green and Lomask, *Vanguard,* pp. 62–68, 89, 176, 204, 283, 287; Stehling, *Project Vanguard,* pp. 64–66, 82–83, 128–29n, 129–30, 132–35; Project Vanguard Staff, "Project Vanguard Report No. 9, Progress through September 15, 1956," Oct. 4, 1956 (Washington, D.C.: Naval Research Laboratory, 1956), pp. 5, 7, seen in NHRC, file 006601, "Vanguard: Project Origins and Progress Reports"; Vanguard Staff, "Project Vanguard Report . . . 1 June 1957," pp. 2-25 to 2-32, 2-34, 2-37 to 2-38, 2-41 to 2-42, 2-45 to 2-50; The Martin Company, "The Vanguard Satellite Launching Vehicle: An Engineering Summary," Engineering Report No. 11022, Apr. 1960, pp. 4, 49–55, 63, cataloged as a book in the NASA History Office; . Kurt R. Stehling, "Aspects of Vanguard Propulsion," *Astronautics,* Jan. 1958, pp. 45–46; Milton Rosen, letter to J. D. Hunley, May 8, 2002; document titled "Vanguard Vehicle Characteristics," n.d. [after Dec. 16, 1959], seen in NASM Archives, folder OV-106015-01, "Vanguard Project, History"; T. L. Moore, "Solid Rocket Development at Allegany Ballistics Laboratory," AIAA paper 99-2931 presented at the Joint Propulsion Conference, June 20–23, 1999, Los Angeles, pp. 5–6; Davis Dyer and David B. Sicilia, *Labors of a Modern Hercules: The Evolution of a Chemical Company* (Boston: Harvard Business School Press, 1990), pp. 2, 9, 257–58, 318–20; Walter A. McDougall, . . . *The Heavens and the Earth: A Political History of the Space Age* (New York: Basic Books, 1985), p. 154, for the two quotations.

60. Congressional committee report, "Project Vanguard," pp. 62, 65–66; Green and Lomask, *Vanguard,* pp. 176–82, 196–98, 204, 210, 213–14, 219, 254–55, 283, 285; Stehling, *Project Vanguard,* pp. 24, 82–83, 103, 106–22, 156–242, 269–81; "Preliminary Report on TV-3," Dec. 18, 1957, 1, found in NHRC, folder 006630, "Vanguard Test Vehicle 3"; Rosen's comments to Hunley by telephone, May 16, 2002; Martin Information Services, "Project Vanguard" [Nov. 23, 1959], seen in NASM Archives, folder OV-106015-01, "Vanguard Project History"; Memo, Chief of Naval Research to Director, Advanced Research Projects Agency, Sept. 25, 1958, seen in NA RG 255, Records of the National Aeronautics and Space Administration, Vanguard Division, Project Vanguard Case Files, 1955–59, entry 35, box 1, ARPA folder; "Space Activities Summary, SLV-1, May 27, 1958," seen in NHRC, folder 006637, "Vanguard (SLV-1, May 27, 1958)"; "Space Activities Summary, SLV-2, June 26, 1958," NHRC, folder 006638, "Vanguard (SLV-2, June 26, 1958)"; "Space Activities Summary, SLV-3, Sept. 26, 1958," NHRC, folder 006639, "Vanguard (SLV-3, Sept. 26, 1958)"; "Space Activities Summary, Vanguard II, Feb. 17, 1959," NHRC, folder 006640, "Vanguard II (Feb. 17, 1959)"; "Space Activities Summary, SLV-5, Apr. 13, 1959," NASM Archives folder OV-106121-01, "Vanguard Launch Vehicle 5"; "Space Activities Summary, SLV-6, June 22, 1959," NHRC, folder 006642, "Vanguard (SLV-6, June 22, 1959)"; file, Homer E. Newell Jr., "Launching of Vanguard III, Sept. 18, 1959," NHRC, folder 006643, "Vanguard III (September 18, 1959)"; "Space Activities Summary, Vanguard III, Sept. 18, 1959," NASM Archives folder OV-106130-1, "Vanguard III Satellite Launch Vehicle 7"; Milton W. Rosen, "A Brief History of Delta and Its Relation to Vanguard," enclosure in letter, Rosen to Constance McL. Green,

Mar. 15, 1968, NHRC, folder 001835, "Rosen, Milton W. (Misc. Bio)"; Chemical Propulsion Information Agency, *CPIA/M1 Rocket Motor Manual* (Columbia, Md.: CPIA, 1994), vol. 1, Unit 412, Minuteman Stage 3 Wing I, Jan. 1964, and Unit 427, Altair I, Mar. 1964 (hereafter cited as *CPIA/M1 Rocket Motor Manual*; all references to vol. 1); Andre Bedard, "Composite Solid Propellants," http://www.friends-partners.org/mwade/articles/comlants.htm (accessed Nov. 22, 2001), p. 9.

61. Milton W. Rosen, "Big Rockets," *International Science and Technology*, Dec. 1962, p. 67; Michael J. Neufeld, "The End of the Army Space Program: Interservice Rivalry and the Transfer of the von Braun Group to NASA, 1958–1959," *The Journal of Military History* 69 (July 2005): 737–57.

62. John Clayton Lonnquest, "The Face of Atlas: General Bernard Schriever and the Development of the Atlas Intercontinental Ballistic Missile, 1953–1960" (Ph.D. diss., Duke University, 1996), pp. 14–16, 21, 23, 28, 34, 37, 41, 208, 220; John L. Chapman, *Atlas: The Story of a Missile* (New York: Harper & Brothers, 1960), p. 8; Thomas P. Hughes, *Rescuing Prometheus* (New York: Vintage Books, 1998), p. 70; Edmund Beard, *Developing the ICBM: A Study in Bureaucratic Politics* (New York: Columbia University Press, 1976), esp. pp. 8, 12, 29, 72, 142, 154, 224, 228.

63. Lonnquest, "Face of Atlas," pp. 29–30, 33–34, 43, 65–82; Neufeld, *Ballistic Missiles*, pp. 68–70, 239, 241, 249–65; Beard, *Developing the ICBM*, pp. 11, 140–43, 165–66; Lonnquest and Winkler, *To Defend and Deter*, pp. 33–43; Iain Pike, "Atlas: Pioneer ICBM and Space-Age Workhorse," *Flight International* 81 (Jan. 1962): 94; unattributed obituary, "Trevor Gardner, Ex-Air Force Aide: Research Chief Who Quit in Dispute in 1956 Dies at 48," *New York Times*, Sept. 29, 1963, p. 86; Hughes, *Rescuing Prometheus*, pp. 81, 83–84; Herbert York, *Race to Oblivion: A Participant's View of the Arms Race* (New York: Simon & Schuster, 1970), pp. 18–22, 84; Paul E. Ceruzzi, *A History of Modern Computing* (Cambridge, Mass.: MIT Press, 1998), pp. 21, 23–24; "History of the Development of Guided Missiles, 1946–1950," Historical Study No. 238, n.d., declassified Nov. 16, 1959, pp. 76–95, copy provided from the Air Force Air Materiel Command's archives by Scott Carlin, to whom thanks; Winter and Ordway, "Reaction Motors . . . Projects," pp. 161–62.

64. Jacob Neufeld, "Bernard A Schriever: Challenging the Unknown," in *Makers of the United States Air Force*, ed. John L. Frisbee (1987; repr. Washington, D.C.: Air Force History and Museums Program, 1996), pp. 281–90; "Historical Timeline of the College of Liberal Arts, Texas A&M University," http://clla .tamu.edu/about/history.htm (accessed May 8, 2002), for the name in 1931 of the institution from which Schriever graduated; Lonnquest, "Face of Atlas," p. 222.

65. Neufeld, "Schriever," p. 290; Lonnquest, "Face of Atlas," pp. 73, 204, 220–23; obituary, "Trevor Gardner," p. 86; interview with Lt. Gen. Charles H. Terhune by Robert Mulcahy, June 6, 2001, at Terhune's home in California, Western Development Division Oral History No. 2, generously provided by Bob Mulcahy, of the Space and Missile Systems Center History Office, pp. 16, 19, for quotations from him; interview of Lt. Gen. Otto J. Glasser by Lt. Col. John J. Allen, seen in the Air Force Historical Research Agency, Maxwell AFB, Ala., K239.0512-1566, Jan. 5–6, 1984, pp. 54–55, for Glasser's quotations.

66. Lonnquest and Winkler, *To Defend and Deter*, pp. 43–44; Hughes, *Rescuing Prometheus*, pp. 103–105; Beard, *Developing the ICBM*, pp. 190–93; "Chronology of the Ballistic Missile Organization, 1945–1990," prepared by the History Office Staff, Aug. 1993, pp. 25–26 (hereafter cited as "BMO Chronology").

67. Davis Dyer, *TRW, Pioneering Technology and Innovation since 1900* (Boston: Harvard Business School Press, 1998), pp. 168–85, 198, 207; Hughes, *Rescuing Prometheus*, pp. 86, 89–92, 97–103, 110–15, 132–35; Beard, *Developing the ICBM*, pp. 171–77; Lonnquest, "Face of Atlas," pp. 144–59; "BMO Chronology," pp. 18–22.

68. On Hall's criticisms, Hall, "USAF Engineer in Wonderland, including the Missile down the Rabbit Hole," undated typescript generously provided by Colonel Hall, and Hall, *The Art of Destructive Management: What Hath Man Wrought?* (New York: Vantage Press, 1984). For the comments of the Convair engineers, Chuck Walker with Joel Powell, *Atlas, the Ultimate Weapon* (Ontario, Canada: Apogee Books, 2005), pp. 136, 257.

69. Lonnquest, "Face of Atlas," pp. 226–31; Hughes, *Rescuing Prometheus*, pp. 119–26; "BMO Chronology," pp. 19, 28.

70. Lonnquest, "Face of Atlas," pp. 232–44; Hughes, *Rescuing Prometheus*, pp. 107–108; Lonnquest and Winkler, *To Defend and Deter*, p. 44.

71. Hughes, *Rescuing Prometheus*, p. 108; interview of Glasser, pp. 44–45.

72. Barton C. Hacker and James M. Grimwood, *On the Shoulders of Titans: A History of Project Gemini* (Washington, D.C.: NASA SP-4203, 1977), pp. 76–78, 87, 104–105; Space Division, "Space and Missile Systems Organization: A Chronology, 1954–1979," pp. 4, 95 (hereafter cited as "SAMSO Chronology"), copy generously provided by Space and Missile Systems Center History Office; Dyer, *TRW*, pp. 231–32.

73. Lonnquest and Winkler, *To Defend and Deter*, p. 39; Hughes, *Rescuing Prometheus*, pp. 93, 102; interview of Glasser, pp. 54–55 ; Lonnquest, "Face of Atlas," pp. 73, 204, 220–23; Pike, "Atlas," p. 92; Richard E. Martin, "The Atlas and Centaur 'Steel Balloon' Tanks: A Legacy of Karel Bossart," paper printed by General Dynamics Space Systems Division, originally delivered at the 40th International Astronautical Congress, IAA-89-738, Oct. 7–13, 1989, Malaga, Spain, pp. 1–2, seen in NASM Archives folder CB-467-000-01, "Bossart, Karel Jan"; Chapman, *Atlas*, pp. 28–35, 86–88; Richard E. Martin, "A Brief History of the *Atlas* Rocket Vehicle," pt. I, *Quest: The History of Spaceflight Quarterly* 8, no. 2 (2000): 54–55; "BMO Chronology," pp. 18–19; Neufeld, *Ballistic Missiles*, pp. 45–50.

74. Chapman, *Atlas*, pp. 28, 50–52, 60–65, 87–88; Martin, "Steel Balloon Tanks," pp. 1–2, 4; Pike, "Atlas," pp. 93–94; Neufeld, *Ballistic Missiles*, pp. 68–77, 116–17; "BMO Chronology," pp. 20–22; Lonnquest, "Face of Atlas," pp. 139–40; Myers, "Navaho," p. 129; John M. Simmons, "The Navaho Lineage," (Rocketdyne), *Threshold: An Engineering Journal of Power Technology*, no. 2 (Dec. 1987): 18–21; Robert A. Smith and Henry M. Minami, "History of Atlas Engines," in *History of Liquid Rocket Engine Development in the United States, 1955–1980*, ed. Stephen E. Doyle, AAS History Series (San Diego: Univelt, 1992), 13:54–55, 63–65; Julian Hartt, *The Mighty Thor: Missile in Readiness* (New York: Duell, Sloan and Pearce, 1961), p. 80.

75. "The Experimental Engines Group," transcript of a group interview with Bill [W. F.] Ezell, Cliff [C. A.] Hauenstein, Jim [J. O.] Bates, Stan [G. S.] Bell, and Dick [R.] Schwarz, (Rocketdyne), *Threshold: An Engineering Journal of Power Technology*, no. 4 (Spring 1989): 21–27, for the quotation; Ezell and Mitchell, "Engine One," p. 57; Edward J. Hujsak, "The Bird That Did Not Want to Fly," *Spaceflight* 34 (Mar. 1992): 102–104; Pike, "Atlas," pp. 175, 178; Sarah A. Grassly, "Ballistic Missile and Space Launch Summary as of 30 June 1969," SAMSO Historical Office, Mar. 1970, p. I-1-1-1, seen at the Air Force Historical Research

Agency, K243.012, 67/07/01–69/06/30; Nicholas and Rossi, *U.S. Missile Data Book, 1994*, pp. 3-2, 3-8; Lonnquest and Winkler, *To Defend and Deter*, p. 216.

76. Armacost, *Thor-Jupiter Controversy*, esp. pp. 50–55; Lonnquest and Winkler, *To Defend and Deter*, pp. 40–41, 47–49; Neufeld, *Ballistic Missiles*, pp. 132–33.

77. *Organization and Management of Missile Programs*, 11th Report by the Committee on Government Operations, 86th Cong., 1st sess., H. Rep. 1121, Sept. 2, 1959, pp. 101 (for quotations), 103–105 (hereafter cited as H. Rep. 1121); "BMO Chronology," p. 23; draft autobiography of Robert C. Truax, kindly provided to the author on computer disk by Captain Truax in 2002, chap. 18, pp. 240–41, chap. 19, pp. 242–44; extract of interview of Adolf K. Thiel by F. I. Ordway, Feb. 20, 1988, pp. 3–4; T.O. 21-SM75-1, Technical Manual, USAF Model SM-75 Missile Weapon System, Oct. 20, 1961, pp. 1-1 to 1-2, 4-1 to 4-6; "Thor, A Study of a Great Weapons System," *Flight* 74 (Dec. 5, 1958): 864; Air Force Missile Test Center, Patrick AFB, Fla., News Release, "Thor Fact Sheet," Apr. 1961, seen in NASM Archives, folder OT-380000-01, "Thor Missile, General"; Paul N. Fuller and Henry M. Minami, "History of the Thor/Delta Booster Engines," in *History of Liquid Rocket Engine Development*, ed. Doyle, pp. 44–45; Grassly, "Ballistic Missile and Space Launch Summary," pp. 1-4-1-1, 1-4-3-1; W. M. Arms, "Thor: The Workhorse of Space—a Narrative History" (Huntington Beach, Calif.: McDonnell Douglas Astronautics Company, 1972), pp. 3-4 to 3-5, B-3 to B-5, seen in the Space and Missile Systems Center History Office, Los Angeles, filed as a separate item in "Standard Launch Vehicles II" ; Nicholas and Rossi, *U.S. Missile Data Book, 1994*, pp. 3–4; Robert L. Perry, "The Atlas, Thor, Titan, and Minuteman," in *History of Rocket Technology*, ed. Emme, p. 153.

78. Hartt, *Mighty Thor*, pp. 129–30, 134–35, 164–69; Arms, "Thor," pp. B-3, B-5 to B-6; H. Rep. 1121, pp. 105–107; *Organization and Management of Missile Programs*, Hearings before a Subcommittee of the Committee on Government Operations, H. Rep., 86th Cong., 1st sess., Feb. 4–Mar. 20, 1959, pp. 339, 381 (hereafter cited as Subcommittee Hearings, *Organization and Management of Missile Programs*); Thiel interview, p. 5; Lonnquest and Winkler, *To Defend and Deter*, pp. 52, 268; News Release, "Thor Fact Sheet," Apr. 1961; Air Force Ballistic Missile Division, Fact Sheet, "Thor," Jun. 25, 1959, NASM Archives, folder OT-380025-01, "Thor IRBM."

79. "BMO Chronology," pp. 19, 28; H. Rep. 1121, pp. 50, 101, 103–105; Grimwood and Strowd, "History of the Jupiter Missile System," pp. 2–13, 17, 25–28, 30–32, 35, 37, 41, 43, 67–71, 5-1 through 5-3; Standard Missile Characteristics, SM-78 Jupiter, Jan. 1962, copied by John Lonnquest at the Air Force Museum at Wright-Patterson AFB; Armacost, *Thor-Jupiter Controversy*, pp. 44–49, 92–93, 119; Lonnquest and Winkler, *To Defend and Deter*, pp. 49, 52; Subcommittee Hearings, *Organization and Management of Missile Programs*, pp. 380–88; Fuller and Minami, "History of the Thor," pp. 44–45.

80. Grimwood and Strowd, "History of the Jupiter Missile System," pp. 58–63, 65–66, 69, 71–73, 82, 157–58, 5-1; Standard Missile Characteristics, SM-78 Jupiter, Jan. 1962; Lonnquest and Winkler, *To Defend and Deter*, pp. 259, 264, 268–69; von Braun, "Redstone, Jupiter and Juno," pp. 117–18; Medaris, *Countdown to Decision*, pp. 137–39; Nicholas and Rossi, *U.S. Missile Data Book, 1994*, pp. 3-2, 3-5, 3-7, 3-8, 3-10; News Release, Air Force Missile Test Center, "Thor"; North American Rockwell Corporation, "Data Sheet, Jupiter Propulsion System," Dec. 15, 1967, copy filed in the NASA History Office.

81. Subcommittee Hearings, *Organization and Management of Missile Programs*, p. 379.

82. Since this section is largely a summary of J. D. Hunley, "Minuteman and the Development of Solid-Rocket Launch Technology," in *To Reach the High Frontier: A History of U.S. Launch Vehicles*, ed. Roger D. Launius and Dennis R. Jenkins (Lexington: University Press of Kentucky, 2002), pp. 238–67, I refer the reader to the extensive endnotes to those pages, keeping references in this section to a minimum.

83. Spinardi, *From Polaris to Trident*, pp. 4–6, 31–34, 99–100, 148–53, 162, 187.

84. Harvey M. Sapolsky, *The Polaris System Development: Bureaucratic and Programmatic Success in Government* (Cambridge, Mass.: Harvard University Press, 1972), pp. 8, 11, 26–28, 35–36, 45–47, 49–51, 55–56, 88; W. F. Raborn Jr., "Management of the Navy's Fleet Ballistic Missile Program," in *Science, Technology, and Management*, ed. Fremont E. Kast and James E. Rosenzweig (New York: McGraw-Hill, 1963), p. 144; James Baar and William E. Howard, *Polaris!* (New York: Harcourt, Brace, 1960), pp. 25–26, 28; J. F. Sparks and M. P. Friedlander III, "Fifty Years of Solid Propellant Technical Achievements at Atlantic Research Corporation," AIAA paper 99-2932 presented at the AIAA/ASME/SAE/ASEE Joint Propulsion Conference, June 20–24, 1999, Los Angeles, pp. 1, 8.

85. Note 84 and Philip Key Reily, *The Rocket Scientists: Achievement in Science, Technology, and Industry at Atlantic Research Corporation* (New York: Vantage Press, 1999), pp. 43–46; K[arl] Klager, "Early Polaris and Minuteman Solid Rocket History," unpublished paper kindly provided by Dr. Klager, pp. 6–8; Fuhrman, "Fleet Ballistic Missile System," pp. 7, 11–16; Robert Gordon et al., *Aerojet: The Creative Company* (Los Angeles: Stuart F. Cooper, 1995), pp. IV-98 through IV-103; Frank Bothwell, "Birth of the Polaris Missile and the Concept of Minimum Deterrence," www.armscontrolsite.com/PolarisIntro.html (accessed Mar. 2001).

86. Fuhrman, "Fleet Ballistic Missile System," pp. 14–15; Spinardi, *Polaris to Trident*, pp. 42–45, 52.

87. *CPIA/M1 Rocket Motor Manual*, Unit 410, Polaris Model A2 Stage 2, Unit 411, 78-DS-31,935, Rocket Motor Mark 6 Mod 0, Polaris Model A3 Stage 2, and Unit 415, 24-DS-5850, XM 94, Altair II; draft paper, Francis A. Warren and Charles H. Herty III, "U.S. Double-Base Solid Propellant Tactical Rockets of the 1950–1955 Era," presented at AIAA History Session, Jan. 8–10, 1973 (no pagination), generously sent to me by Ed Price; Fuhrman, "Fleet Ballistic Missile System," pp. 16–18; Spinardi, *Polaris to Trident*, pp. 63–65, 67–72.

88. Roy Neal, *Ace in the Hole* (Garden City, N.Y.: Doubleday, 1962), pp. 49, 52–62, 73; Hall, "USAF Engineer in Wonderland, including the Missile down the Rabbit Hole," undated typescript kindly provided by Colonel Hall, pp. 44–45; my telephone interview with Hall, Nov. 13, 1998, pp. 3–4; and Hall, *Art of Destructive Management*, pp. 31–38; Klager, "Early Polaris and Minuteman," p. 14, for quotations.

89. Sapolsky, *Polaris System Development*, pp. 21–23, 31, 33–34, 35–37, 39, 45–47, 49–51, 55–56, 64–65, 74, 97–99, 149–50, 157–59, quotation on p. 39; Fuhrman, "Fleet Ballistic Missile System," pp. 2–4; AF Intercontinental Ballistic Missile System Program Office, "Minuteman Weapon System History and Description" (Hill AFB, Utah, May 1996), p. 17; Lonnquest and Winkler, *To Defend and Deter*, pp. 43–44.

90. W. S. Kennedy, S. M. Kovacic, and E. C. Rea, "Solid Rocket History at TRW Ballistic Missiles Division," paper presented at the AIAA/SAE/ASME/ASEE 28th Joint Propulsion Conference, July 6–8, 1992, Nashville, Tenn., pp. 10, 14–15, 17; Gen. Samuel C. Phillips, "Minuteman," in "Rocketry in the 1950's, Transcript of AIAA Panel Discussions," NASA Historical Report No. 36, p. 80, available in the NASA History Office; Klager, "Early Polaris and Minuteman," pp. 17–18; Neal, *Ace in the Hole*, pp. 76, 83, 123, 125, 136–38, 147–51; "Launch on December 63rd: Gen. Sam Phillips Recounts the Emergence of Solids in the Nation's Principal Deterrent," *Astronautics & Aeronautics* 10 (Oct. 1972): 62.

91. Kennedy, Kovacic, and Rea, "Solid Rocket History," pp. 17–18; "Propulsion Characteristics Summary (M-56A1, Wing II)," Nov. 9, 1962; "Propulsion Characteristics Summary (SRJ19-AJ-1)," Jan. 22, 1966, "Propulsion Characteristics Summary (M-56A1, Wing II)," Nov. 9, 1962, and "Propulsion Characteristics Summary (SRJ19-AJ-1)," Jan. 22, 1966 (all three documents from the AF Materiel Command archives); Klager, "Early Polaris and Minuteman," p. 18.

92. Gordon et al., *Aerojet*, pp. IV-104 to IV-105; Lonnquest and Winkler, *To Defend and Deter*, pp. 241–43.

93. Laurence J. Adams, "The Evolution of the Titan Rocket—Titan I to Titan II," in *History of Rocketry and Astronautics*, ed. Hunley, 19:203.

94. Warren E. Greene, "The Development of the SM-68 Titan," AFSC Historical Publications Series 62-23-1, Aug. 1962, I:11–14, 96–99, seen in the Air Force Space and Missile Systems Center History Office, Los Angeles; M. J. Chulick, L. C. Meland, F. C. Thompson, and H. W. Williams, "History of the Titan Liquid Rocket Engines," in *Liquid Rocket Engine Development*, ed. Doyle, 13:4, 20, 23–24; Chandler C. Ross, "Life at Aerojet-General University: A Memoir," 1981, printed by the Aerojet History Group, pp. 47, 72; Gordon et al., *Aerojet*, pp. III-95, III-98; David K. Stumpf, *Titan II: A History of a Cold War Missile Program* (Fayetteville: University of Arkansas Press, 2000), pp. 29–31, 275–77; Adams, "Titan I to Titan II," p. 211.

95. John D. Clark, *Ignition! An Informal History of Liquid Rocket Propellants* (New Brunswick, N.J.: Rutgers University Press, 1972), pp. 42–45; Gordon et al., *Aerojet*, p. III-100; Lonnquest and Winkler, *To Defend and Deter*, p. 231.

96. Stumpf, *Titan II*, pp. 33–35; Lonnquest and Winkler, *To Defend and Deter*, p. 233; Green, "SM-68 Titan," I:74; Adams, "Titan I to Titan II," p. 217.

97. Stumpf, *Titan II*, p. 36; Lonnquest and Winkler, *To Defend and Deter*, p. 230; Green, "SM-68 Titan," I:74–75; MacKenzie, *Inventing Accuracy*, pp. 203–206.

98. Stumpf, *Titan II*, p. 36; "BMO Chronology," p. 68; Green, "SM-68 Titan," I:114.

99. Chulick et al., "Titan Liquid Rocket Engines," pp. 24–29; Stumpf, *Titan II*, pp. 37–40; Aerojet Liquid Rocket Company, *Liquid Rocket Engines* (Sacramento, Calif.: Aerojet, 1975), pp. 4, 8, 20, 22; Adams, "Titan I to Titan II," pp. 214–15.

100. Hacker and Grimwood, *Shoulders of Titans*, pp. 77, 87, 105, 125–26, 134–37, 142–44, 166–69; Stumpf, *Titan II*, pp. 40–44, 72–73, 75–79, 97, 254–65, 281; Lonnquest and Winkler, *To Defend and Deter*, pp. 234–35.

Chapter 2

1. NASA's reviewer #2 reminded me of this important point and helped me articulate it. As in chapter 1, this chapter condenses much longer discussions

of these issues in a separate manuscript organized very differently. So only the most important sources can be referenced in the following notes.

2. Saturn/Apollo Systems Office, "Mercury-Redstone," pp. 2–3 (see chap. 1, n. 54); Loyd S. Swenson Jr., James M. Grimwood, and Charles C. Alexander, *This New Ocean: A History of Project Mercury* (Washington, D.C.: NASA SP-4201, 1998), p. 171.

3. Kuettner, "Mercury-Redstone Launch-Vehicle Development," in *Mercury Project Summary*, ed. Kleinknecht and Bland, pp. 69–79 (see chap. 1, n. 54); Saturn/Apollo Systems Office, "Mercury-Redstone," pp. 1-5, 3-1; NASA Office of Congressional Relations, *Mercury-Redstone III Sub-orbital Manned Flight* (Washington, D.C.: NASA, 1961), p. 5-1; Mitchell R. Sharpe and Bettye R. Burkhalter, "Mercury-Redstone: The First American Man-Rated Space Launch Vehicle," in *History of Rocketry and Astronautics*, ed. Becklake, 17:369 (see chap. 1, n. 54); Saturn/Apollo Systems Office, "Mercury-Redstone," pp. 5-1 to 5-37, 8-5; Ezell, *NASA Historical Data Book*, 2:143–44 (see chap. 1, n. 44).

4. Swenson, Grimwood, and Alexander, *This New Ocean*, pp. 200–205, 274–79, 307–308, 638–39.

5. Ibid., pp. 174–76, 187–89, 255, 308–309, 318–22, 337, 381–84, 640–41.

6. Hacker and Grimwood, *Shoulders of Titans*, pp. 77, 87, 105, 125–26, 134–37, 142–44, 166–69 (see chap. 1, n. 72); Dyer, *TRW*, pp. 231–32 (see chap. 1, n. 67); Stumpf, *Titan II*, pp. 40–42, 72, 78–79 (see chap. 1, n. 94); "Gemini-Titan II Launch Vehicle Fact Sheet," n.d., pp. 6-13 to 6-16, seen in the Air Force Space and Missile Systems Center History Office, photo storage area; Dieter K. Huzel and David H. Huang, *Modern Engineering for Design of Liquid-Propellant Rocket Engines*, rev. and updated by Harry Arbit et al. (Washington, D.C.: AIAA, 1992), p. 366; Chulick et al., Titan Liquid Rocket Engines," p. 31 (see chap. 1, n. 94).

7. Aerospace Corporation, "Gemini Program Launch Systems Final Report," Aerospace Report No. TOR-1001 (2126-80)-3, Jan. 1967, seen at the Air Force Historical Research Agency, K243.0473-7, pp. II.B-1, II.B-22 to II.B-23; Stumpf, *Titan II*, p. 73; Hacker and Grimwood, *Shoulders of Titans*, p. 523; quotation from "Statement of Dr. George E. Mueller, Associate Administrator for Manned Space Flight, NASA, before the Subcommittee on Manned Space Flight, Committee on Science and Astronautics, House of Representatives," Feb. 17, 1964, p. 29, George E. Mueller Collection, folder 13, Speeches, Manuscripts Division, Library of Congress, Washington, D.C.

8. "Gemini-Titan II Launch Vehicle Fact Sheet," pp. 6-9, 6-16 to 6-21; Aerospace Corporation, "Gemini Program," pp. II.C-1, II.C-46 to II.C-55, II.C-58 to II.C-59.

9. Hacker and Grimwood, *Shoulders of Titans*, pp. 268–69, 298–303, 330–31, 383–89, 523–29; Tom D. Crouch, *Aiming for the Stars: The Dreamers and Doers of the Space Age* (Washington, D.C.: Smithsonian Institution Press, 1999), pp. 191–92, 194–98; T. A. Heppenheimer, *Countdown: A History of Space Flight* (New York: Wiley, 1997), pp. 218–24; Aerospace Corporation, "Gemini Program," p. I.A-1; Roger D. Launius, *NASA: A History of the U.S. Civil Space Program* (Malabar, Fla.: Krieger, 1994), pp. 81–82.

10. Steven J. Isakowitz, *International Reference Guide to Space Launch Systems* (Washington, D.C.: AIAA, 1991), pp. 294–95 [hereafter cited as Isakowitz, *Space Launch Systems* (1991) to distinguish it from later editions]; Douglas Missile & Space Systems Division, "The Thor History," Douglas Report SM-41860, Feb. 1964, pp. 66–67, Air Force Space and Missile Systems Center History Office, separate item in file "Standard Launch Vehicles II"; W. M. Arms, *Thor: The*

Workhorse of Space—a Narrative History (Huntington Beach, Calif.: McDonnell Douglas Astronautics Company, 1972), pp. 4-2 through 6-8; Space Division, "SAMSO Chronology," pp. 387–92 (see chap. 1, n. 72), copy generously provided by Space and Missile Systems Center History Office; Goddard Space Flight Center, NASA Facts, "The Delta Expandable Launch Vehicle" [1992], p. 1, NHRC, file 010240, "Delta"; Matt Bille, Pat Johnson, Robyn Kane, and Erika R. Lishock, "History and Development of U.S. Small Launch Vehicles," pp. 198–204, and Kevin S. Forsyth, "Delta: The Ultimate Thor," pp. 103–46, both in To Reach the High Frontier, ed. Launius and Jenkins (see chap. 1, n. 82).

Notes to Pages
54–55

11. J. F. Meyers, "Delta II—a New Era under Way," IAF Paper 89-196, delivered at the 40th Congress of the International Astronautical Federation, Oct. 7–12, 1989, Malaga, Spain, pp. 1–2; Aeronautics and Space Report of the President, Fiscal Year 2001 Activities (Washington, D.C.: Government Printing Office [2002]), p. 140; Boeing, "Delta III Launch Vehicle," http://www.boeing.com/defense-space/space/delta/delta3/delta3.htm (accessed Sept. 11, 2002); Boeing, "Delta IV Launch Vehicles," http://www.boeing.com/defense-space/space/delta/delta4/delta4.htm (accessed Sept. 11, 2002); Peter Pae, "Delta IV's First Launch Provides a Lift to Boeing," Los Angeles Times, Nov. 21, 2002, pp. C1, C4; Forsyth, "Delta," pp. 139–40.

12. "Aerojet to Build Able Star, Bigger, Restartable Able," Missiles and Rockets 6 (Feb. 15, 1960): 34; briefing charts, Able Projects, "Development of Project Able Second Stage, Propulsion System," Air Force Space and Missile Systems Center History Office, folder, "Briefing Charts—Able Projects"; Arms, "Thor," pp. 4-2, 4-3; letter, R. R. Bennett to L. G. Dunn, Mar. 25, 1958, and "Thor Missile 118 Flight Summary," Air Force Space and Missile Systems Center History Office, folder, "Re-entry—(Able-01) (Gen T)"; R. C. Stiff Jr., "Storable Liquid Rockets," paper 67-977 delivered at the AIAA 4th Annual Meeting and Technical Display, Oct. 23–27, 1967, Anaheim, Calif., p. 8; Joel W. Powell, "Thor-Able and Atlas Able," Journal of the British Interplanetary Society (JBIS) 37, no. 5 (May 1984): 221.

13. Powell, "Thor-Able and Atlas-Able," pp. 219, 221, 223–24; Arms, "Thor," pp. 4-4, 4-6, 6-8, 6-9, 6-13 to 6-16, B-5; "The Air Force Ballistic Missile Division and the Able Programs," Nov. 27, 1959, p. 4, Air Force Space and Missile Systems Center History Office, folder, "The Able Programs and AFBMD/STL"; Maj. Gen. O. J. Ritland, "Able Program Final Progress Report," May 25, 1961, p. 2, Air Force Space and Missile Systems Center History Office, folder "Program Progress Report—Able 1961"; E. J. Skurzynski, Project Engineer, Allegany Ballistics Laboratory, Development Progress Report, "Design and Testing of JATO X248 A3, 40-DS-3000," Nov. 11, 1958, NA RG 255, Records of National Aeronautics and Space Administration, Vanguard Division, Project Vanguard Case Files, Hercules Powder—Allegany Ballistics Laboratory Progr. Rpt., box 6; STL, "1958 NASA/USAF Space Probes (ABLE-1), Final Report," vol. 1, summary, pp. 59, 62–63, 84, Air Force Space and Missile Systems Center History Office, separate item in files; Headquarters, Air Research and Development Command (ARDC), "Space System Development Plan, Able 3 and Able 4," June 10, 1959, revised Oct. 26, 1959, pp. III-1 through III-7, III-16 through III-19, Air Force Historical Research Agency K243.8636-17; Report to the Congress from the President of the United States, U.S. Aeronautics and Space Activities, Jan. 1 to Dec. 31, 1959 (Washington, D.C.: The White House, 1960), p. 24; Air Force Space and Missile Systems Center History Office, folder, "Briefing Charts—Able Projects"; ARDC, "Space System Development Plan, Able 3 and Able 4," pp. III-46 through III-59;

briefing chart, "Launch Guidance & Tracking Scheme—Able 3 & 4"; Linda Neuman Ezell, *NASA Historical Data Book: Programs and Projects 1969–1978* (Washington, D.C.: NASA SP-4012, 1988), III:266; R. Weil, STL, "Final Report, Contract No. AF 04(647)-361," Oct. 12, 1961, p. 9, Air Force Space and Missile Systems Center History Office, separate report in files on ABLE 4 & 5; *Report to the Congress, 1960* (Washington, D.C.: The White House, 1961), p. vi.

14. [AFBMD]/WDLPM-4 to [AFBMD]/WDZJP, subject: Proposed AJ10-104 Final Report, Mar. 30, 1960; HQ AFBMD document, "ABLE-STAR (AJ10-104)," Aug. 18, 1961, both documents from Air Force Space and Missile Center History Office, file "Development of AJ10-104 (ABLE STAR)."

15. Weil, STL, "Final Report," pp. 3, 34, 53; Irwin Stambler, "Simplicity Boosts Able-Star to Reliability Record," *Space/Aeronautics,* Aug. 1961, pp. 59, 63–64; BMD document, "ABLE-STAR (AJ10-104)," p. 1-3; "AbleStar is Newest Aerojet Triumph: Restartable Space Engine Orbits Two-in-One Payload," *The Aerojet Booster* 5, no. 1 (July 1960): 2, NASM Archives, folder B7-020030-01, Aerojet General, Publications, "Aerojet Booster"; Gordon et al., *Aerojet*, p. III-135 (see chap. 1, n. 85); Jay Holmes, "*Able-Star* Makes Technological First," *Missiles and Rockets* 6 (Apr. 25, 1960): 44.

16. *Report to the Congress . . . , January 1 to December 31, 1960* (Washington, D.C.: [GPO], 1961), pp. viii, 26, 39; *Report to the Congress . . . , 1962* (Washington, DC: [GPO], [1963]), p. 121; Weil, STL, "Final Report," pp. 31–37, 53; "Historical Reports," Programs Managed by the Directorate of TRANSIT/ANNA, p. 4; *Report to the Congress . . . , 1963* (Washington, D.C.: [GPO], [1964]), pp. 132, 134; *Report to the Congress . . . , 1964* (Washington, D.C.: [GPO], [1965]), pp. 141–42, 147; *Report to the Congress . . . , 1965* (Washington, D.C.: [GPO], [1966]), pp. 145, 150.

17. See, for example, "Twentieth Birthday of Space 'Workhorse,'" *NASA Activities* , May 1979, p. 16, NHRC, folder 010195, "Launch Vehicles: Agena"; "Thor," in "500 Thor Launches," commemorative brochure, Los Angeles, Oct. 21, 1978, George E. Mueller Collection, Manuscripts Division, Library of Congress, box 205, folder 6, "National Aeronautics and Space Administration—Thor"; Jonathan McDowell's table listing Agena missions, http://hea-www .harvard.edu/QEDT/jcm/space/rockets/liquid/US/Agena.new (accessed July 31, 2002), pp. 4–8; Jonathan McDowell, "US Reconnaissance Satellite Programs, Part I: Photoreconnaissance," *Quest: The History of Spaceflight Magazine* 4, no. 2 (Summer 1995): 28–33.

18. "BMO Chronology," Aug. 1993, pp. 29, 31; Dwayne A. Day, "Corona: America's First Spy Satellite Program," *Quest: The History of Spaceflight Magazine* 4, no. 2 (Summer 1995): 10; Michael Yaffee, "Bell Adapts Hustler Rocket Engine for Varied Missions," *Aviation Week,* Nov. 21, 1960, p. 53; A. DiFrancesco and F. Boorady, "The Agena Rocket Engine Story," AIAA Paper 89-2390 delivered at the AIAA/ASME/SAE 25th Joint Propulsion Conference, July 10, 1989, Monterey, Calif., pp. 2, 5; Robert D. Roach Jr., ". . . The Agena Rocket Engine . . . Six Generation of Reliability in Space Propulsion," Bell Aerosystems Company, *Rendezvous* 6, no. 6 (1967): 6, NASA HRC, folder 010680, "Bell Rendezvous."

19. Roach, "Agena Rocket Engine," pp. 6–7; Yaffee, "Bell Adapts Hustler Rocket Engine," p. 57; DiFrancesco and Boorady, "Agena Rocket Engine," pp. 5–6; Day, "Corona," pp. 15–17; Arms, "Thor," pp. 6–28; Satellite Launch Fact Sheet, "U.S. Air Force Satellite Launches," http://www.losangeles.af.mil/SMC/HO/Slfact.htm (accessed Sept. 6, 2002 [hereafter cited as SMC/HO, "Air Force

Satellite Launches"]), p. 3; McDowell, "US Reconnaissance Satellite Programs," pp. 23–24.

20. Yaffee, "Bell Adapts Hustler Rocket Engine," p. 59; McDowell, "US Reconnaissance Satellite Programs," pp. 23–24, 26; DiFrancesco and Boorady, "Agena Rocket Engine," pp. 5–6; Robert M. Powell, "Evolution of Standard Agena: Corona's Spacecraft," in *Corona between the Sun & the Earth: The First NRO Reconnaissance Eye in Space,* ed. Robert A. McDonald (Bethesda, Md.: American Society for Photogrammetry and Remote Sensing, 1997), pp. 121–22; Jonathan McDowell's table listing Agena missions, http://hea-www.harvard .edu/QEDT/jcm/space/rockets/liquid/US/Agena.new (accessed July 31, 2002), pp. 1–2; Arms, "Thor," pp. 6-39, 6-41; Isakowitz, *Space Launch Systems* (1991), p. 295; SMC/HO, "Air Force Satellite Launches," pp. 3–4.

21. Roach, "Agena Rocket Engine," p. 8; Yaffee, "Bell Adapts Hustler Rocket Engine," p. 59; DiFrancesco and Boorady, "Agena Rocket Engine," pp. 5–6; "Final Report of the Survey Team Established to Investigate the Use of Agena for the National Aeronautics and Space Administration," Feb. 15, 1960, JPL Archives, History Collection, box JA-12, Item 2-954A; Dave Feld, "Agena Engine," paper 1412-60 presented at the 15th annual meeting of the American Rocket Society, Dec. 5–8, 1960, Washington, D.C., pp. 1, 5–7, 9, NHRC, folder 010195, "Launch Vehicles: Agena"; McDowell, "U.S. Reconnaissance Satellite Programs," pp. 26–28; Arms, "Thor," pp. 6-39, 6-41, 6-43, 6-44; "SAMSO Chronology," p. 168; Isakowitz, *Space Launch Systems* (1991), p. 295.

22. "SAMSO Chronology," pp. 153, 170, 368; Andrew Wilson, "Burner 2—Boeing's Small Upper Stage," *Spaceflight* 22 (May 5, 1980): 210–11; *CPIA/M1 Rocket Motor Manual,* Unit 427, X248A5, Altair I; David N. Spires, *Beyond Horizons: A Half Century of Air Force Space Leadership* (Peterson Air Force Base, Colo.: Air Force Space Command, 1997), pp. 147, 170; *Report to the Congress . . . , 1965,* pp. 131, 136, 142, 151; *Report to the Congress . . . , 1966* (Washington, D.C.: GPO, [1967]), p. 149.

23. Wilson, "Burner 2," p. 210; "SAMSO Chronology," p. 164.

24. Thiokol Chemical Corporation, "Off-the-Shelf Motor Catalog," n.d., n.p. (coverage of TE-M-364-2 & 3 [Star 37B & 37D]), NASM file B7-820060-01, "Thiokol, General, Rocket Specs"; Boeing News Release S-0416, "Burner II and Burner IIA," Jan. 29, 1970, NASM Archives, folder 0B-840000-01, "Burner II Upper Stage"; Boeing Aerospace Group, Space Division, "Burner II for Synchronous Mission Applications," June 1967, pp. 17–23, NASM Archives, folder 0B-840000-02, "Burner II Upper Stage"; Wilson, "Burner 2," pp. 210–11; "SAMSO Chronology," pp. 186–87, 210, 387, 391–93; Spires, *Beyond Horizons,* p. 151; *Report to the Congress . . . , 1966,* p. 156; *Report to the Congress . . . , 1967* (Washington, D.C.: GPO, [1968]), pp. 125, 128–29.

25. Thiokol, "Off-the-Shelf Motor Catalog," TE-M-442-1, Star 26B; Wilson, "Burner 2," p. 211; "SAMSO Chronology," pp. 185–87, 198, 246, 368, 387–88; John W. R. Taylor, ed., *Jane's All the World's Aircraft, 1977–1978* (London: Jane's Yearbooks, 1978), p. 836; Boeing, "Burner II for Synchronous Mission Applications," p. 39; SMC/HO, "Air Force Satellite Launches," pp. 1–2; Spires, *Beyond Horizons,* p. 148; *Aeronautics and Space Report . . . , Fiscal Year 2000 Activities* (Washington, D.C.: GPO, 2001), pp. 26, 100.

26. V. L. Johnson, "Delta," NASA Program Review, "Launch Vehicles and Propulsion," June 23, 1962, p. 51, NHRC; Philip Chien, "The Reliable Workhorse," *Ad Astra* (Feb. 1991): 38–41; David Ian Wade, "The Delta Family," *Spaceflight* 38 (Nov. 1996): 373–76; "Delta II Becomes New Medium Launch Vehicle," *Astro*

News 29, no. 2 (Jan. 23, 1987), Air Force Historical Research Agency microfilm K168.03-2849; Craig Covault, "Boeing Faces Morale, Leadership Issues as Delta IV Nears Critical First Flight," *Aviation Week & Space Technology* (Aug. 26, 2002): 24; James M. Knauf, Linda R. Drake, and Peter L. Portanova, "EELV: Evolving toward Affordability," *Aerospace America* (Mar. 2002): 38, 40–42.

27. Milton Rosen, "Brief History of Delta and Its Relation to Vanguard," pp. 1–3, in letter, Rosen to Constance McL. Green, Mar. 15, 1968, NHRC, folder 001835, "Rosen, Milton W. (Misc. Bio)"; William R. Corliss, draft "History of the Delta Launch Vehicle," with comments by L. C. Bruno, Sept. 4, 1973, in NHRC, folder 010246, "Delta Documentation (1959–72)," pp. 3-1 through 3-4; Johnson, "Delta," p. 51; J. D. Hunley, ed., *The Birth of NASA: The Diary of T. Keith Glennan* (Washington, D.C.: NASA SP-4105, 1993), pp. 336–37, 357.

28. Corliss, "History of Delta," pp. 2-6, 2-12 to 2-13, 3-4, 3-9; Johnson, "Delta," pp. 54–56, 67–68; Arms, "Thor," pp. 6-49 to 6-50; Schindler's obituary in the *Washington Post*, Jan. 29, 1992; Stuart H. Loory, "Quality Control . . . and Success," *The New York Herald Tribune*, Apr. 21, 1963, p. 4.

29. Ezell, *NASA Historical Data Book*, II:353–55, 368–72, 375; Arms, "Thor," p. 6-49; Rosen, "Brief History of Delta and Its Relation to Vanguard," p. 3; Johnson, "Delta," pp. 62–64; Goddard Space Flight Center, "Delta Expandable Launch Vehicle."

30. See chart 2 in Goddard Space Flight Center, "Delta Expandable Launch Vehicle," p. 9, and Wade, "Delta Family," p. 373; Jyri Kork and William R. Schindler, "The Thor-Delta Launch Vehicle: Past and Future," Paper SD 32 delivered at the 19th Congress of the International Astronautical Federation, Oct. 13–19, New York, 1968, p. 4; Meyers, "Delta II," p. 1.

31. "Thor" brochure from Mueller Collection; Meyers, "Delta II," pp. 1–2; Forsyth, "Delta," p. 117; reliability calculated from Goddard Space Flight Center, "Delta Expandable Launch Vehicle," pp. 4–8.

32. Luis Zea, "Delta's Dawn: The Making of a Rocket," *Final Frontier*, Feb.–Mar. 1995, p. 46; Frank Colucci, "Blue Delta," *Space* 3 (May/June 1987): 42; Meyers, "Delta II," pp. 3–5; Forsyth, "Delta," p. 132.

33. Steven J. Isakowitz, *International Reference Guide to Space Launch Systems*, updated by Jeff Samella, 2d ed. (Washington, D.C.: American Institute of Aeronautics and Astronautics, 1995), pp. 201–205; United States Air Force, Fact Sheet 86–40, "Atlas Space Boosters," Nov. 1986; Convair Division, General Dynamics Corporation, "Atlas Fact Sheet," n.d., p. 5, both fact sheets in NASM Archives, folder OA-401060-01, "Atlas Launch Vehicles (SLV-3)"; General Dynamics, Convair Division, Report A2 TD-2, "Atlas IIB/Centaur Technical Description: A High-Performance Launch Vehicle for Intelsat VI Class Spacecraft," Apr. 1983, foreword, p. xi, Microfiche E 84-10656, Air Force Space and Missiles Systems Center History Office; General Dynamics/Astronautics, "Atlas ICBM Fact Sheet" [Jan. 1962], p. 10, NASM Archives, file OA-401001-01, "Atlas ICBM (SM-65, HGM-16), Articles, 1957"; Spires, *Beyond Horizons*, p. 71.

34. Joel W. Powell, "Thor-Able and Atlas Able," *JBIS* 37 (1984): 225; J. W. Powell and G. R. Richards, "The Atlas E/F Launch Vehicle—an Unsung Workhorse," *JBIS* 44 (1991): 229; Richard Martin, "A Brief History of the *Atlas* Rocket Vehicle," pt. II, *Quest: The History of Spaceflight Quarterly* 8, no. 3 [2000 or 2001]: 40–45; *Project Ranger*, Report of the Subcommittee on NASA Oversight of the Committee on Science and Astronautics, 88th Cong., 2d sess., H. Rep. 1487 (Washington, D.C.: Government Printing Office, 1964), p. 3; R. Cargill Hall, *Lunar Impact: A History of Project Ranger* (Washington, D.C.: NASA

SP-4210, 1977), pp. 25–32, 94–109, 188–90; Convair Division of General Dynamics, "Atlas Family of Space Launch Vehicles: Configuration and Performance Summary," Report No. GDC BNZ-011, revised May 1972, pp. 26, 68, NHRC, folder 010191, "Atlas Launch Vehicles—Technical Reports"; letter, Homer E. Newell, Office of Space Sciences, NASA, to Gen. Bernard A. Schriever, AFSC, Sept. 27, 1962, Jet Propulsion Laboratory Historical Collection, box JA 150, item 5-1179; NASA Agena Program Presentation [made by Marshall Space Flight Center at NASA Headquarters?], Oct. 1, 1962, JPL Historical Collection, box JA36, item 2-2269, pp. 1-4 to 1-7; "Twentieth Birthday of Space 'Workhorse,'" *NASA Activities*, May 1979, p. 16; "Jonathan McDowell's table listing Agena missions.

35. NASA News Release 62-66, "First Launch of Centaur Vehicle Scheduled," Apr. 3, 1962, NASM Archives, folder OA-40107-01, "Atlas Centaur Launch Vehicle"; General Dynamics/Astronautics, "Centaur Primer: An Introduction to Hydrogen-Powered Space Flight," June 1962, NHRC, folder 10203, "Centaur General (1959–89)"; General Dynamics, Space Systems Division, "Atlas/Centaur: Reliable, Versatile, Available," [1985–86?], NASM Archives, folder OA-40107-01, "Atlas Centaur Launch Vehicle"; Virginia P. Dawson and Mark D. Bowles, *Taming Liquid Hydrogen: The Centaur Upper Stage Rocket, 1958–2002* (Washington, D.C.: NASA SP-2004-4230, 2004), esp. chap. 1, 5, 8; "Statement of Krafft A. Ehricke, Director, Advanced Studies, General Dynamics/Astronautics," in *Centaur Program*, Hearings before the Subcommittee on Space Sciences of the Committee on Science and Astronautics, H. Rep., 87th Cong., 2d sess., May 15 and 18, 1962 (Washington, D.C.: GPO, 1962), pp. 5, 61–66; these same Hearings, pp. 4, 9, 105–106, 115–16.

36. NASA News Release 62-66, "First Launch of Centaur Vehicle Scheduled," Apr. 3, 1962; General Dynamics/Astronautics, "Centaur Primer."

37. General Dynamics, Space Systems Division, "Atlas/Centaur"; Ezell, *NASA Historical Data Book*, II:328–31; III:169–70, 305–11; Judy A. Rumerman, *NASA Historical Data Book* (Washington, D.C.: NASA SP-4012, 1999), V:82; Dawson and Bowles, *Centaur*, pp. 222–25; General Dynamics News, Fact Sheet, "Commercial Atlas/Centaur Program," supporting document III-8 in Jeffrey Geiger and Kirk W. Clear, "History of Space and Missile Test Organization and Western Space and Missile Center," Oct. 1, 1987, to Sept. 30, 1988, vol. III, Air Force Historical Research Agency, K241.011.

38. John L. Sloop, *Liquid Hydrogen as a Propulsion Fuel, 1945–1959* (Washington, D.C.: NASA SP-4404, 1978), pp. 191–94; Clarke Newlon, "Krafft Ehricke," in *Rocket and Missile Technology*, ed. Gene Gurney (New York: Franklin Watts, 1964), pp. 86–91; oral history interview [John L. Sloop] with Krafft A. Ehricke, Apr. 26, 1974, pp. 31–33, 51–53, 59, NHRC, folder 010976; John L. Chapman, *Atlas: The Story of a Missile* (New York: Harper & Brothers, 1960), p. 153; Dawson and Bowles, *Centaur*, pp. 5–7, 12–13, 18–22; Dan Heald, "LH_2 Technology was Pioneered on Centaur 30 Years Ago," in *History of Rocketry and Astronautics, Proceedings of the Twenty-Sixth History Symposium of the International Academy of Astronautics*, ed. Philippe Jung, AAS History Series (San Diego: Univelt, 1997), 21:207.

39. Hearings, *Centaur Program*, pp. 5, 7, 9, 43, 47, 51, 63–66, 97; Dawson and Bowles, *Centaur*, p. 40; Irwin Stambler, "Centaur," *Space/Aeronautics* (Oct. 1963): 73–75; W. Schubert, "Centaur," in Office of Space Sciences—Launch Vehicles and Propulsion Programs, "Program Review, Launch Vehicles and Propulsion," June 23, 1962, pp. 173–75, NHRC; Joel E. Tucker, "History of the RL10

Upper-Stage Rocket Engine," in *Liquid Rocket Engine Development*, ed. Doyle, 13:126–31.

40. Tucker, "RL10 Upper-Stage Rocket Engine," pp. 132–37; Hearings, *Centaur Program*, pp. 2, 9, 12–27, 37, 61–62, 66, 104, 115–16; Schubert, "Centaur," p. 131; G. R. Richards and Joel W. Powell, "Centaur Vehicle," *JBIS* 42 (Mar. 1989): 102–103; correspondence by Deane Davis, General Dynamics (retd.), *JBIS* 35 (1982): 17; Heald, "LH$_2$ Technology," p. 206; letter, Hans Hueter, [MSFC] Director, Light and Medium Vehicles Office, to J. R. Dempsey, President, General Dynamics/Astronautics, Jan. 4, 1962, p. 2, NHRC, John Sloop Papers (Centaur Material), box 22, binder, "Centaur Management & Development, Jan 1961–Mar 1962"; Dawson and Bowles, *Centaur*, pp. 34–35, 42–43, 46–51; Philip Geddes, "Centaur, How It Was Put Back on Track," *Aerospace Management*, Apr. 1964, pp. 25, 28–29.

41. Letter with attached account, Deane Davis to Gene [Eugene Emme, then NASA historian], Feb. 6, 1983, NHRC, folder 00190, "Launch Vehicles: Atlas"; Sloop, *Liquid Hydrogen*, pp. 183, 208; Hearings, *Centaur Program*, p. 59; Dawson and Bowles, *Centaur*, pp. 91–98; NASA News Release No. 62-209, "Liquid Hydrogen Program Stepped Up," Sept. 30, 1962, NHRC, folder 010203, "Centaur General (1959–89)"; Joseph Green and Fuller C. Jones, "The Bugs That Live at −423°," *Analog: Science Fiction, Science Fact* 80, no. 5 (Jan. 1968): 30–38; Richards and Powell, "Centaur Vehicle," pp. 106–107; General Dynamics/Convair, "Atlas Fact Sheet," n.d., pp. 12, 14; Ezell, *NASA Historical Data Book*, II:263, 328–31, 399; Asif A. Siddiqi, *Deep Space Chronicle: A Chronology of Deep Space and Planetary Probes, 1958–2000* (Washington, D.C.: NASA SP-2002-4524, 2002), pp. 55, 57, 61, 63, 65, 67–69; Executive Office of the President, *Report to the Congress from the President of the United States* [1965] (Washington, D.C.: GPO, [1966]), p. 161; Executive Office of the President, *United States Aeronautics & Space Activities, 1968* (Washington, D.C.: GPO, [1969]), p. 108.

42. Ezell, *NASA Historical Data Book*, III:222; Dawson and Bowles, *Centaur*, pp. 125, 128, 131, 136, 141–43; Richards and Powell, "Centaur Vehicle," pp. 109–11; Siddiqi, *Deep Space Chronicle*, pp. 93–97; "Atlas Launch Vehicle History," *Astronautics & Aeronautics*, Nov. 1975, no pagination (between pp. 76 and 79); Capt. Nicholas C. Belmont, "Laboratory Tests of Advanced Centaur Components," Jan. 30, 1968, Air Force Historical Research Agency microfilm 32,273, frame 334; Honeywell, "Centaur Inertial Navigation Unit," Mar. 1992, NHRC, folder 010203, "Centaur General (1959–89)"; Air Force Space and Missile Systems Organization, "Centaur D-1 Payload Users Guide," June 30, 1970, pp. 3-1, 3-30 through 3-37, NASM Archives, Bellcom Collection, box 12, folder 5; *CPIA/M1 Rocket Motor Manual*, Unit 576, Star 37E.

43. Dawson and Bowles, *Centaur*, pp. 116–33, 223–24; Richards and Powell, "Centaur Vehicle," p. 111; Ezell, *NASA Historical Data Book*, III:223, 290, 293–94, 304–11, and Rumerman, V:82; Thiokol's *Aerospace Facts*, July–Sept. 1973, p. 12, NASM Archive, folder B7-820030-02, "Thiokol General, Publications, 'Aerospace Facts'"; Siddiqi, *Deep Space Chronicle*, pp. 102–103; Isakowitz, *Space Launch Systems* (1995), pp. 203, 205; Richards and Powell, "Centaur Vehicle," pp. 100, 113–14.

44. Richards and Powell, "Centaur Vehicle," pp. 114–15; Tucker, "RL10 Upper-Stage Rocket Engine," p. 147; Dawson and Bowles, *Centaur*, pp. 224, 232, 238; General Dynamics, Space Systems Division, "Atlas/Centaur"; Isakowitz, *Space Launch Systems* (1995), p. 205; *Aeronautics and Space Report . . . , 1989–1990 Activities* (Washington, D.C.: GPO, 1991), p. 143.

45. Joan Lisa Bromberg, *NASA and the Space Industry* (Baltimore, Md.: Johns Hopkins University Press, 1999), pp. 100–101, 149–59; Richard Martin, "A Brief History of the *Atlas* Rocket Vehicle," pt. III, *Quest: The History of Spaceflight Quarterly* 8, no. 4 [2000 or 2001]: 44–47; Martin, "Brief History of the Atlas," pt. II, p. 44; Dawson and Bowles, *Centaur,* pp. 233–38, 242; Isakowitz, *Space Launch Systems* (1995), p. 205; *Aeronautics and Space Report . . . , 1989–1990 Activities,* pp. 18, 147.

46. Donald F. Robertson, "Centaur Canters On," *Space,* Mar.–Apr. 1991, pp. 22–25; General Dynamics Commercial Launch Services, "Mission Planner's Guide for the Atlas Launch Vehicle Family," Mar. 1989, pp. 1-1, 1-2, A-1 to A-6, NASM Archives, folder OA-401095-01, "Atlas I Launch Vehicle"; Heald, "LH$_2$ Technology," p. 220.

47. Powell and Richards, "Atlas E/F," pp. 229–31; Martin, "Brief History of the Atlas," pt. II, p. 44.

48. Powell and Richards, "Atlas E/F," pp. 230–231; Martin, "Brief History of the Atlas," pt. I, pp. 60–61; Joel W. Powell and G. R. Richards, "The Orbiting Vehicle Series of Satellites," *JBIS* 40 (1987): 417–21, 426; *CPIA/M1 Rocket Motor Manual,* Unit 480, FW-4; Convair Division of General Dynamics, "Atlas Family of Space Launch Vehicles," p. 42.

49. Powell and Richards, "Atlas E/F," pp. 231–33; *Aeronautics and Space Report . . . , 1974 Activities* (Washington, D.C.: GPO, [1975]), p. 44; Norman Friedman, *Seapower and Space: From the Dawn of the Missile Age to Net-Centric Warfare* (Annapolis, Md.: Naval Institute Press, 2000), pp. 228–29, 242, 266–82.

50. Powell and Richards, "Atlas E/F," p. 233; *Aeronautics and Space Report . . . , 1977 Activities* (Washington, D.C.: GPO, [1978]), p. 41; *Aeronautics and Space Report . . . , 1980 Activities* (Washington, D.C.: GPO, [1981]), p. 39; G. Porcelli and E. Vogtel, "Modular, Spin-Stabilized, Tandem Solid Rocket Upper Stage," *Journal of Spacecraft and Rockets* 16, no. 5 (Sept.–Oct. 1979): 338–42.

51. Powell and Richards, "Atlas E/F," pp. 231, 233–34; Thiokol Corporation, *Aerospace Facts,* Spring 1979, p. 25, NASM Archive, folder B7-820030-02, "Thiokol General, Publications, 'Aerospace Facts.'" On the Antares III, *CPIA/ M1 Rocket Motor Manual,* Unit 577, Antares IIIA.

52. Powell and Richards, "Atlas E/F," pp. 231, 234–37; "Star 37S," at www .astronautix.com/engines/star37s.htm, a Mark Wade site (accessed Sept. 6, 2002); *Aeronautics and Space Report . . . , 1981 Activities* (Washington, D.C.: GPO, [1982]), p. 38; Satellite Launch Fact Sheet, "U.S. Air Force Satellite Launches," pp. 1–2, http://www.losangeles.af.mil/SMC/HO/Sifact.htm (accessed Sept. 6, 2002); United States Air Force Fact Sheet, "Defense Meteorological Satellite Program," pp. 1–2, http://www.milnet.com/milnet/pentagon/sats/fsheets/dmsp _fs.htm (accessed Sept. 9, 2002); NASA, "Defense Meteorological Satellites Program," pp. 1–2, http://heasarc.gsfc.gov/docs/heasarc/missions/dmsp.html (accessed Sept. 9, 2002); *Aeronautics and Space Report . . . , 1982 Activities* (Washington, D.C.: GPO, [1983]), p. 87; *Aeronautics and Space Report . . . , 1979 Activities* (Washington, D.C.: GPO, [1980]), p. 89; *Aeronautics and Space Report . . . , 1991 Activities* (Washington, D.C.: GPO, [1992]), p. 160.

53. Space Policy Project, "White Cloud Naval Ocean Surveillance System," http://www.fas.org/spp/military/program/surveill/noss.htm (accessed Sept. 6, 2002); Powell and Richards, "Atlas E/F," pp. 231, 234, 239–40; Isakowitz, *Space Launch Systems* (1995), pp. 204–205.

54. Quotation from Richard E. Martin, "The Atlas and Centaur 'Steel Balloon' Tanks: A Legacy of Karel Bossart," paper printed by General Dynamics

Space Systems Division, originally delivered at the 40th International Astronautical Congress, IAA-89-738, Oct. 7–13, 1989, Malaga, Spain, p. 15, seen in NASM Archives folder CB-467-000-01, "Bossart, Karel Jan"; *Review of Recent Launch Failures,* Hearings before the Subcommittee on NASA Oversight of the Committee on Science and Astronautics, H. Rep., 92d Cong., 1st sess., June 15–17, 1971 (Washington, D.C.: GPO, 1971), esp. pp. 3–5, 14–15, 20–25, 81–89.

55. James R. Hansen, *Engineer in Charge: A History of the Langley Aeronautical Laboratory, 1917–1958* (Washington, D.C.: NASA SP-4305, 1987); James R. Hansen, *Spaceflight Revolution: NASA Langley Research Center from Sputnik to Apollo* (Washington, D.C.: NASA SP-4308, 1995), chap. 7; James R. Hansen, "Learning through Failure: NASA's Scout Rocket," *National Forum* 81, no. 1 (Winter 2001): 18–23; Abraham Leiss, "Scout Launch Vehicle Program Final Report—Phase VI," NASA Contractor Report 165950, pt. 1, May 1982, p. xxxiii, Space and Missile Systems Center History Office, photo room (also available through NASA libraries on microfiche X82-10346); Bille, Kane, and Lishock, "History and Development of U.S. Small Launch Vehicles," pp. 204–13.

56. Hansen, *Spaceflight Revolution,* pp. 214–17, quotation from p. 215; Hansen, "Learning through Failure," pp. 22–23; Bille et al., "Small Launch Vehicles," pp. 210–211; Goddard Space Flight Center, NASA Facts, "NASA's Scout Launch Vehicle," Apr. 1992; Jonathan McDowell, "The Scout Launch Vehicle," *JBIS* 47 (Mar. 1994): 102–107.

57. Hansen, *Spaceflight Revolution,* pp. 197–200, 209–10; Joseph Adams Shortal, *A New Dimension: Wallops Island Flight Test Range, the First Fifteen Years* (Washington, D.C.: NASA Reference Publication 1028, 1978), pp. vii, 706–709, 717, 720; *CPIA/M1 Rocket Motor Manual,* Unit 277, Algol I, Aerojet Senior, Unit 237, Castor, Unit 228, Sergeant, Unit 428, X254A1, Unit 421, X259A2, Antares II, Unit 415 X258B1, Altair II, and Unit 427, Altair I; Thiokol Chemical Corporation, *Rocket Propulsion Data,* 3d ed. (Bristol, Pa.: 1961), TX-12 (Sergeant), TX-33-35 (Scout second stage); "History—Blue Scout," in the archives of the Space and Missile Systems Center History Office, "Blue Scout Chronology," entries for Sept. 9, 1959; Dec. 7, 1959; Mar. 9, 1960; June 30, 1960 (hereafter cited as "Blue Scout Chronology"); Leiss, "Scout Launch Vehicle Program Final Report," pp. 31–32, 53–54, 56, 65, 90, 131; Andrew Wilson, "Scout—NASA's Small Satellite Launcher," *Spaceflight* 21, no. 11 (Nov. 1979): 449–52; Goddard Space Flight Center, "NASA's Scout Launch Vehicle."

58. Shortal, *A New Dimension,* pp. 484–573, 702–706, 708, 712, 716; "Blue Scout Chronology," entries for Aug. 1958; Oct. 14, 1958; Feb. 3, 1959; Feb. 24, 1959; May 8, 1959; May 28–29, 1959; Dec. 2, 1959; Mar. 9, 1960; Sept. 13, 1960; Sept. 21, 1960, and "Blue Scout History," Jan. 1, 1962 through June 20, 1962, contained in the chronology; Gunter Krebs, "Blue Scout Junior (SRM-91, MER-6)," p. 1, http://www.skyrocket.de/space/doc_lau/blue_scout_jr.htm (accessed Nov. 20, 2002); Cliff Lethbridge, "Blue Scout Junior Fact Sheet," p. 1, http://www.spaceline.org/rocketsum/blue-scout-junior.html (accessed Nov. 20, 2002); Mark Wade, "Blue Scout Junior," p. 1, http://www.friends-partners.ru/partners/mwade/lvs/bluunior.htm (accessed Nov. 6, 2002); Frank H. Winter and George S. James, "Highlights of 50 Years of Aerojet, a Pioneering American Rocket Company, 1942–1992," *Acta Astronautica* 35, no. 9–11 (1995): 690; TN 457-72, *Solid Propulsion Systems,* Naval Weapons Center, China Lake, Calif., no pagination, no date in author's notes, seen in China Lake History Office folder KOB, "Solid Propellant Rocket Motors."

59. Mark Wade, "Blue Scout Junior" Web site, pp. 1–2; Krebs, "Blue Scout Junior" Web site, pp. 1–2; "Blue Scout Chronology," entries for Sept. 21, 1960; Nov. 8, 1960; Aug. 17, 1961; Dec. 4, 1961; July 24, 1962; Nov. 21, 1962; Dec. 18, 1962; and the "Blue Scout History" narrative included in the "Blue Scout Chronology" package.

60. McDowell, "Scout Launch Vehicle," p. 101; Mark Wade, "Blue Scout 1," http://www.astronautix.com/lvs/bluecoat1.htm (accessed Nov. 20, 2002), pp. 1–2; Gunter Krebs, "Blue Scout 1," http://www.spaceline.org/rocketsum/blue-scout-1.html (accessed Nov. 6, 2002), pp. 1–2; McDowell, "Scout Launch Vehicle," pp. 101–103, 105–106; "Blue Scout Chronology," entries for Oct. 1960; Jan. 7, 1961; Apr. 1, 1961; May 9, 1961; May 18, 1961; June 6, 1961; Sept. 1961; Oct. 2, 1961; Dec. 18, 1962; and "Blue Scout History"; Gunter Krebs, "Blue Scout-2," http://www.skyrocket.de/space/doc_lau_det/blue-scout-2.htm (accessed Nov. 6, 2002), pp. 1–2; Mark Wade, "Blue Scout 2," http://www.friends-partners.ru/partners/mwade/lvs/bluecout2.htm (accessed Nov. 6, 2002), pp. 1–2; http://www/sciencepresse.qc.cc/clafleur/sat-1967.html (accessed Nov. 20, 2002); General Dynamics/Convair, "Summary of Expendable and Reusable Booster Performance and Cost Data," Report No. GD/C-DCB-65-026, May 26, 1965, p. 3, seen at the Air Force Historical Research Agency, K243.0473-6; *Report to the Congress* . . . , *1967*, p. 127; Goddard Space Flight Center, "NASA's Scout Launch Vehicle"; Leiss, "Scout Launch Vehicle Program Final Report," p. 129.

61. Hansen, *Spaceflight Revolution*, pp. 210–14, quotation from p. 213; Wilson, "Scout," pp. 451–52; Leiss, "Scout Launch Vehicle Program Final Report," pp. 2–3, 50.

62. Hansen, *Spaceflight Revolution*, pp. 210–16; Wilson, "Scout," pp. 452–55; *Report to the Congress* . . . , *1963*, p. 135; Goddard Space Flight Center, "NASA's Scout Launch Vehicle."

63. Wilson, "Scout," pp. 449, 453–57, 459; Leiss, "Scout Launch Vehicle Program Final Report," pp. 2, 53–54, 56–57, 63, 447–48; *Report to the Congress* . . . , *1965*, p. 149; National Aeronautics and Space Council, *Aeronautics and Space Report* . . . , *1972 Activities* (Washington, D.C.: GPO, 1973), p. 89; *Aeronautics and Space Report* . . . , *1974 Activities* (Washington, D.C.: GPO, 1975), p. 128; *Aeronautics and Space Report* . . . , *1979 Activities*, p. 90; Bille et al., "Small Launch Vehicles," pp. 208–209; "BE-3," http://hea-www.harvard.edu/QEDT/jcm/space/book/engines/motor list/be.3.html (accessed Nov. 26, 2002); Gunter Krebs, "Scout-E1," http://www.skyrocket.de/space/doc_lau_det/scout-e1.htm (accessed Nov. 26, 2002); Thiokol, "Thiokol's Solid Propellant Upper and Lower Stages," http://members.aol.com/SLVehicles7/United_States_2/motors.htm (accessed Nov. 30, 2002); Mark Wade, "Star 20A," http://www.astronatuix.com/engines/star20a.htm (accessed Nov. 30, 2002); Gunter Krebs, "Scout," http://www.skyrocket.de/space/doc_lau_fam/scout.htm (accessed Nov. 26, 2002), pp. 2, 5.

64. For Scout, sources in n. 63 and Goddard Space Flight Center, "NASA's Scout Launch Vehicle"; for Saturn V, Ray A. Williamson, "The Biggest of Them All: Reconsidering the Saturn V," in *To Reach the High Frontier*, ed. Launius and Jenkins, pp. 313, 320–21; NASA/Marshall Space Flight Center (MSFC) et al., "Saturn V News Reference," Aug. 1967 (portions of it changed Dec. 1968), pp. iv, 1-2, 9-1; Isakowitz, *Space Launch Systems* (1991), p. 292; Roger E. Bilstein, "The Saturn Launch Vehicle Family," in *Apollo: Ten Years since Tranquility Base*, ed. Richard P. Hallion and Tom D. Crouch (Washington, D.C.: Smithsonian Institution Press, 1979), p. 186; Roger E. Bilstein, *Stages to Saturn: A Technological*

History of the Apollo/Saturn Launch Vehicles (Washington, D.C.: NASA SP-4206, 1980), p. 369.

65. Williamson, "Saturn V," esp. pp. 304–305; Bilstein, *Stages to Saturn*, esp. pp. xv–xvi, 15–16, 36–38, 46–48, 91–92, 95–96, 134, 140–47, 150, 191; Bilstein, "Saturn Launch Vehicle Family," 116; Charles Murray and Catherine Bly Cox, *Apollo: The Race to the Moon* (New York: Simon & Schuster, 1989), pp. 149–51, 180, 313–14; MSFC, Saturn Systems Office, "Saturn Illustrated Chronology (Apr. 1957–Apr. 1962)," pp. 1-2, 9, seen in the National Air and Space Museum Archives, Bellcom Collection, box 13, folder 3; NASA/MSFC et al., "Saturn IB News Reference," Dec. 1965 (changed Sept. 1968), pp. 1-1, 2-2.

66. Bilstein, *Stages to Saturn*, pp. 25–28; MSFC, "Saturn Illustrated Chronology," pp. 1–5; Murray and Cox, *Apollo*, p. 54.

67. Bilstein, *Stages to Saturn*, pp. 28–31; MSFC, "Saturn Illustrated Chronology," pp. 2–4; "The Experimental Engines Group," transcript of a group interview with Bill [W. F.] Ezell, Cliff [C. A.] Hauenstein, Jim [J. O.] Bates, Stan [G. S.] Bell, and Dick [R.] Schwarz, (Rocketdyne), *Threshold: An Engineering Journal of Power Technology*, no. 4 (Spring 1989): 21–27. See also Robert S. Kraemer, *Rocketdyne: Powering Humans into Space* (Reston, Va.: American Institute of Aeronautics and Astronautics, 2006), pp. 122–27.

68. MSFC, "Saturn Illustrated Chronology," pp. 8–10, 12–13, 17–20, 22; Ezell, *NASA Historical Data Book*, II:56–58; Bilstein, *Stages to Saturn*, pp. 188–89; B. K. Heusinger, "Saturn Propulsion Improvements," *Astronautics & Aeronautics*, Aug. 1964, p. 25; *Report to the Congress . . . , 1964* (Washington, D.C.: Executive Office of the President, [1965]), p. 128.

69. Bilstein, *Stages to Saturn*, pp. 77–78, 98–102, 184–85, 324–37; Summary, "Final Report S-IV All-Systems Stage Incident January 24, 1964, May 11, 1964," seen in George E. Mueller Collection, Manuscript Division, Library of Congress, box 91, folder 14, pp. 2–3; Heusinger, "Saturn Propulsion Improvements," p. 25; MSFC, "Saturn Illustrated Chronology," pp. 46–47; NASA/MSFC et al., "Saturn IB News Reference," p. 12-2.

70. NASA/MSFC et al., "Saturn IB News Reference," pp. 1-3 to 2-5, "S-IB Stage Fact Sheet," pp. 3-1, 3-22, unpaginated "H-1 Engine Fact Sheet," 200,000 pounds thrust, pp. 8-1, 12-2; Ezell, *NASA Historical Data Book*, II:56; MSFC, "Saturn Illustrated Chronology," pp. 50, 58, 60; Bilstein, *Stages to Saturn*, pp. 83, 97, 140–41; *CPIA/M5 Liquid Propellant Engine Manual* (Laurel, Md.: Chemical Propulsion Information Agency, 1989), Units 84, H-1 (165,000 and 188,000 pounds thrust) and 173, H-1 (205,000 pounds thrust); extracts from "The Apollo Spacecraft: A Chronology," 1:53–54, in NHRC, folder 013782, "Propulsion J-2."

71. Bilstein, *Stages to Saturn*, pp. 138, 140–45; Hunley, *Birth of NASA*, pp. 149–50, including n. 6; memorandum, NASA/MLP (Tischler) to NASA/ML (Rosen), subj: AGC Proposal, July 8, 1962, in NHRC, folder 013782; MSFC, "Saturn Illustrated Chronology (to Apr. 1962)," pp. 46, 50; Rocketdyne, "Data Sheet, J-2 Rocket Engine," June 3, 1975, in NHRC, folder 013782; memorandum, NASA/MLP (Tischler) to NASA/ML (Rosen), subj: M-1 Engine Review at AGC, July 11–12, 1962, July 24, 1962, in NHRC, folder 013782.

72. NASA/MSFC et al., "Saturn IB News Reference," unpaginated Saturn IB Fact Sheets (a generic one, plus separate fact sheets for AS-203, AS-204, and AS-205); National Aeronautics and Space Council, *Report to the Congress . . . , 1966* (Washington, D.C.: GPO, [1967]), pp. 148, 153, 155; National Aeronautics and Space Council, *United States Aeronautics and Space Activities . . . , 1968* (Washington, D.C.: GPO, [1969]), pp. 95, 99; Bilstein, *Stages to Saturn*, pp. 339–44,

414–16; NSSDC Master Catalog: Spacecraft, AS-202, http://nssdc.gsfc.gov/database/MasterCatalog?sc=APST202 (accessed Aug. 8, 2003); Courtney G. Brooks, James M. Grimwood, and Loyd S. Swenson Jr., *Chariots for Apollo: A History of Manned Lunar Spacecraft* (Washington, D.C.: NASA SP-4205, 1979), chap. 8, section on "Qualifying Missions," http://www.hq.nasa.gov/office/pao/History/SP-4205/ch8–2.html#source11 (accessed Summer 2003); Glen E. Swanson, ed., *Before This Decade Is Out . . . , Personal Reflections on the Apollo Program* (Washington D.C.: NASA SP-4223, 1999), p. 102; Science and Technology Division, Library of Congress, *Astronautics and Aeronautics, 1968: Chronology on Science, Technology, and Policy* (Washington, D.C.: NASA SP-4010, 1969), p. 252; Richard W. Orloff, *Apollo by the Numbers: A Statistical Reference* (Washington, D.C.: NASA SP-2000-4029, 2000), pp. 14–23; Ezell, *NASA Historical Data Book*, III:104–105.

73. MSFC, "Saturn Illustrated Chronology (to Apr. 1962)," pp. 4, 13–14; Bilstein, *Stages to Saturn*, pp. 58–60; Williamson, "Saturn V," p. 315; Ezell, *NASA Historical Data Book*, II:59.

74. Bilstein, *Stages to Saturn*, pp. 58–60, 104–13, 115–16; Williamson, "Saturn V," p. 315; MSFC et al., "Saturn V News Reference," pp. 1-1, 3-1 to 3-5 and unpaginated "F-1 Engine Fact Sheet"; William J. Brennan, "Milestones in Cryogenic Liquid Propellant Rocket Engines," AIAA paper 67-978, delivered at the AIAA 4th Annual Meeting and Technical Display, Oct. 23–27, 1967, Anaheim, Calif., pp. 8–9; Vance Jaqua and Allan Ferrenberg, "The Art of Injector Design," Rockwell International's *Threshold*, no. 4, Spring 1989, pp. 4, 6, 9; "Experimental Engines Group," *Threshold*, p. 21; Murray and Cox, *Apollo*, pp. 145, 147–51, 179–80.

75. Bilstein, *Stages to Saturn*, pp. 116–19, quotation from p. 116.

76. Letter, George E. Mueller to J. L. Atwood, Dec. 19, 1965, and memorandum, MA/S. C. Phillips to M/G. E. Mueller, subj: CSM and S-II Review, Dec. 18, 1965, both from George E. Mueller Collection, Manuscripts Division, Library of Congress, box 84, folder 3; Andrew J. Dunar and Stephen P. Waring, *Power to Explore: A History of Marshall Space Flight Center, 1960–1990* (Washington, D.C.: NASA SP-4313, 1999), pp. 86–87, 90; Bilstein, *Stages to Saturn*, pp. 191–209, 222–33, 269; Barton Hacker and E. M. Emme, notes on interview with Milton W. Rosen at NASA Headquarters, Washington, D.C., Nov. 14, 1969, seen in NHRC, folder 001835, "Rosen, Milton (Miscellaneous Biography)"; Mike Gray, *Angle of Attack: Harrison Storms and the Race to the Moon* (New York: Norton, 1992), pp. 20, 22–34, 65–72, 196–99, 202, 209, 253–55; Murray and Cox, *Apollo*, pp. 166–71, 183, 231–36; National Aeronautics and Space Council, *Report to the Congress . . . , 1967*, p. 131; *Summary of the Problems Encountered in the Second Flight of the Saturn V Launch Vehicle*, Hearing before the Committee on Aeronautical and Space Sciences, Senate, 90th Cong., 2d sess. (Washington, D.C.: GPO, 1968), p. 6, copy in NHRC, folder 010450, "Saturn V, general (1965–1969)."

77. Bilstein, *Stages to Saturn*, pp. 360–63, 366–68; MSFC et al., "Saturn V News Reference," pp. 12-2 to 12-4; Senate Hearings, *Summary of the Problems Encountered in the Second Flight of the Saturn V Launch Vehicle*, pp. 5–6, 16–18, 22–28, 34, 36; Murray and Cox, *Apollo*, pp. 312–14.

78. Dunar and Waring, *Power to Explore*, p. 51; Bilstein, *Stages to Saturn*, p. 263; Stephen B. Johnson, "Samuel Phillips and the Taming of Apollo," *Technology and Culture* 42 (Oct. 2001): 691; interview with Ernst Stuhlinger by J. D. Hunley, Huntsville, Ala., Sept. 20, 1994, pp. 48–49, copy in NHRC.

79. Hunley, *Birth of NASA*, pp. xxi–xxii, xxv, 312–16; MSFC, "Saturn Illustrated Chronology," pp. 8, 14; Arnold S. Levine, *Managing NASA in the Apollo Era* (Washington, D.C.: NASA SP-4102, 1982), pp. 16, 317.

80. W. Henry Lambright, *Powering Apollo: James E. Webb of NASA* (Baltimore, Md.: Johns Hopkins University Press, 1995), esp. pp. xi, 2, 100–105, 108–109 (quotation, p. 101); Levine, *Managing NASA*, pp. 5, 19.

81. Lambright, *Powering Apollo*, pp. 114–16; Levine, *Managing NASA*, p. 19 (quotation); Murray and Cox, *Apollo*, p. 152.

82. Lambright, *Powering Apollo*, pp. 116–17, quotation from p. 117; biographical sketch of Mueller in Levine, *Managing NASA*, p. 308.

83. Murray and Cox, *Apollo*, pp. 152–54, headline from p. 152, quotation from p. 153; Lambright, *Powering Apollo*, p. 117; Ezell, *NASA Historical Data Book*, II:6, 625, 642.

84. Bilstein, *Stages to Saturn*, p. 349; interview with Mueller by Robert Sherrod, Apr. 21, 1971, in Swanson, *Before This Decade Is Out*, p. 108; interview of Lt. Gen. Otto J. Glasser by Lt. Col. John J. Allen, seen in the Air Force Historical Research Agency, Maxwell AFB, Ala., K239.0512-1566, Jan. 5–6, 1984, pp. 75–76.

85. Levine, *Managing NASA*, p. 6, first quotation (from *NASA-Apollo Program Management*, cited there); Bilstein, *Stages to Saturn*, p. 349, next two quotations; memorandum with enclosed press release, AAD-2/Dr. Mueller to A/Mr. Webb through AA/Dr. Seamans, subj: Reorientation of Apollo Plans, Oct. 26, 1963, George E. Mueller Collection, Manuscript Division, Library of Congress, box 91, folder 9.

86. Bilstein, *Stages to Saturn*, pp. 349–51, first quotation from p. 349; Dunar and Waring, *Power to Explore*, pp. 94–95, second and third quotations from p. 94.

87. Jane Van Nimmen and Leonard C. Bruno with Robert L. Rosholt, *NASA Historical Data Book* (Washington, D.C.: NASA SP-4012, 1988), I:610, organizational chart, Nov. 1, 1963; Levine, *Managing NASA*, pp. 5–6, 175; Lambright, *Powering Apollo*, p. 118; Bilstein, *Stages to Saturn*, p. 269.

88. Dunar and Waring, *Power to Explore*, p. 67; Lambright, *Powering Apollo*, p. 118; Johnson, "Samuel Phillips," pp. 694–95, 700; interviews of Lt. Gen. Samuel Phillips by Tom Ray, Sept. 25, 1970, p. 22, July 22, 1970, pp. 8, 12–13, NHRC file 001701; Levine, *Managing NASA*, p. 309.

89. Johnson, "Samuel Phillips," pp. 697, 700–703, quotations from this source; Evert Clark, "The Moon Program's Business Brain Trust," *Nation's Business* (May 1970): 33; Yasuchi Sato, "Local Engineering and Systems Engineering: Cultural Conflict at NASA's Marshall Space Flight Center, 1960–1966," *Technology and Culture* 46, no. 3 (July 2005): 561–83.

90. Johnson, "Samuel Phillips," pp. 700–704; MSFC, *Apollo Program Management*, 3:4–29; Levine, *Managing NASA*, pp. 156–57; navy briefing in Samuel C. Phillips Collection, Manuscripts Division, Library of Congress, box 47, folder 12; Swanson, *Before This Decade Is Out*, pp. 101–102, 108; Phillips's Memorandum to Dr. Mueller, Oct. 3, 1964, in George E. Mueller Collection, Manuscripts Division, Library of Congress, box 43, folder 4.

91. Interview of Gen. Samuel C. Phillips by Frederick I. Ordway, Cosmos Club, Washington, D.C., Jan. 29, 1988, including extracts from Phillips's Wernher von Braun Memorial Lecture, National Air and Space Museum, Jan. 28, 1988, Washington, D.C., pp. 1, 3–4, 7–8 (quotations scattered), Samuel C. Phillips Collection, Manuscripts Division, Library of Congress, box 138, folder 10.

92. First three quotations from interview with Lt. Gen. Samuel C. Phillips by Robert Sherrod, NASA Headquarters, July 2, 1971, NHRC, file 013219; remaining quotations all from Murray and Cox, *Apollo*, pp. 159–60.

93. Roger D. Launius, "Titan: Some Heavy Lifting Required," in *To Reach the High Frontier*, ed. Launius and Jenkins, p. 166; Isakowitz, *Space Launch Systems* (1995), p. 292.

94. Robert F. Piper, "History of Titan III, 1961–1963" (June 1964), pp. 20–30, copy kindly provided by the Space and Missile Systems Center History Office; Launius, "Titan," p. 166 (quotation); Spires, *Beyond Horizons*, p. 81; Levine, *Managing NASA*, pp. 225–26.

95. Piper, "History of Titan III," pp. 101–103; "SAMSO Chronology," p. 110; Harwood, *Raise Heaven and Earth*, p. 356 (see chap. 1, n. 56).

96. "Brainpower First in United's Space Venture," *Business Week*, Mar. 5, 1960, pp. 138–44; "Highlights from the History of United Technologies" (Jan. 1988), pp. 35–42, and a narrative, chronology, and biographic materials, all kindly provided by CSD librarian Karen Schaffer; J. D. Hunley, telephone interviews with Barnet Adelman, Nov. 20, 1996, and Feb. 23, 2000, and with David Altman, Dec. 22, 1999; Wilbur C. Andrepont and Rafael M. Felix, "The History of Large Solid Rocket Motor Development in the United States," AIAA paper 94–3057, presented at the 30th AIAA/ASME/SAE/ASEE Joint Propulsion Conference, June 27–29, 1994, Indianapolis, Ind., pp. 2–3, 7, 19; Russell Hawkes, "United Technology Builds Larger Booster Capabilities," *Aviation Week*, Apr. 10, 1961, pp. 56–65; United Technology Center Pamphlet, "The 120-Inch-Diameter, Segmented, Solid-Propellant Rocket," n.d., seen in the JPL Archives, JPL no. 5, box JA 233, folder 37, esp. pp. 3, 5; CSD booklet, "A Most Reliable Booster System" (1977), unpaginated, section titled "Development of Major Components," copy generously provided by CSD; e-mail comments to Hunley by Bernard Ross Felix, formerly vice president of engineering and technology, CSD, Jan. 8, 1997, telephone interview with him Feb. 10, 1997, and his comments on a draft of Hunley, "Minuteman and Solid-Rocket Launch Technology," Aug. 22 and 23, 2000.

97. G. R. Richards and J. W. Powell, "Titan 3 and Titan 4 Space Launch Vehicles," *JBIS* 46 (1993): 126, 129; Piper, "History of Titan III," pp. 104, 120.

98. Piper, "History of Titan III," pp. 104–105; Richards and Powell, "Titan 3 and Titan 4," p. 126, and *CPIA/M5 Liquid Propellant Engine*, Units 146, AJ10-137, and 154, Titan III Transtage; Dieter K. Huzel and David H. Huang, *Design of Liquid Propellant Rocket Engines* (Washington, D.C.: NASA SP-125, 1967), p. 118.

99. Piper, "History of Titan III," pp. 91, 121, 125–26, quotation from p. 126; *CPIA/M5 Liquid Propellant Engine Manual*, Unit 154, Titan III Transtage; Jason P. Hutton, "Titan Transtage Rockets," http://members.aol.com/_ht_a/hattonjasonp/hasohp/TRANSTG.HTML (accessed June 24, 2003); Huzel and Huang, *Design of Liquid-Propellant Rocket Engines*, revised by Arbit et al., p. 378.

100. Chandler C. Ross, "Life at Aerojet University: A Memoir" (copyrighted by the Aerojet History Group, 1994), pp. 5, 47, 74–75; Stiff, "Storable Liquid Rockets," p. 9.

101. Richards and Powell, "Titan 3 and Titan 4," pp. 126, 130–32; "SAMSO Chronology," pp. 144, 146, 154, 158–59, 164, 166–67, 176.

102. Richards and Powell, "Titan 3 and Titan 4," pp. 130, 134–35; Launius, "Titan," p. 167; Isakowitz, *Space Launch Systems* (1995), p. 293; 45 Space Wing History Office, "The Cape Military Space Operations 1971–1992," http://www.patrick.af.mil/heritage/Cape/Cape2/Cape2-5.htm (accessed June 27, 2003), en-

try for Dec. 13, 1973; "SAMSO Chronology," p. 209; Martin Marietta, "Flight Test Objectives/Performance Analysis Titan 23C-4," pp. 4-1, 4-2; J. Catherine Wilman, "Space Division: A Chronology, 1980–1984," pp. 64, 101, copy provided by Space and Missile Systems Center History Office.

103. "Space Systems Summaries: Titan Launch Vehicle History and Family," *Astronautics & Aeronautics*, June 1975, pp. 76–77; Richards and Powell, "Titan 3 and Titan 4," pp. 133–34, 137; "SAMSO Chronology," pp. 152–53; Wilman, "Space Division Chronology," p. 101; "SAMSO Chronology," p. 361; Donald E. Fink, "Titan 34D Booster Design Completed," *Aviation Week & Space Technology*, May 15, 1978, p. 48.

104. "SAMSO Chronology," pp. 5, 189; Richards and Powell, "Titan 3 and Titan 4," p. 136; "Space Systems Summaries: Titan Launch Vehicle History and Family," *Astronautics & Aeronautics*, June 1975, pp. 76–77.

105. Richards and Powell, "Titan 3 and Titan 4," pp. 136–37; McDowell, "US Reconnaissance Satellite Programs," pp. 31–32.

106. Ezell, *NASA Historical Data Book*, III:38, 41–42; "SAMSO Chronology," p. 225.

107. Dawson and Bowles, *Centaur*, pp. 140–43; Ezell, *NASA Historical Data Book*, III:42; Siddiqi, *Deep Space Chronicle*, pp. 108, 110–12, 115, 117–22; Launius, *NASA*, pp. 101–104.

108. Fink, "Titan 34D Booster," p. 48 (quotation); Richards and Powell, "Titan 3 and Titan 4," p. 138; "SAMSO Chronology," pp. 280, 423; *Aeronautics and Space Report . . . , 1982 Activities*, p. 87.

109. *CPIA/M1 Rocket Motor Manual*, Units 559, Titan III and Titan IIIC Zero Stage, and 578, Titan 34D Stage Zero SRM; "Titan Launch Vehicle History," *Astronautics & Aeronautics*, June 1975, p. 76; *Aeronautics and Space Report . . . , 1986 Activities* (Washington, D.C.: NASA, [1987]), p. 144; Aerojet Liquid Rocket Company, "Propulsion Characteristics Summary," AJ10-138A, Sept. 82, in NASM folder B7-020100-01, Aerojet AJ10 Series; *CPIA/M5 Liquid Rocket Engine Manual*, Units 122 and 154, AJ10-138; Gunter Krebs, "Titan-34D Transtage," http://www.skyrocket.de/space/doc_lau_det/titan-34d_transtage.htm (accessed June 24, 2003), p. 1; Richards and Powell, "Titan 3 and Titan 4," p. 140.

110. Harry N. Waldron, "A History of the Development of the Inertial Upper Stage for the Space Shuttle, 1969–1985," draft monograph (completed 1988), seen at the Space and Missile Systems Center History Office through Dr. Waldron's generosity, pp. 53–54, 95–112, 208–209, supporting document Conclusion-1, pp. 5–8; W. Paul Dunn, "Evolution of the Inertial Upper Stage," http://www .aero.org/publications/crosslink/winter 2003/08.html (an Aerospace Corporation site) (accessed July 3, 2003), pp. 1–3; "Inertial Upper Stage," http://www.fas .org/spp/military/program/launch/ius.htm (accessed July 3, 2003), p. 2; Boeing Aerospace Company, "Interim Upper Stage (IUS)," Jan. 13, 1977, supporting document III-17 in Waldron, "Inertial Upper Stage"; Charles A. Chase, "IUS Solid Rocket Motors Overview," paper presented at the JANNAF Propulsion Conference, Feb. 1983, Monterey, Calif., pp. 13–15, 18, copy provided to the NHRC; Richards and Powell, "Titan 3 and Titan 4," pp. 138–40; *Aeronautics and Space Report . . . , 1982 Activities*, pp. 86–87; *Aeronautics and Space Report . . . , 1989–1990 Activities* (Washington, D.C.: NASA, 1991), pp. 144–45; *Aeronautics and Space Report . . . , Fiscal Year 1992 Activities* (Washington, D.C.: NASA, 1993), pp. 9, 81; Dennis R. Jenkins, *Space Shuttle: The History of the National Space Transportation System, the First 100 Missions* (Cape Canaveral, Fla.: Specialty Press, 2001), p. 244; Isakowitz, *Space Launch Systems* (1995), pp. 292, 294–99.

111. Joel W. Powell and Lee Caldwell, "New Space Careers for Former Military Missiles," *Spaceflight* 32 (Apr. 1990): 124–25; Stumpf, *Titan II*, pp. 265–71; Martin Marietta Astronautics Group, "Titan II Space Launch Vehicle," n.d., seen in NASM Archives, OT-490028-01, "Titan II"; Capt. Jeffrey J. Finan, Titan II 23G-1 Launch Controller, Memo for Record, "Titan II 23G-1 Processing History," Nov. 21, 1988, supporting document III-9 of Geiger and Clear, "History . . . , Oct. 1, 1987–Sept. 30, 1988"; *Aeronautics and Space Report . . . , 1989 90 Activities*, p. 160; *Aeronautics and Space Report . . . , Fiscal Year 1999 Activities* (Washington, D.C.: NASA, [2000]), pp. 14–15; *Aeronautics and Space Report . . . , Fiscal Year 2000 Activities*, pp. 26, 100.

112. Richards and Powell, "Titan 3 and Titan 4," p. 140; Lockheed Martin, "Titan IV," Mar. 2000, seen in Space and Missile Systems Center History Office, photo storage area, Titan IV folder.

113. Martin Marietta, "Fact Sheet, Titan IV," n.d., document III-28 in Geiger and Clear, "History of Space and Missile Organization and Western Space and Missile Center," Oct. 1987–Sept. 1988; *CPIA/MI Rocket Motor Manual*, Unit 578, Titan 34D, Stage Zero SRM, compared with Unit 629, Titan IV SRM, July 1996; Richards and Powell, "Titan 3 and Titan 4," pp. 139–41; Martin Marietta, "[Titan IV] System Critical Design Review," Oct. 14–16, 1986, seen at Space and Missile Systems Center History Office, pp. XII-5, XII-6..

114. Richards and Powell, "Titan 3 and Titan 4," pp. 141–42; *Aeronautics and Space Report . . . , 1989–1990 Activities*, pp. 142, 147; FAS Space Policy Project, "Titan-4 Launch History," http://www.fas.org/spp/military/program/launch/t4table.htm (accessed July 11, 2003); "Titan Launch History Summary," *Aeronautics and Space Report . . . , Fiscal Year 1991 Activities*, pp. 159–60; *Aeronautics and Space Report . . . , Fiscal Year 1992 Activities*, p. 75; *Aeronautics and Space Report . . . , Fiscal Year 1994 Activities*, pp. 11, 70; *Aeronautics and Space Report . . . , Fiscal Year 2000 Activities*, p. 27.

115. These figures result from my corrections to those on the Web site, "Titan Launch History Summary."

116. Knauf, Drake, and Portanova, "EELV," pp. 38, 40; Joseph C. Anselmo, "Air Force Readies Pick of Two EELV Finalists," *Aviation Week & Space Technology*, Dec. 9, 1996, pp. 82–83. See also Launius, "Titan," esp. p. 181.

117. See Jenkins, *Space Shuttle*, and T. A. Heppenheimer, *Development of the Space Shuttle, 1972–1981, History of the Space Shuttle*, vol. 2 (Washington, D.C.: Smithsonian Institution Press, 2002), for details.

118. T. A. Heppenheimer, *The Space Shuttle Decision: NASA's Search for a Reusable Space Vehicle* (Washington, D.C.: NASA SP-4221, 1999), pp. 12–14, 49–54, 73–84, 245–90, 331–422; Jenkins, *Space Shuttle*, pp. 15–101, 139–52, 167–73; Jenkins, "Broken in Mid-Stride," pp. 358–75, Nixon quotation from p. 375; John F. Guilmartin Jr. and John Walker Mauer, *A Shuttle Chronology, 1964–1973: Abstract Concepts to Letter Contracts* (Houston: JSC-23309, 1988) in 5 vols., esp. I:I-1 to I-102, IV:V-5 to V-18, V-23 to V-135, V-193 to V-194, V-237 to V-240, V:VI-45 to VI-46; Roger D. Launius, "NASA and the Decision to Build the Space Shuttle, 1969–72," *The Historian* 57 (Autumn 1994): 17–32; *Aeronautics and Space Report . . . , Fiscal Year 2001 Activities* (Washington, D.C.: NASA, 2002), pp. 142–43; Bromberg, *NASA and Space Industry*, pp. 77–93.

119. Jenkins, *Space Shuttle*, pp. 109–110, 184; Heppenheimer, *Space Shuttle Decision*, pp. 237–39, 242–44; Guilmartin and Mauer, *Shuttle Chronology*, IV: V-34, V-78.

120. Heppenheimer, *Development of the Space Shuttle*, p. 126; Jenkins, *Space Shuttle*, pp. 224–25; Robert E. Biggs, "Space Shuttle Main Engine: The First Ten Years," in *Liquid Rocket Engine Development*, ed. Doyle, 13:75–76; Al Martinez, "Rocket Engine Propulsion Power Cycles," Rockwell International's *Threshold*, no. 7 (Summer 1991): 17.

121. Heppenheimer, *Development of the Space Shuttle*, pp. 127–28, 133–34, 148–71; R. Wiswell and M. Huggins, "Launch Vehicle & Upper Stage Liquid Propulsion at the Astrionics Laboratory (AFSC)—a Historical Study," unpaginated, paper AIAA 90-1839 presented at the AIAA/SAE/ASME/ASEE 26th Joint Propulsion Conference, July 16–18, 1990, Orlando, Fla.; Biggs, "Space Shuttle Main Engine," pp. 80–118; Jenkins, *Space Shuttle*, pp. 225–27.

122. Aeronautics and Space Engineering Board, Assembly of Engineering, National Research Council, Report of Ad Hoc Committee on Liquid Rocket Propulsion Technologies, *Liquid Rocket Propulsion Technology: An Evaluation of NASA's Program* (Washington, D.C.: National Academy Press, 1981), p. 16, George E. Mueller Collection, Manuscript Division, Library of Congress, box 198, folder 9, "NASA, 1981."

123. *CPIA/M5 Liquid Propellant Engine Manual*, Unit 175, F-1 Saturn V Booster Engine, and Unit 195, Space Shuttle Main Engine.

124. Rockwell International, "Press Information: Space Shuttle Transportation System," Jan. 1984, p. 21, seen in NHRC.

125. Jenkins, *Space Shuttle*, pp. 184–86; Heppenheimer, *Development of the Space Shuttle*, pp. 71–78; John M. Logsdon et al., eds., *Exploring the Unknown: Selected Documents in the History of the U.S. Civil Space Program* (Washington, D.C.: NASA SP-4407, 1999), Document II-17, vol. IV:269, 271; Bromberg, *NASA and the Space Industry*, p. 100.

126. Jenkins, *Space Shuttle*, p. 186; Hunley, "Minuteman and the Development of Solid-Rocket Launch Technology," pp. 278–80 (see chap. 1, n. 82); Rockwell International, "Press Information: Space Shuttle," Jan. 1984, pp. 21–22; Heppenheimer, *Development of the Space Shuttle*, pp. 175, 177–78; comments of Bernard Ross Felix, Aug. 22, 2000, on a draft of Hunley, "Minuteman and Solid-Rocket Launch Technology"; Andrepont and Felix, "Large Solid Rocket Motor Development," pp. 7, 14; J. D. Hunley, "The Evolution of Large Solid Propellant Rocketry in the United States," *Quest: The History of Spaceflight Quarterly* 6 (Spring 1998): 31, 37; NASA, "National Space Transportation System Reference," vol. 1, "Systems and Facilities," June 1988, pp. 33a–33c, seen in NHRC.

127. Jenkins, *Space Shuttle*, pp. 227–28; Heppenheimer, *Development of the Space Shuttle*, pp. 178, 183–89.

128. Jenkins, *Space Shuttle*, pp. 186–87; Rockwell International, "Press Information: Space Shuttle," Jan. 1984, p. 46; Heppenheimer, *Development of the Space Shuttle*, pp. 68–69; Dunar and Waring, *Power to Explore*, pp. 292–94, 301, 323; Columbia Accident Investigation Board (hereafter cited as CAIB), *Report*, Aug. 2003, 1:9, first and second quotations, http://boss.streamos.com/download/caib/report/web/chapters/introduction.pdf (accessed Sept. 15, 2003).

129. Jenkins, *Space Shuttle*, pp. 169, 173, 182–83; Jenkins, "Broken in Mid-Stride," pp. 363–64.

130. Heppenheimer, *Development of the Space Shuttle*, pp. 22–27, 246–50; Jenkins, *Space Shuttle*, pp. 189–92, 387; Kenneth W. Iliff and Curtis L. Peebles, *From Runway to Orbit: Reflections of a NASA Engineer* (Washington, D.C.: NASA SP-2004-4109, 2004), esp. pp. 141–51, 157–60, 175–81.

131. Heppenheimer, *Development of the Space Shuttle,* pp. 211–16, 221, 223–27, 229–44, 287–322; Jenkins, *Space Shuttle,* pp. 231–35, 237–40, 395–403; CAIB, *Report,* 1:9, 14 (quotations), 55, 122; Rockwell International, "Press Information: Space Shuttle," Jan. 1984, pp. 23, 36, 54, 75, 438–72; *NSTS 1988 News Reference Manual,* http://science.ksc.nasa.gov/shuttle/technology/sts-newsref/ sts-gnnc.html#sts-imu (accessed Sept. 24, 2003); Isakowitz, "Space Launch Systems" (1991), pp. 252–53.

132. *Aeronautics and Space Report . . . , Fiscal Year 2001 Activities,* pp. 121–29; Jenkins, *Space Shuttle,* pp. 266–75, 294–301, 328–30; Siddiqi, *Deep Space Chronicle,* pp. 143–45; Rumerman, *NASA Historical Data Book,* V:171.

133. Logsdon et al., *Exploring the Unknown,* vol. IV, "Presidential Commission on the Space Shuttle *Challenger* Accident, 'Report at a Glance,' June 6, 1986," pp. 358–59, 363; Jenkins, *Space Shuttle,* pp. 267, 277–81; Launius, *NASA,* pp. 250–51; Stephen P. Waring, "The 'Challenger' Accident and Anachronism: The Rogers Commission and NASA's Marshall Space Flight Center," paper presented at the National Council on Public History Fifteenth Annual Conference, Apr. 22, 1993, pp. 13–14, copy kindly provided by the author; E. S. Sutton, "From Polymers to Propellants to Rockets—a History of Thiokol," AIAA paper 99-2929 presented at the 35th AIAA/ASME/SAE/ASEE Joint Propulsion Conference and Exhibit, June 20–24, 1999, Los Angeles, p. 22.

134. Logsdon et al., *Exploring the Unknown,* vol. IV, "*Challenger* Accident, 'Report at a Glance,'" pp. 363 (quotation), 368; Waring, "'Challenger' Accident," pp. 9–12, 14–15, 18; Jenkins, *Space Shuttle,* pp. 279, 281; Launius, *NASA,* pp. 115–17.

135. NASA, "National Space Transportation System Reference," 1:33a–33b; Jenkins, *Space Shuttle,* p. 288; Spires, *Beyond Horizons,* pp. 221–23, 228–29; Jenkins, "Broken in Midstride," pp. 374–75, 408–409; Launius, "Titan," p. 178; *Aeronautics and Space Report . . . , Fiscal Year 2001 Activities,* pp. 127–29.

136. Launius, "NASA and the Decision to Build the Space Shuttle," p. 34; Ray A. Williamson, "Developing the Space Shuttle," in *Exploring the Unknown,* ed. Longsdon et al., IV:161–91, esp. p. 182; CAIB, *Report,* 1:19 (quotation).

Chapter 3

1. Wernher von Braun, "Reminiscences of German Rocketry," *Journal of the British Interplanetary Society (JBIS)* 15, no. 3 (May–June 1956): 128–31 (all quotations but the first and last ones from p. 131); von Braun, "Behind the Scenes of Rocket Development in Germany, 1928 through 1945," U.S. Space and Rocket Center, Huntsville, Ala., first quotation from p. 11; Dornberger, *V-2,* p. 28, for his quotation (see chap. 1, n. 16).

2. Neufeld, *Rocket and the Reich,* p. 64 (see chap. 1, n. 16); H. A. Schulze, "Technical Data on the Development of the A4 (V-2)," p. 5, prepared by the Historical Office, George C. Marshall Space Flight Center, Feb. 25, 1965, seen in the U.S. Space and Rocket Center, Schulze Collection; Dornberger, *V-2,* p. 50, for the quotations; *Lebenslauf* (curriculum vitae) of Thiel at the time of his doctoral degree, photocopied onto a letter to Frank Winter at NASM, from I. Ritter at the Staatsbibliothek Preussischer Kulturbesitz, Aug. 16, 1976, seen in the folder "Thiel, Walter," CT-168000-01, NASM archives; letter, Martin Schilling to K. L. Heimburg, Aug. 27, 1976, in the same folder.

3. Dornberger, *V-2,* pp. 50, 53, from which all but Schilling's quotations come; von Braun, "Reminiscences," p. 137; letter, Martin Schilling to K. L. Heimburg,

Aug. 27, 1976, in the folder "Thiel, Walter," CT-168000-01, NASM archives, for Schilling's quotation; Ordway and Sharpe, *Rocket Team*, p. 121 (see chap. 1, n. 17); Neufeld, *Rocket and the Reich*, p. 84.

4. Dornberger, *V-2*, pp. 149, 151; [Walter] Thiel, Memorandum, Weapons Test Organization, Kummersdorf—Target Range, "On the Practical Possibilities of Further Development of the Liquid Rockets and a Survey of the Tasks to Be Assigned to Research," Mar. 13, 1937, trans. D. K. Huzel, seen in NASM archives, folder CT-168000-01, "Thiel, Walter." All quotations from Thiel.

5. Martin Schilling, "The Development of the V-2 Rocket Engine," in *History of German Guided Missiles Development: AGARD First Guided Missiles Seminar, Munich, Germany, April, 1956*, ed. Th. Benecke and A. W. Quick (Brunswick: E. Appelhans, 1957), p. 284 (first quotation); Dornberger, *V-2*, pp. 50–52 (for the other quotations).

6. Dornberger, *V-2*, p. 52; Gerhard H. R. Reisig, "Von den Peenemünder 'Aggregaten' zur amerikanischen 'Mondrakete': Die Entwicklung der Apollo-Rakete 'Saturn V' durch das Wernher-von-Braun-Team an Hand der Peenemünder Konzepte," *Astronautik* (1986): 45–46; Neufeld, *Rocket and the Reich*, pp. 78–79; Schilling, "V-2 Rocket Engine," p. 286.

7. Hermann Oberth, *Ways to Spaceflight*, trans. Agence Tunisienne de Public-Relations (Washington, D.C.: NASA TT F-622, 1972), p. 41; Reisig, "Peenemünder 'Aggregaten,'" p. 47; Neufeld, *Rocket and the Reich*, p. 80; Dornberger, *V-2*, p. 52; Schilling, "V-2 Rocket Engine," p. 286.

8. Reisig, "Peenemünder 'Aggregaten,'" p. 47; Neufeld, *Rocket and the Reich*, pp. 80–81.

9. Reisig, "Peenemünder 'Aggregaten,'" p. 47; "History of German Guided Missiles," p. 12, prepared by the Ordnance Research and Development Translation Center, Ft. Eustis, Va., seen at the U.S. Space and Rocket Center, Schulze Collection; the British "Report on Operation 'BACKFIRE,'" prepared by the British Ministry of Supply Technical Officers, 2:18, seen in Technical Library at the Redstone Arsenal, both depositories in Huntsville, Ala.

10. Krafft A. Ehricke, "The Peenemünde Rocket Center," pt. 3, *Rocketscience* 4, no. 3 (Sept. 1950): 60; Schilling, "V-2 Rocket Engine," pp. 289–90; Niederschrift über die Besprechung des Arbeitsstabes Wa A/VP am 3.3.1942, NASM microfilm roll no. 59, FE 692f; letter, HAP to Firma Klein, Schanzlin & Becker, 7.1.1943, NASM microfilm roll no. 36, FE 746c; Niederschrift der Besprechung am 8.8.41 betreffend Aufteilung der Odesse-Turbopumpen auf Aggregate A4; Entwurf, von Braun to Wa Prüf 11, 31.3.41 Betr. Serienanlauf Turbo-Pumpe A4; letter, von Braun to Firma Klein-Schanzlin-Oddesse Betr. Fertigung von 600 Stück Turbopumpen, 27.5.41, last three documents from NASM microfilm roll no. 40, FE 737.

11. Schilling, "V-2 Rocket Engine," pp. 289–90; Reisig, "Peenemünder 'Aggregaten,'" p. 47.

12. Ehricke, "Peenemünde," pt. 3, p. 60.

13. Neufeld, *Rocket and the Reich*, p. 84; Wewerka [first name not given], "Untersuchung einer Kreiselpumpe–Odesse Typ 3/18 brennstoffseitig," July 1941, Arch 33/8; Wewerka, "Untersuchung einer Turbopumpe, Typ TP 1 g," Feb. 1942, Arch 33/9, both reports summarized in Ordnance Research and Development Translation Center, Ft. Eustis, Va., "Accession List of German Documents pertaining to Guided Missiles," II:598, available at Redstone Arsenal Technical Library, Huntsville, Ala.

14. Schilling, "V-2 Rocket Engine," p. 284; Reisig, "Peenemünder 'Aggregaten,'" p. 46; Wewerka, "Der günstigste Erweiterungswinkel bei Lavaldüsen," Feb. 5, 1940, Arch 33/2; Wewerka, "Günstige Bemessung einer Lavaldüse bei zeitlich veränderlichem Aussendruck," Apr. 8, 1940, Arch 33/3, both reports summarized in Ordnance Research and Development Translation Center, Ft. Eustis, Va., "Accession List of German Documents pertaining to Guided Missiles," II:617–18.

15. Schilling, "V-2 Rocket Engine," pp. 284–85, for the quotations from him; "Peenemunde [sic] East through the Eyes of 500 Detained at Garmisch," pp. 184–85, seen in NHRC, folder 002685, for Lindenberg's quotations.

16. Konrad K. Dannenberg, "From Vahrenwald via the Moon to Dresden," in *History of Rocketry and Astronautics,* ed. Hunley, 19:123 (see ch. 1. n. 17).

17. Technical Report Number 10, "Questions by Dr. Martin Summerfield," pp. 3–4 (see chap. 1, n. 47); "Report on Operation 'BACKFIRE,'" pp. 17–34; "History of German Guided Missiles," p. 12.

18. Dornberger, *V-2,* p. xvii; Schilling, "V-2 Rocket Engine," p. 285; Jet Propulsion Laboratory, *Mariner-Mars 1964, Final Project Report* (Washington, D.C.: NASA SP-139, 1967), p. 42n; Technical Report Number 10, "Questions by Dr. Martin Summerfield," p. 1, for the first von Braun quotation and sketch 1; von Braun, "Reminiscences," p. 137, for his second quotation; Dannenberg, "From Vahrenwald," p. 122, for his quotation.

19. Francis A. Warren, *Rocket Propellants* (New York: Reinhold, 1958), pp. 104–105.

20. Technical Report Number 10, "Questions by Dr. Martin Summerfield," pp. 1–2, sketch 1; Schilling, "V-2 Rocket Engine," pp. 287–88.

21. Frank H. Winter and Frederick I. Ordway III, "Pioneering Commercial Rocketry in the United States of America, Reaction Motors, Inc. 1941–1958, Part 2: Projects," *JBIS* 38 (1985): 158–59, 161–64; Swenson, Grimwood, and Alexander, *This New Ocean,* p. 22 (see chap. 1, n. 54); Chapman, *Atlas,* pp. 28–35, 86–88 (see chap. 1, n. 62); Convair, "MX-774 Flight Test Report: Jet Controlled Missile," unpaginated, seen in NASM Archives, folder OM-990774-01, "MX-774 (RTV-A-2, Reports)"; Rosen, *Viking Rocket Story,* p. 63 (see chap. 1, n. 56); Sutton, *Liquid Propellant Rocket Engines,* pp. 220, 224 (see chap. 1, n. 1); Martin, "Atlas and Centaur 'Steel Balloon' Tanks," pp. 1–2 (see chap. 1, n. 73); Martin, "Brief History of the *Atlas,*" pt. I, pp. 54–55 (see chap. 1, n. 73).

22. Interview with Milton William Rosen by David DeVorkin, Washington, D.C., Mar. 25, 1983, pp. 31, 44, copy available through the Space History Division, NASM; Rosen, *Viking Rocket,* pp. 22–23, 58–62, 66, 236–37; Harwood, *Raise Heaven and Earth,* p. 253 (see chap. 1, n. 56); Winter and Ordway, "Reaction Motors . . . Projects," pp. 162–63; Martin Company, "Design Summary, RTV-N-12 Viking, Rockets 1 to 7," Jan. 1954, pp. 5, 6, 99, 104–10 (see chap. 1, n. 57); Keith J. Scala, "The Viking Rocket: Filling the Gap," *Quest: The Magazine of Spaceflight,* Winter 1993, p. 34; comments of Milton Rosen on a draft of the chapter on May 8, 2002, and in a telephone conversation on May 17, 2002.

23. *Project Vanguard, a Scientific Earth Satellite Program for the International Geophysical Year,* A Report to the Committee on Appropriations, U.S. House of Representatives, by Surveys and Investigations Staff, [ca. Feb. 15, 1959], p. 61, found in NASM Archives, folder OV 106120-01, "Vanguard II Launch Vehicle 4"; Vanguard Staff, "Project Vanguard Report . . . 1 June 1957," pp. 2-25 to 2-32, 2-34 (see chap. 1, n. 58); Kurt R. Stehling, *Project Vanguard* (Garden

City, N.Y.: Doubleday, 1961), pp. 129–30; Martin Company, "Vanguard Satellite Launching Vehicle," pp. 49–50 (see chap. 1, n. 59); Kurt R. Stehling, "Aspects of Vanguard Propulsion," *Astronautics*, Jan. 1958, pp. 45–46; letter, Milton Rosen to author on May 8, 2002.

24. Congressional Committee Report, *Project Vanguard*, pp. 62, 65–66; Green and Lomask, *Vanguard*, pp. 176–82, 196–98, 210, 283 (see chap. 1, n. 44); Stehling, *Project Vanguard*, pp. 24 (quotation), 82–83, 103, 106–23; Rosen's comments by telephone to author, May 16, 2002; Space Activities Summary, Vanguard, Dec. 6, 1957, seen in NHRC, folder 006630, "Vanguard Test Vehicle 3"; Ezell, *NASA Historical Data Book*, II:45 (see chap. 1, n. 44).

25. Bullard, "History of the Redstone," pp. 27–35, 55–59 (see chap. 1, n. 30); Wernher von Braun, "The Redstone, Jupiter, and Juno," in *History of Rocket Technology*, ed. Emme, p. 109 (see chap. 1, n. 41); Winter, "Rocketdyne," p. 9 (see chap. 1, n. 51); Kraemer, *Rocketdyne*, pp. 39–43 (see chap. 2, n. 67).

26. "Rockwell International," in *International Directory of Company Histories*, ed. Thomas Derdak (Chicago: St. James Press, 1988), I:78–79; Bromberg, *NASA and the Space Industry*, pp. 19–20 (see chap. 2, n. 45); Gray, *Angle of Attack*, pp. 25–26, 78–79, quotation from p. 25 (see chap. 2, n. 76); Heppenheimer, "Navaho Program," p. 6 (see chap. 1, n. 51).

27. Heppenheimer, "Navaho Program," p. 6; Bromberg, *NASA and the Space Industry*, p. 20; notes from a telephone interview, Feb. 13, 2002, J. D. Hunley with Robert Kraemer, a former NAA engineer, now author of a history of Rocketdyne (see chap. 2, n. 67).

28. Winter, "Rocketdyne," p. 2; Heppenheimer, "Navaho Program," p. 6; Myers, "Navaho," 20:121–32 (see ch. 1, n. 51); Lonnquest and Winkler, *To Defend and Deter*, pp. 3–4, 24–25 (see chap. 1, n. 51); and James N. Gibson, *The Navaho Missile Project: The Story of the "Know-How" Missile of American Rocketry* (Atglen, Pa.: Schiffer, 1996).

29. Winter, "Rocketdyne," pp. 2–4; Ezell Mitchell, "Engine One," p. 54 (see chap. 1, n. 51); Winter, "East Parking Lot Rocket Experiments," p. 2 (see chap. 1, n. 50). Recollections of the (unidentified) employee from Erica M. Karr, "Hoffman . . . the Power behind Rocketdyne," *Missiles and Rockets*, Mar. 23, 1959, p. 26.

30. Winter, "East Parking Lot," pp. 9–10.

31. Ezell and Mitchell, "Engine One," pp. 54–55; Heppenheimer, "Navaho Program," p. 8.

32. Winter, "Rocketdyne," pp. 6–8; Heppenheimer, "Navaho Program," p. 7; Mack Reed, "Rocketdyne Razing Historic Test Stand," *Los Angeles Times*, Feb. 11, 1996, pp. A1, A23.

33. Ezell and Mitchell, "Engine One," pp. 55–63; Winter, "Rocketdyne," p. 9.

34. Winter, "Rocketdyne," p. 8; Heppenheimer, "Navaho Program," pp. 13, 15; Hoffman's biographical sketch, business/professional record, and a sheet listing his responsibilities as chief engineer with Lycoming in NASM Archives, folder CH-480000-01, "Hoffman, Samuel Kurtz."

35. Bullard, "History of the Redstone," pp. 59–60; Ezell and Mitchell, "Engine One," p. 60.

36. "Redstone," http://www.redstone.army.mil/history/systems/redstone/welcome.htm (accessed Jan. 16, 2002), p. 2; Bullard, "History of the Redstone," p. 60; W. R. Stadhalter, Program Manager, Rocketdyne, "The Redstone: Built-In Producibility," n.d., seen in the NASM Archives, folder OR-180000-01, Red-

stone Missile; Chrysler Corporation, Missile Division, "This Is Redstone," n.d. (received Apr. 29, 1966), p. V-6, seen in the Redstone Scientific Information Center, Huntsville, Ala.

37. Stadhalter, "The Redstone," pp. 5–16; Chrysler, "This Is Redstone," p. II-10.

38. Heppenheimer, *Countdown*, pp. 72–73 (see chap. 2, n. 9); Gibson, *Navaho*, pp. 40–41; Myers, "Navaho," p. 129; John M. Simmons, "The Navaho Lineage" (Rocketdyne), *Threshold: An Engineering Journal of Power Technology*, no. 2 (Dec. 1987): 18–19; Chapman, *Atlas*, p. 65 (see chap. 1, n. 62); Clark, *Ignition!*, pp. 32–33, 104–105 (see chap. 1, n. 95); Clarence William (Bill) Schnare, telephone conversation with author, Mar. 14, 2002.

39. Denis R. Jenkins, "Stage-and-a-Half: The Atlas Launch Vehicle," in *To Reach the High Frontier*, ed. Launius and Jenkins, p. 100 (see chap. 1, n. 82); "BMO Chronology,", pp. 21–22 (see chap. 1, n. 66); Smith and Minami, "History of Atlas Engines," pp. 54–55 (chap. 1, n. 74).

40. Smith and Minami, "Atlas Engines," pp. 54–57, 63; Jenkins, "Atlas Launch Vehicle," pp. 100–101; Simmons, "Navaho Lineage," p. 18.

41. Smith and Minami, "Atlas Engines," pp. 55, 63–65; Hartt, *Mighty Thor*, p. 80 (see chap. 1, n. 74); Simmons, "Navaho Lineage," pp. 20–21.

42. Smith and Minami, "Atlas Engines," pp. 55, 60–61, 64–65; *CPIA/M5 Liquid Propellant Engine Manual*, Units 176 (Atlas MA-3 Booster), pp. 1–5, and 178 (Atlas MA-3 Sustainer), pp. 1–5 (see chap. 2, n. 70); "Experimental Engines Group," pp. 25–26 (see chap. 1, n. 75).

43. "Experimental Engines Group," *Threshold*, pp. 21–27, quotations on pp. 21, 22, 25, 26; Ezell and Mitchell, "Engine One," *Threshold*, p. 57.

44. Edward J. Hujsak, "The Bird that Did Not Want to Fly," *Spaceflight* 34 (Mar. 1992): 102–104; telephone comments to author by William Schnare on May 23, 2002, in conjunction with discussion of an oral history interview done with him by James C. Hasdorf, Aug. 5–6, 1975, in Fairborne, Ohio, seen at the Air Force Historical Research Agency, K239.0512-863.

45. Fuller and Minami, "Thor/Delta Booster Engines," p. 41 (see chap. 1, n. 77); Bilstein, *Stages to Saturn*, p. 97 (see chap. 2, n. 64); Ezell, *NASA Historical Data Book*, II:56.

46. Bilstein, *Stages to Saturn*, pp. 97, 99; A. A. McCool and Keith B. Chandler, "Development Trends of Liquid Propellant Engines," in *From Peenemünde to Outer Space, Commemorating the Fiftieth Birthday of Wernher von Braun, March 23, 1962*, ed. Ernst Stuhlinger et al. (Huntsville, Ala.: NASA Marshall Space Flight Center, 1962), p. 296; *CPIA/M5 Liquid Propellant Engine Manual*, Unit 84, H-1, and Unit 85, LR79-NA-11 Thor, May 1965; coverage of the MA-3 previously in this chapter.

47. MSFC, "Saturn Illustrated Chronology (April 1957–April 1962)," pp. 6, 11–12 (see chap. 2, n. 65); Bilstein, *Stages to Saturn*, pp. 97–98.

48. Bilstein, *Stages to Saturn*, pp. 98–102, 188–89; B. K. Heusinger, "Saturn Propulsion Improvements," *Astronautics & Aeronautics*, Aug. 1964, p. 25; Ezell, *NASA Historical Data Book*, II:56–58; *Report to the Congress . . . , 1964* (Washington, D.C.: Government Printing Office, [1965]), p. 128; *CPIA/M5 Liquid Propellant Engine Manual*, Unit 84, H-1.

49. Bilstein, *Stages to Saturn*, pp. 98–104, 414–15.

50. Ibid., pp. 97–99; McCool and Chandler, "Development Trends," 296; *CPIA/M5 Liquid Propellant Engine Manual*, Unit 84, H-1, Apr. 1965.

51. Bilstein, *Stages to Saturn*, pp. 324–37, 414; MSFC, "Saturn Illustrated Chronology," pp. 46–47; NASA/MSFC et al., "Saturn IB News Reference," Dec. 1965 (changed Sept. 1968), p. 12-2.

52. Cf. *CPIA/M5 Liquid Propellant Engine Manual*, Units 84, H-1 (165,000 and 188,000 pounds thrust), and 173, H-1 (205,000 pounds thrust); NASA/MSFC et al., "Saturn IB News Reference," unpaginated "H-1 Engine Fact Sheet," 200,000 pounds thrust; Bilstein, *Stages to Saturn*, p. 97.

53. Bilstein, *Stages to Saturn*, pp. 104–107, first quotation from p. 105; MSFC et al., "Saturn V News Reference," p. 1-1, second quotation; MSFC, "Saturn Illustrated Chronology (to Apr. 1962)," p. 4; Kraemer, *Rocketdyne*, pp. 161–63; Hunley, *Birth of NASA*, pp. 13, 15 (see chap. 2, n. 27); Ronald-Bel Stiffler and Charles V. Eppley, "History of the Air Force Flight Test Center, 1 Jan.–30 June 1960," pp. 69, 180, 183; "History of the Air Force Flight Test Center, 1 Jan.–30 June 1961," pp. 58–59, 71–72, Appendix K; "Test Stand 1B Final Report," July 31, 1961, all seen at the Air Force Flight Test Center History Office on Edwards AFB.

54. Bilstein, *Stages to Saturn*, pp. 107–108, 1st quotation from p. 108; Brennan, "Milestones," p. 8 (see chap. 2, n. 74); *CPIA/M5 Liquid Propellant Engine Manual*, Units 173, H-1 Booster Engines, and 175, F-1, Saturn V Booster Engine.

55. MSFC et al., "Saturn V News Reference," pp. 3-1 to 3-5 and unpaginated "F-1 Engine Fact Sheet"; Brennan, "Milestones," pp. 8–9; *CPIA/M5 Liquid Propellant Engine Manual*, Units 173, H-1 Booster Engines, and 175, F-1, Saturn V Booster Engine; Bilstein, *Stages to Saturn*, pp. 109–10, 416.

56. Vance Jaqua and Allan Ferrenberg, "The Art of Injector Design," Rockwell International's *Threshold*, no. 4, Spring 1989, pp. 4, 6, 9, for first four quotations; Sutton, *Liquid Propellant Rocket Engines*, p. 229, for final quotation.

57. Murray and Cox, *Apollo*, pp. 145, 147–48 (see chap. 2, n. 65); Bilstein, *Stages to Saturn*, pp. 109–13.

58. Murray and Cox, *Apollo*, pp. 148–49, both quotations from p. 149; Bilstein, *Stages to Saturn*, p. 113; "Experimental Engines Group," *Threshold*, p. 21.

59. Murray and Cox, *Apollo*, pp. 150–51, 179–80; Bilstein, *Stages to Saturn*, pp. 115–16; Brennan, "Milestones," p. 9; Louis F. Herzberg, "History of the Air Force Rocket Propulsion Laboratory," 1 Jan.–30 June 1964, I:II-108 to II-158, seen at the Air Force Flight Test Center History Office, Edwards AFB, Calif., filed in one of four unnumbered boxes labeled "Units, RPL [Rocket Propulsion Laboratory]".

60. Fred E. C. Culick and Vigor Yang, "Overview of Combustion Instabilities in Liquid-Propellant Rocket Engines," p. 9 in *Liquid Rocket Engine Combustion Instability*, ed. Vigor Yang and William E. Anderson, vol. 169 of *Progress in Astronautics and Aeronautics*, ed. Paul Zarchan (Washington, D.C.: AIAA, 1995).

61. Murray and Cox, *Apollo*, pp. 146–47; Bilstein, *Stages to Saturn*, p. 109; MSFC et al., "Saturn V News Reference," pp. 3-1 to 3-4; *CPIA/M5 Liquid Propellant Engine Manual*, Unit 175, p. 5.

62. Bilstein, *Stages to Saturn*, pp. 116–19; Herzberg, "History of the Air Force Rocket Propulsion Laboratory, 1 Jan. 30–June 1964," I:IV-346.

63. Bilstein, *Stages to Saturn*, pp. 195–207; Mack R. Herring, *Way Station to Space: A History of the John C. Stennis Space Center* (Washington, D.C.: NASA SP-4310, 1997), pp. 14, 45, 51, 55–56, 93, 96–97, 104, 125–29, 200, 347.

64. MSFC et al., "Saturn V News Reference," pp. 12-1 to 12-2; *Report to the Congress . . . , 1967*, p. 131 (see chap. 1, n. 24); *Summary of the Problems En-*

countered in the Second Flight of the Saturn V Launch Vehicle, Hearing before the Committee on Aeronautical and Space Sciences, Senate, 90th Cong., 2d sess. (Washington, D.C.: GPO, 1968), p. 6, copy in NHRC, folder 010450, "Saturn V, general (1965–1969)."

65. Bilstein, *Stages to Saturn*, pp. 360–61; MSFC et al., "Saturn V News Reference," pp. 12-2 to 12-4; Senate Hearings, *Problems Encountered in the Second Flight of the Saturn V Launch Vehicle*, pp. 5, 16, 27–28, 36; Murray and Cox, *Apollo*, p. 312; National Aeronautics and Space Council, *Report to the Congress from the President, United States Aeronautics & Space Activities, 1968* (Washington, D.C.: GPO, [1969]), p. 96.

66. Senate Hearings, *Problems Encountered in the Second Flight of the Saturn V Launch Vehicle*, 16–17, quotations from both pages of Phillips's testimony.

67. Bilstein, *Stages to Saturn*, pp. 362–63; Senate Hearings, *Problems Encountered in the Second Flight of the Saturn V Launch Vehicle*, pp. 6, 16–18; draft untitled article for the *New York Times*, p. 4 (quotation), in Samuel C. Phillips Collection, Library of Congress, Manuscripts Division, "Manned Lunar Landing Program, Writings by Phillips," 1969, box 118, folder 4; NASA News Release 68-128, "Saturn V Tests Completed," July 18, 1968, p. 2, seen in NHRC, folder 010450, "Saturn V, General."

68. Bilstein, *Stages to Saturn*, pp. 362–63; Senate Hearings, *Problems Encountered in the Second Flight of the Saturn V Launch Vehicle*, p. 18; NASA News Release 68-128, pp. 2–4, 5A; "Minutes of the Saturn V Semi-DCR/AS-502 Evaluation," Apr. 21, 1968, seen in the George E. Mueller Collection, box 92, folder 8, p. 3; Dunar and Waring, *Power to Explore*, p. 97 (see chap. 1, n. 50).

69. Bilstein, *Stages to Saturn*, pp. 366–77; Richard W. Orloff, *Apollo by the Numbers: A Statistical Reference* (Washington, D.C.: NASA SP-2000-4029, 2000), pp. 32–35, 40–43, 72–81, 137–57, 275–76; *Report to the Congress, . . . , 1968*, p. 101.

70. First quotation, Gerhard H. R. Reisig, *Raketenforschung in Deutschland: Wie die Menschen das All eroberten* (Berlin: Wissenschaft und Technik Verlag, 1999), p. 505; second from Neufeld, *Rocket and the Reich*, p. 279.

Chapter 4

1. Neufeld, *Rocket and the Reich*, pp. 230–32 (see chap. 1, n. 16); Slater, "Research and Development at the Jet Propulsion Laboratory," p. 41 (see chap. 1, n. 25); Malina, "Army Air Corps Jet Propulsion Research Project," pp. 160–61, 167 (see chap. 1, n. 25); Frank J. Malina, John W. Parsons, and Edward S. Forman, "Final Report for 1939–40," GALCIT Project No. 1, Report No. 3, pp. 4–10, 22–24, available at the JPL Archives.

2. J. D. Hunley, interview with Martin Summerfield near Princeton, N.J., Sept. 27, 1994, pp. 3–8; Malina, "Army Air Corps Jet Propulsion Research Project," pp. 161–62.

3. Malina, "Army Air Corps Jet Propulsion Research Project," pp. 168, 179–80; Slater, "Research and Development at JPL," pp. 42–45; Summerfield interview, p. 8; Truax, "Rocket Development," pp. 60–61 (see chap. 1, n. 36).

4. Winter and James, "50 Years of Aerojet," pp. 2–3 (see chap. 1, n. 26); Malina, "Army Air Corps Jet Propulsion Project," pp. 194–95; Frank Malina, "A Review of Developments in Liquid Propellant Jet (Rocket) Propulsion at the ACJP Project and the Aerojet Engineering Corporation," report prepared for the Special Office of Scientific Research and Development Committee Meeting, Feb. 17,

1944, esp. p. 2, folder 9.2 of the Malina Collection, Manuscript Collection, Library of Congress; JPL/Monthly Summaries, 1942–1944, entries for May 1–Jun. 30, 1942, and July 1–July 31, 1943 [sic, misprint for 1942], in Malina Collection, folder 8.1.

5. Truax, "Rocket Development," pp. 58–61, 65–66; biographies of Ray C. Stiff Jr., by Aerojet, 1963 and 1969, in NASM archives folder CS-882500-01, "Stiff, Ray C., Jr."; Winter and Ordway, "Reaction Motors," pp. 157–58, 160 (see chap. 1, n. 36).

6. Malina, "ORDCIT," pp. 50 54 (see chap. 1, n. 24); Capt. E. W. Bradshaw Jr. and M. M. Mills, "Development and Characteristics of the WAC Corporal Booster Rocket," JPL Project Note No. 4-30, Feb. 26, 1948, report from JPL Archives; Seifert, "History of Ordnance Research at the Jet Propulsion Laboratory," pp. 18–20 (see chap. 1, n. 25); Bragg, "Development of the Corporal," I:50 (see chap. 1, n. 27).

7. Bragg, "Development of the Corporal," I:61–63; Army Ordnance Corps, "Report No. 20-100, The Corporal," pp. 55–56 (see chap. 1, n. 27).

8. Bragg, "Development of the Corporal," I:67–75, 113.

9. Bragg, "Development of the Corporal," I:105–106; London, "Brennschluss," pp. 353–54 (see chap. 1, n. 39); U.S. Army Ordnance/GE, "Hermes Guided Missile Research," p. 4 (see chap. 1, n. 39); General Electric, "Progress Report on Bumper Vehicle," p. 35 (see chap. 1, n. 42); Starr, "Launch of Bumper 8 from the Cape," p. 4 (see chap. 1, n. 42).

10. Army Ordnance Corps, "Report No. 20-100, The Corporal," p. 2; Seifert, "Ordnance Research," pp. 4, 20; Bragg, "Development of the Corporal," I:44, 108–109, 112, and II:28-2.

11. Army Ordnance Corps, "Report No. 20-100, The Corporal," p. 57; Bragg, "Development of the Corporal," I:116–17.

12. Army Ordnance Corps, "Report No. 20-100, The Corporal," pp. 2–4; Bragg, "Development of the Corporal," I:115–17 and II:19-1; Koppes, *JPL*, p. 39 (see chap. 1, n. 25); Pickering, "Countdown to Space Exploration," p. 393 (see chap. 1, n. 27).

13. Army Ordnance Corps, "Report No. 20-100, The Corporal," pp. 53, 57–59, quotation from p. 58; Bragg, "Development of the Corporal," I:117; Frank G. Denison Jr. and Chauncey J. Hamlin Jr., "The Design of the Axial-Cooled Rocket Motor for the Corporal E," Progress Report No. 4-112, ORDCIT Project (Pasadena, Calif.: JPL, Aug. 29, 1949), pp. 2, 4–11, 18, 21, available in the JPL Archives, JPL Historical Collection, folder 3-999. The project under which JPL developed the Corporal missile for army ordnance was called the ORDCIT project.

14. Bragg, "Development of the Corporal," II:19-5.

15. Ibid., p. 19-6; Army Ordnance Corps, "Report No. 20-100, The Corporal," p. 7; Stephen B. Johnson, "Craft or System?: The Development of Systems Engineering at JPL," *Quest: The History of Spaceflight Quarterly* 6, no. 2 (1998): 19.

16. Interview of H. J. Stewart by John L. Greenberg, Oct. 13–Nov. 9, 1982, seen in the Caltech Archives, pp. 36–37; H. J. Stewart, "Static and Dynamic Stability Estimates for the Corporal (Missile No. 2, XF30L20,000)" (Pasadena, Calif.: JPL, Nov. 10, 1944), Progress Report 4-4, p. 14, seen in the JPL Archives; Bragg, "Development of the Corporal," II:19-6 to 19-7; Seifert, "History of Ordnance Research," pp. 25, 30; Army Ordnance Corps, "Report No. 20-100, The Corporal," pp. 8, 59; Koppes, *JPL*, pp. 51–53.

17. Bragg, "Development of the Corporal," I:165–67, 170; Nicholas and Rossi, *U.S. Missile Data Book, 1994*, p. 3-2 (see chap. 1, n. 27); Army Ordnance Corps, "Report No. 20-100, The Corporal," p. 16.

18. See, e.g., Reisig, "Peenemünder 'Aggregaten,'" p. 74 (see chap. 3, n. 6); J. D. Hunley, interview with Ernst Stuhlinger in his home near Huntsville, Ala., Sept. 20, 1994, pp. 31–33; and a letter, Stuhlinger to Hunley, Mar. 3, 1995, for developments at Peenemünde and Huntsville.

19. Army Ordnance Corps, "Report No. 20-100, The Corporal," pp. 371–73; Koppes, *JPL*, pp. 52–53; Johnson, "Craft or System," pp. 19–20.

20. Vanguard Staff, "Project Vanguard Report . . . 1 June 1957," pp. 2-6 to 2-7 (see chap. 1, n. 58); *Project Vanguard, A Scientific Earth Satellite Program for the International Geophysical Year*, A Report to the Committee on Appropriations, U.S. House of Representatives, by Surveys and Investigations Staff, [ca. Feb. 15, 1959], p. 61, found in NASM Archives, folder OV-106120-01, "Vanguard II Launch Vehicle 4" (hereafter cited as Congressional Committee Report, *Project Vanguard*); Kurt R. Stehling, *Project Vanguard* (Garden City, N.Y.: Doubleday, 1961), p. 301. For a recent account that nicely places Vanguard into its international as well as national context, see Matt Bille and Erika Lishock, *The First Space Race: Launching the World's First Satellites*, ed. Roger D. Launius, Centennial of Flight Series (College Station: Texas A&M University Press, 2004).

21. Vanguard Staff, "Project Vanguard Report . . . 1 June 1957," p. 2-37; document titled "Vanguard Vehicle Characteristics," n.d. [after Dec. 16, 1959], seen in NASM Archives, folder OV-106015–01, "Vanguard Project, History."

22. Bradshaw and Mills, "Development and Characteristics of the WAC Corporal Booster Rocket"; Seifert, "Ordnance Research," pp. 18–20; Bragg, "Development of the Corporal," I:50; Homer E. Newell Jr., *Sounding Rockets* (New York: McGraw-Hill, 1959), p. 63; Clark, *Ignition!*, pp. 21, 26, 41–45, 47–65 (see chap. 1, n. 95).

23. Vanguard Staff, "Project Vanguard Report . . . 1 June 1957," pp. 2-37 to 2-38, quotation from p. 2-37; Vanguard Staff, "Project Vanguard Report . . . September 15, 1956," p. 5 (see chap. 1, n. 59); Martin Company, "Vanguard Satellite Launching Vehicle," pp. 51–55 (see chap. 1, n. 59); Constance McLaughlin Green and Milton Lomask, *Vanguard: A History* (Washington, D.C.: Smithsonian Institution Press, 1971), pp. 89, 204; Stehling, *Project Vanguard*, pp. 132–33; George E. Pelletier, Director of Public Relations, Aerojet, "Details of the Aerojet-General Second-Stage Propulsion System for Vanguard Launching Vehicle," Feb. 11, 1959, in NHRC, folder 006640, "Vanguard II (Feb. 17, 1959)."

24. Vanguard Staff, "Project Vanguard Report . . . 1 June 1957," pp. 2-41 to 2-42; Green and Lomask, *Vanguard*, p. 89; The Martin Company, "Trip to Aerojet-General, Azusa, California, December 18–20, 1956," NA RG 255, Records of the National Aeronautics and Space Administration, Vanguard Division, Project Vanguard Case Files, 1955–59, entry 35, box 1.

25. Green and Lomask, *Vanguard*, p. 204, first quotation; Stehling, *Project Vanguard*, pp. 134–35; memo, Director, U.S. Naval Research Laboratory to The Martin Company, Jul. 25, 1957; memo, The Martin Company to Director, Naval Research Laboratory, Jul. 29, 1957; memo, Director, U.S. Naval Research Laboratory to Bureau of Aeronautics Representative, Azusa, Calif., Nov. 27, 1957, last three sources all from NA RG 255, Records of the National Aeronautics and Space Administration, Vanguard Division, Project Vanguard Case Files, 1955–59, entry 35, box 1; "Project Vanguard," p. 62; Rosen's letter to author on May 8, 2002.

26. Stehling, *Project Vanguard*, p. 134, first quotation; Milton W. Rosen, "Rocket Development for Project Vanguard," [Jan. 23, 1957], p. 5, second quotation, NHRC, folder 001835, "Rosen, Milton W. (Misc. Bio)," date written on original document: "Dod [*sic*] approval 23 Jan 57."

27. Congressional Committee Report, *Project Vanguard*, pp. 62, 65–66; Green and Lomask, *Vanguard*, pp. 176, 283; Stehling, *Project Vanguard*, pp. 82–83.

28. Martin Information Services, "Project Vanguard" [Nov. 23, 1959], seen in NASM Archives, folder OV-106015-01, "Vanguard Project History"; Green and Lomask, *Vanguard*, pp. 204, 219, 285; Stehling, *Project Vanguard*, pp. 156, 182–222, 274.

29. U.S. Naval Research Laboratory, NRL Notice 5400, Transfer of Project Vanguard to NASA, Dec. 4, 1958, NHRC, folder 006633, "Vanguard Documents, Early History"; Green and Lomask, *Vanguard*, p. 223; Stehling, *Project Vanguard*, pp. 237–38.

30. Milton W. Rosen, "A Brief History of Delta and Its Relation to Vanguard," enclosure in letter, Rosen to Constance McL. Green, Mar. 15, 1968, NHRC, folder 001835, "Rosen, Milton W. (Misc. Bio)"; Stehling, *Project Vanguard*, pp. 233–34; John P. Hagen, "The Viking and the Vanguard," in *History of Rocket Technology*, ed. Emme, p. 139 (see chap. 1, n. 41).

31. "Aerojet to Build Able Star, Bigger, Restartable Able," *Missiles and Rockets* 6 (Feb. 15, 1960): 34; briefing charts, Able Projects, "Development of Project Able Second Stage, Propulsion System," Air Force Space and Missile Systems Center History Office, folder, "Briefing Charts—Able Projects"; W. M. Arms, *Thor: The Workhorse of Space—a Narrative History* (Huntington Beach, Calif.: McDonnell Douglas Astronautics Company, 1972), pp. 4-2, 4-3, seen in the Space and Missile Systems Center History Office, Los Angeles, filed as a separate item in "Standard Launch Vehicles II"; letter, R. R. Bennett to L. G. Dunn, Mar. 25, 1958, and "Thor Missile 118 Flight Summary," Air Force Space and Missile Systems Center History Office, folder, "Re-entry—(Able-01) (Gen T)"; Stiff, "Storable Liquid Rockets," p. 8; Powell, "Thor-Able and Atlas Able," p. 221 (see chap. 2, n. 12, for last two sources).

32. Stambler, "Simplicity Boosts Able-Star," p. 59; HQ AFBMD document, "ABLE-STAR (AJ10-104)," Aug. 18, 1961; "AbleStar Is Newest Aerojet Triumph," p. 2, for the quotation (see chap. 2, n. 15, for last three sources); Gordon et al., *Aerojet*, p. III-135 (see chap. 1, n. 85).

33. Powell, "Thor-Able and Atlas-Able," p. 224; [AFBMD]/WDLPM-4 to [AFBMD]/WDZJP, subj.: Proposed AJ10-104 Final Report, Mar. 30, 1960; HQ AFBMD, "ABLE-STAR (AJ10-104)"; Stambler, "Simplicity Boosts Able-Star," pp. 59–63; Holmes, "*Able-Star* Makes Technological First," p. 44 (see chap. 1, n. 15); "Aerojet to Build Able Star," p. 34; Aerojet, Model Specification, Rocket Propulsion System, Liquid Propellant, AGC Model No. AJ10-104, Jan 25, 1961, Space and Missile Systems Center History Office, separately filed item in Able-Star section; *CPIA/M5 Liquid Propellant Engine Manual*, Unit 59, AJ10-104, AJ10-104B (see chap. 2, n. 70).

34. Letter, BMD/WDPCR to Director, Advanced Research Projects Agency, subj.: Development of AJ10-104 (ABLE-STAR) Upper Stage Vehicle as of 31 October 1959, Nov. 9, 1959; letter, BMD/WDLPM-4 to Director, Advanced Research Projects Agency, subj.: Development of AJ10-104 (ABLE-STAR) Upper Stage Vehicle as of 30 November 1959, Dec. 8, 1959, both in Air Force Space and Missile Center History Office, file "Development of AJ10-104 (ABLE STAR)."

35. Weil, STL, "Final Report," pp. 2, 12–25 (see chap. 2, n. 13); Arms, "Thor," pp. 6-21, 6-22, 6-26, 6-27; "Historical Reports," Programs Managed by the Directorate of TRANSIT/ANNA, [AFBMD?], "Thor Able and Thor Ablestar," Mar. 7, 1962, pp. 3–4, Air Force Space and Missile Systems Center History Office, file, "Research & Development—Transit Project (Able-Star except Transit 1A)"; HQ AFBMD Chronology, Space Probes Division, AF Space Boosters, p. 2, Air Force Space and Missile Systems Center History Office, file, "Research & Development—Project Able-5 (Atlas)"; *Report to the Congress . . . , January 1 to December 31, 1960* (Washington, D.C.: [GPO], 1961), pp. 24–25; *Report to the Congress . . . , 1961* (Washington, D.C.: [GPO], 1962), pp. 92, 94, 99; *Report to the Congress . . . , 1962* (Washington, D.C.: [GPO], [1963]), p. 118.

36. Weil, STL, "Final Report," pp. 31–37; *Report to the Congress . . . , 1961,* pp. viii, 26; Spires, *Beyond Horizons,* p. 140 (see chap. 2, n. 22); Leonard Jaffe, *Communications in Space* (New York: Holt, Rinehart and Winston, 1967), pp. 104–105; David J. Whalen, *The Origins of Satellite Communications, 1945–1965* (Washington, D.C.: Smithsonian Institution Press, 2002), pp. 66–67, 111, 160; Arms, "Thor," pp. 6-21, 6-23; "Thor Able-Star" Mark Wade Website, wysiwyg://12/http://www.astronautix.com/lvs/theostar.htm (accessed Sept. 23, 2002).

37. Short biographies of Dr. Klager that he generously provided to author; Gordon et al., *Aerojet,* pp. III-15, III-43, III-46, III-68 through III-69.

38. Clark, *Ignition!,* pp. 42–45; Gordon et al., *Aerojet,* p. III-100; Lonnquest and Winkler, *To Defend and Deter,* p. 231 (see chap. 1, n. 51); G. Harry Stine, *ICBM: The Making of the Weapon That Changed the World* (New York: Orion Books, 1991), p. 229.

39. Stumpf, *Titan II,* pp. 36–37 (see chap. 1, n. 94); "BMO Chronology," p. 68 (see chap. 1, n. 66); Greene, "Development of the SM-68 Titan," p. 114 (see chap. 1, n. 94); Chulick et al., "Titan Liquid Rocket Engines," pp. 24–27 (see chap. 1, n. 94); Aerojet Liquid Rocket Company, *Liquid Rocket Engines* (Sacramento, Calif.: Aerojet, 1975), pp. 4, 8, 20, 22.

40. Chulick et al., "Titan Liquid Rocket Engines," p. 27.

41. Ibid., pp. 24–27; Adams, "Titan I to Titan II," pp. 214–15 (see chap. 1, n. 93); Stumpf, *Titan II,* pp. 37–40.

42. Chulick et al., "Titan Liquid Rocket Engines," pp. 25–29; Harwood, *Raise Heaven and Earth,* p. 320 (see chap. 1, n. 56); Aerojet, *Liquid Rocket Engines,* pp. 4, 20.

43. News Release, "Aerojet Engineers behind Propulsion for the Air Force Titan II," Aerojet-General Corporation, Public Relations, Mar. 8, 1965, seen in NASM Archives, folder OT-490020-16, "Titan II."

44. Stumpf, *Titan II,* pp. 71–73, 86; Adams, "Titan I to Titan II," pp. 220–21; Hacker and Grimwood, *Shoulders of Titans,* pp. 104–105, 140 (see chap. 1, n. 72); Harwood, *Raise Heaven and Earth,* p. 320; Sarah A. Grassly, "Ballistic Missile and Space Launch Summary as of 30 June 1969," SAMSO Historical Office, Mar. 1970, p. I-1-1-1, seen at the Air Force Historical Research Agency, K243.012, 67/07/01–69/06/30.

45. Hacker and Grimwood, *Shoulders of Titans,* esp. pp. 76–78, 104–105; "SAMSO Chronology," pp. 4, 95 (see ch. 1, n. 72).

46. Hacker and Grimwood, *Shoulders of Titans,* pp. 77, 87, 105; Dyer, *TRW,* pp. 231–32 (see chap. 1, n. 67); Stumpf, *Titan II,* p. 72.

47. Hacker and Grimwood, *Shoulders of Titans,* pp. 125–26, 135; Stumpf, *Titan II,* pp. 72, 78.

48. Hacker and Grimwood, *Shoulders of Titans*, pp. 134–37, 142–44, 166–68; Stumpf, *Titan II*, pp. 72, 79; "Gemini-Titan II Launch Vehicle Fact Sheet," n.d., pp. 6-13 to 6-16, seen in the Air Force Space and Missile Systems Center History Office, photo storage area; Huzel and Huang, *Design of Liquid-Propellant Rocket Engines*, p. 366 (see chap. 2, n. 6).

49. Chulick et al., "Titan Liquid Rocket Engines," p. 31; Stumpf, *Titan II*, pp. 40–42; Hacker and Grimwood, *Shoulders of Titans*, pp. 168–69.

50. Stumpf, *Titan II*, pp. 42–44, 72–73, 75–79.

51. "SAMSO Chronology," pp. 131, 133, 139; Piper, "History of Titan III," pp. 104–105 (see chap. 2, n. 94).

52. Richards and Powell, "Titan 3 and Titan 4," p. 126 (see chap. 2, n. 97), and *CPIA/M5 Liquid Propellant Engine Manual*, Units 146, AJ10-137, and 154, Titan III Transtage; Cecil R. Gibson and James A. Wood, "Apollo Experience Report—Service Propulsion Subsystem," NASA Technical Note D-7375, Aug. 1973, p. 7; Piper, "History of Titan III," p. 105.

53. Huzel and Huang, *Design of Liquid-Propellant Rocket Engines*, p. 118.

54. *CPIA/M5 Liquid Propellant Engine Manual*, Units 146, AJ10-137, and 154, Titan III Transtage.

55. Piper, "History of Titan III," pp. 91, 121, 125–26, quotation from p. 126; *CPIA/M5 Liquid Propellant Engine Manual*, Unit 154, Titan III Transtage; Jason P. Hatton, "Titan Transtage Rockets," http://members.aol.com/_ht_a/hattonjasonp/hasohp/TRANSTG.HTML (accessed June 24, 2003); Huzel and Huang, *Design of Liquid-Propellant Rocket Engines*, p. 378.

56. Stiff, "Storable Liquid Rockets," p. 9.

57. Gordon et al., *Aerojet*, p. III-146 for the first and third quotations; *CPIA/M5 Liquid Propellant Engine Manual*, Unit 154, Titan III, Transtage, for second quotation; Richards and Powell, "Titan 3 and Titan 4," p. 126.

58. *CPIA/M5 Liquid Propellant Engine Manual*, Unit 154, Titan III, Transtage; "Titanium Tanks Machined for Titan 3 Transtage," *Aviation Week & Space Technology*, May 11, 1964, p. 69; Stiff, "Storable Liquid Rockets," figs. 37, 38.

59. E. W. Bonnett, "A Cost History of the Thor-Delta Launch Vehicle Family," paper A74-08 delivered at the International Astronautical Federation XXVth Congress, Sept. 30–Oct. 5, 1974, Amsterdam, p. 6; Arms, "Thor," p. 6-66; Isakowitz, *Space Launch Systems* (1995), p. 203 (see chap. 2, n. 33); *CPIA/M5 Liquid Propellant Engine Manual*, Unit 194, AJ10-118F, Second Stage Propulsion System; Unit 122, Titan III Transtage, AJ10-138 (preliminary design completed Nov. 1962); Unit 145, AJ10-118, AJ10-118A/C/D/E; Forsyth, "Delta," p. 126 (see chap. 2, n. 10).

60. Taylor, *Jane's All the World's Aircraft, 1977–1978*, p. 837 (see chap. 2, n. 25); *CPIA/M5 Liquid Propellant Engine Manual*, Unit 194, AJ10-118F-Delta Second Stage Propulsion System, and Unit 208, Delta 2nd Stage Engine.

Chapter 5

1. Thiel, Memorandum, , "Practical Possibilities of Further Development," quotation (see chap. 3, n. 4); on Goddard and Oberth's comments, chapter 1 in this book and Sloop, *Liquid*, pp. 236, 258–64 (see chap. 2, n. 38).

2. Sloop, *Liquid Hydrogen*, pp. 13–14, 20–26, 37–38, 49–58; George H. Osborne, Robert Gordon, and Herman L. Coplen with George S. James, "Liquid-Hydrogen Rocket Engine Development at Aerojet, 1944–1950," in *History of Rocketry and Astronautics*, ed. Hall, pp. 279–318 (see chap. 1, n. 24); NASA

News Release 62-66, "First Launch of Centaur Vehicle Scheduled," Apr. 3, 1962, NASM Archives, folder OA-40107-01, "Atlas Centaur Launch Vehicle"; General Dynamics/Astronautics, "Centaur Primer" (see chap. 2, n. 35).

3. Sloop, *Liquid Hydrogen*, pp. 81–93, 102–12.

4. Ibid., pp. 113, 141–66; Dawson and Bowles, *Centaur*, pp. 17–18 (see chap 2, n. 35); Tucker, "RL10 Upper-Stage Rocket Engine," p. 125 (see chap. 2, n. 39).

5. Sloop, *Liquid Hydrogen*, pp. 191–94; Clarke Newlon, "Krafft Ehricke," in *Rocket and Missile Technology*, ed. Gene Gurney (New York: Franklin Watts, 1964), pp. 86–91; oral history interview (OHI) [John L. Sloop] with Krafft A. Ehricke, Apr. 26, 1974, p. 32, NHRC, folder 010976.

6. OHI, Sloop with Ehricke, pp. 33, 51–53; Chapman, *Atlas*, p. 153 (see chap. 1, n. 62); Sloop, *Liquid Hydrogen*, p. 194; Dawson and Bowles, *Centaur*, pp. 12–13, 18–20; Neufeld, *Ballistic Missiles*, p. 36n (see chap. 1, n. 51).

7. Dawson and Bowles, *Centaur*, pp. 18–20; Sloop, *Liquid Hydrogen*, pp. 178–79, 194–95; "SAMSO Chronology," p. 56 (see chap. 1, n. 72); Spires, *Beyond Horizons*, pp. 57–58 (see chap. 2, n. 22); Convair Division, General Dynamics, "Atlas Fact Sheet," p. 3 (see chap. 2, n. 33).

8. Sloop, *Liquid Hydrogen*, pp. 200–201; "Statement of Krafft A. Ehricke," in *Centaur Program*, Hearings before the Subcommittee on Space Sciences, H. Rep., 87th Cong., 2d sess., pp. 5, 63–66 (see chap. 2, n. 35) (overall document hereafter cited as Hearings, *Centaur Program*).

9. OHI, Sloop with Ehricke, pp. 57–59; Ezell, *NASA Historical Data Book*, II:45 (see chap. 1, n. 44); Hearings, *Centaur Program*, p. 6.

10. OHI, Sloop with Ehricke, p. 59; Heald, "LH$_2$ Technology," p. 207 (see chap. 2, n. 38).

11. Hearings, *Centaur Program*, pp. 4–5, 105–106.

12. Green and Jones, "Bugs That Live at –423°," pp. 8–41 (see chap. 2, n. 41); Martin, "Brief History of the *Atlas*," pt. II, *Quest*, p. 43 (see chap. 2, n. 34); Heald, "LH$_2$ Technology," pp. 209–10; Richards and Powell, "Centaur Vehicle," p. 99 (see chap. 2, n. 40).

13. Hearings, *Centaur Program*, pp. 9, 51, 97; Dawson and Bowles, *Centaur*, pp. 19–20, 34, 51, 74; Irwin Stambler, "Centaur," *Space/Aeronautics*, Oct. 1963, p. 74; John L. Sloop, Memorandum for Director of Space Sciences, Dec. 18, 1961, NHRC, John L. Sloop Papers, box 22, binder "Centaur Management & Development, Jan. 1961–Mar. 62"; W. Schubert, "Centaur," in NASA, Office of Space Sciences, "Program Review, Launch Vehicles and Propulsion," June 23, 1962, pp. 173–75, NHRC.

14. Hearings, *Centaur Program*, pp. 7, 33, 47, 66; Marshall Space Flight Center, bio, Hans Herbert Hueter, fiche no. 1067, Marshall History Office Master Collection, copy in NHRC, file 001055; W. Schubert, "Centaur," in Office of Space Sciences, "Program Review, Launch Vehicles and Propulsion," pp. 121–80.

15. Sloop, Dec. 18, 1961 Memorandum, pp. 1–2, first two quotations; John L. Sloop, Memo for Director of Space Sciences, Dec. 20, 1961, p. 3, NHRC, John L. Sloop Papers, box 22, binder "Centaur Management & Development, Jan. 1961–Mar.," third quotation; Sloop's bio, Sloop, *Liquid Hydrogen*, p. 3.

16. Stambler, "Centaur," pp. 73–75; W. Schubert, "Centaur," in Office of Space Sciences, "Program Review, Launch Vehicles and Propulsion," p. 175, for the quotation.

17. Tucker, "RL10 Upper-Stage Rocket Engine," pp. 126–28, quotations on pp. 126–27.

18. Ibid., pp. 128–29.

19. Ibid., pp. 130–31.

20. Richards and Powell, "Centaur Vehicle," p. 100; Green and Jones, "Bugs That Live at –423°," pp. 21–22.

21. Tucker, "RL10 Upper-Stage Rocket Engine," pp. 132–37, 139; Hearings, *Centaur Program*, pp. 115–16; Schubert, "Centaur," in Office of Space Sciences, "Program Review, Launch Vehicles and Propulsion," p. 131.

22. Richards and Powell, "Centaur Vehicle," p. 101; Heald, "LH$_2$ Technology," p. 213.

23. Richards and Powell, "Centaur Vehicle," pp. 102–103; Isakowitz, *Space Launch Systems* (1995), p. 205 (see chap. 2, n. 33).

24. Richards and Powell, "Centaur Vehicle," p. 103; correspondence by Deane Davis, General Dynamics (retd.), in *Journal of the British Interplanetary Society (JBIS)* 35, no. 1 (Jan. 1982): 17; Heald, "LH$_2$ Technology," p. 206; Hearings, *Centaur Program*, pp. 12–27.

25. Sloop, Memorandum, Dec. 20, 1961, quotations, p. 2; letter, Hans Hueter, [MSFC] Director, Light and Medium Vehicles Office, to J. R. Dempsey, President, General Dynamics/Astronautics, Jan. 4, 1962, NHRC, John Sloop Papers (Centaur Material), box 22, binder, "Centaur Management & Development, Jan 1961–Mar 1962."

26. Letter, Hueter to Dempsey, Jan. 4, 1962, p. 2.

27. Hearings, *Centaur Program*, pp. 9, 61–62; Dawson and Bowles, *Centaur*, p. 35; background, letter, William H. Pickering to Norman L. Baker, President, National Space Club, Dec. 19, 1963, enclosure 1, in Jet Propulsion Laboratory Archives, JPL 133, William Pickering Publications Collection, 1932–71, box 3, folder 29.

28. Geddes, "Centaur," pp. 25, 28–29 (see chap. 2, n. 40); Hearings, *Centaur Program*, pp. 2, 9, 37, 66, 104.

29. Hearings, *Centaur Program*; *Centaur Launch Vehicle Development Program*, Report of the Committee on Science and Astronautics (hereafter cited *Centaur Report*), 87th Cong., 2d sess., H. Rep. 1959, July 2, 1962, p. 11, quotation.

30. *Centaur Report*, p. 12.

31. Letter with attached account, Davis to Emme, Feb. 6, 1983, Davis's quotations from p. 4 of the attachment (see chap. 2, n. 41); Sloop, *Liquid Hydrogen*, p. 208, for Ehricke's quotation. Davis's account is published as "Seeing Is Believing, or How the Atlas Rocket Hit Back," *Spaceflight* 25, no. 5 (May 1983): 196–98, quotations on p. 198.

32. Hearings, *Centaur Program*, p. 59, for the quotations; Dawson and Bowles, *Centaur*, pp. 54–55.

33. "History of the George C. Marshall Space Flight Center," July 1–Dec. 31, 1962, p. 85, (henceforth, "History of MSFC") NHRC, folder 010203, "Centaur General (1959–89)"; Sloop quotations from Sloop, *Liquid Hydrogen*, p. 183; Davis quotations from his letter to Emme; final quotations from Geddes, "Centaur," p. 28, reflecting Hansen's views; Silverstein biography from Virginia P. Dawson, *Engines and Innovation: Lewis Laboratory and American Propulsion Technology* (Washington, D.C.: NASA SP-4306, 1991), pp. 169–70, 177–78, and Hunley, *Birth of NASA*, p. 357 (see chap. 1, n. 33).

34. NASA News Release No. 62-209, "Liquid Hydrogen Program Stepped Up," Sept. 30, 1962, NHRC, folder 010203, "Centaur General (1959–89)"; "History of MSFC," July–Dec. 1962, p. 85.

35. Hearings, *Centaur Program*, pp. 66–68; General Dynamics/Astronautics, "Centaur Primer," pp. 28–29, 41–42; Dawson and Bowles, *Centaur*, pp. 23–24, 27, 43, 53, 60.

36. Dawson and Bowles, *Centaur,* pp. 60–67; Geddes, "Centaur," pp. 27, 29.

37. Dawson and Bowles, *Centaur,* pp. 62–64; Geddes, "Centaur," pp. 27–28; Sloop, Memorandum, Dec. 20, 1961, 2.

38. Dawson and Bowles, *Centaur,* p. 90, table; Green and Jones, "Bugs That Live at –423°," pp. 27–34; Richards and Powell, "Centaur Vehicle," pp. 104–107.

39. Green and Jones, "Bugs That Live at –423°," pp. 26–34; Richards and Powell, "Centaur Vehicle," pp. 104–106; *CPIA/M5 Liquid Propellant Engine Manual,* Unit 115, RL10A-3-1, Centaur and Saturn S-IV Propulsion, and Unit 116, RL10A-3-3, Centaur (see chap. 2, n. 70).

40. Green and Jones, "Bugs That Live at –423°," pp. 30–38; Richards and Powell, "Centaur Vehicle," pp. 106–107; Launius, *NASA,* pp. 83–84 (see chap. 2, n. 9); Isakowitz, *Space Launch Systems* (1995), pp. 203, 205; General Dynamics/ Convair, "Atlas Fact Sheet," n.d., pp. 12, 14; Ezell, *NASA Historical Data Book,* II:263, 328–31, 399; Siddiqi, *Deep Space Chronicle,* pp. 55, 57, 61, 63, 65, 67–69 (see chap. 2, n. 41); *Report to the Congress, . . .* [1965], p. 161 (see chap. 2, n. 41), and *United States Aeronautics & Space Activities, 1968* (Washington, D.C.: GPO, [1968]), p. 108.

41. Isakowitz, *Space Launch Systems* (1995), pp. 203, 205; Richards and Powell, "Centaur Vehicle," pp. 100, 110–11, 113–14; Dawson and Bowles, *Centaur,* pp. 125–31, 222–25; Ezell, *NASA Historical Data Book,* III:290, 293–94, 304–11 (see chap. 2, n. 13), and Rumerman, *NASA Historical Data Book,* V:82 (see chap. 2, n. 37); Pratt & Whitney, "RL10 Engine," available in the NHRC, folder 010192, "Atlas II"; AF Space and Missile Systems Organization, "Centaur D-1 Payload Users Guide," pp. 3-1, 3-30 through 3-37 (see chap. 2, n. 42).

42. Richards and Powell, "Centaur Vehicle," p. 114; Tucker, "RL10 Upper-Stage Rocket Engine," p. 147; Dawson and Bowles, *Centaur,* p. 232; General Dynamics, Space Systems Division, "Atlas/Centaur: Reliable, Versatile, Available" (see chap. 2, n. 35); Honeywell, "Centaur Inertial Navigation Unit," Mar. 1992, NHRC, folder 010203, "Centaur General (1959–89)."

43. Donald F. Robertson, "Centaur Canters On," *Space,* Mar.–Apr. 1991, pp. 22–25; General Dynamics, "Mission Planner's Guide for the Atlas Launch Vehicle Family," pp. 1-1, 1-2, A-1 to A-6 (see chap. 2, n. 46); Heald, "LH₂ Technology," p. 220; Dawson and Bowles, *Centaur,* pp. iv–v, 23–25; Craig Covault, "Atlas V Soars, Market Slumps," *Aviation Week & Space Technology,* Aug. 26, 2002, pp. 22–24; Martin, "Brief History of the Atlas," pt. II, pp. 47–51.

44. Bilstein, *Stages to Saturn,* pp. 41, 44–46 (see chap. 1, n. 50); MSFC, Saturn Systems Office, "Saturn Illustrated Chronology (Apr. 1957–Apr. 1962)," p. 5-8, seen in the NASM Archives, Bellcom Collection, box 13, folder 3.

45. MSFC, "Saturn Illustrated Chronology," pp. 8–10, 12–13, 17–20, 22; Ezell, *NASA Historical Data Book,* II:56–58; Bilstein, *Stages to Saturn,* pp. 188–89; B. K. Heusinger, "Saturn Propulsion Improvements," *Astronautics & Aeronautics,* Aug. 1964, p. 25.

46. Summary, "Final Report S-IV All-Systems Stage Incident," seen in Mueller Collection, from which the quotations are taken, pp. 2–3 (see chap. 2, n. 69); Bilstein, *Stages to Saturn,* pp. 184–85.

47. Bilstein, *Stages to Saturn,* pp. 324–37, 414; MSFC, "Saturn Illustrated Chronology," pp. 46–47; NASA/MSFC et al., "Saturn IB News Reference," Dec. 1965 (changed Sept. 1968), p. 12-2. The Saturn news references are available in various archives, including the NHRC and on the Internet.

48. Bilstein, *Stages to Saturn,* p. 83; NASA/MSFC et al., "Saturn IB News Reference," p. 2-4, unpaginated S-IB Stage Fact Sheet, 3-1, 8-1.

49. Bilstein, *Stages to Saturn*, pp. 140–41; Hunley, *Birth of NASA*, pp. 149–50n6; extracts from "The Apollo Spacecraft: A Chronology," 1:53–54, in NHRC, folder 013782, "Propulsion J-2"; memorandum, NASA/MLP (Tischler) to NASA/ML (Rosen), subj: AGC Proposal, July 8, 1962, in NHRC, folder 013782.

50. Bilstein, *Stages to Saturn*, pp. 141–43; MSFC, "Saturn Illustrated Chronology," pp. 46, 50; Rocketdyne, "Data Sheet, J-2 Rocket Engine," June 3, 1975, in NHRC, folder 013782; memorandum, Eldon W. Hall, NASA/MEE to Dr. Joseph F. Shea, NASA/ME, subj: Transfer of Engine Development Responsibility, July 30, 1962, in NHRC, folder 013782.

51. Bilstein, *Stages to Saturn*, pp. 138, 144–45; memorandum, NASA/MLP (Tischler) to NASA/ML (Rosen), for the quotation (see chap. 2, n. 71).

52. Bilstein, *Stages to Saturn*, pp. 145–46; *CPIA/M5 Liquid Propellant Engine Manual*, Unit 87, engine J-2 (200,000 pounds thrust), Apr. 1965, p. 4.

53. *CPIA/M5 Liquid Propellant Engine Manual*, Unit 87, compared with Unit 116, RL10A-3-3; NASA/MSFC et al., "Saturn IB News Reference," pp. 6-2 to 6-4; Brennan, "Milestones," p. 8 (see chap. 2, n. 74); M. L. "Joe" Strangeland, "Turbopumps for Liquid Rocket Engines," (Rocketdyne), *Threshold*, no. 3 (Summer 1988): 38.

54. Bilstein, *Stages to Saturn*, pp. 150–52; Strangeland, "Turbopumps," p. 42.

55. *CPIA/M5 Liquid Propellant Engine Manual*," Unit 87; Unit 125, J-2, 225K; Unit 174, J-2, 230K; NASA/MSFC et al., "Saturn IB News Reference," pp. 6-1 to 6-5; MSFC et al., "Saturn V News Reference," p. 6-4.

56. Previous two paragraphs based on Bilstein, *Stages to Saturn*, pp. 166–78; NASA/MSFC et al., "Saturn IB News Reference," S-IVB Stage Fact Sheet; MSFC, "Saturn Illustrated Chronology (to Apr. 1962)," p. 50; Ezell, *NASA Historical Data Book*, II:56; Douglas Aircraft Company, "Saturn IB Payload Planner's Guide," n.d., pp. 36, 38, in NASM, Bellcom Collection, box 14, folder 6.

57. Bilstein, *Stages to Saturn*, pp. 182–83, 429; Douglas, "Saturn IB Payload Planner's Guide," p. 38; NASA/MSFC et al., "Saturn IB News Reference," B-5/6.

58. Bilstein, *Stages to Saturn*, pp. 179, 185–86; MSFC et al., "Saturn V News Reference," p. 1-3 and unpaginated Third Stage Fact Sheet; NASA/MSFC et al., "Saturn IB News Reference," unpaginated S-IVB Stage Fact Sheet.

59. MSFC et al., "Saturn V News Reference," pp. 5-10 to 5-11, A-4.

60. Bilstein, *Stages to Saturn*, pp. 186, 353–60.

61. MSFC et al., "Saturn V News Reference," p. 1-6; Bromberg, *NASA*, pp. 56–57 (see chap. 2, n. 45); Heppenheimer, *Countdown*, pp. 207–208, for the first quotation, p. 207 (see chap. 2, n. 9); Gray, *Angle of Attack*, pp. 20, 22–34, 65–72, quotation from Crossfield, p. 66 (see chap. 2, n. 76).

62. Bilstein, *Stages to Saturn*, pp. 209–11; Gray, *Angle of Attack*, p. 89; MSFC et al., "Saturn V News Reference," unpaginated Second Stage Fact Sheet.

63. Bilstein, *Stages to Saturn*, pp. 211–14; MSFC et al., "Saturn V News Reference," Second Stage Fact Sheet and Third Stage Fact Sheet (both unpaginated), pp. 1-6, 8-2.

64. Bilstein, *Stages to Saturn*, pp. 214–16.

65. Gray, *Angle of Attack*, pp. 153–56, quotation from p. 154; Bilstein, *Stages to Saturn*, pp. 217–22.

66. Bilstein, *Stages to Saturn*, pp. 222–23; Gray, *Angle of Attack*, pp. 159–61; Dunar and Waring, *Power to Explore*, pp. 88–89 (see chap. 1, n. 50).

67. Gray, *Angle of Attack*, pp. 196–98; Bilstein, *Stages to Saturn*, pp. 222–24; Dunar and Waring, *Power to Explore*, p. 90.

68. Gray, *Angle of Attack,* p. 198; Bilstein, *Stages to Saturn,* pp. 224–25, 228, 269.

69. Gray, *Angle of Attack,* pp. 198–99; Bilstein, *Stages to Saturn,* pp. 225–26; Murray and Cox, *Apollo,* pp. 166–71, 183 (see chap. 2, n. 65); W. Henry Lambright, *Powering Apollo: James E. Webb of NASA* (Baltimore, Md.: Johns Hopkins University Press, 1995), pp. 107–108; Bromberg, *NASA and the Space Industry,* pp. 58–59.

70. Letter, Mueller to Atwood, Dec. 19, 1965, quotations from pp. 1, 3 (see chap. 2, n. 76).

71. Memorandum, [NASA] MA/S.C. Phillips to M/G.E. Mueller, quotations from pp. 1, 6 (see chap. 2, n. 76); Bilstein, *Stages to Saturn,* pp. 227–28; Gray, *Angle of Attack,* pp. 202, 208.

72. Bilstein, *Stages to Saturn,* pp. 224–33; Gray, *Angle of Attack,* pp. 209, 253–55; Murray and Cox, *Apollo,* pp. 231–36; Bromberg, *NASA and the Space Industry,* pp. 70–71; Lambright, *Powering Apollo,* pp. 174–75.

73. Bilstein, *Stages to Saturn,* pp. 360–61; MSFC et al., "Saturn V News Reference," p. 12-2; Senate Hearings, *Problems Encountered in the Second Flight of the Saturn V Launch Vehicle,* pp. 5, 16, 27–28 (see chap. 2, n. 76); Murray and Cox, *Apollo,* p. 312.

74. MSFC et al., "Saturn V News Reference," pp. 12-2 to 12-4, first quotation from p. 12-2; Senate Hearings, *Problems Encountered in the Second Flight of the Saturn V Launch Vehicle,* pp. 16, 36, including Phillips's comments and second quotation from p. 16; Bilstein, *Stages to Saturn,* pp. 360–61, von Braun quotation from p. 361.

75. Bilstein, *Stages to Saturn,* pp. 361–63; Murray and Cox, *Apollo,* pp. 313–14; "Minutes of the Saturn V Semi-DCR/AS-502 Evaluation," p. 3, Apr. 21, 1968, seen in the George E. Mueller Collection, box 92, folder 8; Senate Hearings, *Problems Encountered in the Second Flight of the Saturn V Launch Vehicle,* pp. 22–27, testimony of George H. Hage, Phillips's deputy director of Apollo.

76. Bilstein, *Stages to Saturn,* pp. 366–72; Orloff, *Apollo by the Numbers,* pp. 32–35, 40–43, 52–62, 72–81, 171–72, 186, 200, 213–14 , 228, 241–42, 254, 275–76 (see chap. 2, n. 73); *Report to the Congress . . . , 1968,* p. 101; Science and Technology Division, Library of Congress, *Astronautics and Aeronautics, 1969: Chronology on Science, Technology, and Policy* (Washington, D.C.: NASA SP-4014, 1970), pp. 434–35; NASA News Release 70-207, "Apollo 14 Saturn Modified," Dec. 4, 1970, NHRC folder 010449, "Saturn V, General (1970–)"; Space Division, North American Rockwell News Release, "Two Saturn Second Stage Modifications to be Tested in Space," n.d., NHRC folder 010450, "Saturn V, General (1965–1969)."

77. Guilmartin and Mauer, *A Shuttle Chronology,* pp. V-55 to V-56 (see chap. 2, n. 118).

78. Heppenheimer, *Space Shuttle Decision,* p. 179 (see chap. 2, n. 118); Bromberg, *NASA and Space Industry,* pp. 88–89, quotation from p. 88; Dunar and Waring, *Power to Explore,* pp. 152–67, 622–24.

79. Jenkins, *Space Shuttle,* pp. 109–10 (see chap. 2, n. 110); Heppenheimer, *Space Shuttle Decision,* pp. 237–39; Brennan, "Milestones," pp. 14–15; Wiswell and Huggins, "Liquid Propulsion at the Astrionics Laboratory" (see chap. 2, n. 121); *CPIA/M5 Liquid Propellant Engine Manual,* Unit 174, J-2 Engine, and Unit 184, J-2S Engine Propulsion System.

80. Heppenheimer, *Space Shuttle Decision*, pp. 240–42; Jenkins, *Space Shuttle*, p. 110; Heppenheimer, *Development of the Space Shuttle*, p. 134 (see chap. 2, n. 117).

81. Jenkins, *Space Shuttle*, pp. 110, 184; Heppenheimer, *Space Shuttle Decision*, pp. 242–44; Guilmartin and Mauer, *Shuttle Chronology*, IV:V-34, V-78; Bromberg, *NASA and Space Industry*, pp. 98–99; Dunar and Waring, *Power to Explore*, pp. 288–89. Quotation from Jenkins, p. 184, and also Dunar and Waring, p. 288.

82. Heppenheimer, *Space Shuttle Decision*, p. 240, for Biggs's quotation; Heppenheimer, *Development of the Space Shuttle*, pp. 126, 136; Jenkins, *Space Shuttle*, p. 224; Biggs, "Space Shuttle Main Engine," pp. 71, 75–76, 81 (see chap. 2, n. 120); Martinez, "Rocket Engine Propulsion Power Cycles," p. 17 (see chap. 2, n. 120); *CPIA/M5 Liquid Propellant Engine Manual*, Unit 174, J-2 Engine, and Unit 195, Space Shuttle Main Engine.

83. Heppenheimer, *Development of the Space Shuttle*, pp. 127–28, 133–34; Wiswell and Huggins, "Liquid Propulsion at the Astrionics Laboratory," n.p.

84. Previous two paragraphs based on Heppenheimer, *Development of the Space Shuttle*, pp. 134–35; Dunar and Waring, *Power to Explore*, pp. 296–97, 625; Jenkins, *Space Shuttle*, p. 225; Biggs, "Space Shuttle Main Engine," p. 77.

85. Biggs, "Space Shuttle Main Engine," pp. 79–80; Heppenheimer, *Development of the Space Shuttle*, pp. 136–37.

86. Material since last note based on Biggs, "Space Shuttle Main Engine," pp. 80–87.

87. Previous three paragraphs based on Biggs, "Space Shuttle Main Engine," pp. 88–91; Heppenheimer, *Development of the Space Shuttle*, pp. 140–42; Martinez, "Rocket Engine Propulsion Power Cycles," p. 22.

88. Biggs, "Space Shuttle Main Engine," pp. 92–96; Heppenheimer, *Development of the Space Shuttle*, pp. 144–47, 429n53.

89. Biggs, "Space Shuttle Main Engine," pp. 87–118; Heppenheimer, *Development of the Space Shuttle*, pp. 148–71; Jenkins, *Space Shuttle*, pp. 225–27.

90. Aeronautics and Space Engineering Board, "Report of Ad Hoc Committee on Liquid Rocket Propulsion Technologies," p. 16 (see chap. 2, n. 122); Rockwell International, "Press Information: Space Shuttle," pp. 9, 51–53 (see chap. 2, n. 124); Jenkins, *Space Shuttle*, pp. 225–27.

91. *CPIA/M5 Liquid Propellant Engine Manual*, Unit 174, J-2 Engine, and Unit 195, Space Shuttle Main Engine.

92. Jenkins, *Space Shuttle*, pp. 186–87; Rockwell International, "Press Information: Space Shuttle," p. 46; Heppenheimer, *Development of the Space Shuttle*, pp. 68–69, quotation from p. 68; Dunar and Waring, *Power to Explore*, p. 293.

93. Dunar and Waring, *Power to Explore*, pp. 292 (first quotation), 294, 301 (second quotation), 323; Jenkins, *Space Shuttle*, p. 186; CAIB, *Report*, 1:9, third and fourth quotations (see chap. 2, n. 128).

94. Jenkins, *Space Shuttle*, pp. 186, 231; Heppenheimer, *Development of the Space Shuttle*, pp. 191–92; Dunar and Waring, *Power to Explore*, p. 292.

95. Heppenheimer, *Development of the Space Shuttle*, pp. 190–91; Jenkins, *Space Shuttle*, p. 229.

96. Jenkins, *Space Shuttle*, pp. 230–31, 422; Rockwell International, "Press Information: Space Shuttle," p. 46; Dunar and Waring, *Power to Explore*, p. 304.

97. Rockwell International, "Press Information: Space Shuttle," pp. 47–49; Jenkins, *Space Shuttle*, p. 421; Heppenheimer, *Development of the Space Shuttle*, p. 194.

98. Heppenheimer, *Development of the Space Shuttle*, pp. 191–92; Dunar and Waring, *Power to Explore*, pp. 304–305, quotation from p. 304; Jenkins, *Space Shuttle*, pp. 231, 421; CAIB, *Report*, 1:14.

99. CAIB, *Report*, 1:52.

100. Ibid., pp. 52, 53, 122, quotations from pp. 52 and 53, respectively.

101. Ibid., pp. 9, 52–53, quotations from pp. 52–53.

102. Ibid., pp. 97, 121, for first and last quotations; Ralph Vartabedian, "NASA Still Vexed by Foam Woes," *Los Angeles Times*, Aug. 16, 2003, pp. A1, A26, quotations (including Pike's) from p. A26.

103. CAIB, *Report*, 1:54, first, third, and fourth quotations from "Foam Fracture under Hydrostatic Pressure," which Osheroff wrote; Vartabedian, "NASA Still Vexed by Foam Woes," p. A26, second quotation, Vartabedian's paraphrase of Osheroff.

Chapter 6

1. Koppes, *JPL*, esp. pp. 18–19 (see chap. 1, n. 26); Malina, "Rocketry in California," pp. 3–6 (see chap. 1, n. 24); Malina, "Army Air Corps Jet Propulsion Research Project," pp. 155, 158 (see chap 1, n. 25).

2. Material since last note from Winter and James, "Highlights of 50 Years of Aerojet," p. 30n1 (supplemental) (see chap. 1, n. 26); FBI file on Parsons, No. 65-59589, p. 8, seen in the FBI archives, Washington, D.C.; Andrew G. Haley, *Rocketry and Space Exploration* (Princeton, N.J.: Van Nostrand, 1958), p. 100; von Kármán with Edson, *Wind and Beyond*, pp. 245–46 (see chap. 1, n. 6); von Kármán with Malina, "Characteristics of the Ideal Solid Propellant Rocket Motor" (JPL Report No. 1-4, 1940), in *Collected Works of Theodore von Kármán* (London: Butterworths, 1956), IV:94–106 (1940–51); Malina, "Army Air Corps Jet Propulsion Research Project," pp. 169–76, 183–87; P. Thomas Carroll, "Historical Origins of the Sergeant Missile Powerplant," in *History of Rocketry and Astronautics*, ed. Kristan R. Lattu, AAS History Series (San Diego: Univelt, 1989), 8:123–26; J. W. Parsons and M. M. Mills, "The Development of an Asphalt Base Solid Propellant," GALCIT Project No. 1, Report No. 15, Oct. 16, 1942, in JPL Archives.

3. Winter and James, "Highlights of 50 Years of Aerojet," pp. 2–3; Malina, "Army Air Corps Jet Propulsion Project," pp. 194–95; Malina, "A Review of Developments in Liquid Propellant Jet (Rocket) Propulsion at the ACJP Project and the Aerojet Engineering Corporation," report prepared for the Special Office of Scientific Research and Development Committee Meeting, Feb. 17, 1944, esp. p. 2, folder 9.2 of the Malina Collection, Manuscripts Division, Library of Congress.

4. Carroll, "Historical Origins," pp. 130–31; Koppes, *JPL*, pp. 13, 36; oral history interview (OHI) of Charles Bartley by John Bluth (then JPL oral historian), Carlsbad, Calif., Oct. 3–4, 1995, pp. 10–28, 34–35, 43–44.

5. Sutton, "Polymers to Propellants," pp. 1–3 (see chap. 2, n. 133); see also Sutton's "How a Tiny Laboratory in Kansas City Grew into a Giant Corporation: A History of Thiokol and Rockets, 1926–1996" (Chadds Ford, Pa.: privately printed, 1997), pp. 3–8 (cited below as "History of Thiokol").

6. Sutton, "Polymers to Propellants," pp. 4–5; Bartley OHI, p. 28; Carroll, "Historical Origins," p. 133.

7. Previous two paragraphs are based on Carroll, "Historical Origins," pp. 132–38; Bartley OHI, pp. 43–46, and Carroll's OHI with John I. Shafer, July 7, 1970, seen in the JPL Archives, esp. pp. 17, 20–21, 30–33. On ABL, see Moore, "Solid Rocket Development at Allegany Ballistics Laboratory," pp. 1–5 (see

chap. 1, n. 59); Joseph W. Wiggins, "Hermes: Milestone in U.S. Aerospace Progress," *Aerospace Historian* 21, no. 1 (Mar. 1974): 34 (hereafter cited as Wiggins, "Hermes").

8. Joseph W. Wiggins, "The Earliest Large Solid Rocket Motor–the Hermes," paper presented at the AIAA 9th Annual Meeting and Technical Display, Jan. 8–10, 1973, Washington, D.C., p. 345 (hereafter cited as Wiggins, "The Hermes" to distinguish it from Wiggins "Hermes"); H. L. Thackwell Jr., and J. I. Shafer, "The Applicability of Solid Propellants to Rocket Vehicles of V-2 Size and Performance," JPL ORDCIT Project Memorandum No. 4-25, July 21, 1948, p. 2 in a portion of the memorandum released to the author by JPL and its NASA Management Office; L. G. Dunn and M. M. Mills, "The Status and Future Program for Research and Development of Solid Propellants," Jet Propulsion Laboratory Memorandum No. 4-5, Mar. 19, 1945, p. 8; M. Summerfield, J. I. Shafer, H. L. Thackwell Jr., and C. E. Bartley, "The Applicability of Solid Propellants to High-Performance Rocket Vehicles," JPL ORDCIT Project Memorandum No. 4-17, Oct. 1, 1947, pp. 11, 23; Paul J. Meeks, David Altman, and John I. Shafer, "Summary of Solid-Propellant Activities at the Jet Propulsion Laboratory California Institute of Technology," Memorandum JPL-11, JPL, Caltech, Aug. 15, 1951, table V, seen in JPL Archives, JPL Historical Collection, folder 3-981 (other JPL reports and memos also from the JPL Archives); Raymond E. Wiech Jr. and Robert F. Strauss, *Fundamentals of Rocket Propulsion* (New York: Reinhold, 1960), p. 78.

9. Karl Klager and Albert O. Dekker, "Early Solid Composite Rockets," unpublished paper dated Oct. 1972, pp. 13–24; Technical Memoir by Dr. H. W. Ritchey [of Thiokol], ca. 1980, p. 6, kindly supplied by Ernie (E. S.) Sutton.

10. Sutton, "Polymers to Propellants," pp. 6–7; Dave Dooling, "Thiokol: Firm Celebrates 30 Years of Space Technology," *The Huntsville Times*, Apr. 22, 1979, pp. 4–5, seen in NHRC, folder 010912, "II Thiokol."

11. Sutton, "Polymers to Propellants," pp. 9, 23; Sutton, "History of Thiokol," p. 58; Wiggins, "The Hermes," p. 345; Shafer OHI, p. 18.

12. Edward N. Hall, "Air Force Missile Experience," *Air University Quarterly Review* 9 (Summer 1957): 22–23; Wiggins, "The Hermes," p. 344.

13. "Memorandum to Dr. L. F. Welenetz," n.d.; A. T. Guzzo, "Progress Report: Development of Standard Operating Procedures for Manufacture of Polysulfide-Perchlorate Propellants," Thiokol Corporation, Redstone Division Report No. 26-51, Nov. 1951, p. 3. Ernie Sutton generously sent me these two and one other early Thiokol document from his collection.

14. Sutton, "History of Thiokol," p. 28; Guzzo, "Progress Report," pp. 3–8; Wiggins, "The Hermes," p. 422.

15. Carroll, "Historical Origins," pp. 140–41; J. D. Hunley, "The Evolution of Large Solid Propellant Rocketry in the United States," *Quest: The History of Spaceflight Quarterly* 6 (Spring 1998): pp. 25, 34n22; F. G. Denison and Larry Thackwell, "Progress of SERGEANT Program," Dec. 20, 1949, report seen in JPL Archives, JPL #5 folder 53, "Sergeant Reports," and documents in JPL #5, folder 49, "Sergeant Reports, 8/49–3/50."

16. Sutton, "History of Thiokol," p. 29; notes of a telephone conversation between P. Thomas Carroll, JPL, and Richard W. Porter, General Electric Company, Aug. 7, 1972, seen in the JPL Archives, JPL History Collection, folder 3-574.

17. Wiggins, "The Hermes," pp. 347–48, 355; notes of telephone conversation between Carroll and Porter.

18. Wiggins, "The Hermes," pp. 357–62.

19. Sutton, "Polymers to Propellants," p. 11; Wiggins, "The Hermes," pp. 363, 388–90.

20. Wiggins, "The Hermes," p. 421.

21. Ibid., pp. 389, 396, 400–401. Quotation taken from Sutton, "Polymers to Propellants," p. 10. See also Wiggins, "Hermes," p. 39.

22. E. W. Price, C. L. Horine, and C. W. Snyder, "Eaton Canyon: A History of Rocket Motor Research and Development in the Caltech-NDRC-Navy Rocket Program, 1941–1946," paper delivered at the 34th AIAA/ASME/SAE/ASEE Joint Propulsion Conference & Exhibit, July 13–15, 1998, Cleveland, Ohio, pp. 2, 4, 8; G. B. Kistiakowsky and Ralph Connor, "Molded Solid Propellants," in *Chemistry: A History of the Chemical Components of the National Defense Research Committee, 1940–1946* (Boston: Little, Brown, 1948), pp. 96–97; Albert B. Christman, *Sailors, Scientists, and Rockets: Origins of the Navy Rocket Program and of the Naval Ordnance Test Station, Inyokern*, in *History of the Naval Weapons Center, China Lake, California* (Washington, D.C.: Naval History Division, 1971), 1:13–14, 35, 100–101, 104–106, 113; John E. Burchard, ed., *Rockets, Guns and Targets* (Boston: Little, Brown, 1948), pp. 14–22, 43–82; e-mail comments on the first draft of parts of this chapter by Ray Miller, May 15, 2002; Constance McLaughlin Green, Harry C. Thompson, and Peter C. Roots, *United States Army in World War II, the Technical Services, the Ordnance Department: Planning Munitions for War* (Washington, D.C.: Department of the Army, 1955), pp. 353–60.

23. Price, Horine, and Snyder, "Eaton Canyon," pp. 1–10, 18, 28; Christman, *Sailors, Scientists, and Rockets*, pp. 167–204, 212; "From the Desert to the Sea: A Brief Overview of the History of China Lake," http://www.nawcwpns.navy.mil/clmf/hist.html (accessed Aug. 18, 2000); Green, Thomson, and Roots, *Planning Munitions for War*, p. 354; C. W. Snyder, "Caltech's *Other* Rocket Project: Personal Recollections," *Engineering & Science* (Spring 1991): 3–13; Goodstein, *History of California Institute of Technology*, pp. 251–59 (see chap. 1, n. 25); Homer E. Newell Jr., *Sounding Rockets* (New York: McGraw-Hill, 1959), pp. 96–97; Shortal, *A New Dimension*, p. 83 (see chap. 2, n. 57).

24. Material since last note from R. Cargill Hall, "Origins and Development of the Vanguard and Explorer Satellite Programs," *The Airpower Historian* 11, no. 1 (Jan. 1964): 111; Moore, "Solid Rocket Development at ABL," pp. 5–6; Hunley, "Evolution," pp. 27–28; Dyer and Sicilia, *Labors of a Modern Hercules*, pp. 2, 9, 257–58 (see chap. 1, n. 59); and author's telephone interview with Daniel W. Dembrow, June 29, 1995; W. A. Noyes Jr., ed., *Chemistry: A History of the Chemistry Components of the National Defense Research Committee, 1940–1946* (Boston: Little, Brown, 1948), pp. 17, 26–33, 127–28; e-mail sent to author by Ronald L. Simmons, July 9, 2002, and the one-page bio he sent a few days later.

25. Vanguard Staff, "Project Vanguard Report . . .1 June 1957," p. 2-50 (see chap. 1, n. 58); Vanguard Staff, "Project Vanguard Report . . . September 15, 1956," p. 7 (see chap. 1, n. 59); report, A. H. Kitzmiller and E. J. Skurzynski, Hercules Powder Company, to R. Winer, subject: MPR—JATO Unit X241 A1 (Project Vanguard) Problem 4-a-81, Sept. 17, 1956, in NA RG 255, Records of the National Aeronautics and Space Administration, Vanguard Division, Project Vanguard Case Files, "Hercules Powder—Allegany Ballistics Laboratory Progress Reports," box 6.

26. Hunley, "Evolution," p. 28; Dyer and Sicilia, *Labors of a Modern Hercules*, pp. 9, 318–20; Brian A. Wilson, "The History of Composite Motor Case De-

sign," AIAA paper 93-1782, presented at the 29th Joint Propulsion Conference and Exhibit, June 28–30, 1993, Monterey, Calif., no pagination; "Lightweight Pressure Vessels," portion of a technical memoir by H. W. Ritchey, ca. 1980, kindly provided by Ernie Sutton.

27. Vanguard Staff, "Project Vanguard Report . . . 1 June 1957," p. 2-52.

28. ABL Report Series No. 40, "JATO X248 A2, A Solid Propellant Thrust Unit with High Impulse, High Performance, Wide Applications," Nov. 1958, p. 7, in NA RG 255, Records of the National Aeronautics and Space Administration, Vanguard Division, Project Vanguard Case Files, "Hercules Powder Allegany Ballistics Laboratory Progress Reports," box 6; Louis A. Povinelli, "Particulate Damping in Solid-Propellant Combustion Instability," *AIAA Journal* 5, no. 10 (Oct. 1967): 1791–96; Code 4120 to Code 4100, subj.: Summary of Conference at ABL and Recommendations, Aug. 13, 1958, in NA RG 255, Records of the National Aeronautics and Space Administration, Vanguard Division, Project Vanguard Case Files, "Hercules Powder—Allegany Ballistics Laboratory Progress Reports," box 6; Green and Lomask, *Vanguard*, p. 287 (see chap. 1, n. 44); Jay Holmes, "ABL's Altair Runs Up 13–13 Record," *Missiles and Rockets*, June 6, 1960, p. 29.

29. Attachment to a letter, Director, U.S. Naval Research Laboratory to Commander, Arnold Engineering Development Center, Sept. 12, 1958, in NA RG 255, Records of the National Aeronautics and Space Administration, Vanguard Division, Project Vanguard Case Files, Arnold Engineering Development Center, box 2, entry 35; ABL Report Series No. 40, "JATO X248 A2," p. 7; Kurt R. Stehling, *Project Vanguard* (Garden City, N.Y.: Doubleday, 1961), pp. 128–29n.

30. Cagle, "History of the Sergeant," pp. 23–25, 31, 43–47, 97 (see chap. 1, n. 28).

31. Ibid., pp. 64–65, 193–94, 199–200, 202–203; Koppes, *JPL*, pp. 63–66, 71–77.

32. Cagle, "History of the Sergeant," pp. 278–79; J. D. Hunley, "The History of Solid-Propellant Rocketry: What We Do and Do Not Know," AIAA Paper 99-2925, presented at the 35th AIAA/ASME/SAE/ASEE Joint Propulsion Conference and Exhibit, June 20–24, 1999, Los Angeles, p. 2; Peter L. Nichols Jr., Robert J. Parks, and James D. Burke, "Solid-Propellant Development at the Jet Propulsion Laboratory," JPL, Caltech Publication No. 105, presented to Ad Hoc Committee on Large Solid-Propellant Rocket Engines, July 17, 1957, p. 11, seen in the JPL Archives, JPL Historical collection, folder 3-525.

33. Koppes, *JPL*, pp. 79–93; JPL, "Explorer I," *Astronautics* (Apr. 1958): 22, 83; Bullard, "History of the Redstone," pp. 140–46 (see chap. 1, n. 30); Grimwood and Strowd, "History of the Jupiter Missile System," p. 81 (see chap. 1, n. 30). (See chapter 1 in this book for details of this development.)

34. Lonnquest and Winkler, *To Defend and Deter*, pp. 209–15, 227–34, 259–64, 268–73 (see chap. 1, n. 51); Nicholas and Rossi, *U.S. Missile Data Book 1994*,, pp. 1-5 and 3-2 through 3-4 (see chap. 1, n. 27).

35. Spinardi, *From Polaris to Trident*, pp. 4–6, 31–34, 99–100, 148–53, 162, 187 (see chap. 1, n. 43); Fuhrman, "Fleet Ballistic Missile System," p. 6 (see chap. 1, n. 44); Sapolsky, *Polaris System Development*, pp. 26–29, 47 (see chap. 1, n. 84).

36. Sapolsky, *Polaris System Development*, pp. 8, 11, 26–28, 35–36, 45–47, 49–51, 55–56; Baar and Howard, *Polaris!* p. 15 (see chap. 1, n. 84); Spinardi, *Polaris to Trident*, pp. 25–26, 28; Philip D. Umholz, "The History of Solid Rocket Propulsion and Aerojet," AIAA paper 99-2927 presented at the AIAA/ASME/SAE/ASEE Joint Propulsion Conference, June 20–24, 1999, Los Angeles, unpaginated (5th page); author's OHI with Grayson Merrill, Annapolis, Md., Jan. 17, 2002, p. 6.

37. Hunley, "Evolution," p. 26, and the sources cited there (including a letter and telephone interviews with Karl Klager); J. F. Sparks and M. P. Friedlander III, "Fifty Years of Solid Propellant Technical Achievements at Atlantic Research Corporation," AIAA paper 99-2932 from the AIAA/ASME/SAE/ASEE Joint Propulsion Conference, June 20–24, 1999, Los Angeles, pp. 1, 8; letter, Charles B. Henderson to author, Oct. 16, 1997; and author's telephone OHI of Henderson, Oct. 15, 1997; Reily, *Rocket Scientists,* pp. 43–46 (see chap. 1, n. 85).

38. Material since last note from Gordon et al., *Aerojet,* pp. IV-98 through IV-103, quotations from Marvin Gold on p. IV-99 (see chap. 1, n. 85); short biographies of Dr. Klager that he generously provided; Hunley, "Evolution," p. 27; *CPIA/M1 Rocket Motor Manual,* Unit 233, July 1960 (see chap. 1, n. 60); and Fuhrman, "Fleet Ballistic Missile System," pp. 11–16.

39. Fuhrman, "Fleet Ballistic Missile System," pp. 12, 40; Nicholas and Rossi, *U.S. Missile Data Book, 1994,* p. 3–6; K[arl] Klager, "Early Polaris and Minuteman Solid Rocket History," unpublished paper kindly provided by Dr. Klager, pp. 6–8; Spinardi, *Polaris to Trident,* p. 52; letter, Commander, U.S. Naval Air Missile Test Center to Commandant, Eleventh Naval District, Dec. 6, 1957, NARA–Pacific Region (Laguna Niguel), RG 181, Naval Air Station Point Mugu, Calif., Central Subject Files, 1957–59, box 35, file A12; Arthur Menken, "History of the Pacific Missile Range, an Historical Report Covering the Period 1 July 1959 to 30 June 1960," in NARA–Pacific Region (Laguna Niguel), RG 181, History of PMR, 1959–74, box 33, p. 11; Eric Pace, "Willy A. Fiedler, 89, a Leading Missile Expert," *The New York Times Biographical Service,* Jan. 1998, p. 139, obituary for Jan. 29, 1998.

40. Fuhrman, "Fleet Ballistic Missile System," p. 13; Spinardi, *Polaris to Trident,* p. 53; Klager, "Early Polaris and Minuteman," pp. 7–8; "Polaris Solid Triumph for Aerojet: Major Breakthroughs Open New Era in Sea Warfare," *The Aerojet Booster,* Feb. 1959, p. 2, *Aerojet Booster* found in NASM Archives.

41. Fuhrman, "Fleet Ballistic Missile System," pp. 14–15; Spinardi, *Polaris to Trident,* p. 52.

42. See Hunley, "Evolution," p. 32, and the sources cited there; a letter from Edward W. Price to author, Oct. 12, 1999; OHI of VAdm. Levering Smith by Leroy Doig III and Elizabeth Babcock, Jan. 15, 1989, copy seen at the China Lake History Office; E. W. Price, "Combustion Instability," NOTS Technical Article 3, TP 2400, Feb. 1960, seen in the China Lake History Office.

43. Fuhrman, "Fleet Ballistic Missile System," p. 16; Hunley, "Evolution," p. 28; Dyer and Sicilia, *Labors of a Modern Hercules,* pp. 9, 318–20; "Lightweight Pressure Vessels," portion of a technical memoir by H. W. Ritchey, ca. 1980; Mike Gruntman, *Blazing the Trail: The Early History of Spacecraft and Rocketry* (Reston, Va.: AIAA, 2004), p. 173.

44. Hunley, "Evolution," p. 28; Dyer and Sicilia, *Labors of a Modern Hercules,* p. 322; *CPIA/M1 Rocket Motor Manual,* Unit 410, Polaris Model A2 Stage 2.

45. Moore, "Solid Rocket Development at ABL," pp. 5–7; Hunley, "Evolution," pp. 27–28; draft paper, Francis A. Warren and Charles H. Herty III, "U.S. Double-Base Solid Propellant Tactical Rockets of the 1950–1955 Era," presented at AIAA History Session, Jan. 8–10, 1973 (no pagination), and generously sent to author by Ed Price; e-mails from Ronald L. Simmons, July 9 and 12, 2002.

46. C. B. Henderson with comments by Rumbel, "The Development of Composite-Modified Double Base Propellants at the Atlantic Research Corporation," Sept. 30, 1998, encl. in letter, Henderson to Hunley, Oct. 8, 1998; three separate e-mails, Ronald L. Simmons to Hunley, July 15, 2002.

47. Fuhrman, "Fleet Ballistic Missile System," pp. 16–17; Spinardi, *Polaris to Trident*, pp. 63–65; *CPIA/M1 Rocket Motor Manual*, Unit 410, 59-DS-32,750, Polaris Model A2 Stage 2; "Modifications Raise Polaris' Range," *Missiles and Rockets*, Oct. 31, 1960, p. 36; bio, Rear Adm. Levering Smith, officer bio files, Naval Historical Center.

48. Fuhrman, "Fleet Ballistic Missile System," pp. 17–18; Hunley, "Evolution," p. 28; "Polaris A3 Firing Tests under Way," *Missiles and Rockets*, Aug. 13, 1962, p. 15; John F. Judge, "Aerojet Moves into Basic Glass," *Missiles and Rockets*, Mar. 18, 1963, p. 34; *CPIA/M1 Rocket Motor Manual*, Unit 376, 64-KS-74,500, Polaris Model A3 Mod 0, Stage 1 with which cf. Unit 375 for Model A2, Stage 1.

49. Fuhrman, "Fleet Ballistic Missile System," p. 18; Spinardi, *Polaris to Trident*, p. 69; "Problems May Cut Polaris A3 Range Goal," *Aviation Week & Space Technology*, Sept. 4, 1961, p. 31; *CPIA/M1 Rocket Motor Manual*, Units 375 and 376.

50. Spinardi, *Polaris to Trident*, p. 69; *CPIA/M1 Rocket Motor Manual*, Unit 411, 78-DS-31,935, Rocket Motor Mark 6 Mod 0, Polaris Model A3 Stage 2, and Unit 410, 59-DS-32,750, Rocket Motor Mark 4 Mod 0, Polaris Model A2 Stage 2; Adolf E. Oberth, *Principles of Solid Propellant Development* (Laurel, Md.: CPIA Publication 469, 1987), p. 2-13; Fuhrman, "Fleet Ballistic Missile System," p. 18.

51. Gordon et al., *Aerojet*, pp. IV-15 to IV-16; Neal, *Ace in the Hole*, p. 73 (see chap. 1, n. 88); Karl Klager and Albert O. Dekker, "Early Solid Composite Rockets," unpublished paper dated Oct. 1972, p. 22; letter, Hall to author, July 15, 2000; and Hunley, "Evolution," p. 25.

52. AF Intercontinental Ballistic Missile System Program Office, *Minuteman*, p. 17 (see chap. 1, n. 89); C. W. (Bill) Schnare OHI with James C. Hasdorf, Fairborne, Ohio, Aug. 5–6, 1975, pp. 145–47, 166 (seen at the AF Historical Research Agency) corroborated and supplemented by Schnare's telephone comments to author on May 23, 2002.

53. Kennedy, Kovacic, and Rea, "Solid Rocket History," pp. 13–14 (see chap. 1, n. 90); Neal, *Ace in the Hole*, pp. 85–86; Robert C. Anderson, "Minuteman to MX: The ICBM Evolution," *TRW/DSSG/Quest* (Autumn 1979): 33–36; "Mobility Designed into Minuteman," *Aviation Week*, Aug. 3, 1959, pp. 93–94.

54. Phillips, "Launch on December 63rd," pp. 14–15 (see chap. 1, n. 90); Kennedy, Kovacic, and Rea, "Solid Rocket History," pp. 10, 15; Frank G. McGuire, "Minuteman Third-Stage Award Nears," *Missiles and Rockets* (Oct. 17, 1960): 36–37; William Leavitt, "Minuteman—Ten Years of Solid Performance," *Air Force Magazine* 54 (Mar. 1971): 26; Lonnquest and Winkler, *To Defend and Deter*, p. 242.

55. Kennedy, Kovacic, and Rea, "Solid Rocket History," pp. 14, 17; Klager, "Early Polaris and Minuteman," pp. 17–18; Neal, *Ace in the Hole*, pp. 136–37.

56. Kennedy, Kovacic, and Rea, "Solid Rocket History," pp. 15, 17; Neal, *Ace in the Hole*, pp. 76, 83, 125, 137–38; Anderson, "Minuteman to MX," p. 38.

57. Phillips, "Launch on December 63rd," p. 62.

58. Ibid.; Neal, *Ace in the Hole*, pp. 147–51; Leavitt, "Minuteman—Ten Years of Solid Performance," p. 26; U.S. Air Force, Astronautics Laboratory, fact sheet, "Air Force Astronautics Laboratory," Feb. 1988, pp. 2–3; Jacob Neufeld's OHI with Colonel Hall, July 11, 1989, p. 22, copy kindly sent to author by Neufeld.

59. Lt. Gen. Otto J. Glasser OHI by Lt. Col. John J. Allen, Washington, D.C., Jan. 5–6, 1984, pp. 75–77, quotations on p. 76, copy in the Air Force Historical Research Agency's file K239.0512-1566; Kennedy, Kovacic, and Rea, "Solid

Rocket History," p. 15. Cf. John Lonnquest, Lonnquest and Winkler, *To Defend and Deter*, p. 246n.

60. Phillips, "Launch on December 63rd," p. 62; Leavitt, "Minuteman," p. 26; AF ICBM Program Office, "Minuteman Weapon System," pp. 14, 17; Sutton, "Polymers to Propellants," p. 13; E. S. Sutton, "From Polysulfides to CTPB Binders—a Major Transition in Solid Propellant Binder Chemistry," AIAA paper 84-1236, presented at the AIAA/SAE/ASME 20th Joint Propulsion Conference, June 11–13, 1984, Cincinnati, Ohio, pp. 6–7; F. J. Mastriola and K. Klager, "Solid Propellants Based on Polybutadiene Binders," reprinted from "Advances in Chemistry Series," no. 88: "Propellant Manufacture, Hazards, and Testing" (American Chemical Society, 1969), pp. 122–23; Oberth, *Principles*, p. 2-8.

61. Sutton, "Polysulfides to CTPB," pp. 6–8; Irving Stone, "Minuteman Propulsion—Part I: Minuteman ICBM Solid Motor Stages Enter Production Phase," *Aviation Week & Space Technology*, Aug. 27, 1962, p. 57; "Propulsion Characteristics Summary, TU-122, Wing I," Feb. 1, 1963, extract from the "Gray Books," generously provided by Bill Elliott of the Air Force Materiel Command History Office; Thiokol Chemical Corporation, "Rocket Propulsion Data," 3d ed. (Bristol, Pa.: Thiokol, 1961), entry for TU-122.

62. Klager, "Early Polaris and Minuteman," p. 16; Irving Stone, "Aerojet Second Stage Must Withstand Heaviest Stresses," *Aviation Week & Space Technology*, Sept. 3, 1962, p. 71; "Propulsion Characteristics Summary, M-56 Wing I," extract from the AF Gray Books, Feb. 3, 1964; *CPIA/M1 Rocket Motor Manual*, Unit 362.

63. Hunley, "Evolution," esp. pp. 27–28; Dyer and Sicilia, *Labors of a Modern Hercules*, p. 322; Irving Stone, "Hercules Stage 3 Uses Glass Fiber Case," *Aviation Week & Space Technology*, Sept. 10, 1962, pp. 162–65, 167; "The Minuteman: The Mobilization Programme for a Thousand Minutemen," *Interavia*, no. 3 (1961): 310; Oberth, *Solid Propellant Development*, p. 2-13; "Propellant Characteristics Summary, 65-DS-15,520," Sept. 29, 1961. Ronald L. Simmons, e-mail to author on July 9, 2002.

64. Anderson, "Minuteman to MX," p. 39; "Propellant Characteristics Summary, 65-DS-15,520," Sept. 29, 1961; "Propellant Characteristics Summary (M-56AJ-3, Wing I)," Apr. 10, 1962; "Propellant Characteristics Summary (TU-122, Wing I)," Jan. 20, 1962; Ogden Air Logistics Center, "Minuteman Weapon System: History and Description" (Hill AFB, Utah: OO-ALC/MMG, Aug. 1990), pp. 27, 33; Lonnquest and Winkler, *To Defend and Deter*, pp. 242, 246.

65. "Propulsion Characteristics Summary (M-56AJ-3, Wing I)," Apr. 10, 1962, and "Propulsion Characteristics Summary (M-56A1, Wing II)," Nov. 9, 1962; Kennedy, Kovacic, and Rea, "Solid Rocket History," p. 16; Stone, "Aerojet Second Stage," p. 68; Klager, "Early Polaris and Minuteman," p. 16; Anderson, "Minuteman to MX," p. 43.

66. Kennedy, Kovacic, and Rea, "Solid Rocket History," pp. 17–18; "Propulsion Characteristics Summary (M-56A1, Wing II)," Nov. 9, 1962; "Propulsion Characteristics Summary (SRJ19-AJ-1)," Jan. 22, 1966.

67. Sutton, "Polysulfides to CTPB," p. 8; Sparks and Friedlander, "Fifty Years at Atlantic Research," p. 8.

68. Gordon et al., *Aerojet*, p. IV-84; Kennedy, Kovacic, and Rea, "Solid Rocket History," p. 18 (source of the quotation); "Propulsion Characteristics Summary (M-56A1, Wing II)," Nov. 9, 1962, and "Propulsion Characteristics Summary (SRJ19-AJ-1)," Jan. 22, 1966; Hunley, "Evolution," p. 29, and the sources it cites.

69. Hunley, "History of Solid-Propellant Rocketry," p. 7; Sutton, "Polysulfides to CTPB," p. 8; Sutton, "Polymers to Propellants," p. 14; "Career Chronology" and "History Questions" generously sent to me by Robert C. Corley via e-mail on June 11 and 21, 2002; "Functional Polymers Products and Research," www.elf-atochem.com (accessed Apr. 10, 2002).

70. "Propulsion Characteristics Summary (M-56A1, Wing II)," Nov. 9, 1962, and "Propulsion Characteristics Summary (SRJ19-AJ-1)," Jan. 22, 1966; Klager, "Early Polaris and Minuteman," p. 18; Kennedy, Kovacic, and Rea, "Solid Rocket History," p. 18; Fuhrman, "Fleet Ballistic Missile System," p. 18; Ogden ALC, "Minuteman Weapon System," Aug. 1990, p. 50; MacKenzie, *Inventing Accuracy*, p. 150 (see chap. 1, n. 17).

71. Lonnquest and Winkler, *To Defend and Deter*, p. 247; Nicholas and Rossi, *U.S. Missile Data Book*, 1994, p. 3-2.

72. Hunley, "Evolution," p. 32; "History of CPIAC [Chemical Propulsion Information Analysis Center]," http://www.cpia.uhu/about/index.php?action= history (accessed July 14, 2006); comments of Edward W. Price on a draft of one of author's manuscripts, Aug. 4, 2000; Schnare OHI, pp. 131–32.

73. Ogden ALC, "Minuteman Weapon System," Aug. 1990, p. 54; Kennedy, Kovacic, and Rea, "Solid Rocket History," p. 20; Wilson, "Composite Motor Case Design"; Gordon, et al., *Aerojet*, pp. IV-104 to IV-105; "Propulsion Characteristics Summary (SRJ19-AJ-1)," Jan. 22, 1966; "Propulsion Characteristics Summary (M57A1)," Jan. 4, 1966; "Propulsion Characteristics Summary (SR73-AJ-1)," Apr. 15, 1969; "Stage III for USAF's Minuteman III," *Aerojet General Booster*, Sept. 1967; *CPIA/M1 Rocket Motor Manual*, Unit 457; Wilbur Andrepont, e-mails of Aug. 9, 1999, and July 22, 2000, to author.

74. Ogden ALC, "Minuteman Weapon System," Aug. 1990, p. 54; Kennedy, Kovacic, and Rea, "Solid Rocket History," p. 20; *CPIA/M1 Rocket Motor Manual*, Unit 412.

75. Lonnquest and Winkler, *To Defend and Deter*, pp. 241–43; Nicholas and Rossi, *U.S. Missile Data Book*, 1994, pp. 3-5, 3-8.

Chapter 7

1. Piper, "History of Titan III," pp. 101–103 (see chap. 2, n. 94); Space Division, "SAMSO Chronology," p. 110 (see chap. 2, n. 10); Harwood, *Raise Heaven and Earth*, p. 356 (see chap. 2, n. 95).

2. "Brainpower First in United's Space Venture," *Business Week*, Mar. 5, 1960, pp. 138–44 (quotation from p. 139); Robert Lindsey, "UTC Chief Sees Tighter Rocket Market," *Missiles and Rockets*, Apr. 18, 1966, p. 22; "Highlights from the History of United Technologies," pp. 35–42 (see chap. 2, n. 96); J. D. Hunley, telephone interviews with Barnet Adelman, Nov. 20, 1996, and Feb. 23, 2000, and with David Altman, Dec. 22, 1999; Michael H. Gorn, *Harnessing the Genie: Science and Technology Forecasting for the Air Force, 1944–1986* (Washington, D.C.: Office of Air Force History, 1988), pp. 48–49, 89–93; and Michael H. Gorn, *The Universal Man: Theodore von Kármán's Life in Aeronautics* (Washington, D.C.: Smithsonian Institution Press, 1992), pp. 90–101, 136–37, 150–54; Hunley, "Minuteman and the Development of Solid-Rocket Launch Technology," pp. 229–300 (see chap. 1, n. 82).

3. Gordon et al., *Aerojet*, p. IV-38 (see chap. 1, n. 85); Karl Klager, "Segmented Rocket Demonstration: Historic Development Prior to Their Use as Space Boosters," in *History of Rocketry and Aeronautics*, ed. Hunley, 20:159–70 (see chap. 1,

n. 13); Andrepont and Felix, "Large Solid Rocket Motor Development," p. 2 (see chap. 2, n. 96); comments of Bernard Ross Felix, formerly vice president of engineering and technology, CSD, on an earlier draft of this chapter, Aug. 22, 2000.

4. Klager, "Segmented Rocket Demonstration," pp. 163–87; Gordon et al., *Aerojet*, pp. IV-38, IV-39; Andrepont and Felix, "Large Solid Rocket Motor Development," pp. 2, 19; Hunley, "Minuteman and Solid-Rocket Launch Technology," pp. 269–72.

5. Andrepont and Felix, "Large Solid Rocket Motor Development," pp. 3, 7, 19; Hawkes, "United Technology Builds Larger Booster Capabilities," pp. 56–65, esp. p. 57 (see chap. 2, n. 96); "Solid-Fueled Rocket Nears Crucial Test," *Business Week*, June 3, 1961, pp. 42–49, esp. p. 49; UTC Pamphlet, "120-Inch . . . Rocket," esp. p. 5 (see chap. 2, n. 96).

6. UTC Pamphlet, "120-Inch . . . Rocket," p. 16; Andrepont and Felix, "Large Solid Rocket Motor Development," p. 7; CSD booklet, *A Most Reliable Booster System* (section titled "CSD Facilities Growth through Titan III") (see chap. 2, n. 96).

7. H. L. Thackwell Jr., "The Application of Solid Propellants to Space Flight Vehicles," apparently unpublished paper, May 1, 1959, no pagination; Thackwell, "Status of United States Large Solid Rocket Programs," AIAA paper no. 65-422 presented at AIAA Second Annual Meeting, July 26–29, 1965, San Francisco, p. 10.

8. UTC Pamphlet, "120-Inch . . . Rocket," p. 16; Andrepont and Felix, "Large Solid Rocket Motor Development," p. 7.

9. Piper, "History of Titan III," pp. 130–31, 136; letter, Brig. Gen. J. S. Bleymaier, System Program Director, SSD/SSB, to Lt. Gen. Donald L. Putt (Ret), United Aircraft Corporation, July 23, 1963, supporting document 24 to Piper's history; UTC Pamphlet, "120-Inch . . . Rocket," p. 13.

10. Hunley, "Evolution," pp. 30–31 (see chap. 1, n. 36), and the sources cited there, esp. *CPIA/M1 Rocket Motor Manual*, Unit 559, Titan III and Titan IIIC Zero Stage (see chap. 1, n. 60); interviews, Hunley with Herman P. Weyland, Paul G. Willoughby, Stan Backlund, and J. G. Hill at Chemical Systems Division, Nov. 18, 1996; Andrepont and Felix, "Large Solid Rocket Motor Development," p. 7.

11. CSD, "A Most Reliable Booster System," n.p., section titled "Development of Major Components"; UTC Pamphlet, "120-Inch . . . Rocket," pp. 3, 5; Richards and Powell, "Titan 3 and Titan 4," p. 125 (see chap. 2, n. 97); Andrepont and Felix, "Large Solid Rocket Motor Development," p. 7; Hunley, 1996 interview with Adelman; e-mail comments to author by Ross Felix, Jan. 8, 1997, telephone interview with him Feb. 10, 1997, and his comments on a draft of Hunley, "Minuteman and Solid-Rocket Launch Technology," Aug. 22 and 23, 2000.

12. CSD, "A Most Reliable Booster System," n.p., section titled "Development of Major Components"; comments of Bernard Ross Felix, Aug. 22, 2000; Andrepont and Felix, "Large Solid Rocket Motor Development," p. 7; Richards and Powell, "Titan 3 and Titan 4," p. 125; "Titan 34D Recovery Program," Aug. 13, 1986, seen in the Samuel C. Phillips Collection, Manuscript Division, Library of Congress, box 21, folder 1, pp. 26, 35; Ballistics System Division, "Titan III Launch System Independent Panel Reviews," Aug. 1986, 1 of 3, Phillips Collection, box 20, folder 8, no pagination; "Titan 34D Flight Readiness Meeting," Vandenberg AFB, Nov. 5, 1986, in Phillips Collection, box 21, folder 5, pp. 10, 12.

13. CSD, "A Most Reliable Booster System," n.p., section titled "Development of Major Components"; Andrepont and Felix, "Large Solid Rocket Motor Development," p. 7; John F. Judge, "Westinghouse Know-How Speeds Flow of 120-in. Cases for Titan III-C's," *Missiles and Rockets,* Sept. 14, 1964, pp. 32–33.

14. *CPIA/M1 Rocket Motor Manual,* Unit 559; "Highlights from the History of United Technologies," p. 42; "SAMSO Chronology," p. 159 (see chap. 1, n. 72).

15. "SAMSO Chronology," pp. 286, 307; Richards and Powell, "Titan 3 and Titan 4," p. 138; CSD, "A Most Reliable Booster System," n.p., section titled "CSD Facilities Growth through Titan III."

16. *CPIA/M1 Rocket Motor Manual,* Units 559, Titan III and Titan IIIC Zero Stage, and 578, Titan 34D Stage Zero SRM; "Titan Launch Vehicle History," *Astronautics & Aeronautics,* June 1975, p. 76.

17. Martin Marietta, "Fact Sheet, Titan IV," n.d., document III-28 in Geiger and Clear, "History of Space and Missile Organization" (see chap. 2, n. 37); *CPIA/MI Rocket Motor Manual,* Unit 578, Titan 34D, Stage Zero SRM, compared with Unit 629, Titan IV SRM, July 1996; Richards and Powell, "Titan 3 and Titan 4," pp. 139–41.

18. Richards and Powell, "Titan 3 and Titan 4," pp. 140–41; Air Force Fact Sheet, "Titan IVB," Jan. 29, 1997, document II-180 in Herbert P. Carlin et al., "History of the Air Force Materiel Command, Oct. 1, 1995–Sept. 30, 1996," vol. V, seen in Air Force Historical Research Agency, K226.01; Hunley, "Minuteman and the Development of Solid-Rocket Launch Technology," pp. 281–83, for details on SRMU.

19. Jenkins, *Space Shuttle,* pp. 184–85 (see chap. 2, n. 110); Heppenheimer, *Development of the Space Shuttle,* pp. 71–78 (see chap. 2, n. 117); John M. Logsdon et al., eds., *Exploring the Unknown: Selected Documents in the History of the U.S. Civil Space Program* (Washington, D.C.: NASA SP-4407, 1999), vol. IV, Document II-17, "The Comptroller General of the United States, Decision in the Matter of Protest by Lockheed Propulsion Company, June 24, 1974," p. 269.

20. Jenkins, *Space Shuttle,* pp. 185–86; Bromberg, *NASA and the Space Industry,* p. 100 (see chap. 2, n. 45); Heppenheimer, *Development of the Space Shuttle,* pp. 71–78; "Comptroller General Decision," p. 271 (quotation).

21. The previous two paragraphs summarize a longer treatment in Hunley, "Minuteman and the Development of Solid-Rocket Launch Technology," pp. 271–78.

22. Jenkins, *Space Shuttle,* p. 186; Hunley, "Minuteman and the Development of Solid-Rocket Launch Technology," pp. 278–80; Rockwell International, "Press Information: Space Shuttle Transportation System" (see chap. 2, n. 124); *CPIA/M1 Rocket Motor Manual,* Unit 556, Space Shuttle Booster; Heppenheimer, *Development of the Space Shuttle,* p. 175.

23. Heppenheimer, *Development of the Space Shuttle,* pp. 175–76.

24. Heppenheimer, *Development of the Space Shuttle,* p. 176; Rockwell International, "Press Information: Space Shuttle Transportation System," pp. 9, 21–22; *CPIA/M1 Rocket Motor Manual,* Unit 613, Redesigned Space Shuttle Booster, June 1993.

25. Heppenheimer, *Development of the Space Shuttle,* pp. 176–77.

26. Comments of Bernard Ross Felix, Aug. 22, 2000, on a draft of Hunley, "Minuteman and Solid-Rocket Launch Technology," which also see, pp. 278–80; Andrepont and Felix, "Large Solid Rocket Motor Development," pp. 7, 14; Heppenheimer, *Development of the Space Shuttle,* pp. 177–78; Hunley, "Evolu-

tion," pp. 31, 37; NASA, "National Space Transportation System Reference," 1:33a–33c (see chap. 2, n. 126).

27. Heppenheimer, *Development of the Space Shuttle*, pp. 178–79; comments of Bernard Ross Felix, Aug. 22, 2000; Rockwell International, "Press Information: Space Shuttle Transportation System," pp. 21–22; *CPIA/M1 Rocket Motor Manual*, Unit 556; e-mail to author from Dennis R. Jenkins, Sept. 17, 2003, correcting data in some of the sources above.

28. Hunley, "Minuteman and Solid Rocket Launch Technology," p. 280; Jenkins, *Space Shuttle*, p. 429; Rockwell International, "Press Information: Space Shuttle Transportation System," Jan. 1984, p. 22; Isakowitz, *Space Launch Systems* (1991), p. 252 (see chap. 2, n. 10); Heppenheimer, *Development of the Space Shuttle*, pp. 179–81.

29. Jenkins, *Space Shuttle*, pp. 425–26; Rockwell International, "Press Information: Space Shuttle Transportation System," p. 21; "Spacecraft Propulsion" in Morton Thiokol, Inc. Aerospace Group, *Aerospace Facts*, p. 4, seen in NASM Archives, B7-820030-02, "Thiokol General, Publications, Aerospace Facts."

30. Jenkins, *Space Shuttle*, pp. 227–28; Heppenheimer, *Development of the Space Shuttle*, pp. 178, 183.

31. Previous two paragraphs based on Heppenheimer, *Development of the Space Shuttle*, pp. 186–89.

32. Hansen, *Spaceflight Revolution*, pp. 197–200 (see chap. 2, n. 55); Joseph Shortal, *A New Dimension*, pp. vii and passim (see chap. 2, n. 57).

33. Shortal, *A New Dimension*, pp. 706–707; *CPIA/M1 Rocket Motor Manual*, Unit 228, Sergeant.

34. Shortal, *A New Dimension*, pp. 707–708; Hansen, *Spaceflight Revolution*, pp. 199–200.

35. Shortal, *A New Dimension*, p. 709; *CPIA/M1 Rocket Motor Manual*, Unit 277, Algol I, Aerojet Senior.

36. Shortal, *A New Dimension*, pp. 708–709; *CPIA/M1 Rocket Motor Manual*, Unit 237, Castor, and Unit 228, Sergeant; Thiokol, *Rocket Propulsion Data*, TX-12 (Sergeant) and TX-33-35 (see chap. 8, n. 36).

37. Andrew Wilson, "Scout—NASA's Small Satellite Launcher," *Spaceflight* 21, no. 11 (Nov. 1979): 449–50; Hansen, *Spaceflight Revolution*, pp. 209–10; Shortal, *A New Dimension*, p. 720; *Report to the Congress . . . , January 1 to December 31, 1960*, p. 91 (see chap. 2, n. 16).

38. Leiss, "Scout Launch Vehicle Program Final Report," pp. 53–54, 56, 65, 131 (see chap. 2, n. 55); Wilson, "Scout," pp. 451–52; *CPIA/M1 Rocket Motor Manual*, Unit 410, Polaris Model A2 Stage 2; Unit 411, Polaris Model A3, Stage 2; Unit 421, X259A2, Antares II.

39. Arms, "Thor," pp. 6–39, 6–41 (see chap. 1, n. 77); Isakowitz, *Space Launch Systems* (1991), p. 295; E. S. Sutton, "How a Tiny Laboratory in Kansas City Grew into a Giant Corporation: A History of Thiokol and Rockets, 1926–1996" (Chadds Ford, Pa.: privately printed by Ernie Sutton, 1997), pp. 53, 92, 98 (page numbers handscribed); *CPIA/M1 Rocket Motor Manual*, Unit 237, XM33E5, Castor, Scout-2nd stage.

40. Arms, "Thor," pp. 6-39, 6-41, 6-43, 6-44; "SAMSO Chronology," p. 168; Isakowitz, *Space Launch Systems* (1991), p. 295; Sutton, "History of Thiokol," p. 98 (handscribed number; p. 16 of the appendices, which have printed numbers); *CPIA/M1 Rocket Motor Manual*, Units 237 and 582, Castor II; Thiokol, "Off-the-Shelf Motor Catalog," n.d., n.p. (coverage of TX-354-4, Castor II) (see chap. 2, n. 24)

41. Leiss, "Scout Launch Vehicle Program Final Report," p. 54; *CPIA/M1 Rocket Motor Manual,* Units 538, X259B4, Antares IIB, and 577, TE-M-762, Star 31, Antares IIIA; Brian A. Wilson, "The History of Composite Motor Case Design," AIAA paper 93-1782, presented at the 29th Joint Propulsion Conference and Exhibit, June 28–30, 1993, Monterey, Calif., no pagination, slides titled "The 70's—Kevlar Is King" and "Composite Motor Cases by Thiokol"; C. A. Zimmerman, J. Linsk, and G. J. Grunwald, "Solid Rocket Technology for the Eighties," IAF paper 81-353, presented at the International Astronautical Federation XXXII Congress, Sept. 6–12, 1981, Rome, Italy, p. 9, "Bidirectional Woven Kevlar," http://www.aircraftspruce.com/catalog/cmpages/bikevlar.php (accessed Dec. 4, 2002); and "Aramid Fiber," http://www.fibersource.com/f-tutor/aramid.htm (accessed Dec. 4, 2002).

42. Gordon et al., *Aerojet,* pp. pp. IV-75, IV-78; *CPIA/M1 Rocket Motor Manual,* Unit 548, Improved Maverick; [ATK Tactical Systems Company], "Maverick Propulsion System and Heavy Warhead," http://www.atk.com/international/tactical-propulsion/maverick.htm (accessed July 9, 2004); Leiss, "Scout Launch Vehicle Program Final Report," pp. 54, 448; *Aeronautics and Space Report . . . , 1979 Activities,* p. 90 (see chap. 2, n. 52).

43. Thiokol Corporation, *Aerospace Facts,* Spring 1979, pp. 21, 25 (see chap. 2, n. 43); *CPIA/M1 Rocket Motor Manual,* Unit 577, Antares IIIA, and Taylor, *Jane's All the World's Aircraft, 1977–78,* p. 837 (see chap. 2, n. 25); *CPIA/M1 Rocket Motor Manual,* Units 457 (Aerojet's version) and 547 (for Thiokol's similar variant).

44. Statement of Maj. Gen. William R. Yost, Director of Space Systems and Command, Control, Communications, HQ USAF, to House of Representatives, Committee on Armed Services, Mar. 1980, supporting document Conclusion-1 to Waldron, "Inertial Upper Stage," p. 3-5 (see chap. 1, n. 110).

45. Previous two paragraphs from W. Paul Dunn, "Evolution of the Inertial Upper Stage," pp. 1–2, first quotation from http://www.aero.org/publications/crosslink/winter 2003/08.html (an Aerospace Corporation site) (accessed July 3, 2003), p. 1; Yost, Mar. 1980 Statement, pp. 5–7, for other quotations; Dave Dooling, "A Third Stage for Space Shuttle: What Happened to Space Tug," *Journal of the British Interplanetary Society (JBIS)* 35 (1982): 559; Boeing Aerospace Company, "Interim Upper Stage (IUS)," Jan. 13, 1977, supporting document III-17 in Waldron, "Inertial Upper Stage"; Waldron, "Inertial Upper Stage," p. 209; Jenkins, *Space Shuttle,* p. 244.

46. Boeing, "IUS," p. 2; Waldron, "Inertial Upper Stage," p. 95.

47. Waldron, "Inertial Upper Stage," pp. 53–54, 95–96.

48. Waldron, "Inertial Upper Stage," pp. 96–112; Dunn, "Evolution of the Inertial Upper Stage," pp. 2–3; Charles A. Chase, "IUS Solid Rocket Motors Overview," paper presented at the JANNAF Propulsion Conference, Feb. 1983, Monterey, Calif., pp. 13–15, 18.

49. Waldron, "Inertial Upper Stage," esp. pp. 208–209; Yost, Mar. 1980 Statement, esp. p. 8.

50. Richards and Powell, "Titan 3 and Titan 4," pp. 138–39; Dunn, "Evolution of the Inertial Upper Stage," p. 3; *Aeronautics and Space Report . . . , 1982 Activities,* pp. 86–87 (see chap. 2, n. 52).

51. Chase, "IUS," pp. 2–5; "Inertial Upper Stage," http://www.fas.org/spp/military/program/launch/ius.htm (accessed July 3, 2003); *Aeronautics and Space Report . . . , 1986 Activities,* p. 144 (see chap. 2, n. 109); "SAMSO Chronology," p. 364.

52. Isakowitz, *Space Launch Systems* (1995), pp. 234–36 (see chap. 2, n. 33); Meyers, "Delta II," pp. 3–5 (see chap. 2, n. 11); Forsyth, "Delta," p. 132 (see chap. 2, n. 10); *CPIA/M1 Rocket Motor Manual*, Unit 583, Castor IV.

Chapter 8

1. Cf. Andrew J. Butrica, *Single Stage to Orbit: Politics, Space Technology, and the Quest for Reusable Rocketry* (Baltimore, Md.: Johns Hopkins University Press, 2003), pp. 47–52.

2. Estimate and general information from Ernest G. Schwiebert, *A History of the U.S. Air Force Ballistic Missiles* (New York: Frederick A. Praeger, [1965]), p. 139; S. Morgan Friedman's "The Inflation Calculator" to compute 2005 dollars from those for 1961 (slightly past the middle of the period Schwiebert's estimate covers from 1955 to about 1964, since costs would have climbed significantly after the early years), http://www.westegg.com/inflation/infl.cgi (accessed June 11, 2005).

3. Costs from Bilstein, *Stages to Saturn*, p. 422 (see chap. 2, n. 64); inflation to 2005 dollars from the inflation calculator cited in the previous note, using the inflator for 1966, the year of highest Saturn costs and also about midway through the development process.

4. See the introduction to this book for references to the works of Layton, Vincenti, and Ferguson.

5. Memorandum, NASA/MLP (Tischler) to NASA/ML (Rosen), July 24, 1962 (see chap. 2, n. 71).

6. See, e.g., chapter 6, Henderson and Rumbel's discovery that aluminum added significantly to specific impulse.

7. Glasser, OHI by Allen, p. 73 (see chap. 2, n. 84).

8. Hugh G. J. Aitken, *The Continuous Wave: Technology and American Radio, 1900–1932* (Princeton, N.J.: Princeton University Press, 1985), quotation from p. 547, but see also pp. 15–16, 522–25, 536–52.

9. E. W. Price, "Solid Rocket Combustion Instability—an American Historical Account," in *Nonsteady Burning and Combustion Stability of Solid Propellants*, ed. Luigi De Luca, Edward W. Price, and Martin Summerfield, vol. 143 of *Progress in Astronautics and Aeronautics* (Washington, D.C.: AIAA, 1992), pp. 1–16; Yang and Anderson, *Liquid Rocket Engine Combustion Instability*, esp. Culick and Yang, "Overview of Combustion Instabilities in Liquid-Propellant Rocket Engines," pp. 3–37 (see chap. 1, n. 53); and the sources they cite.

10. The classic account in this connection is Armacost, *Thor-Jupiter Controversy* (see chap. 1, n. 53).

11. See, e.g., the comments in Hunley, *Birth of NASA*, pp. 9–12, 19–20, 22–23, 111n4, 258 (see chap. 2, n. 27).

12. Charles E. Bartley and Robert G. Bramscher, "Grand Central Rocket Company," in *History of Rocketry and Astronautics*, ed. Donald C. Elder and Christophe Rothmund, AAS History Series (San Diego: Univelt, 2001), 23:267–68, 271, 273–76; letters, Bartley to J. D. Hunley, Aug. 25, 1994, and Bartley to AMERICAN HERITAGE OF INVENTION AND TECHNOLOGY [his capitalization], Dec. 8, 1992, copy enclosed in his Aug. 25 letter.

13. Biographical synopsis of Adelman provided by Karen Schaffer of Chemical Systems Division; J. D. Hunley telephone OHI with Adelman, Feb. 23, 2000; Kennedy, Kovacic, and Rea, "Solid Rocket History at TRW Ballistic Missiles

Division," p. 13 (see chap. 1, n. 90), for Adelman's role on Minuteman. For his contributions to the Titan III, see chapter 7 notes.

14. James M. Knauf, Linda R. Drake, and Peter L. Portanova, "EELV: Evolving toward Affordability," *Aerospace America*, Mar. 2002, pp. 38, 40; Joseph C. Anselmo, "Air Force Readies Pick of Two EELV Finalists," *Aviation Week & Space Technology*, Dec. 9, 1996, pp. 82–83.

15. Craig Covault, "Atlas V Soars, Market Slumps," *Aviation Week & Space Technology*, Aug. 26, 2002, pp. 22–23; "Military EELV Launches Could Save $10 Billion," ibid., p. 23, quotations from this article; Boeing Press Release, "Successful First Launch for Boeing Delta IV," Nov. 20, 2002, http.//www.spaceref .ca/news/viewpr.html?pid=9864 (accessed July 12, 2003). See also "Report: Boeing-Lockheed Rocket Merger Likely to Be Approved," The Aero-News Network, Mar. 31, 2006, http://www.aero-news.net/index.cfm?ContentBlockID= bda56495-731c-4b26-a32e-ad75e5f65d63 (accessed Apr. 11, 2006), and, on the RD-180, Sutton, *Liquid Propellant Rocket Engines*, pp. 505–508, 590 (see chap. 3, n. 21).

16. See, e.g., Andrew J. Butrica, "The Quest for Reusability," in *To Reach the High Frontier*, ed. Launius and Jenkins, 463 (see chap. 1, n. 82).

17. Previous two paragraphs based on http://www.nasa.gov/mission_Pages/ constellation/main/index.html and the link to ARES LAUncH VEHicles (accessed Sept. 15, 2006); John Johnson Jr., "NASA Chief Isolates Likely Cause of Shuttle Trouble," *Los Angeles Times*, Dec. 3, 2005, p. A28; Chris Bergin and Daniel Handlin, "VSE: Less Steroids or Less Apollo," NASA Spaceflight.com, http://www.nasaspaceflight.com/content/?id=4430 (accessed Apr. 11, 2006); "NASA Weighing 2 Rocketdyne Engines," from the *Hartford Courant*, Mar. 23, 2006, http://www.courant.com/business/hc-natbriefs0323.artmar23,0,4988933 .story?coll=hc-headlines-business (accessed Apr. 3, 2006); "NASA Chooses-Moon Mission Engine," the ENGINEER online, http://www.e4engineering.com/ Articles/294605/NASA+chooses+moon+mission+engine.htm (accessed May 24, 2006).

18. CAIB, *Report*, 1:19 (see chap. 2, n. 128). See chapter 3 in this history for the failure rate of early Atlas flights.

A NOTE ON SOURCES

I have based this book to a significant degree on a large variety of archival sources from a number of different repositories. One of the most important was the NASA Historical Reference Collection at NASA Headquarters in Washington, D.C. There I drew upon many reports, letters, interviews, and biographical sketches. A second major archive was that of the National Air and Space Museum (NASM) both on the mall in Washington, D.C., and in Silver Hill, Maryland, where microfilm and microfiche collections, letters, reports, and various other sources helped answer many of my questions, as did interviews on file at the Space Division of NASM. The Goddard Papers and Special Collections of Clark University in Worcester, Massachusetts, proved invaluable in writing the section on Robert Goddard. I found many other sorts of useful material from Record Groups 18, 181, 218, and 255 at the National Archives in Washington, D.C.; College Park, Maryland; and Laguna Niguel, California.

Also extremely valuable in several areas were materials in the Frank Malina, Samuel Phillips, and George Mueller Collections at the Manuscripts Division of the Library of Congress. To supplement captured documents from Peenemünde on microfilm at NASM, materials at the U.S. Space and Rocket Center in Huntsville, Alabama, helped round out the picture of V-2 development. Although because of classification and other restrictions, I was unable to see many files on Polaris and other navy projects at the Naval Historical Center in the Navy Yard, Washington, D.C., biographical and other files there, plus interviews from the Naval Institute in Annapolis, Maryland, allowed me to piece together the history of the Fleet Ballistic Missile program. Extremely helpful in this and other respects were various files and interviews at the China Lake History Office near Ridgecrest, California.

Also crucial were the wide-ranging sources at the Jet Propulsion Laboratory (JPL) Archives in Pasadena, California, including a variety of interviews, reports, and other documents. The nearby California Institute of Technology Archives supplemented materials at JPL with other, similar sources. On John Parsons, the files at the FBI archives in Washington, D.C., were important. In many areas, the holdings of the Redstone Arsenal Technical Library (also called the Redstone Scientific Information Center) proved useful, including not just reference but archival-type materials.

For the air force's missiles and launch vehicles, the voluminous holdings of the Air Force Historical Research Agency at Maxwell Air Force Base, Alabama, yielded a wealth of interviews, reports, microfilm holdings, and other materials. The Air Force Space and Missile Systems Center History Office archives at Los Angeles Air Force Station, California, also proved a treasure trove of reports, white papers, monographs, and microfiche holdings. Supplementing this great variety of materials were numerous interviews I conducted myself and information provided to me by the people I interviewed. Details about all of these materials can be found in the chapter notes for this book. With the exception of published sources available many places, I have placed my sources, including many notes, in the NASA Historical Reference Collection so other scholars can consult them.

Another category of information consisted of congressional reports—some of them found in archives, others in the Library of Congress—that addressed problems faced by missiles and rockets in the process of development. Equally valuable have been many reports by engineers that the International Astronautical Federation, the American Institute of Aeronautics and Astronautics, the American Astronautical Society, and other organizations have published. Some of them are available in libraries or from the societies themselves, but many are extremely difficult to locate. Rocketdyne's publication, *Threshold*, has been uniquely valuable not only for engines that firm developed but also for the nature of engine technology in general. *The Aerojet Booster*, a very rough counterpart for the rival rocket firm, has been far less useful but has added important details on various aspects of Aerojet's rocket development. Lockheed and Thiokol have had similar publications, but I have not found them to be as helpful.

Among other periodical publications, *The Journal of the British Interplanetary Society, Spaceflight, Quest, Missiles and Rockets*, and *Aviation Week* (later, *Aviation Week & Space Technology*) have been enormously useful, but I have employed the last two sparingly because I have found that they frequently contain inaccuracies (or at least disagreements with more official sources). The same can be said in some degree, however, about almost all of the sources I have used. The literature abounds with incompatibilities about details. But used judiciously, *Aviation Week* and *Missiles and Rockets* have filled in a number of gaps in the history of rocket development.

There exist an enormous number of books and articles covering various aspects of launch-vehicle development. No 1 (or 20) of them addresses all the questions I have sought to answer in this volume, but a great many of them have provided useful information. A knowledgeable overview appeared in Wernher von Braun and Frederick I. Ordway III with Dave Dooling, *Space Travel: A History* (New York: Harper & Row, [1985?]), which devotes 281 pages of readable and well-illustrated text to the history of rocketry since the invention of the fireworks rocket and to space travel since 1961. Like it, mainly useful for the big picture, Frank H. Winter's *Rockets into Space* (Cambridge, Mass.: Harvard University Press, 1990) begins much later in the story and focuses more exclusively on rockets but does not provide much technical detail. Both provide worldwide coverage. A third, more recent general history, Roger E. Bilstein's *Testing Aircraft, Exploring Space: An Illustrated History of NACA and NASA* (Baltimore, Md.: Johns Hopkins University Press, 2003), spends more time on aircraft and exploration than on rocket technology but provides useful context.

In a category by itself is Walter A. McDougall's Pulitzer Prize–winning " . . . The Heavens and the Earth": A Political History of the Space Age* (New York: Basic Books, 1985). Full of anecdotes, this is, as the subtitle says, a political history without much technical detail. Thus, it has a totally different focus than my history. Another excellent work is Edmund Beard, *Developing the ICBM: A Study in Bureaucratic Politics* (New York: Columbia University Press, 1976). It focuses on programmatic issues ("bureaucratic politics") much more than the development of technology but provides useful context. Its subject is ballistic missiles, not space-launch vehicles.

More to the point for my own research is Roger D. Launius and Dennis R. Jenkins, eds., *To Reach the High Frontier: A History of U.S. Launch Vehicles* (Lexington: University Press of Kentucky, 2002). It consists of a series of essays on the major U.S. launch vehicles. Despite the uneven quality of the chapters and the shortness of some of them, this valuable addition to the literature was useful to me but mostly a very different sort of book than the present one, with most chapters not going into much technical detail. A much older volume, Eugene M. Emme, ed., *The History of Rocket Technology: Essays on Research, Development, and Utility* (Detroit: Wayne State University Press, 1964), also includes useful essays by knowledgeable people but has less detail than needed for most of my own purposes. A third reference, Steven J. Isakowitz, Joseph P. Hopkins Jr., and Joshua B. Hopkins, *International Reference Guide to Space Launch Systems*, 3d ed. (Reston, Va.: American Institute for Aeronautics and Astronautics, 1999), in conjunction with earlier editions of 1991 and 1995, provides much information (especially from the earlier editions because of the period covered by this book) but far from all the details and explanation one could want in a standard reference.

T. A. Heppenheimer, *Countdown: A History of Space Flight* (New York: Wiley, 1997) provides a coherent narrative imaginatively written by an engineer-turned-historian. Covering the Soviet Union as well as the United States and spaceflight in addition to rocketry, it still contains many useful insights and details, such as those about Rocketdyne. Mike Gruntman, *Blazing the Trail: The Early History of Spacecraft and Rocketry* (Reston, Va.: AIAA, 2004) is similarly broad. Worldwide in scope, it essentially ends with the first Soviet and U.S. space launches in the late 1950s but provides a narrative history of efforts to that time with much technical detail. George P. Sutton has provided a wealth of information about liquid-propulsion technology, not just in the United States but in other countries (especially the Soviet Union and Russia), in *History of Liquid Propellant Rocket Engines* (Reston, Va.: AIAA, 2006). Also valuable for Rocketdyne engines is Robert S. Kraemer with Vince Wheelock, *Rocketdyne: Powering Humans into Space* (Reston, Va.: AIAA, 2006).

To turn to the literature about Goddard and Oberth, there are two indispensable printed primary sources on the American pioneer: Esther C. Goddard and G. Edward Pendray, eds., *The Papers of Robert H. Goddard*, 3 vols. (New York: McGraw-Hill, 1970) and Robert H. Goddard, *Rocket Development: Liquid-Fuel Rocket Research, 1929–1941*, ed. Esther C. Goddard and G. Edward Pendray (New York: Prentice-Hall, 1948). Milton Lehman's *Robert H. Goddard: Pioneer of Space Research* (New York: Da Capo Press, 1988) provides a popular, readable, and useful biography. David A. Clary's *Rocket Man: Robert H. Goddard and the Birth of the Space Age* (New York: Hyperion, 2003) offers a new perspective that is largely favorable though not uncritical (if skimpy on most technical details). On Oberth, see his *Die Rakete zu den Planetenräumen* (1923; repr., Nuremberg: Uni-Verlag, 1960); *Ways to Spaceflight*, trans. Agence Tunisienne de Public-Relations (Washington, D.C.: NASA TT F-622, 1972); and Hans Barth, ed., *Hermann Oberth: Briefwechsel*, 2 vols. (Bucharest: Kriterion Verlag, 1979–84); as well as the informative but uncritical Hans Barth, *Hermann Oberth: "Vater der Raumfahrt"* (Munich: Bechtle, 1991). Those who do not read German can see Boris V. Rauschenback, *Hermann Oberth* (Clarence, N.Y.: West Art, 1994).

On specific missiles and launch vehicles there are many valuable secondary accounts as well as huge gaps in the literature. For the A-4 (V-2), a readable, thoroughly researched, if not highly technical account is Michael Neufeld's *The Rocket and the Reich: Peenemünde and the Coming of the Ballistic Missile Era* (New York: Free Press, 1995), which is critical of the politics and involvement with slave labor on the part of Wernher von Braun and his rocket team. Much more favorably disposed to von Braun are Frederick Ordway III and Mitchell R. Sharpe, *The Rocket Team* (New York: Thomas Y. Crowell, 1979) and Ernst

Stuhlinger and Frederick L. Ordway III, *Wernher von Braun: A Biographical Memoir* (Malabar, Fla.: Krieger, 1994), whereas Walter Dornberger, *V-2*, trans. James Cleugh and Geoffrey Halliday (New York: Viking, 1958) provides some technical details and many anecdotes about the missile and its developers. Serious students of the technology can consult Gerhard H. R. Reisig, *Raketenforschung in Deutschland: Wie die Menschen das All eroberten* (Berlin: Wissenschaft und Technik Verlag, 1999).

On the rocketry developed at JPL, Clayton R. Koppes, *JPL and the American Space Program: A History of the Jet Propulsion Laboratory* (New Haven, Conn.: Yale University Press, 1982) offers a solid, scholarly account that the interested reader can supplement with Frank Malina's many essays—such as "The Jet Propulsion Laboratory: Its Origins and First Decade of Work," *Spaceflight* 6 (1964): 160–65, 216–23—and with monographs such as James W. Bragg's "Development of the Corporal: The Embryo of the Army Missile Program," Historical Monograph No. 4 (Redstone Arsenal, Ala.: Reports and Historical Branch, Army Ordnance Missile Command, 1961) and [Mary T. Cagle], "History of the Sergeant Weapon System" (Redstone Arsenal, Ala.: U.S. Army Missile Command, [1963]). Theodore von Kármán with Lee Edson, *The Wind and Beyond* (Boston: Little, Brown, 1967) yields further perspective on JPL's rocketry work.

For other early missiles, John W. Bullard, "History of the Redstone Missile System," Historical Monograph No. AMC 23M (Redstone Arsenal, Ala.: Army Missile Command, 1965); John B. Medaris with Arthur Gordon, *Countdown for Decision* (New York: G. P. Putnam's Sons, 1960); Wernher von Braun, "The Redstone, Jupiter, and Juno," in *History of Rocket Technology*, ed. Emme; James M. Grimwood and Frances Strowd, "History of the Jupiter Missile System" (Huntsville, Ala.: Army Ordnance Missile Command, 1962); and Michael H. Armacost, *The Politics of Weapons Innovation: The Thor-Jupiter Controversy* (New York: Columbia University Press, 1969) together provide coverage of the Redstone and Jupiter, even if none of them by itself is completely adequate about involved technologies.

More generally, John C. Lonnquest and David F. Winkler, *To Defend and Deter: The Legacy of the United States Cold War Missile Program* (Rock Island, Ill.: Defense Publishing Service, 1996), USACERL Special Report 97/01, provides many details hard to locate elsewhere. John Clayton Lonnquest, "The Face of Atlas: General Bernard Schriever and the Development of the Atlas Intercontinental Ballistic Missile, 1953–1960" (Ph.D. diss., Duke University, 1996) provides by far the best overall account of the development of Atlas, but it is stronger on programmatic than technical details. For the latter, consult Iain Pike, "Atlas: Pioneer ICBM and Space-Age Workhorse," *Flight International* 81 (Jan. 18, 1962): 89–96; Robert A. Smith and Henry M. Minami, "History of Atlas Engines," in *History of Liquid Rocket Engine Development in the United States, 1955–1980*, ed. Stephen E. Doyle, AAS History Series (San Diego: Univelt, 1992), 13:53–66; and Chuck Walker with Joel Powell, *Atlas: The Ultimate Weapon* (Ontario, Canada: Apogee Books, 2005), among other sources. John L. Chapman, *Atlas: The Story of a Missile* (New York: Harper & Brothers, 1960) is good popular history with some information not available in the other sources.

For the Thor missile, which used essentially the same engine as the Atlas and Jupiter, besides Armacost, *Thor-Jupiter Controversy*, Julian Hartt's *The Mighty Thor: Missile in Readiness* (New York: Duell, Sloan and Pearce, 1961) provides a popular but helpful account. Paul N. Fuller and Henry M. Minami, "History of the Thor/Delta Booster Engines," in *History of Liquid Rocket Engine Development*, ed. Doyle, pp. 39–51, covers the evolution of the Thor engines to their use on stage one of the Delta launch vehicle. For these and other engines, I have relied heavily on the Chemical Propulsion Information Agency, *CPIA/M5 Liquid Propellant Engine Manual* (Laurel, Md.: CPIA, 1994), but this source was only available to me as a NASA employee and contains many details that I could not repeat exactly because of export-control laws.

Besides the 1991 and 1995 editions of Isakowitz, *Space Launch Systems*, W. M. Arms, "Thor: The Workhorse of Space—a Narrative History" (Huntington Beach, Calif.: McDonnell Douglas Astronautics Company, 1972) helps piece together the history of the Thor launch vehicle. On Thor and the follow-on Delta launch vehicle, Matt Bille, Pat Johnson, Robyn Kane, and Erika R. Lishock, "History and Development of U.S. Small Launch Vehicles," pp. 198–204, and Kevin S. Forsyth, "Delta: The Ultimate Thor," pp. 103–46, both in *To Reach the High Frontier*, ed. Launius and Jenkins, are good if brief. Bille et al., "Small Launch Vehicles," also covers the Scout for which Abraham Leiss, "Scout Launch Vehicle Program Final Report—Phase VI," NASA Contractor Report 165950, pt. 1, May 1982, Space and Missile Systems Center History Office, photo room (also available through NASA libraries on microfiche X82-10346) is indispensable.

David K. Stumpf, *Titan II: A History of a Cold War Missile Program* (Fayetteville: University of Arkansas Press, 2000) not only provides excellent coverage of the Titan II but also much information about the Titans I and III. Warren E. Greene, "The Development of the SM-68 Titan," AFSC Historical Publications Series 62-23-1, Aug. 1962, is helpful on Titan I, and Laurence J. Adams, "The Evolution of the Titan Rocket—Titan I to Titan II," in *History of Rocketry and Astronautics*, ed. J. D. Hunley, AAS History Series (San Diego: Univelt, 1997), 19:201–23, contains useful technical details about Titans I and II. M. J. Chulick, L. C. Meland, F. C. Thompson, and H. W. Williams, "History of the Titan Liquid Rocket Engines," in *Liquid Rocket Engine Development*, ed. Doyle, pp. 19–35, provides valuable treatment of the principal engines on Titans I–IV.

Graham Spinardi, *From Polaris to Trident: The Development of US Fleet Ballistic Missile Technology* (Cambridge: Cambridge University Press, 1994) has excellent but not exhaustive treatment of technologies for the fleet ballistic missiles, starting with Polaris. R. A. Fuhrman, "Fleet Ballistic Missile System: Polaris to Trident," von Kármán Lecture for 1978 at the 14th annual meeting of the AIAA, Feb. 1978, Washington, D.C., contains much that Spinardi does not cover. James Baar and William E. Howard, *Polaris!* (New York: Harcourt, Brace, 1960) is a good, popular account, and Harvey M. Sapolsky, *The Polaris System Development: Bureaucratic and Programmatic Success in Government* (Cambridge, Mass.: Harvard University Press, 1972) covers some technology as well as programmatics.

There is no good history of Minuteman. Roy Neal, *Ace in the Hole* (Garden City, N.Y.: Doubleday, 1962) cannot be totally relied upon but has much useful information. W. S. Kennedy, S. M. Kovacic, and E. C. Rea, "Solid Rocket History at TRW Ballistic Missiles Division," paper presented at the AIAA/SAE/ASME/ASEE 28th Joint Propulsion Conference, July 6–8, 1992, Nashville, Tenn., provides the Ramo-Wooldridge perspective and some technical details. J. D. Hunley, "Minuteman and the Development of Solid Rocket Launch Technology," in *To Reach the High Frontier*, ed. Launius and Jenkins, pp. 229–300, fits Minuteman into the larger story of solid-rocket development. Also extremely useful on solid-rocket motors in general, not just Polaris and Minuteman, is the restricted *CPIA/M1 Rocket Motor Manual*, vol. I (Columbia, Md.: CPIA, 1994).

Milton W. Rosen, *The Viking Rocket Story* (New York: Harper & Brothers, 1955) and Constance McLaughlin Green and Milton Lomask, *Vanguard: A History* (Washington, D.C.: Smithsonian Institution Press, 1971) competently relate the histories of those important programs but need much supplementation for technical details. More recently, Matt Bille and Erika Lishock have provided a comparative treatment of U.S. and Soviet competition to launch the first satellites in Roger D. Launius, ed., *The Space Race: Launching the World's First Satellites*, Centennial of Flight Series (College Station: Texas A&M University Press, 2004). This book provides excellent context for both the Vanguard and the Juno launch vehicles, as well as coverage of both. For "man-rating" the Redstone, the best source is Joachim P. Kuettner, "Mercury-Redstone Launch-Vehicle Development and Performance," in *Mercury Project Summary including Results of the Fourth Manned Orbital Flight May 15 and 16, 1963*, ed. Kenneth S. Kleinknecht and W. M. Bland Jr. (Washington, D.C.: NASA SP-45, 1963), esp. pp. 69–79. Loyd S. Swenson Jr., James M. Grimwood, and Charles C. Alexander, *This New Ocean: A History of Project Mercury* (Washington, D.C.: NASA SP-4201, 1998) and Barton C. Hacker and James M. Grimwood, *On the Shoulders of Titans: A History of Project Gemini* (Washington, D.C.: NASA SP-4203, 1977) cover modifications to the early Atlas and Titan II missiles to make them launch vehicles for astronauts.

For many upper stages, information is extraordinarily scattered in archival sources, technical reports, and periodical publications such as the *Journal of the British Interplanetary Society*, but now Virginia P. Dawson and Mark D. Bowles have written an excellent history of Centaur, *Taming Liquid Hydrogen: The Centaur Upper Stage Rocket, 1958–2002* (Washington, D.C.: NASA SP-2004-4230, 2004). *Centaur Program*, Hearings before the Subcommittee on Space Sciences of the Committee on Science and Astronautics, H. Rep., 87th Cong., 2d sess., May 15 and 18, 1962 (Washington, D.C.: GPO, 1962) is also valuable on that subject.

Roger E. Bilstein, *Stages to Saturn: A Technological History of the Apollo/Saturn Launch Vehicles* (Washington, D.C.: NASA SP-4206, 1980) comes as close to being the definitive history of the Saturn launch vehicles as any work is ever likely to be, but Charles Murray and Catherine Bly Cox, *Apollo: The Race to the Moon* (New York: Simon & Schuster, 1989) provides much useful material in a history of the larger Apollo Program. Roger D. Launius, "Titan: Some Heavy Lifting Required," in *To Reach the High Frontier*, ed. Launius and Jenkins, pp. 147–85, provides a good introduction to the Titan launch vehicles. G. R. Richards and J. W. Powell, "Titan 3 and Titan 4 Space Launch Vehicles," *Journal of the British Interplanetary Society* 46 (1993): 123–44, provides many other details on the bewildering variety of Titan vehicles.

Between them, Dennis R. Jenkins, *Space Shuttle: The History of the National Space Transportation System, the First 100 Missions* (Cape Canaveral, Fla.: Specialty Press, 2001) and T. A. Heppenheimer, *Development of the Space Shuttle, 1972–1981, History of the Space Shuttle*, vol. 2 (Washington, D.C.: Smithsonian Institution Press, 2002) provide a great deal of technical information about the shuttle, although they do not always agree. Heppenheimer's *The Space Shuttle Decision: NASA's Search for a Reusable Space Vehicle* (Washington, D.C.: NASA SP-4221, 1999) also covers much about shuttle development. John F. Guilmartin Jr.

and John Walker Mauer, *A Shuttle Chronology, 1964–1973: Abstract Concepts to Letter Contracts*, 5 vols. (Houston: JSC-23309, 1988) supplements *Space Shuttle Decision* on many details of the development process.

There are many other sources for various aspects of launch-vehicle technology, including histories of rocket firms, studies of the programmatic aspects of missile and launch-vehicle development, technical reference works, journal articles, and histories of key educational institutions. Space limitations have precluded including them in this essay. The Internet is another source for much technical material on rockets. Internet sites are not always reliable, but on many topics, they are indispensable if used after careful comparison with more traditional sources. For these Web sources and many others not covered in this essay, see the notes to the chapters in this book.

Index

Page numbers for illustrations and their captions are italicized.

A-4 missile. *See* V-2
ABL. *See* Allegany Ballistics
　Laboratory
ablation, 168–69, 196, 272
Able upper stage, 54–55, 157
Able-Star upper stage, 56, 157–59;
　restart capability, 56, 158. *See also*
　Thor/Able-Star launch vehicle
ABMA. *See* Army Ballistic Missile
　Agency under Army, U.S.
AC Spark Plug: inertial guidance for
　Titan, 46
Adelman, Barnett R., 86, 262, 294;
　and founding of United Technology
　Corporation, 260
Advanced Research Projects Agency
　(ARPA), 43, 55, 75, 157–58, 176
AEDC. *See* Arnold Engineering De-
　velopment Center
aerodynamic heating, 5, 215, 219, 242
Aerojet Engineering Corporation,
　17, 224. *See also* Aerojet General
　Corporation
Aerojet General Corporation, 17, 22,
　118, 153, 155, 174, 235, 239–40,
　276–77, 281; and aeroplex binder,
　227; development of Aerozine 50,
　45, 160; early name of, 17; and en-
　gines for Titan I, 44–45; and engines
　for Titan II, 51, 159–68; and engines
　for Titan III, 87, 159, 168; found-
　ing, 17, 147; and JATO devices, 17,
　224; and Minuteman, 43, 247–48,
　251, 252–55, 257; and Polaris, 41,
　240–41, 243–44, 245; and second-
　stage engine for Vanguard, 30,
　153–57; and segmented motors,
　69–70, 261–62; and Transtage, 87,
　168–71; and (other) upper stages
　and motors, 72, 171
Aerospace Corporation, 141, 284;
　relation to Space Technology Labo-
　ratories, 37; and solution of pogo
　problem in Titan II, 165, 166
Aerozine 50, 45, 160
AFB. *See* Air Force Bases
AFSC. *See* Air Force Systems Com-
　mand under Air Force, U.S.
Agena upper stage, 56–57, 58, 116,
　159, *160*, 172, 177; "Ascent
　Agena," 88; and Hustler propulsion

unit, 57; models of, 56–57; success
　rates, 57
AIAA. *See* American Institute of
　Aeronautics and Astronautics
Air Force, U.S., 32, 56, 59, 62, 68, 85,
　90–91, 119, 174, 247, 282; Air Force
　Systems Command (AFSC) of, 37;
　Air Materiel Command of, 35, 122;
　Air Research and Development
　Command of, 33, 37, 176; Blue
　Scout, 71–72; and Centaur, 63, 67,
　175, 178, 183–85; contributions,
　37, 117, 118, 122, 154, 230, 255–56;
　and expendable launch vehicles,
　97, 295; and the Large Segmented
　Solid Rocket Motor Program, 247,
　269–70; MX-774 project of, 32, 37,
　112–13; and product improvement,
　127; Project Suntan, 174–75; and
　Saturn, 138; and segmentation,
　261–62; requirements for the Space
　Shuttle, 95. *See also* Army Air
　Forces; Atlas; EELV; names of Air
　Force organizations below major-
　command level; Navaho, Titan
Air Force Ballistic Missile Division.
　See Ballistic Missile Division
Air Force Bases (AFBs) 79, 88. *See also*
　names of individual bases
alcohol, 51, 104, 112–13, 119, 147
Allegany Ballistics Laboratory (ABL),
　30, 222; beginnings, 233; and
　solid-propellant development, 226,
　234–37, 244–45; and upper stages,
　30, 237, 278
all-up testing, 82, 250; NASA defini-
　tion of, 82
aluminum, 41; damping of insta-
　bilities by, 236, 240; as a fuel, 236,
　240–41, 245, 250–51, 253, 270, 276,
　277; as structural material, 198,
　215, 217, 234
American Institute of Aeronautics
　and Astronautics (AIAA), 22
American Rocket Society, 20; early
　name of, 20; founding, 20; merger
　with American Institute of Aero-
　nautics and Astronautics, 22
Ames Research Center, California,
　85, 96
aniline, 22, 146–47, 150, 154

Apollo. *See* Program Apollo

ARC. *See* Atlantic Research Corporation

Army, U.S., 152, 255–56; and tanks for the Saturn program, 75; Army Ballistic Missile Agency (ABMA), 38–39, 49–51, 74–75, 79, 130–31; Ordnance Department/Corps of, 22–23, 26, 117, 152, 225, 227–29, 237–38

Army Air Corps/Forces, 19, 22, 147, 223; Air Technical Service Command of, 118; and Navaho missile, 118

Arnold Engineering Development Center (AEDC), Tennessee, 79, 96; altitude testing at, 87, 169, 186, 264, 283–84

ARPA. *See* Advanced Research Projects Agency

asphalt, 223–25

Atlantic Research Corporation (ARC), 42; and discovery of aluminum as a fuel, 41, 240; and other propellant development, 244, 252–53

Atlas-Able launch vehicle, 62

Atlas-Agena launch vehicle, 62–63, *130*

Atlas-Centaur launch vehicle, 63–67, *65*, 182, 189; payload, 64

Atlas launch vehicle, 62–69; engines for, 67, 125, *125*, *126*, 295; "man-rating" of, 51; modifications, 51, 62, 66, 67; models, 51, 59, 66, 69, 295; success rates, 62, 66, 69. *See also* Atlas-Able, Atlas-Agena, Atlas-Centaur, Mercury-Atlas

Atlas missile, 32–38, 294; engines for, 38, 67, 122–30; "man-rating" of, 51; models of, 38, 67, 123; operational readiness of, 39; success rate, 38, 297; turbopump problems with, 38–39. *See also* Mercury-Atlas

Atwood, John Leland, 117, 200–201

axial cooling coils (defined, 150), 150

baffles: anti-slosh, 56, 159, 188, 198, 216; anti-vortex, 217; on injectors, 78, 124, *124*, 132, 137–38, 161, 167, 170, 207; materials in, 161; in a turbopump, 210

Ballistic Missile Division (BMD), 37, 71, 247–50. *See also* Ballistic Systems Division, Space Systems Division, Western Development Division

Ballistic Systems Division (BSD), 164–65; replaced part of Ballistic Missile Division, 37. *See also* Space and Missile Systems Organization

Bartley, Charles, 225–26, 228; and associates, 225–26; and Grand Central Rocket Company, 294; and Thunderbird rocket, 226

Bell Aerospace/Aircraft Corp., 57, 118

Biggs, Robert E., 207–209

"Black Saturday." *See under* Western Development Division

Blue Scout. *See under* Air Force, U.S.

BMD. *See* Ballistic Missile Division

Boeing Aerospace Company: and Inertial Upper Stage, 90, 282, 284; acquires McDonnell Douglas, 295. *See also* Boeing Company

Boeing Company, 134, 141, 249; and Burner II/IIA, 58

Bollay, William, 117–20

Bossart, Karel (Charlie), 63; innovations of, 37, 113, 175, 184. *See also* steel-balloon tank

Braun, Wernher Magnus Maximilian von, 3, 14–16, 74, 78, *81*, 102, 107, 118; and all-up testing, 82–83; and Centaur, 184–85; on configuration management, 83–84; conservative design approach, 85; education, 13–14; his group and its culture/ingenuity/tendencies, 23, 82–83, 85, 145, 184; as heterogeneous engineer, 15, 16, 79, *111*; influenced by Oberth, Hermann, 13–14; inventiveness, 120; and liquid hydrogen, 190; at NASA Headquarters, 205; personality, 84–85; and Redstone missile, 26–28, 116; as a student, 13–14; as a systems engineer, 15–16, 79–80; as a technical manager, 15–16, 84, 105–106, 199–200; use of weekly notes, 79–80, 218

BSD. *See* Ballistic Systems Division

BuAer. *See* Bureau of Aeronautics under Navy, U.S.

Bumper WAC project, 23, *24*, 148; ability of WAC to start at high altitude, 23, 148; achievements, 23–24

Burner upper stages, 57–59, 68

California Institute of Technology: Eaton Canyon rocket activities, 222, 233; training of key rocket engineers, 163, 260. *See also* Jet Propulsion Laboratory

Cape Canaveral, Florida, 24, 39, 66, 72, 91, 129, 285; early names of, 24

Carboxy-terminated polybutadiene (CTPB), 43, 279, 285; development of, 252–53

Castenholz, Paul, 126–27, 138, 206–208

cavitation, 107, 148, 204; explained, 107, 121

cavity, internal (within solid propellants), 4, 228, 234, 246, 263; star-shaped, 226, *227*, 229, 230, 234, 238. See also names of solid-propellant rockets/motors

Centaur upper stage, 63–67, *65*, *66*, 175–76; configurations, 65; engines, 64, 66, 177, 179–81, *182*, 185, 187–90; payload capabilities, 64; problems, 177–89; success rates, 66, 67, 189–90; technological contributions of, 67, 190; testing, 64, 177–78, 180–82. See also Atlas-Centaur and Titan-Centaur

CEP. See circular error probable

Challenger explosion, 67, 91, 96–97; and Aerojet booster proposal, 268–69; and tang-and-clevis joint design, 272

Chance Vought Corporation: LTV Missile Group, 73. See also Ling-Temco-Vought, Inc.

Chemical Propulsion Information Agency (CPIA), 256; predecessor organizations, 255–56; and technology transfer, 6, 255–56

Chemical Systems Division (CSD) of United Technologies Corporation, 68, 86, 255. 261; and Inertial Upper Stage, 90, 282–84; and the solid rocket motors for Titan III and Titan IVA, 91, 266–67. See also United Technology Corporation

Chrysler Corporation, 39, 51, 76, 117, 121

circular error probable (defined, 27); for Redstone missile, 27

cold war, 1; end, 295–96; role in missile and launch-vehicle development, 5, 47, 288

Columbia accident, 95, 215, 218–20, 291; and AresI/V, 296

combustion instability, 4–5, 76, 110–11, 230, 234; in Atlas, 124; in Polaris, 242–43; in Redstone, 119; in Saturn F-1, 77–78, 137–39; in Saturn H-1, 132; in Titan II second

stage, 51, 161, 166–67; in V-2, 106; in Vanguard, 114, 236

competition (among rocket-engineering organizations), 5–6, 38, 40. See also interservice and interagency rivalry

computers: early unavailability of, 127; uses of, 143, 192, 193, 203, 207–209, 213, 221, 257. See also guidance/control

Consolidated Vultee Aircraft Corporation (Convair), 78; contracts, 32, 37, 113, 175

Convair. See Consolidated Vultee Aircraft Corporation, General Dynamics

cooling: ablative, 168–69, 196; film (defined, 106); radiative, 168; regenerative (defined, 106), 20, 114, 123, 155, 180, 193, *213*

cooperation (among rocket-engineering organizations), 5–6, 15, 75–76, 96, 99, 142, 154, 292–93; on Centaur, 185–86; between Minuteman and Polaris, 42, 43; on Polaris, 41; on Saturn, 190; between Thor and Jupiter programs, 40. See also information sharing

Corley, Robert C., 253–54

Corporal missile, 17, 148–53; achievements, 152–53; compared with Sergeant, 237–38; compared with V-2, 17, 152; contractors for, 151; deployment date, 152; flight tests, 149–51; operational date, 152

CPIA. See Chemical Propulsion Information Agency

cryogenic propellants (defined, 100); insulation for, 178, 180, 195, 198, 217–18. See under propellants and see also liquid hydrogen and liquid oxygen

CSD. See Chemical Systems Division

CTPB. See carboxy-terminated polybutadiene

cut-and-try engineering (defined, 2), 2, 102, 143, 158, 181, 210. See also trial-and-error procedures, empiricism

Delta launch vehicle, 31–32, 54, 59–62, *61*, 170, *260*; borrowings from Vanguard, 54, 60; characteristics, 61, 62; evolution, 60–61; low-risk strategy, 61; models, 60, 285, 295; modifications, 61; payload

Delta launch vehicle, (*continued*) capabilities, 60; reliability, 61; upper stages, 171

Department of Defense (DoD), 59, 75, 86, 282

DoD. *See* Department of Defense

Dornberger, Walter, 14, 102–103, 105; as a heterogeneous engineer, 15; influenced by Oberth, Hermann, 14

Douglas Aircraft Company, 78; and Corporal missile, 151; and Delta launch vehicle, 60; stages for Saturn vehicles, 75, 190–91, 195–97. *See also* McDonnell Douglas Astronautics Company

Dunn, Louis, 19; as director of the Guided Missile Research Division of Ramo-Wooldridge, 35; as director of Jet Propulsion Laboratory, 17, 18, 19–20, 229

dynamic pressure, 182

EELV. *See* Evolved Expendable Launch Vehicle

Ehricke, Krafft, 107, 175; and Atlas, 63; and Centaur, 63, 175–77, 182–83,

empiricism, 119, 127, 155, 161, 172, 211–12. *See also* cut-and-try engineering, trial-and-error procedures

engineering: as art (or "black magic"), 1, 137–38, 143, 193, 239, 290; and assumptions, 128; as contrasted with "rocket science," 1, 44, 136–37, 274, 290; culture of, 2, 5; as design, 1, 290, 291; as doing rather than just knowing, 1–2, 110, 143, 165, 290; heterogeneous (defined, 6, 16), 15, 16, 33, 44, 98, 239, 288–89; and modifications, 204, 211, 274, 290–91; and mysteries, 104–105, 110, 137, 143, 164, 211, 219, 291; and prediction, 69, 73–74, 87, 98, 141–42, 172, 220, 289; and problem solving, 87, 98, 129–30, 155–56, 203, 210–11, 242–43, 248–50, 284, 292; and redesign, 32, 63–64, 76, 78, 93, 99, 124, 132, 139, 161–62; re-engineering, 167, 170, 188, 203; re-ports and papers, 2, 87, 289; scaling up and, 74, 105, 135, 244, 290; and testing, 69, 87, 130, 172, 180–81, *242*, 248–49, 273–74, *275*, 283, 289, *293*; theory in, 23, 74, 110, 223, 240, 290; and uprating, 132, 133, 136, 194. *See also* "rocket science"

engines: clustering of, 74, *131*, 132, 136; complexity, 87, 104–105. *See also* individual rockets and missiles, engine manufacturers

ET. *See* external tank *under* Space Shuttle

Evolved Expendable Launch Vehicle (EELV) program, 91, 295

Fairchild Space and Electronics Company, 68

Falcon Missile, 228

Fletcher, James C., 207–208, 269

funding for missile and rocket development, 2, 3, 5, 26, 243, 288; constraints for shuttle, 92, 206, 207; early air force, 32–33; for Centaur, 63–64, 177, 184–86; for solid-propellant development, 43, 223, 227

Funk, Ben I., 35, 58

GALCIT. *See* Guggenheim Aeronautical Laboratory at Caltech

Gardner, Trevor, 33

gas generators, *162,* 162, 165, 167–68, 194, 254, 256

GE. *See* General Electric Company

Gemini. *See* Project Gemini

General Dynamics, 51, 67, 129; Astronautics Division (GD/A), 179, 184–86; and Centaur, 63, 64–67, 89, 175–90; and commercial Atlas-Centaur, 67; Convair Division, 63, 78, 175; management issues, 182–183

General Electric (GE) Company, 23–26, 46, 69, 139, 229–31; and first stage engine for Vanguard, 30, 114–16; role in launch-vehicle development, 25, 118. *See* Project Hermes

geostationary transfer orbit, 60

geostationary/geosynchronous orbit, 60, 159, 169

Gillette Procedures, 34

gimballing, 5, 57, 113, 129, 136, 162, 180, 194–95, 212, *271*; contributions of Viking to, 29–30, 113; and Lockseal/Flexseal, 270, 273

Glasser, Otto J., 34, 82, 250; as Atlas project manager and deputy for systems management at WDD, 36–37; on innovation, 291

Glennan, T. Keith, 80, 176, 192

Goddard, Robert H., 7–12, *10*, 14, 22, 113, 173; and assistants, *12;* visited by Frank Malina, 17; education, 9; grants, 8; highest altitude achieved by, 9; influence of, 8, 9, 12, 104; launch of first liquid-propellant rocket, 9, *10, 11;* "Liquid-propellant Rocket Development," 10; "A Method of Reaching Extreme Altitudes," 9; methodology, 9; patents, 8; secrecy of, 8, 20; technological breakthroughs, 8

Goddard Space Flight Center: and Delta launch vehicle, 60, 285

Grand Central Rocket Company, 294; and third-stage engine for Vanguard, 30, 235, 237

Grumman Aerospace Corp., 92

Guggenheim Aeronautical Laboratory at Caltech (GALCIT), 17, 222; and founding of Aerojet, 17. *See also* Jet Propulsion Laboratory

Guidance/control systems, 5, 69, 76, 155, 245, 257, 285; for Centaur, 64–65, 189; for Corporal missile, 18, 151; inertial, 45; for Saturn, 76, 202–203; for Sergeant missile, 18; for Titan missiles, 45, 162–63, 264

Hagen, John: director of Vanguard Project, 30

Hall, Albert C.: contributions to gimballing, 30

Hall, Edward N., 122, 228; designer of Minuteman, 42, 246–47; as heterogeneous engineer, 42; at Western Development Division, 35, 42

Hansen, Grant L., 183, 185

helical cooling coils (defined, 148), 149–50

Henderson, Charles B., 240, 244

Hercules Aerospace Company (formerly, Hercules Powder Company), 268, 295

Hercules Powder Company, 245; and Allegany Ballistics Laboratory, 30; and cast double-base propellants, 234–37; and Minuteman, 43, 247–48, 251; and Polaris, 243–44; and upper stage motors, 42, 235–37, 243–44, 278. *See also* Allegany Ballistics Laboratory

Hermes tactical/test missiles, 25, 26, 230–31. *See also* Project Hermes

Hickman, Clarence, 232–33

high-altitude start, 23, 44, 148, 156, 158

Hoffman, Samuel K., 120, 122

Holmes, D. Brainerd, 80; and problems with Gemini-Titan II, 166

HTPB. See hydroxy-terminated polybutadiene

Hujsak, Edward J., 129

hydrazine, 150, 154, 189, 196, 285

hydrogen peroxide, 107, 113, 114, 180, 189

hydroxy-terminated polybutadiene (HTPB), 68, 90, 268, 279–86; development, 253–54

Hydyne (unsymmetrical dimethylhydrazine and diethylene triamine), 27

hypergolic propellants (defined, 45), 145. *See also under* propellants *and see names of propellants that are hypergolic*

ICBM. *See* intercontinental ballistic missiles

igniters, 231, 256; hypergolic, 44–45, 125–28, 131, 136, 274; pyrotechnic, 109; placement, 119

ignition at high altitude, 23, 44; closures for, 156, 158

Inertial Upper Stage (IUS), 89–90, 91, 286; early name, 281; importance, 282; problems, 90, 281–85

information sharing, 21, 22, 25, 29, 31, 40, 62, 99, 291–92; for Saturn, 76, 79, 82, 143, 195; for Scout, 73. *See also* technology transfer

injection (of liquid propellants), 4; periodization in, 116

injectors, 105, 136–39, 146; design problems with, 77–78, 114–15, 119, 155; impingement in, 78, 110–11, 119, 138, 148, 149, 150, 158; materials for 138, 193; orifice arrangement in, 132, 138; Titan II, 161. *See also* baffles

innovations, 38, 64, 79, 105–106, 109, 223–24, 231, 291; on Atlas, 124, 126; on Centaur, 180; on Saturn, 135–136; in solid propellants, 223–29, 240, 244; on solid-propellant motors/stages, 230–57, 264–65; on Titan II, 162, 166, 168; by U.S. engineers, 27, 78–79, 113, 114, 118–19, 294 (and *see* individual vehicles); on Vanguard, 155. *See also names of innovative technologies*

Integrated Spacecraft System (ISS)
upper stage, 69
interagency cooperation. *See*
cooperation

interagency rivalry. *See* competition
intercontinental ballistic missiles
(ICBMs) (defined, 34), 38, 39. *See
also specific ICBM names*
intermediate range ballistic missile
(IRBM), defined, 38. *See also specific IRBM names*
interservice cooperation, 258. *See
also* cooperation
interservice rivalry, 257–258, 292. *See
also* competition
IRBM. *See* intermediate range ballistic missile
IRFNA. *See* nitric acid, inhibited
red . . . fuming
ISS. *See* Integrated Spacecraft System
IUS. *See* Inertial Upper Stage
IWFNA. *See* nitric acid, inhibited . . .
white fuming

JATO. See Jet Assisted Takeoff
devices
Jet Assisted Takeoff devices, 17, 147,
223–25, *224*, 235; explained, 163,
223
Jet Propulsion Laboratory (JPL),
California, 16–20, 85, 174; characteristics of managers, 19; engine
development, 26, 147–53; first report as JPL, 22; organization, 19,
20; management, 19; early methodology, 19; role in technology
transfer and rocket development,
20, 118, 154, 174, 222–29, 237–38; and
Sergeant test vehicle, 229; size,
19; systems engineering at, 19. *See
also* Aerojet General Corporation,
Guggenheim Aeronautical Laboratory at Caltech (GALCIT), Corporal
Missile, Sergeant Missile, and WAC
Corporal
Johnson Space Center, Texas, 216. *See
also* Manned Spacecraft Center
JPL. *See* Jet Propulsion Laboratory
Juno I launch vehicle, 27–28, *29, 238*
Juno V. *See* Saturn launch vehicles
Jupiter A, 39
Jupiter C, 18, 27, 39, 51, *238. See*
Juno I
Jupiter missile, 32, 38, *289*; compared
with Thor, 32, 39–40; deployment,
39; flight tests for, 39; as launch-

vehicle stage, 27–28; main engine
for, 39, 101, 123; shape of, 39; turbopump problems with, 38–39

Kármán, Theodore von, 16, 17, 117,
146, 149; as JPL director, 19, 222–24
Kennedy, John F., 80, *81*
Kennedy Space Center, Florida, *65,
133*, 205, *221*
kerosene, 63, 77, 114, 122, 132, 135,
174
Killian, James R., Jr., 38
Kindelberger, James H. "Dutch," 117
Klager, Karl, 159, 240–41
Klein, Schanzlin & Becker, 106–107
Kuettner, Joachim P., 50–51

Ladish Company, 94, 170; roll-ring
forging (described, 270), 265–66
Langley Research Center, Virginia,
70, 85, 96, 186; as Langley Aeronautical Laboratory, 276, 277; Pilotless
Aircraft Research Division (PARD)
of, 70, 276; wind-tunnel culture
of, 85
Launch Operations Center (LOC),
82–83. *See also* Kennedy Space
Center
Lauritsen, Charles, 233
launch vehicles: as distinguished
from missiles, 2. *See also names of
individual vehicles*
Lewis Research Center, Cleveland,
Ohio, 78, 193; and Centaur, 89,
185–86, 189; under the NACA,
118, 154, 174; research with liquid
hydrogen, 85; testing at, 185, 189
Ling-Temco-Vought, Inc., 58. *See also*
Chance Vought.
liquid hydrogen, 63; engines using,
63, 93, 173–75, 206; idiosyncrasies
of, 104, 173–74, 177, 178, 191; in
Centaur, 175–90; in Saturn, 135,
190–204; in Space Shuttle, 204–220;
technologies associated with
178–180, 188, 190–95, 197–98, 203,
210
liquid oxygen, 63, 77, 93, 112–14,
173–75; in the V-2, 104, 107; in the
Atlas, 122; in Centaur, 175–90; in
the Redstone, 119; in Saturn, 135,
190–204; in Space Shuttle, 204–20
LOC. *See* Launch Operations Center
Lockheed: Lockheed Aircraft Corporation, 174, 241; and Lockseal
device, 270; Lockheed Martin, 295;

Lockheed Propulsion Company, 294; Missile and Space Division of, 239; Missile Systems Division of, 56–57

Low, George M., 207–208, 214

LTV. *See also* Ling-Temco-Vought, Inc. and Chance Vought Corporation

Malina, Frank J., 16, 17, 22, 145–46, 222–24; as acting director of JPL, 19–20; as chief engineer of JPL, 19; influences on, 21, 22; visit to Goddard, Robert, 17

management systems, 6, 182–84, 294–95; for Apollo, 79–85; Program Evaluation and Review Technique, 47, 84–85; Schriever's system, 35–37, 85; von Braun's weekly notes, 79–80, 218. *See also* systems engineering

Manned Spacecraft Center (MSC), Texas, 82–83, 165, 200, 205. *See also* Johnson Space Center

"man-rating" of launch vehicles, 49–54, 195; of Atlas missiles, 51; of Mercury-Redstone, 50–51; of Titan II missiles, 51–53

Marshall Space Flight Center (MSFC), Alabama, 74, 79, 82–83, 92–93, 163, 197, 199; and Centaur, 178, 183–86; and Michoud Assembly Facility, 214; reorganization, 205; and Saturn F-1, 138, 140, 141; and Saturn J-2, 193, 195, 203; and Space Shuttle, 205–220, 268, 270. *See also* Army Ballistic Missile Agency

Martin Company, Glenn L., 51, 141, 170; and Titan I missile, 30; and Titan II missile, 46, 160–61; and Vanguard launch vehicle, 30–31, 114–16; and Viking rocket, 29–30, 113

Martin Marietta Company, 86, 89, 153, 155; and external tank for Space Shuttle, 94–95, 214–18; part of Lockheed Martin, 295; refurbishment of Titan II missiles as launch vehicles, 90; and solution of pogo problem, 165; and Titan III launch vehicle, 86, 90; and Titan IV launch vehicle, 266

Massachusetts Institute of Technology (MIT), 240

mass fraction (defined, 236), 177, 246, 255, 256, 264, 277, 279–80

McDonnell Douglas Astronautics Company, 68, 92, 285, 295; *See also* Boeing, Douglas Aircraft Company

Medaris, John B., 39

Mercury. *See* Project Mercury

Mercury-Atlas, 51, *52, 101*

Mercury-Redstone, 28, *50*; abort system, 51; "man-rating" of, 28, 50–51, 50–51

Minuteman I missile, 40, 41, 42–44, 246–52; as countercity weapon (deterrent), 45; DoD approval, 42; firing from a silo, 249; operational date, 43, 251; PBAN binder for, 43; range, 43, 251–52; technologies in, 245, 247–49, 251–52

Minuteman II, 43, 252–55; carboxy-terminated polybutadiene in, 43; range, 43; replaces Minuteman I, 43, 255

Minuteman III missile, 43, 255–57; Aerojet third stage, 43, 255; initial operational capability, 43, 257; range, 43

missiles, 5; early costs, 288; relation to launch vehicles, 2, 47, 52, 98. *See also names of individual missiles*

Mississippi Test Facility, *136,* 140, 201, *202,* 203. *See also* National Space Technology Laboratories

MIT. *See* Massachusetts Institute of Technology

Morton Thiokol, 96–97, *293*

MSC. *See* Manned Spacecraft Center

MSFC. See Marshall Space Flight Center

Mueller, George E., 52, 81–85, 200–201, 295; bureaucratic astuteness of, 81; characteristics, 85

MX-774B project, 32, 37; engine for, 112–13; technological contributions of, 113, 114

MX-1593 project, 32–33

Myers, Dale D., 205

NAA. *See* North American Aviation

NACA. *See* National Advisory Committee for Aeronautics

NASA. *See* National Aeronautics and Space Administration

National Advisory Committee for Aeronautics (NACA), 80; culture of, 85

National Aeronautics and Space Administration (NASA), 23, 43, 62, 64, 166, 178–79, 255–56; and Ares

National Aeronautics and Space Administration (NASA) (*continued*) I/V, 296; and Delta launch vehicle, 31–32, 59–60; and the Large Segmented Solid Rocket Motor Program, 270; Office of Manned Space Flight (OMSF) in, 80; and Saturn launch vehicles, 77, 138; and Space Shuttle, 67; management/organizational changes in, 80. *And see* names of field organizations and officials, Projects Mercury and Gemini, and Program Apollo

National Space Technology Laboratories, 208, *213*. *See also* Mississippi Test Facility

Navigation Development System (NDS) spacecraft, 68

Navaho missile, 37–38; legacies from, 117, 118, 122

Naval Ordnance Test Station (NOTS), Inyokern, California, 41, 118, 229; founding, 233; technical contributions of, 72, 154, 233–34, 246, 263

Naval Research Laboratory (NRL), 29; and the Vanguard launch vehicle, 29–30

Navy, U.S., 22, 159, 223; Bureau of Aeronautics (BuAer) in, 22, 24, 118, 227, 228; furtherance of rocketry, 22, 113, 154, 154–155, 225, 240, 255–56; special projects office, 41, 239, 243, 245. *See also* Vanguard, Polaris

Neu, Edward A., Jr., 113; "spaghetti" construction developed by, 21, 123

Neumann, John von, 33

nitric acid, 147, 149, 150; inhibited red- and white-fuming (IWFNA and IRFNA), 153, 154, 158; red-fuming (RFNA), 145–47, 154; white-fuming (WFNA), 154

nitrogen tetroxide, 45, 162, 196

North American Aviation (NAA), 25, 117–22; beginnings, 117; and engines for the Atlas missile, 37, 122–30; and engines for the Navaho missile, 37, 117–18; Space and Information Systems Division (S&ID) of, 197, 200–201. *See also* North American Rockwell, Rocketdyne Division

North American Rockwell, 204; and contract for Space Shuttle orbiters, 95–96. *See also* North American Aviation

NOTS. *See* Naval Ordnance Test Station

nozzles, 3, 57, *136*, 248–49, 282, 284; angles (expansion ratios) of, 123, 158, 169, 180, 226, 238, 254, 273, 283; cooling, 168; designs for, 108, 132, 264–65; erosion in, 230, 248, 254, 274; exit cones for, 281; extendible exit cones for, 169, 266, 283; gimballed, 268, 270; liners for, 241; materials for, 169, 231, 237, 238, 241, 246, 248, 256, 264–65, 272; removable extensions of, 135, 158; submerged, 255, 256, 273; throat inserts in, *227*, 246, 280; vectoring of, 248, 251, 283

NRL. *See* Naval Research Laboratory

Oberth, Hermann, 12–14, 20, 173; collaboration with Max Valier, 13; education, 13; influence of, 12–14; *Die Rakete zu den Planetenräumen* (The Rocket into Interplanetary Space), 13

OMSF. See Office of Manned Space Flight under National Aeronautics and Space Administration

Operation Pushover, 24

Operation Sandy, 24

O-rings, 262, 265, 272

PAM. *See* Payload Assist Module

PARD. *See* Pilotless Aircraft Research Division under Langley Research Center

Parsons, John W., 16, 223–24

Patrick, Joseph C., 225

Payload Assist Module (PAM), 60, 68, 281

Payload Transfer System (PTS), 68

PBAN. *See* polybutadiene-acrylic acid-acrylonitrile

Pendray, G. Edward, 20, 29; and the American Rocket Society, 20; on Goddard, Robert, 20

perchlorates: ammonium, 226–27, 230, 238, 241, 244, 245, 251, 253, 270, 276; potassium, 223–226

PERT. *See* Program Evaluation and Review Technique *under* Raborn, William F. *and under* management systems

Phillips, Samuel C., 83; Apollo Program director, 83–85, 140–141, 199–201; and configuration man-

agement, 83, 295; Minuteman director, 42–43, 83, 249
Pickering, William, 17; roles at Jet Propulsion Laboratory, 19–20
Pöhlmann, Moritz, 106
pogo effect (defined, 51), in Saturn F-1 engine, 78, 140–41; in Titan II, 51, 164–66
Polaris A1 missile, 25, 40–42, 238–43; deployment, 41; flight testing, 41, 242; management of, 295; problem solving, 242–43; range, 42, 243; relation to Jupiter missile, 38, 39, 240, 241; shape, 245
Polaris A2 missile, 42, 243–45; flight testing, 42; operational date, 42; range, 42; shape, 245
Polaris A3 missile, 245–246, 254; operational date, 42; range, 42, 245; shape, 245
polybutadiene-acrylic acid-acrylonitrile (PBAN): low cost, 254; in Minuteman, 43, 250–51; for Titan solid rocket motors, 264; for Space Shuttle SRB, 270
polysulfide polymer, 225–31
polyurethane binder, 227, 240, 245, 251, 276, 277
Pratt & Whitney division of United Aircraft, 78, 174; engines of, 64, 66, 75, 175–92, 206
Price, Edward W., 243; and combustion instability 234, 243; and star-shaped cavity, 226
Program Apollo, 77–85; Apollo fire, 77. See also Saturn, Mueller, Phillips
Project Gemini, 49, 51–54, 58, 164–67
Project Hermes, 22–26; legacy, 25–26, 229
Project Mercury, 28, 49–52,
Project Paperclip, 23; contributions of, 159; previous name of, 23. See also V-2
propellants, 3; advantages of liquids, 40; advantages of solids, 40, 239, 263; castable double-base, 234–37; composite (defined, 222), 223–227; composite-modified double base (CMDB), 244, 251, 278; cryogenic, 4, 173–221; double-base (defined, 222), 225, 226–27, 232–37, 244; extrusion (defined, 225), 232–33; grain (defined, 225); grain configurations, 226–27, 229, 230, 234, 238, 246, 251, 256, 270–71, 277; hypergolic,

4, 45, 145–72; liquid, 4–5, 238–39, 257; solid, 4, 5, 222–87; tanks for, 139, 155, 170, 177–79, 194, 197, 214–220, 235. See also injection (of liquid propellants), and names of individual propellants and vehicles
PTS. See Payload Transfer System
pumps, propellant, 162; axial, 193–94; centrifugal, 107, 135–36, 193, 211; turbopumps and their problems, 107, 123–24, 132–33, 161–62, 179; on Saturn F-1, 139; on Space Shuttle, 207–12

quality control, 178, 198, 219, 228, 249, 284

Raborn, William F. (Red), 41, 239, 245; as heterogeneous engineer, 44; Program Evaluation and Review Technique (PERT) of, 47, 84, 295
Ramo, Simon, 34, 35, 36
Ramo-Wooldridge Corporation, 34–35, 36, 250, 294–95; Guided Missile Research Division (GMRD) of, 35; Space Technology Laboratories of, 35, 165, 248–49. See also Thompson Ramo Wooldridge
R&D (research and development), 187–88
Reaction Motors Inc., 21; merging with Thiokol, 21; MX-774 engine, 112–13; successes, 21; Viking engine, 29–30, 113–14
Redstone Arsenal, Alabama, 18, 26–27, 74, 230, 237
Redstone Missile, 26–28, 120–22; compared with Corporal and Sergeant, 27–28; flight tests, 27; modified as launch vehicle, 28; origins as Hermes C1, 26; product improvement program for, 121
Rees, Eberhard, 83, 199–200, 205
Reisig, Gerhard, 108
René 41, 139
restart (of upper stages), 56, 87, 158, 169, 180, 194, 196
RFNA. See nitric acid, . . . red-fuming
Rocketdyne Division of NAA, North American Rockwell, and Rockwell International, 25, 78, 175, 253; and Atlas engines, 38, 123–30; Experimental Engines Group of, 126–28, 130; and Jupiter engine, 39; and Navaho missile, 37–38; and Redstone engine, 120–22; and Saturn engines,

Rocketdyne Division of NAA (*continued*) 75, 77, 130–43, 192–95, 202–203; Saturn F-1 and Space Shuttle Main Engine compared, 93–94; and Space Shuttle Main Engine (SSME), 93–94, 206–14

Rocket Engine Advancement Program, 122

Rocket Propulsion Laboratory (also known as Edwards AFB "rocket site," other names), 79, 181, 186, 268, 281, 283; Minuteman testing at, 249–50; Saturn testing at, 135; successor to Powerplant Laboratory, 261; technical contributions of, 253, 269–70

rocketry: fundamentals of, 3–5; generic designs in, *162, 227*

"rocket science," 1, 110, 289; engineering not "down to a science," 44–45, 54, 87, 97, 219–20; engineering not mature science, 143, 172, 287, 289

Rockwell International, 208. *See also* North American Rockwell

Rosen, Milton W., 176; and Delta launch vehicle, 31–32, 59–61; as director of launch vehicles and propulsion in NASA, 29; as technical director of Vanguard launch vehicle, 29; and Viking rocket, 29, 113

RP-1. *See* kerosene

Rumbel, Keith, 240, 244

Russia, 190, 295. *See also* cold war, Soviet Union

RV-A-10 Missile, 229–31; characteristics, 230–31; significance, 231, 238

SAMSO. *See* Space and Missile Systems Organization

San Marcos platform (off the coast of Kenya, Africa), 73

Saturn launch vehicles, 74–85, *133, 135, 142;* costs of, 288; engines, 74–78, 130–43, *131, 134, 182,* 190–204, 214; flight testing of, 76–77, 140, 142, 201–204; fuel-line problem, 78; ground testing, 76, 77, 140, 199, 203; [hu]man rating, 54, 195; instrument unit (IU) of, 76, 202–203; pogo in, 140–41; problems with injectors, 76–78; problems with turbopumps, 78, 139; problems from uprating, 74; propellant tanks, 75, *139;* rede-

signs, 76, 78; sizes, 74, 76; stages, 75–78, 130, 132, *136, 139;* use of technologies from other launch vehicles, 74, 75, 78–79, 190, 193; versions, 74, 75, 76, *101,* 190–92

Schilling, Martin, 103, 104, 106, 107–108

Schindler, William R., 60

Schriever, Bernard A., 33–37, 165, 166; and concurrency, 36; education of, 33; as heterogeneous engineer, 33, 34; management system of, 35–37, 294–95; and parallel development, 36; personal characteristics, 33–34; staff of at WDD, 34–35

Schubert, W., 178

Schult, Eugene, 72

Scout launch vehicle, 32, 70–74, 276–81, *280;* acronym, 277; conception of, 70, 276–77; models of, 73; payload capacities, 70, 73; problems, 73; sizes, 74; success rates, 70, 73; tests (ST), *71,* 278; uniqueness of, 4, 70, 278

Seaberg, John D., 174, 176, 178, 184

Sergeant missile, 17–18, 237–38; characteristics, 18; operational date, 237; scaled-down motors, 18, 27–28; technological contributions, 18, 238, *238*

SGS-II upper stage, 68

Silverstein, Abe, 31, 59, 80, 174, 185–86, 190, 192

Sloop, John L., 179, 182–83, 185

Smith, Levering, 41, 231, 245, 256; contributions to Polaris, 41, 239

solid-propellant breakthrough, 40, 43; implications for launch vehicles, 40, 44; interservice cooperation and rivalry in, 43; technology transfer in, 42

Soviet Union: space race with, 28, 53, *289. See also* cold war, Russia, *Sputnik*

Space and Missile Systems Organization (SAMSO), 59, 88, 281, 284. *See also* Ballistic Missile and Space Systems Divisions (BMD and SSD)

Space Shuttle, 91–98, *216,* 221; Air Force requirements, 95; configuration, 92–93, 96; cost constraints, 92, 96, 98; double-delta planform (defined, 96), 96; engines, 93–94, 204–14, *213;* external tank (ET), 92, 94–95, 214–20, *216;* first flight,

212; [hu]man rating, 54; problems with development, 93, 208–12; solid rocket boosters (SRBs) for, 44, 92, 94, *95*, 204, 268–75, *269*, *271*, *275*, *293*; stage-and-a-half concept, 92; success rate, 96; testing of, 96, 208–12, 218; thermal protection system, 96; throttling, 212–13; unusual features, 91–92

Space Systems Division (SSD), 58, 59, 86, 164–65, 264, 279; replaces part of Ballistic Missile Division, 37. *See also* Space and Missile Systems Organization

Space Technology Laboratories (STL). *See* under Ramo-Wooldridge Corporation

"spaghetti" construction, 21, 123, 157

specific impulse (defined, 41), 110, 114, 119, 123, 126, 147, 264, 279, 285; for Centaur, 180, *182*; for Corporal, 152; for early solid propellants, 226–27, 237, 238, 240, 241, 245, 277, 278; for Minuteman, 251; for Saturn J-2, 214; for Space Shuttle, 213–14, 270; for Titans I and II, 163; for Transtage, 170; for Vanguard stage two, 153

Sperry Gyroscope Company, 237–38

Sputnik I, 28, 30, 75, 116, 175, 288

SRB. *See* solid rocket boosters *under* Space Shuttle

SRM. *See* solid-rocket motor *under* Titan III and IV launch vehicles

SSD. *See* Space Systems Division

SSME. *See* Space Shuttle Main Engine *under* Rocketdyne Division

ST. *See* Scout, tests

staged combustion (defined, 93), 207

stages, 92; upper, 3, 98–99, 190–204, *202*; zero, 4. *See also* individual missiles and launch vehicles

Stage Vehicle System (SVS), 68

static testing. *See* testing under engineering

steel-balloon tank structure, 37, 63, 69, 113, 117

steering, 114, 194, 241. *See also* gimballing, thrust vector control

Stiff, Ray C., 147, 163, 170; discovery of hypergolic combustion of aniline and nitric acid, 22, 146; as a manager at Aerojet, 22, 163; other contributions, 163

STL. See Space Technology Laboratories (under Ramo-Wooldridge Corporation)

storable propellants. *See* hypergolic propellants

Storms, Harrison A., Jr., 197–201

strap-on boosters, 57, *61*, 61, 62, 279. *See also* Space Shuttle solid rocket boosters *and* Titan III and Titan IV solid rocket motors

structures, 5, 195, 215–17, 282; cases, 235, 237, 251–52, 262, 265, 267, 268, 270, 273, 279; for combustion chambers, 113–14, 148–50, 155–56; hydrogen embrittlement in metals, 194; materials in, 5, 114, 132, 148–50, 155, 170, 171, 193, 194, 195; welding, 139, 178, 196, 198–99, 231, 265. *See also* steel-balloon tank structure *and names of missiles/vehicles*

Summerfield, Martin, 19, 26, 146, 224; compared with Walter Thiel, 146

SVS. See Stage Vehicle System

swiveling, 113

systems engineering (defined, 15), 20, 47, 70, 183, 199, 205, 218, 294

tang-and-clevis joints, 265, 273; for Space Shuttle and Titan IIIC compared, 272

Teapot Committee, 33

technical institutes, and V-2 technology, 15, 105, 108–109

technology transfer, 43–44, 47, 146–47, 255–56, 265, 281; from JPL, 20, 153, 228, 293; through migration of engineers, 20, 22, 60, 102, 112, 117–18, 143–44, 163, 229, 261, 293–94; from Sergeant, 18, 277–78; joint-venture contracts and, 256; on Saturn, 74, 75, 78–79, 190, 193; in solid-propellant breakthrough, 43, 245, 254; from V-2, 112; from Titan, 272; from Vanguard, 31–32, 157; from Viking, 29–30. *See also* information sharing, cooperation

Teflon, 179, 229

thermal protection: *See under* Space Shuttle *and see* "insulation for" *under* cryogenic propellants

Thibodeaux, Guy, 59, 276, 277

Thiel, Walter, 103–106, 108, 110, 173

Thiokol Chemical Corp., 18, 227, 230–31, 237; development of PBAN, 43, 250–51; founding, 225; innovations, 225, 228–29, 252; and Flexseal, 270, 273; and Minuteman, 247–49, 255; and Scout, 276–77; and Shuttle solid rocket boosters, 94, 95, 269, 269–71, 273–74; technology transfer from JPL, 228; various motor/stage designations, 59, 64, 68–69, 196, 277, 279–81. *See also* Morton Thiokol

Thompson, Jerry, 137–38, 203

Thompson Ramo Wooldridge (later TRW, Inc.), 37; attitude-control engines of, 196; upper-stage engine of, 171; other technical contributions, 141, 253–54, 257. *See also* Ramo Wooldridge Corporation

Thor-Able launch vehicle, 54–55, 55; final launch, 55; success rate, 55. *See also* Able upper stage

Thor/Able-Star launch vehicle, success rate, 56, 159

Thor as launch-vehicle stage, 39–40, 54–60, 279; Thorad, 57, 279. *See also* Delta launch vehicle

Thor-Delta launch vehicle. *See* Delta launch vehicle

"Thor-Jupiter Controversy," 38

Thor missile, 32; engine for, 38, 101, 123, 127; operational alert for, 39; turbopump problems with, 38–39

thrust termination, 242, 251, 257

thrust vector control, 231; jetavator, 241–42, 245; by liquid injection, 246, 252, 254, 262, 264; materials used in, 241–42, 246, 254, 256, 262; on Titan IIIC, 262–63; by vectorable nozzles, 245, 248–249. *See also* gimballing, steering

Titan I missile, 44–45; approval, 44; deployment, 45; high-altitude start, 44; as insurance for Atlas, 44; problems with, 44; range, 45

Titan II launch vehicle, 53–54, 59, 86, 90; engines, 164–168; malfunction detection system, 53; "man-rating" of, 51–53; payload capability, 90; pogo problems, 51, 164–66; and Project Gemini, 46, 51–53, 53

Titan II missile, 45–46; authorization, 45; characteristics, 45; compared with Titan I, 45, 46; as counterforce weapon, 45; deactivation, 46; deployment, 46; development plan for, 45; engines, 159–65, 167–68; flight testing, 46; number of parts, 46; operational date, 46; range, 45; refurbishment as launch vehicle, 90; relation to Titan III and IV, 44; success rate, 164

Titan III launch vehicle, 85–90, 262–63, 285; engines, 159, 168; payload capabilities, 88–89; reliability, 88; solid-rocket motors for, 44, 66, 86, 89, 263–66, 272; success rates, 88, 90; versions, 86–89, 266. *See* Titan-Centaur

Titan IV launch vehicle, 86; A-model, 90–91, 266; B-model, 85, 91, 268, 291; engines for, 159, 168; solid-rocket motors for, 266–68

Titan-Centaur launch vehicle, 65, 66, 89

Transtage, 87–88; engines for, 168–171; restart capability of, 87, 169

trial-and-error procedures, 1, 2, 38, 43, 90, 99, 120, 143, 194, 198, 290, 291; in IUS, 284; to solve combustion instabilities, 5, 138, 243. *See also* cut-and-try, empiricism

Truax, Robert C., 21–22; and jet-assisted takeoff, 22, 117, 147

TRW. *See* Thompson Ramo Wooldridge

turbopumps. *See under* pumps

UDMH. *See* unsymmetrical dimethyl hydrazine

United Technology Center (UTC). *See* United Technology Corporation

United Technology Corporation (UTC), 86; and segmented motors, 86, 262; and solid-rocket motors for Titan, 259–66. *See also* Chemical Systems Division

universities, role in rocket engineering, 43, 79, 138, 141, 154, 174, 210, 233, 243, 255. *See also* technical institutes

unsymmetrical dimethyl hydrazine (UDMH), 153, 155, 159–60

UTC. *See* United Technology Center, United Technology Corporation

V-2 (A-4) missile, 15–16, 23, 24, 24–25, 79, 102–12; accuracy of, 15; influence on the United States, 14–15, 17, 23, 25–26, 102, 113, 118,

150; process of development for, 15, 105; propulsion system for, 103–12

Vandenberg AFB, California, 57–58, 72, 129, 164

Vanguard launch vehicle, 28–32, *31*, 114–16, 153–57; high-altitude start, 44; technological contributions of, 30–32, 54–55, 60, 116, 157, 176, 277; testing, 30, *115*, 156; third stage, 235–37

vernier engines (defined, 5), 162

vibrations and vibration testing, 141, 151, 152, 203, 209, 219, 249

Viking sounding rocket, 28–30, 113–14; contributions to launch vehicles, 29–30, 114

WAC Corporal rocket, 17, 23, 147–48, 233; relation to Corporal missile, 148, 149. *See also* Bumper-WAC

Wallops Island, Virginia, 70, 72, 278

Walter, Hellmuth, 107

WDD. *See* Western Development Division

Webb, James E., 80, 185, 197

Western Development Division (WDD), 33–37, 122, 246; "Black Saturday" meetings of, 36; management control system of, 35–37, 295; replaced by Ballistic Missile Division, 35

WFNA. *See* nitric acid, . . . white-fuming

White Sands Proving Ground, New Mexico, 148, 149

Wooldridge, Dean, 34

Wright Air Development Center, Ohio, 128, 154, 174; Powerplant Laboratory of, 247, 261–62. *See also* Rocket Propulsion Laboratory

Wyld, James H., and regenerative cooling, 20–21

zero stage, 61, 264. *See also* strap-on booster

ISBN-13: 978-1-58544-588-2
ISBN-10: 1-58544-588-6